TRANSITION AND DEVELOPMENT IN CHINA

Transition and Development

Series Editor: Professor Ken Morita
Faculty of Economics, Hiroshima University, Japan

The Transition and Development series aims to provide high quality research books that examine transitional and developing societies in a broad sense – including countries that have made a decisive break with central planning as well as those in which governments are introducing elements of a market approach to promote development. Books examining countries moving in the opposite direction will also be included. Titles in the series will encompass a range of social science disciplines. As a whole the series will add up to a truly global academic endeavour to grapple with the questions transitional and developing economies pose.

Also in the series:

The Political Economy of Asian Transition from Communism
Sujian Guo
ISBN 0 978 7546 4735 5

Globalization and the Transformation of Foreign Economic Policy
Pawel Bozyk
ISBN 978 0 7546 4638 9

The Institutional Economics of Russia's Transformation
Edited by Anton N. Oleinik
ISBN 0 7546 4402 2

Estonia, the New EU Economy
Building a Baltic Miracle?
Edited by Helena Hannula, Slavo Radoševic and Nick von Tunzelmann
ISBN 0 7546 4561 4

The Periphery of the Euro
Monetary and Exchange Rate Policy in CIS Countries
Edited by Lúcio Vinhas de Souza and Philippe De Lombaerde
ISBN 0 7546 4517 7

Transition, Taxation and the State
Gerard Turley
ISBN 0 7546 4368 9

Transition and Development in China
Towards Shared Growth

YUN CHEN
Fudan University, China

LONDON AND NEW YORK

First published 2009 by Ashgate Publishing

Reissued 2018 by Routledge
2 Park Square, Milton Park, Abingdon, Oxon OX14 4RN
605 Third Avenue, New York, NY 10017

First issued in paperback 2021

Routledge is an imprint of the Taylor & Francis Group, an informa business

A Library of Congress record exists under LC control number: 2008013068

ISBN 13: 978-0-8153-9855-4 (hbk)
ISBN 13: 978-1-3511-4428-5 (ebk)
ISBN 13: 978-1-138-35849-2 (pbk)

DOI: 10.4324/9781351144285

Contents

List of Figures *vii*
List of Tables *ix*
List of Photographs *xiii*
Foreword *xv*
Acknowledgment *xvii*

Introduction 1

PART 1: POLITICAL ECONOMY OF TRANSITION IN CHINA: COMPARING THE MAO ZEDONG SYSTEM AND THE DENG XIAOPING SYSTEM

1 The Logic of the Mao Zedong Development System and its Institutional Inefficiency 13

2 Transition towards the Deng Xiaoping Development System: The Wisdom of 'Creative Destruction' 59

3 Advantages and Disadvantages of State-owned Enterprise Reform: Relations with Systemic Reforms of Finance, Administration and Social Security 117

PART 2: POLITICAL ECONOMY OF DEVELOPMENT IN CHINA

4 Relations Between Central and Local Government under the Tax Sharing System: Towards a Constitutional Local Autonomy System 169

5 Political Economy of the Chinese Development Model: The Fact-following Mechanism of Institutional Change in Chinese Society 239

6 Political Economy of the East Asian Authoritarian Development System: Lessons Towards Shared Growth 293

Concluding Remarks: Gradual Way of Transition in China 373

Selected Bibliography 385
Index 403

List of Figures

1.1	Logic of central planning in China	16
1.2	Six big scale economic cooperation districts	22
1.3	The classification of functions of government in centrally planned system	44
2.1	City Structure in China: the "county receives city's guidance" system	78
2.2	Administrative structure of the People's Republic of China	110
3.1	The quadrant reform of state owned enterprises, finance, administration and social security	118
4.1	Characteristics of tax sharing system led by authoritarianism	185
4.2	Structure of items in financial transfer from central government	191
4.3	Logic of development impulse of local government	210
4.4	International comparison of the ratio of administration control costs	212
4.5	Relations between central and local government under the authoritarian development system	223
4.6	Relationship between central and local government under the law-governed system	225
4.7	Framework of local autonomy system in Japan	227
4.8	Multiple layers of controlling space of Chinese traditional society	230
5.1	Complexity of Deng Xiaoping's development system	241
5.2	International comparison of the number of civil servants per 1000 people	251
5.3	Risk transmission mechanism behind the low cost goods competitiveness	268
5.4	New rule for survival and fact following mechanism of institutional change in the Deng Xiaoping development system	284
5.5	Framework of institutional analysis to build the sustainable society in Tokyo	288
6.1	Three kinds of authoritarian system in East Asia	303
6.2	Conceptual figure on productive industrialization ratio and labor force industrialization ratio in Asian countries (1960s–1980s)	320
6.3	Concept of the trap in Southeast Asia.	323

6.4 Realization of shared growth in East Asian NIEs model 326
6.5 Central organization system of the Chinese communist party 341
6.6 Organizational system of Chinese cabinet 342
6.7 Economic development and systemic transition in East Asian NIEs model 368

List of Tables

1.1 The ratio of coastal and inland area on the basic construction investment 18
1.2 The ratio of industrial distribution between coastal and inland areas 18
1.3 Amount of city construction in each period of Chinese provinces and autonomous districts (1947-86) 21
1.4 Ratio of investment in the industrial sector to the total investment (whole industries = 100) 23
1.5 The ratio of non agricultural population to the total urban population in the system of "county receives city's guidance" (10 thousand, %) 32
1.6 Expansion process of the "county receives city's guidance" system 34
1.7 Absolute amount of disparity between agricultural products and industrial products (100 million yuan) 34
1.8 The changing procedure of branch organizations, basic administrative districts in rural areas and autonomous organizations 39
1.9 Production amount of enterprises in the communes 41
1.10 Structure of production and labor in three sectors in China (1952-1977) 46
1.11 Some indicators of labor productivity in agriculture (1953-1977) 49

2.1 Industrial structure of Santai district (Taizhou, Taixin, and Taixian) (1989) 80
2.2 Some indicators of coastal open cities and special economic zone cities 82
2.3 GDP ratios of four major regions 101
2.4 Ratio of basic construction investment amount of eastern, central and western region to the regional total 103
2.5 Fund structure of fixed asset investment (1999 – first quarter of 2003) 104
2.6 Regional structure in industrial production 106
2.7 Some indices of six provinces in the central region 108

3.1 Ratio of employees occupied by enterprise types in urban and rural areas (10 thousand, %) 124
3.2 Situation of deficit operation of state owned manufacturing enterprises within the national budget 125
3.3 Management situation of state owned enterprises controlled by central, provincial and municipal level government in 2006 126

3.4 Profit and growth rate of profit of state owned enterprises 126
3.5 Situation of principal banks in China 128
3.6 Top 15 ranking Asian enterprises (current price, as of the end of December 2006) (million US$) 131
3.7 Distribution of office of foreign owned banks 136
3.8 Locational distribution of office of foreign owned banks 137
3.9 Investment situation of foreign owned financial organizations into Chinese banks (a portion of them) 138
3.10 Deposit structure in Chinese banks (100 million yuan, %) 140
3.11 Four state owned asset management corporations in China 142
3.12 Ratio of bad loans in Chinese commercial banks: Each quarter of the year (2004-2007) 145
3.13 Number of basic level government, committees and family in Chinese rural areas 150
3.14 Indicators of five social insurance funds (2006) 156
3.15 Management purposes pursued by enterprise managers 159
3.16 Participated numbers in basic endowment insurance 160
3.17 Some indicators of basic medical insurance 161
3.18 Member peasants of rural endowment insurance and member migrant peasants of medical insurance and worker's accident insurance (2006) 162

4.1 Two decreases of financial revenue 175
4.2 Comparison of the amount of money paid to the central government: Shanghai and Guangdong 181
4.3 Financial revenue and expenditure for central and local government (100 billion yuan, %) 187
4.4 Self-sufficiency ratio of central and local government 189
4.5 The scale of budget transfer from central government (100 million yuan, %) 194
4.6 Local financial expenditure, financial transfer, and the ratio (100 million yuan, %) 196
4.7 The financial situation of Towns and Villages in Shandong Province (10 thousand yuan, %) 202
4.8 Growth rate of revenues outside the budget of local government (1996-2003) (100 million yuan, %) 206
4.9 Administration control costs in the national finances (100 million yuan, %) 211
4.10 Tendency of the ratio of outside and inside budget revenues in China (100 million yuan, %) 213
4.11 Economic construction expenditure; ratio to total financial expenditure and growth rate (100 million yuan, %) 214
4.12 Japanese situation on tax sharing system (2004) (trillion yen, %) 216
4.13 Economic structure of China 231

5.1 Comparisons between Mao Zedong's ideology and Deng Xiaoping's theory 242
5.2 Corruption perception index: World top 39th list (2005) 252
5.3 Corruption perception index: Asia and Pacific countries (2005) 253
5.4 Corruption perception research of communist party (2004) 254
5.5 The ratio of capital formation and consumption to GDP in China (100 million yuan, %) 258
5.6 The ratio of worker's income and asset income in China 259
5.7 GDP growth and annual average wage growth (index, previous year=100) 260
5.8 Minimum wage criteria of local government 262
5.9 Social average monthly wages in Shanghai 264
5.10 Foreign economic relations of China 267
5.11 The ratio of light and heavy industry to Chinese national industries 270
5.12 Dependence on international market about main ore products 271
5.13 Income disparity between the urban and rural areas in China 280
5.14 Consumption disparity between urban and rural areas in China 281
5.15 Saving and consumption situation of Chinese population (2001-2006) 282

6.1 Real GDP growth rate 297
6.2 Development of regional trade agreements with which China is concerned 299
6.3 Some indicators of East Asian countries and regions 310
6.4 Population below the national poverty lines 311
6.5 Experience of studying abroad of Taiwanese technocrats 313
6.6 Special fields of Taiwanese technocrats 314
6.7 Some indicators on export products of South Korea (1970) 325
6.8 Comparison of employment inducement in manufacturing export of Asian NIEs and Southeast Asia (1975) 325
6.9 The ratio of urbanization in China (100 thousand, %) 328
6.10 Comparisons of labor force industrialization with productive industrialization in China 330
6.11 Job structure of the migrant population in Shanghai (100 thousand, %) 331
6.12 Number of graduates of Universities (prime minister, vice prime minister, state committee, chairperson, ministers) 343
6.13 The executive committee of the central political bureau in the communist party started in 2002 355
6.14 Leaders of next generation 356
6.15 Comparison of high ranking executives of graduates of Peking University and Tsinghua University 358
6.16 Top ten universities from prominent politicians were graduated 359
6.17 Details of eight Democratic Party group 360

List of Photographs

2.1 Deng Xiaoping and his uncle 67
2.2 'Welcome foreign friends' by Deng Xiaoping 68
2.3 'Practice is the only one criterion to verify the truth' by Deng Xiaoping 68

6.1 Actual situation of 'the most terrible case of Dingzihu, eviction rejected family, in history' 336

Foreword

As the editor of this series from the start of 2001, I have heartily desired to have an excellent book on transition and development in China from international perspectives and with an interdisciplinary approach. Finally, and happily, we have a suitable and excellent social scientist (whose wide major fields cover economics, political science and international relations and who meets my desire), Dr Yun Chen, the author of this book.

As of 2007, Dr Yun Chen is an associate professor in the school of International Relations and Public Affairs at Fudan University, Shanghai, China and is one of the most brilliant scholars in the field of transition and development studies all over the world. Between 2002 and 2004 she was a Doctoral Researcher in the School of Economy at Fudan University, and since 2002 she has held many research posts in China and Japan, including a Research Fellow in the Japan Research Center at Fudan University. Since the beginning of 2005 she has been cooperating with me to study issues on transition and development and, since 2006, she has been co-editing with me a book series, the Asian Finance and Development Series, for Ashgate Publishing.

Actually, the current series, entitled transition and development, started with the following awareness of the issues and aims in 2001. World society has suffered two weighty problems since the Second World War: the need for the convergence of east–west and north–south. From the 1970s, it seemed that the socialist countries suffered from inefficient economic systems and the per capita GDP disparity between capitalist and socialist became significant. The change from a centrally planned to a competitive system was the dramatic milestone that drastically accelerated reforms and development, not only for transition and developing countries but also for developed countries. However, scientific frameworks attempting to analyze these drastic changes have always seemed rather limited. The transition and development series looks to understand the global trend. It scientifically analyzes the characteristics of the drastic change in both the international system and the domestic structure from an interdisciplinary perspective, with a view to improving explanation and theories in social science.

In the light of the above awareness of the issues and aims of this series, China is surely an interesting subject to be investigated internationally and in an interdisciplinary way, particularly compared with European transition countries, examples of which are, (1) a gradual way of transition; (2) market socialism; (3) the logic and deficiency of the Mao Zedong development system; (4) comparative analyses with East Asian authoritarian development system; (5) the serious influence of US-centered globalization; (6) substantial disparities closely related with the reform and open door policy led by Deng Xiaoping; (7) relations between central and local government under the one-party system, etc.

We have been considering asking whether the above-stated issues should be analyzed by a particular analytical framework. Might neoclassical economics be an appropriate tool to analyze them correctly? Or might institutional analysis be better compared with neoclassical economics? Might international relations and a political economy approach be a better way?

At this academic and practical stage, on issues as regarding China, we should have a political economy approach that attaches great importance to institutional-related analysis as insisted by the author of this book. The author tries to apply such new interesting frameworks as constitutional economics, evolutionary economics, institutional economics and interaction theory, etc, to understand Chinese issues on transition and development.

For example, for economists classified as neoclassical, this book might be helpful to recognize which issues could be appropriately analyzed by neoclassical economics and which issues could not. For political scientists, this book could be interesting to understand how Chinese political issues might be correctly examined by focusing attention upon institutional aspects related to historical perspectives and a path dependence approach.

In addition to the above scientific aspects, needless to say, this book is suitable for readers who would like to have general knowledge and perspectives on the historical and the main contemporary points regarding China.

I hope this book is widely read and that it leads to a better understanding of the real and complicated situation in the transition and developmental process of China.

Ken Morita
Series Editor of Transition and Development
Professor, Faculty of Economics, Hiroshima University
Japan

Acknowledgment

This book was originally planned to be written jointly with Professor Ken Morita, the editor of this book series. Professor Morita kindly recommended that I write this book on my own and gave me helpful support to complete this work.

Professor Morita was one of my professors when I studied in Japan, and later he has been cooperating with me in studying transition and development. This book is a milestone in our cooperation

I would like to express my deep gratitude and to dedicate this book to Professor Ken Morita with hope for our successful future cooperation.

Yun Chen
Associate Professor, School of International Relations and Public Affairs
Fudan University, Shanghai
China

Introduction

Encounter with 'political economy' and a 'behaviorism' approach

At the beginning of the 1990s, institutional economics became more popular in China than neo-classical economics. In universities in China, they started to give lectures on macro-economics and micro-economics; most students, however, were not interested in such mainstream economics. I do not intend to reject the significance of neo-classical economics for the Chinese economy, as various economic theories need suitable timing for the spread of their particular knowledge and are closely related to the particular stage of transition and socio-economic circumstance in China.

When institutional economics became popular, many economic research centers in China displayed great interest in its approach, and started ambitious attempts to build a new economic theory from Chinese points of view. In the process, they were a bit too on 'worked up' over that approach in discussing a 'Washington consensus', a 'Post-Washington consensus', and a 'Beijing consensus'. I believe, as a younger scholar of the same research field, that a new economic theory and new economic model will be born in China in the future. However, the new theory and new model would be based upon the economic theories developed so far and would not be a completely different discipline. That is because Chinese reform and the open door policy have been a process to return to the 'normal'. It might be that the features are characteristic of China, but China will not be a particular case. Self-discipline requires Chinese scholars should be modest.

My special field as a graduate student was political science. It was 1992 when I entered graduate school this was the year when China was undergoing a great transformation. In Chinese universities in the 1980s and the beginning of 1990s, not only students in the humanities course but also students in the science courses were interested in various philosophies, such as existentialism by Jean-Paul Sartre. On any Chinese university campus, a special course on humanities was always overcrowded and many students attended, even standing outside the classroom and in the corridor. I could never forget the audience's enthusiasm.

This was especially so for students majoring in political science. I was interested in the development of the Chinese political system, but became bothered by two problems. First, China employed the gradual transition and authoritarian system after 1978, whose main goal was economic development. Only advocating the slogan 'democracy and freedom' had a quite limited influence, just like discharging shells without gunshot impacts. Could Chinese political science be theorized correctly in such ways? Second, in fields such as political science and economics, there existed many schools. Which school of thought has the better theory? Which school presents the better interpretation for the actual Chinese situation? It was necessary to spend some time before finding a basis to judge this.

I have reached two solutions after grappling with this problem. First, when we consider Chinese development issues during the transition period, the viewpoints of political economy were important. As argued in this book, a Chinese systemic transition under gradual reform was never led by ideology but was led by a way approved by facts. It means that, if preconditions are satisfied, reasonable results come into existence. As far as economic development is concerned, following the needs of the times, research about the systemic transition in China should be approached by asking which institutional reforms are necessary for sustainable economic development. Second, a behaviorism approach is necessary. In addition to the necessity of a positive approach for political economy, it seems to be necessary to incorporate a psychological approach. This is because, when we focus our attention upon political behavior or economic behavior, the agents are human beings. As far as agents are human beings, we could recognize something in common. Psychological investigations should, we think, also become the bases for the political economy approach. Briefly, everyone – a collective group, or a nation state – has the common aim to exist and develop, and has the need to be legitimate. However, what is the optimum measure for existence and development? According to the solution to this question, an appropriate institutional design varies from one to another. What we should emphasize here is that we should not judge human nature to be good or bad. Only demand that human beings can exist (as Abraham Maslow classified human demands into five stages). In order to meet the demand, human beings take actions. The results of the action could be evaluated to be good or bad from social points of view. How could such a difference in the results of the action appear? We think the difference comes from institutional design. It means that, when results are rather bad, to de-reform is not human nature but institutional. In China, in the Mao Zedong's era, many political movements towards the reform of human nature were carried out; however, they just showed that human nature could not be reformed. Meanwhile, the Chinese systemic transition after 1978 should be recognized as an institutional reform.

When I was a graduate student, based upon this way of thinking, I presented the economic politics approach and published two papers in a domestic academic journal, *Shanghai LiLun Neikan* (*Shanghai Theoretical Study of Political Science: Internal Publication*), in May 1995 and January 1996. In those days, because I recognized that my standpoint of research was political science, I called my field 'economic politics' by reversing the traditional way of saying political economy. In classical political economy, economics and politics were mutually intertwined and came together one after the other. Thus, it was meaningless to recognize which was the subject and which was the adjective. However, most scholars whose way of approach was political economy came originally form economics. My own starting point originally comes from political science, where the special field called 'economic politics' might show the appeal of its own existence and might indicate the desire to contribute something different from economists.

In July and August 2007, a meeting of the society for the study of methodology in political science of Duke University (USA) and Fudan University (China) was held in Shanghai (the first meeting was started in Renmin University of China in the summer of 2006). The aim of the meeting in Fudan University was to impart to young scholars in China the methodology of positive political science, as it had many positive research techniques in political science, such as statistics, sample research theory, game theory, ecological (cross-level) inference, qualitative analysis, *enquête* design, interview technique, case study, public choice theory, and so on. Scholars who took charge of the lectures were Chinese, living in countries and regions such as the USA, Taiwan and Hong Kong, from Professor Emerson M.S. Niou of Duke University on down (as volunteers). We think lectures given by scholars who have been involved in positive research for many years indicate one future course of political science in China and they looked something like the light appearing in a dark sky before dawn. Around 100 scholars participated from universities all over China and enthusiastically audited the lectures. We could easily understand that all the participants shared a common recognition about the future course of development of political science based on positive analysis. This meeting will be continued in the future.

There are various things which I would like to particularly emphasize. First, for a Chinese study of political science, it is surely important for us to reach times of positive analysis. Since the reform and open door policy began in 1978, Chinese society has become complicated due to various evolutions, and many materials and issues to be positively analyzed have emerged. We think that policy proposals according to positive analysis are necessary in order to correctly solve various social problems. Second, when China proceeded on the way to reform and the open door policy, the Chinese living in foreign countries gave helpful assistance at the very beginning, with foreign direct investments (FDI). Currently, around half of inward FDI still occurs from Chinese capital in foreign countries. Economic cooperation is, needless to say, important, and at the same time development of cooperation in the intellectual field should have greater importance. There are some characteristics of the projects led by Professor Niou *et al.* First, voluntary activities coming from a sense of mission and like-minded persons come together rapidly. That is the first good step towards the desired results. Second, Professor Niou *et al.* could become fine intermediaries between China and the external world because scholars who took charge of lectures were Chinese living abroad. Even in the field of academic research, differences of cultural background and accumulated knowledge might become barriers to effective interaction; however, Chinese living in foreign countries could understand these and could become good intermediaries of interaction between China and the external world. Third, regarding the environments that surround China, we have to list lots of tasks, such as what are called the 'Taiwanese problem' and the 'one-country, two-systems' problem of Hong Kong. In order to establish a 'Pan Chinese Community' regardless of its form, it is important for all possible members to join. Such a project, as mentioned above, could kill two birds with one stone. I would like to take this occasion to express my respect for all behaviorists. The meeting in Fudan University in 2007 went well with the behaviorism approach, which seemed to us a meaningful approach.

Some key words in this book: shared growth, East Asian model, and open system

The subtitle of this book is 'Towards shared growth', but there could be two alternative subtitles. The first is 'Could China become an example of the East Asian model?' Because I think that a key term, or essence, of the East Asian model, whose examples are Asian NIEs (newly industrializing economies), is shared growth, both of the above two keywords have the same meaning. The second alternative is 'From a closed system to open system. 'The initial point of the logic of the East Asian model is an 'extroversive' market-oriented economic system (open system). That is quite different from the Mao Zedong system of China before 1978 and Southeast Asian countries' model based upon an import substitution strategy. Explanations about the importance of shared growth and the East Asian model will be given in each chapter, especially in Chapters 5 and 6, and here I would like to emphasize the importance of an open system.

I think that the achievements of an open system in Deng Xiaoping's development system deserve greater attention. Due to the establishment of an open system, Chinese society was partly extricated from disorder. I expect that, provided an open system could be maintained, the Chinese way of gradual transition will proceed successfully. Why is an open system so important? It might be very thought-provoking to think about the second law of thermodynamics or the entropy law on the importance of open systems.

The entropy law was developed by Rudolf Clausius, a German physicist, in 1850, and it presented a very important concept about an open system. The essence of the law is as follows: in an isolated system in which heat and substance can not exchange, energy moves from a higher position to a lower one. As this irreversible process proceeds, energy is transformed to useless energy, which leads to a disordered system, and when entropy reaches a maximum value, the collapse of the system occurs.

According to the second law of thermodynamics (principle of entropy increase), in contrast to evolutionary theory, such theories as declining theory and collapse theory could be developed. The entropy law has been applied not only to natural science but also to social science. *The Entropy Law and the Economic Process* (Georcescu-Roegen, 1971) and *Entropy: A New World View* (Rifkin, 1980)[1] are

1 The Chinese version of Rifkin (1980) was translated by Lv Ming and Yuan Zhou and published from Shanghai Yiwen Chubanshe Publishing in 1987.

typical examples. In addition, the Club of Rome sounded an alarm bell with *The Limits to Growth* (Meadows *et al.*, 1972) which was caused by a similar idea.

The second law of thermodynamics could apply to any isolated system, from the evolution of life to the universe, and thus has philosophical considerations. For a living organic body, if the organic body exists in an isolated situation that has no exchange of energy with the external system, energy is wasted and entropy value increases until it reaches a maximum (meaning death). It is obvious that a living organic body is grown by energy exchange with an external system. The better the exchange of energy with the external world, the longer the life of a living organic body. Because human beings could exchange energy better with the eternal world (for example, the discovery of fire has been helpful in expanding the origin of energy), human beings could reach the peak of all creation.

Moreover, could the second law of thermodynamics be applied to society? An isolated social system could exhaust the available energy, and the utilized energy becomes less and less. Thus, society falls into disorder and decline. It can be concluded, therefore, that an open system is indispensable for sustainable development of the social system. Because the Qing dynasty before the Opium War failed to open the country (to foreign trade and diplomatic relations), China was inferior to Japan after the Meiji Restoration. Both giant empires, the Qing dynasty and Tsarist Russia, had isolated systems (imperial government) and lost the Sino-Japanese War and the Russo-Japanese War, one after the other, to Japan, which had a constitutional government (open system). We should not recognize that large countries (China and Russia) were defeated by a small country (Japan) but should recognize that an isolated system lost to an open system. Thus, the results of both wars were quite reasonable. Because of the defeat in war, the Qing dynasty finally promulgated the fundamental principles of the Imperial Constitution in 1908 and tried to push forward with establishing a constitutional monarchical system. However, it was too late. The Qing dynasty was too decayed to manage to survive against both internal and external pressures. The Qing dynasty collapsed with the Xinhai Revolution.

In addition, we could observe the entropy law between human society and the environment. As a smaller system is involved in a larger system, when the universe is considered as a biggest system, the earth is involved as a subsystem. In the earthly system, we recognize two systems, human society and the natural environment. Moreover, in the human society there are two systems, which are government and private. The government system is entrusted to exercise authority by the private system. The government should act in place of the private, and the actions of exercising authority should be always supervised and replaced through elections. Thus, a popular election system and competitive party system constitutes a mechanism to sustain constant energy exchanges between the government and private citizens. Then how does the government system formed by elections work? It goes without saying that there are three branches (the administrative, legislative, and judicial branches). Among the three branches, the principle of energy exchange should be established. In order to do this, principles of 'the separation of the three branches' and 'mutual restraint' are created. When we think of a nation state as a system, international society might be a group of systems. A good working mechanism of energy exchange among these systems needs a free trade system. In such ways, various systems involved in the universe overlap each other and every system exchanges energy with an external system to retain the ability to survive, like breathing of creatures. It continues eternally.

The entropy law and the theory of evolution might look like opposite theories, however it could be seen as a dialectical existence. There are well known phrases, such as the 'struggles for existence' and the 'survival of fittest', which are connected with the Darwin. The survival and development of human society is the result of the successful ability to adapt to the environment. In order to develop further, it is necessary to reform the structure by breaking down the traditional exclusiveness and by exchanging more with the outside world. At the same time, as symbolized by the Age of Sail, it is necessary to expand as much as possible towards the external world (meaning the development of the origins of energy).

Needless to say, there are various forms of energy in the entropy law. For example, information is a kind of energy.

Information has an important role to alleviate uncertainty (by which a system could keep the order). The concept of information entropy was devised by using the concept of entropy.[2] An increase of information entropy means, in other words, a lack of necessary information to eliminate uncertainty. The higher degree of systemic order indicates the greater amount of useful information (pointing out the minimum entropy). Conversely, a higher degree of systemic disorder expresses a higher value of entropy. A useful amount of information thus displays minus entropy.

We think that problems coming from a centrally planned system, whose characteristics are an isolated system, could be interpreted correctly with the entropy law. As regards a market-oriented system, because it is an open system it has caused two problems to disappear that could not be resolved by an isolated centrally planned system. The first is to have enough information to equilibrate demand and supply by price signals. The second is related to incentive. It is also closely connected with establishing private property rights, for an incentive is indispensable in allocating effectively human and material resources. Institutional design is necessary to realize conditions to make incentives work effectively, including such mobilized mechanisms of energy as securing equality of opportunity, removing equality of result, and giving opportunity for consolation etc. Such an establishment of private property rights indicates the structural reform of the system concerned. It works in a similar function to the evolution of the human body to adapt to the environment (see Chapters 2 and 3). In addition, the establishment of private property rights would proceed beyond economic development towards

2 Although the question about the link between thermodynamics and information entropy, which was originally devised by Claude Shannon in 1948, has been a hot topic of discussion, many scholars argue there is a link between the two.

structural reform of both the social system and political system (see Chapters 4 and 5).

The logic of the entropy law effectively works as mentioned in Chapter 6, entitled 'Political Economy of East Asian Authoritarian Development System'. In the East Asian NIEs, model countries and regions, structural reform gradually caused the countries and regions to adapt to the environment, and the results are symbolically expressed as 'authoritarianism is opposed by authoritarianism' phenomena (which is explained in Chapter 6). These economies succeeded in the peaceful systemic transition. Did China, after 1978, follow the same pattern as East Asian NIEs, countries and regions? That is the purpose of investigation in Chapter 6.

There have existed differences in development in such places as the Chinese continent, Hong Kong, Taiwan, and the Chinese network living in foreign countries, which is closely involved in Chinese transition and development. We think many people recognize negative relations among these because of serious tensions (like the incorporation of Hong Kong on July 1, 1997). However, mainly because there have been differences in development among them, an opportunity was triggered on the Chinese continent to transform the system, and also energy has been given to the Chinese continent to keep the reforms. The mechanism to use this energy is, we think, similar to the entropy law. It seems to be obvious that the Chinese network living in foreign countries and regions, including Hong Kong and Taiwan, is 'social capital' for Chinese development.

Characteristic nature of this book

All good novels look similar to fables. Scholarly research seems to be the same. The dynamic transition and development in China has given us various research materials. Then what kind of fables could we recognize in the research materials?

In this book, I focus attention upon two, which are (1) the collection and verification of materials and (2) the detection of fables entrusted in these materials. To be concrete, the characteristic nature of this book is summarized by the following two points.

The first is the collection and correct classification of positive data on social and economic problems. There is a lack of research regarding the Chinese economy, society and politics and also insufficient circulation of information and materials. Until the end of the 1990s, when I studied in Japan, the situation was basically unchanged. However, due to rapid improvement in IT technology, information resources and development projects (in cooperation with by private participants) such as an internet library have been established one after another. Movement towards the division of labor on collection and correct classification of information has been promoted. In addition, the government has taken actions. Currently, statistical bulletins at provincial and municipal level have been opened to the public through the internet (even though there are differences of speed among regions). When it does become available for us to have more detailed data and case studies, etc, on Chinese transition and development, I surely think we could make new discoveries. In that sense, we could expect the development of Chinese studies to depend crucially upon the substantial development of positive analysis. It would be more than the greatest honor for me if this book could contribute to this development in the correct way.

The second point is that whenever there are universal social and economic problems, we could recognize institutional problems behind them. Thus, it is pointed out, as the characteristic nature of this book, that we should clearly display the aspects of institutional problems and examine the ways for transformation. Needless to say, the accumulation of institutional reforms constitutes the procedure itself of systemic transition. In my own view, the present state of research in political science in China should be adjusted. Currently, idealists in the field of political science tend to be sticklers for principles and their sense of values and to get away from the real world. Conversely, realists of political science who wish to succeed in life become busy rationalizing the government's policy and plans. However, I think there could be a third way, and recommend being an 'idealistic realist'. The well-known scholar of contemporary China, Hu Shi, once advocated that we should assert principles as scarcely as possible, and should study problems as hard as possible. This wise remark of Hu Shi seems to indicate guidelines for current scholars in China.

I would like to mention once again that the Chinese way of gradual transition has been the 'fact-following' type not the 'ideology-led' type. The research itself could contribute to confirming the course of systemic transition in China because Chinese socio-economic problems have become more complicated day by day. I believe that the mission of Chinese scholars in transition and development studies is to master the staying power and studying power to deal with a dynamically changing environment.

Contents of this book and acknowledgments

One of the fundamental judgments of this book is that the implementation of the Chinese systemic transition has been complicated by such fields as politics, economics, internal affairs, foreign affairs, government, and markets. The book points out that various relations, such as politics and economics, internal affairs and foreign affairs, government and market, are in touch-and-go situations, like walking on a tightrope (as expressed in the phrase 'mortal enemies in the same boat'). If they lose their balance, they will fail to carry out the transitions successfully.

In Part 1 of this book (Chapters 1 to 3), I analyze the logic and dismantling procedure of a centrally planned system of 'fallacy composition' by focusing attention upon relations between government and markets, and also make a sketch of dramas of path dependence and anti-path dependence. In Part 2 (Chapters 4 to 6), we investigate the logic of the fact-following mechanism of institutional change of the Chinese systemic transition by attaching great importance to the various relations between the central and local, politics and economics, and internal affairs and foreign affairs.

Each chapter of this book has a long history. This book is the collective work of my researches at various stages. For example, in Chapters 1 and 2 some parts of my research when I studied in Japan are included. Both Chapters 5 and 6 were originally written after I got a position as a scholar in 2002, and were presented at symposia held in China. Chapter 6 was originally published in the proceedings of the annual meeting of the Shanghai Association of Political Science in 2005. These chapters however have been substantially revised. Chapters 3, 4 and 7 are newly written for this book.

In order to complete this newly-born single-authored book, intensive work on new writing and repeated revisions were continued for more than six months. Everyday when I sat in front of my computer both joy and sorrow started. When I show the readers this just-born baby, I feel both nervous and excited.

On the occasion of the publication of this book, I wish to express my respect for the following professors of Hiroshima University when I studied there, Professor Ken Morita (as specifically mentioned in my special acknowledgement, he is the editor of this series, gave me helpful suggestions about the detailed structure of this book and also helped me to make the English manuscript readable), Professor Tsuneichi Toda, the late Professor Makoto Murakami, Professor Shouichi Yamashita, Professor Shuichi Nakayama, Professor Kenji Kitagawa of Hiroshima Kokusai Gakuin University, and also Professor Wang Huning of Fudan University (he is now the Head of Central Policy Research Office of the Chinese Communist Party). The professors to whom I express my respect supported me as supervisors and advisers since I was an undergraduate student. Without their helpful support, I would never have become a successful scholar. I wish to express my gratitude to the school of International Relations and Public Affairs of Fudan University, which has given me the marvelous opportunity for academic work. I would like to express my gratitude for the financial support of the Humanities and Social Science Planning Project of Ministry of Education in China, 'Empirical Study on Economic Development Model in China (2008-2010)', the Philosophy and Social Science Priority Project of Ministry of Education in China, Study of Macro Policy on Energy Saving and Reduction of Pollution Discharge (2008-2010), and the Shanghai Planning Project in Philosophy and Social Science (2007-2009), Empirical Study on Regional Development and Income disparities (2007-2009). I am also deeply grateful to Ms Dymphna Evans and Ms Carolyn Court of Ashgate Publishing Ltd (UK) for their kindness in giving me the valuable opportunity to publish this book, with hope for our fruitful cooperation in the future.

I can never thank my parents enough for their devoted support for my study. Also, I have no words to express my gratitude to most of my friends for their warm and tender support.

When we open the first page of the Bible, we can find the phrase 'Let there be light'. For scholars, to find a meaningful problem explained is the same as the light appearing in the dark. The compiling procedure of this book for me is the procedure of asking what are the problems for transition and development in China. I strongly expect therefore that, after this book is published, I will receive many interesting and challenging problems from some readers. Last but not at least, I want to express my gratitude to every reader who reads this book for the use of their precious time.

PART 1
Political Economy of Transition in China: Comparing the Mao Zedong System and the Deng Xiaoping System

Chapter 1

The Logic of the Mao Zedong Development System and its Institutional Inefficiency

Introduction

China has experienced two different economic systems, before and after the reform and open door policy, since 1978. Before the reform and open door policy, the Chinese economy was under the central planning system and it changed to a market-oriented system after the policy. Those two systems have their own logic for existence and the transformation of the reason for their existence was due to the change in starting point. From 1978, China made a fundamental change in its foundations. Thus, we examine here what were the foundations and the logic for existence for the two economic systems, and why did the change occur in 1978? In Chapters 1 and Chapter 2 of this book I investigate the development performances before and after the reform and open door policy and focus my attention upon each initial condition, institution and policy.

The aim of this chapter is to analyze the Mao Zedong development system. First, I explain the analytical framework for economic development, and then examine the logic of Mao Zedong's Development System, and the actual development strategy and policy. Second, I investigate the characteristics of the Chinese economy in the centrally planned system from the viewpoint of Zheng She He Yi (i.e. the unification of economy and administration), and the closeness of the management system, and then I indicate the problems of lower efficiency, which were associated with Mao Zedong's development system, focusing our attention upon institutional inefficiency. Finally a short conclusion is given.

Analytical framework of economic development

Meanings of development

Hicks (1969) simply declared 'what the development was' insisting that it was a transformation from one circumstance to another. A more concrete way of showing, such a transformation can be classified into the following three aspects: (1) a transformation from a traditional economy to a market economy, which is an interesting issue in development economics; (2) a transformation from central planning to a market-oriented system, whose topic is analyzed in comparative economic systems; and (3) keeping with the dynamic tendency of the times, development from one type of market-oriented system toward another is necessary, a subject investigated in regional economics.

Three factors in development performance

When taking notice of development performance, three factors seem to be closely related with the performance. We can express the relations as,

Development performance = *f*(initial condition, institution, policy)

Koopmans and Montias (1971) formulated the relations in another way, whose model in comparative economic systems was expressed as o = *f*(s, p, e), where o indicates outcome and performance, and s, p, e denote institution, policy and environment respectively.

Myint (1964), Lal (1985), and Ishikawa (1990) also explained the difference in economic performance among the Third World Countries in the 1970s and 1980s through three factors: initial condition, institutions, and economic policy. The initial condition expressed by them was not only the development level in its initial stage, but also overall historical legacies from the past. North (1990) emphasized the path dependency in which present situations showed a tendency dependent upon past experience. Thus, it can be asked if each country and each region has promoted its economic development, by which factors and has been hindered by which factors. As regards China, Eckstein (1977) indicated the existence of a mismatch in that there could coexist radically changed ways and somewhere less changed ways. Both of these resulted from such deep-rooted systemic transformations as socialist reforms in China and other socialist countries.

Revolution is usually less revolutionary than observed superficially. Revolution is manifested by socially serious disorder. However, such a serious social disorder cannot be restored by revolution. On the contrary, serious social disorder might become more serious through revolution. Revolution might not be good medicine because society cannot be adjusted by a 'too radical change', as human beings cannot change so quickly. Inconsistency occurring by revolution can be lating until consistency finally comes about. In Chinese society after the revolution, such a social shock was expressed as a political movement. To the contrary, what is the normal situation with consistency? As the 'bucket' theory says, for buckets that are made of wooden boards, the shortest board decides the capacity of water for the bucket. The same expression seems to be appropriate here, that is to say the 'shortest board' in this sense refers to the subsistence of human beings in society, to whom important conditions consist of living circumstances, education level etc. These might be closely related to Marx's base structure.

Mao Zedong, the leader of the Chinese revolution, introduced the 'revolutionary path' in economic construction after the revolution, which should be interpreted with the concept of 'path dependency'. Although the author believes it would have been best for China if Sun Yat-sen had been the leader to build up the Chinese economy after Mao Zedong won the revolution, it wasn't to be. If path dependency is to explain things correctly, in order to change the path it is necessary to recognize the key ways for the society to change. As the Chinese transformation started in 1978, after 30 years of the Mao Zedong system, the Chinese leaders have employed not a revolutionary process but a gradual reform process, which automatically indicates that the reform takes many years to develop. It should be noted that the Chinese economy has shown remarkable performance, and I think the performance has been a result not of a traditional political and ideological struggle but of a struggle towards better economic construction.

What then are the key factors to change the path? I will investigate this question in Chapter 2.

Logics of a centrally planned economy

In China, after the establishment of a socialist regime, a regional development policy strongly led by centralized system was promoted. This meant the main tasks were, through the budget expenditure of central government, the alleviation of economic disparity among regions, reorganized industrial locations based on economic rationality (more efficient locations among production, material supply and markets), and industrial allocation focusing attention on military considerations. In order to carry out these tasks, a central planning system was built. Then in what way did the Chinese logic in a central planning economy evolve? I examine the issues in the following section (see Figure 1.1).

Foundation of the logic: priority given to military and security aspects

In order to recognize correctly the establishment of the central planning system, we need to correctly recognize the foundation of the logic.

Because a socialist regime could not cover the whole world, and because Sino–Soviet relations worsened at the end of the 1950s, the foundation of the logic for a central planning system in China gave priority to military security. One must be careful in thinking that the priority given to military security occurred because of the ideological conflicts between the east and west.

The funds for building large projects and technology imports at the beginning of the 1950s were obtained from a loan from the Soviet Union. The amount of the loan reached 7.4 billion ruble (around US$2 billion) for the First Five Year Plan period (1952–57). It had also a rather high interest rate and strict conditions requiring repayment within ten years. More serious for China was the interruption of the ruble loan, caused by the worsening of Sino–Soviet relations at the end of the 1950s. It resulted in China's policy of higher accumulation through agriculture and light industry in order to have the funds to implement an industrialization strategy for heavy industry and the chemical industry because foreign capital was not available. Mao Zedong (1977) expressed it at the time as the usual way of

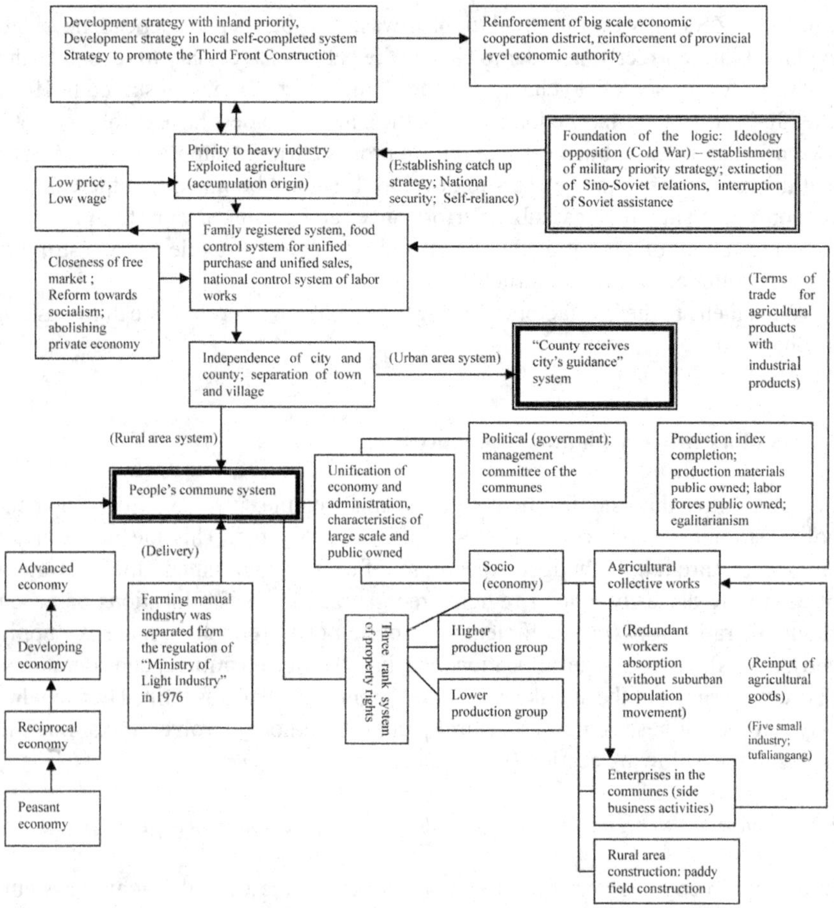

Source: Author.

Figure 1.1 Logic of central planning in China

socialist building, i.e. that the major part of the necessary funding for implementing progress in industrialization and agricultural technology was through accumulation in the agricultural sector.

It was a way of thinking of agriculture as the financial resource for what is called the 'socialist type primitive accumulation'. This policy planted the relations between urban and rural regions in China. That is to say, agriculture was situated as the accumulation resource for heavy industry, with which the three systems (family registered system; food control system for unified purchase and unified sales; national control system of labor works) were enforced.

Under such Cold War circumstances and aggravated Sino–Soviet relations, of the three strategies mentioned below, the priority strategy was allocated to heavy industry (the munitions industry).

Anxiety on their security and nationalist sentiment often caused adventurism among leaders and there occurred several adventurous plans and behaviors closely connected with gratuitous and irresponsible investments. In addition to the Third Front Construction (which will be explained later), in the Great Leap Forward it was advocated that within 15 years China could catch the UK in its crude steel production. Also in the Ten Years Plan of economic development in 1978, a goal was announced indicating that China would reach the level of advanced industrialized countries by the end of 20th century (which was criticized later as the Western Leap Forward).

Expansion of three development strategies

A development strategy is generally indicated as the measures and means to be employed for carrying out development. Strictly speaking, it has such institutions and policies as the basic system to allocate resources (market oriented or central planning), an enterprise system, a social security system, financial and monetary system, industrial policy and foreign policy.

A Chinese development strategy was implemented over 30 years, from 1949 to the end of the 1970s. The strategy was called the 'catch up' strategy and included building up military forces, mainly due to conflicts against the outside world. As regards development strategy, it was by and large classified into the following three areas: (1) development strategy with inland priority; (2) development strategy with heavy industry priority; and (3) development strategy to promote the Third Front Construction. These were recognized to be necessary for newly established Chinese security (see Figure 1.1).

Development strategy of equilibrating arrangement (inland priority)

We can easily reach a conclusion on the strategy, by comparing Table 1.1 with Table 1.2. The ratio of coastal areas in the basic construction investment decreased to 29.4% in the Third Five Year Plan from 44.1% in the First Five Year Plan. Afterwards it was increased to reach 50.3% in the Sixth Five Year Plan during the days of reform and the open door policy.

Meanwhile, a similar change occurred in the ratio of industrial distribution between coastal and inland areas. All of the indicators shown in Table 1.2 display a substantial decrease for coastal areas and a significant increase for inland areas. In particular, as regards industrial fixed assets and chemical fertilizer production, the increase for the inland areas was remarkable.

Assertions on development of inland areas occurred in the 1950s, connected with tasks to have a regional balance in industrial development. These assertions

Table 1.1 The ratio of coastal and inland area on the basic construction investment

Period	Coastal area (%)	Inland area (%)
The First Five Year Plan (1953-1958)	44.1	55.9
The Second Five Year Plan (1959-1962)	40.6	59.4
(1963-1965)	37.5	62.5
The Third Five Year Plan (1966-1970)	29.4	70.6
The Fourth Five Year Plan (1971-1975)	39.5	60.5
The Fifth Five Year Plan (1976-1980)	45.8	54.2
The Sixth Five Year Plan (1981-1985)	50.3	49.7
Average of (1953-1985)	43.7	56.3

Source: Yang WuCao Lei (1991), p.70.

Table 1.2 The ratio of industrial distribution between coastal and inland areas (%)

	Year	Coastal area	Inland area
Number of industrial enterprises	1952	50.3	49.7
	1983	45.9	54.1
Industrial fixed asset	1952	72.0	28.0
	1983	43.2	56.8
Number of employees	1952	60.5	39.5
	1983	46.9	53.1
Total industrial production	1952	69.4	30.6
	1983	59.5	40.5
Coal production	1952	44.0	56.0
	1983	26.3	73.7
Generation of electricity	1952	63.5	36.4
	1983	49.2	50.8
Chemical fertilizer production	1952	100	0
	1983	45.2	54.8
Machinery production	1952	75.9	24.1
	1983	62.8	37.2
Cotton yarn production	1952	82.0	18.0
	1983	57.9	42.1
Light industry production	1952	71.5	28.5
	1983	64.3	35.7

Source: Hamashita (1995) p.35.

were developed by strictly criticizing the unevenly distributed industrial production in traditional Chinese resource allocation, which showed concentration in coastal cities.

Those criticisms of coastal-centered industrialization were as follows:

1. criticism from the viewpoints of economic rationality insisting that the distant location of production facilities from the inland material production and consumption market increased production costs;
2. criticism insisting on a well-balanced development with less regional disparity, saying that the strategy kept extensive inland agricultural areas in economic backwardness;
3. criticism from military points of view, on whether coastal cities were vulnerable to military attacks and were easy to occupy.

Taking into consideration such criticisms, the following clauses were included in a development strategy on regionally balanced arrangements.

1. The advantageous position of large coastal cities intensively receiving heavy and light industry was adjusted.
2. The amount of investment into inland areas was increased to construct production bases in inland area.
3. A policy of closer geographical location of production, material supply and market should be implemented.
4. The arrangement of industrial bases was given priority.
5. The expansion of energy production, mainly hydroelectric power generation, was planned.

The above-mentioned principles, compared with the concrete policies of the First Five Year Plan, showed that industrial development in such coastal cities as Shanghai, Liaoyuan had priority. There were lots of opinions that insisted on utilizing and reinforcing industrial bases already established in coastal areas (Zhu Rongji, 1955). In the Ten Important Relations by Mao Zedong (1977), which was originally announced in 1956 (the well-known speech delivered at the Extension Meeting of the Central Political Bureau of the Chinese Communist Party), as far as the second relationship between coastal industry and inland industry was concerned, Mao Zedong attached greater importance upon inland development towards balanced development, and he even indicated the development of coastal industry, which should assist inland industry. As regards steel production, industrial bases such as the northeast industrial bases, centered on Anshan, Liaoning province (i.e. Fushun coal mine, Yalujiang power station, Fenman power station, and construction of heavy industry production bases in such areas as Dalian, Jilin, Harbin, Qiqihaer, and Shenyang), the reform of industrial production in coastal areas such as Shanghai, Jiangsu, Shandong etc, Central China's industrial bases centered on Wuhan, and northern China's industrial bases, mainly in Baotou, were promoted and newly built.

After 1958 when the Second Five Year Plan started, several big projects were scheduled to be constructed.

1. In the regions of the southwest and northwest, industrial bases were constructed based upon iron ore production and hydroelectric power generation.
2. In Xinjiang, development of oil and metal resources was implemented.
3. In the northeast region, the Daqing oil field was developed.
4. The Panzhihua steel production base in southwest region was constructed.
5. Large-scale coal production bases were developed in Shanxi and Inner Mongolia.
6. Large- and medium-scale hydroelectric power generation plants were constructed upstream of the Yangtze River and Yellow River.

However, such cautious inland development plans contained in the First Five Year Plan were radically changed in the middle of 1958. Development plans to attach greater importance to military security, such as 'prior strategy for inland area', 'development strategy centered in heavy industry within closed local area', 'development strategy to advance the Third Front' etc, were successively scheduled.

After that, the weight of regional development was shifted toward the inland areas. We will have a short look at them considering the urbanization plans in coastal and inland areas as examples.

While inland areas were developed with priority, no urban construction was implemented for ten years from 1966, as shown in Table 1.3, in the vast space of the coastal area, including provinces and districts eastwards from the Jingguang Railway. Existing coastal industrial cities did not receive investment from government expenditure, in which existing facilities and equipment were used without enough maintenance. They soon became outdated, and environments of everyday life in the urban area worsened. These serious circumstances and the necessities to resolve them were important factors for the reform and open door policy, particularly for a development strategy that was the sole direction in the 1990s; this will be analyzed in Chapter 2.

Development strategy centered on heavy industry within closed local areas

The strategy was to establish an autonomous industrial production system for each region, which prospered after Mao Zedong had a tour of inspection to Tianjin in August 1958. He emphasized that each region should construct its own autonomous industrial system in an appropriate way, first in cooperating districts

Table 1.3 Amount of city construction in each period of Chinese provinces and autonomous districts (1947-86)

Area	Province	1947	1949-1952	1953-1957	1958-1965	1966-1977	1978-1986	Total
Coastal	Liaoning, Hebei and Shandong	20	3	2	5		28	58
	Jiangsu and Zhejiang	4	15				10	29
	Fujian, Guangdong and Guangxi	8	12		3		16	39
	Subtotal	32	30	2	8		54	126
Central	Jilin and Heilongjiang	9	2	3	4	2	10	30
	Shanxi, Shanxi, Henan and Anhui	11	18	7	3	1	12	52
	Jiangxi, Hebei and Hunan	4	18		5	1	26	54
	Sichuan, Yunnan and Guizhou	5	8		4	3	16	36
	Subtotal	29	46	10	16	7	64	172
Western	Inner Mongolia	2	2	1	1	1	9	16
	Gansu, Qinghai, Ningxia and Xinjiang	4	4		5	2	19	34
	Tibet				1		1	2
	Subtotal	6	1	1	7	3	29	52
Total		67	13	13	31	10	147	350

Note: City construction period in this table was depending upon the time to become effective of municipal organization, and if the municipal organization was cancelled by returned again later, the period was included as those days concerned.

Source: Japan-China Geography Association (ed.) (1992), p. 23.

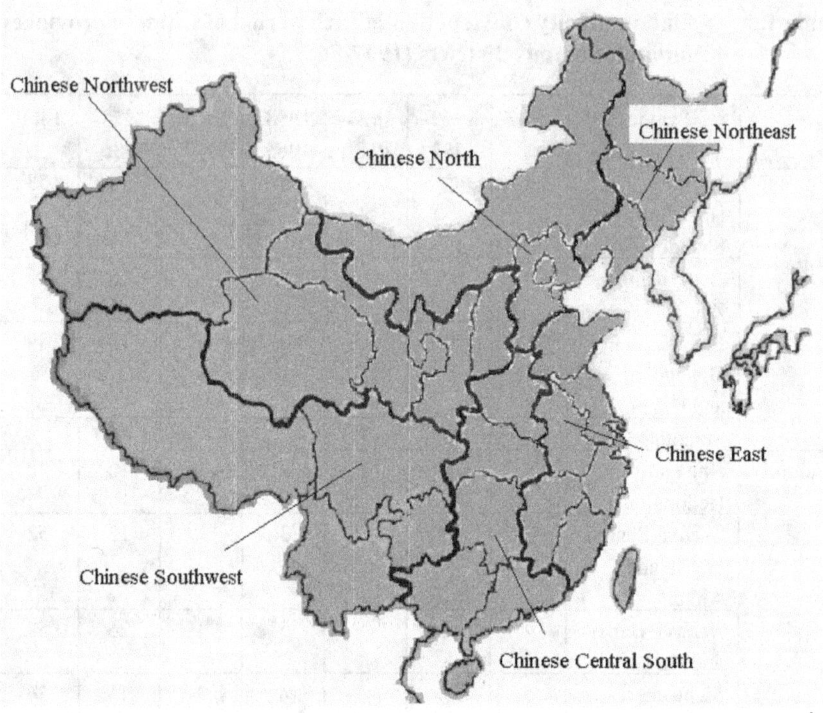

Source: Author.

Figure 1.2 Six big scale economic cooperation districts

and later in many provinces.[1] Based upon the Mao Zedong's comment, a 'large scale economic cooperation district' was designed as such a regional organization unit. Through the 1960s (but starting in 1958), the Chinese central government established a long-term plan with an economic development goal for each region. By considering regional economic areas with a population of 70 million to 100 million people, six or seven large-scale economic cooperation areas were established: the Chinese north, northeast, Chinese east, Chinese central, Chinese south, southwest and northwest. Later, in 1961, the Chinese central and Chinese south areas were unified as the central south area, which led finally to six large economic cooperation areas, as shown in Figure 1.2; i.e. Chinese north, northeast, Chinese east, central south, southwest and northwest. Assuming a large-scale war against foreign enemies, their plan to develop inland areas, allocating military

1 Japan Institute of International Affairs (1974), which had 'The Comments of Mao Zedong concerning the establishment of an independent industrial system located in the local area'.

industry with security considerations, was to let the regions have production systems independent of other regions.

Table 1.4 shows that the ratio of investment in heavy industry to the total investment was more than 45%, except for the First Five Year Plan period, which was higher than in the Soviet Union (the Soviet ratio was less than 40% even in the last of the socialist days). Meanwhile, the ratio of investment in light industry stayed at around 6%. From 1952 to 1978, total investment amount of heavy industry reached 350 billion yuan, however light industry received only 32 billion yuan. In addition, as regards the labor force allocation, the ratio of heavy industry increased to 61% in 1976 from 29.9% in 1952 (and 80.4% in 1958); meanwhile, light industry decreased to 44.2% in 1976 from 64.5% in 1952.

In each large-scale economic cooperation district, a Central Bureau, Big District Economic Committee, and Planning Committee were established to adjust economic cooperation between the interior economic construction and exterior economic construction.

As regards large-scale economic cooperation districts, they had the following problems and results.

(1) Lack of investigations on designated areas Detailed and objective investigations and analyses on large scale economic cooperation districts were not enough. They include the natural environment (like geographical features and climate), regional characteristics (like peoples' everyday lives), resource endowment, accumulative circumstances on industrial production and technology, transportation, and economic influence of the main cities in the district, etc. Thus, in their choice of ways and methods for development for each district, sometimes they were neither appropriate nor unrealistic. In addition, because planning years to attain the goal were too short and the planning goal to be attained was too high, it was very difficult to achieve the goals.

Table 1.4 Ratio of investment in the industrial sector to the total investment (whole industries = 100)

Period	First Five Year Plan (1953-1958)	Second Five Year Plan (1959-1962)	1963-1965	Third Five Year Plan (1966-1970)	Fourth Five Year Plan (1971-1975)	Fifth Five Year Plan (1976-1980)	1953-1978
Light industry	6.4	6.4	3.9	4.4	5.8	6.7	6
Heavy industry	36.1	54.0	45.9	51.1	49.6	45.9	51

Source: Peng Min (ed.) (1989).

(2) Discord on budget expenditure between central and local government A highly centralized system of budget expenditure enabled the central government to promote construction projects planned through a huge amount of budget expenditure. From the beginning of the foundation of China until the end of the 1970s, the Chinese budget system was divided into control by central and local government, in the official sense; however, actually the budget was not only concentrated in central government, but also the range and usage of the local budget was regulated by central government. The local budget was therefore only an implementation section and they had no independent authority over budget expenditure. As for the amount, the budget income and expenditure for local government was not small, but local government did not have any authority over the finance at all. Local government was very cautious about central government's regulation of the actual expenditure and funds were spent as central government designated, except for a very small portion which was the autonomous expenditure.

Thus, two attempts at systemic reforms for decentralization on the authority of the budget and economic control were implemented, in 1958 and at the end of the 1960s and at the beginning of the 1970s, in order for local government and enterprises to have more initiative, and for economic cooperation districts to be reinforced. More practically, central government transferred some directly controlled enterprises to local governments, and the local governments' decision-making power in some basic construction projects was also expanded. Furthermore, central government partly transferred their authority over planning control, budget control, material control and work force control etc.

The above-stated measures were designed for more regional cooperation, for more active regional performance, and so on. The actual results were as follows.

1. Those two attempts of systemic reforms contributed neither to transforming traditional centrally planning system nor to developing large-scale economic cooperation districts. From lessons that suggested further research on natural resources, resource endowments, etc, was necessary, they could recognize circumstances and conditions required for development of the regional economy (for example, southwest planning committee carried out research in cooperation with the Chinese Scientific Organization, several Cabinet committees in China, and many scientists; the Chinese north planning committee also had small scale research). Nevertheless, at the end of the 1960s, productive facilities in the six large-scale economic cooperation districts stopped working, accompanied by the abolition of the districts' organization for decision making.

After all, the purpose of creating a large-scale district was to establish a cooperative district across administrative districts, and such a wider organization could not work as was planned. It was due to the tough hurdle of administrative division, which was deeply rooted in the central planning system. Decentralization attempts – from central to local – were implemented several times; however, because the hurdle of central planning system could not be overcome, the policy for large-scale economic cooperation districts resulted in failure after rather quickly, from 1958 to the end of 1960s.

The political plan for creating economic cooperation districts had another attempt after the reform and open door policy led by Deng Xiaoping. Another attempt had been carried out in different circumstances as the economic system was transformed.

2. The two attempts of systemic reforms partly played a role in strengthening administrative economic districts at the provincial level. After the People's Republic of China began, the administrative districts frequently changed. First, at the end of 1949, the whole nation was united with 50 administrative districts at the provincial level, i.e. 30 provinces, one autonomous region, 12 municipalities directly under central government control, five *Xingshu* (which controlled several counties, and was not a tier government but a dispatch agency of province, it was quite similar to *Dijishi*) administrative districts, one local area (Tibet Difang), and one *Difang* (which was the administrative control system, implemented in Tibet, at the special period of establishment of New China) one *Diqu* (which indicated the administrative control system, implemented in *Changdu*, at the special period of establishment of New China). Afterward, in 1959, they were rearranged to make 29 administrative districts at provincial level, i.e. 22 provinces, four autonomous regions, two municipalities directly under the central government control, and one arrangements committee. In 1967, they were changed again to be 30 administrative districts at the provincial level, with 22 provinces, five autonomous regions and three municipalities directly under the central government. From then until the end of 1987, deep-rooted changes were carried out in county level administrative districts, totaling 2826, but the administrative districts at the provincial level were kept unchanged at 30. In April 1988, the Preliminary Conference of the Seventh National Parliament decided to establish Hainan province, which is the 23rd province and so makes 31 administrative districts at the provincial level (23 provinces, five autonomous regions, three municipalities directly under the central government).

Since 1959, the number of administrative districts at the provincial level has been in the vicinity of 30. Two attempts at systemic transformation (decentralization to the local governments) occurred, in 1958 and from the end of the 1960s to the 1970s, which contributed to each province forming a provincial regional economy as a fundamental unit for the national planning system and for national economic regulation.

In addition to the above, due to China's new development strategy, the authority of the administrative districts at provincial level has been strengthened, as explained below.

Development strategy to promote the Third Front

In the Third Five Year Plan (1966–1970) and the Fourth Five Year Plan (1971–1975), based upon the strategic thinking by Mao Zedong, which was to be prepared for a possible World War (against the USA and the then USSR), great importance was placed on industry building on the Third Front of the interior areas: this was called Third Front Construction.

Geographical position of the Third Front

Although the Third Front was not specifically located, taking into consideration the circumstances on project location and investment scale, we can speculate that the Third Front covered almost all the areas in six provinces and one autonomous region (Sichuang, Guizhou, Yunnan, Shanxi, Gansu, Qinghai, Ningxia) and the western areas of four provinces (Shanxi, Henan, Hubei, Hunan).

The Third Front indicated that the First Front was the front during the War, i.e. the coastal area and the boarder area, and the Second Front was between the First and the Third Fronts. After the period of the Fourth Five Year Plan, the region of the Third Front was expanded slightly. According to the explanation of the 1971 National Planning Committee, the ten provinces and one autonomous region, the northern part of Guangdong province, the northwestern part of Guangxi autonomous region, and the western part of Hebei province were included, but the Ningxia autonomous region was excluded. The Third Front therefore covered the huge interior area south of the Great Wall, north of Shaoguan, west of Jingguang-Railroad, and east of Gansu and Wushao Peak (Wang Chuncai, 1991). However, after 1972, no new construction projects were implemented as part of Third Front Construction for the expanded area.

Policy tasks of the Third Front Construction

The main policy task for the Third Front Construction was to promote a military–industrial system and to establish the major strategy. There were two policy measures to achieve the aims. First, priority investments were given to the Third Front area, especially to the southwest and northwest regions of the inland area. The ratio of basic construction investment occupied by the Third Front area to the national total increased after 1963, and reached its peak at the end of the 1960s and the beginning of the 1970s, but after then gradually decreased. In addition, as well as new investment in the inland area, large-scale transfers from coastal industrial cities of existing equipment, R&D system, engineers and skilled labor, were carried out. For example, from 1964 to 1971, the number of engineers and skilled labor transferred from the coastal area to the inland area was 145,000, and the number of items of equipment reached 38,000.

As a result of implementation of the Third Front Construction, the Third Front area – especially the southwest area – was established as a heavy industry and military industry base, which included steel, machinery, energy, electronics, aviation, and space rockets. However, because almost all enterprises that took responsibility for the above industries were state-owned, after the beginning of 1980s, the traditional Third Front area suffered from the move towards market-oriented reform.

The Third Front Construction and strengthened position of provinces

The reasons why, during the Third Front Construction period, the actual position of provinces was strengthened are explained below.

(1) Implementing system They say that, on February 1965, to implement the Third Front construction, the Centre of Chinese Communist Party and Chinese Cabinet decided to establish the southwest construction committee, and each management section in the respective projects. It was thus said that a management system to construct the Third Front was founded, which consisted of the three levels; centre, southwest construction committee, and management section. The actual membership of the 'Third Front Construction Committee', located in Chengdu, was composed of executive members of Central ministries and committees, the southwest division of the communist party, and executive leaders of each province of Sichuang, Guizhou, Yunnan.

Meanwhile, in each provincial government and each provincial committee of the communist party, the directing group for supporting Third Front construction was founded. For example, in the Guizhou provincial government and provincial committee of the communist party, the provincial directing section for Third Front construction and the provincial party group for Third Front construction were established, respectively.

The Ministry of Material Control, which was founded in 1964, established a 'general directing section for providing materials' in such areas as the southwest, northwest and south central, under whose control a local bureau for materials was built near to the location of important projects, independent of the administrative district. In the southwest area, the local bureau was built in ten places, such as Chongqing, Chengdu, Zigong, Dukou, Guiyang, Liupanshui. In the northwest area there were seven and also seven bureaus were established in the south center area (Zhou Taihe, 1984).

The characteristics of the implementing system were that, first, there was a breaking down of traditional divisions in administration (which was separated vertically and horizontally into divisions); second, there was the build up of organizations that were covering intersections and inter-local governments, which led to close cooperation among the actors concerned and quicker construction. However, such a new system did not work. Because of the traditional central planning system, which had vertically and horizontally separated divisions, and the influence of Cultural Revolution, the southwest construction committee collapsed a few years after its establishment. Also, the local bureau for materials either broke down or was united with traditional material bureaus, almost all of which disappeared (*Dangdai Zhongguo Jihua Gongzuo Bangongshi* (Bureau of Contemporary Chinese Planning Policy), 1987, p. 261).

Even though the implementing system for Third Front construction collapsed, it was continued during the Cultural Revolution. Eventually, all such implementing systems were returned to the traditionally divided system, in which central ministries and committees are vertically divided and provincial level local governments are horizontally divided.

(2) Minor Third Front Construction In May 1965, Mao Zedong appealed the necessities of constructing the Minor Third Front in each province in which the First and Second Fronts were built. Minor Third Front constructions were carried out within each province and neighboring mountain areas, almost simultaneously with (Major) Third Front construction led by central government. As those regions were located in topographically complex areas with inconvenient transportation, everyday living conditions were quite hard. The regions included, for example, Laifu region in Shandong province, Nanping–Sanming–Zhangzhou line in Fujian province, Liaoxi mountain area in Liaoning province, northern part of Taihang Mountains in Hebei province. Details of Minor Third Front construction were adjusted as follows. The first plan, of 1964, was to construct small scale military industry. This was adjusted to establish the self-completed industrial structure based upon steel production base in each province after Mao Zedong's insistence in September 1965 saying that he wanted to have a small scale iron works for each province and the Minor Third Front needed iron works (*Dangdai Zhongguo Jihua Gongzuo Bangongshi* (Bureau of Contemporary Chinese Planning Policy), 1987, p. 233). The plan was adjusted toward forming self-completed industrial structures based upon a steel production base in each province. Such a plan clearly reflected the way of thinking that each local area had to prepare to fight a foreign enemy without help from central government (*Dangdai Zhongguo Jihua Gongzuo Bangongshi* (Bureau of Contemporary Chinese Planning Policy), 1987, p. 234).

In accordance with these new instructions, in June 1966 the National Planning Committee established a plan that, during the Third Five Year Plan, they would construct 101 small-scale iron works. These small scale iron works were located so as not only to support military industry in each province but also to be a part of the local 'five small industries' (i.e. small iron works, small coal mines, small power plants, small machine factories, and small chemical fertilizer factories) to support mechanization in rural areas.

The Minor Third Front construction plan was founded in 1965 and operated for three years, until 1967, and altogether 700 projects were completed. Thirty percent of total investment was absorbed by military industry, the rest included projects in such sectors as steel, machinery, coal, electric power, and transportation. This plan was only 70% completed as of the end of 1967, influenced as it was by the Cultural Revolution, and the final completion was postponed until after 1969. In 1980, conventional weapons factories, completed by Minor Third Front construction, totaled 268, whose total number of workers was 280,000 and whose accumulated investment amount reached 3.2 billion yuan (*Dangdai Zhongguo Jihua Gongzuo Bangongshi* (Bureau of Contemporary Chinese Planning Policy), 1987, p. 265 and pp. 271–272).

Actual construction for the Minor Third Front was mainly carried out in provinces located in The First Front area. In the Chinese north and Chinese east areas, which are the hearts of China, the 'Chinese North Minor Third Front' (Shanxi province), and 'Chinese East Minor Third Front' (Jiangxi province) etc, were constructed.

The Minor Third Front construction case, which was concerned with Shanghai, is analyzed Chapter 6 and it showed horizontally divided characteristics closely related to the central planning system. To investigate the details of the characteristics, it is best to analyze the system in which a county receives a city's guidance as implemented in this period (see later in this chapter).

(3) Establishment of three institutions The three institutions were established to carry out the above-mentioned three strategies from the 1950s to the 1970s. The three institutions meant (1) a family registered system, (2) a food control system for unified purchase and unified sales, and (3) a national control system of labor works (see Figure 1.1).

In the international relations of the 1950s, China was undoubtedly confronted with the Cold War. Entering the Korean War in 1950 led China to decisive opposition to the USA. When China faced the economic blockade by the United Nations, in order to employ a policy for enhancing wealth and military strength, it introduced the Soviet-type heavy industrialization strategy. Actually, as China fully depended upon its rural economy (the rural population occupied 83% of the whole country, and there were huge number of redundant workers because of the lack of arable land), the central government separated the rural population from the urban population and allocated limited resources into capital intensive industries, particularly heavy industry, in urban area.

Many peasants moved to the urban area to establish new industrial cities in inland areas. In particular, in the period of the Great Leap Forward, strengthening of heavy industry was encouraged as before, and both the reform and expansion of large-scale cities were carried out in succession, disregarding financial ability. For three years, from 1957 to 1960, 44 cities were newly established. The increased population in urban areas reached 48.7 million for three years. However, owing to the wrong collective policy in rural areas and serious natural disasters, a food shortage occurred. In addition, in urban areas, such problems as deterioration of the living environment and serious unemployment happened consecutively. The people's commune started in 1958, and its aims were to resolve those serious social, economic and political problems. However, it was effective in restricting peasants' mobility. A family registered system began in the 1950s and was strengthened in the 1960s (Zhou Taihe, 1984). In the adjustment period after the Great Leap

Forward finished and at the period of Cultural Revolution, the separation policy of the urban from the rural was sustained as before.

The Chinese government made peasants stay in rural areas through (1) a family registering system; (2) a food control system for unified purchase and unified sales; and (3) a national control system of labor works, whose purpose was to secure food provision from rural to urban areas, and to establish food security at a time of war and natural disaster. Through such a separation policy of the urban and rural, a rural area was located as a base for heavy industry. Meanwhile, government expenditure was concentrated on heavy industry and investment in the agricultural sector was quite limited, which led to the serious difficulty of producing enough agricultural products. These were the reasons why Mao Zedong advocated productive evolution by self-reliance and collective labor (mass mobilization).

Emphasizing self-reliance was a natural assertion because financial support was impossible. Collective labor progressed from the initial stage, primitive stage and advanced stage, which reached the People's commune system with *Zheng She He Yi* (meaning the unification of economy and administration) and *Yi Da Er Gong* (indicating both characteristics of large scale and public owned).

As long as they had a family registering system in urban areas, it meant that they enjoyed an advantageous situation, such as a basic income level and social security. That is to say, such benefits as housing, food, education, health care were provided by the place of work of state-owned enterprises, people's owned enterprises, etc, as functions of the central planning system. Besides, food rationing and company regulations were effective for separation of the urban from the rural. Because agricultural products were collectively bought, sold and managed by the government, without urban family registration they could not receive food. In addition, jobs in urban areas were allocated by the designation of government. Thus, peasants could not move away from the rural area, and were therefore different from urban citizens who liked to have the government looking after them.

Due to the three institutions, the most basic disparity in China between the urban and rural sectors was firmly established, and peasants suffered inequality in opportunity through birth. In other words, the disparity in this period, typically shown as the difference between urban and rural systems, was systemically and firmly created.

City policy: development of genealogy 'county receives city's guidance'

Change of city policy

We think it is necessary to look back upon the then municipal policy in order to understand correctly the 'county receives city's guidance' system.

After Communist China was founded, the first regulation upon the cities was framed in November 1955, by the local government cabinet, which was the decision on the criteria to use when dividing the area into urban and rural locales. According to the regulation, a city was (1) an area that had more than 1000 permanent residents and in which more than 50% residents were non-agricultural population, and (2) as for an area whose permanent residents totaled between 1000 to 2000, it had to have more than 75% non-agricultural population.

Then, in 1958 and 1959, the Great Leap Forward was employed, and the population that moved from rural to urban areas equaled around 20 million. In Shanghai, for example, from 1957 to 1959, the net increase in population reached 284,000 (*Shanghai Statistical Bulletin*, 1989, p. 103). It could be recognized that, in this period, the remarkable expansion of the suburban area of Shanghai and the establishment of suburban industrial districts in Wusong and Minhang was closely connected with the Great Leap Forward.

Meanwhile, from 1959 to 1961, a serious poor harvest occurred and the inflow of workers from the rural areas could not be absorbed into urban areas, so measures to return to their villages farming people who moved in urban areas after 1957 were carried out in 1961. In addition to the above, in December 1963, the Chinese Central Communist Party and Chinese Cabinet promulgated instructions to adjust municipal and township organization criterion and to downsize the suburban districts. In the 1963 instruction, the policy was established which said that township organization was to be more strictly regulated, and the area that had the criteria of a municipal administration district was radically reduced. As regards the township organization criterion, it said that (1) population was more than 3000 and non-agricultural population occupied more than 70%, and (2) in an area with a population of 2500–3000, the non-agricultural population should be more than 80%. As far as the criterion to reduce suburban districts was concerned, it indicated that (1) all those districts whose farming population was more than 20% were incorporated into the farming administrative district, and (2) even within the area of a municipal administrative district, the population working for agriculture was counted as farming population.

In the light of the above regulation, Shengsi People's Commune, which was once incorporated into Shanghai, was returned again to Zhejiang province, and both suburban industrial districts of Wusong and Minhang were abolished in May 1964. The changes (we think) were caused by the 1964 regulation and the Chinese national circumstances in that period.

Table 1.5 points out the above mentioned change of the municipal policy. In the system of 'county receives city's guidance', the ratio of non-agricultural population to the total urban population was 93% in 1957, which was rapidly reduced to be 66% in 1960, and after that it fluctuated. Since 1983, it decreased to be at around 50%, and reached 46.05% in 1989. This seemed to occur by the wider implementation of the system of 'county receives city's guidance'.

Table 1.5 The ratio of non agricultural population to the total urban population in the system of 'county receives city's guidance' (10 thousand, %)

	National total population (A)	Urban population (B)	Non agricultural population (C)	Ratio of urban population (%, B/A)	Ratio of non agricultural population (%, C/A)	Ratio of non agricultural population to the total urban population (%, C/B)
1957	64653	6798	6322	10.51	9.78	93
1960	66207	11899	7853	17.97	11.86	66
1965	72538	8916	6751	12.29	9.31	75.72
1970	82992	9398	6663	11.32	8.03	70.9
1975	92402	10655	7402	11.53	8.01	69.47
1978	96259	11402	7898	11.85	8.2	69.27
1979	97542	12323	8538	12.63	8.75	69.29
1980	98705	13359	9022	13.53	9.14	67.53
1981	100072	13882	9378	13.87	9.37	67.56
1982	101541	14351	9632	14.13	9.49	67.12
1983	102495	17167	10278	16.75	10.03	59.87
1984	103475	19116	11013	18.47	10.64	57.61
1985	104532	21197	11825	20.28	11.31	55.79
1986	105721	23315	12258	22.05	11.59	52.58
1989	111191	31762	14626	28.57	13.15	46.05

Source: *Chinese Municipal Guidance* until 1986, and *Chinese Urban Statistical Bulletin 1990* as regards 1989, Kaneko (1995), p.160.

The details of the system of 'county receives city's guidance'

In China, they recognize that a 'city' is a region based on industry, and a 'county' on agriculture. Key indices to classify city and county are (1) non-agricultural population and (2) non-agricultural production.

The system saying 'county receives city's guidance' started in 1920s when they established a municipal system. When Hanyang county received Hankou city's guidance in 1926 this was the first case.

Just after the People's Republic of China was founded, the system of 'county receives city's guidance' was the situation of Zishengzimie (which points out the situation of informally occurring and informally disappearing). According to 'a history of administrative district higher level than county of the People's Republic of China', such cities as Wuxi (guided Wuxi county), Xuzhou (guided Tongshan county), and Lanzhou (guided Gaolan county) carried out this system at the end of 1949. After that, cities such as Beijing, Tianjin, Lvda (Dalian), Benxi, Hangzhou,

Chongqing, Guiyang, Kunming implemented the system. Since the founding of the nation, under the separation policy of urban from rural, the distribution of materials and products was cut off in many places. This aim of implementing the system was to secure provisions of vegetables and side dishes etc for urban citizens, but only big cities – like parts of the direct controlled municipalities, the capital cities of provinces and other big cities – carried out this system. In those days, usually one suburban county was guided by one big city, and Lvda which guided two counties was an exception. As of the end of 1957, in the whole of China, only three cities guided four counties, and one city was at county level.

With such movements as the Great Leap Forward, the communes, in order to construct heavy industry and inland industrialization, implemented areas of the 'county receives city's guidance' system. Table 1.6 illustrates the expansion process.

The 'Decision on a system of direct controlled municipalities and rather big cities' guidance for counties and autonomous counties' was adopted by the executive committee of the Chinese Parliament on September 17, 1959, and announced as follows;

> Our project to construct a socialist state has been rapidly developed. Particularly since the year before under the circumstances of a great leap of production in agriculture and industry, and the communes in rural areas, we have attempted to have close links between the urban and rural, with promotion of reciprocal support between agriculture and industry, to secure laborers etc. In order to support such attempts we have decided a system of direct controlled municipalities and rather big cities' guidance for counties and autonomous counties.

This was the initial attempt to legally establish the system, which became much more popular in China afterwards.

Meanwhile, as a city policy, Mao Zedong's slogan about moving from a consumption city to production city was advocated. It was a policy to sustain low wage rates and low price levels in urban areas through purchasing agricultural products in the 'Schere' (disadvantageous terms of trade for agricultural products compared with industrial products). Table 1.7 shows that the amount of disparity between agricultural products and industrial products was 7.4 billion yuan in 1952, 12.7 billion yuan in 1957, and 36.4 billion yuan in 1978, which was the peak year of the disparity. After that the amount decreased to be 28.8 billion in 1982, and 28.6 billion in 1985. At the same time, to establish a principle of 'separation of cities from counties, and separation of townships from villages', three systems were strictly constructed. They were (1) a family registration system, (2) a unified purchase and unified sale system, and (3) a working system. In implementing those systems, in what is called the socialist reform movement from 1949 to 1952, privately owned enterprises were abolished and the free markets for foodstuffs and merchandised commodities were removed.

Table 1.6 Expansion process of the 'county receives city's guidance' system

	Number of city to guide counties	Number of county guided by city					Number of city in county level guided by city
		Total	County	Autonomous county	Qi(*)	Others	
1949	3	3	3				1
1957	3	4	4				2
1958	29	120	118	2			2
1959	37	134	132	2			6
1960	48	234	228	4	2		
1961	39	132	127	3	2		
1961	35	127	123	2	2		
1963	28	111	109	2			
1965	25	79	78	1			
1970	27	85	82	1	2		
1977	42	133	130	1	2		
1982	58	171	165	1	2	3	
1983	126	534	517	5	9	3	8
1984	127	568	549	7	9	3	9
1985	146	658	631	15	9	3	20
1986	151	698	668	18	9	3	31
1988	169	711	680	20	9	2	74
1990	170	700	664	25	9	2	89
1993	184	741	698	32	9	2	179
1994	196	783	741	31	9	2	240

Note: The "Number of city to guide county" included the number of cities by which city in county level was guided. They were Zaozhuang city, Qingdao city in 1990, which added Weihai city in 1993 and Huangshi city, Guangzhou city, Jiangmen city, Foshan city in 1994. Qi indicates the name of a county in Inner Mongolia.

Source: Pu Shanxin et al. (1995).

Table 1.7 Absolute amount of disparity between agricultural products and industrial products (100 million yuan)

	1952	1957	1978	1982	1985
Absolute amount	74	127	364	288	286

Source: Yan Ruiqin et al. (1988).

At the beginning of the 1960s, both failure on agricultural policy by the communes and a natural disaster caused a serious shortage of foodstuffs, which made counties guided by cities return to traditional administrative districts. Until the end of the 1970s, the system 'county receives city's guidance' continued to exist but was inactive.

The purpose of the policy employed from 1949 to the end of 1970s to insulate almost all rural areas from urban areas was simply to allocate scarce resources to capital intensive industry, particularly heavy industry, in urban areas; the above-stated system of 'county receives city's guidance' was not to dissolve the insulation of townships and villages but to compensate for the shortage of foodstuffs and side dishes for urban citizens originally caused by the insulation policy between urban and rural areas; thus, we can say that a more reasonable explanation for it was not 'the promotion of reciprocal support between agriculture and industry' but the development of industry, particularly heavy industry, based upon accumulated resources by the agricultural sector.

The insulation policy of rural areas from urban areas had (we think) negative effects on the growth of urban areas. This was because urban areas were artificially separated from their traditional markets, which meant urban areas lost their roles as centers of the regional economy and of the general distribution network. Goods and materials were distributed, not through urban markets but administrative channels, which were vertically and horizontally divided (Wang Yukun *et al.* 1992, p. 3). In the newly established cities connected with the above-mentioned Third Front construction, they had a much clearer tendency toward insulation.

The actual administration of the system 'county receives city's guidance' was just the expansion of a horizontally divided sphere (and the insulation situation of rural areas from urban areas was never resolved). In this way, no traditional contradiction was resolved. In short, unless the central planning system was transformed, there was no effective solution to the above problem.

In 1983, to improve the isolated situation of rural areas from urban areas, a plan to expand the municipal administrative district by incorporating surrounding counties in their administrative sphere was employed. New circumstances in the system of 'county receives city's guidance' were recognized. We consider the system in Chapter 2.

Rural areas and agricultural policy: development of genealogy of the communes

After the foundation of the People's Republic of China, during the Cold War, a strategy of priority to heavy industry was carried out to the detriment of rural areas. Moreover, the Sino–Soviet conflicts at the end of 1950s made the circumstances of rural areas much more serious.

Appointed tasks for agriculture and rural areas

Central government made peasants stay in rural areas longer, through a family registration system, a foodstuffs allocation system, and a working system to provide foodstuffs to urban citizens from peasants, and also to secure food stocks for war and natural disasters. Through such insulation of rural areas from urban areas, rural areas were placed to accumulate heavy industry. The central budget expenditure for investment was concentrated upon heavy industry and the investment for agriculture was quite limited, which made it difficult to secure enough agricultural products. Mao Zedong therefore advocated development of production by self-reliance and collective production (workforce mobilization).

Emphasizing self-reliance was inevitable because no financial support was available. Meanwhile, as regards collective production, it was transformed from a mutual aid society, early stage cooperatives, mature stage cooperatives, towards *Zheng She He Yi* (the unification of economy and administration) and towards the *Yi Da Er Gong* (both characteristics of large scale and publicly owned) system of the communes. Figure 1.3 illustrates the transformation process. On August 17 1958, the Central Political Bureau held a conference with an enlarged membership in Beidaihe, and decided to build the communes in rural areas. The decision was passed at the Sixth Communist Party Central Committee General Meetings on December 1958 as a resolution on some issues about the communes. After that, a movement toward the communes in rural areas was attempted, in which sideline groups traditionally organized in agricultural collaboration were incorporated into the communes.

The main roles of collective production were the following. (1) By organizing rural areas, the individual peasant was hindered from moving towards urban areas and was bound to the land. (2) By conscripting peasants into establishing fundamental conditions, agricultural capital formation, such as water-use facilities construction and basic redeployment of arable land etc, was carried out. (3) It was a convenient measure to have high accumulation of peasants to accelerate the construction of socialism.

Expanding water-use facilities was an inevitable task for more agricultural production and higher efficiency because agriculture in the Chinese central and Chinese south was characterized as monsoon rice crop, for which water-use facilities were traditionally crucial for production. It was emphasized that small scale water-use construction was available for districts like counties, townships, cooperatives[2] etc. We can easily recognize extremely optimistic goals on each item about basic construction in the 'Seventeen Agricultural Articles'. Their goals were, for example 'by constructing many small scale water-use facilities combined with

2 See Mao Zedong (1997), which had the Mao Zedong's comments about 'uplift of socialism in rural areas in China'.

river valley plan, both floods and drought were generally resolved within seven years', 'both waste fields and bare mountain disappeared within 12 years' etc.[3]

In addition to the primitive accumulation for industry, it was requested that there should be high accumulation for agriculture on its own. In the 'Ways of Production 60 Articles', it was said that, in order to increase the accumulation and to prepare the great leap, allocation of the additional production should be 'three to seven' (allocation to workers occupied three and accumulation in the organization seven), or no allocation to workers was available for one to two years for more accumulation (Japan Institute of International Affairs, 1974).

The 'Ways of Production 60 Articles' also suggested making two kinds of plans, one was a plan to be completed absolutely and was to be announced, the other was a plan that aimed to be completed but without announcement. Mao Zedong raised the level of goals in succession and applied pressures to executive members to struggle for higher goals to be completed. As a result, the commercialized ratio of foodstuffs was maximized to be 40% when a tendency toward the communes was accelerated (Watanabe, 1995).

In addition, as a measure for peasants to accumulate, a labor points system called *Gongfenzhi* (working division system) was put in place. In the labor points system, because labor points were decided in advance and were depending upon actual jobs, no labor incentive worked. In addition, an egalitarian wage system like Dazhai (which meant that each worker's labor point was decided by self-announcement) and that of a public-owned eating house, became popular. However, after all, many of them fell through. Advocating restrictions on bourgeois rights gave a pretext of confiscation of arable land for self-consumption, and livestock and fruit trees for self-consumption.

Procedures toward the communes

The basic administrative districts in China changed with dizzying speed after the foundation of the People's Republic of China. In December 1950, two general rules were proclaimed on the organization of a township people's representative meeting and the organization of a township people's government. They employed a small township system whose base was 100 to 500 families and 500 to 3000 population. On April 24, 1951, by the instruction of the local government cabinet on construction, the township size was reduced and the number of townships increased from 218,642 in 1951 to 275,269 in 1952. Afterwards 68,000 administrative districts in the Chinese north area were united to be 21,00 townships in 1953. When the first national parliament was held in September 1954, in addition to the new constitution, organization laws on people's representative meetings at the local government level and on people's government at the respective level were

3 See Mao Zedong (1997), in which the Mao Zedong's work on 'the request to have opinions about Agricultural 17 Articles' was included.

passed. These laws became the legal bases of township government under the new constitution.

After 1955, as movement toward collective agriculture particularly toward mature stage cooperatives rapidly heightened, township size expanded to be around twice the size. When movement toward the communes was growing in 1958, the number of communes was decreased to be around one quarter compared with the number of townships. Their size was about the same as a district, which was positioned between county and township and in which a branch office of the county government was located. It was said there existed huge communes, one of which was located in each county. Anyway, the communes were established in 94 counties covered by 13 provinces (Liu Zenwei and Wang Zenyao, 1987, p. 99).

After the Great Leap Forward failed and adjusted policies were implemented, both the size and number of the communes were reduced to be the same as those of townships before communes were introduced. However, the size and number of the communes was gradually expanded, and totaled about 53,000 in 1978. The changing procedure of the branch organization (country controlled districts, big production group), basic administrative district in the rural area (township, the communes), and autonomous organization (framers committee) is shown in Table 1.8.

Movement for industrialization in rural areas

Procedure. The communes played a main role in industrialization in rural areas. Such industrialization was carried out by transferring a number of agricultural workers in industry for production of chemical fertilizers, machineries, agricultural chemicals, cement etc. Factories managed by the communes were mainly classified as the following;

a. Enterprises managed by agricultural cooperatives were transferred to the communes.
b. New factories were established which were financed by central government expenditure and by collection from peasants.
c. State-owned enterprises located in farming areas were transferred (Ueno, 1993, p. 42).

Agricultural promotion was attempted for higher accumulation in agriculture. Industrialization of rural areas seemed to be an important factor for agricultural promotion as well as construction of water-use facilities. Industrialization of rural areas was positioned in a 'Resolution by the Sixth Communist Party Central Committee General Meetings' in December 10, 1958. It said that 'the communes had to enthusiastically promote industrialization. Industrial development in the communes contributed not only for progress of industrialization in the whole China but also for decreasing disparities between urban and rural areas through realization of people's ownership in rural areas. Based upon the respective condition of each commune, planned production of such light industry and heavy industry as fertilizer,

Table 1.8 The changing procedure of branch organizations, basic administrative districts in rural areas and autonomous organizations

Year	*Zhuanqu*	*Diqu*	Districts controlled by counties	Township	Commune	Big production group	Peasants committee
1949	195						
1951	201			218642			
1952	163		18144	275269			
1953	152		18930	225884			
1954	152		18621	218721			
1955	153		14959	194858			
1956	144						
1957	140		8505	95843			
1958	121				26593		
1959	119				25450		
1978		173	4022		52534	686666	
1979		171	3619		53229	701288	
1980		170					
1981		168	3791		54368	718022	
1982		170					
1983		138	5909	35514	36268		
1984		135	8119	85290	63		927311
1985		125	7908	79306			948628
1986		119	6165	58417			866130
1987		117	5503	55719			845025
1988		113	3570	43624			882564
1989		113	3502	42869			934346
1990		113	3438	42417			1001272
1991		113	3096	41251			1018593
1992		110	1231	32479			1004349
1993		101	1143	31094			1012756
1994		89	1068	30141			1006541

Note: Statistics about townships from 1951 to 1953 included statistics on administrative villages. Statistics of Tibet from 1951 to 1955 were not available.

Zhuanqu meant a prefecture-level municipality, big city which controlled several counties, existed just before 1970. *Diqu*: indicates prefecture-level municipality, big city which controls several counties, appeared after 1970. The name Zhuanqu was changed to be *Diqu* in 1970.

Source: Pu Shanxin et al. (1995), p.463-464.

agricultural chemicals, farming tools and agricultural machineries, construction materials, processing and general utilization of agricultural products, sugar production, spinning, paper manufacturing, mining, metallurgy and electric power should be developed by correctly transferring the workforce from agriculture to industry.' This resolution was announced at the same time as the above-mentioned Mao Zedong's instruction emphasizing that each region should construct its own autonomous industrial system. After all, even in the rural area, 'Five Small industries' were rapidly developed, in which, in particular 'tufaliangang' (which indicates a method to produce steel in primitive way) in the Great Leap Forward period was publicly advertised. When this movement was at its peak, it was said that, because 18% of the workforce was in rural areas, and 10 to 18% of handcarts and livestock carts and 30% of wooden sailboats were mobilized, a proportion of agricultural products in the good harvest year could not be cropped, and was left in the fields (Zhang Yi, 1988, p. 42).

Under such circumstances, the central government had to regulate the communes' industry and passed the ordinance entitled 'maneuvering ordinance on the communes in rural areas (amendment)' at the Tenth Communist Party Central Committee General Meetings in September 1962. It said that, 'the supervisory committee on the communes could not generally establish any enterprises within the coming few years, and as regards already established enterprises all of them which did not have enough production facilities and did not have people's support should be closed'. Also in November 1962, the Central Communist Party announced a regulation mentioning that the communes and big production groups were neither allowed to manage enterprises nor allowed to found sideline production groups. Because of such results of prohibition on almost all activities, the industry of the communes collapsed in only a few years (Zhang Yi, 1988, p. 44; Fang Weizhong, 1984, pp. 351–352.). As Table 1.9 displays, the production of enterprises in the communes, which were forerunners of Township and Village Enterprises (TVEs), showed a peak of 5.18 billion yuan in 1961 but afterward reduced until 1965.

However, stagnation of sideline production caused a decrease of peasants' income and difficulty of investment into agricultural sector, and also the decrease of enterprises in the communes seriously influenced the production and repair of farming tools. To break the deadlock situation, the Central Communist Party and the Cabinet announced 'the instruction to develop sideline production in rural areas' and allowed the production groups of the communes to manage the main constituents.

Afterwards, the production by enterprises in the communes gradually recovered, which was supported by an agricultural conference in the northern area in 1970 and an agricultural conference on mechanization in 1971. Development of 'Five Small Industries' was instructed and the fund for it was covered by enterprises of the communes themselves and central government expenditure. Also at the 'Conference on lessons of agricultural development from Dazhai', they specifically guaranteed that development of enterprises in the communes contributed to agricultural and industrial development and for stability of people's

Table 1.9 Production amount of enterprises in the communes

Year	Total production of enterprises in the communes	Managed by the communes	Managed by the production group
1958		62.5	
1959		100	
1960		50	
1961	51.8	19.8	22
1962	40.9	7.9	33
1963	40.2	4.2	36
1964	44.6	4.6	40
1965	29.3	5.3	24
1970	67.7	27.6	40
1971	92.0	39.1	52.9
1972	110.6	46.0	64.6
1973	126.4	54.8	71.6
1974	151.3	66.8	84.5
1975	197.8	86.8	111.0
1978	385.3		
1979	424.6		
1980	506.4		

Source: Zhang Yi (1991), p.16-26.

everyday life, and also stimulated development. As indicated in Table 1.9, the production of enterprises in the communes after 1971 successfully recovered.

Characteristics

As stated before, agricultural production of the communes was fully organized by the central government from labor input to purchases. Meanwhile enterprises in the communes in rural areas were clearly recognized and existed outside central planning systems.

The initial purpose of establishing the forerunners of present TVEs, which were sideline business groups of the agricultural cooperatives and enterprises in the communes, was to incorporate widely developed sideline businesses in rural areas into the central planning system.

The ministry of agriculture and forestry in the Cabinet attempted to strengthen the communes in order to develop enterprises in the communes by establishing an enterprise bureau of the communes in 1976 and by transferring manual industry from the ministry of light industry to the communes.

However, although the organized enterprises in the communes could develop by utilizing local materials and workforces, they could not be provided with materials, resources and workforces by central government, as large-scale enterprises in urban areas could be. They were not allowed to compete with enterprises in urban areas and were limited to their activities in rural areas. Industrialization of rural areas, meaning industrial production by enterprises in the communes, was intended just to complement agricultural production and construction in rural areas, it was not allowed to advance into the territory of urban industry.

The organization for the industrialization of rural areas in China (which indicated enterprises in the communes) was a complement to agricultural production and took responsibility for redundant workers in rural areas under the prohibited regulation on labor mobility among towns and villages. In addition, as they existed as part of the development strategy in China (Third Front Construction and *Da-Lian-Gang-Tie-Yun-Dong*, meaning a movement for the way to produce steel), they were organized formerly and forcibly and were not satisfactorily developed because of unstable trends at the time. The products made by them were not merchandise but instead self-sustenance transacted within rural areas.

Harmful effects of the communes and reasons for dissolution

With communes they attempted to realize the collectivization of the workforce and publicly owned production measures, as shown by the slogan of *Yi Da Er Gong* (both characteristics of large scale and publicly owned) system. In short, agricultural collectivization pursued the realization of scale merit in agricultural production. In order for the purpose to be pursued, the communes committee was established, which gave compulsory instructions on four indices (specified kinds of agricultural products, the planted acreage, production quantity, productivity) to subordinate organizations in order (meaning from the communes to higher production groups, and to lower production groups).

Under the communes system, not only land but also all materials, such as livestock and agricultural machinery, were collectively owned. Based upon the collective property of production factors, the workforce was also collectively organized. Such indispensable materials to complete the compulsory instructions on fertilizer and seeds were provided only by the communes. Income distribution to peasants was collectively decided by an administrative committee of the communes. Because it was actually difficult to decide labor points for individual members, distribution was carried out with an egalitarian principle.

Thus, we can sum up the reasons for dissolution, taking into consideration the harmful effects of the communes as the following.

(1) Under the Zheng She He Yi (the unification of economy and administration) system, the basic unit for profit (collective economic organization) had no autonomy and every order was given administratively by a higher organization. Haphazard orders prevailed.

(2) Because motivation of peasants for production was reduced by the egalitarian principle, and supervisory costs for collective labor were high

(also it was impossible to supervise at all times), the implemented period of the communes from 1958 to the end of the 1970s led to stagnation in agricultural production.

(3) Peasants took an excessively heavy burden. In the rural areas such burdens as an executive's allowance was imposed on peasants. It was easily and widely recognized under the Zheng She He Yi (the unification of economy and administration) that the workforce was provided gratuitously, due to the reason of public purpose.

(4) Self-managed land and the free market were criticized as (what is called) the 'tail' of capitalism, and hence this was not available. Peasants thus lost an important source of income for themselves.

(5) Several effects were pointed out (Kobayashi, 1990b, p. 7; Pu Shanxin *et al.*, 1995, pp. 459–466), some of which were as follows: executives of the supervisory section paid too much attention to economic maneuvering and sufficient political instruction was impossible; power was concentrated upon a small number of executives, which led to them abusing their official authority and to oppression against the citizens.

Characteristics of the Chinese economic system under central planning

Basic institutional plan: the Zheng She He Yi (unification of economy and administration)

The Zheng She He Yi (unification of economy and administration) was to be one of the most important characteristics of centrally planned economies. Actually, the administration (central planning authority) could be working for the equilibrium between demand and supply, which was achieved in the market-oriented system, by the market. Meanwhile, it is pointed out that the shortage of information processing ability, corresponding to the flexible socio-economic events, might be the inherent deficiency of a centrally planned economy. Shiozawa (1990), for example, insisted that, unless the central planning economy could solve this deficiency, a general equilibrium situation could not be held.

Actually, the Socialist Calculation Debate had already occurred in the 1930s. Lange (1967), Glushkov and Moev (1976), and Taylor (1994), for example, asserted that trial and error systems could reach the general equilibrium situation even without a price mechanism (government control could reach the economic order more efficiently than a market mechanism). As regards the specific way to reach the situation in which the price equaled the marginal cost, they advocated it was possible by introducing large-scale computers. Moreover, Baran (1960), Dobb (1946) etc., advocated that in order to catch up economic development, a central planning system was necessary. In particular, Dobb (1946) mentioned the validity of central planning by displaying the model of 'owner and dog'. The

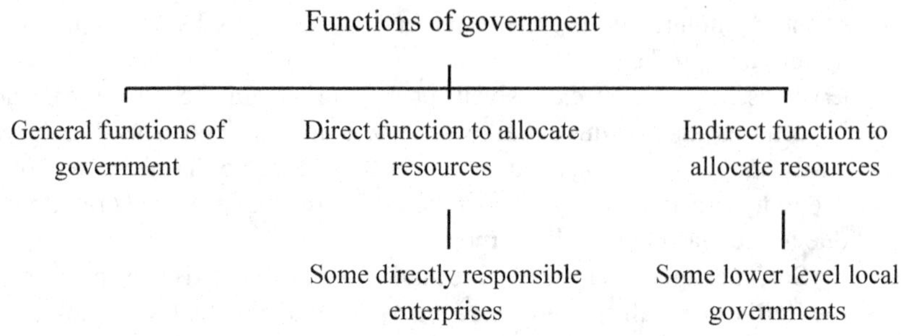

Source: Sheng Hong (1994), p. 215-216, and author.

Figure 1.3 The classification of functions of government in centrally planned system

above assertions were shown later to be a mere figment, however, in those days in China, they believed the validity and possibility of a centrally planned system.

We can indicate that regional development strategies in China until 1978 were closely connected with a traditional investment framework. That is to say, unless government (mainly central government) invested with high concentration, such development strategies as well as balanced regional allocation, formation of local self-completed system, and promotion of Third Front Construction were not carried out.

A fundamental precondition in the traditional investment scheme in China was that enterprises (most of which were state-owned enterprises) were full 'attachments' for central government. The management procedure was said simply to be the following. (1) First, central government decided on specific projects. (2) Investment was financed by central budget expenditure. (3) The administrative section arranged the plan and construction. (4) After the construction, the plant manager was appointed by the administrative section. The administrative section arranged for production and distribution, and paid all the profits (including depreciation) to the finance section. (5) Return to the first process, where central government decides specific projects. Needless to say, the only agent of decision making for investment was central government, and enterprises were just 'attachments' for central government and had no independent authority (see Figure 1.3).

Such a central planning system produced economic activities that were divided both horizontally and vertically by the administrative section. Kojima (1986, pp. 72–75) illustrated actual examples, which include the sailing rights of rivers, cases of multiple construction of factories within the same cities by different administrations, contradictions between urban administration districts and rural administration districts, and useful resources being abolished if the concerned administration had another authority. In order to adjust the contradictions, higher ranking administrations were established, which led to an enlargement of administrative organization. We can recognize therefore that, unless a centrally planned system was radically changed, such contradictions were not resolved.

Characteristics of the managing system; exclusiveness

Kuribayashi (1993) summarized the characteristics of the Chinese economy after the reform and open door policy by using the concept of a two-tiers dual economic structure. He insisted that it was different from the usually observed dual economic structure in urban and rural areas in economic development. In China, within the rural sector, there existed relations between agriculture and non-agriculture, and within the urban sector there existed relations between formal state-owned collective management and informal private-owned small business, and also there existed relations between the rural sector and urban sector (Kuribayashi, 1993). In addition, Chen Zongsheng (1995, pp. 214–262) analyzed the disparity structure in China, after the reform and open door policy started, with the concept of a two-tiers dual-economic structure or three economic sectors (indicating (1) the farming industry, (2) farming non-agriculture, and (3) urban non-agriculture).

Meanwhile, the author of this book called the Chinese economy before the reform and open door policy to be a two-tiers dual-economic structure, based upon investigations which showed that, in China before the reform and open door policy, there was basically a dual structure of urban and rural, and moreover there was a complexly combined sub-dual structure. A centrally planned system usually consists of a two-tiers dual-economic structure (which will be considered later), at the same time, the existence of a two-tiers dual-economic structure showed the closed system of central planning. In addition, the author of this book thinks that the two-tiers dual-economic structure was the mechanism to show the disparity in China in this period. Consider the following.

(1) Dual structure of urban and rural Table 1.10 indicates the structure of production and workers among three sectors for 25 years from 1952 to 1977. As regards the structure of workers, the primary sector increased to 82.5% in 1962 from 77.1% in 1961, after that it was stable. Behind the situation in which many workers stayed in rural areas, there could be recognized the relations between agriculture and industry.

Due to the Great Leap Forward, the unemployment rate in the urban area decreased to 5.62% in 1960 from 13.2% in 1952. However, for three years, 1959–61, a seriously mistaken policy of agricultural aspects was in place because of natural disasters and the communes. Under the serious food shortage and heavy-industry oriented strategy, the industrial sector in urban areas could neither absorb the redundant workers in rural areas nor be available to give additional job opportunities for increased labor forces in urban areas (which showed a

Table 1.10 Structure of production and labor in three sectors in China (1952-1977)

Year	GDP production structure (%)			Labor force structure (%)			GDP per laborer (yuan)		
	Primary	Secondary	Tertiary	Primary	Secondary	Tertiary	Primary	Secondary	Tertiary
1952	50·5	20·9	28·6	83·5	7·4	9·1	198·0	928·0	1030·8
1953	45·9	23·4	30·8	83·1	8·0	8·9	213·0	1127·7	1324·5
1954	45·6	24·6	29·7	83·1	8·6	8·3	216·0	1130·9	1408·2
1955	46·3	24·4	29·3	83·2	8·5	8·3	226·5	1175·0	1440·6
1956	43·2	27·3	29·5	80·5	10·6	8·9	239·5	1148·5	1488·0
1957	40·3	29·7	30·1	81·2	8·9	9·9	222·8	1498·8	1362·5
1958	34·1	37·0	28·9	58·2	26·4	15·4	288·0	687·4	923·7
1959	26·7	42·8	30·6	62·1	20·5	17·4	236·1	1148·3	965·1
1960	23·4	44·5	32·1	65·7	15·7	18·6	200·5	1596·9	970·2
1961	36·2	31·9	32·0	77·1	11·0	11·9	223·6	1380·0	1281·2
1962	39·4	31·3	29·3	82·0	7·8	10·1	213·1	1767·3	1286·9
1963	40·3	33·0	26·6	82·4	7·5	10·1	226·7	2027·9	1223·7
1964	38·4	35·3	26·2	82·1	7·8	10·1	245·4	2383·9	1360·6
1965	37·9	35·1	27·0	81·5	8·3	10·2	278·6	2534·5	1583·8
1966	37·6	38·0	24·4	81·4	8·6	9·9	289·3	2763·9	1539·0
1967	40·3	34·0	25·8	81·6	8·5	9·9	284·1	2295·5	1499·5
1968	42·2	31·2	26·7	81·6	8·5	9·9	278·9	1984·9	1449·5
1969	38·0	35·6	26·5	81·5	9·0	9·5	271·7	2303·1	1632·0
1970	35·2	40·5	24·3	80·7	10·1	9·2	285·5	2622·0	1727·8
1971	34·1	42·2	23·8	79·6	11·1	9·3	291·3	2595·3	1741·5
1972	32·9	43·1	24·1	78·8	11·8	9·4	292·9	2566·2	1793·8
1973	33·4	43·1	23·5	78·6	12·1	9·3	314·9	2644·3	1885·7
1974	33·9	42·7	23·4	78·1	12·4	9·5	323·9	2565·6	1842·2
1975	32·4	45·7	21·9	77·1	13·2	9·6	330·1	2700·5	1782·8
1976	32·8	45·4	21·7	75·7	14·2	10·1	328·9	2418·5	1636·8
1977	29·7	47·1	23·4	74·4	14·6	11·0	321·6	2630·9	1726·9

Source: *Chinese Statistical Bulletin*, 1993, 1996, and 2001.

negative growth rate in three continuous years from 1960). During the period of the serious unemployment situation in urban areas from the beginning of 1960s to the middle of 1970s, central government carried out the large scale movement of urban young people toward rural areas and border areas (*XiaFang*), the aim of this was to alleviate the serious unemployment in the urban area. Such a strange policy contributed to the decrease of the unemployment rate of 2 to 5% annually which reached 5.3% in urban areas in 1978. However, we can insist that the above-stated reverse movement of population went against the modernization policy of population movement.

Table 1.10 shows the following facts, that for 26 years from 1952 to 1977, as far as the primary sector was concerned, the decreased ratio of total production reached 17.7%; however, the decreased ratio of total labor force equaled only 9.1%. As regards the secondary sector, the respective increased ratio reached 26.2% in total production and only 7.2% in total labor force. From 1952 to 1977, the per capita GDP growth rate in agriculture was 62.4%, and per capita GDP growth rate in industry reached 284%, which pointed out the remarkable lower development in agriculture than industry due to the closed dual structure between urban and rural areas.

The low job opportunity and low wage rate of the industrial sector was significantly effective for development in the tertiary sector. According to the survey carried out by the Chinese Statistical Office in 74 cities, the changing process occurred in the number of commercial shops, restaurants, and service shops per 10,000 population as follows. The number of commercial shops, restaurants, and service shops per 10,000 population was 47.6 in 1949, 67.2 in 1952, 26.4 in 1957, 13.2 in 1962, 9.5 in 1965, and 10.8 in 1978, which was a substantial decrease. Compared with 1952 and 1978, the ratio of the total labor force in the tertiary sector slightly increased to be 11% in 1978 from 9.1% in 1952.

China is still an agricultural country, and in the Mao Zedong's era the ratio of agriculture was much higher. The higher the ratio of agriculture in industrial structure, the more effective influence was given to the industrial sector by the agricultural sector. Tang Anthony (1968) examined empirically and asserted (with his rank correlation analysis on the effects of agricultural production to industrial production in the 1950s) that the Chinese effects of agricultural production on industrial production were substantial, which was different from the USSR.

(2) The dual structure of heavy industry and light industry A primitive approach for the expansion of heavy industry was to set low price foodstuffs and the price ratio of agricultural products to industrial products (what is called *Schere*). Thus, consumption by peasants in the rural area and workers in the urban area was kept to an extremely low level. A huge amount of profit for the Ministry of Light Industry through the *Schere* was paid to the government along with commerce and industry tax, which became the primitive accumulation for heavy industry expansion. That actual circumstance was a result of the strategic priority for heavy industry.

Meanwhile, what was said to be a self-circulation mechanism within heavy industry was created. That is to say, such collectively distributed materials by the state as steel and machine tools, and such controlled materials by the main administrative section as coke and ferroalloy were circulated with low prices within heavy industry because their materials were given priority.

(3) Centrally controlled enterprises and local enterprises Most large- and medium-scaled state-owned enterprises in the central and western areas were established by the state in the 1950s and 1960s or transferred from coastal areas. Because the majority were controlled by central government, they were regulated

by an administratively higher ranking organization. However, they could not have any advantageous treatment by local government. Meanwhile, a centrally planned strategy, such as Third Front Construction, produced an structure of centrally controlled enterprises insulated from the regional economy. Centrally controlled enterprises could not demonstrate advantages in the financial and technological sphere. This was a bad effect coming from an administratively divided (locally and centrally) system.

(4) Military industry and ordinary industry Major parts of the newly constructed industry in inland areas were military. In order to keep them confidential, there was a closed production system and no competition in military industry. Thus, after the 1980s, reforming the military industry was a serious policy task.

(5) Rural industry and urban industry Rural industry (enterprises in the communes) activities were strictly limited within rural areas. The industries could develop by utilizing local materials and workforces, but they were not allowed to receive state allocated materials, resources and workforces, as were large scale enterprises in urban areas. Industrialization in rural areas, i.e. industrial production by enterprises in the communes, was simply to complement agricultural production and rural area construction; construction that could not invade areas of urban industrialization.

(6) Industrial center of inland area and periphery area Most cities in which inland state-owned enterprises were located were constructed in the boom period of the Third Front Construction. Specific distribution said that each of them was isolated from each other and, although many industrial districts and industrial centers were formed, most of them could not lead to development of surrounding areas, thus they were the same as enclaves, which had no linkage with surrounding and less developed rural areas. They certainly built a huge industrial accumulation in inland areas; however, they neither contributed to the progress of everyday life nor increased income level. It seems to be a kind of dual structure.

A centrally planned system incorporated a variety of dual structures, in other words it showed the exclusiveness of the central planning system.

Deng Xiaoping's reform and open door policy has been to resolve such a variety of dual structures. At the same time however, the reform and open door policy has been also a transition attempt, which has caused a new kind of dual structure. For example, at the end of 1980s, it often indicated the dual structure of a price system. The Chinese procedure of reform and open policy has therefore been an arena against new and traditional dual structures.

Inefficiency of development and the analysis of the reasons

The Mao Zedong strategy had a serious defect. That is to say, three factors of population, cost, and market were neglected (Kobayashi, 1990a, p. 182.). Needless to say, such a serious defect was not only in Mao Zedong strategy's but also in the central planning system.

As a matter of fact, the inefficiency that occurred was closely related with the characteristics of a centrally planned system such as the above-mentioned Zheng She He Yi and exclusiveness. We recognize it as the following.

Inefficiency of development

Table 1.10 indicated that, in China, around 80% of the labor force stayed in the agricultural sector until the 1970s. During that period, in Chinese rural areas, they implemented such agricultural promotion policies as the green revolution, e.g. the improvement of species, promotion of Five Small Industries by a self-reliance policy, and construction of water-use facilities by mobilizing free labor forces. However, the Chinese agricultural production level remained very low, people's everyday life was never improved and it was difficult to reach minimum subsistence level. Table 1.11 shows some indicators of labor productivity in agriculture. From 1953 to 1977, the growth rate of per capita GDP and per capita food production remained low, and both indicators of the absolute amount of commercial food production and commercialized ratio were reduced. These were, we think, caused by a redundant population in rural areas whose situation was never improved for many years. Although the reasons were different, a similar phenomenon was displayed with rural areas in post-war Southeast Asian countries that suffered from a population explosion (see Chapter 6 on the Southeast Asian development model).

Table 1.11 Some indicators of labor productivity in agriculture (1953-1977)

Year	Per capita production (yuan)	Per capita food production (kilogram)	Commercial food production (kilogram)	Commercialized ratio of food production (%)
1953	201	897	188	21·0
1957	207	949	165	17·4
1962	208	749	121	16·1
1965	272	827	143	17·3
1970	283	854	150	17·5
1975	329	950	147	15·4

Source: Xu Dixin (ed.) (1988), p.296.

According to Maddison (2001), the growth of labor productivity in several countries from 1950 to 1973 (making US labor productivity equal 100), revealed that in Japan it rose from 16 to 48, in the USSR from 24 to 28, Czechoslovakia from 29 to 34, Hungary from 21 to 28, Poland from 19 to 24, South Korea from 10 to 14, and Taiwan from 9 to 18. Meanwhile in China it decreased from 7 to 6. In comparison with labor productivity in other countries, it reduced for 23 years.

What was the main reason for the inefficiency of development in the Mao Zedong system? We investigate by focusing our attention upon institutional inefficiency.

Fel'dman–Domar model and institutional inefficiency

From the viewpoints of industrial policy, the main characteristic of the three big development strategies in the central planning period was to attach greater importance to heavy industry.

The theoretical background of the development strategy to give priority to production goods has been the Fel'dman–Domar model, originally by Fel'dman (1928) and later improved by Domar (1957). The Fel'dman–Domar model has similarity with the unbalanced growth theory asserted by Hirschman (1958). The unbalanced growth implied that the forerunner sector developed by priority investment establishes the external economy, which induces investment in other sectors, which again creates an external economy, which again induces additional investment, whose see-saw pattern will make the whole economy develop. That assertion also emphasized that the continuous unbalanced growth was effective for economic development, which criticized the multi-sector balanced growth model insisted upon by Nurkse (1953). As in Hirschman (1958), it indicated that the production sector of final demand goods was more realistic than the basic material production sector or intermediary production sector for industrial production because final demand causes more demand pressure due to backward relations.

Meanwhile, the Fel'dman–Domar model emphasized that priority investment in the production sector compared with consumption sector leads to more expansion of the economy in the long run. Conditions for their development model were, for example, (1) no depreciation, (2) a closed economy, (3) consumption level was above subsistence minimum, and (4) no institutional inefficiency (constant capital coefficient) etc (Ishikawa, 1980).

Under the open economy, international trade becomes more active based upon the comparative advantage principle. Needless to say, small open economies, such as Singapore and the Netherlands, are expanding with their comparative advantage. However, larger economies (such as larger population and larger land area economies) have a more independent economic structure. International economic circumstances have a variety of unstable factors, and depending upon such unstable factors is too risky. In addition, input–output relations have positive effects upon economic growth. In China we think that developing heavy industry led to Chinese economic expansion, but actually that is not so likely.

What does the Fel'dman–Domar model suggest for the Chinese economy?

We think there are the following two points. (1) First, as regards a consumption level above the subsistence minimum in Chinese farming areas during the Mao Zedong's era, because of the failure in agricultural policy, it is said that twenty to thirty million people starved to death. The high accumulation model of the Mao Zedong's era should be recognized as it was below the subsistence minimum. (2) As far as no institutional inefficiency is concerned, in the China of the Mao Zedong's era, due to wrong statistical reports, waste of resources, delayed technological progress, and low labor motivation etc, the marginal capital coefficient remarkably decreased. What caused this institutional inefficiency?

What are some of the reasons why the above two disadvantageous circumstances occurred in China?

(I) Based upon the concept of transaction costs, in a centrally planned system (in the communes system in China) the supervising cost was enormous, and reasons for the institutional inefficiency were not regulated by appropriate supervision. Institutional inefficiency inevitably resulted. Lin Yifu (1992) insisted that the reasons for the collapse of the people's commune were due to the enormous cost of supervision. In the collective labor system, the labor incentive of workers was closely related to the strictness of supervision. Meanwhile, different from industrial production, farming labor is difficult to strictly supervise because agriculture is dispersed in geographical space and also because agriculture has seasonal characteristics. In the communes, although a labor points system, called the *Gongfenzhi* (working division system), was introduced, it was a preliminary evaluation and, under the weak supervision system, hard work could easily be overlooked. As a result, egalitarianism in the distributing institution became popular. Because the people's commune system had no incentive for laborers to work hard, it was reasonable for collective labor to decrease the efficiency. Conversely, because the family contract system after 1978 resolved the supervising problem of agricultural production by institutional progress, it substantially contributed to agricultural development in China (Lin Yifu, 1992).

(II) Because greater importance was attached to national defense, investment efficiency in heavy industry was slight and a self-circulating system of heavy industry was formed. Nakagane (1999) pointed out that the tendency toward heavy industry carried out in this period in China became, what is to say, its self-purpose, and much investment in the heavy industry sector was not effective for overall economic growth. Nakagane (1999) investigated the reason and reached the conclusion that it came from the institutional inefficiency. In other words, the induced effects expected by the unbalanced growth model could not be gained because of institutional inefficiency, and in order to get the induced effects of unbalanced growth, reforming the centrally planned system might be necessary.

Heavy industry was just like the existence of an only child, and such other industries as light industry and agriculture might be servants. The low marginal capital efficiency of Chinese state-owned enterprises was basically unchanged, even after the reform and open door policy started.

(III) We recognize the soft budget system in China. Undoubtedly it was impossible not to consider the construction cost of national economy. Why were they attaching less importance to the construction cost? We think it was because, in the central planning system, all agents of the whole economy could manage without considering costs. As a matter of fact, nobody was responsible for inefficient investment, which led to the soft budget constraint by Kornai (for example, Kornai, 1986, 1990).

What caused the soft budget constraint in China? The traditional system of investment expenditure in China was explained by a unified system of parliament and administration, who could monopolize all the systems based on exclusive authority and without supervision. Characteristic of budget expenditure under such system was a lack of responsibility for any investment. In the non-responsible system, enterprises had poor incentives for more efficient investments without cost constraints. At the same time, national management section, which ordered a national goal in quantitative attainment, had little interest in maintenance and renewal of existing facilities. Because the direct and short-term effect on production expansion by enlarging the scale of enterprises and the establishment of enterprises was clearer, they had more interest in them and less interest in efficiency progress.

The high accumulation model and institutional inefficiency

The development strategy with prioritized heavy industry, which was strongly promoted during the very serious economic situation after Communist China, was established and is said to be the high accumulation model (Minami and Ono, 1987; Watanabe, 1996). The enormous farming area was actually identified as the origin of accumulation for heavy industry development.

The high accumulation model was carried out in rural areas. Under the communes system, as well as collective production, they introduced non-paid service by the general public in such cases as construction of water-use facilities. Nurkse (1953) used a model of a redundant workforce, which said that, as less developed countries were in a vicious circle of poverty, and they had difficulty in capital accumulation, they accumulated capital by introducing a volunteer base workforce with below zero marginal productivity of labor.

The Great Leap Forward in China seemed to be the actual practice of Nurkse's assertion. However, we should ask whether or not such mobilization was efficient. Also when we ask that question, we have to consider the institutional inefficiency.

Appropriate technology theory and institutional inefficiency

It is insisted that an appropriate technology or intermediate technology is crucial in economic development theory. With intermediate technology it is pointed out that, although it has an essence of modern technology, it is appropriate for regional circumstances like factor endowment (Ishikawa *et al*., 1974). Because technology and workforce are a substitute for each other in factor combination, they say that, in countries or regions with a redundant workforce, there is a cost advantage in developing intermediate technology rather than using the most advanced technology. In rural areas in Mao Zedong's era, they emphasized improvement of a species based upon experience. Advocates of 'Five Small Industries' (which indicate small iron works, small coal mines, small power stations, small machine factories, and small chemical fertilizer factories) in rural areas had the same kind of emphasis. According to Sigurdson (1977), the intermediate technology was an approach to alleviate the technological disparity between urban and rural areas by transferring the technology of the urban modern sector to rural areas.

We think the viewpoint of intermediate technology is reasonable. At the same time however, technological progress has occurred dynamically, which has led to economic development. By introducing intermediate technology, it is desirable that the quantity of population is decreased and the quality of population is improved. In Mao Zedong's era, they cut off the national economy in many separate fields. The communes in this period were recognized to be the origin of the accumulation of heavy industry development under the policy of separation of city and county, and separation of suburban area and township, and although farming industry was implemented, it stayed within rural areas (Watanabe, 1996). The possibility of technological progress was quite limited and the technology level in such fields – which used traditional technology and intermediate technology – as agriculture and light industry remained stagnant. The above-stated low labor productivity in China seemed to be evidence of this. Actually, no alleviation measure about disparity including technology between urban and rural was carried out.

Moreover, the population policy in Mao Zedong's era, as shown in the slogan 'honorable mother', indicated both production power and military power. A population increase was (mentally) encouraged, but seemed to damage the incentives for technological progress.

As stated above, each bit of the Fel'dman–Domar model, high accumulation model, and optimum technology theory, proposed a viewpoint that takes into consideration the characteristics of the less developed countries concerned. In centrally planned China, institutional inefficiency was encountered and China was caught in the trap of inefficiency. A lack of a general consideration and a systematic way of thinking seemed to lead to the failure of the China in Mao Zedong's era.

Characteristics of regional economy: appearance of the administrative economic district

The actual situation of the regional economy

As mentioned before in this chapter, upon the establishment of large scale economic cooperation districts, which was carried out in 1958 and 1961 in the whole of China, the Shanghai municipality directly under the central government, Jiangsu, and the Zhejiang province in the Yangtze River Delta were designated a portion of the Chinese eastern economic cooperation district.

The Third Front Construction was a good example of the big scale economic cooperation district system (see the previous section about the Third Front Construction). The example of Shanghai is as follows. (1) During the Third Front Construction period from 1964 to 1973, 304 projects, 411 factories, 92,000 employees and workers were moved to the inland Third Front area (Fang Weizhong, 1984, pp. 179–180). (2) In the Minor Third Front Constructions, Shanghai was involved and there were the two which were (i) Chinese East Minor Third Front, and (ii) Shanghai logistical base. Shanghai constructed 19 military enterprises in Jiangxi province, which was located in Chinese East Minor Third Front district. Until 1977, in the 16 counties and cities in Anhui province and Zhejiang province which were located at Shanghai logistical base, they established 83 enterprises and organizations, whose total investment amount reached 500 million yuan (Sun Huairen, 1990, pp. 469–470, 512–513).

Although those enterprises were located in other provinces, by the horizontally divided and vertically divided administrative sections, which were characteristic of a centrally planned system, they were controlled by the Shanghai municipal government until the 1980s. In the management sense, along the administrative channel, such activities in which materials were transported into Shanghai and products were transported from Shanghai etc, were implemented (Yan Hao, 1988, pp. 146–148).

It was easily recognized that linkages between industrial centers and surrounding areas were not established enough and the regional economy was separated by administrative barriers.

Systemic background: administrative economic district

The characteristics of the regional economy, which were coming from the centrally planned system, were summarized as the 'administrative economic district'.

The administrative economic district was the special combination of administrative district and economic district, which was available in only a centrally planned system. State-owned enterprises were strictly controlled by the national administration, which pointed out that management authority, like the allocation of resources and products, was concentrated in the national administration. It was therefore the case that enterprises were actually just production and sales divisions at the end of the administrative organization, and management authority of enterprises was not secured (thus, it was said that enterprise was inseparable from administration).

The supervising government for enterprises varied from one ministry, committee, province, city, county, and district to another ministry, committee, province, city, county, and district. After all, enterprises were surrounded by *Tiaotiao* and *Kuaikuai*. *Tiaotiao* showed the vertically divided situation in which any organization controlled by a supervising authority (such as a ministry and committee) was fully regulated by the authority from the top to the bottom, and other authorities and local government could not be committed at all. Meanwhile, *Kuaikuai* indicated the horizontally divided situation in which any local government controlling a certain regional area excluded the governmental intervention of other administrative areas and other vertical divided administrative sections. These were, needless to say, characteristics of the centrally planned system.

Thus, although the large economic cooperative districts, which were established by provincial association, existed from the 1950s, and their role was often emphasized, they could not work well as the unified entity because of vertically and horizontally divided situations. At the end of the 1960s, six big economic cooperative districts disappeared over the whole nation. The district-level that actually worked well enough was the administrative economic district at the respective levels. Currently, in the investigations of economic districts, it is said that such existences as the presentation of the principle that economic districts correspond to administrative districts, and the expectation for economic districts at the provincial level to have enough work etc, show that a centrally planned system as the condition of the existence of administrative economic districts could work to some extent. Because the disappearance of an administrative economic district means the disappearance of a centrally planned system, the degree of disappearance of the administrative economic district displays the *merkmal* of the degree of development of reform and open door policy in China.

Accompanied with the market oriented reform of the 1980s, the transformation of the administrative economic district started. Those transformations were divided into the two stages in the 1980s and in the 1990s, which corresponded to the reform speed. In the 1980s, it was the transformation period of administrative economic districts, and in the 1990s it was recognized that, in some regions of market-oriented reform, like the Yangtze River Delta, there could exist initial conditions to establish regional economic zones in place of administrative economic districts (Chen Yun and Tsuneichi Toda, 2001).

Conclusion

There is a saying, 'existence has its own *raison d'être*' (in Chinese they say *Cun Zai Jiu Shi He Li De*), originally asserted by Hegel, the German philosopher. It is interpreted that it might be difficult to change a result if the *raisons d'être* could not be eliminated. Also, it is easily recognized that, if such a *raison d'être* continues to exist, path dependence could be established. In 1949, China was in a complicated situation, both internal and external, and the socialist system was established. The definition of a socialist system has never been so simple. Initially, China introduced the Soviet type socialist system, this was because the Chinese Communist Party administration, which started as the revolutionary party, had no experience in building a nation, so introducing the Soviet model was the only selection. Mao Zedong, who had a strong personality, did not want simply to copy the Soviet model. In fact, the Ten Important Relations announced in 1956 were advocated with the characteristics of Mao Zedong's personality.

At the end of the 1950s, Sino–Soviet relations worsened, although various Soviet legacies remained, the Chinese way of development was changed to a Mao Zedong type socialist system. One of the reasons for the deterioration in Sino–Soviet relations came from the great power's consciousness of China. During the days of the Cold War, what the USA requested of Japan was similar to the requests Khrushchev demanded of China. However, Japan was completely different from China, and Mao Zedong decisively refused Khrushchev's requests. After that Mao Zedong advanced the slogan of self-reliance for the Chinese people, and the Chinese people were in sympathy with this (people in China had similar ideas to their leader, Mao Zedong). To establish the self-reliance model, the Daqing model[4] and Dazhai model[5] were made for industry and agriculture respectively, and became the examples of Chinese socialist construction.

By then, the unique personality of Mao Zedong had been substantially effective for China for many years. The Cultural Revolution was the strange political movement – why did such a large scale political movement occur? Was the personality of Mao Zedong like a monkey (said to be similar to the personality of Sun Wukong, the main character in the classical *Chinese* epic novel, *Xiyouji – Journey to the West*) leading the strange political movement (for the biography of Mao Zedong, see Terrill, 1999)? Or should we suppose that to take on the burden of 4000 years of Chinese history needed extraordinary strength. Thus, it might be natural for China to drive the historical burden away. In other words, we could recognize that the Cultural Revolution was evidence that the Chinese

4 At the end of 1963, in Hei Longjiang province, the Daqing oil field was discovered and the days when China depended upon oil imports were finished. The Daqing oil field was completed successfully, in all the processes, from inquiry to oil production, within a very short period with unbelievable hardships. In 1964, Mao Zedong used a slogan with the aim of 'industry should follow the Daqing', by praising the spirit of Daqing oil field workers. After that, the slogan spread throughout the whole nation.

5 Dazhai was traditionally a poor mountain village in Xiyang county, Shanxi province. In the 1950s, in the mountain village concerned, which was arranged as a production group under the farming cooperatives and the people's commune, they reclaimed land from the foot of the mountain and successfully made it into terraced fields. The fields recorded a succession of good harvests, as *Renmin RiBao* (*People's Daily*) on December 28, 1963 and February 10, 1964, announced in the special report and the editorial, which highly evaluated the Dazhai spirit and Dazhai achievements. Mao Zedong also advocated 'agriculture should follow the Dazhai' which was parallel to 'industry should follow the Daqing'. During the process, Chen Yonggui who was a secretary of a village party branch played the serious role of the leader, and later he was promoted to Vice Premier of the Chinese Cabinet, recommended by Mao Zedong (Chen Yonggui was a true peasant and it was said he could read only around 1000 Chinese characters and he could write much fewer than 1000 Chinese characters).

Communist Party was not able to inherit the 4000 years of Chinese history. The reason for the strange political movement seemed to be coming from the character of the Chinese Communist Party. The early stage leaders of the Communist Party included many intellectuals; however, later more leaders, from workers and peasants, gradually occupied the positions. Those leaders who took root in the earth of China succeeded in rousing national sentiment and led their revolution to victory. Unfortunately, however, they had weak transcendence, and in the victory of revolution there were enough traces of a peasant uprising at the end of the dynasty.

Meanwhile, Mao Zedong's development system for 30 years surely contributed to presenting Chinese nation building as the 'negative legacy'. As it is said that 'failure is a stepping-stone to success', the Chinese people were immune to the negative legacy. That is to say, the Chinese people were no longer interested in Mao Zedong's type of socialist system. Socialism as the ideology could still be fascinating. However, the main problem is how to reach utopia. We think the welfare state system has been fairly stimulating. Recently in China, the North European model, represented by Swedish model, has been actively discussed, behind which the people's interest and fretfulness against the hidden problems of the Chinese development model are recognized. Although socialism still has rationality as the goal, the actual important task has been to find the best way to reach the goal.

Chapter 2
Transition towards the Deng Xiaoping Development System: The Wisdom of 'Creative Destruction'

Introduction

A well-known policy measure in China, called the 'reform and open door policy', has been implemented through the gradual transition process. This indicates the expansion and deepening of Chinese transition, in which there has been an expansion of the open areas, from an open coastal strategy in the 1980s to an omni-directional open strategy in the 1990s, with a deepening of democratic and market oriented system.

On the reform and open door policy in China, many arguments have been discussed from various viewpoints. For example, Murrell (1992), Lin Yifu *et al.* (1999) comparatively analyzed the differences in patterns, factors and performances between a gradual transition process in China and Hungary and a radical transition in Poland and Russia. In addition, Fan Gang (1993), Ogawa and Watanabe (1995), Aslund (1994), Winiecki (1993), Berliner (1994), Kornai (1990), among others, investigated the costs and benefits related to the respective transition methods.

In this chapter, we concentrate our attention on the Deng Xiaoping development system, for which we would indicate that the key concept of the system was the wisdom of *creative destruction*. In order to succeed with gradual transition, it is important to have a leader who can reset the logic of initial reform, have a reasonable priority of reforms, and a systemic point of view.

This chapter consists of the following five sections and the conclusion. In the next section, we explain the transition and strategy towards a market-oriented system and construction of a policy system, and in the following three sections, we examine the three main issues of Chinese transition, which are (1) rural reform, (2) urban reform, and (3) the open door policy, and then investigate the relations between them. In the sixth section, we consider the recent situation of inland development strategy and analyze the possibility of inland development. Finally, a short conclusion is given.

Transition towards a market-oriented system: reset of the logic of initial reform and construction of strategy and the policy system

Reset of the logic of initial reform

As shown previously, the two economic systems (i.e. before and after 1978) have a respective foundation of logic for their systems. The logic of transformation was thus the transformation of the foundation. But why has such a transformation occurred?

Such a transformation was caused by various factors, and we are going to focus our attention upon the following three factors: (1) the huge disparity between China and the rest of the world, owing to 30 years of central planning in China, from the nation-building to the open-door policy; (2) characteristics of a slackly centralized Chinese system; and (3) Deng Xiaoping's wisdom.

First, we should have a short look at the circumstances in China in 1978.

A self-circulating mechanism under the centrally planned system brought about, for China, a serious pathology, expressed by political disturbance and economic backwardness. The Cultural Revolution showing serious defects in the political and economic system was redressed, which was how the reform and open door policy all started. The Chinese economy in 1978 suffered from not only huge disparity in GDP level compared with advanced industrialized economies but also problems in distortion of industrial structure and regional structure. It has been said that, in order to reduce the serious problems, there is no other way except a deep-rooted transition of the socio-economic system.

Second, we think the characteristics of a slackly centralized system in China were effectively related with such transformation. Brus (1972) classified the socialist economic system into the following three categories: (1) war-time communism; (2) collective socialism; and (3) decentralized socialism. Later he added one more type of socialism – market socialism – in which, under the public property system, the decision-making authority regarding investment was left to markets and enterprises.

The Chinese centrally planned economy carried out in the Mao Zedong's era from the 1950s to 1970s had the characteristics, as indicated by Nakagane (1979), of a 'slackly centralized system' (a centralized system without enough institutions). These seemed to be roughly the same characteristics as the 'decentralized socialism' described by Brus (1972). In the Mao Zedong's era, a drastic plan for a local decentralization system was carried out in order to realize a development strategy with a locally self-completed industrial system. Meanwhile however, because of Mao Zedong's dogmatic way of thinking (for example, as Mao Zedong believed in the motive power theory of contradiction, it might be assumed he was repulsed by institutionalization), there was no such stabilized mechanism of the policy in Mao Zedong's era in China. Generally speaking, such Chinese characteristics in Mao Zedong's era as a slackly centralized system and local decentralization system gave substantial effects to Chinese society after the open door policy was started (Nakagane, 1999).

To be sure, because China, as an agricultural country, was different from the USSR, an industrial country, China has been less organized than the USSR and the first wave of Chinese reform and the open policy began in rural areas (see the latter part of this chapter). In addition, in urban areas, again different from the USSR, there in China were lots of collective-owned enterprises as well as state-owned enterprises. The 'less organized' society means there were many openings within the organization, which were spaces in which to develop new opportunities. In other words, because of the less organized society, China has always included flexibility. The slackly centralized system was an institutional condition for China in order for creative destruction to be possible.

Third, the fact that Deng Xiaoping was a powerful leader was very important. The Chinese people praised him as a magnificent planner for reform and for the open door policy. On February 14, 1981, Deng Xiaoping wrote in the preface for his *Collective Works of Deng Xiaoping*, published by Pergamon (UK), that he was a son of the Chinese people, and he heartily loved his Chinese mother country and Chinese people. The sentiment of loving one's mother country is a natural extension to loving one's home town, which might be instinctive for human beings. However, as far as the life of Deng Xiaoping was concerned, we could recognize, in his rational mind, that this was not simply a natural extension. The details on Deng Xiaoping are as following.

Comparison of the characters of the two leaders: Mao Zedong and Deng Xiaoping

Many people correctly recognize Deng Xiaoping's remarkable contribution to Chinese reform and the open door policy. In connection with this, an interesting question to be analyzed is why Mao Zedong could not do what Deng Xiaoping could do. In other words, even though there was not a significant difference in their wisdom (Mao Zedong was endowed with prominent gifts in a variety of fields, such as military strategy, calligraphy, poetry etc), what brought them to such a different way of thinking? According to the author of this book, there were some philosophical factors that should be investigated as relating to life experience and wisdom.

Deng Xiaoping (1904–1997) came from Guangan county, Sichuang province and was accepted by a preliminary school to study in France. In 1920, when he was young, he visited France with Zhou Enlai and others and experienced the real world by studying and working. At the beginning of 1926, he visited to Moscow to study at the Moscow Eastern University and at Sun Yat-Sen University, and he returned to China in the spring of 1927. After that, he was engaged for many years in intelligence work for the Chinese communist party in the enemy-occupied region in China (Zhou Enlai did the same work). He acquired the ability to work, side by side with the enemy. In intelligence work, such abilities as being suited to the occasion, as finding a means of survival, were in high demand. They became part of Deng Xiaoping's character. After he returned to China, he lost his position twice and miraculously came back each time. Deng Xiaoping had a magnificent character, including both as a result of his experiences in the outside world and his excellent observational ability. In addition, he was a person of conviction, from which we think he obtained his optimism and patience.

Six years' study in France was significant as it gave him an impression of the western world. His experience of staying in Western Europe and the Soviet Union, we think, contributed to his well-balanced sense of the 'outside' world. It displayed a significant contrast with Mao Zedong, who was terrified by the unknown 'outside' world. Deng Xiaoping did not agree with Mao Zedong's ideas, saying that a World War might occur as occasion demanded. To the contrary, he recognized that both peace and development were two major subjects for the world. After Zhou Enlai and Mao Zedong passed away, one after another, Deng Xiaoping expressed his political capability, based upon his wisdom, to lead China to an open system.

Deng Xiaoping's view on development and the ideal of Chinese ancient politics

In September 1985, on the way back to Beijing from the visit to North Korea, Deng Xiaoping went to Benxi city, Liaoning province, to inspect it. Then he said the following;

> The world is ceaselessly changing day by day. New problems and challenges have constantly come into existence. We should not close the door. We should not be late permanently without recognition. Our country was counted as a poor country, the Third World, and was classified as a less developed country. (Deng Xiaoping, 1994)

Deng Xiaoping reached the conclusion from his experience and observation that a less-developed poor country could not be respected by other countries and could not be entrusted by the people of his own country. In 1978, just before the new China started, Deng Xiaoping said, with deep regret, that we were too poor, too less developed, and he was very sorry for the Chinese people. On June 30, 1983, when Deng Xiaoping talked with his friends from foreign countries, he mentioned that socialism has to eradicate poverty, poverty had no relations with socialism and also poverty had nothing to do with communism.

One of Deng Xiaoping's wise remarks was that some people could become richer than others earlier; he also predicted that, when the reform and open door policy started, shared growth should be emphasized to be the main aim, and in the near future it would really be the central goal. As regards the Chinese development stage, he stressed the development stage theory whose chief concept was the '*Xiaokang*' (comfortable) society, coming originally from the ideal of Chinese ancient politics.

At the end of 1979, Deng Xiaoping first declared the concept of '*Xiaokang*'. At the beginning of 1980, he emphasized that the '*Xiaokang*' would be realized within two decades. In 1981, he explained the strategic idea, called the two-stage schedule, which indicated within two decades the Chinese economy would double in size. In September 1982, the above idea was included in the Report of the Twelfth National Representative Meeting of the Chinese Communist Party. In 1987, three years in advance, China realized the first doubling of the Gross National Product. Thus, in April 1987, Deng Xiaoping first mentioned a three-stage development plan when he talked with a Spanish friend. In October the same year, the plan was included in the Report of the Thirteenth National Representative Meeting of the Chinese Communist Party.

The details of the three-stage development plan were as follows. The aim was, in the first stage, to realize a doubling in the per capita GDP in the 1980s. The base per capita GDP in 1980 (when Chinese per capita GDP was only US$250) would double to be US$500. In the second stage, until the end of the 20th century, the second doubling of per capita GDP would be realized, which meant a per capita GDP of US$1000. With such a level of per capita GDP, China would be in the 'comfortable society'. From the poor country it was, China would become the *Xiaokang* China. Then, the Chinese total GDP level would reach US$1000 billion. Even though the per capita GDP level was still low, the national total level would become substantial. In light of this aim, the most important stage was the third one. From the start of the 21st century, within 30 to 50 years, the third doubling in the per capita GDP would be realized, which would lead to a per capita GDP of US$4000. In such a stage, China would surely reach the middle level of a developed country. That would be our ambition (Deng Xiaoping, 1993).

The 'comfortable society' emphasized by Deng Xiaoping might have close relations with the 'Datong ideal' (egalitarian ideal) for Chinese people. The first Confucian writing insisting on a 'Datong world' (egalitarian world) was the *LiJi LiYunPian.* The Confucius way of saying, classified human society into three, which were (1) '*Luanshi*' (chaotic), (2) '*Xiaokang*' (comfortable), and (3) '*Datong*' (egalitarian). As regards the 'Datong' (common prosperous) society, it was described as

> in the egalitarian society, everybody worked for the public. Wise and capable persons were selected, and confidence and friendship were of great importance. Thus, people think of everybody as parents and children with care and affection. Every elderly person reaches a happy end of life, every person in his prime has the sphere of activity, every young person has his own characteristic field, a person without family and disabled person is taken care by the society. Men have appropriate jobs and women have happy families. They respect the results of work, but do not occupy them. They work hard but not for themselves. There is no conspiracy, no thief, no revolt, which leads to a peaceful and comfortable society. They do not need to close doors in the society.

Altogether, there are 80 chapters in the scripture of Taoism, from the same era as Confucius, and although there is a little bit of a passive ideology, saying 'towards a simple life with abolishing useless wisdom', in the 'small country and small number of population', a comfortable and harmonized society is described. After this, the 'egalitarian society' ideology became the supreme ideal of politics of ancient China. In contemporary China, '*Tian Chao Tian Mu Zhi*' (which meant the equal area of arable land system) was promulgated by Hong Xiuquan, the leader of '*Taiping Tianguo* (Peaceful Heaven) Movement' was an expression of the 'egalitarian society' ideology.

Kang Youwei completed the ten volumes of '*Da Tong Shu*' (Theory of Egalitarianism). In addition, his pupil Liang Qichao pointed out in such works as *Jun Zheng Min Zheng Xiang Shan Zhi Li*, which combined western political theories with the three societies' theory – meaning *Ju Luan Shi* (chaotic), *Xiao Kang Sheng PingShi* (comfortable), *Da Tong Tai Ping Shi* (egaritarian) – asserted by GongYangJia, one of the hundred schools of those days when every scholar could express his own opinion, at the time of the 'Chinese spring and autumn' (from 770 AD to 476 AD), as follows. It was the historical necessity for the society to evolve gradually from sorrow to joy, from wrong to right, from war to peace, from barbarianism to civilization, which also indicated this as a historical process, from *Duo Jun Shi* (lots of monarchs existing, in *Ju Luan Shi* – chaos) to *Yi Jun Shi* (only one monarch existing, *Xiao Kang Sheng PingShi* – comfortable), furthermore from *Yi Jun Shi* to *Min Zheng Shi* (the society of people's sovereignty, *Da Tong Tai Ping Shi* – egalitarianism). It was also said that the *San Ming Zhu Yi* ideology by Sun Yat-sen was influenced by the *Datong* ideology (towards a shared society).

In the *Theory towards People's Democracy*, written by Mao Zedong in 1949, Mao Zedong insisted that the way towards a shared society was through revolution. It has been generally asserted that the People's commune, whose characteristic was *Yi Da Er Gong* (meaning that the communes were, first, large scale and, second, under public ownership), started in 1958 and was the reflection of Mao Zedong's ideology towards a shared society. The comfortable society mentioned by Deng Xiaoping could be interpreted as the society of one stage before a shared society.

Deng Xiaoping's view of the world: the two big themes for the world are peace and development

In 1985, as regards the international situation, Deng Xiaoping mentioned the following; the current big global issues, meaning global strategic issues, were (1) first, the peace issue, and (2) second, the development issue. The peace issue was the East–West problem and the development issue was the North–South issue. Generally, these were summarized as four words: east, West, North, and South. After that he always emphasized, at any National Meeting of Communist Party Representatives, that peace and development were two major issues.

Deng Xiaoping displayed the same slogan 'Five Principles of Peaceful Coexistence' as in the Mao Zedong's era, and developed the contents of it. In particular, it was meaningful that, beyond the social system and ideology, he attempted to have friendly and cooperative relations with every country. Deng Xiaoping once said to a visitor from the USA that it was an old-fashioned ideology to think that such capitalist countries as USA would be abolished by our ideology. He did not think of international relations from ideological points of view. Sino–US relations had the characteristics of North-South relations, pointing out that the USA was the greatest developed country and China was the biggest developing country. People had to find shared interests between the countries. He kept mentioning the following to the visitor from US; you have a problem in developing more and to do so you need to cooperate with developing countries. Unless developing countries grow, more development for USA will be difficult. It is necessary for you to have a peaceful situation.

Meanwhile, as far as Chinese relations with socialist countries were concerned, Deng Xiaoping recommended these countries do not stick to historical affairs, saying that past discrepancies between both countries should not be obstacles to friendship and peaceful relations. In order to realize normal relations between China and the Soviet Union, he advocated to Soviet leaders that both sides should finish with the past and develop the future together.

Four modernization theories as goals of the reform and open door policy

The purposes of reform and open door policy date back to the presentation of four modernizations.

At the first meeting of the Fourth National Parliament on 13 January 1975, Zhou Enlai, the Prime Minister of the Cabinet, presented a plan of four modernizations in the government policy report, officially for the first time. The four modernizations indicate the goal of leading China to be the front runner in the world in four fields: industry, agriculture, national defense, and science and technology. As regards the plan, the national economy was scheduled to be developed in two stages, from 1966–1980 and 1980–2000. However, a concrete plan was not be clarified at that time. With the process of reform, and the open door policy starting in 1978, we think that the evolution of the four modernizations could be understood as the evolution of the resolution measures for an increase in labor productivity, an increase in personal consumption, the resolution of dual structures (see Chapter 1), the transfer of advanced technology, and the alleviation of economic disparity, and so on.

The initial plan of the four modernizations was originally proposed in *Hurrah for Mao Zedong* in 1955.[1] This was consistently said to be the overall goals for social construction after the People's Republic of China was founded. It has been necessary for the concrete development strategy and development policy plan to

1 Mao Zedong (1974), which has 'The Summary of The Sixth General Meeting of the Seventh Communist Party Central Committee Expanded General Meeting of September 1955'.

use enough of the huge land resources. In China, which experienced the failure of a central planning system, they wished to have the new leader and the evolution of a strategic plan.

On the natural gifts of the ideal leader

Compared with Mao Zedong, Deng Xiaoping could be said to be a more rational leader. Deng Xiaoping recognized dialectically the relations between himself and society, and between China and the rest of the world. Meanwhile, Mao Zedong had a more emotional portion in his leadership, with a self-centered wish for realization, through which Mao Zedong found it easier to lose the balance between the above two relations.

By returning to the first question, the reason why Mao Zedong could not do what Deng Xiaoping could do, a simple answer is as follows. We think, even with the same wisdom, Mao Zedong's necessary life experience as a leader of China had a serious deficiency compared with Deng Xiaoping. The necessary character for a leader of a newly developed China requires both life experiences with an open society during his younger days and the observational ability. The relatively closed life experience of Mao Zedong, we think, led to his relatively closed way of thinking (Deng Xiaoping was the opposite, which might be said as a kind of path dependency). Generally speaking therefore, a person in a high position within a closed system tends to lose flexibility towards the outside world and also tends to be more exclusive. One can point out the synergy between a closed system and closed character of the leader. The stronger the character, like Mao Zedong, the closer the relations. Mao Zedong visited the Soviet Union twice after the foundation of the People's Republic of China.[2] However, Soviet leaders that had the same strong character as him, Stalin and Khrushchev, did not get on with Mao Zedong. After the two visits to the Soviet Union, Mao Zedong visited no other country. At the end of the 1950s, Sino–Soviet relations drastically worsened.

Taking into consideration the above-mentioned events, cooperation between socialist countries unfortunately could not be recognized. The CMEA (Council for

---

2 For two years from the beginning of 1947 to the beginning of 1949, Mao Zedong requested Stalin to visit China five times. Stalin refused to visit China despite all Mao Zedong's requests. In December 1949, Mao Zedong realized his visit to Soviet Union. Mao Zedong and his staff left Beijing on 6 February by train, and reached Moscow on 16 February. The purposes on the Chinese side were the following: (1) by abolishing the unequal treaty between China and the Soviet Union, completed in 1945 between the Soviet Union and the Nationalist Party of China, a new Sino–Soviet Friendship Allied Treaty could be completed; (2) through Soviet support, a quick recovery of the Chinese national economy could be attempted, and (3) on 21 December Stalin's 70th birthday was celebrated. Needless to say, their main purpose was to follow the experience and performance of the Soviet Union's socialist construction. On 2 November 1957, Mao Zedong for a second time visited the Soviet Union, this time by airplane, to participate in the 40 years commemorative ceremony of the victory of the October revolution. He had a meeting with Khrushchev.

Mutual Economic Assistance) among socialist economies, which was a counter organization against the western GATT and IMF, seemed to be an international open system; however, it had a deep-rooted closed system based upon a central planning system.

The relationship between a closed system and closed-mind leader should reach a kind of equilibrium. Without this equilibrium, the system cannot survive.

In China, as the country has a long history, we can see a repetition of prosperity and economic decline. Hence, China has become a country with various kinds of complexes, such as the Boxer Rebellion complex and foreign capital complex (Sugimoto, 2006). Thus, in 1978, the purging such complexes, led by reform and the open door policy, was Deng Xiaoping's magnificent contribution to Chinese society. We think a more significant contribution by Deng Xiaoping than economic progress was to create an open-minded mentality for the Chinese people, through which China could go ahead with autonomous reform in its mental structure.

Deng Xiaoping himself was a magnificent planner for reform and the open door policy became an initial condition of Chinese development after 1978, in place of Mao Zedong.

Deng Xiaoping (late in life)

Deng Xiaoping in 1921 (right) and his uncle Deng Shaosheng

Photo 2.1 Deng Xiaoping and his uncle

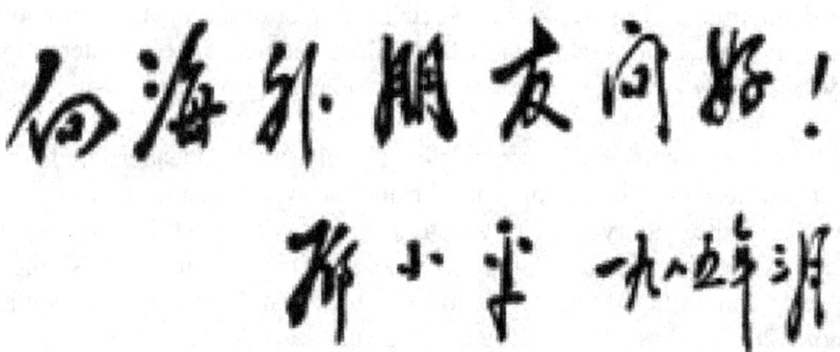

The title for the first issue of the overseas edition, Peoople's daily newspaper, by Deng Xiaoping, 'Welcome foreign friends', March 1985

Photo 2.2 "Welcome foreign friends" by Deng Xiaoping

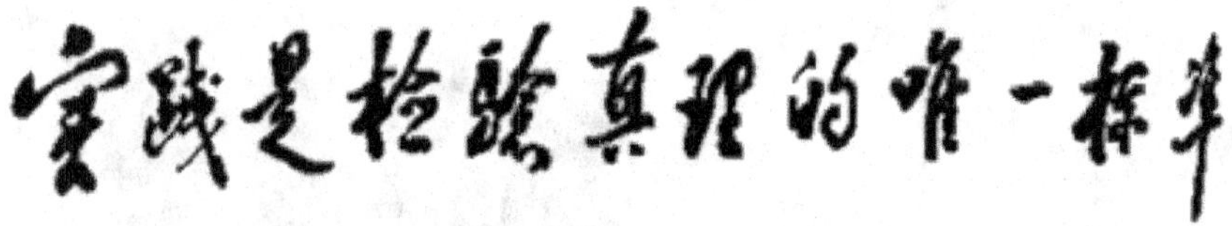

The title for a memorial of collected newspapers on criterion for the truth published in a daily newspaper, Guangming (bright future) by Deng Xiaoping, 'Practice is the only one criterion to verify the truth', 11th May, 1988

Photo 2.3 "Practice is the only one criterion to verify the truth" by Deng Xiaoping

Deepening of economic transformation: from a centrally planned system to a market socialism system

As stated in Chapter 1, after the introduction of a Soviet-type model, the Chinese central planning system could not be sustained because of exclusiveness and inefficiency. A systemic transformation was attempted at the end of 1970s, helped by Deng Xiaoping's ability as a leader. However, details of the economic system were not clear in its early stage, but were gradually clarified. We follow the locus of systemic transformation in China based upon the principles expressed at the National Conference of the Communist Party.

The proposition of a planned commercial economic system

At the Twelfth National Conference of the Communist Party (autumn, 1982), the basic principle was to have a planning economy first and a market economy subordinate to this.

In the 'decision about systemic reform of the economy by the central committee of Chinese communist party' at the Third Meeting of the Twelfth National Conference of the Communist Party in 1984 it was expressed as follows: a commercial economy was an indispensable stage for socio-economic development, and it was clarified for the first time that the Chinese socialist economy was a planned commercial economy based upon the principle of public ownership. In the decision, they said it was necessary to overcome the traditional concept of conflict between a planning economy and a commercial economy, because it could have benefits of both increasing the efficiency of enterprises and of a well-balanced development of the national economy.

Two days after the passing of the decision, at the Third Meeting of Central Advisory Committee,[3] Deng Xiaoping appreciated the decision, saying that the present official document regarding economic system was very fine, because it had an interpretation about the concept of socialism, in which completely new words were presented (Deng Xiaoping, 1993, p. 91). We could recognize the reason why Deng Xiaoping commented on it. It was said in Marx and Engels' socialist theory there was neither commercial production nor commercial exchange. Meanwhile Stalin once recognized in *Economic Problems on Soviet Socialism*, which indicated positive results for 35 years after Soviet socialism was constructed, that there could exist commercial production and commercial exchange. However, they were limited to consumer goods, and producer goods were not commodities even if they were goods. According to the rule of commercial value, the adjustment mechanism on consumer goods could work in the distribution channel but it could not work for producer goods.

On 23 October 1985, Deng Xiaoping said to a foreign visitor that there was no fundamental contradiction between socialism and a market economy. The problem was about the possibility of whether or not social production was developed using such an economic mechanism.

At the Thirteenth National Conference of the Communist Party in 1987, it was decided that a socialist planned commercial economy was a system in which the plan and the market were united. In addition, at the Fourth National Meeting of the Chinese Communist Party in June 1989, after the settlement of the Tian'an'men Affairs (the June 4 Incident), they decided to continue the reform plan, mentioning

3 The Central Advisory Committee of Chinese Communist Party was established by the decision of the Twelfth Communist Party Conference in 1982, and was abolished by the decision of the Fourteenth Communist Party Conference. The Central Advisory Committee was the transitional organization to successfully implement the change of high ranking leaders of the communist party.

that the economic system was to establish and combine a planned economy and market mechanism in order to develop a planned commercial economy.

Towards a socialist market economy system

After the Tian'an'men Affairs, China was strictly under international sanctions. With a variety of difficulties, in February 1992, Deng Xiaoping announced in the southern speech in his southern tour at Shenzhen, Guangdong province, the start of the open door policy led by him. The speech in the southern tour was on a new idea about relations between the plan and the market. He insisted on the following: as regards a planned commercial economy, the essential difference between socialism and capitalism was not whether more emphasis was put on planning or on the market. A planning system does not equal socialism, because capitalism also includes a plan, and the market does not equal capitalism because socialism also includes a market. Both the plan and market were economic measures. He announced a domestic and international Chinese way for the open door policy to progress.

At the Fourteenth Communist Party Meeting in 1992, they passed the decision on 'a few problems regarding systemic building of a socialist market economy',[4] in which the concept of a socialist market economy was officially presented. The fundamental policy framework of a socialist market economy was as follows: (1) construction of a modern enterprise system; (2) reform of the foodstuff distribution system and liberalized foodstuff prices; (3) reform of the financial system; (4) unification of the corporate tax system; and (5) reform of the social security system.

The above five systemic reforms were closely connected and, undoubtedly a systemic policy plan was necessary for full transformation (see Chapter 3).

After that at the Fifteenth Communist Party Meeting in 1997 they passed the decision about 'a few problems concerning reform and development of state-owned enterprises', with which they attempted to have multiple investment agents based on the public ownership principle and wrote clearly to promote a modern enterprise system.

At the Sixteenth Communist Party Meeting in 2002, delegations on central state-owned enterprises and on central financial organizations were formed respectively and led, in total, to 38 delegations, which was two more than the previous 36 delegations. The Meeting passed the amendment of the Chinese Communist Party and formerly permitted private enterprise owners to become members of the party, by which we could recognize that the Chinese Communist Party has changed to be the people's party. However, it should not be overlooked that lots of party members have never agreed with it. There are various reasons for this. For example, although it is the communist party, capitalist people have been

4 Selected important documents of each National Representative Meeting since the Fourth General Council of the Thirteenth Communist Party Conference, 2003.

members. This has undoubtedly caused an ideological contradiction. In addition, capitalist members are not only members but also receive such political advantages as being selected to be representatives of their respective level parliament. Thus, ordinary party members might have dissatisfaction and complaints about this state of affairs. However, a much deeper-rooted psychological reason could exist, which is the socially generalized psychology of complaints against newly rich people in social circumstances that contain severe disparities.

Because the Chinese system is formerly called 'market socialism', and because the 'socialism' cannot be consistent with a Chinese market-oriented economy, it might be a strange way of expressing the system. It should be, we think, recognized that, in the gradual movement of the Chinese reform process, the word 'socialism' has been necessary so as not to cause a hot debate on ideology. It would be a strategic practice led by Deng Xiaoping, who said that not arguing was one of his inventions. The author might interpret it that the market socialism has been a Chinese expression of an East Asian authoritarian system (see Chapter 6 on this concept).

As stated above, the Tian'an'men Affairs in 1989 might be recognized as a failure or a backward aspect of Chinese reform. However, Chinese transition has never stepped back and has been improved towards a more market-oriented system. Thus, we should understand the Tian'an'men Affairs in 1989 could be vicissitudes of systemic improvement, but not serious countercurrents. We think is might be an affair for a moment coming from losing a balance through the process of systemic transition in a large-scale country, China.

Undoubtedly, the Tian'an'men Affairs in 1989 were unhappy and tragic events; however, they were not Chinese exceptions. In most countries and regions in the East Asian model, the authoritarian system has been attacked by student movements and suffered many accusations. We could not help evaluating this as inevitable costs, like transition costs, during the process of transition, although the affairs might be re-evaluated in the future.

Three principles of reform and open door policy

Chinese reform and the open door policy after 1978 was supported by the following three principles, which were (1) reform of rural areas and agriculture; (2) 'the quarter centered' ('the trinity plus one') reform concentrated upon the transition of urban economic regions and of state-owned enterprises; and (3) the open door system toward international circumstances. The tendency of the reform was toward construction of a market oriented economic system.

We investigate in this chapter the change of development strategies and development policies regarding the above three principles and investigate the change of national economy and regional economy after the transition.

On the reform of rural areas and agriculture

The reform of agriculture and rural areas triggered the Chinese transition toward a market economy. However, taking into consideration the low value added in agriculture, and external conditions such as limited labor mobility, more development in rural areas and agriculture has been difficult without urban and industrial development. We thus need the second reform in agriculture.

Process

The first step of Chinese economic reform started in rural areas. This was the resolution of the communes and the progress of the family contract system. The resolution of the communes was radically implemented, and it has been shown that, at the end of 1983, 95% of the peasants introduced private-owned management and, at the end of 1984, around 97% of all farming families carried out a family contract system. In addition, the unified purchase and unified sale of agricultural products by central government was abolished in 1985. The movement towards a market-oriented system in the rural economy was expanded with successful results.

At the beginning of the 1980s, just after the reform and open door policy started, the majority of peasants who moved from rural areas found job opportunities in the non-agricultural sector, such as TVEs (Township and Village Enterprises). The main reasons for their movement to the non-agricultural sector in rural areas were the following: (1) because of such institutional barriers as the family registered system and food allocation system, it was very difficult for them to get jobs in the urban area; and (2) due to the lack of receiving capacity in urban areas, coming from an immature social infrastructure and the redundant workers in the state-owned sector, the central government politically recommended the *LiTuBuLiXiang*, indicating the 'even leaving farmland, staying in homeland' policy.

However, in October 1984, the 'official notice from the cabinet on the problem for peasants to move to the suburban area and transfer their family registrations' was promulgated, and on the condition that they are not dependent upon food allocation from the nation, their movement to a smaller suburban area than the county level was officially permitted. Also accompanying the promotion of reform and open door policy, the economic development in China was accelerated and labor demand in urban areas, especially in construction sector, was increased. Moreover, because the free market for agricultural products was growing, it was not so difficult to get food, which was independent of the government food allocation. Based upon such various social backgrounds, after the middle of the 1980s, in not only local small urban areas but also big urban areas, the number of peasants who moved to an urban area to find job opportunities by staying with their family registrations in the homelands rapidly increased. The number, when the Chinese economy expanded in 1988, reached 2.09 million in Shanghai, 1.31

million in Beijing, and 1.3 million in Guangzhou, and so on, in each of which their population equaled 20 to 40% of the original population (Zhou Taihe, 1984).

Earlier literature suggested that, in the first half of the 1980s, agricultural production in China substantially increased, which led to the decreased disparity between urban and rural areas, however, in the second half of the 1980s, agricultural production shrank and the disparity between the urban and rural increased. That is to say, the temporary agricultural land reform, which was said to be a family contract system at the beginning of 1980s, was effective but quite limited. Thus, in order to prevent the Ricardian trap and to alleviate the disparity between the urban and rural, new institutional establishments seemed to be necessary.

New tendency

In the decision about 'a few problems concerning policies on agriculture and rural areas' by the Chinese Communist Party, passed at the Fourth National Conference of the Fifteenth Communist Party Meeting in October 1998, the Party considered a reform policy of rural areas for 20 years. They presented a goal to establish new rural areas with the characteristics of socialism up to 2010, and emphasized the necessity of keeping the distribution system for the long run, combining distribution of labor with distribution of capital according to the coexistence of public ownership and private ownership, including the family contract system.

At the Sixteenth Communist Party Meeting in 2002, the Party stressed important works to establish a 'comfortable society' (meaning a slightly affluent society, as explained previously) by increasing peasants' income and developing a farming economy. In other words, the jobs were implemented by strengthening the basic position of agriculture, by adjusting the economic structure of agriculture and rural areas, by protecting and increasing the general ability in agriculture, and by reinforcing the competitiveness of agriculture (taking into consideration opening the agricultural market by joining the WTO). Agricultural management has to progress from industrial viewpoints and develop the market in rural areas. As regards policies for urbanization, the Party insisted on maintaining cooperative development among large- and middle-scale cities and local districts. For the development of local districts, based upon the present prefectures, townships and villages with satisfying conditions, population and industry had to be reasonably allocated. In addition, development of local districts should be combined with development of TVEs and with development of agricultural services.

However, even if such plans were announced, because of the rapid progression of urbanization in China from 1999, illegal occupations of arable lands (most of which were closely related with local government, leading to a boom in development districts and development of real estates) occurred frequently. In addition, a serious disadvantageous situation of decreased food production in four consecutive years happened. The disadvantaged called people's attention to the 'three agricultural related problems'. Thus, it has been pointed out that, if a current agricultural country, such as China, encounters the situation in which arable land in the farming area reaches its limit, then the marginal productivity of the land is decreased, and economy would suffer from the Ricardian trap. To raise the motivation for agricultural production for peasants, the agricultural tax, which was collected at a higher percentage than taxes in the industrial and service sectors, was abolished in 2005.

Consideration

Chinese transition started in rural areas and has now returned to agriculture and rural areas. We think this has necessarily happened because the development strategy with priority has had to adjust to a bad reaction (indicated as a disparity) produced by its own function.

We consider the reason why the transition started in rural areas, and what the effects of were of rural area reforms.

First, it is no exaggeration to say that rural areas are on the verge of collapse because they were placed as a source of primitive accumulation for 30 years. When peasants in Xiaogang village, Fengyang county, Anhui province, voluntarily began the family contract system by taking risks, there was an easily recognized tension with traditional institutions[5]. This might be an expression of institutional inefficiency.

As a matter of fact, after the people's commune started, peasants were not fully unresisting. In the basic rural areas in China they took such collective measures as hidden production. For example, for the production of 100 kg of potatoes and sweet potatoes, the village collected only 50 kg and the rest of the total production stayed with the peasants. They recognized that a way to increase peasants'

5 At present, Xiaogang village consists of two natural villages. Geographically it is located in the eastern part of Anhuishengfengyang county, which belongs to Xiaoxihe Town. It is 5 km from Jinjiu Railway (between Beijing and Kowloon, Hong Kong), 7 km from provincial road no.307, 20 km from two ports of Huai River, Mingguang and Linhuai (Huai River valley is positioned between the two big river valleys of Yangtze River and Yellow River). The present scale of the village is 90 families, a population of 373, including 180 in the workforce, the total area of arable land is around 10667 ares including 7100 ares contracted arable land, 28.6 per capita area.

Xiaogang village before 1978 (which was called as Xiaogang production group then) was well known as a *Shankao* village (which means a village depending upon the following three; (1) food sold by an upper organization, which is called *Fanxiaoliang*, indicating that central government purchases food once and then sells it back to farmers when poor harvest happens; (2) aid as regards budget deficit; (3) debt regarding production), and almost all families could do nothing except beg, after the autumn every year. On November 24, 1978, 18 farmers of Xiaogang village gave, in secret, a written oath and started a family contract system before all other villages in China, after making up their mind to carry out the contract of land, and even risking being imprisoned. It might be historically by chance, but just after the farmers' written oath, the Eleventh Communist Party Conference was held and they announced the open door policy in China. Xiaogang village became the birthplace of Chinese agricultural reform by their courageous behavior.

incentive for production was the family contract system. For example, in 1956, in Yongjia county, Wenzhou city of Zhejiang province, they had hidden experiments which resulted in the production volume in the family contract system reaching three to four times more than in the collective production system. In 1959 and 1962, because serious poor harvests occurred in addition to the wrong agricultural policies, many people died of hunger, during when Deng Xiaoping supported the family contract system experiments in Anhui province by using the 'black cats and white cats assertion'. Moreover, after 1976, hidden family contract systems were carried out in such provinces as Anhui and Sichuan (for example, Du Runsheng, 1998).

The above-mentioned cases suggest to us that China has been managed by a slackly centralized system and, when political excitement and class struggle disputes were superficially run around the whole nation, the Chinese people, particularly peasants, were reliably rational. Political and the ideological excitement was fairly easily broken when humans were faced by the subsistence minimum. Chinese peasants' simple rationality, which did not disappear even in the days of a central planning system, could construct a bridge over the initial stage of the reform and open door policy, which started later, in 1978.

Second, food production in rural areas was a necessity for everyday life; however, as far as value added points of view are concerned, agriculture was not a key industry, which meant that experiment and failure could be permitted. It was indicated that Chinese systemic transition was easier because China could start with the agricultural sector. As experience in China and Vietnam clearly showed, agricultural reform was less difficult than non-agricultural reform, because of the easier effects.

Third, we think Deng Xiaoping correctly recognized that, judging from such conditions as a redundant population in rural areas and the technology level in agriculture, the development stage of Chinese agriculture after 1978 reached the peasant economy. Aspiring to the idealistic commune system and large-scale production by mechanization was dangerous, so rather, in order to raise workers' incentive, the family contract system was introduced.

Urban reform: institutional revision and change of urban economic regions

The evolution, all over the nation, by transforming from a coastal open strategy in the 1980s to an omni-directional open strategy in the 1990s has been an important policy measure to deepen the freer mobility of production factors as well as to rearrange the functional regional economy, through destroying administrative barriers among regions. At the same time, one of the important aims of urban reform was undoubtedly to reform the state-owned enterprise system, which would mainly take responsibility for urban industry. In this section we consider the liberalizing measures of production factor mobility and the change of urban economic regions.

Liberalizing measures of production factor mobility

The effective functioning of a market economy needs to mobilize production factors and utilize them efficiently; thus, the liberalization of production materials, capital, technology and human resources and the successful establishment of the market would be necessary.

In the 1990s in China, extroversive development through such measures as promotion of price liberalization, establishment of the capital and labor market, and deregulation of foreign capital inflow to place. At the end of 1991, each industry in the real estate, distribution, transportation, bank, insurance, and trading sectors, in which foreign capital was not allowed, were partly liberalized. Also in the service sector, the Chinese government has been enthusiastic in introducing the know-how of foreign capital as the service sector puts in a great deal of effort. These efforts were initially limited to some cities in coastal areas, such as Shanghai Pudong East Area, Beijing, Tianjin, and Dalian, however, after the experimental stage was finished, the area was gradually expanded. For example, as regards the area in which foreign banks were permitted to conduct business in Chinese yuan, it was strictly limited to only Shanghai Pudong area. However, the area was extended to 18 cities in 2004 and 25 cities in December 2005 (see Chapter 3 on the details).

To alleviate the serious shortage of materials all over the nation because of price distortion, with the Eighth Five Year Plan the Chinese government increased the investment amount for mineral resources development compared with the previous Five Year Plan period. Also, since 1991, energy and materials prices, which had such a serious price distortion that the government always had to make up for the deficit, were raised. In 1992, market transaction amounts of coal and oil substantially increased. The main aim of the distortion adjustment was to mobilize private activities into resource development by stimulating production expansion through raising profitability, in addition to other aims of decreasing the government budget deficit and emphasizing consumers' economizing behavior.

After the presentation of the market socialism system in 1992, in 1993 the price and management of most agricultural products (including food) was transformed into an open system with a price mechanism in a free market. All the coupon systems, such as food provision, which was indispensable to purchase foods, were abolished. The per capita fixed amount allocation system was replaced by a free purchasing system in the market.

Reform and tasks of the 'county receives city's guidance' system

In the previous chapter, the characteristics of the 'county receives city's guidance' system in the centrally planning era were introduced in the administrative economic district. In this chapter, we look at the later development, after 1980s. The new efforts to establish a regional economy, including both industry and agriculture were closely connected with the above-stated liberalization measures of production factor mobility.

(I) Process of change

In the 1980s, in the relatively economic developed areas they carried out the system in which 'the city included counties'. This meant that the leading cities, which had developed economies, contained the surrounding counties and the respective advantages – which indicated such urban advantages as political, economic, cultural, technological and informational and such rural advantages as resources, lands and labor forces – were combined to reach and find a new type of urban regional economy, with its respective size and characteristics.

In 1982, the Central Chinese Communist Party promulgated the 52nd document, which was the announcement on the trial of the 'county receives city's guidance' system by reforming the district system. At the end of 1982, it carried out the trial, initially in Jiangsu province, and later from 1983 it was promoted in the whole nation one province after another; for example, in Liaoning province (1984) and in Guangdong province (1988).

As Table 1.6 in Chapter 1 of this book showed, in 1994, in the 29 provinces, autonomous districts and cities under direct control of central government (except Hainan province), the above-mentioned system was carried out, and altogether 196 cities (93.77% of cities under direct control of central government and of local government level) contained 741 counties, 31 autonomous counties, nine *qi* (meaning autonomous administrative organizations of minority race, which corresponded to the county), and two special zones.[6] The number of counties which received city's guidance totaled 45.13% of the administrative organization at county level, except for cities of county level and districts controlled by cities. In addition, 240 cities of county level were entrusted the control to the cities. On the average, each city has 4.02 counties to guide.

Figure 2.1 shows the city structure to implement the 'county receives city's guidance' system in China.

(II) Problems and limits: Santai district case

At the time when this reform to 'county receives city's guidance' system was tried, the system was given positive evaluation all over the nation. Leaders of provinces and autonomous districts thought that, through such a systemic trial, the separation between urban and rural would be broken down and a new type of relations between urban and rural, with Chinese characteristics, established, which would lead to the decreased disparity between the two areas. Meanwhile, central cities were pleased to secure their demands for vegetables, side dishes, industrial materials, and to expand the supply market of their industrial products. In addition, counties wished to introduce technologies, human resources, capital and equipment depending upon the power of cities.

---

6 Different from *Jingji Tequ* (Special economic zones) in coastal area after 1979, there were *Tequ* for the purpose of forestry, mining industry and tourism.

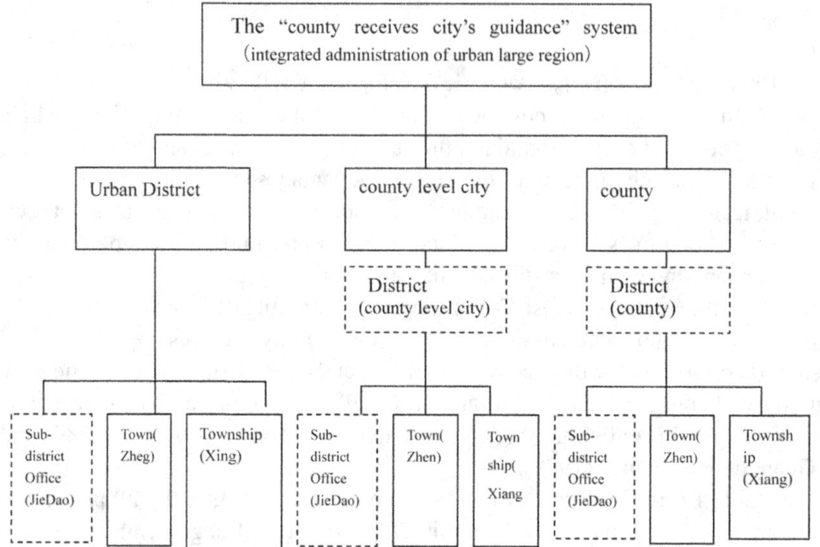

Note: (1) municipalities in this system are roughly classified into two groups: "municipalities directly under the central government" and "municipalities directly under the control of the province".

(2) parts of the dotted line are not administrative institutions, but agency of upper administrative institutions.

Source: Author.

Figure 2.1 City Structure in China: the "county receives city's guidance" system

Analysis of their motives of cities and counties suggested that the 'county receives city's guidance' system was evaluated as a haphazard policy carried out in an incomplete system of the factor market and goods market because the market system was immature. Both city and county had an immature market system in which the transaction costs of the market with uncertainty and externality became higher, and thus through direct intervention of administrative organization they had transactions in order to exchange necessities with each other.

In short, in 1983, the systemic transition of the Chinese economy started, and actual economic reforms were implemented. The situation of 'county receives city's guidance' system in this period showed the change of the central planning system and the system played a substantial role in the rearrangement of the regional economy. In addition, it clearly indicated the limit or transitional character of centrally planned economies.

From the viewpoint of regional breakdown, the more the market-oriented system was developed, the more the contradictions between city and county in the 'county receives city's guidance' system became clear. That was because it undoubtedly cost less for a county's economic activities to use a market system than an administrative system under a higher level city's guidance.

We could recognize the 'Research on the problems of administrative district system in Santai district (Taizhou, Taixin, and Taixian) of Jiangsu province' (Liu Junde, 1996, pp. 302–320) as helpful evidence of the above-mentioned situation.

The Santai district of Jiangsu province was the third-level economic district within the province, whose center was Taizhou. According to the 'county receives city's guidance' system, all of Santai (Taizhou, Taixin, and Taixian) were under the system of administrative regulations, which were guided by Yangzhou city. This produced the distortion between the administrative district and economic district of the urban area. The research mentioned specific contradictions and problems as follows.

First, Santai district traditionally and objectively existed as an urban area economic district, which however had no appropriate administrative organization to regulate the three cities. In addition, Yangzhou city, which was formerly the higher administrative organization to guide the three cities, had substantial difficulties to overcome. As Table 2.1 displays, a strictly homogeneous structure of industries was recognized among the three cities. Therefore, it was difficult to attain optimum size production in Santai district and there always occurred keen competition for materials and products among the cities.

Second, because the three cities in Santai district suffered from disadvantages in budget allocation, project arrangement etc, given by Yangzhou city, their relations with Yangzhou city worsened. Thus, in addition to the economic loss, an atmosphere of tension and caution was brought about.

Third, the above-stated research suggested that the position of Taizhou city, which was a relatively larger city, and also the economic center, was gradually declining. It resulted in substantial effects against economic development of the surrounding region.

When tough conflicts among the cities continued, in 1996 the Taizhou city (of the local level) was ratified by the cabinet and was established. As the lower government of Taizhou city, there were four cities of county level, Xinghua, Jingjiang, Taixing, Jiangyan (former Taixian) and two districts, Hailing, Gaogang, whose total land area and total population reached 5,790 square kilometers and 5.04 million respectively.

Briefly, the aim of the 'county receives city's guidance' system was to adjust the separation between the urban and rural, coming from the traditional isolation policy of local areas; however, a limit to the system became clear. In order to realize the aim of the 'county receives city's guidance' system (urban economic region), it should become available to break away from an administratively isolated situation among districts and to have free mobility of capital, products, and (with various conditions) human resources. However we should point out that, in order to create the organic system closely connected with economic activities, which means economic agents (enterprises) exclude administrative intervention and work with the market mechanism, it might be fairly difficult to reach the goal of the 'county receives city's guidance' system under the situation of an immature market-oriented system.

Table 2.1 Industrial structure of Santai district (Taizhou, Taixin, and Taixian) (1989)

	Total industrial production (10,000 yuan)	Machinery (%)	Electronics (%)	Chemical (%)	Building materials (%)	Spinning (%)	Food (%)
Taizhou	1648448	35.0	3.9	13.0	1.4	27.8	4.5
Taixin	314327	30.3	3.8	16.9	6.0	6.9	5.1
Taixian	126494	36.4	1.7	8.7	7.6	24.2	7.8

Source: *Statistical Bulletin* of each region, and Liu Junde (1996).

Therefore, we expect that, without the drastic reform of state-owned enterprises, local government intervention to economic activities would be inevitable. It shows that such administrative economic districts would continue to exist.

Kojima (1986) doubted that – even within one area in which the 'county receives city's guidance' system, free mobility of capital, products and human resources was possible – in multiple areas which had the above system, it was similarly possible. The doubt of Kojima clearly indicated the tasks of the system. Actually, because of unilateral implementation of decentralization (at the stage without a local autonomous system in a constitutional sense, which shows immature legislation about decentralization regarding financial authority and public works obligation between central and local government) and an immature market oriented system, an administrative blockade occurred among local governments and had serious effects on the Chinese economy after and including the 1980s.

The Chinese economy in the 1980s was classified into the three periods: (1) the period in which a financial contract system was carried out from 1979 to 1984; (2) the period in which a serious material supply shortage occurred, from 1985 to 1988; and (3) the period in which market demand was seriously depressed due to the restraint policy, after 1989.

In such periods, the following two economic phenomena were remarkable. First, the rise of local economy protectionism (usually called *Zhu Hou Jing Ji*, 'little empire economy', which means – because of complicated administrative barriers – the market situation of cutting into pieces) was substantial, i.e. local government enclosed the resources within their region. This undoubtedly caused the tendency to split the national economy into pieces. Second, local governments entered into the manufacturing sector simultaneously in order to get higher profits. Needless to say, this led to the high speed economic growth in 1980s, but it also aggravated the distorted industrial structure because of overgrown downstream industries and it made the competition to get materials in the whole nation much keener.

(III) Investigation

The above-stated circumstances indicate that a negative legacy of the Chinese economy coming from the central planning system in which the economy has been managed by administrative measures has substantially existed. The actual form of an economic district after the reform has surely been different from an administrative economic district before the reform. However, it is said to be an administrative district economy (on the concept and analysis of administrative district economy, see Liu Junde, 1996, pp. 93–132). The administrative intervention against economic activities has still been an important aspect for the Chinese economy. It might be appropriately and delicately expressed to say there has been change in the characteristics of the Chinese economic activities from the administrative economic district to the administrative district economy.

By implementing the 'county receives city's guidance' system, in order not to confuse the urban population statistics, the concept of a non-agricultural population has been used. Table 1.5 of Chapter 1 displayed that, in 1989, of the total urban population of 317.62 million, the non-agricultural population reached 146.26 million, and the ratio of non-agricultural population to the urban total was only 46.05%. These figures suggested that the urban administrative economic districts that controlled such counties significantly retained the characteristics of traditionally independent rural economies. The fact might show one aspect of the characteristics of the 'county receives city's guidance' system.

At present what is the Chinese economy like? Table 2.2 shows some indicators (2005) of cities in coastal open areas and special economic zones (in which the 'county receives city's guidance' system has been carried out). As regards the ratio on the indicators occupied by city and district (except county), while the land area had 3.39%, and population 46.25%, the ratio of non-agricultural population occupied 50.01%, the number of employees 75.6%, and GDP 63.86%, by which we recognize both secondary and tertiary sectors have been concentrated in the city and district.

The 'county receives city's guidance' system introduced the new administrative stratum entitled 'local level city' in the Chinese administrative structure. Since the beginning of the 21st century, strong counties all over China (the list of 100 strong counties is announced by Statistical Office every year) have appeared, and the 'county receives city's guidance' system has been regarded as a burden and has received serious dissatisfaction and resistance. Thus, it was easily expected that the system would disappear sooner or later (see also Chapter 4 on the above issue).

The immaturity of the relations between the government and market has caused the local economy protectionism, *Zhu Hou Jing Ji*. In other words, resolving the local economy protectionism to create an urban economic region needs indispensably better establishment of a market economy system, particularly state-owned enterprise reform (see Chapter 3 on the detail of this important problem).

Table 2.2 Some indicators of coastal open cities and special economic zone cities

	Coastal open cities			Special economic zone cities		
	Whole region	City and district (except county)	Ratio (%)	Whole region	City and district (except county)	Ratio (%)
Land area (10 thousand square kilometers)	14.05	3.39	24.13	0.73	0.71642	98.14
Total population (the end of year) (10 thousand)	9563.99	4423.04	46.25	916.04	908.8	99.21
Non agricultural population (10 thousand)	4783	3477	72.69	854	852	99.77
Non agricultural population (Ratio, %)	50.01	78.61		93.23	93.75	
Employees (10 thousand)	1414	1069	75.60	301	301	100.00
GDP (100 million yuan)	34817.196	22234.581	63.86	7243.8003	7238.9426	99.93
Primary industry	1857.4379	409.279	22.03	94.5461	92.5187	97.86
Secondary industry	17350.472	10594.223	61.06	3857.2635	3855.9738	99.97
Tertiary industry	15609.286	11231.079	71.95	3291.9907	3290.4501	99.95

Source: *Chinese Statistical Bulletin* 2006 and author's calculation.

Evolution of the reform and open door policy in China

The driving force of the above-stated various urban reforms was closely connected with the reform and open door policy.

In the Chinese transition, starting in 1978, an open district toward foreign countries was a novel policy attempt to have a transformation into a new economic structure, which was intended to improve the disadvantages in the traditional economic system by first reforming the regions with advantages on economic fundamentals and geographical position (mainly urban areas) through pursuing the advantage of a latecomer less developed country. The open districts were established as an experiment for a market-oriented system, and four windows (which pointed out capital, technology, management and knowledge), for national economy and respective regional economy were also established.

Deng Xiaoping evaluated in 1984 that the special economic zone was a window, for technology, for management, for knowledge, and for foreign policy (Deng Xiaoping, 1987). This assertion for four windows clarifies the characteristics of special economic zones. Actually it is not only special economic zones but also all kinds of various open economic districts, which been successively established, have the same characteristics.

As Myint (1971) asserted, an open economy has better effects for economic development than a closed economy. The open economy defined by Myint meant an outward-looking economy, looking towards foreign countries. In China, however, there existed a multi-tiers dual economic structure from the 1950s to 1970s; thus, the open economy in China broke down the multi-tiers dual economic structure.

In the following section, we consider the evolution of the reform and open door policy in China.

Tempo of the reform and open door policy and correspondence of open strategic areas

As the establishment of an open economic district was concentrated in the coastal area in the 1980s, it was said that the open strategy in this period was a coastal open strategy. In the 1990s, however, transformation towards an omni-directional open strategy was recognized.

(I) Initial stage (1978–1984) We think the Chinese regional development strategy to give priority to the coastal area was indispensable for the Chinese situation in those days. To reform the national and regional economy needed lots of capital, for which expanding international trade was their most urgent task. However, the traditional Chinese system of international trade was too closed, too autonomous, and too rigid to meet the necessity. For example, as the central planning system put the first priority upon the general equilibrium in the domestic economy, international trade was quite limited, particularly in exports whose exchange rate was distortionally determined. Thus, international economic policy progressed ahead of domestic economic reform, which produced special economic zones.

First, we look at the preceding experiments in the special economic zones and 14 open coastal cities.

At the end of the 1970s, there still existed ideological conflicts. Such special economic zones as Shenzhen, Zhuhai, Xiamen, Shantou were created as enclaves and attracting complicated attention. In both provinces of Fujian and Guangdong in 1979, a special policy on international trade was permitted. First, the provinces were planned as the exportable goods base, but later, in May 1980, the Central Chinese Communist Party decided to change the name to *special economic zone.*

The main reason for the change was to emphasize the substantial difference from the export processing zone, which was established in capitalist countries such as South Korea. However, later, when the special economic zone was called an 'experimental zone' and the 'window of capital, technology, knowledge, and foreign policy', the 'special economic zone' covered a wider range of economic contents compared with the 'export processing zone'.

In 1983, Hainan Island became the open district. Also, in 1984, 14 coastal cities (which were Dalian, Qinhuangdao, Tianjin, Yantai, Qingdao, Lianyungang, Nantong, Shanghai, Ningbo, Wenzhou, Fuzhou, Guangzhou, Zhanjiang, Beihai, – later 15 cities including Weihai) were designated as open districts. Each respective city was given permission to establishing an economic development zone of national level.

Second, as regards the experiment of urban economic reform, urban economic reform started a little after rural economic reform. According to such reform, in addition to the above-mentioned four special economic zones (1980), 14 coastal open cities (1984), cities located in three delta open regions (1985), i.e. regardless of coastal and inland, in around 300 cities all over China, 58 general experimental cities for economic reform (later increased to be 72 till 1994), ten cities called independent cities from provincial plan (later expanded to 14 in 1984–1985, which were given the provincial standard of financial authority) were designated in succession. It was reasonable to be open not only to foreign countries but also open to other regions within China because Chinese reform and the open door policy were intended to break down the chain of dual economic structures stated above.

The main reform tasks the Chinese government faced at this stage were the extension of autonomy in enterprise management and the transformation of government functions. In essence, they were reforms of planning, finance, price, loan, distribution, and wage system.

Of the cities, the cities of special economic zones, coastal open cities, and delta region cities were located in coastal areas, while the general experimental cities of urban economic reform were mainly located in inland areas. Of the 72 general experimental cities, 24 were provincial capitals of the highest administrative districts. Independent cities from the provincial plan were located regardless of whether they were in coastal and inland areas. The geographical distribution of designated areas showed that urban reform in those days attached greater importance not only to the open coastal region but also to active economy in inland areas.

Although experimental cities in economic reform were selected by both coastal and inland areas, the results of both areas were significantly different. Coastal open areas went ahead, because of the difference between them regarding pressure and motivation in the reform process. The special economic zones has played a central role in international trade and inward foreign direct investment, thus they have the usual recognition that special economic zones should receive special treatment for their special position. In addition, an important situation regarding special economic zones has been that their economic activities should approach international standards, because they are receiving technology, finance, management and knowledge which will expand their market-oriented rules and ideas.

Moreover, in the case of the economic technology development zones newly established in suburban areas of special zones and coastal open cities, these have no direct relations with the traditional economic system and they can have quick results on their activities, focusing their attention upon developing processing industry and industrial technology, from which they can get a higher rate of profit.

However, in the case of general experimental cities for economic reform in inland areas, because they had insufficient recognition on the necessity of reform, and because resistance from vested interest groups of traditional economic system was hard, and because there was no direct relations with the international market, motivation and pressure toward reform was rather weak. Moreover, as it was supposed to be 'general', the systemic reform was extended over almost all aspects, so the reform was extremely difficult, as expected.

In short, it was very difficult for them to have successful results in each experimental city at the beginning of 1980s when the Chinese transition toward a market oriented system started. It can be said, however, that both coastal and inland open experimental cities have accumulated helpful lessons and experiences, which led to success in the next reform steps.

(II) Diversification of open areas (1985–1990) We can point out the characteristics of open economic districts during 1985 to 1990, saying that they designated not a single city but a huge area, including city and rural areas, to be open economic zones. An international strategic development plan for 'the big circle' was an attempt to create a newly successful circle by breaking down traditional dual economic structures, like dividing agriculture and industry, light industry and heavy industry, coastal areas and inland areas etc. For example, in 1985, three such delta areas – Yangtze River Delta, Yellow River Delta, and Minjiang Delta – and the two peninsular areas of Shandong and Liaodong were designated as open districts with integration among agriculture, industry and trade. At present, therefore, the coastal open economic area has covered 260 cities and prefectures, and such provinces and autonomous district as Guangdong, Jiangsu, Zhejiang, Liaoning, Fujian, Shandong, Hebei and Guangxi Zhuang autonomous region, which has formed a huge open area from north to south.

It is recognized that Chinese reform and open strategy has extended from point to line, and from line to surface. In 1988, the Hainan special administrative district was also raised to the province and special economic zone.

(III) International strategic development plan for the big circle Based upon experimental results and suggestions, Wang Jian (1988) presented the well-known 'International Strategic Development Plan for the Big Circle', whose main assertion

was what is called the comparative advantage strategy. In short, the progress of industrialization towards the export of labor-intensive products was developed, whose absorption of the workforce contributes to absorbing redundant workforces in rural areas. Hard currency gained by exports was allocated to material industry and to infrastructure. The main player of that strategy was TVEs, located in the coastal area. To make the competitive position of enterprises better, there were three capital enterprises, i.e. 100% foreign-owned, a joint venture with foreign enterprises, and a cooperative with foreign enterprises, which contributed to higher quality, technological progress, improvement of enterprise management, and development of sales networks, etc. It was also insisted that, to avoid the resource war with the inland economy, the improvement of trade should be developed, getting the materials section and sales section overseas.

From 1985 to 1990, it was a characteristic during the period that the target area to be nominated as an open economic district was a huge area, including both urban and rural in place of a single city. The international strategic development plan for the big circle was a trial to create an advantageous circle to abolish the traditional multi-tiers dual economic structure, which consisted of a primary and secondary sector, light and heavy industry, coastal and inland area. For example, in Delta and Peninsular areas, which were coastal open areas, they advocated the unified model of trade, industry and agriculture.

Fei *et al.* (1986) classified economic development into the following four stages, from the viewpoint of the development experience of East Asian countries: (1) the premodern stage; (2) the first stage of import substitution; (3) the first stage of being export oriented; and (4) the second stage of import substitution and export oriented. Okawa and Kohama (1993) changed these to the following four: (1) the first stage was the initial import substitution stage in which industrial consumption goods were replaced from import to domestic production; (2) the second stage was the first export promotion stage in which export structure was changed from primary commodities oriented to industrial consumption goods; (3) the third stage was the second import substitution stage in which industrial production goods were replaced from import to domestic production based upon the backward linkage effect argued by Hershman; (4) the fourth stage was the second export promotion stage in which export structure was replaced by industrial consumers products to durable consumers products and industrial production goods.

Various studies were implemented on the question of which stage was China at in the development. Generally speaking, China employed import substitution policies on both consumers' and producers' products, and traditionally exported oil and agricultural products. However, after the second half of the 1980s, export structure was changed so that consumer products were the main exportables. For example, in the form of entrusted manufacturing, the export of watches and clocks drastically increased from the second half of the 1980s; and, in 1992, export quantity became more than the quantity of domestic products. Thus, as a whole, we think China was at the first export promotion stage (Nakagane, 1999).

The reform and open door policy since the 1980s has contributed to the substantial change of Chinese industrial structure. As will be mentioned later in this book, the locational disparity of growing industries among regions has been clearly reflected in regional disparities.

(IV) Transformation towards an omni-directional open strategy (1990–the present) Through such an accumulation of gradual reforms in the 1980s, the non-state-owned sector – like TVEs, privately-owned enterprises, foreign-owned enterprises – grew rapidly as the main player of a market-oriented economy. To the contrary, many state-owned enterprises could not adapt to the transformation with a deficit operation.

As the second step of reform after 1985, reforming the state-owned sector in the urban area was started; however, because of resistance by the conservatives and the vested interest groups, the reform was delayed. Thus, on the one hand planning and official prices controlled by the authority were working, while the market mechanism and market prices rapidly occupied more activities on the other. Inconsistency in the reform processes toward a market-oriented system reached a disturbance in production and distribution, which sometimes caused two-digit inflation.

The northeast area, Shanghai, and the southwest area, in which state-owned enterprises and military industry were concentrated, suffered seriously from the disturbance in production. State-owned enterprises had no experience of sluggish demand because they were always in a shortage economy without the necessity of technological innovation and without competition. The second stage of Wang Jian's strategy, which indicates that hard currency gained by exports should be allocated for reforming the state-owned sector, such as basic material industry and infrastructure construction, is nearing. It indicates the stage in which development benefit should be efficiently returned to society.

At the beginning of the 1990s, the open door policy in China reached a new stage. The main area of regional development has been moved to Shanghai. It has also shed light on the development and open policy of huge inland areas, including the southwest area through the Yangtze River from Shanghai. The development strategies at this stage, which focused attention upon open economic zones, were the following: (1) a formal decision on the development of the Shanghai Pudong area in 1990; (2) a decision to speed the development of the Shanghai Pudong area; and (3) an omnidirectional open policy, often called the 'opening policy of three borders' which came about in 1992.

It meant a development toward an omnidirectional open strategy from the traditional coastal development strategy, in which, as well as coastal areas, 36 cities (five cities in the Changjiang-coastal area, 13 cities in the borderland area, and 18 inlands cities and provinces) have been appointed as strategic regions for development. They have been given the same advantageous policy measures as coastal open cities.

Designation of three border open cities and inland open cities

(I) Development of Shanghai Pudong area In 1990, it was decided to designate the development of the Shanghai Pudong area (which is located on the opposite shore of Shanghai across the Huangpu River) as a national project. The plan shows the Pudong area is to be developed as a world trade and financial center, second to Hong Kong, and is linked with the development of the Yangtze River Delta area, with which inland economic development is attempted. From the beginning therefore, greater attention has been attached to the introduction of tertiary industry and High-Tech industry. Because the Pudong new area is a large-scale area, at present based upon four important development areas: (1) Lujiazui financial and trade district, (2) Jinqiao export processing district, (3) Waigaoqiao bonded area, (4) Zhangjiang High-Tech development area, there already is considerable accumulation.

(II) Development of river valley area Accompanying the development of the Shanghai Pudong new area is the economic development of the Yangtze River valley area, in which the Yangtze River flows through a wedge-shaped inland area and which has Shanghai as the apex. Five cities of Wuhu, Jiujiang, Wuhan, Yueyang, and Chongqing were designated as open cities in 1990.

(III) Development of borderland areas In March 1992, in the government policy report of the fifth meeting at the Seventh National Parliament, Prime Minister Lipeng emphasized that they would develop an open door policy of inland border and racial regions in good order. After that, the opening of the 13 cities located in border areas was decided. They were such cities as Huichun, Suifenhe, Heihe, and Manzhouli in Heilongjiang province; Erlianhaote in Inner Mongolia autonomous district; Yili, Tacheng, and Hekou in Xinjiang autonomous district; Ruili, and Wantingin in Yunnan province; and Fengxiang, and Dongxing in Guangxi province etc, each of which was designated as an open border city (a base city for border trade). As the result, at the time of writing, more than 100 bases for border trade have been established (Maruyama, 1994). The 13 cities in the inland border areas, permitted at the national level, were given the authority to manage international trade and also were given a permission to construct collaboration districts in border trade and given advantageous treatments on tax – the same as for coastal development districts.

The open economic districts have been characterized as a politically important factor to decrease disparity between coastal and inland areas, by providing opportunities for development to transform a poverty situation in border racial districts.

(IV) Designation of inland open cities In 1992, the following 18 provinces and cities were designated as inland open cities to attempt technological progress: Harbin (Heilongjiangsheng Province), Changchun (Jilin province), Hohhot (Inner Mongolian Autonomous Region), Shijiazhuang (Hebei province), Taiyuan (Shanxi

province), Yinchuan (Ningxia Hui Autonomous Regions), Xining (Qinghai province), Lanzhou (Gansu province), Xi'an (Shanxi province), Zhengzhou (Henan province), Hefei (Anhui province), Chengdu (Sichuan province), Nanchang (Jiangxi province), Changsha (Hunan province), Guiyang (Guizhou province), Nanning (Guangxi zhuang Autonomous Region), Urumqi (Xinjiang Uyghur Autonomous Region), Kunming (Yunnan province).

Characteristics of the distribution of various open economic zones at the national level

To be designated as an open city means a possible establishment of economic development at the national level. We can recognize the following characteristics from a geographical distribution of various development zones within cities. Those characteristics show that various development zones (1) are concentrated in the eastern and central area; (2) in the eastern area, they are concentrated in three delta areas and two peninsular areas; (3) as regards provincial distribution, they are concentrated in such provinces as Shanghai (city), Jiangsu, Zejiang, Shandong, Liaoning etc; (4) concerning geographical distribution, they are concentrated in the Yangtze River Valley area especially the midstream and downstream areas; (5) in inland areas they are concentrated in provincial capitals; (6) the number of open economic zones located in the border area in western part was much less than in the border areas in the eastern part, which might be related with the development level of trading countries.

In short, open economic zones in China have progressed in eastern coastal areas from point to line, from line to surface, and then omnidirectionally, from coastal area to inland area. In addition, they were qualitatively changed, to be allowed, for example, to establish a bonded district, and to introduce foreign capital of financial, commercial and real estate sectors. Generally, various open economic zones were recognized as experimental, toward a market oriented system.

Foreign economic relations of China in the reform and open door policy

Deng Xiaoping evaluated the special economic zone as the four windows in Beijing in 1984, after he visited Guangdong and Fujian. The open area, as a matter of fact, played a role in the window of foreign policy in addition to knowledge, management and technology. We recognize the following changes for Chinese foreign economic relations.

1. After the Chinese open door policy started, in April 1980, the IMF (International Monetary Fund) decided on the representative rights of China, and in May 1980, the Board of Directors of the World Bank decided on the restoration of representative rights of China in the World Bank, International Development Association, and International Financial Corporation. Moreover, although being a member of the Asian Development

Bank was delayed, mainly due to the Taiwanese problem, it occurred in February 1986. In April 1987, China was selected to be a member of the council. China thus returned to almost all international organizations.

2. Besides the coastal open strategy, China actively implemented the receiving ways and measures of multilateral and bilateral aid through strengthening the economic and technological cooperation with various organizations of the United Nations Development Programme and other international organizations. That is to say, as regards aid-receiving areas from foreign countries, they attached greater importance to technological development and human resources development projects. In 1989, China finally and straightforwardly accepted the fact that it was an aid-receiving country (*Renmin Ribao* (*People's Daily*), January 4, 1989).
3. Judging by the process of establishment the 'Taiwanese compatriot investment district' in Guangdong, Fujian, Hainan etc, until the second half of 1980s from the start of special economic zone policy in 1979, it could be recognized that establishment and management of open economic districts in China have become important measures to promote relations between both coastal sides of the Chinese Continent and Taiwan.
4. China formerly applied to participate in the GATT (General Agreement on Trade and Tariff) in 1986, which enforced China promoting domestic price reform, establishing a market-oriented system, including a factor market, transforming industrial structure and enterprise management mechanism etc. It is expected that the current reform process implemented in China would contribute to improving the investment environment for foreign investors by providing the same treatments for domestic enterprises and reforming the foreign exchange regime.

Meanwhile, as the advantageous policies with regional priority in the 1980s were cautioned to be against the nationwide unification of trade policy, the Chinese purpose to return the member of GATT was one of the factors to promote the transformation towards an omnidirectional open strategy in the 1990s. Finally, in December 2001, after a long period (more than 20 years) of negotiation, China became a member of the WTO (formerly GATT). Chinese economic development, up to present, has been substantially helped by close linkage with the international economy. Chinese economic development needs world economic development, but also world economic development needs Chinese economic development. However, as trade conflicts are symbolically expressed, the Chinese economic development model has seriously been depending upon a low production cost scheme. Thus, because we could easily recognize various side effects regarding the Chinese economy, the policy measure to break away from the low production cost scheme has become the serious task of this period (see Chapter 4).

Possibility of the development of the inland area

Since the end of the 1990s, considering the balance of regional development, the targets on the regional development policy have shifted, gradually, towards the western, northeastern, and central areas. The main strategies were, for example, the 'go-west' policy in 1999, the industrial regional promotion strategy in the northeast area in 2001, and the central region promotion strategy in 2004. What, then, is the possibility of development in the inland area?

Trend of development in inland areas until the 1990s

(I) Policies to attract domestic and foreign capital These are the policies to introduce capital and technology from outside regions, whose motivations are to get markets and resources to inland provinces. To attract them, foreign investors were given permission to participate in the development of inland resources with product allocation schemes as well as the opening of local markets. For example, as regards inland oil fields, in which traditionally foreign investors were not allowed to participate, particularly the Xinjiang, Tarim oil field, foreign investors were allowed to put in a tender for rights to develop the oil field area in 1992. In addition, they encouraged enterprises in coastal areas to invest in material production on the condition that the resource supply to manufacturing industry in the coastal area was given priority. For example, it is said that a case where an enterprise in Guangdong province invests in an electric power development project in Yunnan province and collects electric power as its bill, is worth attention.

(II) Economic cooperation activities among areas As with earlier cases of formation of the cooperative organization among inland areas, cases in southwest region were considered. Examples include: seven regions' cooperation among five provinces and autonomous regions, and two cities were established in 1983 whose members were Yunnan province, Sichuan province, Guizhou province, Guangxi Zhuangzu autonomous region, Tibet autonomous region, and Chongqing city and Chengdu city. In June 1993, an Economic Cooperation meeting was carried out by the northwest five provinces and autonomous regions, Shanxi, Gansu, Qinghai, Ningxia, and Xinjiang.

Attention has been paid to the fact that each province in the central economic area has attempted to develop omnidirectional foreign economic relations with the east (western market), south (Southeast Asia), and west (Russia and Central Asian countries) through creating economic cooperation with coastal areas and border areas.

Sichuan province, for example, which is located upstream of the Yangtze River and has largest population, has employed the omnidirectional development strategy. This indicates an economic cooperation policy with the coastal area along the Yangtze River on the one hand, and a development policy of border trade through economic cooperation with border areas on the other.

Such cooperative activities produced a leading role for government and independence of enterprises. The Sichuan province government decided on measures, with ten articles in 1993 and 1994, to support enterprises engaged in border trade. They included such contents as helping business, personnel service, facilities for traffic permits to border areas, financial support, three years exemption from income tax, and so on. With such a support policy from the Sichuan province government, more than 1000 enterprises established branches and agents in Shenzhen, Zhuhai, Hainan, etc. In addition, several hundred enterprises joined the border trade in the provinces of Yunnan, Guangxi, Xinjiang, Heilongjiang, whose transaction amount from January to September 1992 reached more than 100 million yuan. A specific example of this is that, through cooperation of six prefectures in Neijiang city and one prefecture in Leshan city, the seven prefectures economic cooperation enterprise was established in 1988, and Chuanlianghongxiang management department was started in Heihe city, Heilongjiang province, in 1992. In the area from Sichuan province to Xinjiang Autonomous Region, 39 construction enterprises and more than 70 commercial and engineering enterprises invested in the development of mines, agriculture and stock raising, and hotels (Yang Deyin, 1993, p. 46).

(III) Cooperation between growing region and underdeveloped regions Cooperation here means that multiple local governments concluded a contract for a particular field to develop their cooperative activities. Cooperation between a growing region and an underdeveloped region includes such various types as technology transfer, human capital promotion, trade support, joint management with capital cooperation, joint development, etc. Needless to say, free mobility among regions by enterprises, private persons and various types of organization will become more active.

i. Compensation of the development benefit from eastern coastal regions to central and western regions. Since an open door policy started, central government has increased its investment expenditure into the coastal region on the one hand, and on the other has given such advantageous measures to the region as tax reduction, and benefit transfer. Development of the coastal region has been completed at the cost to the central government budget and other regions. Taking into consideration such details, supporting measures to develop resources in central, western and poor regions, by establishing a development fund for poor regions contributed to by the coastal region, have been embodied. After the projects are completed, some of the materials and processed products are returned to the regions concerned proportional to the initially provided amount.
ii. More flexible measures are implemented regarding the poverty relief fund to the central and western regions. These measures mean that, for example, the burden of a poverty relief fund for the central and western regions is allocated to the provinces and municipalities directly under the central

government in the eastern regions, which is invested in a limited number of proper provinces and autonomous districts. The investment attaches great importance on development of TVEs, for which a mechanism of TVEs in eastern region is introduced to try to overcome the poverty situation in rural areas of the central and western region.

iii. By contributing part of the finance and workforce from poor provinces, the 'window' is established in coastal and border open regions to start export and import businesses and tertiary businesses. Through such cooperation, poor provinces could learn advanced control methods, management mechanisms, and about international markets embodied in the coastal open region. In addition, such cooperation could provide information for introducing capital, technology, and human resources in poor regions to improve the market oriented system.

(IV) Problems they face Economic cooperation among western border provinces and central inland provinces has developed based upon the formation of three development zones of the northeast, northwest, and southwest. In addition to their trade, economic cooperation has extended to investment, labor cooperation, and tourism, which need further transition.

To resolve the obstacles for development of border trade, it is indicated for respective issues for example, that (1) as regards preventing the export of goods of inferior quality, regulations such as the stricter enforcement of the penal regulations, and the implementation of stricter regulations by examination offices and customs houses on border trade, are necessary, and (2) as far as putting right disorder in border trade is concerned, it is necessary for reliable official organizations to carry on transactions, to establish an export–import bank for border trade, and to found branches and agents for international trade finance (Maruyama, 1993, p. 373).

At the same time, when they wish to expand international economic activities in inland areas, the difficulty of transportation becomes a serious obstacle. Various inland provinces have put a great deal of effort into improving their local airports. For example, putting Beihai, Qinzhou, Fangcheng in Guangxi Zhuangzu autonomous region, in a good condition as open cities and free trade bases, to which both the Chengkun railway and Nankun railway have been extended from Chengdu in the southwest in order to link the southwest area for the utilization of the trade port there.

New inland development strategy after the end of the 1990s

Such a new trend has been concentrated upon the three, which have been the go-west development strategy, the industrial region promotion strategy in northeast area, and the central region promotion strategy. A simple explanation of these is given below.

(I) Setting forth a new development strategy in inland areas As regards the go-west development strategy, we can say the following. The west area in China is indicated to be 12 provinces, autonomous regions, and direct-controlled cities, i.e. Chongqing,[7] Sichuang, Gguizhou, Yunnan, Tibet, Shanxi, Gansu, Ningxia, Xinjiang, Inner Mongolia and Guangxi[8] etc. The total land area shows 6,850,000 square kilometers (71.4% of the whole of China), a total population of around 369 million (28.6% of the whole of China), GDP in 2003 reached 2,295.466 billion yuan (19.6% of the whole nation). Within the area, there are 55 minority races, whose ratio to the minority race population of the whole of China is 71.5% (according to the fifth national census in 2000). All the five minority race autonomous regions (of provincial level) are located in the western area.

Although the western area is rich in natural resources, for various reasons, such as nature, history, society, particularly since the 1980s when the oceanic civilization started, the coastal open strategy has become main plan, and the economic development of the western area has fallen behind. Per capita GDP of the west in 2003 was 6216 yuan, which is only 38% of the east.

In June 1999, Jiang Zemin presented the plan of the go-west development strategy in the old city, Xian. In January 2000, the Cabinet created a 'leaders group for western area development', which was a start of the development of the west. After that, various policies were announced, which were development plans in the western area. For example, official documents promulgated by the Cabinet were as follows; 'a few policy measures on implementation of development in the western area', 'a few opinions on implementation of Tuigeng Huanlin, Tuigeng Huancao (which meant the policy of returning the arable lands to previous forest and grassland) policy', 'a few opinions on measures to make Tuigeng Huanlin, Tuigeng Huancao policy more successful' etc. Meanwhile, official documents announced by the 'leaders group for western area development' was the 'practical opinions on policy measures about development in the western area'. In addition, the national planning committee (now changed to be the national committee on reform and development) and the leaders group for the western area development,

---

7 Chongqing is a newly promoted municipality directly under the central government in 1997 (which is the fourth city after Beijing, Shanghai, and Tianjin), after the Shanxia Dam construction was decided.

8 Guangxi autonomous district was classified as an eastern region before the go-west development strategy was presented. That was because, under the coastal development strategy, the eastern region as a target of the strategy was designated to be provinces including the coastline. Guangxi autonomous district has undoubtedly a coastline and moreover two port cities, Zhanjiang and Beihai were designated as coastal open cities. However, the economic development level of Guangxi, as one of the five minority race autonomous districts, was much less than other coastal provinces. After the beginning of the 1990s, Guangxi autonomous district could not erase the image of being a less-developed region. After the go-west development strategy was presented, Guangxi autonomous district, which has similar characteristics to the western region has been joined as a western region in a statistical sense.

jointly announced a 'general plan of development in the western area during the period of Eleventh Five Year Plan'.

In the 'practical opinions on policy measures about the development in the western area', the following 18 headings were included; (1) expansion of the total investment scale; (2) fundamental construction projects are taken as the first priority; (3) extension of the financial scale transferred to the western area; (4) extension of the possibility for financial loan; (5) improvement of the investment environment of the soft side (meaning that reform of state-owned enterprises, attracting the non-state-owned sector, simplifying of application procedure by reforming governmental function); (6) advantageous treatment on the taxation system; (7) advantageous treatment on land use; (8) advantageous treatment on ore resource development; (9) reform of the price system (such as expanding the ratio of market price system and special ticket pricing system on newly constructed railways); (10) expanding the field of foreign investors' activities; (11) expanding the system to cooperate with foreign investors; (12) deregulation upon foreign investor's activities; (13) active participation in international trade (meaning that, when enterprises in the western area get involved in foreign economic activities, deregulation on the rights of foreign trade and technological cooperation was decided, deregulation on urgent imports of engineering facilities was decided, various advantageous treatments on border trade were kept); (14) promotion of support in regional cooperation; (15) policy to attract human resources; (16) playing a leading role in development of science and technology; (17) increasing investment in education; (18) enforcement in the foundation of such social activities as culture and health.

We could recognize that the go-west policy indicated a large-scale development project for the western region with a large amount of financial expenditure for industrial infrastructure building, agricultural infrastructure building, education expenditure, such as 'Transport water from south to north' project (meaning the infrastructure building to transport water from southern region to northern region). In addition, many important national projects were related with western development, projects such as construction work of a temporary drainage canal for Changjiang's sanxia dam, the railway construction between Qinghai and Tibet, 'transport electric power from western to eastern region', the 'transport natural gas from western region to eastern coastal area' project and the eastern route of 'Transport water from south to north' project. In order to implement such projects, issuing long-term construction treasury bonds amounted to 660 billion yuan for five years from 1997. Such finance, including bank loans and other induced investments, reached 3,280 billion yuan, with which a trial calculation was made, which indicated it would leading to 1.5–2.0% annual GDP growth rate and 7.5 million jobs being created.

(II) Industrial regional promotion strategy in the northeast area (2002) In the northeast region, three provinces of Heilongjiang province, Jilin province, Liaoning province are standing in a line from north to south, which share common

characteristics geographically, historically, and culturally. When classifying China in the three areas as eastern, central and western, Liaoning province is also classified as a coastal region. In Liaoning province they have actively progressed their open door policy from the 1980s. However, the area in Liaoning province, except Liaodong Peninsula, for example the provincial capital, Shenyang, was located inland, and the industrial structure was constructed by mainly state-owned enterprises. Liaoning province, therefore, has two sides. Both Heilongjiang province, and Jilin province are classified as the central area.

The northeast area in those days failed to keep up with reform and the open door policy and was in the similar situation to Shanghai at the beginning of 1990s because they were bases of state-owned and heavy industry. Moreover as the area concerned is endowed with resources and lots of cities with heavy industry, which were dependent upon mining resources and manufacturing, the cities became superannuated. In most mining districts, workers' houses turned into slums. In addition, due to the deficit operation of state-owned enterprises, restructuring was indispensable and lots of workers suffered from great difficulties.

The northeast area was thus seriously dependent upon the central planning system for many years, which seems to be significantly related with workers' consciousness of this area. They are traditionally dependent on state-owned enterprises and are less active in finding new jobs by adapting an independent spirit. This style of behavior might have connections with a regional culture in the northeast area. In particular, male workers in the northeast do not want to lose their '*Mianzi*' (matter of honor). Even if they just spend their time at home without job, they do not want to work for small-scale service or in manual labor (which is fairly different from southern Chinese consciousness). Thus, the northeast situation might be said to be a strange mix of the regional culture of northeast with a central planning system.

Liaoning province occupied the top position in the whole of China in the total industrial production for many years during the central planning days. It was praised as '*Liao Lao Da*' meaning Liaoning was number one. During the period of the First Five Year Plan, central government investment in industrial construction in Liaoning province amounted to 4.64 billion yuan, which occupied 18.5% of Chinese total industrial investment. Of 156 national important projects, Liaoning province has 24 of them. Related investment with central government allocated 730 projects, of provincial and city level, to Liaoning province. The whole area of the northeast was given a position of being a manufacturing base for energy, material and large-scale equipment production. Those are indispensable for the establishment of an independent national economy with self-rehabilitation.

However, since the end of the 1990s, the total industrial production of Liaoning province decreased to tenth position in the whole of China. The often cited figures are: (1) the GDP of Liaoning province at the beginning of the open door policy was twice that of Guangdong province; however, at present, the GDP of Guangdong province is twice as large as the GDP of Liaoning province. (2) In 2001, the total

GDP of the three provinces in the northeast area reached 1,062.66 billion yuan, which equaled the one province of Guandong.

Central government support policy for the industrial region promotion strategy in the northeast area has included such reform policies as a change from value added tax in the production stage to value added tax in the consumption stage, exemption from taxation etc. Local government also has attempted to construct more cooperation with enterprises and governments in coastal open areas, which have started their strategies since the 1980s, to introduce market-oriented reform initiatives from the outside.

At the 16th Chinese Communist Party Meeting in autumn 2002, Prime Minister Wen Jiabao proposed the plan for industrial regional promotion strategy in the northeast area for the first time. In 2003, he had three tours of inspection to the northeast area and asserted that the industrial regional promotion strategy in the northeast area would be an essential strategic move to construct modernization, which would become an important policy goal for regional development. In China they expected the northeast area to be the fourth center of growth, in addition to Pearl River Delta, Yangtze River Delta, and Bo Hai Bay.

Upon finishing his second tour of inspection to the northeast area, Wen Jiabao attended the northeast area promotion meeting in Changchun, Jilin province. He presented the following policy goals: (1) reform of economic structure (indicating industrial structure, ownership structure, state-owned economy structure) was a fundamental line for northeast area promotion; (2) reinforcement of reforming industrial technology was an important step for northeast area promotion; (3) planning a sustainable growth path was a long-term goal for northeast area promotion; (4) expanding job search and social security system was an important social network for northeast area promotion; (5) development of science and technology, and education system was an important condition for northeast area promotion; (6) development of reform and open door policy was an engine for northeast area promotion.

(III) Central region promotion strategy (2004) The central region promotion strategy presented in 2004 is the next topic to be considered here. After the slogan on the go-west development strategy was announced, the central region was worried about its position of being neither east nor west (which was shown through the region being embarrassed by its falling behind in development). In March 2004, Wen Jiabao mentioned, in the government policy report at the Tenth National Parliament, that by keeping the promotion plan for the go-west development strategy and industrial region promotion strategy in the northeast area, and by promoting the rise of the central region, by also encouraging more advanced development in the eastern region, a new scheme will occur for cooperative development through mutual promotion and the complementing of the advantages of the east, central, and western regions. And so the strategy for the rise of the central region was officially announced. In December 2004, at the leaders' group meeting on central government economic policy, they again referred to the

rise of the central region. In March 2005, in the National Parliament, the Prime Minister Wen Jiabao requested an immediate setting forth of a more concrete plan and measures for the rise of central region.

At the time of writing, some scholars are calling the rise of the central region the establishment of the fifth center of Chinese growth. We should be careful, however, as this is a slightly different concept regarding the central region. In the central region promotion strategy, the central region does not include Heilongjiang province and Jilin province because those two provinces have been included in the industrial region promotion strategy in the northeast area. The central region – the policy designated area – includes six provinces, i.e. Hebei, Hubei, Shanxi, Hunan, Anhui, Jiangxi.

In the Central region, needless to say, there are important transformation arteries such as Jingjiu Railroad (which connects Beijing and Jiulong in Hong Kong). However, the western part of Jingjiu Railroad is covered by the construction of the Third Front region,[9] where lots of former state-owned enterprises have been located and they have the same problems as the northeast region. In addition, the eastern part of Jingjiu Railroad has been easy to appoint as the center of construction of the Minor Third Front region, [10] but it has been seriously suffering from traditional administrative regulation. Even though not the same as the 'little empire economy' (which means that, because of complicated administrative barriers, the market was in a situation of being cut into pieces) in the 1980s, protection measures have been employed for the labor force and for raw materials not to be flexibly distributed. We easily recognize the western difficulty of integrating into the economy in the eastern region. Systemic transition has therefore been the necessity for regional economies in China to work reasonably. It means the way to develop the inland economy in China might not be easy.

---

9 In the period of the Third Five Year Plan (1966–70) and the Fourth Five Year Plan (1971–75), based upon the strategic way of thinking by Mao Zedong, which was to be in preparation for a possible World War (against USA and the then USSR), they placed great importance on industry building on the Third Front of the interior areas, which has been called Third Front Construction. Third Front means the huge interior region, which includes south of the Great Wall, north of Shaoguan, west of Jingguang-Railroad, and east of Gansu and Wushao Peak. As a result of Third Front Construction, in the Third Front, particularly in the southwest region they established an industrial base for heavy industry and military industry, including steel, machinery, energy, electronics, aircraft, space rockets etc. Needless to say, as those industrial productions have been taken by state-owned enterprises, since the 1980s the traditional region of the Third Front has suffered from the delayed market-oriented transition.

10 Different from the above-mentioned major Third Front (of note 9), the building plan of Minor Third Front indicates the region meeting the condition of 'mountains, diffused, caves'. For example, the Minor Third Front constructions in which Shanghai was involved indicated, as it were, the Minor Third Front in East China (Jiangxi province) and the base behind Shanghai (Anhui province and Zhejiang province).

Concrete details of the central region promotion strategy have never been clear, because, since the omnidirectional development strategy started, they have requested a more independent policy than the regional advantageous policy that has been necessary. Central government has been worrying about what they support for six provinces in the central region. Meanwhile, in February 2005, at the policy forum on the central region promotion strategy being held under the auspices of Cabinet Development Research Center, the following eight plans were considered. However, are still 'paper plans' and it is uncertain whether or not they will be realized and in which way. The eight plans are the following. (1) Promotion plans and construction of infrastructure, including transportation, river improvement, agricultural water supply etc, in which the particularly construction of a main artery of transportation and the network of arteries going through the eastern and western areas has a pressing need. (2) Reinforcement of measures against environmental pollution. (3) By reinforcing the agricultural support policy, general productivity in agriculture is improved. (4) The promotion and reform policy of the industrial regions in the central area should be implemented (a transplant of policies carried out in the northeast area might be probable). (5) The promotion of potentially advantageous industries (such as energy, material production, processing industry of agricultural products, refining industry, equipment manufacturing, transportation equipment manufacturing, high-tech industries, tourism, etc). (6) An attempt at reforming value added tax is implemented in the central region. (7) The promotion policy of urbanization in the central region. (8) Supporting policy against poverty in the central region.

In 2005, the urbanization ratio in the central region was only 25%, which was much lower than the national average of 35%. In the six provinces of the central region, they expected development of the core city and its 'ripple effect' over the surrounding regions. The regions upon which attention was focused were: the Wuhan urban area, Wuhan and the surrounding eight cities; ChangZhuTan urban belt area (Changsha, Zhuzhou, Yingtan); Zhongyuan city group (as one and a half hours from Zhengzhou by train, economic region centered by Zhengzhou, capital of Henan province, nine cities as Luoyang, Kaifeng, Xinxiang, Jiaozuo, Xuchang, Pingdingshan, Luohe, Jiyuan and Zhengzhou are included. There is also a plan of two hours economic region).

Currently, six provinces in the central region have formed a common recognition regarding the following important construction goals. There are five strategic goals: (1) one big urban area (Wuhan urban area); (2) two economic belts (the economic belt along the horizontally expanded Yangtze River and along the vertically extended Jinguang Railway); (3) three plains (Jianghan plain, Huanghuai plain, and Boyanghu plain, which are the production bases of foodstuffs, cotton, and oil products); (4) four high-tech industries (the optical electronic information industry, new materials, high-tech manufacturing, biology, bio-pharmaceutical industry); (5) five main industries (automobiles, steel, spinning, hydroelectric power generation, and tertiary industries such as finance, real estate, commerce, and tourism).

Evaluation of policy measures

The above-stated development strategies in the coastal, western, northeast, and central region have covered all China. It can be said that they have realized an omnidirectional development strategy in the true sense. Among these strategies, the main goals have similarities and differences. A coastal development strategy was carried out as an experiment for the reform and open door policy. The western development strategy focused attention upon resource development and infrastructure construction. The northeast development strategy was concentrated on restructuring the policy of state-owned heavy industry. The central development strategy put greater importance on three agricultural problems.

Under each development strategy, a complete policy system design was presented. In addition, the 'learning by doing' characteristics were clear. Although inland development was promoted, disparity among regions was still expanded.

Table 2.3 indicates the GDP ratios of four major regions. As the table shows, (1) for ten years from 1995 to 2005, the GDP ratio of ten provinces and cities under direct control of central government in the coastal eastern region increased from 48.27% to 52.1%, which indicated that, generally, their regional economic power was strengthened. The Bohai Rim Region (Beijing, Tianjin, Hebei, Shandong) expanded its GDP ration to 16.34% from 15.22%, the Yangtze River Delta (Jiangsu, Zhejiang and Shanghai) increased it to 20.68% from 19.33%, and the China south region (Guangdong, Fujian, Hainan) extended it to 15.08% from 13.72%. (2) Three provinces in the northeast region declined to 8.67% in 2005 from 10.3% in 1995. (3) Six provinces in the central region decreased to 18.82% in 2005 from 20.63% in 1995. (4) Western twelve provinces, municipalities directly under the central government, autonomous districts, declined to 16.93% in 2005 from 18.37% in 1995.

What was the main problem causing the disparity? We think it is necessary to reconsider policy measures.

(I) Reconsider the leading role of investment Since the go-west development strategy was presented, we recognize investment has contributed mainly to economic development. However, it will take many more years to complete the implementation of policy measures effectively.

For five years from 1999 to 2003, the fixed asset investment amount reached 3,810.97 billion yuan in the western region, 11,328.05 billion yuan in the eastern region, and 4,229.35 billion yuan in the central region, and the ratios to the national total amount was 19.1%, 56.8%, and 21.2% respectively. The eastern region received much more investment than the other regions.

Table 2.4 displays the ratio of the basic construction investment amount of the eastern, central and western regions, respectively, to the regional total. Compared with the national average, the ratio of the eastern region was lower than the national average; meanwhile, each of central and western regions ratios was higher, in particular the western region was the highest. It should be pointed out that, in the

Table 2.3 GDP ratios of four major regions (%)

Area	Province	1995	1998	2000	2003	2004	2005
1. Total of east coast ten provinces and municipalities directly under the central government		48.27	48.71	49.94	51.36	51.55	52.10
The Bohai Rim Region	Sub total	15.22	15.41	15.71	16.22	16.66	16.34
	Tianjin	1.60	1.61	1.69	1.81	1.80	1.87
	Hebei	4.94	5.14	5.24	5.24	5.37	5.10
	Shandong	8.68	8.65	8.79	9.18	9.49	9.36
Yangtze River Delta Region	Sub total	19.33	19.18	19.72	20.74	20.89	20.68
	Shanghai	4.27	4.46	4.68	4.61	4.56	4.63
	Jiangsu	8.94	8.70	8.83	9.19	9.44	9.26
	Zhejiang	6.12	6.02	6.21	6.93	6.89	6.79
South China Region	Sub total	13.72	14.12	14.51	14.41	14.01	15.08
	Guangdong	9.34	9.57	9.94	10.05	9.83	11.31
	Hainan	0.63	0.53	0.53	0.50	0.47	0.45
	Fujian	3.75	4.02	4.03	3.86	3.71	3.32
2. Total of central six provinces		20.63	21.18	20.36	19.44	19.66	18.82
	Anhui	3.48	3.39	3.13	2.93	2.95	2.72
	Jiangxi	2.09	2.24	2.06	2.09	2.14	2.05
	Shanxi	1.90	1.93	1.69	1.81	1.86	2.11
	Henan	5.21	5.26	5.29	5.20	5.40	5.35
	Hebei	4.15	4.47	4.40	3.99	3.87	3.30
	Hunan	3.81	3.88	3.80	3.42	3.44	3.29
3. Total of northeast three provinces		10.30	9.99	10.02	9.56	9.27	8.67
	Liaoning	4.85	4.69	4.80	4.43	4.21	4.05
	Jilin	1.96	1.88	1.87	1.86	1.81	1.83
	Heilongjiang	3.50	3.42	3.35	3.27	3.25	2.79
4. Total of western 12 provinces, municipalities directly under the central government and autonomous districts		18.37	17.69	17.13	16.94	16.90	16.93
	Inner Mongolia	1.45	1.44	1.44	1.59	1.66	1.97
	Guangxi	2.79	2.30	2.11	2.02	2.03	2.06
	Chongqing		1.73	1.63	1.66	1.63	1.55
	Sichuan	6.13	4.33	4.13	4.03	4.02	3.73
	Guizhou	1.09	1.02	1.02	1.00	0.98	1.00
	Yunnan	2.09	2.17	2.01	1.82	1.81	1.76
	Tibet	0.10	0.11	0.12	0.14	0.13	0.13
	Shanxi	1.74	1.67	1.71	1.77	1.77	1.86
	Gansu	0.96	1.05	1.01	0.96	0.95	0.98
	Qinghai	0.29	0.27	0.27	0.29	0.29	0.27
	Ningxia	0.29	0.27	0.27	0.28	0.28	0.31
	Xinjiang	1.45	1.35	1.40	1.39	1.35	1.32

Source: *Chinese Statistical Bulletin*, annual.

eastern region, the basic infrastructure construction has already been carried out; meanwhile, in both the central and western regions, the infrastructure building has been carried forward. The detail suggests that the investment was spent on more than 60 important infrastructure constructions, horizontally through the regions. For example, the 'transport water from south to north' project (meaning the infrastructure building to transport water from the southern region to the northern region, which needed to construct a canal across the valley), the 'transport electric power from western to eastern region' project, the 'transport natural gas from western region to eastern coastal area)' project, infrastructure construction for inland agriculture, education, and so on.

However, as far as the absolute amount of basic construction investment was concerned, from 1999 to 2003, the eastern region occupied the highest ratio, at 45.4% of national total, and the central and western region shared 22.7% and 22.8% respectively.

From 1999 to the first quarter of 2004, the number of various fixed asset investments all over the nation, whose total was 4,285, was made up of 982 by the western region, 2,171 by the eastern region and 1,132 by the central region, the total amount of which reached 895.2 billion yuan. Table 2.5 shows the fund structure of fixed asset investment of each respective region, which indicated that (1) as regards the national budget, each of the eastern, central and western regions had about one third (the western had a little higher than others, at 37.8%); (2) in the total amount of bank loans, 260.6 billion yuan, the eastern region occupied 55.9%, while the western region had only 18.2% and the central region received 25.9%; (3) in the total amount of credit, 3.013 billion yuan, the eastern region had 47%, the central region 9.4%, and the western region 43.5%; (4) in the total amount of foreign capital, 106.504 billion yuan, the eastern region had 85.5%, the central region had 10.7% and the western region had only 3.4%; (5) as far as their own money, 459.37 billion yuan, was concerned, the eastern region received more than half, 51.7%, while the central and western regions had 27% and 21.3% respectively; (6) in the others in Table 2.5 whose amount was 53.91 billion yuan, the eastern region received 70%, and central and western regions occupied, respectively, about 15%. Also in the others, some amounts were originally coming from the bank, thus if we count that 5% came from the bank, in the total fixed asset investment amount around one third came from the bank.

On the whole, investment in the eastern region had different sources, which were bank loans, foreign capital, own money, and credit, investment in the central region mainly came from the national budget and credit. Meanwhile, the central region received more bank loans than the western region in addition to the national budget.

Table 2.4 Ratio of basic construction investment amount of eastern, central and western region to the regional total (%)

	1999	2000	2001	2002	2003	1999–2003 Total
National average	41.72	40.79	39.82	40.61	41.22	40.83
Eastern	36.32	34.35	32.61	33.20	28.99	32.56
Central	43.00	42.73	42.75	45.65	43.39	43.57
Western	48.96	48.83	47.38	45.48	51.69	48.64

Source: *Chinese Statistical Bulletin*, annual.

As regards the problems on the go-west development strategy, they were as follows,[11] and were shared with problems occurring in other regions' development strategies. (1) The investment environment necessary for economic development (both hard and soft) has been ten to 15 years behind the coastal region, in which in particular such aspects as consciousness, institution, and human resources had a large difference. (2) Even the national budget expenditure increased, although private-owned capital was not increased so much. That is to say, the situation was 'hot public, cool private'. (3) The main industries to lead to the overall development have never been developed. The government investment was mainly for infrastructure construction and ecological system protection, but not for manufacturing development – particularly not for the advantageous industry in the western region. Because of the delayed development in industry in the western region, there were not enough sectors to receive the redundant workforce in rural areas. (4) The leakage effects in big projects were recognized, and their reason was thought to be due to the project's purpose to resolve the energy shortage in the eastern coastal regions. In addition, enterprises in the eastern region mainly made successful bids. Most national projects have never been closely connected with the regional economy. There is a kind of 'dual structure'.

The situation was different from the Third Front Construction period in the 1960s and 1970s. The above-mentioned projects seem to contribute to job creation for the local economy, the progress of environmental investment in the western region, and the accumulation of related industries For the huge inland area, however, some more factors might be necessary to realize such contributions for the regional economy.

For the promotion of the northeastern region, the central government announced, at the end of 2003, the 100 projects in the first period and, altogether, 61 billion

11 See for example, 'a research on economic structural adjustment in western region and development of specially advantageous industry' published by Research center of Development in Western Region in Chinese Social Science Agency, in September, 2005.

Table 2.5 Fund structure of fixed asset investment (1999 – first quarter of 2003) (%)

	National budget	Ratio (%)	Bank loan	Ratio (%)	Credit	Ratio (%)	Foreign capital	Ratio (%)	Own money	Ratio (%)	Others	Ratio (%)
National average	1184552		26056092		301279		10650370		45936864		5390761	
Eastern	363760	30.7	14552469	55.9	141820	47.1	9143222	85.8	23742623	51.7	3766674	69.9
Central	373602	31.5	6760174	25.9	28316	9.4	1142292	10.7	12418513	27.0	846933	15.7
Western	447190	37.8	4743449	18.2	131143	43.5	364856	3.4	9775728	21.3	777154	14.4

Source: Author's calculation with research carried out by National Statistical Bureau, Enterprise Research Group in October, 2004.

yuan investment. However, after that the central government seemed to reconsider the investment-led method of development. Are investment expenditures necessary to promote the northeast region? As a matter of fact, at the end of the 20th century, central government invested more than 100 billion yuan into the northeast region to resolve the problem of collecting bills for state-owned enterprises in the region. Central government has still kept compensating for the budget deficit. Also, as bank loans have been given to the region, the northeast region has never suffered from less finance than the other regions.

Rather more finance was given to the northeast region than other regions. The way of thinking that, if system and consciousness is kept unchanged, then more efficient investment and more development would be difficult, has prevailed. Market-oriented reform is the most important way for the northeast region to develop.

A regional development bank plan was considered to carry out more efficient investment from the central budget. The main aim of the bank is to select better projects for development as well as bank loans. Such consideration on systemic transformation needs to examine the 'public oriented culture' in the northeast region in addition to the state-owned sector problem.

(II) State-owned sector problem and the 'public oriented culture' In the systemic transition years of China, regional development of inland areas has had a more serious burden coming from former central planning days than the coastal area, which is a different issue from the neo-classical way of development. From viewpoints of comparative economic systems, in all the regions of the western, northeast, and central, the state-owned sector has occupied a much higher ratio than the eastern region. Reforming the state-owned sector is, needless to say, a more serious burden for them.

Table 2.6 points out the regional breakdown of structure in industrial production, which showed that the ratio of the state-owned sector in the eastern region was 10% less than the national average in 1999 and 9% less in 2003; contrarily, in the central region, it was 18% and 22% more respectively than the national average and in the western region 26% and 25% more respectively than the national average. As regards the ratio of stock company, foreign-owned enterprise, and others, both central and western regions had much less.

Heilongjiang province in the northeast region (classified as in the central region) has been in a typical state-owned system. It has recorded various kinds of firsts. For example, the number of restructured workers, which was 878,000 – the most in the whole nation; the per capita consumption in townships and villages in the province showed only 4462 yuan, which was least over all China; the number of citizens receiving minimum social security in townships and villages in the province was 1.46 million, which was the most in China. Heilongjiang is a typical province depending upon resources; it has four of the biggest coal-towns, two of the biggest forest-towns, and one of the biggest oil-towns (Daqing). The GDP growth rate of Heilongjiang province in 2002 was in the tenth rank in China; however, the Daqing oil field produced 43.6 billion yuan, which occupied 44% of manufacturing products and 94% of profits in the whole province. Most townships and villages in the northeast region are suffering from serious problems such as ecology-related ones and subsidence coming from excessive mining.

In the state-owned enterprises-led region. whose characteristics are the *Zheng She He Yi* (unification of economy and administration), there exists what is called a 'public-oriented culture'. A state-owned enterprise, which is an appurtenance of the government, needs to have negotiations for survival, but whose behavior is not compatible with a market-oriented system that attaches great importance to confidence and integrity. It means an extreme expansion of transaction costs, which leads to less attractive circumstances in the northeast region for foreign capital.

For example, for five years from 1999, in Jilin province, they had more than 3000 cases of cancellation of inward FDI projects. However, for the same period, the number of ratified projects of inward FDI reached in roughly 2000. It is difficult to say that Local governments in the northeastern region have never been enthusiastic about attracting inward FDI, but they had no successful result. In 2001, the inward FDI received in the three provinces of the northeastern region in reached 3.19 billion yuan, occupying 6.4% of the national total. This was only one seventh of the Chinese east, and one quarter of Guangdong province. In 2002, considering inward FDI in Jilin province, the total FDI, pledged base FDI amount and actual base FDI amount were 27.3% less, 0.8% less, and 6.1% less respectively than the previous year.

(III) Cause of the three agricultural problems: another theory of accumulated poverty The position of six provinces in the central region is shown in Table 2.7. They occupied 10.7% area, 28.1% population, 22.5% GDP, 30.8% food production of the national total. Henan, of the six provinces, in particular has one quarter of the whole China's wheat production. In Henan province, 1.8 billion yuan has been invested to develop the wheat flour processing industry and the frozen food processing industry.

Six provinces in the central region have been given an important role as a food production base. They could not thus attach less importance to agricultural production and greater importance on industrialization. Promotion of the central

Table 2.6 Regional structure in industrial production (%)

	1999				2003			
	Whole China	East	Central	West	Whole China	East	Central	West
State owned	49	39	67	75	38	29	60	63
Collective	17	19	17	9	7	7	8	4
Stock company	7	6	9	10	13	10	18	21
Foreign owned	14	18	5	4	19	23	9	6
Others	13	18	2	2	23	31	5	6

Source: *Chinese Statistical Bulletin*, annual.

region has been closely related with the three agricultural problems. Also, without the development of agriculture and rural areas, the economy of six provinces in the central region is undoubtedly unable to develop.

The six provinces in the central region have a huge farming population, which is one third of the whole of China. The structure of workforce in the six provinces is such that the ratio of agricultural workers to the total workforce is 53.7% and the share of agricultural products to total GDP is 16.9%, a figure that is 3.2% more and 2.1% more, respectively, than the national average. The industrialization policy is necessary to absorb the redundant workforce in rural areas; at the same time peasants in the central region who cannot find any job opportunity have started to move to the cities in the coastal region across provinces and cities.

Considering the number of ‘immigrant labor’ who are working in outside provinces and cities, the greatest number (100 million workers) is recognized in Sichuan province, which is a big province, in population, of the western region. The second to the sixth provinces in rank were Anhui province, Hunan province, Jiangxi province, Henan province, Hubei province, in order, all of which are located in the central region. In particularly, it is said that the ‘immigrant labor’ coming from Anhui province reaches eight million.

In order to resolve the three agricultural problems typically shown in the central region, the most important measure is to develop the local economies. However, rural areas in China have suffered from a serious budget deficit. An announcement by the ministry of agriculture said that the average debt amount of towns and townships in 1998 reached four million yuan and the national total debt amount of towns and townships equaled 200 billion yuan, and average debt amount of villages and the national total amount in 1998 showed 200 thousand yuan and 150 billion yuan. The sum total of the towns, townships and villages was said to be 350 billion yuan debt for the rural area in China. The accumulated debt situation for some of the towns, townships and villages has deteriorated. For example, in 2000, before the tax reform was started in Hunansheng, it was 8.54 billion yuan and in

Anhui province it was 5.02 billion yuan.[12] Other provinces in the central region are in a similar situation.

On June 25, 2003, the Chief of the Board of Audit, Jinhua, reported at the Third Meeting of Tenth National Parliament that, of altogether about 2,800 counties in 2001 in the whole of China, the number of counties with a budget deficit reached 731, which was around 30%. Most of the counties were located in the central and western region (*Xinhua Net*, June 25, 2003).

In the rural area, therefore, the burden for peasants has been most serious and the financial debt situation has been worst. In Hunan province and Hubei province, before the tax reform was started in 2000, for example, the average tax burden per 6.667 ares was 300 yuan, in which the highest burden was more than 400 yuan. Although tax reform was carried out after then, the tax burden for peasants in central region is still highest. The tax burden per 6.667 ares for peasants in Dongting Lake is, for example, in the vicinity of 120 yuan.

After the agricultural tax, among others, was abolished in 2005, the budget imbalance problem for towns, townships, and villages as a basic administrative organization has been more serious. It means they lost their traditional financial resource and central government has never compensated the lost budget income. It has caused unwilling misappropriated use of other financial resources, such as educational funds, which has often led to unpaid income for school teachers in rural areas all over the nation.

In 1997, the then prime minister Zhu Rongji presented the three reforms, in which he raised the administration reform. The administration problem became more serious in the more basic administrations. There are various reasons for the debt problem in rural areas, which has complicatedly related the cause and effect of the administration system, the budget system, and the finance system. One of the important reasons seems to be too many civil servants. Because of the poverty, the position as a civil servant or as a quasi civil servant (employed from necessity) becomes very popular. To employ too many civil servants results in a greater burden for peasants, which worsens the government budget situation. It seems to be correctly explained by the circular accumulative causation of Myrdal (1968).

(IV) Reform plan of administrative districts: is Shenyang a municipality directly under the central government? Is Wuhan a Special Economic Zone? Around 2004, the proposal for Shenyang to be a municipality directly under the central government was widely discussed. The main reason for this was Chongqing's improved economic performance that, after the city was promoted to be a municipality directly under the central government in 1997, its economic

12 Guo Shutian, former director of the policy legislation section in the Ministry of Agriculture, enumerated the three agricultural problems after the beginning of 1990s, in addition to decreased production of food and decreased income of farmers. These were (1) burdens for farmers, (2) misuse of land resources, (3) debt problems of townships and villages. See *Diyi Caijing Ribao*, October 14, 2005.

Table 2.7 Some indices of six provinces in the central region

	Situation and Performance	Ratio to the national total (%)
Area (2004)	1027.5 (thousand square kilometer)	10.7
Population (2004)	363.1 (million)	28.1
GDP (2003)	2634.8 (billion yuan)	22.5
Export (2003)	13.15 (billion US$)	3.3
Food production (2003)	144.68 (million ton)	30.8

Source: National Statistical Bureau.

performance was significantly improved. The number of first-rank administrative districts in China is much less than in the USA, which has about the same land area. The number of such districts in China is 31, which is about 60% of the number in the USA. This seems to be closely connected with the vertical division of the administrative levels into five parts (see the Figure 2.2). The fewer the number of first-rank administrative districts means that, in a gradually transformed country such as China, in which much central planning exists, various inefficiently accumulated administrative strata have seriously damaged the autonomous system at lower level local government. Among scholars, there have been deep-rooted arguments for necessities to expand municipalities directly under the central government.

They insisted, as beneficiaries of Shenyang being a municipality directly under the central government, on the following: (1) the same amount of total investment could be more efficiently and intensively allocated toward redevelopment of cities for their rebirth, and (2) it is expected to have a ripple effect on surrounding regions. It is planned for Shenyang city because, as Shenyang has a well established base for heavy industry, equipment manufacturing should be a key industry. The southern area in China that has developed with light industry would become a big market for such equipment manufacturing. As a specific example, privately owned enterprises in the spinning industry in Shaoxing, Zhejiang province, imported spinning machines with 20 billion yuan.

In addition, after a development strategy of 'the rise of the central region' was presented in 2004, it was argued that Wuhan should become a central core city in the central region and should be given a special policy similar to special zones.[13]

13 Statement by Wang Maolin who was a deputy director of legal committee in executive committee of National Parliament, at the strategic forum on the rise of central region on May 14, 2005.

Population movement and the change of the relations between urban and rural, and between coastal and inland in China

Relations between coastal and inland areas can be said to be similar to relations between the urban and rural in a broad sense. As labor mobility from rural to urban (immigrant labor) also indicates mobility from inland to coastal, the underdeveloped regions are the rural and inland regions. As regards theories on labor movement, we can depend on the dual structure model of Lewis (1954) and Todaro (1969).

(I) The Lewis model and the applicability to China The Lewis model, which was originally developed by Lewis and was later developed by Fei and Ranis, is well known as the dual economy model (Ranis and Fei, 1961, and Fei *et al.*, 1986). It shows, as a kind of redundant labor model, that, provided free mobility exists, labor mobility occurs from the agricultural sector (traditional sector) to the industrial sector (modern sector), which also indicates that the industrial structure shifts from the primary sector to the manufacturing sector. After the transformation point, the wage rate of unskilled labor in urban area starts to increase.

The Lewis model could not be applied to China in Mao Zedong's era because the precondition (labor mobility) did not exist. There are pros and cons to the applicability of Lewis model to industrialization and urbanization in the Deng Xiaoping's era. The positive side of applicability tells us that there is a farming population of around 800 million in China that might display the unlimited supply of labor, however, over recent years, a negative side of applicability suggests that, in Guangdong province for example, labor shortage has been experienced for four consecutive years. According to various sources of information, most immigrant labor moved to the Yangtze River Delta area which has more advantageous conditions for them. Why has such labor movement occurred?

In the Yangtze River Delta, they have a better wage rate and have established better social networks, which receive favorable reception by immigrant labor. In particular, skilled labor with embodied technology have enjoyed advantageous measures. Many factories suffered from a labor shortage in the Pearl River Delta, and tried to find enough workers after the New Year (according to the lunar calendar) holidays were over, but found it difficult. Regional disparity within China therefore caused labor re-mobility of immigrant labor. Local government in Guangdong province finally tried to adjust, and raised the minimum wage rate after ten years of leaving it unchanged.

This came from a kind of competition among provinces and regions. The Chinese economy as a whole has never reached the transformation point, but because of competition among regions, wages were moving up. At the same time, the whole of China still has a huge number of redundant workers, most of whom are not mobile. Even after institutional conditions (the family registration system) were alleviated, 'unpatriotic personal treatment' against the immigrant labor, which was reflected in social security and children's education, has existed as a deep-rooted condition. As

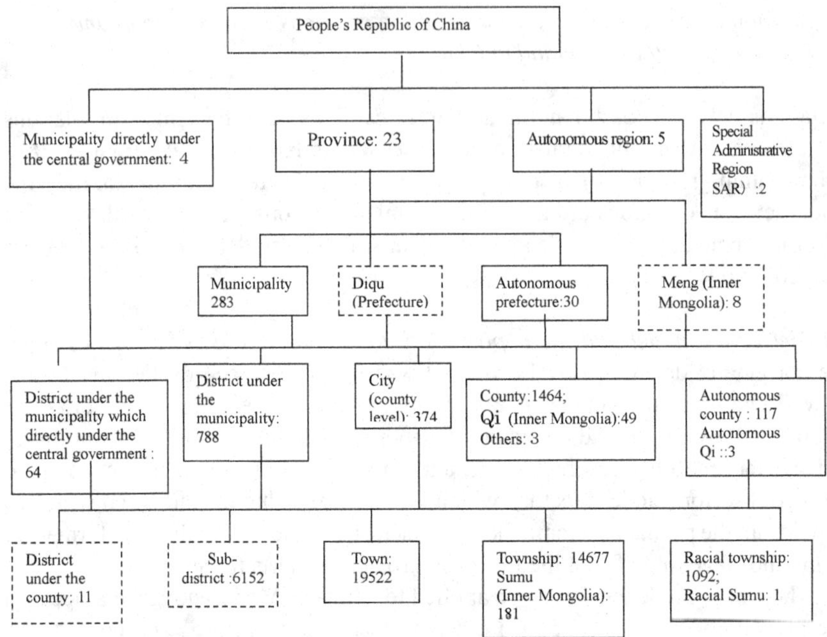

Note:(1) parts of dotted line are not administrative institutions, but the agency of upper administrative institutions.

(2) Both municipality and district are former Zhuanqu Special district, most of which have implemented the "county receives city's guidance" system since 1980s.

(3) Both town and township are the former people's commune.

(4) Most "districts under the counties" have been removed.

(5) Statistical data were as of December 31, 2005.

Source: Pu Shanxin et al. (1995), p.49, and Chinese Administrative Structure Net. (http://www.xzqh.org.cn/ONEWS_zq.asp?id=1150).

Figure 2.2 Administrative structure of the People's Republic of China

well as a mental burden for the mobile population (immigrant labor) they suffered also from much discrimination. The high survival costs in urban area have surely hindered labor mobility. In China, recently, there has bee the opposite movement tendency, from urban to rural, from coastal to inland. Although some of this is negative returning, the majority seem to be positive, those wishing to be entrepreneurs in their hometowns through their accumulated technology and experience.

(II) Todaro model and the applicability to China Todaro's model is constructed of three sectors: rural, formal urban, and informal urban. The Todaro model leads us to the following conclusion; the reason for labor mobility comes from cost and benefit considerations, and the key concept for mobility is expected income, which is

calculated as the product of wage rate in the urban area by employment probability.

As important and meaningful is the suggestion by Todaro's model for China, we think that the huge disparity between urban and rural makes employment probability less important for the decision to move to the urban area. This explains the excessive mobility of labor from rural areas. Todaro cautioned on the possible phenomena of the coexistence of a huge number of unemployed workers in urban areas and labor shortage in rural areas. An excessively inflowing population in the urban area can be absorbed in the informal sector and their living conditions might deteriorate, which can lead to slums in urban areas. Under such a huge disparity between urban and rural, essentially positive policy measures, like employment promotion policy in urban area and education promotion policy in rural area, might have opposite effects, because those policy measures make a signal for the rural population, saying that employment probability becomes higher. A policy proposal suggested by Todaro tells us that, in order to reduce unemployed workers in urban areas, they should develop an effective promotion strategy for rural areas to increase peasants' income.

The new reform and open door policy in China started in the 1980s, has depended upon economic rationality and is based on Deng Xiaoping's idea to first develop the coastal region with advantages in industrial foundation. However, the imbalance of regional development (regional disparity problem) has been constantly considered. Deregulation of labor mobility was carried out and we think the conditions that apply in Todaro's model exist in China.

As regards regional disparity and the disparity between urban and rural areas in China, The World Bank announced the Gini coefficient in China was 0.376 in 1992, 0.403 in 1998 and 0.447 in 2001. Income disparity shows how many times more urban per capita income is than rural per capita income, although this disparity reduced in 1978–85. After that the trend fluctuated and was followed by an expansion, reaching and income disparity of more than three times in 2002 and 2003. The disparity situation in China is said to be significant.

The Chinese open door policy after 1978 has been successful (because the high speed of economic growth has continued for more than 20 years); however, a variety of complications that accompanied the high-speed economic growth have been recognized. A typical example is economic disparity (as well as environmental pollution, resource shortage, etc). Unless such negative phenomena can be resolved, China will suffer from serious difficulties related to agriculture and farming problems. We expect therefore, in the next development stage, that three agricultural problems become important. (At the time of writing, central government has publicly announced its position to attach greater importance to three agricultural problems).

Conclusion

Gradual transition process in China: the wisdom of creative destruction

(I) Criteria for judgment: the Chinese gradual way of transition The Chinese transition started at the end of 1978 with the open door policy, led by Deng Xiaoping, and called the gradual way of transition. As a whole, the Chinese method of transition has been recognized as gradual reform; however, in China, there were some radical transition parts. For example, because the family contract system in rural areas, which started at the end of the 1970s, was fairly radical, within five years the rural scenery was transformed and, 900 million people's lives changed completely. Because of the dissolution of the People's commune, at the end of 1983, 95% of the rural families began to manage private business and, at the end of 1984, around 97% of rural families carried out the family contract system. In addition to the above, the unified purchase and unified sale of agricultural products by central government was abolished in 1985, which contributed to the promotion of a market-oriented system of the rural economy and led to the substantial success of the Chinese transition. In addition, price reform implemented at the end of 1980s showed the radical method of reform, which seemed, however, to be less successful. The real estate bubble, which occurred after 2003, was a phenomenon that also came from the radical reform. Such examples are particular cases whose characteristic nature is radical; however, generally speaking, we should recognize that in general Chinese transition has been gradual.

(II) Characteristics of the Chinese gradual transition As stated above, the Chinese way of gradual reform has followed the process of expanding gradually from rural areas (family contract system) to urban areas (state-owned enterprises), from coastal areas to inland areas. In addition, as regards the reform of enterprise and industry in the urban area, first, opportunities were given to foreign-owned enterprises and private enterprises to develop, and then we think these gradually became development models for state-owned enterprises.

Meanwhile, in the 1980s, both the open door policy and regional development policy were gradual reforms, and the main measures of the open door policy were decentralization from the central to the local. Once designated as open cities and open regions, they could autonomously establish the 'development district of national level' and could independently authorize investment by foreign capital, which contributed to regional economic development.

Under the new coastal open strategy, which started by designating open areas like special economic zones and also by promoting TVEs and implementing a family contract system in rural areas in the 1980s, the growing industries in the growing regions were labor intensive. In summary, they were the Guangdong model (making use of foreign capital) and the Jiangzhe model (led by TVEs, which were geographically covered by the southern part of Jiangsu province and the northern part of Zhejiang province) (Chen Yun and Tsuneichi Toda, 2001; Wu Junhua, 1995).

In the 1990s in China, the omnidirectional open strategy was promoted. Inland areas as well as coastal areas were designated as open regions. Policy process was mentioned above.

We think that the advantage of employing the gradual way of transition was to abolish the time- and energy-consuming ideological discussions by realizing the merits contributed by transition, which started from the sectors and regions that were easiest to reform. Deng Xiaoping mentioned in the speech in his southern tour the following; 'We do not argue, which is one of my inventions, and not to discuss is to save valuable time, if discussion starts, the situation would become complicated, time would be consuming, and we have nothing. It might be better to challenge something new, and to experiment drastically, without discussion'.

The author of this book would conclude that the Chinese gradual way of transition has been to establish creative destruction.[14] As is said, 'look before you leap'; that is, before abolishing something make something to be substituted. Under such a strategy, although China has adopted the principle of market socialism, the role of the state-owned sector has become less and foreign-owned and private-owned enterprises have played more important roles. The activities of foreign-owned and private-owned enterprises have also contributed to the restoration of state-owned enterprises, some of which are, we believe, understood to be creative. Therefore, we recognize the process through which the state-owned sector, compared with former days, has become less important in the whole economy (Chen Yun and Ken Morita, 2005).

(III) Social distribution of development benefits Chinese reform and the open door policy have been said to be a transformation from an inland civilization to an ocean civilization. A coastal region has a geographical advantage and an inland region has to wait to receive the open door policy measures. The great importance of regional development in China has been shifted toward the reform of industrial structures and of the ownership system, from the open door and inward FDI attractive policies. Since the end of the 1990s, the efficient reform of state-owned enterprises and the well-balanced regional development between coastal and inland areas have become the main tasks in China.

Although China expanded the disequilibrium development strategy, it has employed an omnidirectional open policy. Transformation of the strategy requests that local areas attempt self-reliance, in addition to the financial support and advantageous policies supplied by central government. Cooperative relations among regions, in particular, have become an important topic to be considered from

---

14 Jefferson and Singh called the process 'creative reduction' suggested by the innovation theory of Schumpeter, because they thought that, in the transition process in China, state-owned enterprises would be declining through competition with the non-state-owned sector, which could dynamically be expanding. See Jefferson and Singh (1997).

the viewpoints of complementing of each advantage and the social distribution of development benefits among regions.

The necessity and possibility of the gradual way of transition in China: comparisons with Central and Eastern Europe

It is not easy how to evaluate the adaptability of the Chinese gradual way of transition compared with the former socialist countries in Central and Eastern Europe. China has employed a gradual transition while former socialist countries in Central and Eastern Europe such as Poland and the Czech Republic have selected a radical transition. What are the main reasons of each method of transition? We consider here the reasons why China has needed a gradual transition and why, in China, it has been possible to choose this gradual way.

(I) On the necessity of a gradual way of transition First of all, a transition pattern is closely related to the complexity and urgency of the surrounding circumstances. The more complex, the less urgent, the more gradual transition is necessary. China is an very big country, with 9.6 million square kilometers of land area and a population of 1.3 billion; China is also the biggest less-developed and transition country in the world and therefore has large-scale variety. In addition, China has been suffering from an inconsistency problem. Thus, in the development pattern, we think a gradual way of transition would be applicable in China; however, at the same time, a radical way of reform was partly employed and in a timely way.

We should understand that because China is a big country, it causes difficulties for Chinese transition whilst also enabling Chinese strength to endure the external pressure. As far as China has gone into a gradual way of transition and as far as the Chinese government could give the Chinese people a more advanced way of everyday life than previously, then the internal pressure for a more radical way of transition will reduce. Smaller countries – in land area and population – cannot be simply compared with China but could have the rationality of a respective pattern of transition and development.

Meanwhile, for the smaller countries, it might be more likely to be supported by foreign countries and international society towards a more rapid transition (such as post-war Japan). However, in China, it might be impossible to carry out the systemic transition without self-reliance (meaning without an internal incentive). No other country could finance a giant country of this size, and hence self-reliance would be the only way for China. Through a gradual transition, China has been planting the incentives for transformation within Chinese society little by little; it would not be good for the external world to let China employ radical measures. Keeping up helpful external pressures to promote reform should be encouraged. As far as Chinese society after 1978 (and especially after 2001) is concerned, as China has been closely connected with international politics and the international economy, the country has received external pressures. In Chapter 5, we argue in detail about the characteristics of the Chinese development model and the fact-following mechanism of institutional change.

(II) On the possibility of a gradual way of transition: comparisons with Central and Eastern Europe As mentioned previously about the start of the logic and the beginning of gradual reforms in 1978, complicating factors were at work – in particular, the following three should be emphasized: (1) the huge disparity between China and the rest of the world, which came from implementation of a central planning system for 30 years, from the establishment of the new nation to the reform and open door policy; (2) a slackly centralized system has been the characteristic nature of China; and (3) the wisdom of Deng Xiaoping.

There are other reasons for successful Chinese gradual transition. The following two are remarkable compared with the situation of Central and Eastern Europe.

First, there are large differences in traditional culture or popular culture between China and these areas. Gradual reform automatically displays the maintenance of an authoritarian system (led by the communist party). There are substantial differences in patience in authoritarianism between east and west. As regards Central and Eastern Europe, they had the popular feudal system before the Middle Ages, under which local decentralization had a long tradition. Thus, a socialistic centralization system was heterogeneous for them from the beginning. In particular, from the practical stage of socialism, not the theory stage, the immaturity of the system was exposed much more clearly, and the admired utopia was ruined. In Central and Eastern Europe, they tried to break away from socialism in the early days, from the end of the Second World War, for example Hungary in 1956.

Meanwhile, in China around the days of the third century BC (after the Qin dynasty and the Han dynasty built big empires), they established a country in which people endured an autocratic system. People were apt to understand not that liberty was given from birth but that authority was given from birth. Needless to say, they desired to have wise authority, as expressed by Qingtian Dalaoye (wise bureaucrats like a blue sky), and lots of traditional plays described such wise governors and bureaucrats, for example Bao Zheng (999–1062) and Hai Rui (1514–1587) who every Chinese knows.[15] Even these days such plays gain the sympathy of the Chinese people.

Second, in Europe, each country is not as big, and also most of them have a land border with others. In such an environment, they have substantial learning effects on each another. A rebellious mind and radical transformation are easily diffused throughout Europe, when they occur in one country or region. There are in Europe existing environments in which people are mutually encouraged. However, in the world's largest unified nation (China), it is difficult to have such

---

15 Bao Zheng (999–1062) was a prime minister of the Song dynasty (1271–1368), and Hai Rui (1514–1587) was of the Ming dynasty (1368–1644). (Hai Rui was from Hainan Island and was of Hui nationality. For only a few years did he work for central government, and he lived in lots of places. He was basically a local bureaucrat.)

effects. Once you have been the largest unified nation for many years, a kind of super stable structure has been established. According to Jin Guantao and Liu Qingfeng (1984), the structure among the peasant economy, Confucian culture, and political authoritarianism have been created to supported one another. Thus, even dynastic changes were carried out every decade, or every several hundred years without exception, and a newly established dynasty had no new basic framework and so was a copy of the previous dynasty. We think Eckstein's (1977) assertion is plausible that, although the peasant revolution was a peasant uprising in the dynastic period in China, it was not so revolutionary.

Chapter 3
Advantages and Disadvantages of State-owned Enterprise Reform: Relations with Systemic Reforms of Finance, Administration and Social Security

Introduction

As mentioned in Chapter 2, the three main problems regarding the reform and open door policy in China relate to the urban reform issue. There are many things to be transformed in the urban reforms, and one of the most important problems in China has undoubtedly been the reform of state-owned enterprises, which would be responsible for urban industries.

Traditionally, state-owned enterprises were the products of the *Zheng She He Yi* (unification of the economy and administration), for whom reforming has never been easy. Thus, this difficult issue has never been started the reform process (which is completely different from family contract system, TVEs reformation, and inward FDI, which began in the 1980s). We think that, in order to reform state-owned enterprises, quadrant reform might be required, with finance, administration and social security. The basic policy framework of market socialism mentioned in Chapter 2 showed the necessity to reform consistently the above issues.

In addition to the separation of government from enterprises, financial organizations, such as banks, have to be free from the attachment position of government. State-owned banks were, needless to say, state-owned enterprises in the financial sector; however, because of the importance of the financial sector, the reform of the banking sector has been delayed compared with other sectors. Traditional state-owned enterprises worked for employees to take care of all the aspects of everyday life. Thus, unless the welfare benefits could be separated, these enterprises could not become ordinary companies in a market economic sense. When we argue the reform of state-owned enterprises, we have to consider them from viewpoint of a systemic approach (see Figure 3.1).

This chapter starts by pointing out the problems of state-owned enterprise reforms, considering the several stages of reforms necessary. From the second to the fourth sections of this chapter, we discuss reform of finance, administration and social security, respectively, each of which was reformed in cooperation with state-owned enterprises, and also try to analyze their current situation and to find a possible way for development. Finally, a short conclusion will be given.

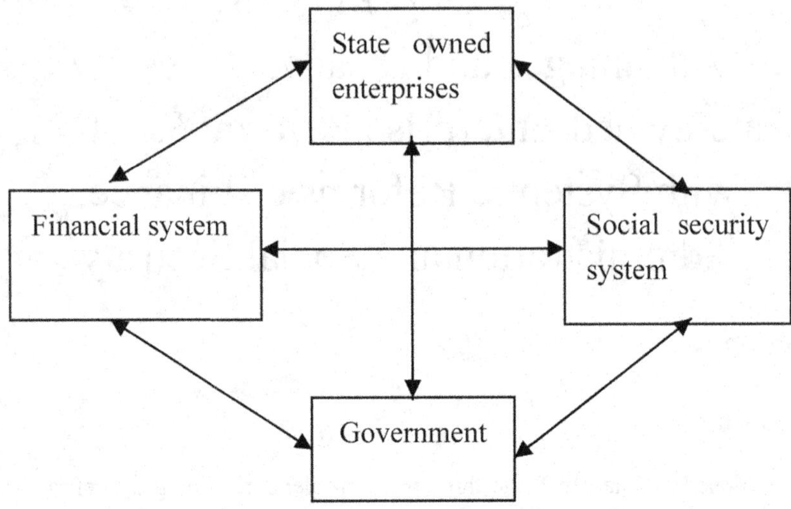

Source: Author.

Figure 3.1 The quadrant reform of state owned enterprises, finance, administration and social security

Reform of state owned enterprises

The necessity behind reforming state-owned enterprises has been, first of all, to increase efficiency. In addition, the previous literature on regional disparity in China showed that geographical differences among regions in which state-owned enterprises were established had substantial effects upon the economic disparity between regions. It thus suggests that the reform of state-owned enterprises has been crucial for promoting economic development and for alleviating regional disparity in the Chinese economy.

Several stages of the reform of state-owned enterprises

We recognize that, in 1992, Chinese policy of reform of state-owned enterprises was changed. Before 1992, the country was at the stage of policy adjustment, indicating the contract system, separation of property from management, and *Fang Quan Rang Li* (see below), but after the Fourteenth Communist Party Meeting in 1992, the stage of property rights reform of state-owned enterprises was started. The Party tried to transform the enterprise management mechanism through joint-stock privatization and grouping of state-owned enterprises. Details of the development stages are given in the following (see Sasaki, 1993, pp. 14–15, Kawachi *et al.*, 1987, pp. 124–141, and Kawai, 1996, pp. 15–44).

First, from 1979 to 1986, the main issue for the reform was the *Fang Quan Rang Li*, which pointed out the beginning of an enterprise profit reserving system and the expansion of rights to use the reserved profit. The concept of profit after tax, which divides profit into tax, was established.

Second, during the period from 1987 to 1993, the main task was the separation of property rights from management rights. In order for enterprises to be more independent, various rights were given to them. By the industrial enterprise act on people's property rights in 1988, and the ordinance on the management mechanism transformation act in 1992, the following rights were given to enterprises: (1) decision making rights on production and management; (2) price decision rights; (3) products sales rights; (4) materials purchase rights; (5) export and import rights; (6) negotiation rights to foreign capital; (7) usufruct of reserved money; (8) rental and alienation rights of fixed assets; (9) cooperation and takeover rights; (10) employment and dismissal rights; (11) personnel management rights; (12) wage rate and bonus decision rights; (13) internal organization establishment rights; and (14) veto power against compulsory assignment. Meanwhile however, as far as the actual implementation on independent rights of an enterprise is concerned, there may be significant room to consider this further. According to the then Overseas Economic Cooperation Fund (OECF) research, there could be recognized substantial differences between rules and reality (Wada, 1997).

Third, in the period after 1994, it was necessary for the organization system of state-owned enterprise to be reformed, including property rights, towards the establishment of a modern enterprise system. 'A modern enterprise system' means the following: (1) it adjusts the debt structure of enterprise asset, and puts the capital system in order; (2) it makes the managing authority on the assets of state-owned enterprises clear and adjusts the relationships on asset authority, (3) it makes both the enterprise system and joint stock system the main systems of the organization, and it adjusts the property rights structure of enterprises; (4) it utilizes surplus assets and implements asset value management; (5) it establishes the corporate system of enterprise and it makes the allocation system of enterprises more reasonable (*Yokohama Kogyoukan* (Yokohama Industrial Office, 1996).

Through the modern enterprise system, government will not directly intervene in the management of state-owned enterprises, by which an enterprise could become independent in the market and would be required to pay corporation tax. As a matter of fact, China has actively enacted legislation on enterprise activities since the beginning of the 1990s, in order to establish normative management environments for enterprises. For example, China legislated such acts as the Corporate Act of the People's Republic of China (enacted in 1993 and amended in 1999), the TVEs Act of the People's Republic of China (enacted in 1996), the Joint Venture Act of People's Republic of China (enacted in 1997), and the Private Capital Corporate Act of People's Republic of China (enacted in 1999).

Important contents of reforms of state-owned enterprises

Since 1994, great importance regarding the state-owned enterprise reform towards the modern enterprise system was placed on (1) corporate governance and (2) loan structure. The change of the loan structure indicated that corporate finance changed from the traditional government budget transfer to financial intermediaries. Enterprises therefore became serious about costs; we will consider this later in this chapter.

As far as corporate governance is concerned, the reform of joint-stock privatization of enterprises and the establishment of a normative board of directors etc has been given great importance. This new board of directors had a very important feature, which was that independent directors were selected from outside the enterprise. Therefore, in 2004, the two regulations – the directive opinions about the establishment of a board of directors in state- and wholly-owned enterprises, and the managing style of including independent directors on the board of directors in state- and wholly-owned enterprises – were submitted by the State-owned Assets Supervision and Administration Commission of the State Council (SASAC). They regulated that central state-owned enterprises had to be occupied by more than half of their number of independent directors invited from outside. In 2005, new boards of directors were inaugurated in the six large-scale state-owned enterprises, such as the Shanghai Baoshan iron works. On the meaning of the establishment the new board of directors, the head of the commission, Li Rongrong, evaluated that it was the greatest news since the founding of SASAC in 2003.

Meanwhile, Li Yining pointed out that final goal of the reform of state-owned enterprises in China was to introduce the joint-stock privatization.[1] In 1997, at the Fifteenth Communist Party Representative Meeting, they formerly confirmed that joint-stock privatization of state-owned enterprises was a form of socialism. It contributed to the joint-stock privatization reform of state-owned enterprises and to being listed. In 2004, of altogether 2903 state-owned middle-scale enterprises, which occupied 66.9% of the total assets of state-owned enterprises, 1464 enterprises finished their joint-stock privatization reform, whose ratio of completion reached 50.4%. In addition, more than 1000 enterprises were listed in the stock markets, both at the domestic and foreign level. Until the end of 2004, the number of listed enterprises whose stocks were controlled by centrally state-owned enterprises equaled 168, and their total amount of stock prices reached 33.34% of the total amount of all listed enterprises. The number of listed enterprises in Hong Kong's stock market was 60, and their total amount of stocks which could be tradable in the stock market occupied 19.37% of the total amount of tradable stocks in the Hong Kong market.

1 In May 1980, at the symposium on employment problems held under the auspices of the policy research office of the Chinese Communist Party Secretariat and National Ministry of Labor Personnel, Li Yining mentioned the reform through privatization. In 1985, Li Yining submitted formerly the above opinion, and later in various opportunities he insisted on the privatized reform through joint-stocks. It is thus called 'Li stocks'.

Strategy characteristics in the state-owned enterprise reforms

We think there are three strategy characteristics in the state-owned enterprise reforms.

First, in 1993, corporation law was established and the enterprise held a position of being a corporate body. In 1996, a policy plan, entitled *Zhua Da Fang Xiao*, was employed, which indicated that large-scale state-owned enterprises were still controlled by the government; however, small and medium sized state-owned enterprises were encouraged to be transformed into various property rights, including being privately owned. The head of SASAC, Li Rongrong, mentioned in 2005 that the number of state-owned industrial and service enterprises was 138,000 and the number of employees reached 43 million, of which there were 169 centrally controlled enterprises and 10.53 million employees. Thus, if the current speed of reform was sustained, the number of enterprises that were state-owned and controlled by state-owned enterprises could be decreased by 4000 to 5000.[2]

Second, we could recognize a trial of management of enterprise groups. Since 1991, the Chinese cabinet has implemented an experiment of management control, in which they authorized eight enterprise groups, such as the Dongfeng Motor Company, to be test cases for state-assets-receiving management. The enterprise groups, independent of administrative control, have adopted a management system in which the main enterprises unify the affiliated enterprises. It could be recognized that the experiment was aimed at the optimum size and optimum efficiency of enterprise behavior.

Third, the strategies of *Yin Jin Lai* (meaning the introduction of foreign capital into Chinese domestic enterprise) and *Zou Chu Qu* (indicating the strategy of encouragement for state-owned enterprises to invest abroad, including mergers) were implemented.

China started actively inviting a policy of foreign capital at the end of 1979, when special economic zones were established. Because international M&A (mergers and acquisitions) has been an important measure for FDI, China has been ready to carry out M&A after careful preparations. Joining the WTO in December 2001 was a helpful incentive.

The State-owned Assets Supervision and Administration Commission of the State Council (SASAC), which was established in 2003, has the clear intention that, in order to be more competitive, a state-owned enterprise has to compete with multinationals, with reciprocal interactions among internal and external enterprises.

The Chinese government founded the QFII (Qualified Foreign Institutional Investors) in 2003 to give helpful stimuli for the reform of state-owned enterprise and for capital market development. Up to the end of 2006, 32 enterprises were accepted by QFII and the total investment amount in the stock market reached around 60 billion yuan.

2 Statement by Li Rongrong, at the press conference held on December 22, 2005.

We will have a short look at the policy on state-owned enterprise mergers by foreign capital.

By both regulations – the provisional regulation on utilizing foreign capital for state-owned enterprise reform in September 1998 and the provisional regulation on the state-owned enterprise merger case by foreign capital in August 1999 – the Chinese government fundamentally authorized that foreign capital and state-owned enterprises could be merged. However, as a complex inspection procedure was necessary, the state-owned enterprise merger case by foreign capital was not developed.

In November 2001, before China joined the WTO, a few opinions about foreign capital investment problems in listed state-owned enterprises were promulgated, and later, on November 4, 2002, by the announcement on the problems of the transfer of state-owned stocks and corporate stocks of listed enterprises to foreign capital, the Chinese government formerly authorized that foreign enterprises could merge with listed state-owned enterprises (by purchasing non-tradable stocks etc). In addition, through the provisional measures about the regulation on domestic stock investment by QFII on November 8, 2002, the Chinese government provided that foreign capital could invest in A stocks in China through consignment banks. The provisional measures on mergers and acquisitions of Chinese enterprises by QFII in March 2003 were to establish this rule. These regulations request that the ratio of foreign-owned stocks should be less than 20%.

At the same time, in addition to the traditional *Yin Jin Lai* strategy (pointing out the introduction of foreign capital into domestic enterprises), the Chinese government requested that Chinese-owned enterprises actively invest abroad, behind which a huge amount of foreign currency reserves seem to be closely related to the strategy. Generally, large-scale state-owned enterprises that have attempted the improvement of technological development by rich financial capacity are quite active for outward FDI. (As seen in the case of the takeover of Ssanglong Motor by Shanghai Automotive Industry Corporation) we expect a future tendency to purchase foreign enterprises that have excellent technology but poor managerial resources.

The head of SASAC, Li Rongrong, emphasized the *Zuo Da Zuo Qiang* (meaning towards big and strong) of central-government controlled state-owned enterprises. Li Rongrong expressed his opinion at a press conference at the end of 2006, that they had to establish a catch up plan to reach other international corporations, by growing 30 to 50 internationally competitive enterprise groups in China, taking into consideration the Chinese government schedule, which showed that the 169 central-government controlled state-owned enterprises were to be reduced to 80 to 100 through strategic mergers and acquisitions specializing in important sectors of the national economy.

Results of the state-owned enterprise reform

When SASAC was created on April 6, 2003, the roles of the commission were to sustain and to grow the value of state assets. The head of the commission, Li Rongrong, positively evaluated that the state-owned enterprise reform in China will become more competitive, with better quality of assets, although the number of state-owned enterprises will decrease. Statistics pointed out the following: (1) in 1998, Chinese state-owned enterprises and state-owned holding companies totaled 238,000 which decreased to 150,000 (40% less); (2) as regards profit, it increased to 495.1 billion yuan in 2003 from 21.4 billion yuan in 1998, which meant a 22-fold increase; (3) also the total amount of enterprise assets expanded to be 19.7 trillion yuan in 2003 from 14.9 trillion yuan in 1998, which showed a 35% increase; (4) the same situation was recognized on the net assets of state-owned enterprises, which grew to be 8.4 trillion yuan in 2003 from 5.2 trillion yuan in 1998, whose growth rate reached 60%; (5) in 2004, a tax payment amount of 169 central government controlled state-owned enterprises equaled 9.2 trillion yuan, which was 110 billion yuan more than the previous year; (6) until October 2004, the number of state-owned manufacturing enterprises was 31.5,000 which occupied 15% of total manufacturing enterprises (altogether 210,000), however tax payment occupied 63% of total tax payment amount. Meanwhile, in the top 500 enterprises all over the world, as reported by a Chinese journal, *Caifu* (*Fortune China*), 15 Chinese enterprises were included, all of which were state owned.

Table 3.1 indicates the ratio of employees occupied by enterprise types in both urban and rural areas. The ratio of the state-owned sector decreased to 22.7% in 2006 although it was 78.3% in 1978. In addition, the ratio of the collectively-owned sector declined to 2.7% in 2006 from 21.5% in 1978. The ratios of privately-managed and privately-owned enterprises increased to 14.0% and 10.6% respectively in 2006 from 0.3% and 0.2% each in 1990. The proportion of Hong Kong and Macao enterprises and foreign-owned enterprises increased to 5.0% in 2006 from 0.4% in 1990. It clearly showed that job opportunities mainly from the state-owned sector were replaced by those from the privately-owned sector.

Problems on state-owned enterprise reform

Meanwhile, we have to recognize that there could always be with problems regarding the process of state-owned enterprise reform.

First, there was the issue of state assets that were purchased by enterprise managers (the MBO method). Because of the lack of social norms on this, the problem of state-asset loss was serious and was heavily criticized by Chinese citizens. Especially in 2002 and 2003, such state asset problems occurred intensively and were concentrated at the municipality, city and county levels. Thus, in December 2003, the SASAC promulgated the two regulations that were opinions on the norm of institutional reform measures of state-owned enterprises and provisional measures on the transfer and management of state-

Table 3.1 Ratio of employees occupied by enterprise types in urban and rural areas (10 thousand, %)

Year		Enterprise in urban areas											Enterprise in rural areas			
	Total (10 thousand)	Sub total (10 thousand)	State owned sector (%)	Collectively owned sector (%)	Joint-stock cooperative (%)	Joint-managed company (%)	Limited company (%)	Joint-stock company (%)	Private company (%)	Hong Kong Macao company (%)	Foreign owned company (%)	Personal company (%)	Sub total (10 thousand)	TVEs company (%)	Private company (%)	Personal company (%)
1978	40152	9514	78.3	21.5								0.2	30638	9.2		
1980	42361	10525	76.2	23.0								0.8	31836	9.4		
1985	49873	12808	70.2	26.0		0.3					0.0	3.5	37065	18.8		
1990	64749	17041	60.7	20.8		0.6			0.3	0.0	0.4	3.6	47708	19.4	0.2	3.1
1995	68065	19040	59.1	16.5		0.3		1.7	2.5	1.4	1.3	8.2	49025	26.2	1.0	6.2
1996	68950	19922	56.4	15.1		0.2		1.8	3.1	1.3	1.4	8.6	49028	27.6	1.1	6.7
1997	69820	20781	53.1	13.9		0.2		2.3	3.6	1.4	1.4	9.2	49039	26.6	1.2	7.2
1998	70637	21616	41.9	9.1	0.6	0.2	2.2	1.9	4.5	1.4	1.4	10.5	49021	25.6	1.5	7.9
1999	71394	22412	38.2	7.6	0.6	0.2	2.7	1.9	4.7	1.4	1.4	10.8	48982	25.9	2.0	7.8
2000	72085	23151	35.0	6.5	0.7	0.2	3.0	2.0	5.5	1.3	1.4	9.2	48934	26.2	2.3	6.0
2001	73025	23940	31.9	5.4	0.6	0.2	3.5	2.0	6.4	1.4	1.4	8.9	49085	26.7	2.4	5.4
2002	73740	24780	28.9	4.5	0.6	0.2	4.4	2.2	8.1	1.5	1.6	9.2	48960	27.1	2.9	5.1
2003	74432	25639	26.8	3.9	0.7	0.2	4.9	2.3	9.9	1.6	1.8	9.3	48793	27.8	3.6	4.6
2004	75200	26476	25.3	3.4	0.7	0.2	5.4	2.4	11.3	1.8	2.1	9.5	48724	28.5	4.2	4.2
2005	75825	27331	23.7	3.0		0.2	6.4	2.6	12.7	2.0	2.5	10.2	48494	29.4	4.9	4.4
2006	76400	28310	22.7	2.7	0.6	0.2	6.8	2.6	14.0	2.2	2.8	10.6	48090	30.5	5.5	4.5

Source: *Chinese Statistical Bulletin*, 2007, and author's calculation.

Table 3.2 Situation of deficit operation of state owned manufacturing enterprises within the national budget

	1985	1988	1989	1990
Number of enterprise	39158	38480	38030	377774
Number of deficit operation enterprises	4185	4712	6212	11898
Ratio of deficit operation enterprises (%)	10.69	12.25	16.33	31.50
Amount of profit and tax revenue (100 million yuan)	1182.06	1557.68	1558.91	1270.76
Amount of enterprise deficit operation (100 million yuan)	26.78	63.08	136.60	286.03

Source: Chinese Statistical Office, *Statistical Summary of 1991.*

owned enterprise assets. It emphasized the need to establish a state-owned asset management organization at local city level and declared, as a matter of fact, the freezing of the MBO method.

Second, it has started to argue about the profit problem on state assets. Since 1994, Chinese state-owned enterprises have paid tax by legal regulation; however, they have never paid any dividends to the National Treasury (i.e. the Ministry of Finance, SASAC, and other central government sectors). There have been several reasons for this. Since 1994, state-owned enterprises actually entered into the serious period of reform. Because substantial burdens related to institutional reform were taken by state-owned enterprises, some state-owned enterprises were on the verge of collapse and could not pay any dividends. As shown in Table 3.2, the ratio of state-owned enterprises with deficit operation to all enterprises increasing to 31.5% in 1990 from 10.69% in 1985. This means that the state-owned enterprises, which once monopolized the market, are now in less advantageous circumstances and a more market-oriented situation. It might be indispensable that state-owned enterprises were exempted from paying any dividends to the National Treasury.

However, the recent situation suggests that institutional reform of state-owned enterprises was favorably carried out and some state-owned enterprises have broken away from management difficulties, and have achieved a huge amount of profit with monopolistic advantages. The World Bank's *China Quarterly Update* in May 2006 indicated that the net earning rate of assets of state-owned enterprises grew to 12.7% in 2005 from 2% in 1998. At the beginning of 2007, Li Rongrong showed at the policy meeting on supervising of state-owned assets in China that the total profit of centrally state-owned enterprises (who totaled 159 in 2006) reached 754.7 billion yuan (18.2% more than the year before), and also that the total profit

Table 3.3 Management situation of state owned enterprises controlled by central, provincial and municipal level government in 2006

	Number of enterprise	Profit (100 million yuan)	Growth rate of profit (%)
Total	1190	9600	6.1
Enterprises controlled by central government	159	7546.9	18.2
Enterprises controlled by provincial, municipal level government	1031	2097.2	38

Source: Material of Chinese State owned Assets Supervision and Administration Commission of the State Council (SASAC).

Table 3.4 Profit and growth rate of profit of state owned enterprises

	1998	1999	2002	2003	2004	2005	2006
Profit (100 million yuan)	213.7	1145.8	3786.3	4769.4	7368.8	9047.2	9600
Growth rate of profit (%)		436.2		26.0	54.5	22.8	6.1

Source: Material of Chinese State owned Assets Supervision and Administration Commission of the State Council (SASAC).

of locally state-owned enterprises controlled by 1031 provinces, municipalities and cities equaled 209.7 billion yuan (38% more than the previous year). The sum total of these reached 960 billion yuan (6.1% more than in 2005) (see Table 3.3). Table 3.4 shows that total profit of state-owned enterprises in 1998 amounted to 21.4 billion yuan only.

The above mentioned profit growth rate showed an improvement of corporate governance and also suggested the close relations with the corporate characteristics of monopolistic enterprises, which were usually called in China 'special interest groups'. The typical examples are enterprises in the business of oil, gas, electric power, water supply, telecommunication, superhighways, etc (most of which are listed companies). Not only are executives working for the above enterprises, whose annual income was reported to be seven million yuan, but also employees receive a much higher income than the social average wage rate. For example, Chinese citizens were surprised to hear that ordinary employees working at the tollgate of superhighways and ordinary recorders of electric power meters were paid annually 100,000 yuan (compared with the annual average income of citizens in Shanghai in 2005, of around 25,000).

In 2005, the *China Quarterly Update* from the World Bank indicated that Chinese state-owned enterprises did not pay any dividends to the National Treasury, which drew the attention of the world (actually the World Bank delivered the similar recommendation to the Chinese government in 2002). Currently, centrally controlled state-owned enterprises have around 12 trillion yuan of assets and their net profit reached 600 billion yuan. If they calculate the dividend rate to pay to the National Treasury as one third, at least 200 billion yuan should be paid to the National Treasury. The above-stated World Bank update pointed out that, if the Chinese government could have used the money, health and educational expenditure in 2004 could increase by 85% more than it actually did. The *Quarterly Update* also insisted that, if the Chinese government could have used the money to improve the social welfare system, the Chinese people could allocate more money to the stock market and consumption and not to saving, which could contribute to the expansion of domestic demand.

With a similar argument to the *Quarterly Update*, Li Rongrong mentioned, at the annual meeting of Chinese enterprise managers in 2005, that a state-owned enterprise should pay dividends to the owners and also that the way to pay the dividends should be controlled by the owners. We can recognize here some signs that the Chinese central government would remove the authorities on profit from state-owned enterprises. In a report announced in December 2006, the International Monetary Fund (IMF) supported the opinion, insisting that the Chinese government should collect dividends from state-owned enterprises. The reasons mentioned by the IMF were, as well as those stated above, that collecting dividend money could contribute to settling down the investment boom by decreasing enterprise liquidity.

The above two important problems have, we think, been closely related to wider disparity problems in Chinese society. It might be easy to understand that the Chinese people were led to a serious response. In order to carry out the shared growth, it is necessary to have policy adjustments appropriate for social circumstances. This should be the national ability of China in the transition period.

The reform towards an independent financial system

When they discussed the problems about the Chinese financial system, they traditionally insisted that state-owned enterprises were ringleaders. As a matter of fact, a huge amount of bad loans of state-owned banks were caused by state-owned enterprises. To reform and list the state-owned banks, around two trillion yuan worth of bad loans were separated from state-owned banks from 1999 to 2004,

Table 3.5 Situation of principal banks in China

Name	Established year and month	Main location	Remarks	Main stockholder of the listed bank	Number of Offices (2005)	Number of Employees (2005)
Total					82453	1800381
The People's Bank of China	1948.10	Beijing Headoffice, Shanghai Second Headoffice (2005.8)	To be nominated as central bank (1983.9), to be legally settled as central bank (1995.3)		2167	138538
Industry and Commercial Bank of China	1984.1	Beijing Headoffice	State owned commercial bank, listed at Hong Kong market (2006.10) and recorded the biggest IPO in the world	Chinese government owned China SAFE Investments Limited	18764	427383
Agriculture Bank of China	1951.8	Beijing Headoffice	State owned commercial bank	unlisted	28234	478895
Bank of China	1953.1, (originally started in 1905).	Beijing Headoffice	State owned commercial bank, listed on Hong Kong market (2006.6) and Shanghai market (2006.7)	Chinese government owned China SAFE Investments Limited	11019	229740
Construction Bank of China	1954.10	Beijing Headoffice	State owned commercial bank, listed on Hong Kong market (2005.10) and recorded the biggest IPO in the world	Chinese government owned China SAFE Investments Limited	14088	300288

Table 3.5 continued

Name	Established year and month	Main location	Remarks	Main stockholder of the listed bank	Number of Offices (2005)	Number of Employees (2005)
Agricultural Development Bank of China	1994.4	Beijing Headoffice	Policy bank	unlisted	2176	59598
China Export-import Bank	1994	Beijing Headoffice	Policy bank	unlisted	16	908
China Development Bank	1994.3	Beijing Headoffice	Policy bank	unlisted	38	4708
Bank of Communi-cations	1908 (created) 1986.7 (rebuilt)	Shanghai Headoffice	First listed state owned commercial bank, Hong Kong market (2005.6) and Shanghai market (2007.5)	Chinese Ministry of Finance	2607	57323
Shanghai Pudong Development Bank	1993.1	Shanghai Headoffice	Joint-stock commercial bank, listed on Shanghai market (1999)	Shanghai local government Owned "Shanghai international group"	375	10082
CITIC Industrial Bank	1987	Beijing Headoffice	Joint-stock commercial bank	unlisted	418	14577
China Everbright Bank	1992.8	Beijing Headoffice	Joint-stock commercial bank	unlisted	416	9734
China Minsheng Bank	1996.1	Beijing Headoffice	Joint-stock commercial bank, listed on Shanghai market (2000.12)	Private enterprise (feed production), "New Hope group"	242	9447
Huaxia Bank	1992	Beijing Headoffice	Joint-stock commercial bank, listed on Shanghai market (2003.9)	Capital Iron and Steel Company	294	7761

Table 3.5 concluded

Name	Established year and month	Main location	Remarks	Main stockholder of the listed bank	Number of Offices (2005)	Number of Employees (2005)
China Merchants Bank	1987.4	Shenzhen Headoffice (Guangdong province)	Joint-stock commercial bank, listed on Shanghai market (2002.4)	Hong Kong Securities Clearing Company Nominees Limited (subsidiary of Hong Kong Stock exchange)	454	20653
Guandong Development Bank	1988.9	Guangzhou Headoffice (Guangdong province)	Joint-stock commercial bank	unlisted	500	12284
Industrial Bank of Fujian	1988.8	Fuzhou Headoffice (Fujian province)	Joint-stock commercial bank	unlisted	329	9918
Shenzhen Development Bank	1987.12	Shenzhen Headoffice (Guangdong province)	Joint-stock commercial bank, listed on Shenzhen market (1988.4)	US owned investment company, Newbridge Asia AIV,L.P.	240	7142
Evergrowing Bank	1987 (as Yantai housing savings Bank 2003, (rebuilt and change of name)	Yantai Headoffice (Shandong province)	Joint-stock commercial bank	unlisted	76	1402
China Zhejiang Bank	2004.8 (rebuilt)	Hangzhou Headoffice (Zhejiang province)	Joint-stock commercial bank	unlisted	NA	NA
Bohai Bank	2005.12	Tianjin Headofficd	Joint-stock commercial bank	unlisted	NA	NA

Note: As State owned Assets Supervision and Administration Commission of the State Council (SASAC, established in March 2003) has no authority to control state owned financial institutions, China SAFE Investments Limited was founded on December 16, 2003, as the wholly state owned investment company and has been in charge of state owed banks as the investor.

Source: Author (based upon such materials as *Chinese Statistical Bulletin, Chinese Financial Bulletin).*

Table 3.6 Top 15 ranking Asian enterprises (current price, as of the end of December 2006) (million US$)

Rank	Company	Market	Total amount (current price)
1	HSBC	Hong Kong	212,034
2	Industry and Commercial Bank of China	China	199,353
3	China Mobile Limited	Hong Kong	172,262
4	Construction Bank of China	Hong Kong	142,998
5	Bank of China	China	123,708
6	Samsung Electronics Co. Ltd	South Korea	97,091
7	China Petrochemical Corporation	China	81,701
8	Taiwan Semiconductor Manufacturing Company	Taiwan	53,490
9	Hutchson Whampoa Limited	Hong Kong	43,331
10	Oil and Natural Gas Corporation (India)	India	42,045
11	China National Offshore Oil Corporation	Hong Kong	41,168
12	Reliance Industries Ltd.	India	39,996
13	Hon Hai Precision Industry	Taiwan	35,559
14	Singapore Telecommunications Ltd.	Singapore	33,887
15	PetroChina Co. Ltd.	Hong Kong	29,894

Source: Mizuho Securities Co., Ltd.

most of which were produced by state-owned enterprises. For 13 years from 1995 to 2002, four state-owned banks supported around 6,000 state-owned enterprises for their mergers and for their failure adjustments, whose lost money reached 315.5 billion yuan; in addition, other loans amounted to more 800 billion yuan.[3] Also state-owned banks have their own problems, because state-owned banks are state-owned enterprises. In other words, therefore, the current situation in China has to be understood as caused by a central planning system that incorporated enterprises, banks and social welfare.

Several stages in the reform of the financial system

By looking back at the reforms in China, we recognize that financial system reform has been improved simultaneously with state-owned enterprise reforms. These were divided into three stages.

First, the period from 1978 to 1984 was the reconstruction period of the banking system. In September 1983, the People's Bank of China was designated as the central bank.

---

3 Statement by Xie Ping, the chairperson of the board of directors of China SAFE Investments Limited, see *Anbound Meiri Jingji* (*Anbound Business Daily*), December 28, 2005.

Second, from 1984 to 1992, the People's Bank of China initially established its functions as the central bank, and also the transformation of other state-owned banks into commercial banks was ready to start. The Chinese financial system in this period was under the influence of the central planning system. Therefore, because state-owned banks had the same character of problems as state-owned enterprises, and because the response to market-oriented reform was delayed, the financial order was distorted and the Chinese economy suffered from serious inflation.

Third, after 1993, there was the overall preparation stage of the financial system. In order to establish the macro-economic adjustment ability of the central bank, the arrangement of banking functions was fully carried out, in which it was attempted to strengthen the functions of the People's Bank of China as the central bank. In 1995, through the implementation of the People' Bank Act, the legal position of the People's Bank of China as the central bank was founded. In August 2005, the People's Bank of China established the second head office in Shanghai. This was similar to the New York Branch of the US Federal Reserve System, whose functions are the supervision of the market and market intervention when necessary. It was also recognized that such a policy decision contributed to establishing an international financial center in Shanghai.

At the same time, in 1994, the four major state-owned banks – which were (1) Bank of China, (2) Industrial and Commercial Bank of China, (3) China Construction Bank, and (4) Agricultural Bank of China – were given the clear position as commercial banks. In addition, separation of commercial banks from policy banks was attempted and such policy banks as the China Development Bank, Agricultural Development Bank of China, and China Export-Import Bank, were newly founded in 1994.

At present, in addition to the Bank of Communications, three of the four major state-owned commercial banks have been listed on the stock market, both domestic and foreign (see Table 3.5). Table 3.6 indicates the top 15 enterprises in terms of current price in Asia, in which the Industry and Commercial Bank of China (the second rank), the Construction Bank of China (the fourth rank) and the Bank of China (the fifth rank) has been remarkable.

Needless to say, for state-owned commercial banks to be listed on the stock markets, both domestic and foreign, it is necessary to adjust the bad loans as a prerequisite condition. We will consider the problems later in this chapter.

After the 1980s, it was approved to establish joint-stock commercial banks that could be financed by multilateral ways. The number of joint-stock commercial banks doing business in the whole of China reached 13, of which five were listed on the domestic stock markets (see Table 3.5). However, the total listed banks, except for the four state-owned commercial banks, have common characteristics and a relatively low ratio of the largest stockholder; an example of which is that the ratio of Shenzhen Development Bank and China Merchants Bank is around 17% respectively, and the ratio of China Minsheng Bank is only 6%. Thus, to become the largest stockholder they had keen competition, including from foreign capital.

In addition, both city banks (118 banks at the end of 2006) and rural banks have been reorganized. The reorganization started in 2003, and the plan was to reorganize around 30,000 rural credit associations into three kinds of corporation: rural commercial banks, rural cooperative banks, and rural credit associations.

Until October 2005, all over China, the number of banking and financial organizations reached more than 30,000. The are: one central bank, three policy banks, five state-owned commercial banks (including the Bank of Communication), 12 joint-stock commercial banks in the whole nation, 115 city commercial banks, 626 city credit associations, 30,438 rural credit associations, 57 rural cooperative commercial banks, 238 foreign bank business organizations, four financial asset management banks, 59 trust banks, 74 enterprise group financial organizations, 12 financial leasing banks, five automotive financial banks, and a postal savings organization in urban and rural areas.

Such a banking sector reorganization was accompanied by financial legislation. After 1994, such acts as the People's Bank of China Act (established in 1995 and revised in 2004), the Commercial Bank Act of the People's Republic of China (established in 1995 and revised in 2004), the Draft Act of the People's Republic of China (established on January 1, 1996), Insurance Act of People's Republic of China (established in 1995 and revised in 2002), were legally designated in succession.

In 1997, the Asian financial crisis occurred, and in November of the same year the Central Communist Party and Chinese Cabinet held the Financial Meeting in China and decided that they would thoroughly implement the reform of the financial system within three years. The Asian financial crisis became a favorable wind for the reform of the Chinese financial system, and also internationalization of the Chinese economy had substantial effects on the reform of the governance system within China. These phenomena seemed to promote Chinese systemic transition (see the following section of this chapter, also see Chapters 5 and 6 of this book).

Advancement of foreign-owned banks

Chinese advancement of foreign-owned banks has had a long history of more than 100 years. Especially at the beginning of 20th century, Shanghai had overwhelming economic power as the center of Chinese finance, trade and industry. Shanghai held about 43% of the total number of domestic banks and 89% of total assets. Both total volume of trade and industrial production were shared by about 50% of the whole nation. In the Bund, 113 financial organizations from all over the world had offices, which showed that Shanghai was the financial and trade center of the Far East. In 1949, after the new socialist China was founded, almost all offices of foreign banks and trade companies moved to Hong Kong. There were only six financial organizations that still stayed in China including HSBC, The Bank of East Asia (BEA), the Bank of Overseas Chinese Bank, and Standard Chartered Bank.

(I) Three stages of the open door policy in finance After the reform and open door policy started in 1978, there were three stages in the Chinese open door policy of the financial sector (Chinese Bank Regulatory Commission, 2007b).

The first stage was from 1980 to1993. The purpose of attracting foreign-owned banks was mainly to introduce foreign capital and to improve financial services for foreign-owned enterprises. The establishment of the Beijing Office of the Japan Export-Import Bank in 1980 was the first case. In 1981, the Nanyang Commercial Bank established the Shenzhen Branch, which was the first business organization of a foreign-owned bank. After that, the open area of the banking business gradually expanded, from special economic zones in coastal open areas and to core municipalities of the region. At the end of 1993, foreign-owned banks founded 76 business organizations in 13 municipalities and cities to contribute to the foreign currency business of foreign-owned enterprises and foreign-nationality citizens, whose assets reached around US$8.9 billion.

The second stage was from 1994 to 2001. The active business of foreign-owned enterprises in China was followed by business expansion of foreign-owned banks. In 1994, the regulation act on foreign-owned banks and Chinese and foreign cooperative banks in special economic zones in the People's Republic of China was revised by the regulation act of foreign-owned financial organizations in the People's Republic of China, which was the start of the foreign-owed banks' business activities all over China. In 1996, the provisional regulation measures on the experiment of yuan business by foreign-owned financial organizations in the Shanghai Pudong area was promulgated, through which foreign-owned banks located in the Shanghai Pudong area were authorized for yuan business. At the end of 1997, the number of business organizations of foreign-owned banks reached 175, which meant that, for four years, 99 business bases were expanding and the total assets was increased more than three times. However, after the Asian financial crisis occurred, it was recognized that the location adjustment by foreign-owned banks, and the increase of business organizations was only 15 business organizations of foreign owned banks were increased from 1998 to 2001. In order to promote the development of foreign-owned banks, Shenzhen was authorized to be the second municipality after Shanghai in which yuan business was possible. In addition, the business area for foreign-owned banks could be extended; for example, business areas of foreign-owned banks in Shanghai and Shenzhen were expanded into Jiangsu and Zhejiang provinces, and Guangdong, Guangxi and Hunan provinces respectively.

The third stage was from 2002 to 2006. China could finally join the WTO in December 2001, which surely contributed to attracting foreign-owned financial organizations. In various agreements of the WTO, the GATS (General Agreement on Trade in Service) is closely related with financial services. In particular, the third part of the GATS (from article 16 to 18) was concerned with the following details, which were authorized by member countries. The authorized details accepted by China were, (1) from 2001, foreign-owned banks could have any foreign currency businesses for three kinds of enterprise (wholly foreign-owned enterprise, jointly-owned enterprise, cooperative enterprise); (2) from 2003, foreign-owned banks could have any foreign currency businesses for Chinese enterprises; (3) from 2004, foreign-owned banks could have any yuan businesses for Chinese government and Chinese enterprises; (4) from 2007, any yuan businesses by foreign-owned banks would be completely free in any organizations and in any areas in China.

Based upon the above procedures, during the five-year period to be ready for the full opening of the financial sector, the number of business organizations of foreign-owned banks expanded from 190 to 312, an increase (excluding mergers) of 122. The municipalities that were authorized in yuan business increased from four (Shanghai, Shenzhen, Tianjin, Dalian) to 18 in 2004, and became 25 in December 2005.

Customers of the yuan business were extended from foreigners and foreign-owned banks to Chinese people and Chinese enterprises. In addition, because such regulations as (1) the provision for debt amount in terms of yuan to be less than 50% in terms of foreign currency, and (2) the abolishment of restrictions on deposits in foreign currency, it became possible for foreign-owned banks to have business in financial commodities, consigned business on domestic security investment, consigned business on insurance, and so on. In order to be helpful for banking reform in China, the percentage of capital received from foreign financial organizations was adjusted. In China, therefore, successful attempts by foreign-owned banks to have domestic treatment were steadily implemented, as was agreed with the WTO.

Since the end of the 1990s, China presented such inland development strategies, one after the other, as a go-west policy (1999), an industrial region promotion strategy in northeast area (2002), and the central region promotion strategy (2004) (see Chapter 2). The open policy in the banking sector has been incorporated in those strategies. For example, by moving up the planned schedule, foreign-owned banks could have yuan business in the municipalities in the central, western and northeastern region (in Xian, Shenyang, Harbin, Changchun, Lanzhou, Xining). In addition, they attempted to implement less complicated procedures in establishing business organizations.

(II) Business performance of foreign-owned banks First, as regards the number of financial organizations, it was said that (1) until the end of December 2006, wholly-owned foreign banks and cooperative foreign-owned banks registered in China totaled 14, had 19 branches and other attached offices; (2) 74 foreign-owned banks, coming from 22 countries and regions, established 279 branches in 25 municipalities and cities; (3) 186 foreign-owned banks, coming from 42 countries and regions, founded 242 offices in 24 municipalities and cities.

Second, as shown in Table 3.7, the regional distribution of foreign-owned banks was such that the highest ratio (53.8%) was for Asia, followed by Europe (24.7%) and North America (10.3%). As far as nationality and regional breakdown was concerned, Hong Kong had the highest number and ratio of the total, which indicated 102 business organizations and 32.7%.

Table 3.7 Distribution of office of foreign owned banks

	Number of offices	Ratio (%)
Total	312	100
Asia	168	53.8
Hong Kong	102	32.7
Japan	19	6.1
Singapore	17	5.4
Europe	77	24.7
UK	21	6.7
France	15	4.8
North America	32	10.3
USA	26	8.3
Canada	6	1.9

Source: Chinese Bank Regulatory Commission (2007b).

Third, the scale of assets has been expanding. As of the end of December 2006, total asset amount (US$103.3 billion) and total amount of loans in foreign currency (US$35.9 billion) of foreign-owned banks in China occupied around 1.8% and 20% respectively of the financial organizations in the banking sector in the whole of China. Meanwhile, the ratio of bad loans of foreign-owned banks in China equaled 0.7%.

Fourth, in some particular regions, foreign-owned banks have been in powerful existence. For example, in Shanghai, the total asset amount and total amount of loans in foreign currency of foreign-owned banks reached 12.4% and 54.8% respectively. Table 3.8 displays the regional distribution of the business organization of foreign-owned banks in China. As it clearly shows, Shanghai occupied the highest ratio at 32%, which was followed by Shenzhen (13%), Beijing (12%), Guangzhou (9%), Tianjin (5%) and Xiamen (5%). Besides, because of the association strategy for inland promotion as stared above, the number of business organizations of foreign-owned banks located in the central, western and northeastern region reached 30 (whose ratio equaled to 10% of the national total).

Fifth, we could recognize that foreign capital has actively participated in Chinese financial organizations. China has actually improved the opening up policy of the financial sector, as it pledged to the WTO to carry out the policy within five years after participation. On the condition that the Chinese government would keep the control of stocks of large-scale banks, the introduction of strategic

Table 3.8 Locational distribution of office of foreign owned banks

	Shanghai	Shenzhen	Beijing	Guangzhou	Tianjin	Xiamen	Others	Central, Western, and Northeastern Regions
Number of offices	100	40	37	28	17	16	74	30
Ratio (%)	32	13	12	9	5	5	24	10

Source: Chinese Bank Regulatory Commission (2007b).

investors has been promoted. As a matter of fact, foreign-owned banks have been active in reorganizing small- and medium-sized banks in urban and rural areas in addition to state-owned commercial banks and joint-stock commercial banks (see Table 3.9). At the end of December 2006, 29 foreign-owned investment organizations inflowed their capital into 21 Chinese banks, and the total amount reached US$19 billion.

The details were as follows. The peak year of investment into state-owned commercial banks by foreign capital was 2005, when Chinese open policy in the financial sector was ready. The Bank of America (USA) invested US$3 billion in the Chinese Construction Bank in 2005. The Bank of China also received altogether US$3.1 billion by investment groups, including the Royal Bank of Scotland (UK). Actual investment amounts in the financial sector in 2005 reached US$12.1 billion, which was around twice that of the year before. However, although, in January 2006, Goldman Sachs (USA) etc invested altogether US$3.8 billion into the Industry and Commercial Bank of China, according to the Chinese Ministry of Commerce the actual amount of inward FDI into the financial sector, such as banks, security and insurance, in 2006 decreased to US$6.45 billion, which was 46.6% less than the previous year. It seemed to be a reaction against the previous peak year.[4]

(III) Change of deposit structure in Chinese banks There was a view insisting that Chinese transition in the financial system was endogenously implemented (Lin Yifu, 1999 and Zhang Jie, 1998). We basically agree with that view; however, we think one should be careful when considering that changes of the external environment played an important role in the transition of the Chinese financial system. The development of the private sector resulted in substantial changes for deposit structures in Chinese banks, which moved from a traditional government and enterprise-led deposit structure to the household-led deposit structure. The

4 The material published by Chinese Ministry of Commerce in April 2004, see *Fuji Sankei Business i*, April 9, 2007.

Table 3.9 Investment situation of foreign owned financial organizations into Chinese banks (a portion of them)

Year and month	Foreign capital	Ratio of foreign owned capital (as of 2006.10) (%)	Chinese	Remarks
2003.1.	Citigroup	3.8	Shanghai Pudong Development Bank	Around 72 million US$ investment. 85 per cent IBM acquisition jointly with Chinese Life Insurance(Group) Company (2006.11)
2004. 8	HSBC	19.9	Bank of Communications	Around three billion US$ investment
2004. 12	US owned investment company, Newbridge Asia AIV,L.P.	17.89	Shenzhen Development Bank	
2005. 6	Bank of America	9	Construction Bank of China	
2005. 8	Royal Bank of Scotland	10	Bank of China	
2005. 7	Temasek (Singapore)	6	Construction Bank of China	
2005. 8	Temasek (Singapore)	5	Bank of China	
2005. 8	Merrill Lynch	1	Bank of China	
2005. 9	Standard Chartered Bank	19.9	Bohai Bank	
2005. 9	UBS	1.3	Bank of China	
2005. 10	Deutsche Bank	14	Huaxia Bank	
2006. 1	American Express	1	Industry and Commercial Bank of China	
2006. 2	BNP Paribas	19	Nanjing City Commercial Bank	
2006. 3	Goldman Sachs	6	Industry and Commercial Bank of China	

Source: Mizuho Securities Co., Ltd., and various media information.

situation surely had significant effects on the behavioral pattern of banks in China. It means that profit-oriented bank behavior has become extremely important in China. In addition, the tendency has been promoted by the possibility of multiple finance, by listing on the stock market.

The change towards a private-oriented deposit structure has been remarkable. The deposit structure in 1979 expressed the ratio of household, enterprise and government to be 23%, 34% and 43% respectively (Xie Ping and Wu Xiaoling, 1992). In 1985, the ratios were changed to 35.28%, 48.48% and 8.62% respectively, and in 2006 the respective ratios became 48.17% (household), 33.76% (enterprise) and 3.26% (government). The extreme increase of the household sector was substantial (see Table 3.10).

As stated above, the rapid change of the private-led deposit structure and multiple tendency of banking capital in China, indicated the successful movement of the Chinese systemic transition in the financial sector towards a market-oriented regime and internationalization. In addition, it is thought that the debates on extra-national treatment or non-national treatment as regards Chinese banks and foreign-owned banks would not easily come to an end.

Various problems of state owned banks: focusing upon the adjustment of bad loans

Partly because of the Asian financial crisis, in China the new financial reforms were started in 1999. Particular problems in the Chinese financial system were pointed out as (1) a low efficiency in capital allocation and (2) a high ratio of bad loans and a low ratio of owner's equity of Chinese state-owned banks etc.

As regards the low efficiency problem of capital allocation, the problem of the serious shortage of financial services given to private enterprises was recognized, despite the fact that, for the past 30 years, private enterprises have contributed to Chinese economic development. The main target for state-owned banks to support was state-owned enterprises (which has been because (1) the relations come from administrative channels and (2) most privately-owned enterprises are small and medium sized and do not have sufficient collateral), and non-state owned financial organizations have not been developed for many years. Privately owned banks and rural cooperative trust banks, which reached a definite size, were forced to close, and also credit associations – both in urban and rural areas – were forced to merge into state-owned financial institutions. This was due to the policy to restrain the activities of private capital in the financial sector. Although that was coming from the importance of the financial sector to the national economy, it took substantially disadvantageous effects against macro economic performance. For example, when the Chinese economy suffered from recession in 2000, the expanding fiscal policy was employed to promote private investment. However, because financing to private enterprises was restrained, the scheduled goal failed to be carried out (Yu Yongzhen, 2006).

Table 3.10 Deposit structure in Chinese banks (100 million yuan, %)

	1985		1990		1995		2000		2005		2006	
	Total amount (billion yuan)	**Ratio**	**Total amount (billion yuan)**	**Ratio**	**Total amount (billion yuan)**	**Ratio**	**Total amount (billion yuan)**	**Ratio**	**Total amount (billion yuan)**	**Ratio**	**Total amount (billion yuan)**	**Ratio**
Deposits	427.3		1164.5		3878.3		12380.4		28716.9		33545.9	
Enterprise deposits	207.2	48.48	399.8	34.33	1452	37.44	4409.40	35.62	9614.4	33.48	11323.9	33.76
Treasury deposits	36.8	8.62	38	3.27	100.3	2.59	350.80	2.83	799.6	2.78	1092.7	3.26
Deposits of overnment Agencies and Organizations	32.6	7.62	61.5	5.28	89.9	2.32	222.40	1.80	1205.2	4.20	1504.6	4.49
Urban and Rural savings deposits	150.7	35.28	604.3	51.89	2215.8	57.13	6433.20	51.96	14105.1	49.12	16158.7	48.17
Agricuture deposits		0.00		0.00		0.00	264.30	2.13	620.4	2.16	741.4	2.21
Entrust and Trust etc. Deposits		0.00		0.00		0.00	287.40	2.32	346.2	1.21	346.2	1.21
Other Deposits		0.00	60.9	5.23	20.2	0.52	412.90	3.34	2026.1	7.06	2026.1	7.06

Note: Financial institutions includes central bank, policy bank, wholly state owned commercial bank, postal service savings institution, other commercial banks, urban cooperative banks, rural credit associations, urban credit associations, foreign owned banks, investment trust companies, leasing companies, and financial companies etc.

Source: *Chiniese Statistical Bulletin*, annual.

The situation on the ratio of owner's equity was as follows. For many years, the ratio of owner's equity in Chinese state-owned banks was much less than 8% (which was the international criterion). In September 1999, before bad loans were separated, the average ratio of owner's equity in the four state-owned banks was 4.36% (Mi Jianguo *et al*., 2001). At the beginning of 2004, there were only eight city commercial banks whose ratio of owner's equity reached 8%. At the end of 2005, the number had increased to 53; however, the number of financial institutions whose ratio of owner's equity reached 8% was never half the total (the average ratio of the owner's equity of city commercial banks was only 2.7%). As far as the asset size of city commercial banks with more than an 8% ratio of owner's equity was concerned, their ratio to the total assets at the beginning of 2003 was only 0.6%, which however expanded to be around 75%) (Chinese Bank Regulatory

Commission, 2007a). City commercial banks mean regional commercial banks under the control of local government. A state-owned commercial bank is able to be supported by the central government budget; however, city commercial banks have to basically adjust in self-reliance to bad loans. Local government sometimes supports with the budget, but more often the administrative interventions disturb the normal management of commercial banks.

In order to raise the ratio of owner's equity of a state-owned commercial bank, there could be measures such as an advantageous tax policy, cramming public money, separation from bad loans, and so on.

As regards re-examination of the tax policy, the situation is as follows.

The tax payment is, needless to say, closely connected with the bank's profit. The main tax payments for Chinese domestic enterprises are income tax and business tax. In 1997, the income tax ratio decreased to 33% from 55%, and in 2001 business tax ratio declined to 5% from 8%. However, the tax burden for Chinese commercial banks has still been heavier than for foreign commercial banks. In particular, the business tax burden has been serious for them (in such advanced industrialized countries as the USA, Japan, the UK, and France, there was no business tax payments). Moreover, the collection of business tax covers wider business activities, but not inter-bank business (in Germany, the tax collection base of business tax is profit). As far as income tax is concerned, foreign-owned banks could receive various advantageous tax treatments in addition to lower income tax of 15% (which is less than half for Chinese domestic banks).

The following measures might be available for Chinese commercial banks to be more competitive with a fair tax burden. (1) The business tax ratio could be further reduced to be 3%. (2) Tax collection activities should be much smaller; for example, from a current calculation formula, interest payment should be excluded and only value added should be part of the tax collection. (3) Equal tax rates should be carried out for both domestic and foreign-owned banks. On March 16, 2007, the Corporate Income Tax Act of the People's Republic of China was revised, and since January 1, 2008, income taxes for both domestic and foreign enterprises would be unified at 25%. This means that the extremely advantageous treatments for foreign-owned enterprises, since the 1980s, would finally be abolished.[5]

In addition, such measures as cramming public money and separation from bad loans were employed by state-owned banks to raise the ratio of owner's equity. The following measure for establishing four state-owned Asset Management Corporations is a typical example.

(I) Appearance of four state-owned asset management corporations Three times the Chinese government carried out financial support for state-owned banks for

5 However, industrial sectors like the high-tech sector, which the Chinese government encourages, could enjoy an advantageous tax policy.

Table 3.11 Four state owned asset management corporations in China

Name	Establishment	Duties	Character
China Cinda Asset Management Corporation (connected with Bank of China)	1999.4	They purchase bad loans of financial institutions, and manage and dispose; they keep asset value with maximum effort, and raise the collective ratio of bad loans of banking sector.	Wholly state owned financial assets management corporation with independent legal person.
China Huarong Asset Management Corporation (connected with Industry and Commercial Bank of China)	1999.10		
China Great Wall Asset Management Corporation (connected with Agriculture Bank of China)	1999.10		
China Orient Asset Management Corporation (connected with Construction Bank of China)	1999.10		

Source: Various press news.

adjustment of bad loans and for raising the ratio of owner's equity.

The first such support was in 1997, when the Ministry of Finance issued particular bonds and crammed public money with 270 billion yuan for the four state-owned commercial banks.

The second attempt at support was to establish the four state-owned Asset Management Corporations – which were called Cinda, Huarong, Orient, Great Wall – whose main purpose was to adjust the bad loans, because the bad loans problem was the chief task of the financial reform that started in 1999. Initially, the four Asset Management Corporations had one-to-one business relations with the four state-owned commercial banks, but later the framework was abolished (see Table 3.11). In 1999 and 2000, the separation of bad loans in state-owned banks was led by the central government and the amount separated from state-owned banks reached 1.4 trillion yuan.

The third support attempt was the joint-stock privatization reform of the Construction Bank of China, and the Bank of China, which started in 2004. To support the listing of the Bank of China, the Construction Bank of China, and the Industry and Commercial Bank of China, central government separated risky bad loans of 730 billion yuan in 2004 and 2005. In addition, lost loans, which amounted to 450 billion yuan, were written off. Bad loans belonging the Bank of Communications, which amounted to 60 billion yuan, were separated. After the adjustment of bad loans, the ratios of owner's equity of the Bank of China, the Construction Bank of China and the Industry and Commercial Bank of China reached 8.62%, 11.95% and 9.12% respectively (Li Yang, 2006).

After 1999, the four state-owned Asset Management Corporations altogether adjusted 2.6 trillion yuan of bad loans. Let us have a short look at the adjustment methods.

The four state-owned Asset Management Corporations have duties in which they purchase bad loans separated from state-owned banks and implement appropriate adjustment. The money to purchase the bad loans in 1999 was produced in the following ways. First, there was 40 billion yuan provided by the Ministry of Finance (including both Chinese yuan and foreign currencies), of which 10 billion yuan were allocated to each of the four state-owned commercial banks. Thus, the Ministry of Finance was only one stock holder of the four Asset Management Corporations. Second, there was 570 billion yuan borrowing money from the central bank. Third, there was 820 billion yuan, money collected by issuing the financial bonds of Asset Management Corporations (Wu Chuanzhen and Yuan Li, 2005). The main duty of Asset Management Corporations after purchasing bad loans was to collect money from debtor enterprises, which have various difficulties. However, some legal frameworks are, at present, disadvantageous for the Corporations. For example, because the enterprise bankruptcy law has never had enough protection for creditors, there have appeared state-owned enterprises and local governments who tried to be free from financial loans through bankruptcy. In addition, there have been attempts to prevent reconstruction and sale of the state-owned enterprises controlled by governmental sections and local governments. As a matter of fact, all four Asset Management Corporations had no experience, and clearly hesitated to carry out the task on the bad loans. In 2000, only Cinda Asset Management Corporation attempted the method whereby credits were exchanged with enterprise stocks.

Foreign-owned investment banks started their mergers and acquisitions behavior by focusing their attention upon profitability. Domestic commercial banks also participated in the activities. Traditionally, Commercial Bank Law has prohibited commercial banks from asset transaction behavior, deeming it irregular procedure. The Construction Bank of China and the Bank of China introduced experimental managements. At the end of 2004, according to the statistics of the Chinese Bank Regulatory Commission, except for the way in which credits were exchanged with enterprise stock, the Asset Management Corporations altogether adjusted 675 billion yuan of bad loans. According to the statistics of PricewaterhouseCoopers, the purchasing amount of foreign-owned investment banks reached US$6.016 billion, whose ratio was 10%. At the end of 2006, the adjustment amount of bad loans by the four Asset Management Corporations equaled 1.21 trillion yuan, in which the cash collection amount reached 211 billion yuan. The cash collection amount was 28.6 billion yuan more than the target amount of the Chinese government.

The separation procedures of bad loans from state-owned banks carried out by the four Asset Management Corporations were always accompanied by problems. For example, the Asset Management Corporations are actually state-owned enterprises controlled by central government (although they are called private corporations), and central government is actively involved in personnel and organizational activities. However, the sectors in which the Asset Management Corporations behave are competitive. This expresses the undoubted systemic contradiction between the appropriate governance of Asset Management Corporations and the incentive of their activities.

At the beginning of 2005, the National Board of Audit announced the results of its inspection into the four Asset Management Corporations after their five years of activities, and it said that the 'bad loan money' caused by an inadequate internal control system reached around 70 billion yuan. The problems indicated by the National Board of Audit were as follow. (1) The inspection procedure into purchasing bad loans was not very strict and there was no legal certificate on financial credit. At the same time, some state-owned commercial banks abused the national policy of separation from bad loans. It indicated that they escaped the responsibility of bad loans, which were caused by their own wrong management decisions, through forged documents. (2) The lack of public information with such 'black box' operations, and credit adjustment by unfair low prices, caused the loss of national assets. (3) Some finance managements of the Asset Management Corporations were recognized to be lacking norms and rules, and so the misappropriation of funds often happened, and unreasonable amounts of wage, bonus and other allowances were displayed (*Di Yi Cai Jing Ribao* (*China Business News*), January 20, 2005). In fact, such bad situations had already been pointed out by the Chinese Bank Regulatory Commission before the National Board of Audit.

Initial duties, which were given to the four Asset Management Corporations after they were established, were (1) to purchase the bad loans of financial institutions; (2) to manage and adjust the bad loans of financial institutions; (3) to fully keep the asset value; and (4) to raise the recovering ratio of bad loans in the banking sector. The initial schedule said that their duties were to be completed in ten years and they would be closed. However, when the end of bad loans adjustment was approaching, all four Asset Management Corporations gradually prepared to transform their organizations. In the procedure for adjusting bad loans, the four Asset Management Corporations were deeply involved in such financial service activities as securities, trusts, banks, and leases in which, moreover, they had relatively good results (Yuan Yuanyuan, 2007). The scheduled target of the four Asset Management Corporations had been general financial service enterprises, for which they needed the views of the Ministry of Finance, the only stock holder when they were established in 1999. In addition, the legislative establishment is important. For example, the Asset Management Corporation Act promulgated at the end of 2000 should be revised. Financial service activities are the sectors with complexity and high risks and current Asset Management Corporations have never had enough governance in a modern corporate system. Thus, it might be necessary carefully to prepare transparency, a risk monitoring system, and evaluation criteria, which are currently insufficient. We think it could be possible to realize the multiple source of capital through joint-stock privatization reform, the same as state-owned bank reform. Some Asset Management Corporations have already implemented this and the Ministry of Finance has agreed with the above.

Table 3.12 Ratio of bad loans in Chinese commercial banks: Each quarter of the year (2004-2007) (%)

	2004				2005				2006				2007
	I	II	III	IV	I	II	III	IV	I	II	III	IV	I
1.Main Commercial Banks					12.7	8.79	8.7	8.9	8.26	7.8	7.64	7.51	7.02
State owned commercial banks	19.2	15.59	15.71	15.57	15	10.12	10.11	10.49	9.78	9.47	9.31	9.22	8.2
Joint-stock commercial bank	7.1	5.16	5.03	4.94	4.9	4.66	4.51	4.22	3.92	3.09	2.91	2.81	2.78
2.Urban commercial banks					11.5	10.43	9.74	7.73	7.59	6.72	6.07	4.78	4.52
3.Rural commercial bank					6.1	6.38	5.8	6.03	6.96	6.64	6.58	5.9	5.32
4.Foreign owned banks					1.2	1.14	0.92	1.05	0.95	0.87	0.81	0.78	0.62

Note: (1) In 2006, there was institutional expansion in urban and rural commercial banks, and it is impossible to simply compare with 2005.

(2) In 2007, there was reorganization in state owned commercial banks and joint-stock commercial banks, and it is impossible to simply compare with 2006.

Source: Chinese Bank Regulatory Commission Home Page, (*http:*//www.cbrc.gov.cn/chinese/info/twohome/index).

(II) Change of the ratio of bad loans in Chinese commercial banks What are the results of financial reform in China which started in 1999?

Table 3.12 indicates the ratio of bad loans in Chinese commercial banks. Each commercial bank decreased the ratio of bad loans, and the state-owned commercial banks decreased the ratio to be 7.02% in the first quarter in 2007 from 19.2% at the first quarter in 2004. However, the ratio of bad loans of state owned commercial banks was the highest of all the commercial banks, which was followed by rural commercial banks (5.32%), urban commercial banks (4.52%), and joint-stock commercial banks (2.78%). The lowest ratio was for foreign-owned banks (0.62%).

As mentioned above, the reform process of the financial system in China, which was dynamically implemented, has been improved, but with many unresolved tasks. The process progressed in the same way as painting pictures, initially they were sketched with pencil and then, after the framework was made, they moved into the stage of expressing the detail. Needless to say, while it might be difficult initially to reach perfection, it should be necessary to prepare carefully in order to minimize costs.

Reform of the administration system

We could recognize the reform of state-owned enterprise to be related to the administration system under the slogan of 'separation of enterprise from administration'. Since the 1980s, the autonomous rights of a state-owned enterprise traditionally controlled by central government have been expanding towards independent corporate bodies. Accompanied with this movement, in China since the 1980s, five large-scale administrative reforms have been carried out, whose main task was to adjust the government function and to simplify the administrative organizations.

Movement towards administrative reorganization

The first reform was carried out in 1982. In 1981, the governmental sections in the Chinese cabinet numbered 100, which was the highest figure since the start of the new China. According to the reform plan to simplify the organizations, which was signed at the Fifth Parliament in March 1982, the number of governmental sections was reduced from 100 to 61, and the number of personnel was decreased from 51,000 to 30,000.

A second reform was implemented in 1988. In April 1988, the new reform plan was signed in the Seventh Parliament, and greater importance was attached to transformation of the governmental function, meaning that governmental sections closely connected with systemic transitions were the main targets to be reformed. The results showed that governmental sections in cabinet were reduced from 45 to 41; organizations under the direct control of central government were decreased from 22 to 19; and non-standing organizations decreased from 75 to 44. In the 32 governmental sections, altogether 15,000 personnel cuts were carried out, meanwhile in the other 30 governmental sections, altogether there was an increase of 5300 personnel. The net effect therefore was that 9700 people were cut from the central organizations, and this was followed by local government administration reforms.

The third reform was carried out in 1998. In March 1998, at the Eighth Parliament, they signed the reform plan, according to which the number of governmental sections in the Chinese cabinet and organizations under the direct control of central government declined from 86 to 59, and also personnel cuts of 20% were obtained. Meanwhile, both the Taiwan Office of the cabinet and Newspaper Office of the cabinet were newly established.

A fourth reform was implemented in 1998. In 1997, the new administration reforms were greatly promoted, led by the then prime minister Zhu Rongji. In March 1998, the reform plan of the cabinet organization was signed at the National Parliament. In the organization reform plan, which was connected with the reform of state-owned enterprises to establish a modern corporation system, it was clearly written that the functions of the governmental sections converged to macro-economic policy, social management, and public service. Through the reforms, the number of organizations in the cabinet was reduced from 40 to 29, and a personnel cut was implemented to halve the number (from 32,000 to altogether 16,000).

Needless to say the most difficult task to be carried out in each organization reform was the personnel cutting measures, accompanied with the simplification of governmental sections. In the central organization reforms in 1998, the strict policy that the fixed number of personnel should be halved was implemented. Various measures of personnel dispersion were introduced. For those personnel younger than 30, the government would pay school expenses for them to study at university but would not take care of their job opportunities after graduation. For some government officials older than 50, the central government recommends they have earlier retirements with much more retirement money. Such measures as changing social status, which indicated that a government official changes job from government to the third sector controlled by the government, were employed. Since 1999, similar organizational reforms and personnel cuts in the local governments have been started, whose results thus reached 1.15 million personnel cuts in the number government officials all over China.

The fifth and final reform was realized in 2003, and the details are considered in the following section.

Characteristics of the reform in 2003

According to the reform plan signed at the Tenth National Parliament in March 2003, the number of organizations was to be similar (28 from 29) and a personnel cut was not carried out. The main characteristics of the 2003 reforms were the following. (1) Through reorganization of existing governmental sections, the functions of macro-economic policy were reinforced, and (2) accompanying the development of new market-oriented reform, several higher standard independent organizations were newly established.

(I) Reinforcement of macro-economic policy adjustment functions As regards the macro-economic policy adjustment functions, it was important to establish the National Development and Reforms Commission (NDRC). The forerunner of the Commission was the National Planning Commission, which was established in 1952, and which changed its name to the National Development and Planning Commission (NDRC). This was founded in 2003 by partly taking over the function of the National Economy and Trade Commission, and the function of the Systemic Reform Bureau in the Chinese cabinet (in China, higher ranking bureaus have the functions of guidance and practical affairs). The organization concerned, which has a powerful authority on industrial policy, has been considered to be the Chinese version of the Japanese MITI (former Ministry of International Trade and Industry).

The Ministry of Commerce was established by partly taking over the traditional function of the Ministry of International Economy and Trade, Economy and Trade Commission, and National Planning Commission. Thus, such mergers have realized unification of the regulating functions of internal trade and external trade. The name of the Ministry of Commerce seemed to be a conscious reference to the US Ministry of Commerce.

The China National Family Planning Commission was changed to the National Population and Family Planning Commission of China (NPFPC). The change of name suggested that the population problem in China was not only to quantitatively restrain it but also to strategically consider such various factors as quality, age structure, gender structure, regional disparity etc.

(II) Establishment of higher ranking independent organizations First, the State-owned Assets Supervision and Administration Commission of the State Council (SASAC) has taken the position of a special organization at ministry level, which has been different from an ordinary administrative organization and ordinary business organization. Traditionally, the supervising authority on state-owned enterprises was dispersed around such institutions as the National Economy and Trade Commission (the authority on the ordinary management), the Central Industry and Enterprise Commission (the authority on the personnel affairs), the statistical evaluation division and the state-owned asset supervising division of the Ministry of Finance, and the National Planning Commission (the authority on investment decision). These were called the 'five dragons for riparian works' (the dragon is the deity of water; however, when five dragons are appearing simultaneously, the situation is undoubtedly confused). The new special organization was founded by merging the above institutions, whose functions are as follows: (1) to be the investor which is representative of the Chinese nation; (2) to be responsible for supervising state assets (the assets amounted to 11 trillion yuan whose half assets were occupied by 195 centrally controlled enterprises) and for adjustment of the economic structure and for state-owned enterprise reform; (3) to be responsible for keeping state assets intact and for expanding (excluding financial related enterprises).

Second, the Chinese Bank Regulatory Commission was established in 2003, whose purpose has been for the Chinese central bank to concentrate on monetary policy. It is responsible thus for issuing a license on market entry to financial institutions, and for such practical businesses as supervising their jobs and managing illegal activities. Other independent institutions established included the State Food and Drug Administration (SFDA), whose forerunner was the national supervising administration on drugs. The necessity to supervise the function on food and drugs, which is closely involved in people's health and welfare, is urgent as dangerous affairs on food and drugs have occurred quite often.[6] For the

6 However, in May 2007, the former chief of national supervising administration on food and drug, Zheng Xiao Yu, was sentenced to death and accused of taking a bribe of

same reason, serious coal mining accidents have often occurred, and the State Administration of Work Safety (SAWS) was promoted to be the institution under the direct control of the Chinese cabinet, which was traditionally under the control of the Commission of the National Economy and Trade.

In addition to the above, the China Securities Regulatory Commission (CSRC, 1995) and China Insurance Regulatory Commission (CIRC, 1998) were established ahead of the Chinese Bank Regulatory Commission (CBRC, 2003).

The above-stated waves of governmental institutional reforms seemed to be the funeral services for the centrally planned economy (whose services, however, were not carried out only once, but were implemented several times, based upon a gradualism principle).

(III) Actual situations of institutional reforms in basic level governments Actually, since the 1950s, the name, scale, and supervising institution regarding town and village level government have frequently changed. For example, from 1950 to 1958, the number of town- and village-level governments all over China changed from 280,000 small-scale townships to 26,000 large-scale communes; where, for example, one commune controlled up to 4615 families and 20,000 people. From 1986 to 1996, the total number of towns and villages in the whole of China reduced from 91,138 to 45,454, and the total number of peasant committees also decreased to 740,000 from 94,000.

Table 3.13 shows that, after 1998, institutional reforms on towns and villages in the whole of China were implemented. During the period 1998 to 2005, the total number of towns and villages all over China decreased from 45,500 to 35,500, which signaled that four towns and villages per day were abolished. The number of peasant committees reduced from 740,000 to 640,000. In addition, for ten years from 1993 to 2003, executives of rural areas decreased to 2.59 million from 4.56 million (Zhang Xinguang, 2006). Although such reforms were carried out, we are not optimistic about the results. As often mentioned about the current situation, even though there are 10,000 threads at the top, there is only one needle at the bottom. Also, it is pointed out that, in China, there are countermeasures at the bottom that correspond to the policy from the top – this has been the tacit ironclad rule in China. The same seems to be correct concerning institutional reforms. Regardless of whether they are central or local, and although the number of governmental offices was reduced, the number of employees of these offices gradually expanded (around 70% of government revenues out of the budget were used to pay for these employees – see Chapter 4 for details). That is, even though the name changes, the actual situation remains unchanged. The repetition of administrative institutions,

---

around six million yuan from a pharmaceutical company (the death sentence was carried out on July 10, 2007). By then, there were several high-ranking officials of the administration concerned who had unsuspended sentences and were accused of taking a bribe. We should recognize that the actual situation of serious corruption occurred in administrative offices that should be in charge of social management.

Table 3.13 Number of basic level government, committees and family in Chinese rural areas

	1995	1996	1997	1998	1999	2000	2002	2003	2004	2005	2006
Town level government	2.98	2.75	2.63	2.64	2.56	2.40	1.92	1.84	1.78	1.66	1.66
Village level government	1.73	1.8	1.84	1.91	1.92	1.97	1.98	1.96	1.92	1.89	1.89
Farmers committees	74.02	74.01	73.94	74	73.74	73.47	69.45	67.86	65.27	64.01	64.01
Number of farming family	23282	23438	23406	23693	23811	24149	24569	24793	24971	25223	25223

Source: *Chinese Statistical Bulletin*, annual.

which says 'simplification – expanding – re-simplification – re-expanding', might be more serious at the more basic level of government.

(IV) Driving forces towards institutional reforms: consideration of outside pressure and inside pressure I am impressed by the following two things regarding the institutional reforms in China after the 1980s. First was the repetition indicating the 'simplification – expanding – re-simplification – re-expanding' cycle, which expressed the same situation as 'a cat chasing its own tail'. Even though people work hard, as this is just a repetition, they produce no progress. The author of this book thinks that the main reason for such strange phenomena has been caused by soft budget constraint. Because each level of parliament (the people's representative meeting) cannot express any opinions against the government budget situation, and the government can expend the budget without any checks, institutional expansion might be inevitable. (According to the Public Choice Theory, government behaves to maximize its self-interest similar to other interest groups).

Second, an adjustment tendency for governmental functions to concentrate on macro-economic policy was recognized. In the institutional reforms in 2003, the characteristics became clearer. The opportunity to transform traditional governmental attitude came from external pressure, and this external pressure was the successful result for which China was working towards. In December

2001, China realized its desire to participate in the WTO. The WTO participation caused unexpected external pressure on Chinese administrative institutions. The administration license act was rapidly enacted in August 2003 (and was implemented in January 2004). Additionally, legislative establishment to normalize the market-oriented economic order was quickly promoted. Each governmental section of the Chinese cabinet adjusted the regulations related to respective policies, whose number was in total 2300. Of these 2300, 830 were abolished and 325 were revised, and 1195 administrative authorized cases were cancelled.

In order to promote thoroughly the separation of enterprise from administration, an attempt was made to separate enterprises and business organizations (which are different from traditional state-owned enterprises, and are similar to the third sector) established by the new investment from central and local governmental organizations (financial independence). However, this caused much dissatisfaction by employees who had disparities in treatment and retirement money compared with former colleagues in various regions in China. It was strictly forbidden that military forces, armed police, and governmental institutions could get involved with commercial activities (in compensation for this, the salary of professional soldiers was raised and various conditions of the military forces were improved, which became one of the main reasons for the increase in military expenditure).

The question to be asked was why the government took such self-restraining actions even though the government would basically maximize its self-interest.

A reasonable interpretation seems to be that, because a more developed Chinese economy, through WTO participation, would lead the Chinese government to become more of a beneficiary, the government has partly transformed itself in exchange for the benefits. Currently, there have been lots of new pretext cases authorized by the administration in every region in China, which suggests that the fundamental framework to restrain the government's behavior for maximizing its self-interest desire has never been established. The fundamental framework is, needless to say, the legal control.

The actors, who behave in the legal controlled system, are various kinds of market agents, including government. However, in countries with a development-oriented system, such as China, it is necessary to regulate governmental behaviors under a legally controlled system. If it is not possible, China would probably fall into the trap of the disadvantages of a late comer (delayed institutional innovation). The establishment of appropriate institutions for a constitutional society has been the most important challenges for China after the WTO participation.

Reforms of the social security system

After 1998, behind the accelerated construction of the social security system in China, we can recognize at least two factors. (1) First, as traditional state-owned enterprises took on the burden to provide social welfare for employees, which was usually called 'from the cradle to the grave', state-owned enterprise reform means that such social welfare functions were separated from the enterprises and moved to society. Therefore, various kinds of social security system had to be rapidly constructed. (2) Second, both the Chinese high propensity to save and the domestic demand shortage phenomena have appeared in connection with an insufficient social security system. We think that to establish a sufficient social security system would be indispensable for expanding domestic demand.

Historical details of social security system construction in China

Going back in Chinese history, and focusing our attention to the social security system, suggests that since the Song days both government and private organizations have been involved in rescue facilities, and it seems to the author that those activities were closely connected with the Confucian relief ideology and the development of Lixue[7]. In the days of Yuan Ming Qing, they basically succeeded in this ideology and activity. Concrete examples of the 'rescue facilities' in the Song days were the facilities for the poor and for solitary aged persons, institutions to support burial (public cemeteries), and rescue institutions for little children (Guo Wenjia, 2003). In the new China after 1949, they had three stages in the social security system.

(I) The period of the central planning system The labor insurance act established at the beginning of the 1950s was implemented for 30 years. Characteristics of this period were 'low wage, high employment rate, high benefit, and high welfare'. The nation-state had eternal responsibility for employees of state-owned enterprises, covering everything in the employees' life and death. However, the target of the social insurance was limited to enterprise workers and government employees in the towns and villages, which excluded the farming population (which occupied around 80% of the total population). Various social relief measures provided from the national budget were irregular and of a limited amount.

(II) For 15 years from 1978 to 1993 Since the 1980s, after the open door policy was begun, China has started experimenting with endowment, unemployment, and medical care. During this period, a contract system was usually introduced in state-owned enterprises. However, in order to dissolve the disparity of the social insurance premium among workers of old and new enterprises and to sustain the insurance treatment for employees with difficulties in making a living, the central government proposed the social security system should include multiple differences regarding the endowment insurance system reform for enterprise employees in 1991. The regulation was to recommend enterprises and employees

7 It was the idealistic philosophical thought that started in the North Song days. Various schools of it developed their original theories. Representative thinkers were, for example, Zhou Dunyi in the middle of North Song days, Zhu Xi in the South Song days, and Wang Yangming in the middle of Ming days.

join the supplementary endowment insurance, by implementing a socially unified provision system for endowment, unemployment and medical care.

Regarding the collection of funds, its principles were, (1) insurance treatment was fundamentally the same for anybody according to national unified regulation; (2) the cost burden could be transferred among social cooperatives and among generations; (3) *Yi Zhi Ding Shou, Xian Shou Xian Fu, Lue You Ji Lei* (meaning that, deciding on the levying criteria is dependent upon expenditure, revenue is used for expenditure, a gradually accumulating fund) etc. As far as the problem of the system was concerned, because there existed the vested interest of enterprises and local governments, the levying fund money was extremely difficult and the phenomenon of enterprises escaping from paying insurance premiums by became common. Also, adjusting the fund money difference among regions was remarkably difficult. Generally speaking, the social insurance fund level was low and the ability to manage and avert risks was weak. At the same time, the inflexibility of social insurance treatment became more serious. As regards social insurance treatments among enterprises, the phenomenon of 'one is on the same level with others' became popular, to which there was no effective restraint mechanism. Thus, in many regions, non-payment of endowment insurance, medical expenses, and basic living expenses of temporary layoff workers occurred quite often, and many poor families suffered from difficulties in making a living.

(III) The period after 1993 In the period after 1993, accompanied with the measures stating that 'one center, two secures, three security lines' through state-owned enterprise reform, the building of a social security system that consisted of endowment insurance, medical insurance and unemployment insurance was carried out. The details of which are as follows.

First, the measures indicating 'one center, two secures, three security lines' were implemented. The decision on a few problems about the construction of a socialist market economy examined at the Third Conference of the Fourteenth Chinese Communist Party Meeting, held in 1993, included the idea to construct fully the social security system. That is to say, construction of the social security system appeared closely connected with implementation of a modern enterprise system for state-owned enterprises. After that, the Ministry of Labor and Social Security announced the plan and concrete details of 'one center, two secures, three security lines'.

'One center' pointed out the establishment of a re-employment service center for restructured workers all over China for the restructured employees produced by state-owned enterprise reform. In 1998, state-owned enterprises in the whole of China altogether dismissed 12.19 million workers, of whom 6.09 million workers were re-employed. Of the remaining 6.1 million workers, 95% (5.8 million workers) were registered at the re-employment service center. Until 2005, the number of restructured workers from state-owned enterprises who wished to be re-employed reached around 19 million. Those restructured workers who could establish their own enterprises could receive exemption from taxation for three years and advantageous tax measures after three years.

'Two secures' expressed the total payment of basic living expenses for restructured workers from state-owned enterprises, and of endowment insurance for retired employees. As regards the former, it was prescribed that all the state-owned enterprises that had restructured workers had to establish the re-employment service center for restructured workers and also had to give basic living expenses, social insurance payment and opportunity for vocational training to restructured workers. Profitable operation enterprises had to finance the money by themselves; however, deficit operation enterprises were prescribed to take a burden of one third each of government budget, enterprise and society. At the end of 2005, the restructured workers who received basic living expenses reached 24 million. Because the main purpose was to establish an independent unemployment insurance system of enterprises, the re-employment service center for restructured workers was a provisional institution to support the jobless workers for three years after their dismissals (most of the service centers were founded from 2002 to 2005).

Regarding the latter (on the endowment insurance for retired employees), it was secured by reinforcement of fund money collection, establishment of a fund-adjusting system of provincial-level government, investment in each level of the government budget (especially in the case of central government, by expanding fund money for Industrial regions in the central and western regions) and so on.

'The three security lines' indicate securing (1) basic living expenses for restructured workers from state-owned enterprises, (2) unemployment insurance, and (3) minimum living expenses for citizens in towns and villages. According to the Twelfth Document of the Chinese Communist Party in 1999, those three lines were increased by 30%, respectively, from July 1999 (related to which, the endowment payment was also increased by around 15%). Undoubtedly, those measures had another aim of expanding domestic demand.

Second, the social security system, which consisted of endowment insurance, medical insurance and unemployment insurance, was built. In the announcement of the deepening of the endowment insurance system reform for enterprise employees by the cabinet in 1995, a plan to combine a socially unified provision account with a personal account was incorporated. In addition, in the prescription about the establishment of a unified endowment insurance system for enterprise employees by the cabinet in 1997, the basic model of endowment insurance was further clarified. Under the principle of a jointly shared burden by the three sectors (enterprise, personal, and government), various insurance systems – such as endowment, medical and unemployment – were promoted. Moreover, trial and error reform of the housing system was implemented.

The above-stated principle of a jointly shared burden by the three sectors means that, in establishing a socially unified provision account and personal account, the three sectors (enterprise, personal, and government) joint share the burden. Actually, the socially unified provision account was mainly shared by government, and the personal account was covered by the premium paid by the enterprise and individual person. Some parts of premiums paid by enterprises were transferred to personal accounts, and other parts were transferred to socially unified provision accounts. The money received by employees after retirement comprised 20% of regional average wage and a certain ratio of accumulated funds in the personal account.

The money from a socially unified provision account was chiefly used to adjust the endowment payment all over the region. However, because of an aging society and longer life expectancy, the Chinese endowment suffered from serious pressures. From December 2005, as far as enterprise endowment insurance was concerned, transferring partly the premium paid by an enterprise into a personal account was stopped.

Structure and current situation of the social security system in China

The Chinese social security system includes advantageous measures for particular targets (persons and institutions), social rescue and housing security (on the housing system reforms, see Chen Yun, 2007a) etc, as well as social insurance. The social insurance consisted of five portions: basic endowment, basic medical, unemployment, worker's accident, and educational insurance. As regards wider regional adjustment of the fund money, regarding the basic endowment insurance, a socially unified provision system at the provisional level was established, in addition to which, in 2000, the national council for social security fund was founded, which was the adjustment fund at the central government level. Meanwhile, the other four elements – medical, unemployment, worker's accident and educational insurance – were adjusted in the fund by a socially unified provision system at the municipality level.

The social security fund in a wider sense in China consists of the national council for the social security fund as strategic reserves, the social security fund of each region controlled by the Ministry of Labor and Social Security, enterprise pension, endowment insurance partly supplemented by regional government, and medical insurance fund. The details are as follows.

First, in August 2000, the institution entitled the National Council for Social Security Fund was established. The management of this fund was carried out by the board of directors of the National Council for the Social Security Fund. This fund was intensively controlled by central government, whose main aim was the strategic reserves for the days of an aging society. According to the US Population Research Bureau, the years required to increase the ratio of the aged (older than 65 years old) from 7% to 14% were 115 years in France, 66 years in USA, 30 years in Japan, and 25 years in China. The 'only one child' policy started at the end of the 1970s and contributed to controlling the population explosion in China, but rapidly brought about the aging society.

The provisional method of investment management of the national council for social security fund announced on December 13, 2001, said that sources of money of the national council for social security fund consisted of the central government budget, revenues from non-marketable stock reforms of state-owned enterprises,

Table 3.14 Indicators of five social insurance funds (2006)

	Endowment	Medical	Unemploy-ment	Worker's accident	Educational
Members (10 thousand)	18766 (1279 increase)	15732 (1949 increase)	11187 (539 increase)	10268 (1790 increase)	6459 (1051 increase)
Revenue (100 million yuan)	6310 (23.9% increase)	1747 (24.3% increase)	385 (15.8% increase)	122 (31.7% increase)	62 (41.9% increase)
Expenditure (100 million yuan)	4897 (21.2% increase)	1277 (18.3% increase)	193 (6.9% decrease)	68.5 (44.2% increase)	37 (36.8% increase)
Accumulated balance (100 million yuan)	5489	1752	708	24	97

Note: The figures in parentheses are changing numbers and changing ratios compared with previous year.

Source: Jointly announced report by Ministry of Labor and Social Security, and Chinese Statistical Office, *Statistical Bulletin on the development of labor and social security projects in 2006.*

and fund money collected by the methods ratified by cabinet, investment revenues, stock assets, etc. At the end of 2005, the fund money size of the national council for social security fund reached 201 billion yuan.

Second, the social security fund of each region is the fund that is managed with jointly invested money by enterprises, individuals, and the government budget, which consists of five portions: endowment insurance, basic medical insurance, unemployment insurance, worker's accident insurance, and educational insurance.

In 1998, the Chinese cabinet promulgated the decision about the basic medical insurance system for town and village employees and, in 1999, started to promote the insurance policy in the whole of China. At the end of 1998, the participant ratio of basic endowment insurance was 73% and the participant ratio of unemployment insurance was 56%. Because of the low participant ratio, the Chinese cabinet promulgated in January 1999 both a provisional act of social insurance premium levy, and an unemployment insurance act, which contributed to an improved situation. The unemployment insurance act prescribed that (1) all enterprises located in towns and villages had to participate in unemployment insurance, (2) the premium was jointly shared by employer, employee, and government, (3) employees could receive unemployment allowance after being made unemployed for, at the most, 24 months.

Management authority of the social security fund of each region was entrusted to local government, and was operated with the regulation by the Ministry of Labor and Social Security. Most provinces and municipalities put into force the basic adjustment institution of endowment insurance within the region. After 1999, basic fund operation was limited to savings and deposits of state-owned banks and national bond purchase. In 2005, the total revenue of the Chinese social security fund reached 696.9 billion yuan and total expenditure was 540.1 billion yuan. Until the end of 2005, the total accumulated fund of the five insurances equaled 606.61 billion yuan, whose largest amount of insurance was the endowment insurance fund. Table 3.14 shows some indicators on the five social insurance funds.

Third, the enterprise pension means both (1) the basic endowment insurance, which is participated by enterprise and employees, and which is enacted by the law, and (2) the supplemented endowment insurance system, which people participate in of their own free will. Before 2004, there was no unified prescription and each region was managed and operated separately and differently. In Shanghai and Shenzhen, they founded social insurance centers by which the enterprise pension was operated by the center. Enterprise sectors such as electric power contributed to the unified collection and management of the respective business sector. On January 6, 2004, the Ministry of Labor and Social Security announced the operational method of enterprise pensions, which, the author believes, contributed meaningfully to the formal establishment of a Chinese enterprise pension system. After then, an enterprise pension was operated by the prescription prepared by governmental institutions such as the Ministry of Labor and Social Security, Chinese Securities Regulatory Commission (CSRC), Chinese Bank Regulatory Commission (CBRC), and Central Bank. After the operational method of an enterprise pension was carried out, the total amount of accumulated funds of the enterprise pensions, which were followed by prescription, reached around 68 billion yuan (it was said that the previous amount reached around 100 billion yuan). At the end of 2006, 24,000 enterprises participated in an enterprise pension system and the number of employees who paid the premium was 9.64 million. The total amount of accumulated funds of enterprise pensions reached 91 billion yuan.

Problems to be resolved

By such procedures, the safety net provided by basic social security was established. However, there are still many problems to be resolved.

(I) The balance of endowment insurance deteriorated and a budget crisis occurred As regards the endowment insurance fund; in 1997 in five regions they recorded the deficit in the whole of China, and the deficit budget regions expanded to 21 in 1998 and 25 in 1999. As of June 1998, the total amount of non-payment endowment insurance over all China reached 14.6 billion yuan and an accumulated deficit of the endowment insurance fund in 1999 equaled 18.7 billion yuan. After the Twelfth Document of the Chinese Communist Party in 1999 was announced, the central budget paid the non-payment endowment insurance money in one lump sum through a budget transfer method. However, after that payment, a new deficit was brought about and the situation was repeated. According to the prescription,

basic living expenses for restructured workers were paid by one third by each; however, because enterprises and individual persons did not pay, the government budget payment occupied 70%.

(II) Misappropriate social security fund problems in local areas occurred frequently As mentioned above, after 1999, the basic fund operation of the social security fund in local areas was limited to savings and deposits of state-owned banks and national bond purchase. However, as a matter of fact, misappropriated fund problems frequently occurred all over China. Because fund managers could gain better profit than with national bonds, they invested institutionally (not personally) the fund money into other financial commodities and real estate etc. The interest rate set by the social security fund is around 6 to 8%, which is similar to the bank loan interest rate. In recent years, in order to control the overheated macro-economic situation, (because the monetary policy authority has employed a tight money policy, and receiving a bank loan has become more difficult) privately owned enterprises have suffered from capital shortage problems. Compared with the usual interest rate of a loan from the state-owned enterprise fund (which is around 15%), the social security fund has become an advantageous source of money.

A formal announcement by central government indicated that, since 1998, altogether US$2 billion of social security fund money was misappropriated. The Deputy Minister of Ministry of Labor and Social Security, Liu Yongfu, reported that, in addition to institutional misappropriation, the amount personally embezzled reached US$42 million for the past ten years.

The above system has been operated for the past 15 years without an effective supervising mechanism, in which a huge amount of fund money has been managed within the closed system. We think the roots of the problem should reach the system, meaning that the social security section of local government plays both the roles of manager and investor of the fund. Due to the system, corruption problems related to the fund money have become more serious. The Shanghai social security fund case, disclosed in September 2006, might be just the tip of the iceberg. Before then, the premium collection situation of the Shanghai social security fund was ranked at the higher position, and the Shanghai fund was popular for its 'high efficiency and timely payment'. The case might show a serious payment risk problem of the social security fund across China. Moreover, in the extension of the risk management issue, we think it is necessary to be cautious about the danger of a serious social crisis.

(III) Excessive distribution problem of state-owned enterprises The excessive distribution problem of state-owned enterprises appeared as a fact that the ratio of premium payment in wages increased. Research results by Li Peilin and Zhang Yi (2003) covering 508 enterprises in 10 Chinese municipalities and cities reported that the ratio of premium payment and welfare expenditure to the total wages of the state-owned enterprises and state-owned holding companies reached 57.66% and 50.33% respectively, meanwhile the same ratio of three kinds of enterprise (wholly foreign

owned enterprise, jointly owned enterprise, cooperative enterprise), and collectively owned enterprises, and privately owned enterprises was 20.29%, 18.74%, and 18.18% respectively. The ratios of premium payment of five social insurances which were paid by enterprises reached, by present institutional prescription, 29.8% (endowment insurance 20%, medical insurance 6%, unemployment insurance 2%, worker's accident insurance 1% and educational insurance 0.8%). As a matter of fact, the ratios in 16 provinces reached more than 30%. Examples of various foreign countries have caused many to insist that the premium payment burden of state-owned enterprises should be placed at the upper limit (for example, it is placed at 29% in Japan and around 24% in European countries).

What is the purpose of Chinese state-owned enterprises? Private enterprises in the competitive situation in the market oriented economy usually pursue profit maximization and market share maximization; however, state-owned enterprises usually concentrate their attention upon a revenue increase by employees. Thus, the excessive distribution tendency of state-owned enterprises has been recognized as being easier than in privately owned enterprises. Table 3.15 shows the purpose of management of various enterprise types investigated by the Chinese Entrepreneur Research Association (1997).

Why have such differences occurred? We think they have been coming from the soft budget constraint of state-owned enterprise. They have no incentive to pursue profit maximization and market share maximization, in place of this they have another incentive: one of self-interest maximization. The internal management mechanism within state-owned enterprises has been said to be a 'big iron pot', in which executive interest maximization has never been separated from employee interest maximization. It thus has raised the distribution ratio to employees. As mentioned previously in this chapter, currently, large-scale state-owned enterprises (which have become special interest groups) actually pay much higher wage rates than the socially averaged wage rate. Why have they paid a higher wage rate? Industrial sectors that are occupied by Chinese state-owned enterprises have become

Table 3.15 Management purposes pursued by enterprise managers

	State owned enterprise	Collective owned enterprise in urban area	Town and village enterprise	Wholly foreign owned enter-prise	Foreign owned joint enter-prise	Private owned enter-prise	Joint-stock enter-prise
Revenue increase of employees	73.6	73.1	58.5	47.0	57.3	53.3	58.4
Growth of enterprise	66.3	61.9	66.1	64.7	60.9	40.1	60.5
Profit maxi-mization	59.8	60.1	55.8	70.6	67.1	53.4	71.5

Source: Chinese Entrepreneur Research Association (1997).

smaller. This points out that almost all state-owned enterprises that still exist are large-scale monopolistic enterprises. Having monopolistic profit and unreasonable corporate governance etc might be factors leading to excessive maldistribution. Therefore, thorough reforms of state-owned enterprises (meaning the return to ordinary enterprises) would weaken the excessive maldistribution phenomena.

(IV) The excessive maldistribution problem of state-owned enterprises In 1997, the Chinese government unified the basic endowment insurance for enterprise employees of towns and villages in the whole of China, and employed a method to combine the social contribution by enterprises and government into personal accounts. They prescribed that individual workers who met the following conditions could receive endowment pension money: the conditions were (1) employees who attained the legal retired age (i.e. having turned 60 years old for male workers, 55 years old for female executives, and 50 years old for ordinary female workers); (2) individual employees paid premium money for more than 15 years . In 2003, the average monthly endowment pension money of retired employees equaled 621 yuan.

Meanwhile, as Table 3.16 indicates, the number of employees in the urban area who participated in basic endowment insurance in 2006 was 187.7 million, of whom the number of employees in active service was 141.3 million and retired employees 46.4 million. The respective increased number was by 101.1 million

Table 3.16 Participated numbers in basic endowment insurance

	Active employees (A)	Retired employees (B)	B/A (%)
1989	4816.9	893.4	18.55
1990	5200.7	1086.6	20.89
1991	5653.7	1681.5	29.74
1992	7774.7	1839.4	23.66
1993	8008.2	2079.4	25.97
1994	8494.1	2241.2	26.39
1995	8737.8	2358.3	26.99
2000	10447.5	3380.6	32.36
2001	10801.9	3380.6	31.30
2002	11128.8	3607.8	32.42
2003	11646.5	3860.2	33.14
2004	12250.3	4102.6	33.49
2005	13120	4367	33.29
2006	14131	4635	32.80

Source: *Chinese Labor Statistical Bulletin*, 2005, and jointly announced report by the Ministry of Labor and Social Security, and Chinese Statistical Office, *Statistical Bulletin on the development of labor and social security projects in 2006.*

Table 3.17 Some indicators of basic medical insurance

	Active employees (A)	**Retired employees (B)**	**B/A*100**
Members (10 thousand)			
1994	374.6	25.7	6.87
1995	702.6	43.3	6.16
1996	791.2	64.5	8.15
1997	1588.9	173.1	10.89
1998	1508.7	369.0	24.46
1999	1509.4	555.9	36.83
2000	2862.8	924.2	32.28
2001	5470.7	1815.2	33.18
2002	6925.8	2475.4	35.74
2003	7974.9	2926.8	36.70
2004	9045	3359.2	37.14
2005	10021.7	3761.2	37.53
2006	11580.3	4151.5	35.85
Annual growth rate (%)			
1995	87.6	68.0	
1996	12.6	49.0	
1997	100.8	168.4	
1998	-5.1	113.2	
1999	0.0	50.7	
2000	89.7	66.2	
2001	91.1	96.4	
2002	26.6	36.4	
2003	15.1	18.2	
2004	13.4	14.8	
2005	10.8	12.0	
2006	15.6	10.4	

Source: *Chinese Labor Statistical Bulletin*, 2007.

and 2.68 million. Thus, the ratio of employees in active service to those retired was three to one. Actually, the ratio of retired employees to those in active service was 18.55% in 1989, which increased to be around 30% at the end of the 1990s. The pressure of an aging society would undoubtedly have been stronger. It is anticipated that, in 2010, the ratio of active employees and retired employees will become two to one, and in 2030 will become one to one.

In addition, the basic medical insurance case has a similar situation (seen Table 3.17). The ratio of retired employees to active employees was expanded to 37.53% in 2005 from 36.83% in 1999 and 6.16% in 1995. Also, after 2000, the growth rate of retired employees who have enjoyed receiving insurance money has been more than the growth rate of active employees. (In 2006, the situation slightly improved.)

It is necessary to examine countermeasures to this tendency. At the present time, as regards the retirement age, there is a five year difference between male employees and female employees. This difference should be eliminated and, from the viewpoint of an aging society and longer life expectancy, it might also be examined whether the retirement age should be higher than 65 years old. In addition, after the transition period is over, the condition that the employee must have paid endowment insurance money for more than 15 years might be reconsidered. From foreign countries examples, some opinions insist that 30 years (not 15 years) might be appropriate.

Table 3.18 Member peasants of rural endowment insurance and member migrant peasants of medical insurance and worker's accident insurance (2006)

	Rural endowment insurance	**Medical insurance (migrant peasants)**	**Worker'saccident insurance (migrant peasants)**
Members (10 thousand)	5374	2367	2537
Provided members (10 thousand)	355		78

Source: Jointly announced report by Ministry of Labor and Social Security, and Chinese Statistical Office, *Statistical Bulletin on the development of labor and social security projects in 2006.*

(V) Social security problems for peasants It has become necessary to investigate the effects on the employment problem given by such factors as urbanization, globalization of the economy, multiple forms of employment etc. In particular, due to urbanization, the social security problems of migrant peasants and peasants whose lands were requisitioned have become more serious.

As shown in Table 3.18, at the end of 2006, the population paying rural endowment insurance reached 53.74 million, and 3.55 million peasants received endowment money. The total amount of endowment money paid to the peasants equaled three billion yuan and the accumulated fund balance reached 35.5 billion yuan. The Chinese population in the rural area is around 780 million, of whom the ratio of the member population of endowment insurance in rural areas is only about 7%. The ratio has been rather low. The situation seems to oppose the government plan entitled Planned Policy of Birthrate, the purpose of which is to restrain the population birthrate in rural areas. In other words, it is necessary to recognize that the saturation level of endowment insurance in rural areas would be closely connected with the result of the Chinese population policy in the future.

Meanwhile, the total population of migrant peasants is said to be 120 million; however, the ratio of migrant peasants with medical insurance to those with worker's accident insurance is still only less than 20%. Another problem is that, because the insurance accounts of migrant peasants could not be moved to other areas (Shanghai municipal government has established a general insurance system for migrant peasants), migrant peasants who transfer to other provinces find it difficult to receive insurance benefits. However, as the Min Gong Huang problem in the Chinese south region (it has been suffering from a shortage of migrant peasants for the labor force) has become more serious, it was attempted to establish new insurance institutions. As far as this problem is concerned, it is expected to be improved in the near future.

The source of money for the social security system: on the non-marketable stock reforms of state-owned enterprises

The sources of money in the social security system include government, workplace, individual persons, and fund-operating revenue. At the time of writing, as regards the burden taken by each of them, the following plan is established. (1) An enterprise's burden is occupied by 25% of wage payment (endowment insurance 15%, medical insurance 6%, unemployment insurance 2%, worker's accident insurance 1%, and educational insurance 1%); (2) an individual person's burden is occupied by more than 11% of wage earnings (endowment insurance 8%, medical insurance 2%, unemployment insurance 1%); (3) the ratio of government burden is occupied by less than 30% of wage payment, and government ordinary expenditure is covered by tax revenues. However, as far as the burden of institutional transformation coming from enterprise reforms is concerned, they have decided on the plan to be managed by the release of non-marketable stocks of state-owned enterprises and by issuing national bonds.

At present, the national council for the social security fund has requested to be allocated a share from state-owned enterprises whose stocks were listed on both (domestic and foreign) stock markets after their reforms (particularly their joint-stock privatization). It clearly shows that the tasks for the social security fund to enrich the function are closely connected with state-owned enterprise reforms.

Then, at which stage is the advance of state-owned enterprises into the capital market?

The Chinese stock market suffered from an institutional deficiency for many years. To be concrete, at the beginning of the 1990s when joint-stock reform of state-owned enterprise was carried out, three kinds of stocks were issued, which were state-owned stocks, corporate stocks, and general public stocks. Of the three, state-owned stocks and corporate stocks were frozen, not to be traded at the market, and only general public stocks, whose share was around one third, were permitted to be tradable. Such institutional prescription, which led the stock market to have a dual structure, came from the gradual method of transition. It seems to be the results coming from the then deep-rooted ideology saying that socialism should have public ownership.

Undoubtedly, such a dual structure in joint-stock reforms has substantial side effects, which are as follows. (1) The structure caused the advantageous situation of state-owned stocks, which was harmful to the intrinsic rationality of corporate governance. The stock market became the market mainly for state-owned enterprises to finance the necessary money, and state-owned enterprises were not properly responsible. Listed state-owned enterprises had no incentive to increase their asset value. The delayed advance into international capital markets resulted from the nature of such state-owned enterprises. (2) When lots of state-owned stocks and corporate stocks are not traded on the market, the efficient allocation of state-owned assets could not be realized. (3) Because only general public stocks (which occupy one third of total stocks) are tradable and the size of capital market could not be expanded, speculative behavior on the stock market can become more active, which would cause erratic stock prices.

Towards combining the reform problems of a dual structure of stock markets with the social security system, the tradable reform of state-owned stocks and corporate stocks was started.

In June 2000, the then minister of finance, Xiang Huaicheng, mentioned that the Chinese government would develop financial measures towards a substantial social security system at the appropriate time and some portion of state-owned assets are used to enrich the social security fund. On June 12, 2001, the Chinese cabinet formerly promulgated the provisional method on the management to allot to the social security fund by decreasing state-owned stocks (hereafter the provisional method). The main part of it was article five, which prescribed that when new stocks or additional stocks were issued, state-owned stocks equal to 10% of the total amount should be sold and be allotted to the social security fund.

However, during the slump period of the stock market, on October 22, 2001, the Chinese Securities Regulatory Commission suddenly ordered it to stop executing the provisional method. Also on June 23, 2002, the Chinese cabinet decided to suspend the reform, to decrease the ratio of state-owned stock at the domestic stock market. That is, they gave notice of suspending the provisional method for state-owned enterprises listed on the domestic stock market (except state-owned enterprises listed at the foreign stock market).

Thus, it took around one year to suspend the provisional method from its promulgation. The deep-rooted reasons for the suspension were the following; first (1) state-owned stocks gave remarkable shocks for the stock market because the state-owned stocks occupy two-thirds of the total. Wariness to the stock market became serious and market confusion occurred. The Chinese capital market itself has unquestionably still been weak, and institutional, technical and psychological arrangements have never been enough. Second, (2) reaching a balance between stockholders of tradable stocks and non-tradable stocks might be serious. To be more specific, the problem is said to be the way of transforming non-tradable stocks into tradables (at which ratio and which price?). This was the most serious technical difficulty when non-tradable state-owned stocks were reduced.

In order to overcome the difficulty, opinions on the reform plan of non-tradable stocks were requested from the whole society. As the result, it was decided that the main method was to pay dividends on three non-tradable stocks per ten tradable stocks. The stockholders' interest was compensated to some extent and a compromise was reached. On 29 April, 2005, the Chinese Securities Regulatory Commission released the announcement on the trial problem of non-tradable stocks reform of listed enterprises, which opened the way towards new reforms of non-tradable stocks. The stock market response to the method seemed to be constructive. The general index of the Shanghai Stock Exchange rapidly increased from 998 in June 2004 to 4000 as of May 2007. According to the statistics of SASAC, until November 30, 2006, 179 holding companies of altogether 190 whose stocks are held by centrally controlled enterprises, have started or have already reformed the non-tradable stocks.

Meanwhile, Li Rongrong mentioned positive opinions in the press conference at the end of 2006 on the management to allot portions of state-owned enterprise profit to the social security fund, however he gave an additional explanation saying that allotted portions could be paid by money, not by stocks, because SASAC wished to maintain absolute authority to control the substantial number of state-owned enterprises.

Concluding remarks

In this chapter, we insist on advantages and disadvantages of state-owned enterprise reform related with systemic reforms of finance, administration and social security. The socio-economic system established in the days of the centrally planned economy caused the institutional inefficiency, which could be recognized as the 'fallacy composition'. Through the reform centered on state-owned enterprises, the social welfare function and central government intervention etc, which were originally accompanied by state-owned enterprises, were removed. In addition, the social security system, which was originally unified, was given segmentation and diversity. Meanwhile, state-owned banks, which are the state-owned enterprises of financial sector, also broke away from the function of the accountant of government finance, and differentiated themselves to be independent central banks, commercial banks and policy banks. The phenomena, called 'reforms induce reforms', were brought about, and the days of 'fallacy composition' were replaced by the days of division of labor.

Special points to be noted are: (1) before the state-owned enterprise reform started, the non-state-owned sector in rural and urban areas had already developed, and this became the successful model for the state-owned enterprise reform; and (2) the state-owned enterprise reform was delayed because of serious difficulties; however, once the reform was put into practice, the reform process had positive chain reactions.

The reforms that successfully occurred in enterprises, banks and government are called 'market oriented reforms'. As a matter fact, such reforms should be recognized as the return to an ordinary function. Moreover, we think that the returning process towards an ordinary enterprise, ordinary bank and ordinary government might consist of a Chinese systemic transition itself.

A traditional state-owned enterprise was accompanied by a large government. By the deepening of state-owned enterprise reform, the huge government undoubtedly collapsed. At the present time, although the Chinese government still has an authoritarian system, it has to establish, sooner or later, equal relations with society under the system of division of labor and cooperation.

What kind of impacts by growth of the private sector and substantial appearance of privatized society are caused by the form of government? Could modernization of the political system be led by the modernization of the economy? Such important tasks, closely connected with the Chinese systemic transition, will be investigated in chapters of Part 2.

PART 2
Political Economy of Development in China

Chapter 4
Relations Between Central and Local Government under the Tax Sharing System: Towards a Constitutional Local Autonomy System

Introduction

From historical perspectives, Chinese relations between central and local government always displayed multiple layers whose cyclical pattern expressed "decentralization in the centralized system" and "centralization in the decentralized system". In the dynastic days in China, we could recognize the multiple layers of controlling space meaning "imperial power control" and "co-existence of official authority, tribal authority, rank authority", however, after the new Chinese nation was established, under the centralized system of the Mao Zedong's era, the phenomenon of Xiaogang village in Anhui province showed the gap still existed among basic government 30 years after the new nation was founded based upon the huge space of the farming area. It points out the multiple layers of controlling space have continued. After the Deng Xiaoping system started in 1978, we can insist that it is a tendency towards the wise authoritarianism system (which means the East Asian model with a rather high rate of economic growth shared among people, however it might be too early to decide whether or not China has the same pattern of shared growth). The multiple layers principle has been said to occur in another form. Before the tax sharing system was carried out in 1994, it was what is called the days of centralization in a decentralization system, after 1994 however the relationship between central and local government has changed to be the days of decentralization in the centralized system.

Actually, both centralization and decentralization are just the means of control, it is necessary for the effective centralization and decentralization to establish a more fundamental institutional framework. That is we think the constitutional government is indispensable for nation building. There are several characteristics of constitutional government, whose most important ones are (1) existence of a constitution expressing peoples' rights, and that (2) the government which carries it out should have the separation of the three branches of government. The latter of the separation system is further divided horizontally into a three branches system and also vertical relations between central and local government.

When advanced industrialized countries regulate the central and local government relations, the following two are important. They are (1) provisions on nation's structure indicating single government or federal government, and (2) provisions for specifying a local autonomy system. The majority of experts assert that, for a large scale country with diversified characteristics like China, a federation might be appropriate. Although we will not examine more about the federation issue, either single government or federal government has implemented a local autonomy system all over the world. We think thus that China should introduce the local autonomy system in a constitutional sense. The problem to be considered is the opportunity.

Central government aims towards a sound macro economic situation, meanwhile local government tries to maximize local benefit, which suggests to us conflicts between central and local government. The reform and open door policy in China was started by decentralization of power. However, it has never been enough.

Establishing new stable relations between central and local government should we think near introducing a local autonomy system in a constitutional sense. Reasons to need such new stable institutions are, (1) to reduce huge transaction costs, and (2) to realize efficient management of public services by attempting to have a symmetric system of financial authority and service obligation. The institutional change is neither to deny target benefit nor to change target benefit for central and local government respectively, but is to realize maximization of public benefit (the cooperation of local benefit with nation wide benefit) through institutional change.

The purpose of introducing tax sharing system in 1994 was to restore the redistribution function by central government which became weaker due to overdoing decentralization of power. In those days, the term "nation's ability" was often used to express weak central government financial control. Urgent tasks therefore were to check wealthy local government activities which had their own ways, and to alleviate regional disparities by a financial redistribution system.

Although the tax sharing system in 1994 was said to be successful as an initial attempt, various problems were also exposed. A tax system with such tax sharing system might be easily recognized to have limit unless it is related with institutional reform at a higher stage. What is the institutional reform at a higher stage? We think it is towards local authority in a constitutional sense. Does Chinese economic modernization through economic construction lead to political democratization? Will China be led to the East Asian model?

From historical perspectives on foreign countries' circumstances, we have concluded to say that the four features (private property rights system, parliamentary system, constitutional government, and local autonomy) have been closely related with each other. Accompanied with improving market oriented reform, in China they established protection of private proper rights in the Chinese constitution. It might be undoubtedly a strong driving force towards establishing constitutional government in China.

A private property system is a driving force for systemic transition. Because of an open door policy of gradual reform China has found it necessary to expand private property rights, and it might be reasonable to reach institutional reform. However, if they cannot appropriately resolve the disparity problems as well as extensions of a market oriented system and privatization, a gradual way of transition might collapse. In a less developed country like China which has huge population, huge area, various issues might tend to be easily put together and the disparity issue should be carefully adjusted. Shared growth is an important key to nip revolutionary movement in the bud.

Does Chinese economic modernization through economic construction after 1978 lead to political democratization? Will China be led to the East Asian model?

This chapter is divided into seven sections. In the first section, we have a short look at the actual situation about development after the 1980s. In the second section, we consider advantages and disadvantages of a financial contract system in the 1980s, and backgrounds of implementation of tax sharing system. We introduce in the third section the purpose of tax sharing system, and the details and institutional frameworks of tax sharing system. In the fourth section, we analyze the problems on current tax sharing system, in particular, (1) on asymmetry problem of financial authority and public service obligation of lower rank local government than provincial level, (2) without norm problem and regional disparity problem in financial transfer pattern led by administration power, and (3) incomplete tax collection authority problem of local government.

In the fifth section, problems in the relations among governments and social effects from viewpoints of tax sharing system are investigated. Former problems are analyzed by focusing attention upon the booming tendency of the Beijing representative bureau; the latter ones by concentrating on accumulated debt problems of rural lowest level government, especially on (1) general tendency for local government to depend upon land finance and (2) weakening of rural lowest level government. In the sixth section, the logics of land finance dependence are examined, taking into consideration the four factors which are (1) weakening of local assembly, (2) soft budget system and self-expansion of government organization, (3) government's view for GDP as almighty, and (4) effects of current tax sharing system.

In the seventh section, we analyze relations between central and local government in the future and recommend a local autonomy system. We reach the recommendation by considering first, the problems of relations between central and local government under the authoritarianism system by summarizing four views which are problems of irresponsible local government, problems of administration structural reform, problems of workers mobility, problems of bureaucracy, and second, impacts of establishing private property system for constitutional government in China based upon general characteristics of a local autonomy system, the Chinese tradition of "imperial power cannot extend over the local area"; finally historical perspectives of Chinese attempts to establish constitutional government and a retrospect on peasants autonomy system.

Causational drama of local freedom

Classification of relationships between central and local government

As regards the structure of relations among governments within nation states, there are horizontal relations of the three branches of government and vertically structural relations of central and local government. The structural relations are classified into the following three kinds.

First is the centralization system, which is the system that central government sends bureaucrats to local government and has unified control.

Second is the decentralization system. Central government transfers some authorities to local government, and local government has partial autonomy under the local control. However, as it is the transferred authority, when the situation is changed, central government can take the power back with enough authority and legal grounds.

Third is the local autonomy system in a constitutional sense. The constitution and other special laws prescribe regional administration authority belongs to local government. Citizens of each local region vote directly for the head of local government and members of assembly, and financial authority and service obligation is divided into respective levels of government by the law.

In the country with a huge area like China, institutional structure between central and local government is undoubtedly important. After 1978, China has proceeded into a gradual way of transition and development led by government. Relations between central and local government have been kept in the level of decentralization. Relations between them are the initial condition of economic development and also evolved accompanied with economic development.

Setting forth the reform and open door policy: adjustment of relations between central and local government

(I) Preceding decentralization of power (combination of vertical and horizontal administrative order) Vertical administrative order means a nation state as a top and local government as a bottom vertically combined administrative order, and a horizontal administrative order indicates horizontally spreading administrative order within respective provinces and respective administrative districts. Such vertical and horizontal administrative combinations displayed fundamental characteristics of a traditional centrally planned economy.

Since 1979, in such coastal regions as Guangdong province and Fujian province, which were given special policies and flexible measures by central government, principles of combining vertical and horizontal administrative order whose latter is principal were carried out through (1) autonomous discretion rights in drafting and implementing economic plans, (2) extension of financial and foreign exchange reserves, (3) transferring authority of monetary policy, wage policy, and price policy etc.

(II) Improvement of the foreign trade system and decentralization Expanding the region for reform and open door policy was accompanied by expansion of authority of local government. Authority of approving the amount of foreign capital by local government in 1980 was five million US$ for Guangdong and Fujian province, three million US$ for other provinces, autonomous districts and direct controlled cities (first rank administrative districts). The authority was drastically expanded in September 1984 which was spreading to lower rank governments. The maximum limit of approving foreign capital amount was as following; it was 100 million US$ for Guangdong and Fujian province, 30 million US$ for Shanghai and Tianjin municipality, ten million US$ for Beijing city, Liaoning province, Dalian city, and Guangzhou city, five million US$ for other provinces, autonomous districts and major cities, two to three million US$ for middle and small size cities in Guangdong, Liaoning, Jiangsu provinces, 1.5 to two million US$ for counties in Guangdong province and Shanghai city. It led to the result saying that the respective level local governments attempted actively to attract foreign capital (Ma Chengsan, 1995, Imai, 1985).

Decentralization of power has been carried out even in border region at an early stage. At the beginning of the 1980s, both frontier small trade and Bianmin Hushi were resumed in various places. In December 1984, in order to give definite structure for frontier small trade which was disorderly and to improve economic management, a "provisionary administration law on the frontier small trade" was ratified in the cabinet and was announced by the Ministry of International Trade (Chinese Ministry of International Economy and Trade (ed), 1985, p.75). By the law, any businesses concerning frontier small trade like opening the trading place, medical inspection of commodities, customs office etc., have been managed by provinces and autonomous districts for themselves which are located near to neighboring countries.

(III) Transfer to the local of state owned enterprise directly controlled by central government Since the end of the 1980s, local governments have become acting controllers of most state owned enterprises which were traditionally controlled by central government and have become actual owners. Thus, local government owned enterprises have been the main constituents of Chinese state owned enterprises. Local governments control on the state owned enterprises are so strong that enterprises behave in accordance with local government policy. Local governments have often employed protection policies for the state owned enterprises. For example, although most banks in China have been state owned, local governments could intervene in personnel matters of banks which were located in the local areas concerned until the beginning of 1990s. It meant local government could have serious effects on enterprise management through controlling power to the banks. In 1994, by establishing the People's Bank of China Act, legally local government has lost the power to appoint the president of the bank located in the local area;

however local government's influence over the bank has still been powerful.

The tendency towards decentralization of power after the 1980s might have relations with such traditional legacies as loose centralization system in Chinese characteristics which was left from the Mao Zedong's era and various attempts to decentralize power. Such Chinese traditions could be said that they established the base to promote competition among regions, sectors, and enterprises in Chinese society after the reform and open door policy on the one hand, and they caused the rise and improvement of local protectionism in 1980s on the other. They have also we think significant impacts on the disparity formation mechanism among regions with complex relations to industrial policy, fiscal policy and monetary policy during the transition period.

(IV) Pluralization of development investment The investment actor which was unified in central government became plural after the reform and open door policy in 1978. They have been central government, respective local government, state owned enterprise, collective owned enterprise, three kinds of enterprise (wholly foreign owned enterprise, jointly owned enterprise, cooperative enterprise), private investor, and foreign business actors etc. The ratio of nation state investment (mainly central budget expenditure) occupied to fundamental construction investment was traditionally 80-90 per cent, however it decreased year by year since the reform and open door policy started. Table 4.1 indicates that the ratio was reduced to 37.5 per cent in 1985, 20.8 per cent in 1989, and 10.2 per cent in 1992. In place of the tendency, such plural ways of investment as bank loan, finance from issuing securities and stocks, inviting foreign capital, were expanded.

In addition to the pluralization of development investment actors, local budget system, fixed asset investment system, FDI inflow, each of which was closely involved with investment, has been changed. The question asking about which effects are related with the changes to regional disparity in China is the topic investigated in this chapter.

Occurrence of a development zone boom

It is expected that, by designating an open city or open area in various forms in China, they establish such development zones as an 'industrial technology development zone', 'High-Tech industry development zone', 'reservation zone of collecting customs duty', 'Taiwan brotherhood investment zone', and 'sightseeing resort development zone' etc., by receiving advantageous measures within cities. They expect that the zones work as new growing regions for urban development and industrial development.

Establishment of an industrial technology development zone was restricted to particular coastal areas in the 1980s, however in the 1990s accompanied with open border policy, inland and border areas were allowed to establish. There are 30 industrial technology development zones at national level in China. Compared with

Table 4.1 Two deceases of financial revenue

	The ratio of financial revenue (%)		The ratio of financial revenue to GDP (%)
	Central government	Local government	
1978	15.52	84.48	31.2
1980	24.52	75.48	25.7
1985	38.39	61.61	22.4
1989	30.90	69.10	15.8
1990	33.79	66.21	15.8
1991	29.79	70.21	14.6
1992	28.12	71.88	13.1
1993	22.02	77.98	12.6
1994	55.70	44.30	11.2
1995	52.17	47.83	10.7
1996	49.42	50.58	10.9
1997	48.90	51.10	11.6
1998	49.50	50.50	12.6
1999	51.10	48.90	13.9
2000	52.20	47.80	15.0
2001	52.40	47.60	16.8
2002	54.96	45.04	18.0
2003	54.64	45.36	18.5
2004	54.94	45.06	19.3
2005	52.3	47.7	17.2
2006	52.8	47.2	18.4

Source: *Chinese Statistical Bulletin* 2007.

special economic zones which are comprehensive development zones, industrial technology development zones are basically industrial export complexes.

In China there were two times development zone booms in the end of 1993 and after 1998. At the end of 1993, with Deng Xiaoping's speech in the southern tour nation wide development boom occurred, some of which were successful. The well known successful case was an industrial technology development zone located at Kunshan city (Jiangsu province), which was constructed by self effort without any permissions and support by central government and attracted inward FDI by providing independent advantageous measures. Meanwhile, at the beginning of 1991, central government changed the position that the Kunshan city case was illegal and approved the Kunshan case as a new model for regional development with a self effort strategy.

In China, regardless of the region, coastal or inland, province or town and village, a development zone boom occurred anywhere, which were counted as 1,000 or 2,000 (in case of Jiangsu province, for example, almost all towns and villages proceeded with development zone construction). Except in some development zones approved as national level development zones like the above mentioned Kunshan industrial technology development zone, in respective development zones at local level, corporate income tax was imposed as 15 per cent around the same as in national approved development zones although usually corporate income tax was 30 per cent. The difference between 30 per cent and 15 per cent was transferred to local government.

The development zone boom played a role for respective local governments to have active measures, meanwhile excessive expectation for development by foreign enterprises was brought about. In various places several disturbances occurred, for example, disordering development by changing farming land to development zone, and providing excessive advantageous measures to attract foreign capital. Central government needed to strengthen their control.

After 1998, attached to rapid development of the urbanization process, the second development zone boom happened. Also after 2003 a real estate development boom in various places occurred with synergy effects. Central government had to take an action against disordering excessive development which was effective for the macro economic situation. Reforming the land policy was the main target for central government.

By the then policy putting in order the development zones, of the total 6,866 various development zones in the whole of China, 70 per cent of them were abolished and 70 per cent of the planned area was condensed. However, it was difficult to say it was successful. Afterwards illegal developments were continued. According to the inspections from October 2004 to May 2005, the illegally expropriated number of places and land area occupied 61 per cent and 50 per cent respectively. In Zhejiang province, when the development zone boom in 2003 was recognized, various development zones equaled 758. However, after putting in order new policy they were radically reduced to 134, which was 1.33 per county (*Shijiazhuang Ribao* (*Shijiazhuang daily report*), May 24, 2004).

Central government was compelled to attempt the vertical control of land in 2004 and also took a measure to allocate land collecting rights to higher administration. Those attempts were not effective. Disordering developments were done not only by county and city, or town and village governments but also provincial governments were also in impulsive developments. As a matter of fact, in 1998 the "land regulation law" was amended to allocate the land commandeering rights of collectively owned land (rural area land) to provincial governments. It could not however stop the illegal development of land.

On 24 July, 2006, the Chinese cabinet issued the "announcement on national institution about land inspection" which said that, in the Ministry of National Resources, they established a general secretariat on land inspection in China and established nine national land inspection bureaus. Central government tried to make land inspection independent from local government. However, a fully independent land inspection section has so limited human power that it might be difficult for them to go around huge Chinese land and to stop disordering development. Also it might be questionable to think who supervises the highly centralized land inspection section? Various problems remain unsolved.

Short summary

Although it was a decentralization to make the local area active, the center was the Chinese south in the 1980s and was Shanghai in the 1990s, a strange circle of decentralization and centralization occurred. In Chinese, it is said that decentralization leads to disorder, disorder leads to centralization, centralization leads to death, death leads to decentralization again and has been repeated. It is difficult to see much prospect of stable relations between local and central government.

As is well known, the tax system is crucial to relations between the local and center. In China as a matter of fact tax sharing systems has been introduced to stabilize relations between them since 1994. The separation of the taxation system was given attention as an important system to contribute to new stable relations of central government with local government, which was to apply the brakes to the "little empire economy" in the 1980s. We think it is necessary to consider the evaluation on tax sharing system 14 years after it was introduced (as stated above, the development zone boom in local areas occurred before and after tax sharing system was carried out). Also it is necessary to examine the prospects for the future and to think about the possibilities of further development.

Background of implementation for tax sharing system: advantages and disadvantages of the budget contract system in 1980s

Weakening of the central budget

Since the 1980s, China has experienced high speed economic growth. For ten years from 1980 to 1990, average annual GDP growth rate reached 9.5 per cent. However, high speed economic growth did not bring about financial revenue increase for central government. The ratio of financial revenue to GDP was drastically decreased to 12.6 per cent in 1993 from 31.2 per cent in 1978 when reform and open door policy started. Also the ratio of central government financial revenue to total financial revenue was kept decreasing to be 22.02 per cent in 1993 from 38.39 per cent in 1985. They said it was the two deceases, shown in Table 4.1.

Under the weakening of the central budget, from the end of the 1980s to the beginning of the 1990s, central government borrowed money from local government twice, which was not paid back at all. At the beginning of the 1980s, just after the "*Da bao Gan*" (one set contract system) was implemented, central government asked local government for a loan for two consecutive years to finance the financial expenditure. In the middle of the 1980s central government financed about 10 billion yuan from the local budget (meaning ten per cent more than the originally collected amount) under the pretext of the energy and transportation fund. In 1989, central government with more budget deficit increased five per cent more income than the original plan from the local budget; also under the pretext of a budget adjustment fund. In every year of those days at the national financial meeting, central government created measures to increase financial revenue compared with the local budget on the one hand, local government tried to expand their ratio to central government's based upon several reasons. After all the national financial meeting became an arena for negotiation between central government and local government.

In the first half of 1993 before the tax sharing system was carried out, the national budget deficit reached its peak. Central government complained about the shortage of money in such policy measures as subsidy for foodstuffs purchase, national important projects fund, circulating capital for state owned enterprises. The Ministry of Finance borrowed money from the bank when the national budget was in deficit. However, when Zhu Rongji was responsible for monetary policy, he declared that, even if the budget was in serious deficit, financial authority should not have over-borrowing. Actually on the 23rd July 1993, at the national budget and tax meeting, Zhu Rongji asserted that, without the reform of the current budget system, central budget was certainly to fall apart before 2000.

Causes of the weakening: pluralization and destabilization of the financial system

Causes of the national budget's weakening were related with a background of reform and open door policy. In order to increase independence of local government, they carried out much decentralization, in which budget authority and investment authority was included.

Both pluralization and destabilization have always existed in the Chinese financial system. Before the tax sharing system was implemented in 1994, the Chinese financial system experienced institutional changes at least 15 times for around 40 years, of which the shortest financial system lashed for only one year. In the 1950s to 1970s, the following institutional changes of financial system were repeated; (1) from 1950 to 1952 and from 1969 to 1970, "*Tong Shou Tong Zhi*" (unified income and unified expenditure) was carried out, meanwhile, (2) in other years, "*Fen Lei Fen Cheng*" (in which they classified the various kinds and decided their distribution with certain ratios) or "*Zhong He Fen Cheng*" (in which they allocated total financial revenue with certain ratios) was implemented.

Since the 1980s the financial system was recognized to have the three stage reforms. They were (1) "*Hua Fen Shou Zhi, Fen Ji Bao Gan*" in 1980, which indicated that income and expenditure was divided and a contract system was introduced at each local government level. The cabinet promulgated the provisional regulation on implementation in financial system of "*Hua Fen Shou Zhi, Fen Ji Bao Gan*" and carried out a financial contract system in the whole nation, except the three municipalities directly under the central government, Beijing, Shanghai and Tianjin. (2) "*Hua Fen Shui zhong, He Ding shou zhi* and *Fen Ji Bao Gan*" in 1985, which showed that based upon various taxes, each level local government implemented the contract system. Before then in 1983 and 1984, the tax system to state owned enterprises was reformed which was called tax reform from profit.[1] (3) "*Shou Ru Di Zeng Bao Gan*" in 1988, whose details were classified into the following six; "*Di Zeng Bao Gan*", "*Zhong He Bao Gan*", "*Zhong He Fen Cheng*" plus "*Zeng Zhang Fen Cheng*", "*Shang Jie Di Zeng Bao Gan*", "*Ding E Shang Jie*", and "*Ding E Bu Zhu*". Those various kinds were said to be "one province one system".

Generally speaking, the financial system since the 1980s has been basically a contract system. This financial contract system has the common characteristics recognized in such other contract systems such as family contract system of arable land in rural areas, contract system in management of state owned enterprises.

Wu (1995) classified the national financial system before the tax sharing system into the following four; (I) First was the "*Shou Ru Fen Cheng*" system which was most widely carried out. Both central and local government decided their ratios depending on their money paid to the authorities. The contract system was introduced in the 16 provinces which were Hebei, Shanxi, Jiangsu, Zhejiang, Liaoning, Anhui, Shandong, Henan, Hubei, Hunan, Sichuan, Sanxi, Gansu, Jilin, Helongjiang, Jiangxi. Such provinces as Jiangxi, Jilin which had deficit were subsidized with a fixed amount. (II) Second was the supporting system for less developed minority race regions. In addition to the five minority race autonomous districts which are Inner Mongolia, Tibet, Xinjiang, Guangxi, Ningxia, the other three provinces, Qinghai, Yunnan, Guizhou in which minority race people lived intensively also introduced such supporting systems. Central government subsidized a fixed amount to each province and each district. (III) Third was "*Da Bao Gan*" at the experimental zone for reform and open door policy. Target provinces of this policy were Guangdong, Fujian, and Hainan (which was raised to the status of province in 1988). This system displayed that, as far as they pay the money to the central government, more money of financial revenue could be reserved to the local government. Particularly for Fujian (which was a rather less developed province) it was permitted to reserve all the financial revenue to local government besides subsidy from central government reached 150 million yuan. (IV) Fourth was "*Ding Shou Ding Zhi*" for Beijing, Shanghai, and Tianjin. It indicated that income and expenditure was combined, a fixed amount of which was allocated between central and local government, and the amount could be revised every year. What was different from the above mentioned (V) was that local government financial revenue paid to central government was not granted without assessment of

1 Reform of "tax reform from profit" means changing a collecting way from profit by state owned enterprises to tax. Collecting money from profit has been kept, however various discussions are insisted recently, an example of which is that state owned enterprises should pay a dividend to the state as well as profit.

central government. In 1978, financial revenue of the three municipalities directly under the central government occupied 27 per cent of national financial revenue, meanwhile financial expenditure of the three municipalities reached ten per cent of national financial expenditure. The three municipalities directly under the the central government contributed most for central government budget situation.

Problems of the financial contract system

During the transition in China, carrying out the financial contract system seems to be necessary. It can be positively evaluated that the system broke the socialistlitarian scheme traditionally recognized in each section in China in the 1980s. Expanding of autonomy in the local budget system contributed to regional economic development. 'The harder work, the more payment' system has given incentive for workers. However, the financial contract system combined with a traditional vertically and horizontally divided administrative system has given significant distortion both for the national and regional economy. Some examples of the detail were as following.

(1) Because of the impulsive investment by local governments, excessive investment and an overheated macro economic situation was brought about. Control of state owned enterprises was divided vertically (each level government) and horizontally (control section for each industry), respective of which each pursued its self interest. Under the system called 'Baoyingbubaokui' (meaning that, when it was successful they got benefit, but when it failed they were irresponsible), each actor both vertical and horizontal tried to expand itself. An investment boom led by governments caused the overheated macro economic situation in China in 1993.

(2) Because a regional blockade and regional protectionism in production and distribution was produced, the formation of a unified market in China was hindered. In 1993, regional battles such as on wool, cotton, mulberry were hardly expanded, which were later called the 'little empire economy'. They seem to be related to the financial contract system with 'The harder work, the more payment' system.

(3) In various kinds of contract system, basic figures on balance between income and expenditure, the amounts of money paid to the central government, and the amounts of subsidy etc, were decided by negotiation between central and local government. They were usually less transparent with more transaction costs. Such negotiations were always done in any case, in any way, and in any time which reached the peak at the national financial meetings in the middle of and at the end of the year.

(4) As there were too many differences in financial system among regions, problems of fairness came up to the surface. By taking Shanghai municipality directly under the central government and Guangdong province as examples, Wu (1995) compared the amounts of money paid

to the central government of the above type (IV) (Shanghai) and type (III) (Guangdong) and showed, at the end of the 1980s, 70 per cent by Shanghai and 30 per cent in Guangdong (see Table 4.2).
(5) During the financial shortage of central government with a budget deficit, depending on bank loans was kept. It accelerated remarkable inflation in China which was 18.8 per cent in 1988 and 18.0 per cent in 1989.

Table 4.2 Comparison of the amount of money paid to the central government: Shanghai and Guangdong

	Item	1987	1989	1990
Shanghai	Budget revenue (100 million yuan)	241	158	163
	Reserved money (100 million yuan)	70	49	54
	Ratio of paying to the central government	70	69	67
	Amounts of money paid to the central government(100 million Yuan	171	109	109
Guangdong	Budget revenue (100 million yuan)	93	110	129.35
	Reserved money (100 million yuan)	63.1	74.5	90.7
	Ratio of paying to the central government	32.2	32.3	30.0
	Amounts of money paid to the central government(100 million Yuan	29.9	35.5	38.7

Source: Takai and Fujino (eds) (1996), p.35.

Implementation of tax sharing system: aims, details and institutional framework

Aims

It is said that tax sharing system started in Europe in the 19th century. At the end of the Qing dynasty in China the initial experiment of tax sharing system was carried out. Nowadays most developed countries have introduced tax sharing system.

The aims of implementation of tax sharing system in China in 1990s were as following; (1) the above mentioned various bad effects were removed, (2) the tax system in China was unified, (3) negotiations among provinces (which brought about huge amount of transaction costs) were finished, (4) a central government function for income distribution to alleviate disparity was strengthened.

Details

In the 1980s, central government had a plan to reform the financial system and to introduce a tax sharing system. A policy decision section of central government tried to carry out the reform plan at the beginning of 1987 which was considered carefully for a long time about the triple reform on price, tax and budget. Macro economic circumstances to accept them were not enough. For example, a reformed plan of state owned enterprises was still ambiguous. As a matter of fact, just after the part of the draft got abroad, the triple reform plan met with strong opposition from several provinces. Finally at the end of 1986, it miscarried.

In 1990, in 'the opinions about the ten years' plan of social development and the eighth five years plan on national economy' delivered by the then prime minister Li Peng, the opinion insisted that during the eighth five years plan tax sharing system was carried out and was incorporated. In the same year the Ministry of Finance presented an intermediary experimental plan called tax sharing system and contract system.

At the beginning of 1992, after Deng Xiaoping's speech in the southern tour, a tax sharing system plan was presented once again. In the announcement of the fourteenth Chinese communist party national meeting, it was written to be 'divided allocation of tax and profit and tax sharing system will be gradually implemented'. In the same year, central government selected nine provinces, municipalities directly under the central government, and autonomous districts like Liaoning province as experimental regions for tax sharing system.

In 1993, the third general meeting of the fourteenth Chinese communist party passed 'the resolution on some serious problems of a socialist market economy', in which the reform for tax sharing system was formerly written. At the end of April in 1993, in the central government a team to reform the tax sharing system was established whose main attention was focused on institutional design for value added tax. It was because value added tax was the biggest one which occupied 43.7 per cent of total tax income and 75 per cent of circulate tax.[2] During April and August 1993, the team to reform the tax sharing system made around 40 plans leading to a final one as the central government plan. The crucial principle of the central government plan was such a mild-mannered plan it is said to be 'by protecting local benefit they attempt for a central budget to increase income in moderate way'.

To carrying out the plan, central government has to persuade each local government. For more than two months from September 9 to November 11, 1993, Zhu Rongji visited altogether 17 provinces, municipalities directly under the central government and autonomous districts leading a party of 60 members of the Bureau of Reforming Economic System, Ministry of Finance, National Bureau

2 Circulate tax means a tax whose subject is goods including value added tax, business tax, consumption tax, land value added tax, customs duty, and some other items of local tax.

of Tax, and Banks, to investigate, interpret, persuade, and negotiate. In not only advanced regions but also less developed regions they dealt with opposite views on the plan. In such provinces as Guizhou, Yunnan etc. because their local budgets largely depended upon beverage and tobacco and increased portion of consumption tax fully became central government's tax income, it undoubtedly had an effect on local financial revenue. Also in Xinjiang, as they were in a less developed region, they requested more portion of value added tax and consumption tax. After the two months negotiation, in order to respond to local governments' hard requests, they had to do a series of adjustments, compromise, and concession. However, central government officials said that basic principle of tax sharing system put up a stubborn defense. Negotiation between central and local government led to the results on tax sharing system and converged in the following three; (1) central government returned all the money of basic portion of tax income to the local government, (2) central government and local government shares respectively 75 per cent and 25 per cent of increased value added tax, (3) in order to encourage regional economic development and to collect money paid as taxes, the central government returned a fixed amount of money to local government according to an increased portion of the financial revenue of central government with an elasticity coefficient, 1 : 0.3.

Institutional framework

Details of the tax sharing system started on January 1st, 1994, were as following; (1) first was decentralization, which meant the division of service obligation and extent of financial expenditure between central and local government, (2) second was the tax sharing system indicating dividing of income between central and local government whose details showed classification of 24 taxes into the three, (I) central tax (which included value added tax, corporate income tax, and consumption tax), (II) local tax (which displayed business tax, city construction tax, tax on added cost on education, personal income tax, cultural business construction tax, and royalties etc), (III) shared tax between central and local (which expressed value added tax, three to one between central and local, stock exchange tax, fifty to fifty between central and local, business tax, and resource tax etc), (3) third was to establish a financial transfer system among governments with a certain standard. In addition to a traditional fixed amount subsidy, subsidy to particular activities, and revenue submitted from local government, according to an increased portion of central financial revenue a fixed amount of money was returned to local government with a 1:0.3 elasticity coefficient, (4) fourth was to implement drawing up a new budget system and financial regulation. Through "the higher government, the higher budget" system, it was to complete the hard budget system, (5) fifth was to establish differential regulations between national tax and local tax. A tax collection system for each national tax and local tax was formed respectively (as regards shared tax, the national tax organization first collected and then returned to the local their portion).

Problems on the current tax sharing system

The current tax sharing system has been carried out since it started 14 years ago. It is the longest lived financial system China has ever had since its foundation. For ten years from 1994 to 2003, annual average growth rate of the financial revenue was 17.4 per cent, of which the growth rate of central budget and of local budget was 16.1 per cent and 19.3 per cent respectively. Both the ratio of total financial revenue to GDP and the ratio of central financial revenue to total financial revenue were raised. The former ratio was increased to 18.4 per cent in 2006 from 12.6 per cent in 1993, and the latter was rapidly expanded as 54.94 per cent in 2004 from 22.02 per cent in 1993 (see Table 4.1).

In light of initial aims of tax sharing system, the implemented system of tax sharing left problems to be resolved (because of a Chinese gradual transition, those problems were brought about when times passed by). Institutional evolution has been pursued.

Asymmetry problem of financial authority and service obligation in local governments lower than the provincial level

Tax sharing system in 1994 was to carry out the tax sharing system and decentralization as regards financial authority and service obligation among central government and provinces. However, among provinces and the lower level local governments they could not decide any frameworks on them. The tax sharing system vertically decided under the authoritarianism reached the result saying that more authoritative higher government plundered the financial authority of lower governments' rights. Such actual transfer of financial authority among governments which showed asymmetric problems on financial authority and service obligation has made the problem more serious. It means the tendency indicating that financial authority is concentrated upwards and service obligation is shifted downwards has become clearer (see Figure 4.1).

(1) Changes on division of tax items and financial deterioration problem for basic level governments Nowadays, as regards financial relations among each level (particularly lower than provincial level) governments, legal grounds could not be created and the traditional vertical authoritarianism structure among central and local government was unchanged. They are the fundamental reasons for deterioration of the financial situation in local governments (particularly in basic level governments). The details are as following.

First, after the implementation of the tax sharing system started, some portions of tax items which were traditionally for local financial revenue (for example, fixed asset investment adjustment tax, agricultural and stock farming tax) were revoked. Meanwhile, in the tax sharing system, there were 13 kinds of local tax however such taxes as land value added tax, agriculture and livestock slaughter tax, banquet tax, and inheritance tax have been at the stage of consideration. The

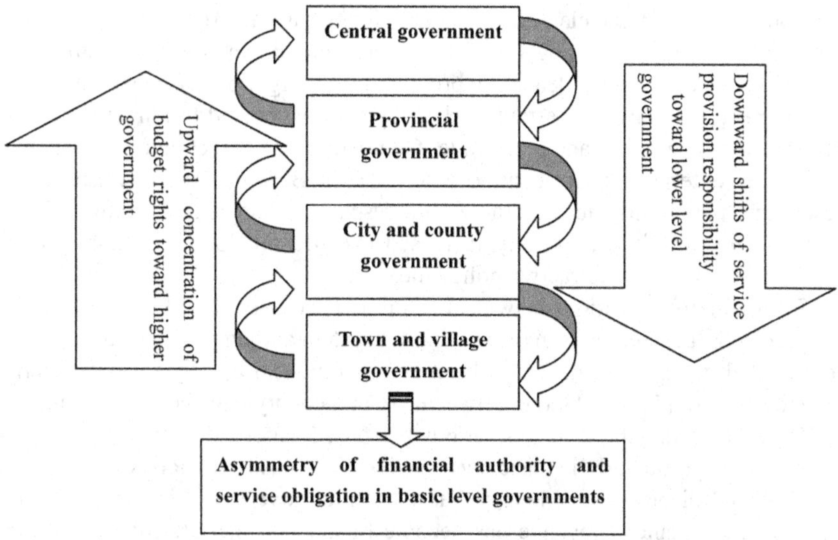

Source: Author.

Figure 4.1 Characteristics of tax sharing system led by authoritarianism

main tax items in the local tax are business tax (except the portion of overall tax payments in railway, bank head office, and insurance company), real estate tax and contact tax (which is paid by recipient in property rights transfer like real estate) etc.

Second, lots of local tax items are showing a tendency to change toward shared tax between central and local. For example, income tax was traditionally a local tax, however since 2002 it has changed to be shared tax between central and local. As of 1994 shared tax had only three which were value added tax, resource tax, and stock exchange tax, however as of 2006 it expanded to be 12. The ratio of the shared tax amount occupied to national total tax income amount increased to 70 per cent in 2003 from 55 per cent in 1994. Because of big disparity among regions in China, regional structure of tax items indicated significance. Therefore to make more tax items shared might be necessary, but expanding the ratio of shared tax might make the fundamental work of tax sharing system ineffectual as a side effect. It makes the local government budget more unstable.

Third, as shown in the stock exchange tax case, allocation of shared tax is easily expected to be more advantageous for central government. Traditionally the shared portion of stock exchange tax was fifty to fifty, but from January 1, 1997, it became to be four (central) to one (local), and in 2003 it changed to be 98 per cent (central) to two per cent (local).

Fourth, we think the classification of tax items has had problems. Because the main tax items for local budget have been corporate income tax and circulate tax (business tax and value added tax in production), it might be reasonable that local governments have tried to establish development zones and to attract capital in order to increase the financial revenue. Competition to attract enterprises is just to transfer enterprise from location A to location B, which surely wastes huge resources (particularly fertile arable land resources) and it is doubtful if local financial revenue is successfully increased (as after all local governments are burdened with various attractive policy measures).

Fifth, although relations between central and province have had some norms for their activities, relations in the tax sharing system among province (or city) and lower level government have still been ambiguous, and usually several patterns have been recognized (relations between city and county have been the same).

Because of the above stated various reasons, financial deterioration in local government (particularly in basic level government) has been more serious.

Table 4.3 displays the tendency that the central government financial revenue ratio of total financial revenue has become higher and the ratio of expenditure has become lower. It shows that central government attains the goal of financial centralization which means that local government has become substantially dependent upon central government financial transfer when local government does expenditure. The self-sufficient ratio (expressing the ratio of financial revenue to financial expenditure) of central and local government shown in Table 4.4 clearly points out the tendency.

The Ratio of central finance to overall national finance was increased to 54.9 per cent in 2002 from 22 per cent in 1993, and also provincial government expanded the ratio to 28.8 per cent in 2000 from 16.8 per cent in 1994 led by the Wang Zhenzhong (2006) calculated the self-sufficient capacity of finance reaching the following results that, for 17 years after 1987 financial self-sufficient capacity of local government was gradually decreased (especially it was remarkable after the tax sharing system was implemented). The self-sufficiency ratio for local government showed 0.59 in 2004 from 1.03 in 1987 which was four per cent less annually, of which the annual decreasing rate of the provinces was 1.6 per cent, 5.1 per cent of big city (which has county at lower level), 3.4 per cent of county, and four per cent of town.

Table 4.3 Financial revenue and expenditure for central and local government (100 billion yuan, %)

Year	Income inside budget			Expenditure inside budget			Income outside budget			Expenditure outside budget		
	Total amount	Ratio of Central	Ratio of Local	Total amount	Ratio of Central	Ratio of Local	Total amount	Ratio of Central	Ratio of Local	Total amount	Ratio of Central	Ratio of Local
1982	1212.3	28.6	71.4	1230.0	53.0	47.0	802.7	33.7	66.3	734.5	30.9	69.1
1983	1367.0	35.8	64.2	1409.5	53.9	46.1	976.7	37.2	62.8	875.8	34.3	65.7
1984	1642.9	40.5	59.5	1701.0	52.5	47.5	1181.5	39.6	60.4	1114.7	37.7	62.3
1985	2002.8	38.4	61.6	2004.3	39.7	60.3	1530.0	41.6	58.4	1375.0	40.9	59.1
1986	2122.0	36.7	63.3	2204.9	37.9	62.1	1737.3	41.2	58.8	1578.4	40.6	59.4
1987	2199.4	33.5	66.5	2262.2	37.4	62.6	2028.8	40.8	59.2	1840.8	40.3	59.7
1988	2357.2	32.9	67.1	2491.2	33.9	66.1	2360.8	38.4	61.6	2145.3	39.3	60.7
1989	2664.9	30.9	69.1	2823.8	31.5	68.5	2658.8	40.3	59.7	2503.1	39.0	61.0
1990	2937.1	33.8	66.2	3083.6	32.6	67.6	2708.6	39.6	60.4	2707.1	38.3	61.7
1991	3149.5	29.8	70.2	3386.6	32.2	67.8	3243.3	42.6	57.4	3092.3	40.9	59.1
1992	3483.4	28.1	71.9	3742.2	31.3	68.7	3854.9	44.3	55.7	1649.9	43.6	56.4
1993	4349.0	22.0	78.0	4642.3	28.3	61.7	1432.5	17.2	82.8	1314.3	15.1	84.9
1994	5218.1	55.7	44.3	5792.6	30.3	67.7	1862.5	15.2	84.8	1710.4	13.2	86.8
1995	6242.2	52.2	47.8	6823.7	29.2	70.8	2406.5	13.2	86.8	2331.3	15.1	84.9
1996	7408.0	49.4	50.6	7937.6	27.1	72.9	3893.3	24.3	75.7	3838.3	27.0	73.0
1997	8651.1	48.9	51.1	9233.6	27.4	72.6	2826.0	5.1	94.9	2685.5	5.4	94.6
1998	9876.0	49.5	50.5	10798.2	28.9	71.1	3082.3	5.3	94.7	2918.3	4.8	95.2
1999	114444.1	51.1	48.9	13187.5	31.5	68.5	3385.2	6.8	93.2	3139.1	5.3	94.7
2000	1339523	52.2	47.8	15886.5	34.7	65.3	3826.43	6.5	93.5	3529.01	6	94.03
2001	1638604	52.4	47.6	18902.58	30.5	69.5	4300	8.1	91.93	3850	6.70	93.30
2002	18903.64	55.0	45.0	22053.15	30.7	69.3	4479	9.82	90.18	3831	6.8	93.2
2003	21715.25	54.6	45.4	24649.95	30.1	69.9	4566.8	8.31	91.69	4156.36	7.92	92.08
2004	26396.47	54.9	45.1	28486.89	27.7	72.3						

Notes for Table 4.3

Notes (1): As regards income inside budget, it did not include (I) financial transfer, (II) debt income inside and outside the country, (III) debt payment and interest payment inside and outside the country, and basic construction expenditure depending upon loans from foreign countries, but it include (IV) interest payment on debt inside and outside the country after 2000.

Notes (2): As regards income outside budget, (I) the limits of the income and expenditure outside the budget were adjusted from 1993 to 1996, which were different from each year previously, and (II) after 1997 fund outside budget did not include government fund (cost collection), which could not be compared with years before.

Source: Chinese Statistical Bulletin, annual.

As a result of vertically financial plunder, the financial situation of county, town and village government has deteriorated. In a certain county of Hebei province, the following story was written in their inside document regarding "measurement explanation on financial system adjustment in county"; "when personal income tax changed from local tax to shared tax between central and local in 2002, responding to it local government like provincial power. Meanwhile, as regards lower level government than province (except province), the ratio to overall national finance was radically reduced to 17 per cent from 60 per cent.

As a result of vertically financial plunder, the self-sufficient ratio of financial situation of county, town and village government has deteriorated. According to Table 4.4, the self-sufficient ratio of such government as province, city, county, and town was increased from 1992 to 1994, but after 1994 the ratio was gradually decreased.

Provinces and cities adjust the distribution ratio as regards four tax items which were value added tax, corporate income tax, personal income tax, and business tax). Before the reform in 2002, as regards the incremental portion of the four tax items, the ratio which counties and towns had was 25 per cent of value added tax, 100 per cent of corporate and personal income tax, 100 per cent of business tax. However the ratios of them after 2002 were decreased to ten per cent of value added tax, 15 per cent of corporate income tax, 20 per cent of personal income tax, and 80 per cent of business income tax. Because total financial revenue coming from value added tax and, corporate and personal income tax occupies 86 per cent of county financial revenue, it is easily expected that after this expansion of tax income will be difficult. The financial situation of county and town governments would not be more than in 2002, or if it is increased, it might not be more than three per cent. However, it is forecasted that the financial capacity of service obligation to be necessary for economic development will be far more than present capacity (Zhang Xinguang, 2004).

(II) Lack of legal framework: downward shift of responsibility They could not have any unambiguous legal regulation on public service provision responsibility and financial expenditure, which brought about the asymmetric phenomena

Table 4.4 Self-sufficiency ratio of central and local government

	Central	Local (average)	Province level	City level	County level	Town level
1980	0.43	1.56				
1985	0.97	1.02				
1990	0.99	0.94				
1991	0.86	0.96	0.61	1.32	0.71	1.35
1992	0.84	0.97				
1993	0.73	1.02	0.68	1.36	0.78	1.4
1994	1.66	0.59				
1995	1.63	0.62	0.48	0.72	0.48	0.95
1996	1.7	0.65	0.54	0.73	0.49	1
1997	1.67	0.65	0.54	0.73	0.5	1
1998	1.57	0.65				
1999	1.41	0.62				
2000	1.27	0.61				
2001	1.49	0.59				
2002	1.53	0.56				
2003	1.6	0.57				
2004	1.84	0.59				

Note: Self-sufficient ratio means the ratio of financial revenue to financial expenditure. Local (average) indicates the average value of province, city, county and town.

Source: *Chinese Statistical Bulletin*, annual.

between them. It has caused the tendency expressing an upward movement of financial authority and downward movement of service provision given by government.

Since the end of the 1990s, state owned enterprises with deficits have become a serious burden for each level government and jurisdiction over most of them has been in the lower level local governments' hands. It might be a kind of shifting of the responsibility. Central government sometimes came out with policy (for example, policy to raise the monthly salary of government employees), however because the policies had no (or insufficient) financial capability, local government finally had to take on more serious financial burden.

(III) Disorder of administrative organization lower than province: inside circumstances of administrative district change in counties and, towns and villages The Chinese constitution says that in local governments there have been three levels, which are province, city and county, town and village. Actually however there has existed municipality between province and, city and county (see chapter one and two on the history of municipality). Accompanied by development of urbanization, many counties and cities of county level belonging to cities of local level were changed to be districts controlled by cities which were

controlled by cities of local level. Also towns and villages were changed to be sub-district bureaus in urban area. Although it is due to urbanization, a more deep-rooted reason existed in the battle for financial authority. Financial authority of counties and cities of county level are directly controlled by the province, however the districts controlled by cities are controlled by cities of local level. The changes of districts in towns and villages have been the same which indicate that towns and villages have independent financial authority but sub-district bureaus are not first rank government but branch organization. They are described in *Liao Wang Dong Fang Zhou Kan* (*Weekly Journal of Eastern Region*), on April 7, 2004, about the arena on "abolishing city and establishing district" battles which happened in the middle of the 1990s and lasted for more than ten years between Taizhou (municipality), Zhejiang province, and Huangyan (city of county level). Such conflicts as on financial authority and administrative permission rights among local governments without legal framework had substantial impacts on the regional economy. (In the example above, after Huangyan changed from a city of county level to a district, economic development of the region has undoubtedly decreased). After Huangyan was adjusted from a city of county level to a district, they continued to request autonomous authority and due to compromise of Taizhou in 2003 the battles finally reached convergence which said that Huangyan could keep autonomous financial authority and administrative permission rights even if Huangyan was a district.

Financial transfer pattern led by administrative power: without norm problem and regional disparity

Initially one of the purposes of implementing a tax sharing system was to alleviate economic disparity in China (like regional disparity and income disparity etc.) through redistribution by fiscal policy. It was recognized there were significant problems with it. Even under the tax sharing system huge scale financial transfer from central government was carried out, but regional disparity problems were still serious.

(I) Structure of items in financial transfer from central government Items of financial transfer from central government under the tax sharing system includes "return of tax income", "subsidy for former financial system", "subsidy for accounts" which are a compromise with the traditional system. Financial transfer in a true sense is classified into general financial transfer and financial transfer for particular purpose, but the present situation to operate has many problems. The structure of items in financial transfer from central government shows the following five (see Figure 4.2).

i. First is return for tax income, which occupies the biggest ratio of financial transfer. The amount of return for tax income in 1994 for example was

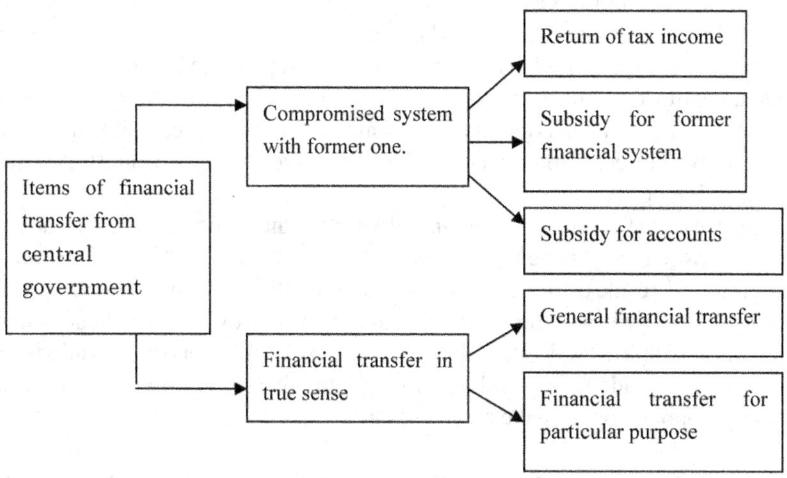

Source: Author.

Figure 4.2 Structure of items in financial transfer from central government

calculated depending upon the amount of 1993. The basic amount of two big local taxes (consumption tax and value added tax) are calculated with the following equation.

$$R=C+0.75V-S$$

where R means the basic amount of return for tax income, C shows consumption tax income, V indicates value added tax income, S points out transfer income between central and local government. For the year after 1994, the amount of return for tax income is calculated to be included as following; in addition to the basic amount of previous year, an incremental portion is calculated by an elasticity coefficient with 1: 0.3. The equation for calculation is,

$$R_n = R_{n-1}\left(1+0.3\frac{(C+0.75V)_n-(C+0.75V)_{n-1}}{(C+0.75V)_{n-1}}\right)$$

The financial transfer system as it is a return for tax income is to keep traditional former system, and because the richer region can get more, it is understood that the redistribution function actually does not work.

According to Table 4.5, financial revenue of China in 1993 equaled 434.9 billion yuan, which recorded a remarkable growth rate, 24.8 per cent. It was not only more than 10.6 per cent in 1992 and 7.23 per cent in 1991 but also five per cent more than the year after 1994, 19.99 per cent. The main reason for the remarkable growth was due to the above mentioned tax sharing system. That is to say, each local region tried to collect tax as much as possible in order to expand the basic amount of 1993. There were such several cases as additional collection of nonpaid tax, beforehand collection from enterprises of next year's tax, the possible reason of which seems to be relations between government and enterprises during the transition period.

What was the reason why the initial year for the basic amount was not 1992 but 1993 when the financial year was not finished at that time? This was the compromised result of the central government with local government (in which first opposite view was presented by Guangdong province the most benefited province of reform and open door policy). Although opposite opinions were insisted upon inside the central government, the then prime minister Zhu Rongji overcame opposition to make a concession.

ii. Second is the fixed amount subsidy, which points out that, when local financial revenue is below the expenditure, central government subsidizes it. It is the same system as general financial transfer of foreign countries. In China this has less weight in the financial system. In 2005 in China, the ratio of general financial transfer to total amount of financial transfer in a wide sense (including return for tax income and subsidy for former financial system) and in a narrow sense (excluding return for tax income and subsidy for former financial system) was only 9.8 per cent and 15.3 per cent respectively.
iii. Third is various conditional particular purpose transfers of finance, for which a supervisory section has an influential voice. Under the current system, they are several hundred kinds and they reach several hundred million yuan annually. They include for example relief funds to natural disaster, aid for less developed areas etc. Such financial transfer money in drawing up the budget of central government could not be used for any other purposes except the previously determined one. The ratio of particular purpose transfer of finance to total amount of financial transfer in a wide sense and in a narrow sense in 2005 was 30.73 per cent and 48.07 per cent respectively, both of which occupied high ratios.
iv. Fourth is subsidy for accounts. It shows that, at the end of financial year, the portion of the loss for local government during the financial year due to enterprises related and new policy related was subsidized by central government.
v. Fifth is subsidy for the former financial system. Since before 1994, central government has established subsidies for local governments of various levels for a certain period of transition. In 2005, the ratio of the total amount of return for tax income and subsidy for the former financial system to total amount of financial system in a wide sense was 36.08 per cent, which was higher than the ratio of particular purpose transfer of finance (30.73 per cent).

The problem China has faced is that, as the basic amount for return for tax revenue was based upon local tax revenue in 1993, each province had undoubtedly a different base. Also as regards the fixed amount subsidy, the basic amount for it was depending upon a certain year in the past, thus there still has existed a problem saying that 'both ratio and amount vary from one province to another'. The deep-rooted origin of the without norm financial transfer surely seems to be closely related with an administration led development system.

(II) Scale of budget transfer from central government With the tax sharing system, the budget transfer amount from central government was much expanded. The amount in 1990 equaled about 58.5 billion yuan, which was raised to 466.5 billion yuan in 2000 and rapidly increased to 826.1 billion yuan in 2003 (see Table 4.5).

(III) Financial transfer pattern led by administrative power: problems and Expression In China, legal grounds for financial transfer from central government have still been ambiguous. The Chinese Ministry of Finance decided on 'the scheme of expenditure by financial transfer during the transition period'. After the tax sharing system has been carried out, the ratio of financial transfer to local financial expenditure has become rapidly higher, which recorded 41.2 per cent in 1994, and after then gradually decreased to 29.4 per cent in 2000, and afterward tended to increase again. In 2005, local general budget revenue of the whole of China was 1,487.6 billion yuan and local general budget expenditure reached 2,502.2 billion yuan. That is to say, around 40.6 per cent of local general budget expenditure depended upon various financial transfers from central government.

When a huge amount of financial transfer is carried out, these regulations could not deal effectively with the transfer. After 1994, due to lack of legal grounds, the financial transfer pattern led by administrative power has become usual. The details have been reported as following.

(I) Priority for sectional benefit: diversion problem of financial fund At the end of 2002, although the budget balance of 129 central sections recorded 64.6 billion yuan, when the Ministry of Finance settled the balance in 2003, they included only 5.7 billion yuan in their sectional balance and the rest, 58.9 billion yuan, was as a matter of fact settled in each government section. In 2003, the total amount of the basic construction fund in the central budget (which the national development and reform committee controlled) was 16.2 billion yuan, of which 7.6 billion yuan (shared 25 per cent of the total) was settled inside the section. The defense and science industry committee also settled 6.3 billion yuan inside the section which occupied 38.8 per cent of the total budget and was 16.2 billion yuan.

According to the 2003 account of financial fund expenditure situation by the national board of audit, of 19 financial transfer items for particular purpose, the

Table 4.5 The scale of budget transfer from central government (100 million yuan, %)

Year	Consolidated revenue								Consolidated expenditure							
			Central government total revenue								Central government total expenditure					
	Amount	Growth rate	Amount	Growth rate	Revenue from central level government	Growth rate	Revenue from submitting of local government	Growth rate	Amount	Growth rate	Amount	Growth rate	Expenditure from central level government	Growth rate	Expenditure for Allocation to local government	Growth rate
1990	2937.10		1474.61		992.42		482.19		3083.59		1589.75		1004.47		585.28	
1991	3149.48	7.23	1428.55	-3.12	938.25	-5.46	490.30	1.68	3386.62	9.83	1645.56	3.51	1090.81	8.60	554.75	-5.22
1992	3483.37	10.60	1538.15	7.67	979.51	4.40	558.64	13.94	3742.20	10.50	1766.94	7.38	1170.44	7.30	596.50	7.53
1993	4348.95	24.85	1557.82	1.28	957.51	-2.25	600.31	7.46	4642.30	24.05	1856.69	5.08	1312.06	12.10	544.63	-8.70
1994	5218.10	19.99	3476.55	123.17	2906.50	203.55	570.05	-5.04	5792.62	24.78	4143.52	123.17	1754.43	33.72	2389.09	338.66
1995	6242.20	19.63	3866.63	11.22	3256.62	12.05	610.01	7.01	6823.72	17.80	4529.45	9.31	1995.39	13.73	2534.06	6.07
1996	7407.99	18.68	4264.95	10.30	3661.07	12.42	603.88	-1.00	7937.55	16.32	4873.79	7.60	2151.27	7.81	2722.52	7.44
1997	8651.14	16.78	4830.72	13.27	4226.92	15.46	603.80	-0.01	9233.56	16.33	5389.17	10.57	2532.50	17.72	2856.67	4.93
1998	9875.95	14.16	5489.13	13.63	4892.00	15.73	597.13	-1.10	10798.18	16.94	6447.14	19.63	3125.60	23.42	3321.54	16.27
1999	11444.08	15.88	6447.34	17.46	5849.21	19.57	598.13	0.17	13187.67	22.13	8238.94	27.79	4152.33	32.85	4086.61	23.03
2000	13395.23	17.05	7588.29	17.70	6989.17	19.49	599.12	0.17	15886.50	20.46	10185.16	23.62	5519.85	32.93	4665.31	14.16
2001	16386.04	22.33	9173.70	20.89	8582.74	22.80	590.96	-1.36	18902.58	18.99	11769.97	15.56	5768.02	4.50	6001.95	28.65
2002	18903.64	15.36	11026.60	20.20	10388.64	21.04	637.96	7.95	22053.15	16.67	14123.47	20.00	6771.70	17.40	7351.77	22.49
2003	21715.25	14.87	12483.83	13.22	11865.27	14.21	618.56	-3.04	24649.95	11.78	15681.51	11.03	7420.10	9.58	8261.41	12.37

Note for Table 4.5

Note: Revenue in this table excludes the foreign and domestic debts revenue, expenditure excludes payment for the principal and interest of foreign and domestic debts and expenditure for capital construction financed by foreign debts.

Source: Ministry of Finance (People's Republic of China), http://www.mof.gov.cn/1162.htm.

total fund amount which was poorly controlled reached 11.2 billion yuan. In 11 of the 19, they found the changes in the use of fund, whose amount was 3.3 billion yuan (adjustment ratio reached 11 per cent). From the financial transfer fund which was controlled by 41 central sections, 1.4 billion yuan was diverted to be used for housing for personnel, plus various allowances etc.

(II) "Soft budget" problem for the government Weakening of the local assembly means weakening of the supervising system for local government. Regardless of local or central government, it cannot help indicating an institutional problem that governmental organization has existed out of the supervision by assembly and parliament. This is closely connected with the system led by administrative power. In other words, it is an important characteristic feature of an authoritarianism development system. Not only the above mentioned sections of central government but also the variety of local governments at each respective level have manifested an imperfect supervision system. According to the inspection of 17 provinces by the national board of audit, in the 2002 settlement of accounts at provincial level, they were recorded to be 93.6 billion yuan as subsidy revenue from central government which occupied only 22.5 per cent of the actual total subsidy amount 414.9 billion yuan. Four provinces did not include subsidy revenue from central government at all.

Also as mentioned above, because basic governments of county and town level have suffered from a serious budget deficit, the financial transfer fund for particular purpose from central government has been usually used to cover the deficit. In a certain poor county of Dabieshan, of the total financial transfer fund from central for ten years, of 240 million yuan, 60 per cent of them were used to compensate for the budget deficit (Zhang Xinguang, 2004).

(III) Derived problems caused by enormous free discretion rights in the financial transfer fund for particular purpose As regards the financial transfer fund for particular purpose, authority to examine, control and allocate them is so widely spreading that the duplicated control overlapping each other is remarkable. In 2002, in order to improve the environment in education of elementary and junior high schools, the central government financial section transferred the finance with ten particular purposes. The controlling sections were spreading over such sections as the Ministry of Finance, Ministry of Education, former National Planning Committee (at present Reform and Development Committee) etc. Also regarding

Table 4.6 Local financial expenditure, financial transfer, and the ratio (100 million yuan, %)

Year	Local Financial Expenditure (A)	Financial Transfer (B)	Ratio (B/A) (%)
1990	3083.6	585.28	19.0
1991	3386.6	554.75	16.4
1992	3742.2	596.50	15.9
1993	4642.3	544.63	11.7
1994	5792.6	2389.09	41.2
1995	6823.7	2534.06	37.1
1996	7937.6	2722.52	34.3
1997	9233.6	2856.67	30.9
1998	10798.2	3321.54	30.8
1999	13187.5	4086.61	31.0
2000	15886.5	4665.31	29.4
2001	18902.58	6001.95	31.8
2002	22053.15	7351.77	33.3
2003	24649.95	8261.41	33.5
2005	25022.2	10146.7	40.6

Source: calculated by Table 4.3 and Table 4.5.

the financial transfer on a relief fund for natural disasters, it had 15 items (whose amount equaled 4.1 billion yuan), and the controlling sections were spreading over the Ministry of Finance, former National Planning Committee, Ministry of Civil Administration (on labor and public welfare), Ministry of Agriculture, Ministry of Education. As far as the controlling items for each ministry is concerned, the actual system to control them was further spreading over more divisions within each ministry.[3]

Of all the amount of the financial transfer fund from central government in 2003 which reached around 800 billion yuan (whose ratio to central financial expenditure and to local financial expenditure was 52.7 per cent and 50 per cent respectively), the amount of return of tax revenue equaled about 300 billion yuan and the amount which played a real redistribution function by central government reached the vicinity of 500 billion yuan. The financial transfer was further classified into general transfer expenditure and transfer expenditure for particular purposes.

General transfer expenditure has been carried out with some norms, but as regards transfer expenditure for particular purposes, we can indicate various

3 From the report presented by the head of National Board of Audit, Li Jinhua, at the Third Meeting of National Parliament, see New China net on June 25, 2003.

problems. In 2003, for example, the amount of expenditures unaccounted in transfer expenditure for particular purposes was about 230 billion yuan.

Because of the lack of norms in financial transfer, there have been subjectivity and arbitrariness everywhere in government offices and bureaucrats. The funds without norm easily bring about ample scope for sectional benefits and give rise to corruption for self benefits by bureaucrats. For example, to take a bribe from transferred governments under the pretext of controlling cost has occurred frequently. In addition to the above, in order to get the fund money, local governments in each level have opened the Beijing representative bureau and have competition in entertainment among bureaucrats. The tax sharing system started in 1994 has changed the main player to take the initiative from local government to central government through centralization of financial authority. Local governments therefore have been forced to depend upon central government offices which represent sectional benefits.

There is competition to get fund money, but less developed regions usually have lower power to petition, thus they get less financial transfer money. As a result, the current system has a possibility to make the disparity among regions more serious. For example, in 2002, when the Ministry of Finance allocated fund money to construct elementary and junior high schools and to social security, they gave subsidy money to developed regions and developed units beyond the extent regulated by national documents, which amounted to 500 million yuan. Regarding the three items of social security funds, they subsidized 408 million yuan to four provinces by violating the rules. Besides as regards the subsidy to construct special schools of vocational education, even the rules say the priority to subsidize is given to less developed regions such as the central western region and farming area, of the total 44.5 million yuan given to ten schools, 25 million yuan (reached 56 per cent) was subsidized for two schools in more developed regions.

Also when financial transfer was implemented, it was done even when they did not have enough research and did not have enough information on present circumstances. In 2002, for example, in wage subsidies to simplify administrative organization, although a certain province did not carry out any organizational reforms in lower than city level administrations, the Ministry of Finance transferred 590 million yuan to them as wage subsidies, all of which were used to compensate for a provincial budget deficit.[4]

Sectional benefit priority or financial situation without appropriate supervision as mentioned above has become usual under the development system led by governments. Those seem to be necessary outcomes.

Incomplete problems on tax revenue rights of local government

On the tax revenue rights of local government, they include legislative power, collective power, interpretation power, reduction and exemption etc. In China

4 The same report by Li Jinhua as note 3 of Chapter 4.

however, the tax revenue rights of local government have been limited to collection of local taxes. It could be pointed out that with such limited power active policies by local governments are seriously damaged. However, under the soft budget system on financial funds, if local governments are given such rights as establishing new taxes and issuing local government bonds, it is extremely difficult to think who is supervising and who is responsible.

Problems and social effects of relations among governments with tax sharing system

Problems of relations among government

(I) A boom tendency in the 'Beijing representative bureau' phenomena Under the present tax sharing system in which lower governments petition higher governments, it is inevitable to have conflicts on funds and loans between lower and higher level governments. As stated above, the lower local governments, have lower self-sufficient financial power and are the more dependent upon higher governments. The greater part of financial transfer from central government is concentrated upon provincial government. As after that in accordance with administrative channel it is allocated to lower government, it is often robbed and misappropriated during the transfer. It has become characteristic political scenery in China that, in order to get the funds, each province establishes the bureau in Beijing and each government like city and county opens the bureau at the capital city of the province.

At the beginning of 2006, a secretary of the Chinese communist party central committee for discipline inspection, Wu Guanzheng, put his finger a good three times on the various kinds of corruption that happened at the Beijing representative office of local government at the Sixth general meeting of the central committee for discipline. After then the Chinese cabinet executive bureau for administration convened executives of the Beijing representative bureau of local government and held the meeting on political activity of integrity. At the meeting, they decided that the Chinese cabinet executive bureau for administration would submit concrete policy measures for them, however as of 2007, no concrete measure has been submitted (Zhang Xiangdong and Gou Xinyu, 2006).

The history of the 'Beijing representative bureau' dated back to the 1950s. In the central planning era, they did nothing unless they had the details of the central authority's view. However, in the transition days these phenomena have deteriorated. In Beijing in 1991 more than 186 Beijing representative bureaus of higher than city government level were established and after the tax sharing system started in 1994 the number of them have rapidly increased. In 2006, in addition to 52 local governments of higher than deputy provincial level (which indicate ordinance-designated cities,[5] Shanghai Pudong New Area etc. counted altogether 11), 520 city level local governments, more than 5,000 county level local governments have established Beijing representative bureaus. If including such liaison offices as sections of each province, various governmental and non-governmental associations, state owned enterprises, universities etc., the number of them seems to be more than 10,000. Recently, not only state owned enterprises but also large-scale private enterprises have sent employees assigned to the Beijing representative bureau.[6]

The tendency towards Beijing representative bureau phenomena was closely connected with the time when the tax sharing system was carried out in 1994. The main purposes of the representative bureau are (1) to establish a human network with each section of the Chinese cabinet in order for the convenience of getting administrative permission and various burdens (especially for financial transfer for particular purposes), (2) to entertain executives who visit Beijing from their districts, (3) to send back the people to visit Beijing from their hometown to make complaints etc.

A fundamental reason for the boom of Beijing representative bureaus seems to be a transformation of governmental functions. As far as in China the tax sharing system was implemented and both an upward shift of financial authority and without norm of financial transfer are recognized, it is necessary for local government to have an effect through the Beijing representative bureau. In taking macro economic adjustment policies, they have attempted to do a policy mix of 'administrative', 'legal', and 'economic' measures; however the main tool of them has been the administrative ones. It is remarkably observed that each functional section of the Cabinet has tried to expand its own self interest. After China joined the WTO (World Trade Organization), they have employed one after another such regulations as 'platforms to fully promote the administration under legislative control', 'administrative permission law'. 'public servant law', it has been difficult to actually carry these out. For example, formerly, they passed the regulation saying that provisions which are legally permitted by administration are changed to be examined and recorded, however each central section has never wished to lay beneficial provisions aside or it has established additional administrative permitted items accompanied with macro economic controls.

When they try to find deeper-rooted reasons, they easily recognize that there is no supervising power against administrative authority. Recently, the Chinese mass media have endeavored to expose various affairs, but the mass media have no authority to punish them. Although normally the Chinese National Parliament should play this role, it should be said that the National Parliament is rather

5 They are about the same as Japanese ordinance-designated cities.

6 Statement by Bao Yujun, the president of the Chinese Private Economy Research Association, at the 59th International Forum of Chinese (Hainan) Reform and Development Research Institute, see *JinJiGuanChaBao* (*Economic Observers' Report*), November, November 27, 2006.

helpless. Also because party organization has been unified to administration, it is doubtful whether or not they can actually supervise.

As the Chinese economy has been growing, the corruption perception index (CPI, which is reported by Transparency International as *Global Corruption Report*, annually) has been deteriorated. Of altogether 163 countries and regions, China was the 66th rank in 2003, which became lower at 78th in 2005, and was a little better in 2006 as the 70th rank.

The East Asian model shows that shared growth has been the origin for legitimacy of an authoritarianism system. For China it has been said to be the same. However, at present, corruption has become a serious obstacle to realize the goal of shared growth. We think it has been a very important task in the institutional design that they incorporate any effective supervisions and restrictions against government organizations through a separation of powers.

(II) The accumulated debt problems of basic level governments in rural areas As far as the actual situation in which the financial authority is concentrated upon higher and service obligation, the responsibility is shifted onto lower level and it has been reflected as the accumulated debt problem for the most basic local governments (county and lower towns and villages).

County and, town and village governments are in the bottom position of the administrative structure, and in the most serious asymmetry of financial authority and service responsibility. As regards (1) service responsibility, county and, town and village governments have responsibility in many services like compulsory education, public health, infrastructure construction, social security, militiamen training, welfare service for particular purpose, environmental protection, administrative control etc. Especially, in the compulsory education which central and provincial governments usually should have more responsibility, such level governments have done less expenditure. Expenditure on the compulsory education in urban area has been assured by the national budget, meanwhile the compulsory education expenditure in rural area has been covered by towns and villages' budget after all. For around ten years from 1990 to 2000, in the education expenditure of Xiangyang county Hubei province, each level of financial expenditure occupied 40.7 per cent, of which towns and villages' expenditure shared 34.6 per cent, county expenditure 6.25 per cent and more higher than province only 0.1 per cent (Chen Xiwen, 2003, p.19).

Regarding the financial authority, after the commune system collapsed, in 1985 a financial system of towns and villages was established in the whole of China. The financial revenue has consisted of funds inside the national budget, funds outside the national budget, and funds in their hands. The funds inside the national budget include corporate income tax, livestock slaughter tax, city maintenance and construction tax, market transaction tax, vehicles number plate tax, contract tax distributed by higher rank government, meanwhile the funds outside the national budget show agricultural added costs and official business added costs distributed by higher rank government. Until 2004, the main financial revenue consisted of the three which were agricultural tax and added costs, fund finance for each provision, and financial transfer from central government. However, after 2004, the situation has been changed.

In March 2004, Prime Minister Wen Jiabao made a declaration in the government policy report at the second meeting of the Tenth National Parliament that from 2004 step by step the rate of agricultural tax would be reduced by one per cent in annual average to become zero within five years. At the end of 2005, in 28 provinces they were already exempted from agricultural tax. In 2006 the "agricultural tax ordinance" was formally abolished. For example, in Ningxia autonomous district, after the agricultural tax was exempted in 2005, the per capita peasant's burden has been 20 yuan less.

Also after agricultural tax was exempted, various agricultural added costs could not be collected. According to the *Chinese Financial Statistical Bulletin*, before agricultural tax was exempted in 2002 and 2003, total revenue from agricultural tax in the whole of China reached 71.8 billion yuan and 87.2 billion yuan respectively, of which the three agricultural taxes (agricultural tax, stock peasants' tax, and agricultural special products tax) occupied 50-60 billion yuan. However, expenditure to maintain basic farming administration was much more than the amount and the origin of the fund was to collect various added costs closely connected with the agricultural tax. Therefore, the amount which central government should transfer after agricultural tax was exempted has become 160-180 billion yuan. That is about three times more than agricultural tax income. As a matter of fact, the financial transfer amount from central government was 66.2 billion yuan (26 per cent more than the year before) in 2005, and since 2006 78.2 billion yuan has been transferred every year. When including financial transfers from each level of local government, the total amount of financial transfer in 2006 reached 103 billion yuan. However, because, in addition to the limited amount of financial transfer, some portion of the money has been usually robbed by higher level government, it might be inevitable that the financial ability of rural areas is remarkably reduced.

As Table 4.7 indicates, after 1998 both ratios of financial revenue and expenditure occupied by towns and villages to the whole province of Shandong have been reduced. Moreover the ratio of revenue tends to be more than the ratio of expenditure, which shows that such local regions as towns and villages are in an unfavorable position for distribution of financial transfer.

At present, we understand that both proceedings and regulations in rural area are ambiguous, the income of peasants is low, and the way of one item and one discussion cannot contribute to infrastructure construction in rural areas. Even it is said that in China there has been a peasant's self-governing system, the function of it varies from one system to another and lots of peasant's committees cannot work at all (especially in poor regions). Also it might become a problem with the consistency between peasant's self-governing committee whose member is selected by direct election and the higher government of towns and villages. When village executives are seriously worrying whether they prefer peasants' intentions or direction by higher government, they often prefer higher government's direction because the higher government has financial authority. We should say that a peasant's self-governing system which is inconsistent with financial authority, service obligation, personnel authority, has by nature many defects.

In addition to the above, relations between peasant's self-governing committee and the party branch of the village have been delicate. The party branch of the village has to follow upper level administration (that is to say party committee of town and village). The organization act of the peasant's committee (revised in 1998) also specifies that the roles of the party branch of the village are protector and supervisor in carrying out peasant's autonomy system. The two jobs above are difficult to be compatible. The upper level town and village government and party committee tends to support and strengthen the party branch of the village as they wish to control the village more than at the present time. Actually however a peasant's self-governing committee has appeared to divide the power of the traditional party organization of the village. It is naturally thus a tense relationships between them that has been brought about. Then which is recognized to have more authority, the head of peasant's self-governing committee or the party branch secretary of the village? According to a questionnaire survey to heads of peasant's self-governing committees implemented in Zhejiang province in 1998, only 15.3 per cent of the response said that the head of the committee was more authorized than the party branch secretary because the head was selected by direct election. To the contrary, 55.9 per cent of the response answered that the party branch secretary was more authorized than the head of the committee

Table 4.7 The financial situation of Towns and Villages in Shandong Province (10 thousand yuan, %)

	Total financial revenue of Shandong province	Total financial expenditure of Shandong province	TV level revenue	TV level expend-iture	Self sufficient ratio of TV	Ratio of revenue of TV to the whole province	Ratio of expend-iture of TV to the whole province
1998	3523912	4878175	832245	919644	0.90	23.62	18.9
1999	4044829	5500034	1305613	—		24.3	—
2000	4636788	6130774	1022660	1179892	0.87	22.1	19.2
2001	5731793	7537781	1220782	1410166	0.87	21.3	18.7
2002	6102242	8606484	1266068	1693192	0.75	20.7	19.7
2003	7137877	10106395	1509750	1864671	0.81	21.2	18.45
2004	8283306	11893716	1443496	2085945	0.69	17.43	17.53
2005	10731250	14662271	1829933	2305746	0.79	17.05	15.73

Note: TV means towns and villages.

Source: As regards figures of 1998-2003, Yin (2004),p.48, and figure of 2004-2005, see tables of Financial settlement of accounts of Shandong province.

because the communist party was the center of leadership. At the same time, a questionnaire to executives of town and village government, asking if the head of the peasant's self-governing committee who was selected by direct election came under pressure to the party branch secretary of village, indicated that 61.7 per cent of executives said 'no' and 37.5 per cent said 'yes' (Lang Youxing and Lang Yougen, 2005). In that sense, peasant's self-governing system in China might be said to be '30 per cent autonomy'[7]. Also, third, there are still no legal grounds for final decision-making authority which is head of the committee or party branch secretary. For example, the organization act of peasant's committee (revised in 1998) prescribes that the 'basic level organization in villages of the Chinese communist party should play central leading roles based on the charter of the communist party' (article three). Such provision has possibility actually for peasant's autonomous system to become a mere name. The party branch of the village has tried to control policy decision authority in various ways. Fourth, as peasant's autonomous system has been implemented for many years, new changes have appeared. For example, a reverse pattern came into existence. It meant that a person who was elected as a head of a peasant's self-governing committee was selected as a party branch secretary of the village. According to an official party document of Weihai city (Shandong province), they decided a regulation saying that, the party branch secretary was not only encouraged to compete for the post of head of the peasant's self-governing committee but also, when the branch secretary fails, he or she could not be reappointed to the post of branch secretary. Similar rules have been provided in the whole nation. Meanwhile, the civil administration section of respective level government could not straightforwardly oppose the tendency towards unification of party and administration because of a promoting institution of peasant's autonomy, but has shown a cold attitude against it.

In 2003, the ex-US President, Jimmy Carter gave a speech saying that 'in my own observation, peasant's election in China has already had remarkable success.'[8] Although it might be too early to finally conclude, the author positively appreciates the above stated tendency of pressure that the party branch secretary has to take the office of head of the peasant's self-governing committee by fair competition. The reason why the author positively appreciates this is that the tendency has similarity with the Taiwanese case of professional technocrats as it is described in Chapter 6. Party organizations are in a position to appoint capable executive bureaucrats. In the long run, we conclude that only able persons who have thorough knowledge of socio-economic management of regions should be concerned in party executives. That is a concrete expression of the 'East Asian model' in which a gradual way of transition is going through the process.

---

7 Because around two thirds of sources of revenue of local government depended upon financial transfer from central government, the Japanese local autonomy system was derided as '30 per cent autonomy' for many years.

8 Speech at Peking University on September 9, 2003, entitled "From May 4th Movement to village elections: China's quest for democracy."

It is the current situation that because of poor financial authority and a less developed regional economy, lots of towns and villages gain few funds. At most they can pay civil servant's salaries. They cannot afford to build to agricultural infrastructure construction and maintenance, environmental protection, social security, anti-poverty measures. After all, the ways left for the lowest level government in rural areas are, to cover the shortage money, (1) by cutting down on services normally provided, (2) by borrowing money illegally, (3) by going to land finance, or (4) by exploiting peasants with various measures.

Therefore, the accumulated debt problems for the lowest level local government (like county, lower towns and villages) have been serious. We can have a short look at an example of Jiangxi province located in the central region. According to a research carried out in the 1,759 towns and villages (total number of them was 1,930) within Jiangxi province at the end of 1998, financial revenue of towns and villages in the year 1998 amounted to 4.12 billion yuan, total credit amount equaled 1.8 billion yuan and the total debt amount reached 4.7 billion yuan, and debt amount per town and village was 2.7 million yuan (except average credit amount per town and village which was 997 thousand yuan, the average debt amount reached 1671 thousand yuan). The number of towns with no debt was only 37, with less than one million debts shared 48.3 per cent, with less than one to two million debts shared 6.1 per cent. The debt structure of towns and villages indicated as (1) loan and interest payment from bank, and credit unions (whose ratio was 29.95 per cent), (2) loan and interest payment from enterprises and private persons (which shared 28.7 per cent), (3) security for enterprises under the control (whose ratio was 21.8 per cent), and (4) other arrears (which shared 19. 6 per cent). Those accumulated debts became far beyond repayment possibility to most towns and villages' governments which actually collapsed (Xiao Tangbiao, 2004).

A research about peasants' burden in all 81 counties reported that average net debt amount reached 7.08 million yuan (Zhang Xiuying and Liu Jinling, 2004, p.17). A research team of the 'financial situation of counties and towns, and peasants' income increase' at the cabinet development research center, which investigated Xiangyang county (Hubei province), Yanling county (Henan province), Taihe county (Jiangxi province), said that; (1) the financial situation of Taihe county showed the best of all the three counties, even which was typically depending on finance. It barely managed to cover civil servant's wage, (2) the economy of Yanling county was so serious that they could not pay civil servant's wage and they could not provide any public service, (3) the economic situation of Xiangyang county can be expressed only as beggar finance which has been the worst. Moreover, because basic government's confidence has radically become much less, it is difficult to borrow money (Chen Xiwen, 2003, p.17).

In 2002 the National Board of Audit had an inspection of 49 counties (cities) of ten provinces in the central western region, whose result said that the accumulated deficit in the 49 counties (cities) equaled 16.3 billion yuan and reached 2.1 times more than available financial revenue in 2002. At the end of September 2002, 42 counties (cities) out of the 49 experienced altogether 1.8 billion yuan overdue wages, which was equivalent to around three times more than overdue wages at the end of 1998.[9]

On economic and social influence

(I) Generalization of dependence upon land finance of local government Given the background of the continued development zone boom and real estate development boom which has been heated since 2003, there has existed "an asymmetry of financial authority and service obligation" which local governments have shouldered after tax sharing system was carried out.

According to an investigation by the Development Research Center of the Cabinet, in 2003 land conveyance revenue of Shaoxing, Zhejiang province, reached 1.92 billion yuan which occupied 69.3 per cent of revenue outside the budget. The land conveyance revenue of Jinhua, Zhejiang province was around 2 billion yuan, whose ratio to the revenue outside budget reached 60 per cent. However, we should indicate other background factors than tax sharing system on dependent phenomena upon land finance of local government, which are shown later.

(II) Enterprises and citizens (peasants in particular) have become victims of illegal tax burdens Table 4.8 points out the growth rate of funds outside the budget of local government in 1996-2003. Revenue outside the budget includes administrative service cost, government type fund, and land conveyance. Accompanied with reforming the revenue outside the budget, the norm in collecting tax becomes necessary. However, it has never been improved.

The current situation has given us doubt if fundamental policy for central government to alleviate peasants burden is realistic. That is to say, even without agricultural tax, they should be worried that various types of illegal tax collection would be rampant. Recently, it has been changed so that compulsory education costs are expended by county budget not by towns and villages budget. However, because of poor county revenue, finance of compulsory education costs have still been heavily dependent upon added costs for education paid by peasants although financial transfer has been partly implemented.

The ratios shown in the previous Table 4.3 on fund revenue and fund expenditure between central and local government point out that local government occupied much more ratios in both of them. As regards the ratio of local government and central government on the fund revenue outside the budget, they were 33.7 per cent and 66.3 per cent respectively in 1982, which were changed to 92.08 per cent and 7.92 per cent in 2003 (although, as from 1997 some portions of fund outside the budget have changed, it is impossible to simply compare them but we

9 The same report by Li Jinhua as note 3 of Chapter 4.

Table 4.8 Growth rate of revenues outside the budget of local government (1996-2003) (100 million yuan, %)

	1996	1997	1998	1999	2000	2001	2002	2003
Actual result	2945.68	2680.92	2918.14	3154.72	3578.79	3953	4039	4187.43
Growth rate	41.0	-9.0	8.8	8.1	13.4	0.4	2.2	3.7

Source: *Chinese Statistical Bulletin* 2005 and author's calculation.

can recognize the tendency). The more weight of them has been put upon local government. The same tendency is recognized in expenditure.

As far as financial authority on the funds inside the budget are centralized into central government, local government can be autonomous only in funds outside the budget. A recent trend says to us that the ratio of administration service costs in funds outside the budget has become smaller, meanwhile the ratio of land conveyance money larger rapidly.

(III) Weakening of basic government in rural areas Basically, because of an ambiguous legal foundation, a symmetry between central government and local government on authority and obligation is difficult to establish. Under the asymmetric situation on the service obligation and financial authority, it is not optimistic for basic local government circumstance on public service provision. Unless this situation is reformed, a weakening of basic government might be easily realized (as regards this topic, see for example, Yu Jianrong, 2001, Wu Yi, 2002, He Xuefen, 2003, Huang Zongzhi, 1994, Gu Wenfeng, 2006, and Cao Jinqing, 2000).

Both relations between basic government and peasants, between basic government and higher level government have become serious phenomena and what is called loss of cooperation. They have gradually changed from "taken up type government" to "floating type government" (Zhou Feizhou, 2006). However, meanwhile, we think it has produced a space for grown up and growth of voluntarily private organizations. For example, Xie Lizhoug (2001) and Lu Huilin (2004) analyzed occurrence and function of voluntary organization of "the aged association" at the border region located in Mindong district of Fujian province.

We think that, even if an authoritarian system is necessary in the transition of China, a weakening phenomena of basic level government in rural areas might make such gradual systemic transformation difficult to sustain. The Yang Balang village case which was reported by the Chinese Central TV on March 2, 2000, was a typical case expressing the above difficulty. The Yang Balang village is under Heping township, Dehui city of Jilin province located at northeast area in China whose population is only less than 1,000. After 1993, in the Yang Balang village, peasants lapsed into serious opposition to village executives and it was difficult for government officials sent by the upper level government to collect agricultural tax etc. to enter the village. Thus they called the village "Baiqu" (white district). In China, the occupied districts by the Communist Party before 1949 were called "liberation district" or "Suqu" (Soviet district) (from 1931 to 1937, the China Soviet Republic was founded in Ruijin of Jiangxi province, from which the name of the Soviet district came), and to the contrary the governing districts by the Nationalist Party were usually called "Baiqu". That is to say, "Baiqu" indicates the region that Communist administration does not reach. Serious oppositions were caused by an accumulation of various affairs. For example, executives to manage the village collected lots of tax and money from peasants but gave no explanations on what the money was spent for although peasants requested it. Such affairs which damaged peasant's interest illegally occurred often. Even if peasants complained about them, no government sections for troubleshooting existed. Then peasants who complained against such illegal affairs rejected duties of food delivered to the authorities. They went too far that they did neither deliver food to government nor pay various agricultural taxes and other costs. Moreover, in order to prevent force approaching the village by executives and police, they hung a big bell at the entrance of the village and turned them away in one united body. As the results, Yang Balang was the village in which nobody could approach for eight years and it meant that neither village party organization nor peasant's self-governing committee could work at all. Executives of upper level government of towns and cities did not know what they would do for the Yang Balang village which was fully separated from the Chinese system for eight years. Needless to say, in the Yang Balang village as a lawless district, they did not provide public services and the economy became poorer. Public order was also seriously damaged. For example, houses of peasants who were ostracized were often set on fire. After the articles about Yang Balang village were reported all over China, at the beginning of 2001, a working group whose chief was the mayor of Dehui started to restore the order. Members of the group were sent to the Yang Balang village, however they were surrounded by hostile peasants and could not find any place to stay. Moreover, the house of peasants who finally accepted the group members was caught in a fire suddenly at night. It was undoubtedly an incendiary fire. The working group listened humbly to the voice of peasants' opinion and tried to break an impasse. After half a year passed, signs of restoration of order began to appear in the village. A regular meeting of party organization was held after eight years' interval, and peasants began to pay agricultural tax. Also some peasants went to compulsory work for construction of irrigation.

Even though the Yang Balang village case might be an extreme case, other similar cases could be recognized. It could be understood rather as the epitome of Chinese rural society after the 1990s. Analyzing the Yang Balang village case showed us that a reason for serious opposition came from corruption and incompetence of basic level administration and restoring the order was caused by contrary actions. However, it was a pity that, after the case was reported all over the nation, the working group was finally established to solve the problems which were claimed by peasants for many years. It is necessary to learn a lesson from the case that institution building is crucial to prevent any recurrence of a similar case. We suggest the need to implement the constitutional local autonomy system in that sense (see later in this chapter).

Logic of the dependency symptom on land finance of local government

Previously in this chapter, we understand the development boom after 1980s. Also the development boom occurred at around 1994 when a tax sharing system was carried out. That is to say, the investment impulse of local government in the second half of the 1980s was never overcome by implementing a tax sharing system. Then what are the logics of dependency on land finance of local government?

As far as the performance prospects as GDP growth rate, financial revenue etc. are institutionally provided, local government has become a kind of interest group. Although the Communist Party has succeeded in centralization of power, under the reform and open door policy started in 1978, market oriented reform has been progressed and decentralization has been improved. Traditional relations of guidance-obedience between central government and local government were radically changed, and self assertion of local government has been stronger. Central government at present is suffering from both completing successful macro economic regulation to develop more the fourth rank economy in the world and from applying the brakes to unregulated development activities by local governments.

To find any successful solutions, it is necessary to analyze the causes and effects. According to the author's way of thinking, logics of local government are summarized as following. A fundamental institutional reason which is weakening of local assembly leads to the following three administrative characteristics; (1) "soft budget constraint" to the government budget, (2) government's view for GDP as almighty, (3) tax sharing system led by authority. The details of them are as follows.

Weakening of Parliament: financial decision authority, tax collection authority

The executive committee of the Sixth National Parliament in 1984 promulgated the following consignment legislation ordinance. It said that "in the reform process of tax revenues from profit of state owned enterprises and of the industrial and commercial tax system, through proposition by cabinet, authority to promulgate and trial tax revenues ordinance related with cabinet in the form of draft is given to cabinet. After the draft is revised based upon actual circumstances, it is submitted to the executive committee of the National Parliament. The above mentioned tax revenues ordinance established by cabinet is not applied to joint venture companies between Chinese and foreign capital and foreign owned enterprises." As a result, 80 per cent of tax revenues ordinance related laws in China were promulgated in such forms as ordinance and preliminary provision (cabinet also gives authority of establishing concrete provisions to ministries and sections like the Ministry of Finance) . Laws related with tax system promulgated by National Parliament were only three.

According to the Chinese Constitution, Article 62, each level of the government's financial budget and settlement of accounts have to be examined and ratified by the National Parliament. However, as regards authority of collecting tax, there is no provision saying that the authority belongs to the National Parliament. Therefore, it is not necessary to have permission of the National Parliament to decide new tax clauses, to adjust existing tax clauses and existing tax rates. Because of imperfect decision authority of the National Parliament on finance and budget, it is natural that independence of the parliament is not established.

As is mentioned later, less development of the national assembly is closely related with less establishment of private property rights. In another way of saying, sound establishment of private property rights needs the national assembly to perform this duty. Analyzing the current situation in China indicates that less development of national assembly has brought about the following three serious problems.

Soft budget constraint to the government budget and self expanding of government organization

Because of less development of the national assembly, in place of traditional state owned enterprises, a soft budget constraint to the government budget has become clearer accompanied with economic growth. It has led to self expanding of government organization to be possible, and expansion of administration control costs in the financial expenditure has become a serious problem.

Although China tried to reform administrative organization twice in 1993 and 1998, the self expansion tendency of government organization has never been improved.

We can have a short look at an example of Shanxi province. Statistics said that public employees who are paid by budget revenues in 2002 reached 1.37 million (except service persons) which occupied 4.14 per cent of the total population. It means 24 workers keep one public employee on average.

An investigation on social psychology of Shanxi done by Shanxi province government shows that highest score was gained by "strong public centered mind" and "public special privilege mind". Also in the job selection among university students of Shanxi province, the most priority was given to public or related service organization (which occupied 67.35 per cent), whose reason was the "special privilege" (whose ratio was 54.08 per cent) (Li Honggu and Wang Jiayao, 2005).

Since the beginning of the 1990s, the ratio of administration control costs to financial expenditure inside the budget was in upward tendency from 12.2 per cent in 1991 to 19.4 per cent in 2004. Administration control costs' total amount grew with a two digit rate whose peak years were 1993 (36.9 per cent) and 2000 (37

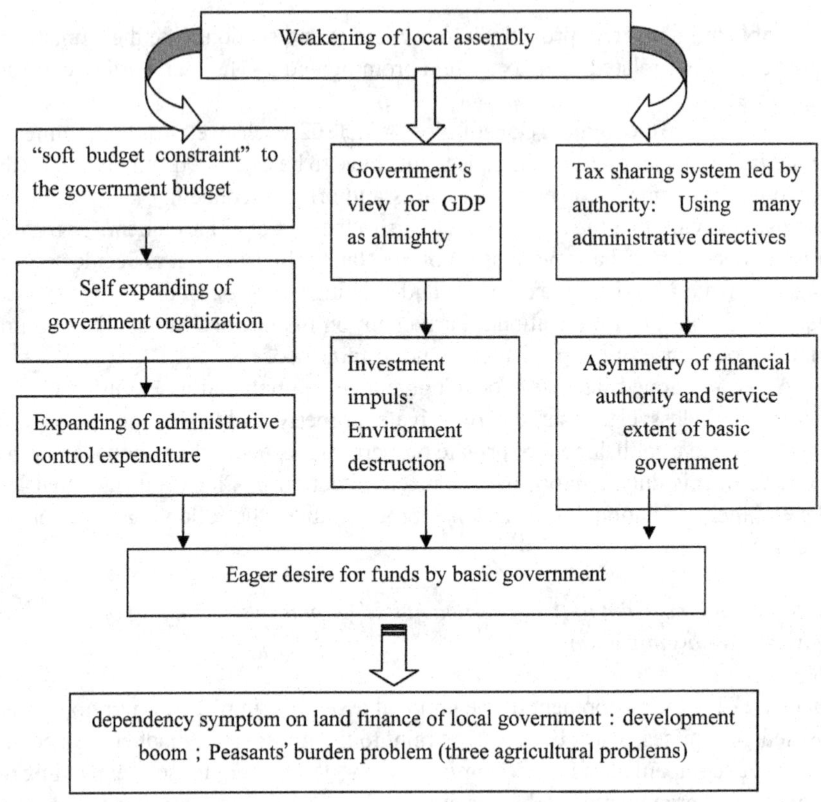

Source: Author.

Figure 4.3 Logic of development impulse of local government

per cent). In 2003 it reduced to 14.38 per cent but it increased to 17.7 per cent in 2004. (See Table 4.9)

As far as administration control costs in the financial expenditure outside the budget (which is basically used for personnel expenses etc., and the biggest expenditure of the outside budget) are concerned, the situation has become much more serious. The absolute amount of them increased from 125.4 billion yuan in 1996 to 283.7 billion yuan in 2003, whose ratio to the financial expenditure amount outside the budget was expanded from 32.7 per cent to 68.2 per cent respectively. If towns and villages unified financial revenues are included, administration control costs are undoubtedly extending.

The ratio of the total amount of administration control costs inside and outside the budget to overall financial expenditure decreased from 42.7 per cent in 1996 to 30.7 per cent in 2003, however except for 1997 and 1998 the absolute amount expanded. Compared with other countries' situation, the Chinese ratio was much more than the USA (ten per cent) and France (8.6 per cent), and a little higher than Indonesia (29 per cent) (see Figure 4.4).

Originally the outside budget fund is the same nature as the inside budget fund, but because of "outside budget", supervision would be less hard. A significant part of administration control costs of local government particularly of basic government are covered by the outside budget fund. Since the middle of the 1990s, reform to incorporate outside budget funds inside has been attempted and the ratio of inside budget funds to the total financial revenues (the total of inside budget and outside budget fund) has been expanded from 67. 4 per cent in 1996 to 85.6 per cent in 2003 (see Table 4.10).

Table 4.9 Administration control costs in the national finances

(100 million yuan, %)

	Administration control costs inside budget			Administration control costs outside budget			Total expenditure of administration control costs	Ratio of total adm-istration costs
	Total expend-iture	Growth rate	Ratio	Total expend-iture	Growth rate	Ratio		
1978	52.9		4.7					
1980	75.53		6.1					
1985	171.06		8.5					
1989	386.26		13.7					
1990	414.56	7.3	13.4					
1991	414.01	-0.1	12.2					
1992	463.41	11.9	12.4					
1993	634.26	36.9	13.7					
1994	847.68	33.6	14.6					
1995	996.54	17.6	14.6					
1996	1185.28	18.9	14.9	3838.32		32.68	5023.60	42.7
1997	1358.85	14.6	14.7	2685.54	2.1	47.67	4044.39	33.9
1998	1600.27	17.8	14.8	2918.31	24.1	54.42	4518.58	32.9
1999	2020.6	26.3	15.3	3139.14	14.3	57.85	5159.74	31.6
2000	2768.22	37.0	17.4	3529.01	22.5	63.05	6297.23	32.4
2001	3512.49	26.9	18.6	3850	12.4	64.94	7362.49	32.4
2002	4101.32	16.8	18.6	3831	6.2	69.30	7932.32	30.6
2003	4691.26	14.4	19.0	4156.36	6.8	68.25	8847.62	30.7
2004	5521.98	17.7	19.4					

Source: *Chinese Statistical Bulletin* 2005, and author's calculation.

Meanwhile, however, the outside budget fund of basic local government has never shrunk. Especially financial revenues for them coming from land conveyance occupied a significant ratio of the total revenues. The above stated expansion of administration control expenditure has been seriously related with the dependency symptom on land finance of local government.

Government's view for GDP almighty and investment impulse of government

Although Chinese government has advocated "scientific view on development" and "green GDP" and has recognized the wrong result of Government's view for GDP as almighty, at present they have no effective way to reform it. Basically such performances as the GDP growth rate, financial revenues, capital invitation have still become criteria to evaluate local government attainment.

Table 4.11 points out the economic construction expenditure, whose ratio to total financial expenditure and whose growth rate is also indicated. The ratio to total financial expenditure has reduced to be 38.42 per cent in 2003 from 60.1 per cent in 1996. The growth rate was kept in the vicinity of ten per cent till 2001, but was rapidly shrunk to 1.6 per cent in 2002 and 3.6 per cent in 2003. It undoubtedly shows an increase of the market mechanism end decrease of government

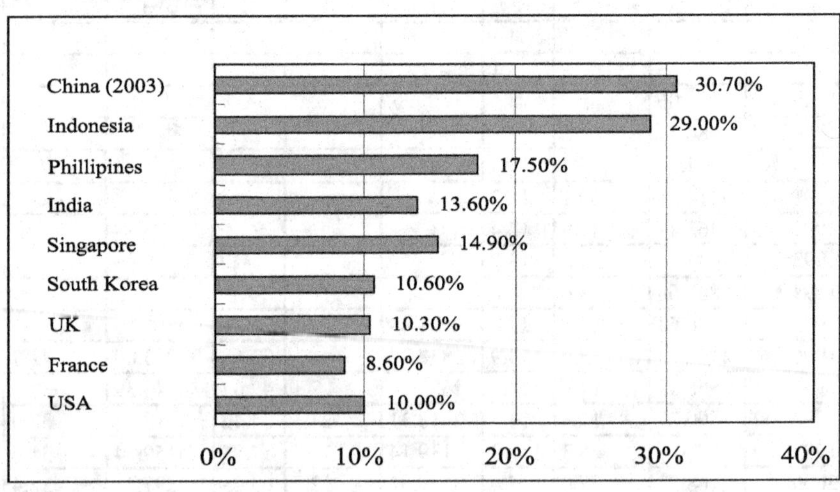

Note: Ratios of the countries except China are in 1994.

Source: *Chinese Financial Statistical Bulletin 1997*, and author's calculation.

Figure 4.4 International comparison of the ratio of administration control costs

Table 4.10 Tendency of the ratio of outside and inside budget revenues in China (100 million yuan, %)

	Total financial revenues	Inside budget revenues		Outside budget revenues	
		Amount	Ratio	Amount	Ratio
1978		1122.09			
1980		1228.83			
1985		2004.25			
1989		2823.78			
1990		3083.59			
1991		3386.62			
1992		3742.2			
1993		4642.3			
1994		5792.62			
1995		6823.72			
1996	11775.87	7937.55	67.4	3838.32	32.6
1997	11919.1	9233.56	77.5	2685.54	22.5
1998	13716.49	10798.18	78.7	2918.31	21.3
1999	16326.81	13187.67	80.8	3139.14	19.2
2000	19415.51	15886.5	81.8	3529.01	18.2
2001	22752.58	18902.58	83.1	3850	16.9
2002	25884.15	22053.15	85.2	3831	14.8
2003	28806.31	24649.95	85.6	4156.36	14.4
2004		28486.89			

Source: *Chinese Statistical Bulletin* 2005, and author's calculation.

intervention. Also it displays that around 40 per cent of financial expenditure has been paid for economic construction and expenditure, for social welfare and education has been relatively less. Transition of the government function is still very important, however it should be recognized that, unless a market mechanism is developed, transition of government function is difficult.

The inside budget fund generally showed a similar tendency, whose growth rate increased to be 14.8 per cent in 2004. Meanwhile, the outside budget fund recorded the fundamental construction expenditure as 37 per cent growth rate in 1999, which displayed however a negative growth rate in other years (although in 2003 it had a positive growth rate of 3.8 per cent).

Table 4.11 Economic construction expenditure; ratio to total financial expenditure and growth rate (100 million yuan, %)

Year	Total financial revenues (inside and outside) (A+B)	Total expenditure for economic construction (C+D)	Growth rate of total expenditure for economic construction	Ratio of total expenditure for economic construction	Total amount of inside budget fund (A)	Eonomic constructio costs			Total amount of outside budget fund (B)	Fundametal construction expenditure		
						Amount (C)	Growth rate	Ratio		Amount (D)	Growth rate	ratio
1978					1122.09	718.98		64.1				
1980					1228.83	715.46		58.2				
1985					2004.25	1127.55		56.3				
1989					2823.78	1291.19		45.7				
1990					3083.59	1368.01	5.9	44.4				
1991					3386.62	1428.47	4.4	42.2				
1992					3742.2	1612.81	12.9	43.1				
1993					4642.3	1834.79	13.8	39.5				
1994					5792.62	2393.69	30.5	41.3				
1995					6823.72	2855.78	19.3	41.9				
1996	11775.87	4724.01		60.1	7937.55	3233.78	13.2	40.7	3838.32	1490.23		38.8
1997	11919.1	4149.36	-12.2	53.1	9233.56	3647.33	12.8	39.5	2685.54	502.03	-66.3	18.7
1998	13716.49	4573.49	10.2	51.7	10798.18	4179.51	14.6	38.7	2918.31	393.98	-21.5	13.5
1999	16326.81	5601.28	22.5	50.2	13187.67	5061.46	21.1	38.4	3139.14	539.82	37.0	17.2
2000	19415.51	6174.56	10.2	47.8	15886.5	5748.36	13.6	36.2	3529.01	426.2	-21.0	12.1
2001	22752.58	6822.56	10.5	45.4	18902.58	6472.56	12.6	34.2	3850	350	-17.9	9.1
2002	25884.15	6933.7	1.6	40.6	22053.15	6673.7	3.1	30.3	3831	260	-25.7	6.8
2003	28806.31	7181.91	3.6	38.42	24649.95	6912.05	3.6	28.0	4156.36	269.86	3.8	6.49
2004					28486.89	7933.25	14.8	27.8				

Source: *Chinese Statistical Bulletin* 2005, and author's calculation.

Institutional reform of tax sharing system and suppression of the development impulse by local government

We can recognize the institutional reform of the current tax sharing system suppresses the development impulse of local government. It is considered as concrete measures exemplified by following two aspects:

(I) On the necessity of change in the tax item structure As mentioned above, current tax sharing system which is a product of compromise is still immature. In the Chinese system we can recognize in it that tax items transfer between central and local, and change of divided ratios of shared tax is generally observed. In advanced industrialized countries, usually income tax, various turnover tax (value added tax and business tax), resource tax belong to central government, meanwhile less flexible taxes like property tax, fixed property tax, real estate tax etc. belong to local government. The Japanese tax sharing system has such characteristics (see Table 4.11).

According to Table 4.12, central government mainly collected income tax, turnover tax (chiefly consumption tax in Japanese case), and inheritance tax. The county collected county citizen tax, business tax, and local consumption tax, and city, town and village mainly collected city, town, village citizen tax and fixed property tax. Although some small portions of tax items were shared between central and local government, most of them were exclusively occupied. The structure of tax revenues showed that higher level administration had more weight upon income tax and basic level administration had more weight on property tax.

The Chinese division of tax items should follow the Japanese lesson. For example, such taxes as income tax, value added tax, resource tax are classified into central tax, and business tax belongs to province tax, property tax is classified into county tax. Through such reforms, it is expected to apply the breaks to the development impulse of local government. At present, value added tax is collected at the production and distribution stage in order to reduce collection cost. Because the production stage value added tax has become an important factor to stimulate a development impulse for local government, various proposals to change the production stage value added tax to consumption stage value added tax are presented.

The current division of taxes between governments indicates that financial revenues are easily concentrated in urban area. For example, turnover tax occupied around 60 per cent of total tax re0venues. As industrial and commercial enterprises are intensively located in urban area, it is natural for tax revenues to concentrate in urban area. Moreover, because turnover tax can be transferred, even citizens living in rural areas actually pay tax through consumption, it might not become financial revenues for local governments in farming areas. However, since 2002, Chinese income tax has had a growing ratio. Central government which has been conscious of the disparity among regions has revised the income tax to be shared tax from local tax.

Table 4.12 Japanese situation on tax sharing system (2004) (trillion yen, %)

		Income Tax	Consumption Tax	Property Tax etc.	Total
Central Government		Income tax (15.1) Corporation tax (11.4)	Consumption tax(10.0) Light oil tax (2.9) Liquor tax (1.7) Refuse tax (0.9) Auto weight tax (1.1) Energy tax (0.03) etc.	Inheritance tax (1.4) Registration and license tax (0.5) etc.	
		Individual 31.4% Corporate 23.8%			
		Subtotal: 55.2 (26.5)	Subtotal: 39.5 (19.0)	Subtotal: 5.4 (2.6)	(48.1)
Local Government	County	Corporate business tax 4.1) Individual county tax (2.3) Corporate county tax (0.9) County interest tax (0.3) Individual business tax (0.2)	Local consumption tax (2.6) Auto tax (1.7) Light oil transaction tax (1.1) Auto acquisition tax (0.5) County tobacco tax (0.3) etc.	Real estate acquisition tax (0.5) etc.	
		Individual 18.9% Corporate 34.5%			
		Subtotal: 53.4 (7.7)	Subtotal: 43.0 (6.2)	Subtotal:3.6 (0.5)	(14.5)
	City, town, village	Individual residence tax (5.5) Corporate residence tax (2.2)	Tobacco tax (0.9) Auto tax (0.1) etc.	Fixed property tax (8.8) Urban planning tax (1.2) Special land possession tax (0.01) Office tax (0.3)etc.	
		Individual 28.7% Corporate 11.6%			
		Subtotal: 40.3 (7.7)	Subtotal: 5.5 (1.0)	Subtotal: 54.3 (10.3)	(19.1)
	Local subtotal average	45.9 (15.4)	21.7 (7.3)	32.4 (10.9)	(33.5)
Total		(41.9)	(26.2)	(13.4)	(81.6)

Note: Tax revenues in parentheses indicate 2004 fiscal year.

Source: Ministry of Internal Affairs and Communications (Japan).

(II) Normalcy of financial transfer In order to raise the normalcy of financial transfer, establishment of a legal system became an urgent task. As a matter of fact, this problem became important several years ago. In December 2003, in the legislation plan of the executive committee of the Tenth National Parliament, they had a clause of "financial transfer expenditure law". On 14th December, 2003, the Ministry of Finance held an international symposium to prepare the legislation. Towards the institutional reform we consider the following way of thinking is important;

I. The criterion of financial transfer should be changed from a "cardinal number method" to a "factor criterion method". In order to carry out the change, it is necessary to frame a "standard formula of financial transfer". That is to say, central government calculates the "financial transfer" to realize fair and homogeneous public service for each region, taking into consideration various factors such as regional land area, population structure (whose factors should be simple and easily understood), based upon which central government makes the criteria for financial transfer to compensate for the difference with actual financial revenues for local government.

A traditional cardinal number method is a system to keep a vested interest for local government. By changing to a "factor criterion method", it becomes clear that the financial transfer from central government has been in reverse relations with regional economic development and it is expected government's view for GDP as almighty (about which it is insisted in some local areas that statistical figures are doubtful) could die down.

II. As regards donations for minority race autonomous districts, less economic developed area, and go-west development areas, if considering efficiency of capital expenditure, not only financial transfer but also bringing up market mechanism should together be carried out.

Summary

Behind the background of universal social, economic and political phenomena, institutional factors surely exist. For example, in the national land development and regional development, the phenomena which, relate to local government, land finance and real estate development boom occurred have been coming from institutional factors. In the previous section, we have had a short look at the logic of development impulse for local government. We think it is necessary to build up the institutions to resolve such serious problems as poor basic government and poor rural areas.

Chinese reform and open door policy started from decentralization, and local government has given liveliness to the Chinese economy as a new player of a market oriented economy. However, because of the transition period, there could be often recognized that local government led benefit could not reach the whole of Chinese benefit. Gradual transition in institutions is necessary for Chinese society to maximize its welfare. It should be asked what the desirable relationships between central and local government will be.

Reestablishing relationships between central and local government needs to improve national welfare and successful macro economic adjustment. The author of this book suggests the gradual introduction of a constitutional local autonomy system.

Considering the future relationships between central and local government: towards a constitutional local autonomy system

Compared with the Mao Zedong system, we can say the Deng Xiaoping system led to high speed economic growth and is a "wise authoritarianism system". However, as far as the authoritarianism is concerned, the current tax sharing system has also deep-rooted characteristics of authoritarianism.

What kinds of relationships exist between current tax sharing system (started in 1994) and regional economic growth? It undoubtedly varies a little from one objective region and selective index to another. Generally speaking, however, as of 1994, China broke away from the financial contract system in the 1980s and had inherent reasons to carry out tax sharing system. Also it cannot be rejected to say that tax sharing system has been gradually improved from a financial contract system in an institutional sense. However, as mentioned above, although tax sharing system in 1994 tentatively overcame institutional bad effects till then, it has also brought about new problems. In the light of a local autonomy system in a constitutional sense, the current tax sharing system is a partial and superficial institution. It is still only half way towards the initial goal of tax sharing system.

Therefore we think that such a financial system as tax sharing system is necessary to link one of these days with more fundamental and a much higher institution (that is to say, a local autonomy system). If not, it might be difficult to be effective. This section is given to extract the problems between central and local government, and later to insist on the possibility of implementation of the local autonomy system in China.

Relationship between central and local government under the authoritarianism development system

We have the following four conclusions of the problems on the relationship between central and local government under the authoritarianism development system.

(I) Problems of irresponsible local government For citizens in urban area, the three problems of housing problem, medical problem and educational problem

have become the three big burdens for Chinese people. They are followed by the three agricultural problems which become serious tasks for current days. As stated above, central government tends to force the responsibility to provide public service (service provision rights) upon lower governments in place of upward shifting the financial authority. It has become generalized that local government (particularly basic government) which has been faced by a serious budget deficit tries to maximize its own self interest and throw away the responsibility to the "market system". Accompanied with an unhealthy government system, the market has become also an unhealthy system. It means market cannot be responsible to resolve the problems. In this period when a theory of new public management was introduced from the US and Europe into China, such irresponsible behaviors were carried out under the name of city management, education industry, marketization of housing system reform, marketization of medical reform etc.

The fundamental reason why those problems occurred is lack of institutions to make local government responsible to Chinese citizens. In China the same mechanism is working to worsen environment problem. (On the details, see Chapter 5 of this book.)

(II) Problems on structural reform of administration As a matter of fact, various proposals insisting on reform towards simpler administrative structure with vertically three stages from with vertically five stages focusing attention upon the disadvantageous aspects. However, without introducing a local autonomy system in a constitutional sense it might be difficult to have radical effects.

On the tax sharing system which has become clear there are many problems, some experts asserted that they should divide Chinese regions into the two as following; one block divides provinces vertically into two stages, another divides the whole area horizontally into more developed and less developed stages, of which in less than province level and less developed areas tax sharing system should not be introduced. However, against the above assertion, some experts insisted that all the efforts to unify the Chinese financial system came to nothing which backed to a "one region, one institution" negotiation era. At present, related to the problems of tax sharing system, reforming the administration districts has been focusing attention.

As far as reasons why the present tax sharing system has produced various confusions are concerned, it is often pointed out the complexity of Chinese administration levels and the vertical structure of five ranks has been the bases of them. Many opinions indicate that it is impossible to completely implement the tax sharing system under the vertically divided five ranks administration structure. An idea usually mention to solve the problem is to reform the five ranks administration structure to the three of central, province and, city and county, which means the flat administration rank structure. Actually, "stronger county, more authority" phenomena has been realized. It indicates that more experiments to give more authority to a stronger county have been carried out. Another idea is saying that county level government collectively manages financial authority of towns and villages governments. Through such ideas, the united county level regional economy has been more improved with better formed three rank administration structure of central, province, and city and county.

Is that a truly better solution?

If local government is not given consistent rights and obligations with financial authority, public service obligation, and personnel authority, the current budget difficulty of towns and villages will be just transferred to county level budget difficulty. It might be probable, if cities of local level are abolished, the autonomous authority of city and county will surely be raised. However, problems still remain.

Particularly, conflicts between ordinary cities and province capital city have been remarkable as the dramas like "Tale of Two Cities" (Charles Dickens, 1989) are presented in each place. Conflicts between ShenZhen and Guangzhou Ningbo and Hangzhou, Qingdao and Jinan,Dalian and Shenyang are typical examples. Also the same conflicts are recognized between the national capital, Beijing, and a municipality directly under the central government, Tianjin. It means that under the present system there have been lots of conflicts between political and administration centered cities and economic centered cities (most of which are port towns). Latter cities advocate more autonomous authorities, meanwhile former cities try to keep their vested interests. Thus, a new institutional framework to introduce social norms into vertical and horizontal relations among governments is necessary.

(III) Problems of free movement of population When looking at the poor public service situation provided by the lowest level governments in Chinese rural areas, some scholars remember Tiebout (Tiebout, 1956, pp.416-424) (1956), which indicates if human resources move freely, they move to a region which provides public services and the best tax system. Through such mechanism, local government is under a competitive situation which leads to equilibrium among regions (Ping Xinqiao, 1995). Concretely, for example, population in rural areas move into urban areas towards self interest maximization to pursue better public services, which increases per capita public expenditure in rural areas and raises the public service level. To the contrary, in urban areas per capita financial expenditure decreases which leads to a financial hardship situation. Urban area local government therefore selects more financial transfer amount to rural area because they try to block the huge number of population inflow, which undoubtedly contributes for better public service in rural area. In the long run, finally, equalization of public service between rural area and urban area is realized. Some scholars insist as above and advocate the necessity of human mobility among regions by abolishing thoroughly the traditional family registration system.

However, the theory of free movement of population which leads to equalization of public service has the following problems.

I. Local governments also try to maximize their self interest which is reasonable. However, under the present relations between central and local government, local governments' self interest means better public service provision. As analyzed above, local governments have no direct incentive to provide better public service with the "soft budget system", "GDP almighty sentiment", and "authoritarianism tax sharing system". Executives of towns and villages are not elected by citizens. Although executives of peasants' autonomous committees are as a rule selected by peasants, because financial authority is controlled by higher level government, they attach greater importance upon implementing various orders given by higher level government, not upon responsibility for peasants.
II. Even if most rural areas in China have redundant workers, the majority of outflowed workers are younger ones. Younger workers drain might make regional agriculture and other industries in rural areas decline more, which leads to less financial revenues for the region. It might be less probable to increase per capita financial expenditure in rural area and to improve public services.
III. It might be doubtful to expect that local government of urban areas (higher level government) can expand the scale of financial transfer to rural areas in order to block the huge number of inflowed population from rural areas. Moving population into urban area is not only from the surrounding rural area (controlled by higher level government) but also from rural areas in the whole of China. Expansion of financial transfers from urban to rural areas is not realized by simple liberalization of population movement without entire institutional reform.

In China, even after "the forced sending back home system" was finished in 2003[10], institutional regulation against the population movement was already abolished. However, there still have existed hindering economic factors. Actually, for example, no equalized treatments with urban citizens are given to them in such aspects as education, job search, social welfare. Also they have suffered from mental fatigue, which has become the dark side of a social psychological aspect in China. This "dual structure" between urban citizens and outside citizens has brought about lots of human rights problems and has become effective restraint

10 The Chinese Cabinet promulgated "The way of accommodate and deportation to urban beggars" in 1982. This way was made bad use of regulation against the mobilized population without temporary residential certificate, not only for regulation to urban beggars. It was abolished as an opportunity when the Sun Zhigang affairs occurred, which indicated that, after Sun Zhigang coming from Hubei province graduated from Wuhan Science and Technology Institute, he got a job in Zhuangzhou. Just after a little more than 20 days he got the job, on March 17, 2003, around 10p.m., he went to the street and was arrested due to being without the temporary residential certificate. After then he was attacked by some inmates at the prison and died. The press report on it roused public opinion.

against the rapid movement from the rural to urban. They are rather usual cases as a matter of fact that, after staying in urban areas for a fixed period of time, they return to the home town to start a new business.

Also in urban areas, various new policies to treat the moving population from rural areas have been planned. New treatments for such problems as education problem, medical insurance problem, are started. In Shanghai for example a general insurance system to the moving population from rural area has been carried out. However, taking into consideration the Todaro model, in the situation of significant disparity between the urban and rural, improving living condition in urban areas attracts much more movement of farming population into urban areas. If it occurs for a long period, both unemployment in urban areas and workforce shortage in rural areas might be possible at the same time.

Generally speaking, considering equalization of public service provision as an aim, we think it is not good policy to improve freer movement of population. As Todaro suggested, a strategy to develop rural areas should have priority. Since reform and open door policy started, less developed rural areas and inland areas undoubtedly have taken more burdens. It is reasonable thus to examine appropriate policy to return the benefit gained in earlier developed areas. As far as urbanization is concerned, it is important to carefully consider the speed and consistency. The appropriate industrial policy to treat the current size and quality of redundant workers is necessary on the one hand, and under the government led development system first priority should be given to establish responsible to local basic government for rural society on the other. Fei Xiaotong (1988) correctly advocated that "there is one prerequisite in rebuilding homeland China. We have to establish our government for the people" (Fei Xiaotong, 1988, p.168).

(IV) *Problems of bureaucracy* There is a Chinese characteristic in the relations between central and local governments under the authoritarian development system, which shows that policies putting right distorted development in local areas are often implemented by the unified way of politics and economy. Injustice and corruption occurred under the authoritarian development system (like cozy relations between government and business in the real estate development) and has surely been produced by the system structurally. When central government decides the targets to be punished, they expose political problems of the chief of local government (like they exposed the corruption) and change the development pattern of the regional economy. The serious matter happened in 2006 which was known as the "Shanghai top executive Chen Liangyu affair" and was dealt with the above stated procedure (see Figure 4.5).

In the democratic system, a chief of local government is elected directly and is replaced by a new chief by election. Even when they failed to carry out economic policy and social welfare policy, they can come back politically by the following election. However, in the authoritarianism system, a downfallen chief of local government who receives a penalty in unified system of politics and economy has no possibility to come back. It means the privileged persons have more serious risks. Who are modest in using their power when they acquire special privileges? As is well known, countries and regions of the East Asian model employed the way of authoritarianism. In such countries and regions as postwar Taiwan, South Korea, Singapore, and Hong Kong, various types of wise authoritarianism were established, in which elite specialists worked in good jobs. In China in which for a significantly long period an authoritarian development system will be maintained, it is crucial that such elite specialists should be ensured.

At present in China, in official organizations in central government especially related with financial and monetary organizations, lots of scholarly bureaucrats have been selected, also scholarly bureaucrats have invited scholarly bureaucrats (see chapter six about the details). However, selection of local governments' officials has proceeded in a traditional pattern, in which institutional reform has run into difficulties. In present China lots of local governments' bureaucrats who are promoted with the seniority system have no experience to study at university and are provided within the system, in which many ex-soldiers who have royalty and discipline are included. Chen Liangyu was an ex-soldier.

It is natural to recognize that, as financial and monetary sections in central government are very important to develop towards more advanced economy, bureaucrats working for such sections need to be internationalized. Meanwhile,

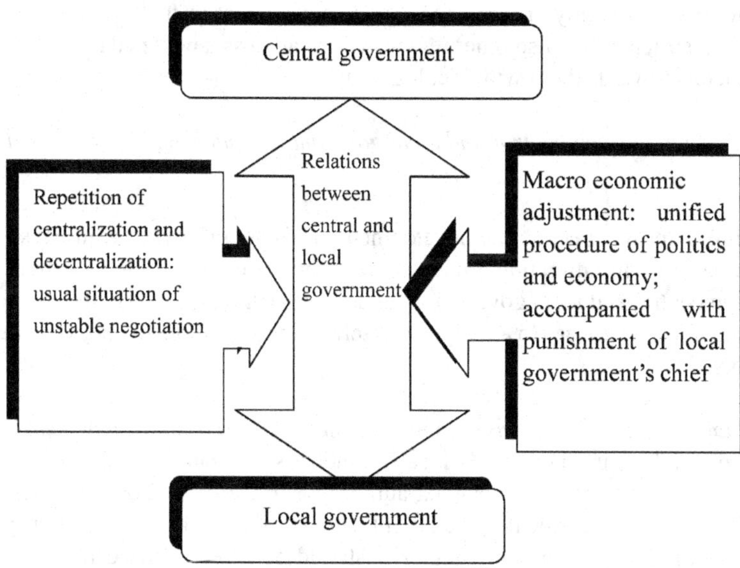

Source: Author.

Figure 4.5 Relations between central and local government under the authoritarian development system

although local government's bureaucrats who were absorbed in making China into a world factory which has been developed mainly by low cost depended manufacturing (see chapter five on it) they are not knowledgeable in finance and money, but they can attract foreign capital through competition with preferential treatment and can form a regional economy.

However, the situation has been changing. Particularly, big cities like Shanghai which need to transform their industrial structures and urban structures have problems of a human resource shortage coming from bureaucrats' supply system. An advanced economic structure needs an advanced political system. During the transition days, elite specialists work as intermediaries between the two systems. They exist like enclaves, who have links with the outside world not only in technical aspect but also in ideological aspect. They are knowledgeable persons about the future tendency of socio-economic development. Moreover, as they have higher goal for their lives, they do not attach greater importance upon personal interest. Such human resources cannot be mass produced within a traditional system. Thus usually human resources who went abroad to study (or to do other purposes) for longer period can carry out the jobs (Deng Xiaoping and Zhou Enlai etc. were pioneers in that sense).

We think that changing focus paid attention to capital and also an inviting policy to human resources (especially international students with Chinese nationality); an inviting policy is indispensable for an authoritarian development system to transform it. Not only the regions which are necessary to have an advanced industrial structure but also other regions which are less developed need to change bureaucrats towards them with ideologies and beliefs.

Relationship between central and local government under the law-governed system

We think improving economic development needs an improving political system. In the days of omnidirectional open strategy, because the traditional relationship between central and local government under authoritarianism system would reach the limits, it is necessary to attempt to establish a new relationship between central and local level.

(I) Characteristics of local autonomy system in a constitutional sense We recommend the introduction of a local autonomy system in a constitutional sense. It indicates that as regards financial authority, service obligation, and personnel authority, each level local government should have consistent authority and responsibility, and supervising authority should be given to the Chinese people. Through such change of institutional incentive, if central government has no treatment for various conflicts as mentioned above, each local government would have gradually autonomous controlling power against them (see Figure 4.6).

The birthplace of a local autonomy system is England. Before the Duke of Normandy (ducs de Normandie, 1035-1087) unified England, they had a tradition to discuss public services within the region at the citizens' meeting in the villages and parishes in England. Establishment of the local autonomy system was shown in England by implementing the "Municipal Corporation Act" of 1835 and the "Local Government Act" of 1888. After then, the local autonomy was transmitted to the European Continent. The self-governing city of the Middle Ages in Europe was at the forefront of them. In those days, some cities with developed industry and commerce citizens tried to build the castle within the castle by establishing city construction, in order to compete with feudal lords. Those phenomena continued until centralized monarchy came into existence in the 16th century. After the French Revolution in 1789, an important institutional change occurred, in which a way of selection of local assembly member became election by popular vote. Later with improvement of institutional unification and democratization, a local autonomy system was established in France. In Germany, led by Baron Stein in 1808, the "Prusse Law of Local Authority" was established and citizens' suffrage was substantially approved.

What are the characteristics of local autonomy?

We here have a short look at the Japanese local autonomy case. The Shoup three principles were employed when the local autonomy system of postwar Japan

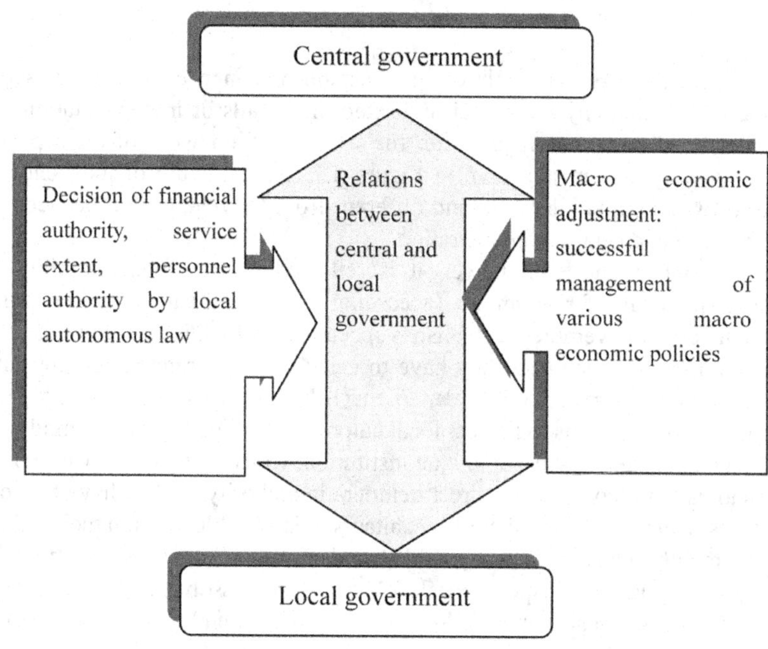

Source: Author.

Figure 4.6 Relationship between central and local government under the law-governed system

was introduced. In 1949, the Shoup recommendation was presented after the US delegation on tax system led by C. Shoup visited and stayed in Japan for four months, which contributed to establishing the crucial tax system for postwar Japan and for forming a new relationship between central and local government. The three principles reflected traditional viewpoints of a local autonomy system, which are as following.

I. Principle on definite responsibility of administration.
In the postwar Japan, a three stages vertical administration structure which indicate "central, county, and city and towns" have been established, each of which has definite responsibility for administration.

II. Principle of efficiency.
The second principle is on the way to allocate service responsibility among the three stage administrations. Principally, the most efficient administration level should be responsible for providing public service, which also should be given enough financial authority.

III. Principle to respect local autonomy.
The third principle said that most basic local government should be responsible for as much public service as possible.

In Japan, such principles have been established in a constitutional sense, and the local autonomy law which indicated the details of implementation was passed at the Japanese Diet just after the war. The framework of the Japanese local autonomy system is shown in Figure 4.7. The structure of independence of authority is both similar with and different from the relationship between the National Diet and central administration.

As the inhabitants gain power, it is reflected by the vote, eligibility for election, and local referendum etc. (according to the local autonomy law, article 95, when central government establishes special law which is applied to the only local government concerned, they have to carry out local referendum and must have approval of a majority in order to enact the law. This institution has been established with the aims to respect local autonomy and local citizens' mind)

Direct claim rights is also a unique institution, which was established in order for inhabitants to have widely direct democratic authority. If they have the joint signatures with a certain number of inhabitants, it is possible to claim their right. It includes mainly such claims as to establish and abolish local ordinance (article 74, local autonomy law), to inspect (article 12 and 75), to dissolve the local assembly (article 76), to designate a chief of local government, assembly member and other executives (article 81 and 86).

The local autonomy system has established the bottom-up way of policy decision system from the lower to the higher based upon right an obligation among "people, local public authority, and central government". In the postwar Japan,

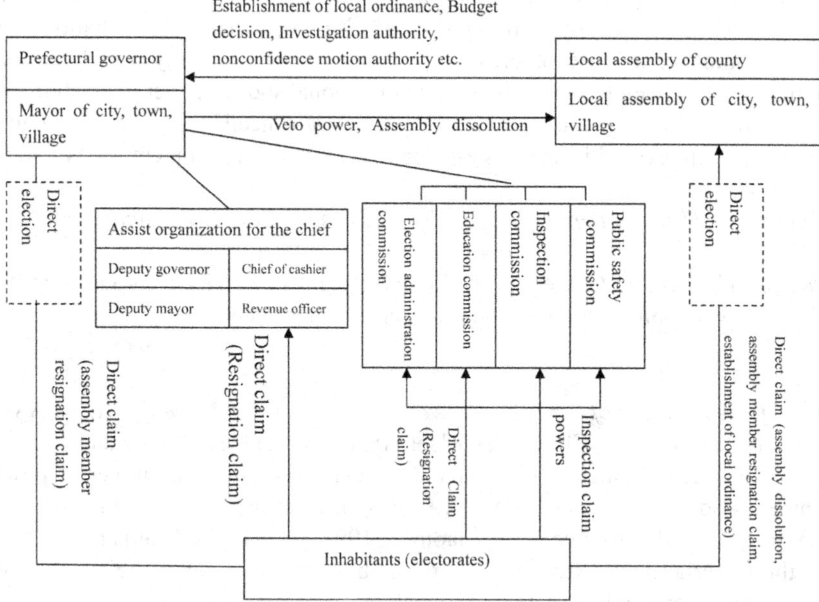

Source: Tanaka (1993), p.104.

Figure 4.7 Framework of local autonomy system in Japan

because of the local authority system, they finally succeeded in applying the breaks to the development impulse of local government. Moreover, reformist local self-governing bodies came into existence one after another, which had more advanced ideology on environmental protection than central government and carried out concrete measures led to national legislation of better law. We recognize the strained competitive relations between central and local government in Japan.

As the same more precise legislation on property rights of enterprises is a crucial part for reforming state owned enterprises, policy decision mechanism, with respecting opinions of local citizens, which has clearer relations on financial authority; service obligation, personnel authority between central and local government; all those are indispensable to establishing responsible government. Is it possible in China to have a local autonomy system?

(II) Special attention to be paid on local autonomy system In China where few experts introduced local autonomy, the term local autonomy easily reminds Chinese people of little empire economy, segmentation etc. However, from the viewpoints of the history of the 18th century European continent introducing a

local autonomy system in Germany and France, a local autonomy system was advocated as a measure to promote patriotism for a newly born nation state, and to improve a sense of civic responsibility. That is to say, to secure local citizens' participation, for public service in regional society under the institutional framework, is an important measure for western advanced industrialized countries to bring up modern citizens. It is especially meaningful for contemporary China.

On the possibility of implementing a local autonomy system in China

We consider here the Chinese possibility of implementing a local autonomy system from the viewpoints of both traditional and actual aspects.

(I) *On the tradition of "imperial power cannot extend over local area"* A well known sociologist in China, Fei Xiaotong, mentioned that "the basic structure in the Chinese hometown is a far different structure from imperial power. Imperial politics is loose and weak for actual everyday life of the people. It is an insubstantial existence" (Fei Xiaotong, 1998, pp. 24-63). That is to say, "One is the imperial power from the top to the bottom, the other is the tribal power from the bottom to the top, both of which exist side by side and have interaction. Those powers make a local village control model come into being, which is said that, even if the emperor is idle, the whole country is ruled over" (Fei Xiaotong, 1998, pp.95-301). Wen Tiejun once called it "central government's power cannot reach lower government than county", and Qin (2004) furthermore indicated it as "central government's power cannot reach lower government than county, lower level governance than county depends upon family organization, all the family organizations are autonomous organizations, autonomous models are supported by ethics, and towns and high ranking officials of them take the responsibility for the ethics" (Qin Hui, 2004, p.3). Weber also mentioned about bureaucracy in traditional China that "as a matter of fact formal imperial politics did no more than urban or sub-urban area. ...outside urban and sub-urban area controlling power of imperial politics deeply weakened and finally disappeared" (Weber, 1993, p.110).

It indicates that traditional Chinese society was divided in imperial politics (controlling space from central to county) and local politics (autonomous space lower than county) (see Figure 4.8). Under the tradition of "central government's power cannot reach lower government than county", public service had to be provided by local government all by itself-sufficient parents had family's duty and providing workforce for infrastructural construction and this was local government's duty. However, as regards tax collection and judicial power, imperial power did not lose the jurisdiction at lower than county level. Therefore, official bureaucrats of the Chinese nation were delegated powers until county level, and lower level governments than county had lots of lower ranking government officials.

Before 1949, China had local autonomous experience of towns and villages. At the end of the Qing dynasty, they promulgated the local autonomy rules of towns and villages. In liberation areas under the control by the communist party, they carried out local autonomy. For example, in 1946, according to the ordinance of election at the Suwanbian district, towns and villages were the basic form of local autonomous government. Wei Guangqi (2004) considered the Chinese county system in the first half of the 20th century and described the ruling space in which authoritarian governance and autonomous governance were intermingled.

Chen Shaofang shows that at the rural society in Qing dynasty, the following powers and authorities co-existed; (1) official authority (which was intervened by Bao Jia Zhi Du,[11] family organization system (2) tribal authority (based upon blood relationship), (3) rank authority (by monopoly of knowledge and culture), and (4) feudalistic enlightenment power going back to the imperial power (Chen Shaofang, 2006, pp. 83-88).

The dual structure of imperial politics and local politics might be thought of as a reasonable combination from the viewpoints of Chinese national circumstances. First, on the necessity, we think that ancient China had private property rights, in which both tax collection rights (tax paying and tax collecting for national control) and social stability (judicial power) were important. In the days of

---

11 Bao Jia Zhi Du was a governing way to basic level society continued from Chinese dynastic eras with discontinuity, whose characteristics were to make a family as a unit and to mobilize power of the same family groups. It could be recognized as a reflection of Confucian ideology to unify the nation's relations and same family's relations. In the Han era, they prescribed to be one Wu for every five families, one Shen for every ten families, one Li for every 100 families, however in the Tang ear, they changed the prescription to be one Lin for every four families, one Bao for every five Lin, one Li for every 100 families. In the Yuan era, the prescription of Jia was appeared which indicated to be one Jia for every 20 families. In the Qing era, Paijia system, which was based on the decimal system, was created which pointed out as one Pai for every ten families, one Jia for every ten Pai, one Bao for every ten Jia. At the beginning of the foundation of the Republic of China, the Paijia system was abolished, however in some local areas, similar system with the above existed fragmentarily. In 1927 after the Nanjing Nationalist Government was established, with the county organization law, they prescribed to be one township (town for every 100 families in a district, one Lv for every 25 families in a township (town, one Lin for very five families in a Lv. The Republic Bao Jia Zhi Du was deeply connected with the Nationalist-Communist civil war. By direct instruction of Chiang Kai-shek, the Nationalist Party governments attempted the Bao Jia Zhi Du of Republic version for the first time in 1931 at Jiangxi province in which Jinggangshan as the base of Communist Red Army was located. They implemented it in the whole nation in 1934. To be concrete, they prescribed to be one Jia for every ten families, one Bao for every ten Jia, and to become township (town for more than ten Bao. They also used jointly four principles of "Guan, Jiao, Yang, Wei" (pointing out management, education, economy, and military). They emphasized both local autonomy and self-defense, and in order to control Communist Party supporters (sympathizers) they introduced the guilt-by-association system among families of which Bao and Jia consisted.

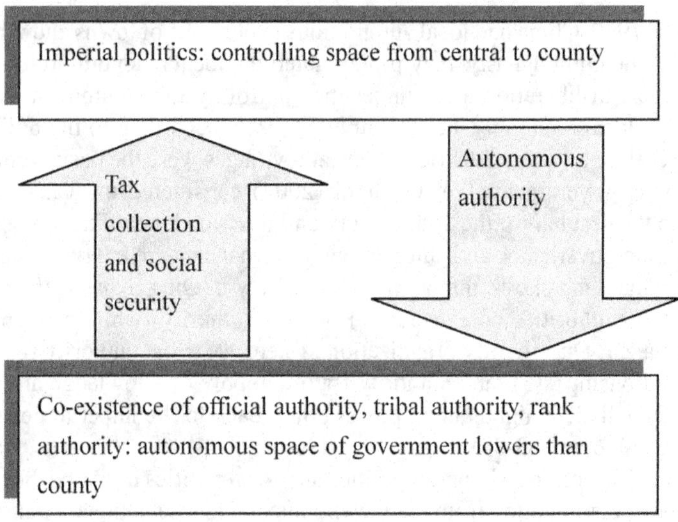

Source: Author.

Figure 4.8 Multiple layers of controlling space of Chinese traditional society

normal situations, imperial power needed nothing from local society. Second, on the possibility, as China before the new country was founded was an agricultural country with a peasant economy, it is natural that they did not have a highly organized system like the industrialized USSR. In China, from then, they failed to establish the people's commune system and moved to a collective economic system. We understand that if neither industrial structure nor agricultural structure changed, it was impossible to regulate local society with centralized power. Table 4.13 points out the economic structure of the former society of China. Although the figures vary from one expert to another, China was undoubtedly an agricultural country. What was emphasized is that China was the agricultural country not only from viewpoints of production but also from workforce structure (see Chapter 1 on the detail). It expresses that China was a typical case of an Asian agricultural country which has redundant workers.

Table 4.13 Economic structure of China **(%)**

	Perkins' estimation		**Liu and Yeh estimation**	
	1914-18	1933	1933	1952
Agriculture	61.8	59.2	57.0	47.9
Manufacturing	17.6	19.8	20.2	26.2
Service	20.7	21.0	22.8	25.9
Total	100	100	100	100

Note: Manufacturing includes transportation. Perkins' estimation was shown in 1957 price, and Liu and Yeh estimation in 1952 price.

Source: Perkins (1969), Liu and Yeh (1965), Nakagane (1999).

After the days of the Western Zhou Period (around BC 1027–BC 771), China experienced cycles of breaking up and integration, and feudal system in the true sense was abolished in China and a centralization system established by the First Emperor of the Qin dynasty, Shi Huangdi, became the fundamental system of the dynasty. The image saying that China was a highly centralized country became popular among the world, and Wittfogel (1961) interpreted the reason of oriental despotism with the "theory of water". Meanwhile, some experts recognize China not to be a highly centralized system but to be a slackly centralized system. For example, Nakagane (1999) mentioned that the Mao Zedong system was similar to wartime communism, but from viewpoints of a characteristic mixture of centralization and decentralization in the decision making system and of characteristics of a central planning system in China, it should be called a slackly centralized system[12]. The viewpoint of Nakagane might be interpreted by the dual structure of controlling space as mentioned above.

Is it possible to think that multiple strata of controlling space in traditional Chinese society have been changing with a deep-rooted link to a modern local autonomy system? As a matter of fact, since the 1980s in Chinese rural society, peasants' autonomy has been restored as an institution.

(II) History of the constitutional system and local autonomy system in China At the end of the 19th century, the colonized powers of western advanced industrial countries approached East Asia. Those were globalization days in which whole Asian countries were involved by such movements as war, interaction processes each other etc. In the former China before 1949, they established eight constitutions (or eight drafts of constitution)[13]. During the days of disorders, some drafts

12 Nakagane is the first expert in naming the Chinese economic system as a slackly centralized system. See also Nakagane (1979).

13 Rulers of Qing dynasty were surprised to hear the results of the Sino-Japanese War in 1895 and the Russo-Japanese War in 1905. They recognized with the results of the wars that the main reason why the then small-scale country, Japan, won the wars against the

miscarried and others were short-lived. However, the way to going back from them was leading to Chinese constitutionalism. Under the constitutional spirits, most constitutions (drafts) authorize local autonomy principles.

At the end of the Qing dynasty, citizens actively took action. After announcement of the outline, a constitutionalism group demonstrated in the whole nation three times to hold the national parliament promptly. Together with the establishment of a national parliament at the middle of 1909, a local assembly was held in each province, in which lots of landowners with a flowering of culture and wealthy persons became members of assembly. In 1911, after the Wuchang Uprising occurred, the Qing dynasty publicly announced the article 19 of important problems of the constitution in order to make a concession to largely restrict the monarch's power. This procedure closely resembled the United Kingdom in the 17th century which showed the procedure of reformism. However, in China at the beginning of the 20th century, they did not have enough time to reform. Both international and domestic circumstances were growing more and more tense, and too many economic and social contradictions were accumulated. The reform process of the last Chinese dynasty, Qing dynasty, was finally finished by the revolution. It might be said as a kind of disadvantage of backwardness.

(III) Peasants' autonomy system in new China: current situation and suggestions

The democratic evolution in China started in rural areas, as the family contract system in agricultural production started as the first step of reform and open door

---

two large empires, China and Russia, was institutions of the nation, which meant that the results of wars were the results of difference between autocratic government and constitutional government. Some months after the Russo-Japanese War was finished, the needs of constitutional government were aroused all over the nation. Qing dispatched five ministers like Zai Ze Duanfang to Europe and USA, and they returned one year after. Qing government promulgated the official preliminary draft of constitution on September 1, 1906, the fundamental principles of the Imperial Constitution in 1908, and the 19 important articles of constitution in 1911.

After Sun Yat-sen took office as the temporary president of the Republic of China, they promulgated the temporary constitution of the Republic of China on March 11, 1912. On October 31, 1913, the Chinese parliament in which the majority of them were occupied by the National Party promulgated the constitutional draft of the Republic of China, however, Yuan Shikai ordered dissolution of the nation and the draft of constitution miscarried. On May 1, 1914, the temporary constitution of the Republic of China was promulgated, led by Yuan Shikai and the parliamentary system was changed to be a presidential system. During the disorder among military cliques, on October 10, 1923, the first formal constitution, constitution of the Republic of China, of the Chinese history was promulgated. Also on May 5, 1936, at the cabinet of the National Party, the constitutional draft of the Republic of China was prepared but, because of the full outbreak of the war between China and Japan, it was aborted again without the approval of parliament. In 1946 a national meeting was held led by the National Party in which the constitution of the Republic of China (at present Taiwanese constitution) was signed, which was implemented on January 1, 1947.

policy in the Chinese economy. Article 111 of the constitution of the People's Republic of China in 1982 prescribed that executive, deputy executive, and committee member of rural committees for peasants were elected by direct vote. In the middle of the 1990s, more than 90 per cent of peasants' autonomous committee carried out elections. In more than 50 per cent of villages, peasants representative meetings started and were regularly held, which got involved in public service of village and supervised executives of the village (Research Group on the Peasants' Autonomous System in Chinese Rural Areas, 1995).

Wang explains that peasants' autonomy was an institutional compromise (Wang Shaoguang, 1997, chap. ten.). During the days of the people's commune, because various resources were concentrated upon the communes and executives, such jobs as food production, sale to the nation, agricultural tax collection etc. were intensively settled. However, under the family contract system, various resources were dispersed among each family and it became difficult to carry out the orders (like collecting food, agricultural tax, agricultural costs, conscription, family plans etc.) from central government and to provide public services in rural society. At the beginning of the 1980s, therefore, in rural area peasants' committees came into existence which were voluntarily established basic organizations in rural society. Those days each area had a name which was not unified and was restricted to covering the extent of providing service, however, after then they were moving towards maturity level.

Basic government in China has been towns and villages, and farming villages are autonomous organizations which have no financial authority. Financial revenues of farming villages consist of some portions of agricultural tax and costs, and of collecting revenues from peasants with the principle of one event one tax. Former revenues are used for daily expenditure of farming villages (including executives' salary), and latter revenues for public service for rural society and infrastructure construction (like road, bridge, elementary school building construction, establishing enterprises). Before peasants' autonomous committees were established, as immoderate behaviors of executives in farming villages were not appropriately supervised; peasants gave a shriek in various ways at collecting funds, which led to establishing the committee. One of the buzzwords in farming villages was that "be careful about fire, thief, and executive" pointed out, conflicts between executives and peasants were accumulated and displayed a limit to the traditional executives and peasants' model. It is interpreted that, although the economic system in rural areas was changing, the political system remained, the gap between them became more serious.

After a peasants' autonomous committee was established, it was reported that executives' behaviors were well supervised, opportunities to exchange opinions on explanations and necessities about financial expenditures were formed, and peasants became more cooperative. Wang Shaoguang (1997) positively evaluated that democratic decision making system raised the absorbing ability of national finance. The details of evaluation on positive democratic system were as following; (1) first was to secure public interest. Executives wanted to use the finance for constructing official buildings, purchasing passenger cars, but rather often peasants changed them to finance school construction, rural economic development. (2) Second was to check the details of financial revenues and expenditures by a peasants' representative meeting which could contribute to prevent the corruption. (3) Third was to improve their unity by making opportunities to express various opinions. Also Wang Shaoguang(1997) was given the idea from effects of the peasants' autonomous committee (from Dutch and British examples in 18th century) suggesting that, opposing the uncooperative attitude of local government after the tax sharing system was introduced, by establishing special organization and by participating central decision making procedure, local representatives could have voting rights. Wang Shaoguang (1997) was emphasizing that in order for central government to improve financial controlling ability, they should allow local government to participate in the policy decision process.

We partly share the views of Wang Shaoguang (1997). The democratic process in China should be born endogenously and as a matter of fact a democratic tendency in China has been kept in step with the economic development process. Chinese transition and development has been characterized as gradual way which we think is positively evaluated as appropriately embedded in Chinese society. However, what should be indicated is that emphasizing the nation's ability does not lead to the final solution of various problems in relations between central and local government. By emphasizing the nation's ability, in China after 1994, they realized the upward shift of financial authority, which at the same time the by-product, downward shift of responsibility to provide public service, came into existence. We should not be optimistic to think that establishing a special organization, in which local representatives participate and vote on policy decision procedure in central government, is just a democratic procedure within the government and that it is easy to change the current situation. Actually, before implementing the tax sharing system, a central meeting on economy and finance has been held every year. At the meeting they have no voting rights, however they have insisted on their self interest, about some of which the central government has been forced to compromise.

Both nation's ability and special organization are authoritarian development systems without peoples' participation. If expansion of control space is necessary, it is not desirable for Chinese political and economic development to expand the control space in exchange with pressing autonomous space. As gradual way of transition in China means creative destruction, institutional reforms should be improved to be advantageous for local autonomy.

Based upon Chinese tradition that "imperial power cannot extend over local area" and former Chinese experience on autonomy of towns and villages, various proposals were submitted to expand locally autonomous institutions. Generally speaking, they are classified into two types which are (1) towns and villages government becomes the branch office of county government and (2) autonomy of towns and villages expands. The former opinion asserts that, through strengthening the peasants' autonomy system, towns and villages government should gradually disappear, meanwhile the latter insists that towns and villages should be promoted to be higher rank autonomous governments. Such a way of thinking, which says that sub-township is a lower rank than town and township, and town and township are lower rank than county, has Chinese characteristics. Essentially, such local governments as city, town, township, sub-township are administrative units which should be classified by population, industrial structure etc. They are independent of each other and direct elections should be carried out there.

(IV) Possibility of expansion of private property rights and of establishment of constitutional government

I. Private property rights as a base of constitutional government

Local autonomy and constitutional government cannot be separated from each other. The main existence of constitutional government is the parliamentary system. The history of originating a parliamentary system suggests to us that a private property system becomes an important social base for the system. Because of private property, the nation state has the nature of taxing the nation. Also because of private property, private assets are dispersed around the regions and country which makes tax collection extremely difficult. Yang Xiaokai (2004) asserts that constitutional government and a republican form of government was born before the popular election system, and private property system is a base of constitutional government. Pipes (1999) also explained that the private property system of land was the base of constitutional government and parliamentary system of United Kingdom.

We should recognize that parliament was established as a place of collective negotiation between king and people. For example, in the United Kingdom, parliament was the institutional mechanism which was needed to establish to oppose reckless tax collection by the king. When the negotiation mechanism called a parliament did not work well, revolution occurred. All of the three revolutions happened in the United Kingdom, France and United States of America, the reason for them was reckless tax collection behavior of the king. From their history, we can recognize close relations among the four, private property rights, parliament, constitutional government, and local autonomy.

It is understand the reason why, in the fundamental principles of the imperial constitution established in 1908 at the end of Qing dynasty, a locally autonomous system was introduced because of the relations between private property rights and constitutional government. Also in the seven drafts of the constitution planned after then, all of them allowed the local autonomy system.

II. Recommendation of a constitutional one-party system

Returning to contemporary China, suffering from the disadvantage of backwardness (meaning that a reforming way was dispelled by the way of revolution) led to the communist revolution which established a communist China in 1949.

In China during 1949-1978, as there was the public property rights system, the fundamental condition for a constitutional government system did not exist. Because of public property rights, the national ability to have financial revenue was inexhaustible (whose typical example was the scissors shaped price system). Of the four constitutions established after 1949, any of them have no concrete regulation on a tax collection system. The current situation, in which the decision authority of the assembly on tax collection rights and government budget has been extremely incomplete, has seemed to be related to the public property rights system after 1949.

However, the Chinese communist party which has monopolistic controlling power denied voluntarily the Mao Zedong development system in 1978 and was transformed into Deng Xiaoping development system led by wise authoritarianism (which indicates the East Asian model showing the authoritarian system with economic growth sharing the benefits among the people). As stated above, in the Chinese rural areas after 1978, because of implementation of a family contract system, production process and assets accumulation has shown the dispersion and tax collection costs for the nation have been remarkably increased, which caused a peasants' autonomy system endogenously.

In China gradually privatization, a market oriented system, and private property rights have been improved in a legal sense. By the constitutional revision in March 2004, the principle saying that legally private owned assets are protected has been established. Also at the National Parliament held in March 2007 they signed the real right law. It could be interpreted as actual expression of the constitutional revision.

The logic of internal politics of the four; private property rights, parliament, constitutional government, and local autonomy, seems to suggest that China will after all introduce gradually a parliament system, constitutional government, and local autonomy system in a true sense. As the first step, we recommend the constitutional one-party system. First of all, the National Parliament has complete decision authority on the national budget, which should have appropriate supervision for the government. It is necessary then that party leadership should change the activity from the front to behind the scenes. Official party document should be limited to circulate within the party, and if it is necessary to change the principle of society, the change should be done through the parliament. Also the reform of party affairs as the People's party carried out in Taiwan in 1950s should be implemented. It should be recognized as a blood renewal movement under the one-party politics.

To unite the constitutional one-party system from the top with the local autonomy system from the bottom becomes a driving force for the Chinese political system to be more reasonable. The adhesiveness of them is we think a private property rights system which is a necessary product of a market oriented reform.

Concluding remarks

Deficiency of tax sharing system in China is the product of an authoritarian development system on the one hand, it has a relationship with an incomplete market oriented economic system on the other. As regards in particular the relationship between government and market, government and state owned enterprises, it is necessary to transform government functions and to reorganize the system, and to establish a legal system for a market economy.

In the extension of the above, the consistency problem of political system with economic system should be considered. For example, to reform the soft budget system is, we think, necessary for a local assembly to return.

Under the way of gradual reform, the key issue to examine systemic transition problems in China is that economic development will bring about endogenously the adjustment of the political system. Although undoubtedly the structural reform of relations between central and local government in China representatively indicated by tax sharing system is halfway through the transition now, we could expect in the extension the change of political economy in China.

Chapter 5
Political Economy of the Chinese Development Model: The Fact-following Mechanism of Institutional Change in Chinese Society

Introduction

In Chapters 5 and 6 we investigate, from both economic and political viewpoints, the important topic of asking whether China could join the East Asian model countries.

An authoritarian development system is summarized as its characteristics given as 'a high rate of economic growth and low degree of political participation' (actually it is necessary simultaneously to attain both a shared and a high rate of economic growth). The main task of China in the systemic transition has been the 'economic construction', not the 'institutional democratization'. However, the transition of the economic system, mainly coming from such economic construction, has been covered not only by the economic aspect but also by much more 'embedded' aspects, such as social and political ones. As a result, the logic saying that authoritarianism was rejected by authoritarianism itself came into existence (as regards an authoritarian system in East Asia, see Chapter 6). We think the Chinese reform of democracy in the gradual transition has never been of the 'ideology preceding' type, but rather of the 'approval after the fact' type. In this chapter, in the light of various characteristics of the East Asian model, we examine the important topic of whether China could join the East Asian model countries.

This chapter has seven sections. In the second section, we give an outline of the complexity of the Deng Xiaoping development system. In the third section, we examine the establishment and characteristics of the Chinese development system from the viewpoints of the East Asian development model. In the fourth section, we investigate the characteristics of the whole national system in the Chinese economic development model, whose attention is paid, first, to the risk transmission mechanism behind the competitiveness of low-cost products, and second, to the task of transforming from price competitiveness to technology competitiveness. In the fifth section, various problems of systemic transition are discussed, which are, for example, a driving force of systemic transition, the advantages and disadvantages of backwardness, the capability of challenge and counter-challenge of civilization. In the sixth section, we consider the evolution of a fact following mechanism of institutional change, whose main attention is given to: (1) the protection of workers' interests and the establishment of a new type of trade union, (2) the clearer sign of problems on peasants' representative rights, (3) the necessity of establishment of environmental rights. A short conclusion is given in the final section.

Complexity of Deng Xiaoping's development system

The characteristics of the Chinese economic development model after 1978 (Deng Xiaoping development system) are summarized as the following: (1) whole nation's system (a kind of extreme development oriented system); (2) reform and open door system (opposite of the closed system in Mao Zedong's era); and (3) the market oriented system (transition from a central planning system). That is to say, Deng Xiaoping's development system is a kind of authoritarian development system. In addition, it has interactions with the reform and open door system, with the whole nation's system, and the market-oriented system (see Figure 5.1).

The market-oriented system in China has consisted of the mobility of production factors, the establishment of a price mechanism and the recurrence of state-owned enterprises towards normal enterprises. Fundamentally, a market-oriented system is superior to a central planning system in such senses as symmetry of information and motivation for workers, and a competitive principle contributes to efficiency of enterprise management and welfare improvement of the society (consumer sovereignty).

The market oriented system is fairly consistent with reform and the open door system; however it rather contradicts the whole nation's system (for example, a serious difference between consumers' sovereignty and producers' sovereignty). During the transition period in China, such systems, which are fundamentally difficult to make consistent, coexisted in various ways.

On the market-oriented system and open system

The open system might be only one way to abolish the Entropy Law mentioned in the introduction of this book. For economic development, it is said that an open policy is a kind of effective stimulus model. Through its open system, lots of information can be exchanged, which is encouraging demand and supply to be extended. It makes the market size increase. The division of labor and the transaction network have been developed at a global scale, which contributes to technological progress and efficiency improvement. It could be understood that the division of labor insisted on by Adam Smith (1776) expanded to be a global scale. Meanwhile, such economies as a primitive community, a traditional economic system, a central planning system and an industrialization strategy based upon import substitution have closed characteristics and the results are completely the opposite.

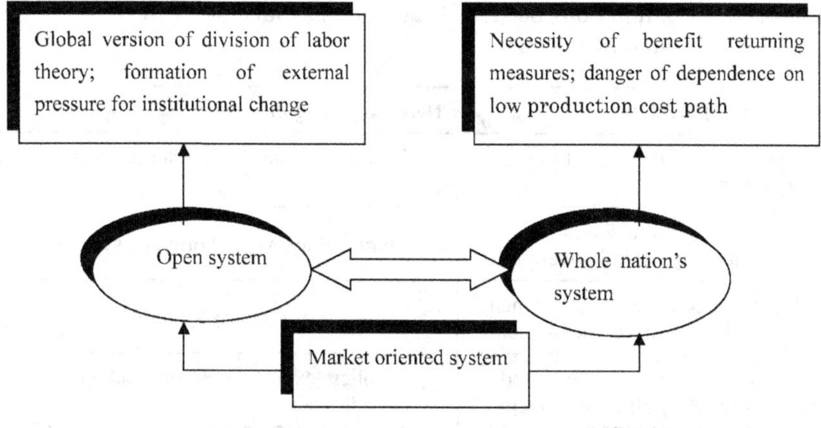

Source: Author.

Figure 5.1 Complexity of Deng Xiaoping's development system

At the same time, an open system creates external pressure towards institutional change, which is as effective as providing a measure of substitute institution under the lack of incentive (see the following section).

On the market-oriented system and whole nation's system

The whole national system in China was established in Mao Zedong's era. The catch-up strategy, which was developed in post-war emerging nation states, seems to include the whole nation's system. It might be reasonable, to a certain extent, that the whole nation's system is necessary under the condition of resource shortage on the one hand. However, it might be dangerous on the other. If any benefit returning measures are not carried out in a certain period in a certain way, the whole national system would reach the limit and might collapse. For example, in the Mao Zedong development system, exclusiveness was fully occupied in each sector, in which the possibility to return the benefit was suppressed. If it is implemented for many years, a sacrificed sector (such as agriculture and rural areas) cannot be maintained. The whole national system is just like a wartime system, and it is unrealistic to be depending upon it for a long period. Thus, it seems to be indispensable that the Chinese economy, which had an exclusive central planning system for 30 years, was in danger of collapse. (See Chapter 1 for the details.)

The Chinese economic development pattern after 1978 has the aspect of being the whole nation's system. Because the Chinese way of transition is gradual, the aspect of the whole nation's system is not radically eliminated. Also, it is reasonable for the Chinese way of a national system that, after 1978, China was confronted with a resource shortage. Around 30 years after the reform and open door policy

Table 5.1 Comparisons between Mao Zedong's ideology and Deng Xiaoping's theory

Mao Zedong ideology	Deng Xiaoping theory
Egalitarianism, Government looking after system	Anti-egalitarianism, The harder the richer system
Administrative centralization, Centralization by central government	Decentralization, Market oriented system
Public property system (state owned system and collective owned system)	Various ways of property system
Self-rehabilitation under the closed system (import substitution strategy)	Open policy (export promotion, foreign capital inflow)
Idealism	Pragmatism
Populist line (AnGang Constitution was the example)	Experts governing country
Priority to politics	Priority to economy
Radicalism	Gradualism
Human-governed system	Law-governed system

Note: The origin of the AnGang Constitution was as follows. In March 1960, Mao Zedong gave instructions to establish the system saying 'two participants, one reform and three unions' regarding the management of the Anshan iron and steel works. The 'two participants' meant that executives participated in labor and laborers participated in management, 'one reform' showed that unreasonable prescriptions and institutions were reformed, and 'three unions' indicated that the three of laborer, executive and engineer were united. By the state-owned industrial enterprise policy act (commonly known as industrial 70 articles), they decided that this management system was formerly approved and an employee representative meeting system under the directives by communist committee of the factory was established. The aims of the act were displayed that the administration and management sections of the enterprise was supervised and the bureaucratic system was overcome, and the democratic management system of the enterprise was improved. As a matter of fact, we should recognize the aspect indicating that the AnGang Constitution was presented as the opposition to the Soviet style management method, in which a factory manager took whole responsibility, after the Sino–Soviet relations deteriorated.

Source: Author.

in 1978, China had various measures of benefit returning (for example, go-west development strategy, industrial region promotional strategy in the northeast area (2002), central region promotion strategy (2004) etc), but the country still has the necessity to return the benefit measures, as regional disparity and income disparity have been expanding, and environmental destruction has been worsening (see Chapter 2 about the details). We should point out the danger of dependence on a low production cost path in the Chinese high rate of economic growth led by foreign demand under the national system.

The problems are indicated as the following. (1) Both domestic demand shortage and trade conflict occur at the same time. (2) The negative externality of excluding environment costs occurs, which means that national health is damaged and the development model of energy and resource consumption is easy to come to a deadlock. (3) The producers' sovereignty might cause such economic effects as overinvestment and an asset bubble – low technology plus competitiveness of Chinese products.

Generally speaking, under the Deng Xiaoping development regime, the Chinese market-oriented system has the complexity of an open system and the whole nation system, which has caused both sides of FDI inflow and foreign trade expansion, plus various side effects. In order to change the situation, the traditional dependence on a low production cost path should be modified. In the extension of the change, the existence of a new fact following mechanism of institutional change could be recognized in a crossed form of economics and politics (see the following section).

Establishment of an open system in China

Change of institutional environment in China

Since the People's Republic of China was established in 1949, international circumstances had effects on Chinese development. Initially, due to the outbreak of the Korean War in 1950, the USA strengthened the defense of Taiwan. After the Cold War between the East and the West became decisive, China preferred a pro-Soviet model and fully introduced the Soviet-type socialist development model. The personal prestige of Mao Zedong, established in wartime, was powerfully effective after the war. However, at the end of 1950s, Sino–Soviet relations suddenly deteriorated and Mao Zedong advocated the development strategy of independent autonomy and self-rehabilitation to the nation. The Chinese development model was changed from a Soviet-type to a Mao Zedong type. The Mao Zedong ideology (populist line, spiritualism, egalitarianism) was clearly reflected in the Mao Zedong development system afterwards.

After 1978, China entered the socialist construction period of the Chinese way. The main purposes of development strategy in China were changed towards modernization of the economy, improvement of peoples' everyday lives, and advancement of the international position. Since improving the international position of China has become one of the purposes for the nation, China finished the socialist construction in the closed system model and pushed forward with its open system.

Comparisons between Mao Zedong's ideology and Deng Xiaoping's theory

The Chinese development system after 1978 was still been within an authoritarian development system, which is sometimes called a 'development dictatorship' by foreign scholars. However, Deng Xiaoping's development system was definitely different from the system of Mao Zedong's era. Table 5.1 shows comparisons between Mao Zedong's ideology and Deng Xiaoping's theory.

We think that the Deng Xiaoping development system after 1978 was a kind of East Asian development model, because both of them have fairly similar characteristics.

The most important characteristic of the East Asian model is what is called the economic development model led by government. Suehiro (1998) defined the development oriented system to be 'a development model in which, under the slogan of economic development, both a high rate of economic growth and strengthening of national power are realized by mobilizing and regulating human, material and financial resources towards particular aims of the nation (which is generally the industrialization) whose priority is put on national and racial interests not on regional and private interests. Details of the East Asian model are as follows. (1) The market plays the main role and government actively intervenes in the economic development process, which could be said to be a kind of mixed economic system. The government establishes infrastructure, such as road building and harbor facilities construction, through extensive government expenditure, which raises the demand in a macro economic sense. In addition, the government indicates its intention, with various middle and long-term economic plans, to attempt the equilibrium development of the nation. Five years plans such as the post-war Japanese general national development plan (from 1965), India (from 1951), Thailand (from 1960), South Korea (from 1962), Indonesia (from 1969), and also the NEP new economic plan of Malaysia (from 1971) were typical examples. (2) Considering the export oriented open policy, the necessary technology, capital, human resource, management method etc are gained through promoting international trade and inward FDI. The establishment of Japanese MITI in 1949 was the institutional preparation for an export oriented industrialization strategy, and the foreign capital introduction act of South Korea in 1965 and investment encouragement act of Malaysia in 1968 etc were to establish legal environments for attracting foreign capital. (3) Achieve a higher level of education and higher level of educational investment. (4) Achieve a higher rate of saving and a higher rate of investment, which could be recognized as closely connected with Confucian culture, as referred to in the following. (5) Achieve shared growth, which means a good balance between economic growth and income distribution. As far as relations between economic growth and income distribution are concerned, it has been usually accepted that the inverted-U shaped hypothesis insisted on by Kuznets (which expressed that the first disparity was expanding accompanied with economic development, and reached the peak period, after then disparity was reduced – Kuznets, 1955; Williamson, 1965)[1] was scientifically confirmed. The post-war East Asian model has appeared to disprove the hypothesis (World Bank, 1993). Why was the shared growth possible? Was the successful result led by land reform or compound factors that were characteristics of the East Asian model? If there were compound factors, what kind of mechanism (in which various factors had logical relationships) was working? In this chapter we investigate the Chinese development model and expose problems of the Chinese development model in the light of the East Asian model. We think that it is extremely important to examine logical relationships among various factors (because it has close connections with a priority of reforms). (6) Achieve an efficient administrative organization, which means the existence of a modern bureaucratic system in a rational and institutional sense, as Weber (1968) insisted. As the post-war Japanese miracle of high speed economic growth was said to be a 'miracle of MITI' (Johnson, 1982), the efficient administrative organization has been the governmental agency of an actively intervening mechanism for economic development. In Chapter 6, we examine the role of a professional technocrat organization in the transition process of Taiwan. (7) Achieve the common cultural background of Confucian society. Weber (1958) emphasized the important influence of religious culture in the development of capitalism. Weber (1964) concluded that western protestant ethics played positive roles, meanwhile eastern Confucianism was negative because Confucianism had neither an ideology of contract with God nor a tension with this world. In addition to the above, even causational analyses were not the same, there were lots of investigations insisting that Confucianism was a serious factor of economic backwardness. However, after the 1970s, the success of the East Asian model gave evidence of positive relations between Confucianism and the spirit of capitalism, which seemed to be an inverted Weber hypothesis. Some scholars presented the concept of Neo-Confucian Countries, in which the reason for high-speed economic growth in East Asian region was connected with Asian ethics (for example, because of attaching greater importance upon human relations, human networks were utilized – Kahn, 1979).

Yu Yingshi (1991), a historian, argued that, in China, the main reason why they could not have advanced capitalism was not due to a lack of ethics of asceticism but due to the lack of a rationalized process of politics and law. Fang, an economist, also insisted that Chinese traditional culture attached too great an importance upon ethics compared with western culture and Chinese culture had stronger attributes of informal institutions (such as traditional practice, moral ethics, ideology). Thus, Chinese traditional culture (whose center was Confucianism), with stronger attributes of informal institutions, has hindered the development of a capitalist economy. Meanwhile, the economic success of the Chinese people in foreign

1 See Kuznets (1955). Kuznets reached the conclusion by considering income disparity among households, and Williamson verified the hypothesis by arguing that income disparity among regions within a country could hold the same inverted-U shaped hypothesis. See Williamson (1965).

countries was interpreted to be coming from the combination of cultural virtue (diligence of the inside) and legal order (of the outside). Therefore, the method of institutional evolution in China after this would be the successful introduction of a legal mind, whose arrival point might be rationalized institutions. The role of rationalized institutions seems to be the protection of property rights, the removal of asymmetric information, the reduction of transaction cost etc (Fan, 1997, Nakagane, 1979).[2]

The above-stated discussions might be closely related with constitutional economics.[3] We basically recognize the importance of legal order; however, in the days of a wise authoritarianism system, which East Asian model countries experienced, political aspects and socio-economic aspects were divided into two, and at least in the political aspects the elite group kept up social order in place of the law. It might be recognized by comparing the Southeast Asian model with the East Asian model that the way of organizing a bureaucratic system in the transition period might be a serious turning point of success or failure.

Problems in the Chinese development model: comparisons with the East Asian model

Compared with the East Asian model, the Chinese model has clearly more problems to be resolved. In the light of characteristics of the traditional East Asian model, a deep-rooted problem for the Chinese development model has been 'inconsistency'. For example, (1) although governmental active intervention has been implemented, a rationalized institutional bureaucratic system has never been established. (2) Although high speed economic growth was carried out, the shared growth problem has still been serious. (3) Although export oriented industrialization and trade strategy policy has been improved, it has caused higher dependence upon foreign demand, which has brought about trade conflict issues with foreign countries and lack of domestic demand. Such conflicts and contradictions, which

---

2 See Fan (1997). Fan also argued that in Chinese society lots of informal institutions were popular, which made Chinese society more flexible, and made the basis for institutional reform easier. The argument seemed to be similar to the slackly centralized system of Nakagane (1979).

3 Research topics of constitutional economics are the economic effects of the constitution and constitutional government. One of the crucial tasks for this is the dilemma of government activity, because for economic development a government role is indispensable but at the same time government activity is the most serious barrier for economic development. In McKenzie (1984), the concept of constitutional economics was presented for the first time. However, we recognize that after the 1970s such schools as public choice school, legal economics school, neo-economic history school, and the Austrian school substantially contributed to development of constitutional economics. Constitutional economics has been continued from the ideologies and theories of Spinoza (1632–1677), David Hume (1711–1776), Adam Smith (1723–1790), Friedrich von Hayek (1899–1992), James Mcgill Buchanan (1919–) etc.

are coming from inconsistency, have been closely linked to each other and have been amongst most serious problems for the Chinese development model. We can look at them in the following.

(1) Can China simultaneously realize economic growth and fair distribution? The Chinese development model in which both an open system and development oriented system are consistent has enjoyed high speed economic growth. For more than 25 years during 1978–2004, the annual average growth rate in China reached 9.6%, and for more than half of those years China experienced more than 10% growth rate. However, Since Mao Zedong advocated the ten main relations[4] in 1950s, as the present three agricultural problems are called, serious disparity in Chinese society has never disappeared. Shared growth has been the most concerned aim (see later in this chapter).

(2) Can China keep up both economic development and a better environmental situation? Environmental problems are involved in human rights (and called environmental rights) regarding the nations' health and everyday quality of life. In addition, as far as the production aspect is concerned, is it possible to change from an energy- and resource-consuming economic growth pattern to an energy- and resource-saving growth pattern with regard to sustainable growth? (See later in this chapter.)

(3) Export-oriented industrialization and trade strategy and the current situation of foreign demand dependence Foreign demand dependence is a reflection of the economic disparity problem in China, which is both sides of the same coin as the shared growth issue (see later in this chapter).

(4) Chinese task for human resource advancement and current situation of education For many years, in China, both the ratios of public education expenditure to GDP and to budget expenditure have been low. According to

4 At the beginning of 1956, for one and half months, Mao Zedong received the reports of 34 sections of central government on the main tasks for establishing socialism. After then, the political bureau had meetings several times. Based upon these meetings, Mao Zedong summarized the tasks to be the following 'ten relations', which were reported by Mao at the extension meeting of the central political bureau on 25 April, and at the supreme conference of the cabinet on 2 May. The ten relations were: (1) relations among heavy industry, light industry and agriculture; (2) relations between industries of coastal areas and industry of inland areas; (3) relations between economic construction and defense construction; (4) relations between national production organization and personal producers; (5) relations between central and local; (6) relations between Han race and minority race; (7) relations between party and non-party; (8) relations between revolution and anti-revolution; (9) relations between right and wrong; (10) relations between China and foreign countries. Mao Zedong's lecture was to emphasize the characteristics of the Chinese construction of socialism compared with the Soviet model.

UNESCO statistics in 1996, as regards the ratio of public education expenditure to GDP, the world average was 4.8% and the advanced industrialized countries and less developed countries was 5.1% and 3.6% respectively. Also, the ratio of public education expenditure to budget expenditure was 12.7% (world average), 12.3% (advanced industrialized countries), and 14.8% (less developed countries). The Chinese ratio of public education expenditure to GDP and to budget expenditure was only 2.3% and 11.9%. In comparison with the world average and less developed countries, each Chinese ratio was lower.

UNESCO (2003) showed that 70% of the around 800 million adult illiterate population were concentrated on India (34%), China (11%), Bangladesh (6.5%), and Pakistan (6.4%). It says that characteristics of the East Asian model, which expressed a high education level and high educational investment, have been weakly recognized in China. Thus, accompanied with transformation of the Chinese development model, we expect human resource advancement to become necessary.

Problems of a bureaucratic system

Such important problems as complexity of administrative strata, organizational reform problems towards a more simplified system, low policy making ability on several complex socio-economic problems (such as housing, transportation, rural areas, environment problems), corruption etc, should be correctly indicated as very important. Huge scale bureaucracy was necessary for a central planning system, and under the authoritarian system of a unified party and administration the party organization itself became bigger and a dual structure of government occurred. As regards the problems of a bureaucratic system in China, we will concentrate our attention here upon the following.

First, the main characteristic of Chinese bureaucracy has been indicated as being a high ratio of administration management cost to financial expenditure within central budget.

As the result of the above-stated situation, the ratio of administration management cost to financial expenditure within the central budget increased to 19% in 2003 from 4.7% in 1978. Meanwhile, the ratio of public enterprise expenditure, agricultural investment, educational investment, was 11%, 5%, and 2.7% respectively. On the contrary, the ratio of administration management cost in the USA, France, Canada, Japan occupied 9.9%, 6.5%, 7%, and 2.38% respectively.[5] (On the problems of a soft budget constraint and self-expanding government organizations, see Chapter 4).

As regards separation of party and administration, although it has been the slogan for the reform since it was advocated in 1980s, it has never been realistic under a party and nation system in a real sense (it means an only one party system

5 The lecture on viewpoints of scientific development given by Professor Li Junjie of the Central Party School, which was held in March 2007.

as a matter of fact, in which the only one party forms the core of national politics even if the party is not selected by national election). Taking into consideration the mechanism of a market oriented system, party affairs reform, which was carried out by the Nationalist Party in Taiwan in 1950s, might become necessary in China. This is because, in the market-oriented system, which has progressed day by day its division of labor, the system of rule of law (and rule of experts) will become indispensable. If the party system is too different from the surrounding organizations, corruption in the party organization is widespread in the whole of China and the Chinese economy is easy to be disordered.

As far as the advancement of reform of party affairs is concerned, it has been inactive. Although we can recognize the tendency towards the rule of experts (see Chapter 3), it has never reached the radical reform of Communist Party system. That is to say, traditional characteristics of the reform of party affairs have been, after all, possible to a certain degree, but the subtraction of party affairs has never been possible. We think it is easy to understand the difficulty of reform of party affairs because the executive leaders of the party have been the most powerful vested interest group in China. Recently, in 2006, in each province they reformed the party to reduce the number of secretaries and deputy secretaries. The reform plan, which states that the numbers of deputy secretaries (there were some provinces with more than ten deputy secretaries) are to be decreased to two, has been carried out. The purpose of it is to check the power of the secretary. That is to say, the total number of secretaries and deputy secretaries is diminished and their share at the party committee of managing directors is decreased. It means, thus, that the traditional situation of a secretariat meeting (in which secretary and deputy secretaries participate, and the secretary takes the initiative), whose resolution automatically becomes the resolution of the party committee of managing directors, will change.

However, the author thinks that the impact of the above reform plan against the secretary initiative system has never been so serious. The important things to reform regarding party affairs seem to be the following. First, following the course of the idea of the rule of technocrat, the structure of communist party leaders should be shifted towards such an idea. It is indispensable that a huge number of full-time party leaders are not in the center of politics (see also Chapter 6). Second, the difficult problem to be overcome for many years has been to establish an effective system in which the party secretary can be supervised, because the party secretary occupies the peak position of party organization in any level. The effects of such traditional measures as reforming the horizontally organized system of the party discipline inspection committee (the deputy secretary of the party organization of the same governmental level has been responsible for the discipline inspection committee as its secretary, and thus it is impossible for the deputy secretary to supervise his or her superior, the party secretary) to a vertically supervised system have been limited. It has seemed to be necessary because the secretary and other members of discipline inspection committee are self-interest oriented persons. If the communist party system does not become more transparent (by such a system as the introduction of direct election), it will be difficult to prevent corruption.

In the corruption affairs that were disclosed by the middle of 2008, a large number indicated the participation of the secretary of the discipline inspection committee. This should not be overlooked in China.

As long as the Chinese Communist Party has governed the country, the healthy movement of party organization system should be the most important. The author's way of thinking suggests that, if the maintenance of the authoritarian system is a precondition for the reform of the party, the only one way is to bring the direct election of the secretary into the basic level of party organization (and then the level of direct election will become gradually higher). In China, democratization of inside the party has been constantly emphasized; however, thus far, effective measures have never been employed and the corruption coming from systemic defect has never been eliminated. As far as the Chinese Communist Party has been the center of politics, democratization inside the party would have enormous effects on the whole of society. How, then, should the democratization inside the party be realized? What the author wishes to emphasize is that the most effective measure is direct election.

As far as Japan is concerned, they attained a more simplified administration (see Figure 5.2). Japan has the smallest number of civil servants per 1000 people, i.e. 33.6, on the contrary, France has the largest which reached 89.7. Although Japan employed the post-war economic growth path led by government, it has a small number of civil servants. It seems to be evidence that an efficient administrative organization surely exists, as the East Asian model emphasizes.

Regarding the problems on bureaucracy, see also Chapter 6 of this book.

The second characteristic of Chinese bureaucracy has been pointed out to be a serious corruption problem. Chinese corruption was systemic corruption: thus, the only way to solve the problem was reconstruction of the institutions. In April 2005, the Public Service Law of the People's Republic of China was signed, into which, however, the final private property report system of public services was not incorporated. We think this has to be a serious defect. The private property report system of public services started in Sweden in 1776 and has been introduced in most countries and has contributed to the prevention of corruption

In China, both secretariats of the Chinese communist party and the Chinese cabinet jointly promulgated the 'regulation on income report of executives in higher rank than county level of party administration' on May 25, 1995. This was the first regulation of the income report of the executives in China, but because there were too many inborn defects in institutional building, it was not correctly carried out. Meanwhile, the attempted ordinance of public service promulgated in 1993 entered the stage to formally make a law 12 years after the attempted ordinance. However, the private property report system was miscarried, although the people and scholars hoped it was signed. It seemed to indicate that bureaucrats in China have had a serious effect on regulation as the vested interests group.

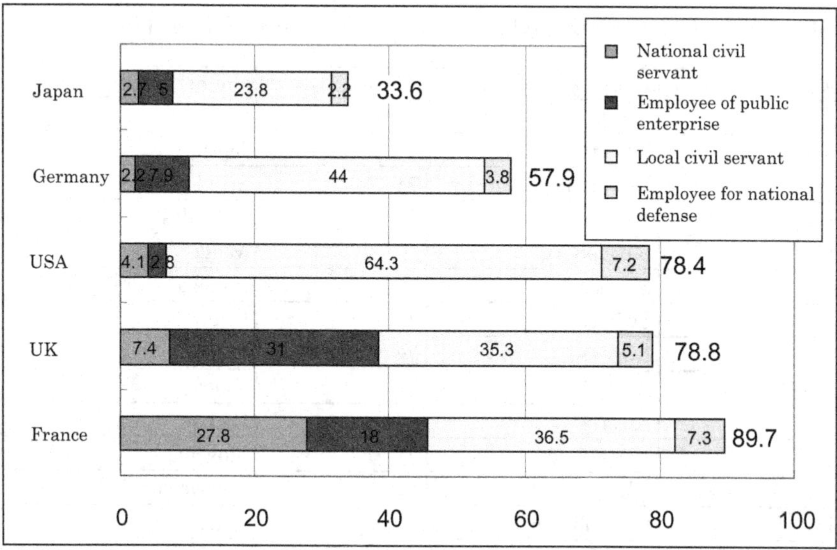

Source: Ministry of Public Management, Home Affairs, Posts and Telecommunications (Japan).

Figure 5.2 International comparison of the number of civil servants per 1000 people

Undoubtedly the corruption problems in China have been closely related with the authoritarian bureaucratic system. If Chinese society cannot solve the corruption problems, China might fall into the 'Soft State' as Myrdal (1968) insisted. The Soft State is pointed out to be an inefficient and a corrupt bureaucratic system. Weber (1964) called the mixed system of official business with personal affairs, from the Qin dynasty to the Qing dynasty in China, to be 'patrimonial bureaucracy'. In the global competitiveness report of the World Economic Forum, they have an evaluation of corruption problems. Undoubtedly, corruption has been an extremely important problem for Chinese competitiveness – as shown later.

(I) International comparison of corruption problems Tables 5.2 and 5.3 show the corruption perception index – the research results in 2005 of Transparency International.[6] Table 5.2 shows the world ranking, in which four countries, Singapore (5th rank), Hong Kong (15th rank), Japan (21st rank), and Malaysia (39th rank) are included in the rank of East Asian countries and regions. The table of the Asian and Pacific countries shows that Asian NIEs and Japan occupied

6 This is the international anti-corruption NGO founded in 1993, the head of which is located in Berlin and whose branches are established in more than 100 countries and regions. The corruption perception index of each country is a result generally evaluated by various public opinion polls, experts' researches, opinions of business persons etc.

Table 5.2 Corruption perception index: World top 39th list (2005)

Rank	Country	Rank	Country
1	Iceland	21	Chile
2	Finland		Japan
	New Zealand	23	Spain
4	Denmark	24	Barbados
5	Singapore	25	Malta
6	Sweden	26	Portugal
7	Switzerland	27	Estonia
8	Norway	28	Israel
9	Australia		Oman
10	Austria	30	UAE
11	Netherlands	31	Slovenia
	UK	32	Botswana
13	Luxembourg		Qatar
14	Canada		Taiwan
15	Hong Kong		Uruguay
16	Germany	36	Bahrain
17	USA	37	Cyprus
18	France	39	Jordan
19	Belgium		Malaysia
	Ireland		

Source: Transparency International (www.transparency.org).

the less corrupt rank, but China's position was 78th in the world and 12th in the region (the Chinese rank in the world was 66th in 2004 and 70th in 2006). Such countries as Japan and NIEs, which were successful in shared growth, also showed successful solutions against the problems of political corruption.

(II) Seriously corrupted fields The central discipline inspection committees in China entrusted, in 2004, the integrity of research to each local discipline inspection committee and statistical group, whose research was implemented in ten regions, Beijing, Helongjiang, Hebei, Jiangsu, Jiangxi, Hubei, Guangxi, Guangdong, Sichuan, Xinjiang (see Table 5.4). According to the results, the degree of concern of corruption was third (32.2%) after employment (51.42%) and social security (34.67%).

Meanwhile, as far as seriously corrupted fields are concerned, the first was construction (38.54%), which was followed in second place by public peace, public prosecutor, and law courts (38.53%), in third place by the medical field (29.24%), fourth place by the educational field (26.13%), and the fifth place by the organizational personnel field (21.2%).

Table 5.3 Corruption perception index: Asia and Pacific countries (2005)

Rank of the region	Rank of the world	Country
1	2	Netherlands
2	5	Singapore
3	9	Australia
4	15	Hong Kong
5	21	Japan
6	32	Taiwan
7	39	Malaysia
8	40	South Korea
9	55	Fiji Islands
10	59	Thailand
11	77	Laos
12	78	China
13		Sri Lanka
14	85	Mongolia
15	88	India
16	107	Vietnam
17	117	Nepal
18		Philippines
19	130	Cambodia
20	137	Papua New Guinea

Source: Transparency International.

We recognize that corruption in China varies from one region to another. (1) In the developed regions, corruption of unified phenomena between government and business has frequently occurred. As mentioned above, people understand that corruption connected with the field of construction projects has been most serious. (2) In some less developed regions, the phenomena of selling government posts have been remarkable (expressed as the organizational personnel field corruption) as it quite often happened that high ranking local government officials, such as party secretariats, sold government posts. (3) In the lowest level rural areas, because neither a developed economy nor resources such government posts exist to be sold, peasants would become direct victims (of bribery).

(III) Social risk of corruption problems Under the authoritarian system, the side-effects of the corruption might raise a degree of social mobilization that would be possible to go beyond the ability to ensure the institution. In that case, it might be indispensable to bring about social disorder (as Samuel P. Huntington asserts with the formula saying that social stability = ability to ensure the institution to give

Table 5.4 Corruption perception research of communist party (2004)

Rank	Field of concern	Ranking of degree of corruption
1	Unemployment problem 51.42%	Construction process 38.54%
2	Social security problem 34.67%	Public peace, prosecution, court 38.53%
3	Government integrity, anti-corruption problem 32.2%	Medical 29.24%
4	Medical system reform problem 31.46%	Education 26.13%
5	Education problem for the younger generation 28.77%	Organizational personnel 21.2%

Source: Xinhua Net, Beijing, January 26, 2004.

citizens satisfaction/degree of social mobilization). For example, the Tian'an'men Affairs in 1989 might be related to the phenomena of social corruption, especially the serious corruption phenomena of rent seeking (meaning that they utilized the dual price structure at the end of the 1980s, the price difference between commodities controlled by the planning authority and commodities without any control, and got profit from the price difference. In particular, the corruption of government officials who authorized the allocation of lower price commodities was pointed out).

Meanwhile, corruption problems do not become remarkable or become tolerable for the people under definite conditions. Those conditions are as follows.

i. At the early stage of economic development, when the economy is expanding and job opportunity is secured, and the level of everyday life is improving, it might be easily recognized that corruption is a lubricant for economic development. (In particular, for the former socialist economies, because every regulation was rather strict, such a tolerant recognition became more generalized). For example, Myrdal (1968) called the money to be used for corruption in less developed countries 'speed money'. The money seemed to be effective for raising the efficiency of the bureaucratic system.
ii. After the middle stage of economic development, when economic development is satisfactory and income distribution is relatively fair, most people are not so interested in corruption problems, although they might be targets for the intelligentsia and student movements. (Examples were Taiwan and South Korea in the authoritarianism days). Undoubtedly, both Taiwan and South Korea successfully adjusted high speed economic growth and a disparity problem, which realized the shared growth. However, is it possible to generalize the East Asian model, like Taiwan and South Korea,

to much wider regions? In particular, in such countries with as great a variety as China, it seems to be difficult to follow the East Asian model. Actually, in China, corruption problems are hindering the shared growth. For example, a real estate bubble in various regions in China has been closely related to the corruption of local government officials. It has caused not only macro economic distortion (like financial risk and excessive investment) but also lots of Fangnu (meaning those who have no possibility of buying a house and have a huge amount of debt) in the micro economic sense, and this could damage the welfare level of the people. It could also be asserted that the soaring prices of real estate in urban areas expanded the business costs, which would decrease the competitiveness of economic activities (Chen Yun, 2007a).

iii. The corruption problems do not become remarkable or become tolerable for the people when the people are in closed circumstances and a full asymmetric information situation exists. In China, with a gradual policy of reform, such situations have become less and less. Because TVs and mobile phones have become more and more popular, even in rural areas, it becomes difficult for people to be isolated from information (if people can be isolated from information, it means the regional economy concerned is suffering from expansion). Ironically, if the economy does not expand, corruption is not a beneficial activity. However, if the economy is developed, TVs and mobile phones are popular, and are convenient tools to expose corruption. Thus, corruption has become a more risky business.

Because of the authoritarian system, it is not strange that accompanying systemic corruption exists. In addition, because of the systemic corruption, we think it is not fully resolved without a systemic transformation. However, is it possible to produce, from the present system, a driving force to transform the system? By considering the countries of the East Asian model, the process to realize shared growth is the process to fight against corruption. We thus think in China, it is necessary to learn from the experience of Taiwan and South Korea, who experienced an authoritarianism development system (see Chapter 6).

The East Asian model also has such characteristics as a high rate of saving and a high rate of investment, which it shares with China in the form of the whole nation's system.

The characteristics of the whole nation's system in the Chinese economic development model

Background of the establishment of the whole nation's system

The whole nation's system has a long history in China. As far as the whole national system is concerned, it reminds us easily of the physical education system in

China. The origin of the whole national physical education system was after the establishment of the new nation of China. The government official of the general bureau of national physical education, Li Zhijian, mentioned that the whole national system was to have a maximum goal of national interest, it was to be a constructive system and to have a managing mechanism to establish important projects at both national level and world level by mobilizing physical and mental resources in the nation (Ke Yan, 2002). In China it is believed that the country achieved its 1054 world records and 1498 world champions because of the whole nation's physical education system.

The history of the national physical education system started in 1984 after the Los Angeles Olympic Games finished. When the national physical education committee established the Olympic strategy, some executives indicated that the rapid rise of advantageous games for China was contributed to by the nation's physical education system. The contents of the nation's system were (1) a 'one stop shop' training system, (2) a national athletic competition system, and (3) a long-term training system of the national team. Because such a system comprising physical education, competitive organization and management method was similar with the development model of 'two bombs and one satellite' (meaning the atomic bomb, the hydrogen bomb and a man-made satellite), it was called the 'whole nation's system'. Afterwards the whole nation's system has been pointed out as the overall system of physical education in China (Liang Xiaolong et al., 2006).

Generally speaking, after less developed counties carried out their national independence, in order to for these nations to develop it is necessary for them intensively to allocate limited resources into particular fields. Because world records and world champions are effective in raising national pride, they are selected to be the goals of the resource allocation. As a matter of fact, after the new China was established, the whole nation's system was not limited to the physical education system, but was spread out over other social fields including economic development.

In the 1980s, when US–Japan trade conflicts were serious, the Japanese people were satirized by international society as worker bees living in rabbit hutches. That is to say, mobilizing national virtue, diligence and saving, to increase investment, which decreases production costs. The Japanese national system was suggested to be the origin of international trade conflicts. Such Japanese styles as peoples' way of life, peoples' everyday life situation, government-led industrial policy, and so on, were targets of criticism. We think that China has shared and evolved the form of the East Asian model coming from Japan on a much bigger scale.

Characteristics of the national development system

The national system in China was established towards a development strategy centered on heavy industries before 1978 (see Chapter 1), and after 1978 China has tried to transform the heavy-industries-led strategy several times but has never fully broken away from it.

The fundamental characteristics of the national development system after 1978 were as follows. (1) The first is the supremacy of the nation and the people's interest, which means that regional- and self-interest step back. Employment of the disequilibrium development strategy has good reasons (see Chapter 2). (2) The second characteristic is a development strategy led by strong government. A typical example is the positive financial policy led by a huge amount of government investment. (3) The third characteristic is producers' predominance over consumers, which might be a continuation of producers' sovereignty from the days of a central planning system. The details are given below.

(1) Economic growth led by investment Table 5.5 indicates the ratios of capital formation and consumption to GDP. After the reform and open door policy started in 1978, the investment ratio in China gradually decreased but, from 1982, began to increase. During 1987 and 1992, the ratio fluctuated and finally reached 42.6% in 1993. In 2000 the ratio was 35.3% and after then it had an upward tendency which was recorded as 42.5% in 2006. However, the type of economic growth led by investment has various problems. Through the overinvestment, the macro economic situation was overheated, and because domestic demand was limited, excess capacity of production had to shift to foreign markets. Meanwhile, the ratio of consumption gradually decreased to 58.1% in 1995 from 67.1% in 1981. Afterwards, the ratio returned to 62.3% in 2000, but still decreased to 49.9% in 2006.

Generally speaking, the growth of capital formation and consumption in China had no balance between them. The weakening of consumption was closely connected to domestic demand shortage and the stagnated import rate of expansion, and the domestic capacity of production meant it was necessary to export more.

One of the characteristics of the East Asian development model was a high rate of saving and a high rate of investment. At the initial stage of economic development, such a high rate tendency could be evaluated as a positive factor for economic development. However, from the middle and long-term points of view, the expansion of domestic demand might become an important task in order to maintain the balance of demand and supply (particularly taking into consideration trade conflicts). We should pay attention to the facts, which say that that only countries and regions that successfully realized shared growth could maintain firm domestic demand. The East Asian model countries such as Japan and NIEs are good examples.

(2) Predominance of asset income There have been internal relations between the GDP structure in expenditure and the GDP structure in distribution.

Since the reform and open door policy started in China, the ratio of asset income to GDP has been continuously high. Table 5.6 shows that the ratio of asset income to GDP was 18.3% in 1992, which increased to 20.59% in 1996. It was reduced again to 11.41% in 2004. The ratio of worker's income to GDP stayed around

Table 5.5 The ratio of capital formation and consumption to GDP in China (100 million yuan, %)

Year	GDP (100million yuan)	Final consumption	Total amount of Capital formation	Goods and service net export	Capital formation Ratio to GDP(%)	Consumption Ratio to GDP(%)
1978	3605.6	2239.1	1377.9	-11.4	38.2	62.1
1979	4092.6	2633.7	1478.9	-20	36.1	64.4
1980	4592.9	3007.9	1599.7	-14.7	34.8	65.5
1981	5008.8	3361.5	1630.2	17.1	32.5	67.1
1982	5590	3714.8	1784.2	91	31.9	66.5
1983	6216.2	4126.4	2039	50.8	32.8	66.4
1984	7362.7	4846.3	2515.1	1.3	34.2	65.8
1985	9076.7	5986.3	3457.5	-367.1	38.1	66
1986	10508.5	6821.8	3941.9	-255.2	37.5	64.9
1987	12277.4	7804.6	4462	10.8	36.3	63.6
1988	15388.6	9839.5	5700.2	-151.1	37	63.9
1989	17311.3	11164.2	6332.7	-185.6	36.6	64.5
1990	19347.8	12090.5	6747	510.3	34.9	62.5
1991	22577.4	14091.9	7868	617.5	34.8	62.4
1992	27565.2	17203.3	10086.3	275.6	36.6	62.4
1993	36938.1	21899.9	15717.7	-679.5	42.6	59.3
1994	50217.4	29242.2	20341.1	634.1	40.5	58.2
1995	63216.9	36748.2	25470.1	998.6	40.3	58.1
1996	74163.6	43919.5	28784.9	1459.2	38.8	59.2
1997	81658.5	48140.6	29968	3549.9	36.7	59
1998	86531.6	51588.2	31314.2	3629.2	36.2	59.6
1999	90964.1	55636.9	32951.5	2375.7	36.2	61.2
2000	98749	61516	34842.8	2390.2	35.3	62.3
2001	108972.4	66878.3	39769.4	2324.7	36.5	61.4
2002	120350.3	71691.2	45565	3094.1	37.9	59.6
2003	136398.8	77449.5	55963	2986.3	41	56.8
2004	160280.4	87032.9	69168.4	4079.1	43.2	54.3
2005	188692.1	97822.7	80646.3	10223.1	42.7	51.8
2006	221170.5	110413.2	94103.2	16654.1	42.5	49.9

Note: Differences between the total of each item and GDP are due to errors in calculation.

Source: *Chinese Statistical Bulletin* 2005.

Table 5.6 The ratio of worker's income and asset income in China (%)

	1992	1996	2001	2002	2004
Workers income	59.88	58.76	59.53	60.21	47.14
Net total amount of production tax	13.11	15.1	18.05	17.16	14.93
Asset income	18.3	20.59	13.57	13.64	11.41
Total revenue of initial distribution	91.29	94.45	91.15	91	99.82

Note: Because of other factors, the total does not reach 100%.

Source: *Chinese Statistical Bulletin*, annual.

59% till 2001, and increased to 60.21% in 2002. However, it rapidly decreased to 47.14% in 2004. Compared with the Chinese ratio, in Japan, the ratio of worker's income has been in the vicinity of 70%.

Generally, because less developed countries seriously suffered from a shortage of initial capital for development, they took capital as more important, and so took various advantageous measures regarding foreign capital, which caused a higher ratio of asset income to GDP. To the contrary however, a worker's income usually occupies a lower ratio of income distribution. In order to verify the phenomena further, we consider Table 5.7.

Table 5.7 points out that, since the 1990s, the wage rate expansion of state-owned enterprises exceeded the wage rate growth of collectively owned enterprises and others. The disparity was remarkable during the years of 1996–2005. As usually indicated, state-owned enterprises have distributed more for workers, and are particularly remarkable compared with others (meaning private-owned and foreign-owned enterprises).

However, on the other hand, it is interesting that, since the 1980s, per capita wage expansion has been more than GDP growth (except for 1997–2000). In order to recognize correctly the 'low wage rate dependence' structure in the Chinese development model, we should consider the wage rate disparity between regular employees and irregular employees as well as the above-mentioned wage rate disparity among different types of enterprise (the excess distribution of the wage rate in the state-owned sector is effective to expand the wage rate as a whole). The wage rate of irregular employees is not included in Table 5.7. Focusing our attention upon the wage rate of irregular employees, in the following section, we will investigate the detail of the dual structure of wage rates in the Chinese manufacturing sector.

Table 5.7 GDP growth and annual average wage growth (index, previous year=100)

	GDP index	Per capita GDP index	Employees average real wages			
			Total	State Owned	Collective owned	Others
1978	111.7	110.2	110.5	110.1	112.5	
1980	107.8	106.5	119.4	118.6	123.3	
1985	113.5	111.9	122	121.6	123	163.9
1990	103.8	102.3	112.7	113.4	108.7	135.7
1991	109.2	107.7	112.6	111.7	113.4	153
1992	114.2	112.8	118.5	119.1	112.8	150
1993	114	112.7	124.8	123.4	114.4	240.2
1994	113.1	111.8	135.4	135.8	120.4	179.7
1995	110.9	109.7	121.7	117.4	115.5	140
1996	110	108.9	112.1	111.7	105	119.4
1997	109.3	108.2	103.6	106.2	101	123.6
1998	107.8	106.8	100.2	95.8	83.1	156.9
1999	107.6	106.7	106.2	105.1	94.2	119.8
2000	108.4	107.6	107.9	106.3	95.5	121.3
2001	108.3	107.5	111	109.8	94.1	122.9
2002	109.1	108.4	111.2	107.1	95.8	129.6
2003	110	109.3	112	108.3	100.2	124.7
2004	110.1	109.4	114.6	111.2	101.1	125.2
2005	110.4	109.8	117.1	111.4	103.5	130.8
2006	111.1	110.5	117.6	113.2	108.9	126.2

Source: *Chinese Statistical Bulletin* 2007.

(3) Dual structure of wage rates China became a member of the WTO in December 2001, and it also expanded its exports mainly by price competition, which was undoubtedly coming from low wage rates. What we should pay attention to is that the workers that support 'made in China' are not only from urban areas but also from rural areas (migrant workers), the total number of which reached 120 million. By such worker mobility, the dual structure in the industrial sector is established, the result of which indicates that, in some cities, there are rather developed economies and a high average income level, but also the minimum level of monthly income is extremely low. In the Pearl River Delta area, the monthly

income of migrant workers is only 500–600 yuan and they have to work 12 hours per day (Ma Guochuan, 2005).

In January 2004, the Ministry of Labor and Social Security promulgated the 'regulation on a minimum wage rate'. The regulation said that, when each government makes criteria for a minimum wage rate, it is possible to have three kinds of calculation (weight method,[7] Engel coefficient method,[8] and social average wage method[9]) and each government has to adjust the criteria at least every two years. As a matter of fact, in some regions they have never adjusted it for many years. In addition, there are differences of economic development among regions, which lead to regional differences in the minimum wage rate among the regions. As shown in Table 5.8, the highest minimum wage rate is given in Shenzhen (810 yuan per month), which is followed by Shanghai, Ningbo, Guangdong (750 yuan per month), and the lowest minimum wage rate is given in Gansu province which is 430 yuan per month. In each district and region, taking into consideration the disparity within the district and region, various kinds of minimum wage rates were established. Another problem is that, whether or not the social insurance premium paid by private persons is included in the minimum wage rate varies from one region to region. Thus, it is very difficult simply to compare figures. For example, in Shanghai and Beijing it is not included but in Shenzhen it is included.

In Guangdong province, since September 1, 2006, the wage rate has been raised. That was the seventh adjustment of the minimum wage rate in Guangdong province, whose growth rate was the highest, at 17.8%. The new criteria are classified into five kinds according to regional development levels (which are 780 yuan, 690 yuan, 600 yuan, 500 yuan and 450 yuan per month respectively). However, because the judgment of which criterion to employ is fully dependent upon each local government, the local government has a tendency to employ a lower wage rate by considering an enterprise's response. For example, in Guangzhou, they attempted to employ the second highest (690 yuan) but because of strong social opposition saying that, if Guangzhou employs the second highest, then the first highest has no significance, they had to abandon it (Jingji Cankao Bao (Economic Information Daily) September 4, 2006).

7 The weight method means that, first, they recognize a 'poor family' as when the family has a minimum income, of a certain proportion; then, in order to calculate per capita average cost of living they multiply the average dependent coefficient per worker and add the adjustment value, which leads to the minimum wage. The adjustment value varies from one area to another because there are differences in the own expense ratio of such payments as social insurance and housing common fund in respective areas.

8 The Engel coefficient method indicates that, based upon basic data, they calculate per capita minimum food expenditure, from which the Engel coefficient is subtracted. Then they multiply the dependent coefficient and add the adjustment value, which reaches the minimum wage.

9 In the social average wage method they decide a certain portion of the social average wage, in the local area concerned, to be the minimum wage. The internationally standard portion seems to be 40–60%.

Table 5.8 Minimum wage criteria of local government

	The date of inquiry	Minimum wage criteria (yuan per month)
Beijing	2005.7.1 2006.7.1	580 640
Tianjin	2005.7.1 2006.4.1	590 570 670 570
Hebei	2004.7.1 2006.10.1	520 470 420 580 540 480 440
Shanxi (Capital:Datong)	2004.7.1 2006.10.1	520 480 440 400 550 510 470 430
Inner Mongolia	2004.7.1 2006.10.1	420 400 380 560 520 460 440
Liaoning	2004.11.11 2006.7.1	450 400 350 590 480 420
(Dalian)	2005.1 2006.8.1	500 450 380 700 600 500
Jilin	2003.9.1 2006.5.1 2007.7.1	360 330 300 510 460 410 650 600 550
Heilongjiang	2004.3.1 2006.5.1	390 360 325 305 280 250 235 620 590 475 450 420 400 380
Shanghai	2005.7.1 2006.9.1	690 750
Jiangsu	2005.11.1	690 550 480 400
Zhejiang	2005.12.1 2006.9.1	670 610 560 490 750 670 620 540
(Ningbo)	2003.9.1 2005.12.1 2006.9.1	520 480 670 610 750 670
Anhui	2004.10.1 2006.10.1	410 390 370 360 350 340 330 320 310 290 520 500 460 430 390 360
Fujian	2005.7.1 2006.8.1	600 550 480 470 430 400 350 320 650 600 570 550 480 400
(Xiamen)	2005.7.1	600 550 480
Jiangxi	2004.9.1 2006.10.1	360 330 300 270 550 510 470 430
Shandong	2002.10.1 2005.1.1 2006.10.1	410 380 340 310 290 530 470 420 380 350 610 540 480 430 390
(Qingdao)	2001.7.1 2002.10.1 2005.1.1 2006.10.1	370 340 410 380 530 470 610 540
Henan	2005.10.1	480 400 320
Hubei	2005.3.1	460 400 360 320 280
Hunan	2005.7.1 2006.7.1	480 440 420 400 380 350 600 500 480 450 420 400
Guangdong	2004.12.1 2006.9.1	684 574 494 446 410 377 352 780 690 600 500 450

Table 5.8 ***Continued***

(Shenzhen)	2005.7.1 2006.7.1	690 580 810 700
Guangxi	2004.10.25 2006.9.1	460 400 360 320 500 435 390 345
Hainan	2004.7.1 2006.7.1	500 400 350 580 480 430
Chongqing	2004.5.1 2006.9.1	400 380 350 330 580 510 450 400
Sichuan	2004.10.18 2006.9.11	450 400 340 280 580 510 450 400
Guizhou	2004.10.1 2006.10.1	400 360 320 550 500 450
Yunnan	2004.10.1 2006.7.1	470 405 350 540 480 420
Tibet	2004.11.1	495 470 445
Shanxi (Capital:Xian)	2005.7.1 2006.10.1	490 460 430 400 540 500 460 420
Gansu	2004.1.1 2006.8.25	340 320 300 430 400 360 320
Qinghai	2004.10.1 2006.7.1	370 360 340 330 460 450 440
Ningxia	2004.2.1 2006.3.1	380 350 320 450 420 380
Xinjiang	2004.5.1 2006.5.1	480 440 380 370 360 350 330 320 300 670 620 580 550 520 500 480 460 440

Note:

(1) Each local government established various kinds of minimum wage taking into consideration disparities within the region.

(2) Latest statistics as of the end of 2006.

(3) Cities in parentheses are lower level administrations of province, autonomous district and municipality directly under the central government of the above lines. And the inimum wage criteria of Shanxi are of provinces, neither of Datong nor of Xian.

Source: Ministry of Labor and Social Security of PRC web site, newspaper articles etc.

What has been the actual wage rate in the labor market? The rural area research group of the statistical bureau in Guangdong province carried out large-scale sample research in the second quarter of 2005. The result showed that the average monthly wage rate for rural workers was 905 yuan. Meanwhile, the research result by the labor market service center of Guangzhou city on 200,000 workers of 245 labor intensive sector enterprises announced that the medium ranking monthly wage rate reached 934 yuan (which was 38% higher than the then minimum wage rate). Meanwhile, the hourly wage in Guangzhou city was more than 10 yuan which was twice more than the minimum hourly wage of 4.66 yuan.

Table 5.9 Social average monthly wages in Shanghai

	Annual salary (yuan)	Monthly salary		Monthly minimum wage	
		yuan	growth rate (%)	yuan	growth rate (%)
1993	5652	472		210	
1994	7404	617	31	220	4.8
1995	9276	773	25.3	270	22.7
1996	10668	889	15	300	11.1
1997	11424	952	7.1	315	5
1998	12060	1005	5.6	325	3.2
1999	14148	1179	17.3	370	13.8
2000	15420	1285	9	445	20.3
2001	17764	1480	15.2	490	10.1
2002	19473	1623	9.7	535	9.2
2003	22160	1847	13.8	570	6.5
2004	24398	2033	10.1	635	11.4
2005	26820	2235	9.9	690	8.7
2006	29569	2464	10.29	750	8.7
2007	34707	2894	17.4	840	12

Source: *Shanghai Statistical Bulletin*, annual, and Bureau of Labor and Social Security of Shanghai government.

Table 5.9 indicates the tendency of the minimum monthly wage of Shanghai. Shanghai was the first local government to introduce a minimum wage system in China, and the system was adjusted 14 times for the 13 years from 1993 to 2006 and it reached 10.3% of annual average growth rate. According to the announcement by the Bureau of Labor and Social Security in the Shanghai government, if the social insurance premium paid by private persons is included, the minimum wage in Shanghai reaches 44.3% of the average monthly wage of workers in Shanghai (2,662 yuan) (a figure that came from the calculation method of social average wages, which through the international criteria said that the minimum wages was to be in the vicinity of 40–60% of local monthly average).

The average monthly wage in Beijing in 2005 was 2734 yuan. This calculation showed that the minimum monthly wage in Beijing reached only 24%, but if the social insurance premium paid by private persons is included, the minimum wage in Beijing was said to be more than 40%.

As regards the dual economy model insisted on by Lewis (1954), in China before the reform and open door policy, because of strict regulations on free labor mobility, like the family registration system, it might not be appropriate to apply the model to China in the period. However, after the reform and open door policy, accompanied with the abolition of the three big scale systems, it has sometimes been indicated that the dual economy model has become applicable. Actually, it has been remarkable that the excessive labor force in rural areas has moved towards urban areas. The dual structure of wage rate in China seems to reflect such social reality.

(4) Producers' sovereignty In order to publicize and protect the consumer's rights and interests, the Chinese government has decided that March 15 is the 'day of consumers'. The existence of such a day points out the weaker position of consumers than producers and managers. At the end of 2004, the Social Survey Institute of China (SSIC) (which was established in 1985) implemented a questionnaire survey over about one month, from November 22 to December 15, in cooperation with more than 30 media, whose result indicated that the following ten businesses were recognized to be the most super normal profitable ones: (1) telecommunication (87.6%); (2) real estate (including housing management) (54.5%); (3) insurance (51.3%); (4) electric power (48.7%); (5) education (38%); (6) medical care (29.8%); (7) banks (22.5%); (8) railway (19.8%); (9) transportation (17.1%); and (10) supermarkets (15.7%) (Jinghua Shibao (Beijing Times), December 21, 2004.)

Most of the above ten businesses have the characteristic of being monopolistic industries. Both real estate (including housing management) and insurance are not recognized as being monopolistic, but actually they are. The real estate industry moved from the initial pattern of a conference system to an auction system to acquire land for business and housing use. However, real estate is still an industry with a strong cozy relationship between administration and business, whose function is similar to a monopolistic industry. Insurance is now at the first stage of development; its legal system is less developed, and consumers do not have enough knowledge and there could exists asymmetric information. This lead to producers' sovereignty. As regards the supermarket case, it is rather special in China because supermarkets have already been popular. What does the 'violent' behavior of supermarket managers, who are sometimes reported (to be the rough body to check suspicious customers in a rough manner and to request a special admission fee to delivery traders), indicate? When, in an urban area, traditional shops are closed, the supermarket style of business is widely accepted by consumers because of wider variety of goods, the method of selection (picking goods in their own hands), discounted prices, and so on. Supermarket managers are proud of being the winners these days, but they have no intention of respecting customers and producers. Many traditional state-owned shops have been replaced by supermarkets, whose advantage is that they have much more shops than newcomers to the supermarket industry. However, managers and employees of state-owned shops still have a state-owned mind and a less market-oriented mind. They are unwilling to do a service and so also act arrogantly.

According to the principle of survival of the fittest, the existence of such phenomena is allowed by the environment. In other words, removing such phenomena might be necessary depending upon the promotion of a market-oriented system. Under the promoted evolutionary system, unless each enterprise and sector could suitably evolve, they would undoubtedly die out.

Generally speaking, under the whole nation's system, the Chinese economy has been depending upon a lower cost path. If the side effects coming from the path are accumulated, they would surely be factors to hinder sustainable development. We examine the risk transmission mechanism behind the lower cost competitiveness in the following section.

Risk transmission mechanism behind the lower cost competitiveness

Since the reform and open door policy started, the Chinese economy has kept expanding by more than 9% annual average growth rate. Statistics by the Ministry of Commerce show that the Chinese degree of dependence upon foreign trade (meaning the ratio of total amount of export and import to GDP) rapidly increased to be around 70% in 2006 from about 15% at the beginning of 1980s, 48.9% in 2002 and 60.1% in 2003, which seemed to be caused by Chinese participation in the WTO in December 2001. Also the process was correlated with the expansion process of inward FDI into China (see Table 5.10).[10]

Countries that have a big economic scale are generally led by domestic demand. For example, such countries as the USA, Japan and India have the degree of dependence upon foreign trade, from 14% to 20%. A significantly low degree of dependence of Japan upon foreign trade would be impressive because Japan is thought to be a trading nation. As a matter of fact, the absolute amounts of Japanese exports and imports have been large; however, the total GDP amount has been also large, which makes the degree not so big. The less degree of dependence upon foreign trade in Japan indicates the large amount of domestic demand.

Behind the Chinese high-speed economic growth, depending upon foreign demand, there exist characteristic risks in China (see Figure 5.3). The price competitive advantage in China has been caused by lower production costs, which has meant neglecting workers' rights and interests and environmental protection. Under the national system, producers are in a superior position to workers and consumers. In the short-run, producers contribute to the nation state by expanding the economy through exports and foreign reserves (as the whole nation's system attaches greater importance to the contribution), but in the log-run, such a vicious transmission mechanism in China hinders, it is believed, sustainable development of the Chinese economy and society.

10 Some experts indicate that the degree of external dependence is related to the trade pattern. During the decreasing tendency of the ratio of ordinary trade, improvement trade has become a major pattern of Chinese international trade. Also it is pointed out that, in recent days, the ratio of domestic material provision has been increased and the characteristics of major material import and major goods export have been weakened.

Table 5.10 Foreign economic relations of China

Year	Total amount of exports and imports (100 million yuan)	Export amount	Import amount	Net exports	FDI (actual base, 100 million yuan)	Yuan exchange rate (per one US$)	Degree of dependence on foreign trade (%)
1978	206.4	97.5	108.9	-11.4	-	1.72	9.8
1979	293	136.6	156.4	-19.8	-	1.55	11.3
1980	3	181.2	-178.2	359.4	-	1.494	12.6
1981	381.4	220.1	161.3	58.8	-	1.075	9.7
1982	440.3	223.2	217.1	6.1	-	1.893	14.9
1983	416.1	222.3	193.8	28.5	6.36	1.976	14.5
1984	436.2	261.4	174.8	86.6	12.6	2.327	17.4
1985	535.5	273.5	262	11.5	16.6	2.937	22.8
1986	696	309.4	386.6	-77.2	18.7	3.453	25
1987	738.5	394.4	344.1	50.3	23.1	3.722	25.7
1988	826.5	475.2	351.3	123.9	31.9	3.722	25.6
1989	1116.8	525.4	591.4	-66	33.9	3.765	24.9
1990	1154.4	620.9	533.5	87.4	34.9	4.783	29.8
1991	1357	719.1	637.9	81.2	43.7	5.323	33.4
1992	1655.3	849.4	805.9	43.5	110.1	5.515	34.3
1993	1957	917.4	1039.6	-122.2	275.2	5.762	32.6
1994	2366.2	1210.1	1156.1	54	337.7	8.619	43.6
1995	2808.6	1487.1	1321.5	165.6	375.21	8.351	40.1
1996	2898.8	1510.5	1388.3	122.2	417.26	8.314	35.5
1997	3251.6	1827.9	1423.7	404.2	452.57	8.29	36.2
1998	3239.5	1837.1	1402.4	434.7	454.63	8.279	34.2
1999	3606.3	1949.3	1657	292.3	403.19	8.278	36.4
2000	4742.9	2492	2250.9	241.1	407.15	8.278	43.9
2001	5096.5	2661	2435.5	225.5	468.78	8.277	43.3
2002	6207.7	3256	2951.7	304.3	527.43	8.277	48.9
2003	8509.9	4382.3	4127.6	254.7	535.05	8.277	60.1
2004	11545.5	5933.2	5612.3	320.9	606.3	8.277	59.8
2005	14219.1	7619.5	6599.5	1020	603.25	8.192	63.9
2006	17607	9691	7916	1775	694.7	7.972	69.1

Notes: (1) Degree of dependence on foreign trade means the ratio of the total amount of exports and imports to GDP).

(2) From July 21, 2005, the Yuan exchange rate has been transformed into managed float system.

Source: *Chinese Statistical Bulletin* 1991, 2005 and 2007, *Chinese National Economy and Social Development Statistical Bulletin* 2006.

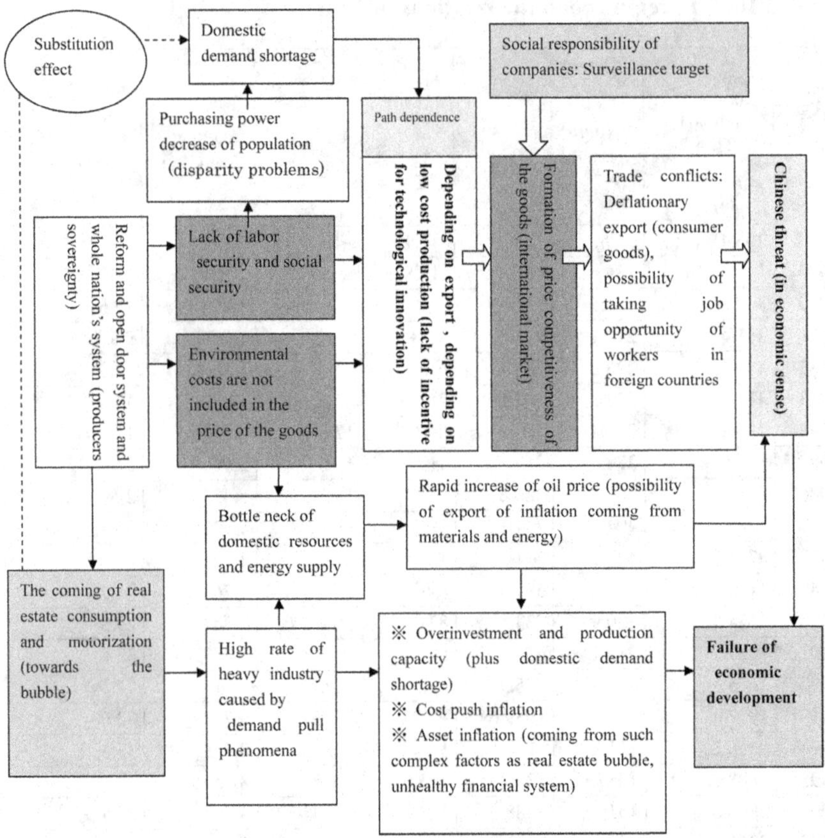

Source: Author.

Figure 5.3 Risk transmission mechanism behind the low cost goods competitiveness

As for the harmful effects, we point out first the occurrence of both domestic demand shortage and trade conflict. Low labor wages and poor social security systems make the consumption instincts of lower-income people (particularly in rural areas) conservative, which causes low real purchasing power and a domestic demand shortage. Because the lack of domestic demand is serious, an expanding economy depends more upon foreign markets. Thus foreign trade conflicts and legal cases happen. To be specific, cheap consumer goods from China might absorb the markets of those countries importing from China, and the job opportunities for workers of those countries importing from China could be lost. We can recognize many cases in which people in trading partner countries rebel against China. For example, on September 16, 2004, in Elche, located in the southeast area of Spain, which is famous for shoes production, there occurred arson attacks, the targets of which were Chinese (Wenzhou) origin shoes shops and warehouses. These attacks were understood as the result of various trade conflicts that Chinese products have brought about in foreign countries.[11]

In addition, the Chinese way of management (depending upon lower costs) has already faced the limit for the sustainable development path. Actually, the economic growth path, neglecting workers' rights and interests and environmental protection, has been the target of monitoring by international society. Since 1995, when the world's large wholesalers (which receive the SA 8000 social responsibility certification) make purchases in China, in the light of production regulation clause, they have attempted to make Chinese producing enterprises improve by regularly inspecting their social responsibility.

Second, we indicate the negative externalities that neglect the environmental costs. Producers neglecting the environmental costs contribute fewer production costs, which has been an important part of the price competitive advantage for Chinese products. However, it also produces negative externalities: (1) first, serious environmental pollution cases have often occurred and have gradually damaged people's health in China; (2) the poor situation of environmental legislation has given no incentive for enterprises to progress and introduce environmental technology and to improve production and management processes. As a result, the bottleneck of resource and energy consumption in Chinese economic development has come into existence, which has brought about soaring prices for oil and other raw materials. In other words, unless China can solve the incentive problems, it is impossible to change from price competition to technology competition, which we discuss later. Such circumstances might become suitable targets against the 'the menace by China' in an economic sense caused by the above-mentioned two results, regardless of the recognition of the Chinese government and Chinese people.

Third, the producers' sovereignty has economic effects. Under the whole nation system, the days of 'own home' and 'own car' have rapidly come to Chinese society. The consumption boom has directly pushed the industrialization of China.

Table 5.11 points out the ratio of light and heavy industry to Chinese national industries. The ratio of heavy industry reached 56.9% in 1978, after that the ratio was gradually decreased to its lowest level of 50.6% in 1990. It was increased until 1995, and then reduced again to 50.8% in 1999. However, the ratio expanded to 60.2% in 2000 and 69.5% in 2006. It is easily recognized that, from the Sixth Five Year Plan to the Tenth Five Year Plan, particularly in the period of the Tenth Five Year Plan, heavy industry substantially developed in China.

We should be careful, however, of the following.

i. First, the details of industrialization are not so optimistic. The Chinese

11 However, one year after then, on December 17, 2005, the shoe makers association of Elche city visited Wenzhou city and both of them jointly announced the Wenzhou Declaration to build friendly competitive relations.

Table 5.11 The ratio of light and heavy industry to Chinese national industries

Year	Light industry	Heavy industry	Year	Light industry	Heavy industry
1978	43.1	56.9	2000	39.8	60.2
1980	47.1	52.9	2001	39.4	60.6
1985	47.1	52.9	2002	39.1	60.9
1990	49.4	50.6	2003	35.5	64.5
1991	48.4	51.6	2004	33.5	66.5
1992	46.6	53.4	2005	31.0	69.0
1993	46.5	53.5	2006	30.5	69.5
1994	46.3	53.7	Sixth Five Year Plan period (1980-1985)	48.9	51.1
1995	46.2	53.8	Seventh Five Year Plan period (1986-1990)	48.7	51.3
1996	48.1	51.9	Eighth Five Year Plan period (1991-1995)	46.8	53.2
1997	49.0	51.0	Ninth Five Year Plan period (1996-2000)	48.9	51.1
1998	49.3	50.7	Tenth Five Year Plan period (2001-2005)	33.7	66.3
1999	49.2	50.8			

Notes:

(1) In the years from 2000 to 2004, they recorded industrial enterprises production amount of more than a certain scale, in other years they pointed out the total industrial production amount.

(2) In 2005 and 2006, and the period of the Tenth Five Year Plan, the ratio was calculated with industrial value added (of whole industries).

Source: *Chinese Statistical Bulletin*, annual, and *Chinese National Economy and Social Development Statistical Bulletin 2005 and 2006.*

economic development model, focusing more attention upon low-stage processing of machinery has been a development model of resource and energy consumption. Chinese dependence on strategic resources from foreign countries has been more serious. The statistics of the Chinese Statistical Office reported that, in 2003, imports of steel, aluminum oxide (AL203), iron ore (and refined ore) were growing by 51.8%, 22.6%, and 32.9% respectively. According to the estimation by experts, the Chinese degree of dependence upon oil import in 2020 would reach 60%. Although Chinese GDP had a 4.4% ratio of the world GDP, the ratio of Chinese consumption of crude oil, coal, iron ore steel, aluminum oxide (AL203), and cement to the world total of consumption was 7.4%, 31%, 30%, 27%, 25% and 40%. In 2006, the Chinese economy recorded a 10.7% growth rate, which indicated that China sustained a two-digit growth rate for four consecutive years. China also paid serious compensation for resources and energy. Chinese GDP in 2006 occupied around 5.5% of total world GDP, however Chinese energy consumption corresponded to 2460 million tons standard coal consumption, which reached 15% of the world total. Steel consumption reached 388 million tons (occupying 30% of the world total) and cement consumption was 1240 million tons (reaching 54% of the world total).[12]

Table 5.12 displays the dependence on international markets for main ore products. It expresses the increasing tendency of import dependence on oil, iron, manganese, copper, lead, and zinc.

ii. Second, since the 1980s, overproduction and overinvestment problems in China came into existence several times and, particularly after joining the WTO, a combination of factors (both internal and external) might cause cost-push inflation by increasing the prices of raw materials and energy and also such phenomena as an unhealthy financial system, a housing bubble, and car consumption, might bring about an asset bubble phenomenon in the domestic economy. Unless China can solve these serious problems, the Chinese economy would be damaged by them. Different from the usual type of inflation, asset inflation is more dangerous. Asset inflation in Japan,

Table 5.12 Dependence on international market about main ore products

	Degree of dependence on imports (%)		
	2000	2010 (anticipation)	2020 (anticipation)
Oil	31	41	58
Iron	33	34	52
manganese	16	31	38
Copper	48	72	82
Lead	0	45	52
Zinc	0	53	69

Source: Chinese Cabinet Development Research Center.

12 Statement of Makai, the head of the National Development and Reform Committee, at the High Ranking Forum 2007 of Chinese Development. See HP of National Development and Reform Committee, http://www.sdpc.gov.cn.

which existed during the bubble economy from the end of 1980s to the beginning of 1990s, serious damaged the Japanese economy. In order to restore the economy from its low level, it was necessary for Japan to lose around the equivalent of ten years in the 1990s (in Japan it was said to be the lost decade).

Leaders in China have recognized the problems. Central meetings on economic policy in 2005 prescribed the improvement of consumers' capacity as the important duty in 2006. In addition to redressing income disparity, a transformation was necessary from the position from attaching greater importance on real estate industry (of the leading effects for economic development) to putting more weight upon consumption expansion (to contribute to economic growth). Although it has looked as government's return towards a more reasonable policy from the development oriented regime, the institutional base to carry out the policy measures has never been enough.

Tasks to transform the Chinese-made goods from price competition to technology competition

A friend in a foreign country said to the author of this book that in China you have 1.3 billion population, so selecting 11 players to play soccer should be easy. China therefore should be a major power in soccer! As a matter of fact, in China there are lots of soccer fans, and officials of the national bureau of physical education and of Chinese soccer association are enthusiastic for the Chinese soccer team to be world class. However, ironically, the Chinese whole nation system of physical education has been successful for China to get lots of medals but has never contributed for a successful health sports country. Similarly, while the Chinese whole nation's system of the economy is successful for the country to become a large scale economy and a large scale trading country, China undoubtedly is neither an economic empire nor a trading empire. Thus the Chinese position of the international competitiveness ranking has never been improved.

Both the World Economic Forum (WEF) and International Institute for Management Development (IMD) of Lausanne are the two authorized institutions to evaluate the international competitiveness. According to the world competitiveness ranking report of 2005 by the WEF, China occupied 49th position, moving three rankings down from the year before. Also, in 2006, China moved five ranks down, to be in 54th position[13] (of altogether 125 countries and regions). In addition, the IMD World Competitiveness Yearbook (by IMD) reported in May, 2005, that China decreased its position from 24th place to 31st in 2004. However, according

13 As, in 2006, they introduced the new evaluation system, the 2005 ranking was adjusted to the new system, and China was adjusted to 48th position.

to the IMD report in 2006, China rapidly increased its position to 19th place (of altogether 60 countries and regions).[14]

As stated above, the two institutions gave rather different evaluations on the Chinese international competitiveness in 2006. Generally speaking, they say that evaluation by WEF attaches greater importance upon soft competitiveness (indicating macro-economic management, technology innovation, public institution – quality of government); meanwhile, evaluation by IMD puts greater importance on hard competitiveness (showing the four indices as the economic development situation, government efficiency, enterprise efficiency and infrastructure construction). The difference of evaluation between the two institutions might also be coming from the method of how to apply the hard data and questionnaire survey. We think that it is necessary to examine more about the better evaluation of China in 2006 by IMD than WEF and whether it could be stable or not. For China during the transition period, it could be more meaningful to attach greater importance to soft competitiveness, because such indices as efficiency of the market mechanism, legal environment, financial efficiency, corporate governance, health and environment, education have been remarkable as weak aspects of competitiveness in China.

As regards the competitiveness problem in China, we can recognize the following two characteristics related to the low cost path dependence. (i) First, for Chinese economic growth depending upon exports (see Table 5.10), the major contribution has been from foreign-owned enterprises. Around 60% of the total was exported by foreign-owned ones. Of the increase in exportable goods whose quantity regulation was abolished in 2005, 70% was shared by foreign-owned enterprises. The foreign enterprises locate the production stage in China; meanwhile, other stages of enterprise activities such as R&D, production design, spare parts and components production, marketing, distribution, etc, are implemented mainly outside of China. (ii) Second, a lack of general competitiveness by Chinese enterprises comes not only from a lower ratio of exports but also from low value added activities of material processing. The value added occupies only 15–20% of the total value added. For example, Chinese major exports of textiles are processed products for foreign big-name brands, of which Chinese enterprises take around 10% processing of the total value added. As stated above, most machinery processed products in China are lower-stage processed, they consume lots of resources and energy. Such a development pattern in China might be difficult to be sustainable.

Generally speaking, the current Chinese development model, with such characteristics as low wage and low social security, and neglecting environment protection, could not reach the goal of industrial advancement (to be an economic empire).

---

14 Japan, Taiwan, Malaysia, India, Thailand and South Korea in Asia occupied the position as 17th, 18th, 23rd, 29th, 32nd, 38th, respectively.

Various problems of systemic transition

Economic development theory is a field to investigate the mechanism of the social system as a whole, related to development and backwardness. Development economics correctly recognize close relations between development performance and initial conditions. Such initial conditions, as given by neoclassical economics, are institutionally related ones that might be crucial factors that hinder the development of less developed countries. Almost all less developed countries have been faced by a serious institution-building process. A neoclassical economic approach might not be appropriate to analyze the problems of less developed countries.

Two driving forces in the systemic transition

In the systemic transition of former socialist economies, two driving forces are important. (1) The first is the existence of a charismatic leader at the initial stage of transition. At the initial stage, the institutional framework for the new days cannot be ready, and if they introduce the institutions from foreign countries, the transition economies cannot be changed to appropriately accept them. For large countries, such as China, it is particularly important to have the internal logic for a gradual systemic transition rather than a radically surgical form of transition. At the initial stage of transition, the wisdom of the charismatic leader might work in place of legal institutions, which could be said to be an authoritarian development system. (2) Second, we should say that transition at the later stage has to depend upon institutional evolution. During the process of transition, leaders become older, have less powerful leadership, and the socio-economic system might be more complex, whose adjustment is difficult through simple patterns. The role of the legal institution therefore becomes much more important than less authorized leaders. The establishment process of legal institutions is also the process of systemic transition.

Advantage and disadvantage of backwardness

As regards economic development of less developed countries, we recognize the advantage of backwardness in an academic sense. The advantage of backwardness means that less developed countries could introduce directly the latest technology through technology transfer, the costs of which are much lower than initial development. At the same time, under the same conditions of finance, resource and technology, less developed countries could implement the catching up and getting ahead strategy more easily because of cost advantages in labor and land etc.

However, we also consider the disadvantage of backwardness. Constitutional economics paid attention to the disadvantage at an earlier stage, also in China, the late Professor Yang Xiaokai presented this issue in a relatively earlier period. Yang Xiaokai (2001) insisted that, because less developed countries have imitated space of advanced technology from developed countries, technology imitation is easier than institution imitation. That is also because institution imitation is usually confronted with resistance by vested interest groups, which cause difficulty to be carried out. However, excessive imitation of technology is possible to suppress the imitated space of institutions. Thus, less developed countries are satisfied with the short-run advantage of backwardness (technology imitation) and are negative about institutional reform (institutional imitation), which leads to final failure.

We fundamentally agree with the viewpoints of Yang Xiaokai; however, we also assert that it might be reasonable to attach greater importance to technology imitation at the initial stage of economic development, and at the later stage more weight should be put upon institution imitation (institutional evolution). The reasons for this are as follows.

At the initial stage, less developed countries have the advantage of low labor cost and a low land price. However, at this stage they have never had basic conditions to accept institutional imitation. For example, because they do not have enough recognition of new economic systems and do not have enough experience of managing new economic systems, they could not have enough effects of systemic transition. (Even if China has a radical way of transition, like Poland, it might be difficult to be successful.) A lower-level economic structure needs a lower level of institutional reform. Peasant economies and processing industries are consistent with autocratic governments and authoritarian governments. They need therefore no institutional evolution.

However, advancement of industrial structure is improved and the necessity of institutional evolution is gradually remarkable. Taiwan, regarding autocratic systems, has given enough freedom in the economy (although in the politically it still has centralization and an anti-democratic system). Because, without institutional evolution, economic growth will be confronted with a serious limit, a legal crisis of authoritarianism will occur. Institutional transformation will come into existence in an extension of the advancement of the economic structure.

Generally speaking, as institutional evolution is accompanied with economic evolution, it is very important to introduce the evolution appropriately. Too early causes problems as does too late. North and Weingast (1989) presented a question, asking why the Industrial Revolution occurred first in England in Holland. According to their explanation, England established a constitutional system after the 'Glorious Revolution' in 1688. The constitutional system promoted technological progress (such as patent rights protection), which led to the Industrial Revolution. The Rights Act promulgated in 1689 established the constitutional monarchy, which substantially restricted the rights of the King. For example, without approval by Parliament, the King cannot establish any law, cannot abolish any law, cannot collect any tax and cannot have any military force. Meanwhile, the Act prescribed that people could have freedom of suffrage and Parliament could have the freedom of public speaking.

In England after the Glorious Revolution, such topics as internal administration, peace keeping, public finance, colonization, commerce, development of the parliamentary system, and struggle through the parliament were the most important matters of concern for the government and society. However, in the Western Europe and other regions of the world in the 17th century, the monarchy was the general way of administration. In France, Spain, Austria, Sweden, and Germany, for example, they established the centralized autocrat system whose ruling ideology was that God gave rights to the monarch. Russia and China had had an absolute monarchical system for many years.

The Industrial Revolution required much more institutional security than traditional manual industry. In England, the origin of constitutional monarchy was founded in the 13th century. It was particularly meaningful that article 39 of the Great Charter in 1215 prescribed the protection of personal liberty and private property. England thus had the institutional conditions to reach the Industrial Revolution via the Glorious Revolution in 1688.

At present, in China, which has been suffering from a risk transmission mechanism behind the low-cost competitiveness, the transformation of an economic development model has been promoted. Innovation has been submitted as the most important slogan for the new industrial promotion strategy in China. In order to carry it out successfully, putting the institutions in appropriate conditions is necessary. We can recognize the fact following mechanism of institutional change, which is explained in the following section.

Ability in the challenge and counter-challenge of civilization

The Chinese way of management, depending upon low production cost, has been confronted with serious tasks. We should remind ourselves that Toynbee (1957) suggested that progress of civilization was accomplished by the repetition of challenge and counter-challenge. Without challenge, civilization has not progressed naturally. When there are appropriate conflicts between the civilization base and environmental circumstance, the capacity of the civilization base is stimulated to lead to progress. From the viewpoints of Chinese economic development, what is important is to have an active and dynamic ideology to respond effectively to various internal and external factors upon economic development (such as the soaring price of oil and appreciation pressure on the yuan exchange rate). It seems to be more important for civilization to progress to improve the counter-challenge ability than to dichotomize absolute beneficial factors and absolute improper factors.

A reasonable example of it would be Japan.

Japan during the high-speed economic growth in the 1960s was notorious as a major country of environmental pollution. Japan, which was suffering from lawsuits about environmental pollution, held the Diet on environmental pollution in 1970 and signed the acts on environmental regulation, actively struggling against the environmental pollution problems. Through such strict procedures with environmental legislation, particularly in the 1990s, Japan has grown to be an advanced country and established the waste management society. A reasonable example can be interpreted by the theory of induced technology and institutional innovation by Hayami (1995, chapter 6).

Also in Japan in the 1970s, the country twice faced a crisis coming from the oil shocks. Against the challenge, Japan developed an innovative technology to save energy consumption and promote the advancement of industrial structure. At present, Japan has developed to be one of the most advanced countries in the world in energy saving technology (Chen Yun, 2006a). We think that the counter challenging ability to respond reasonably against crises and to successfully and internally assimilate has been a traditional Japanese advantage, which has been suffering from resource shortage. To the contrary, China has traditionally had shortcomings in this aspect because the nation has been proud of its huge resources. The difference between Japan and China might be caused by this path dependence.

Putting the legislative circumstances in the appropriate condition to overcome the environmental pollution and oil crisis is just the institutional evolution. The Japanese ability of institutional evolution seems to be a beneficial characteristic caused by the resource shortages. It might be the same mechanism as saying that persons who are hard of hearing have good vision. The social ability of institutional evolution thus progresses similar to the instinct of creatures. In addition, the Japanese example indicated the above mechanism that they opened the country through the Meiji Restoration and established a constitutional system. As Darwin insisted, it is not the strong but those appropriate to environmental change that can survive.

Evolution of a fact-following mechanism of institutional change

The interaction between the internal society and external society in the reform and open door policy, forms a kind of transmission mechanism. We think that, by the good effects and the bad reactions of the whole nation's system, economic problems and political problems have interacted in a complex way. We also think that institutional transition of the economy is necessarily transmitted into the institutional transition of the politics. The institutional change between internal and external, economy and politics, seems not to be improved artificially but to be carried out endogenously by the survival rules of the economy and enterprises.

In China, meanwhile, the national system has been effective in the athletics field and in the economics field, but it has also had several restrictions. The reform and open door policy after 1978 expressed the original functions and impacts, which are different from Mao Zedong's era. As stated previously, with various problems caused by the whole nation's system, current Chinese society has faced the time to transform its development model. The key concept for transformation is to change the low cost path of neglecting workers' rights and interests, and environmental pollution by producers.

When the low cost path is changed, in order to have new competitiveness, enterprise and government have to try to move towards technological progress and the advancement of the industrial structure. The process means the transformation of the development model of the resource and energy consumption type.

Microscopic viewpoints: necessity to rouse the social responsibility of enterprises

In the second half of 2002, China grew to become the main FDI receiving country of the world. Under the circumstance of economic globalization, Chinese trading behavior must follow international trade rules.

Since the middle of the 1990s, developed countries have tried to combine human rights issues and trade issues under the banner of surveillance of human rights problems in less developed countries. For example, in the WTO multilateral negotiation, developed countries emphasized the workers' rights and interests criteria issue repeatedly and insisted on taking sanctions against violating countries. However, because of opposition by less developed countries, the developed countries failed to do this. Since 1995, however, when general trading companies from developed countries (which already have the SA8000 certification of social responsibility of enterprises) conducted deals with Chinese companies, they strongly requested Chinese partners to take social responsibility. This has been a serious experience for Chinese companies.

We should have a short look at the background of social responsibility of enterprises. Economic globalization means the mobility of resources and capital all over the world, which is mainly contributed by multinational corporations. Initially, some multinational corporations had a tendency of attaching less importance to workers' security and welfare security, corresponding to the delayed legal establishment of the host less developed countries, in order to get more advantages and more profits. For example, in the 1980s, in such Asian countries as Indonesia, the Philippines, and Thailand, various problems, such as low wages, compulsory overtime work, sexual discrimination, lack of health security in jobs, prohibition of joining trade unions etc, occurred quite often. After the problems were disclosed, inside the developed countries, consumers, NGOs, trade unions, student organizations etc, applied pressures against multinational corporations to take social responsibility, including workers rights and interests.

The movements for social responsibility of enterprises, have combined with international trade unions, consumers' movements, environmental protection movements, women's rights movements etc, have improved since the 1990s. Based upon the spirit of the Universal Declaration of Human Rights by the United Nations and based upon the decent treatment of working people by the International Labor Organization, the Basic Code of International Confederation of Free Trade Unions which was signed in December, 1997, some developed countries and international organizations decided to implement and establish the social responsibility of enterprises. For example, the Ethical Trading Initiative Base Code in UK, The Fair Trade Charter for Garments sponsored by the Clean Clothes Campaign in

Europe, SA8000 sponsored by Social Accountability International (SAI) in USA, Workplace Code of Conduct by Fair Labor Association in the USA.

Multinational corporations are usually managed in a well-established supervising system in developed countries. However, as regards international management, their managements carried on as they liked without any supervising systems. Finally, they were caught by civil society. Profit oriented enterprises might damage human rights and social fairness without surveillance by a mature civil society. Correction against the colonial policies of western countries became possible after human rights consciousness was developed inside the countries concerned.

After China became a member of the WTO, foreign countries transacting business with Chinese enterprises have requested various conditions on workers' rights and interests related to the social responsibility of enterprises. Chinese enterprises initially paid attention to workers' rights and interests in response to partner companies' requests, and gradually they naturally recognized the rules for surviving.

Macroscopic viewpoints: necessity to correct disparities

In order to alleviate trade conflicts with foreign countries China has to solve the task of expanding domestic demand. At present we think there are barriers to this, such as the following.

(1) Purchasing power problems of the farming population Although China has a population of 1.3 billion, the enormous size does not automatically mean a large market size, because a population without purchasing power means no market. To change, China has to improve measures to correct disparities between the urban and rural in order to increase the income and purchasing power of the farming population, whose size is around 800 million.

Both disparities of income and consumption between urban and rural areas are substantial. Moreover, the latter disparity is more than the former. Table 5.13 shows how many times more is the per capita income of the urban population compared with the rural population. According to the Table 5.13 (except for the years 1978–1985) we can see the increasing ratio of per capita income of urban to rural. That is to say, the ratio of urban to rural decreased from 1978 to 1985, after then the ratio fluctuated, and since 1996 it showed an increasing tendency, which reached, in 2006, 3.28 times more per capita income of urban than of rural. As regards consumption, the tendency is indicated to be similar. Table 5.14 shows that the ratio of urban to rural initially decreased from 2.9 times in 1978 to 2.2 times in 1985, but after that it expanded to reach 3.8 times in 1995, after which the ratio remained stable.

We should note that, from the 1980s to the present, the urban population can receive various welfare benefits. The per capita annual average reached 3000–4000 yuan. In 2005, the per capita social security expenditure for workers in urban

Table 5.13 Income disparity between the urban and rural areas in China

	Per capita income of rural population (yuan)	Per capita income of urban population (yuan)	Ratio Urban/Rural
1978	133.6	343.4	2.57
1985	397.6	739.1	1.86
1990	686.3	1510.2	2.2
1995	1577.7	4283	2.71
2000	2253.4	6280	2.79
2001	2366.4	6859.6	2.9
2002	2475.6	7702.8	3.11
2003	2622.2	8472.2	3.23
2004	2936.4	9421.6	3.21
2005	3254.9	10493	3.22
2006	3587	11759.5	3.28

Source: *Chinese Statistical Bulletin* 2007.

areas (including private enterprises and retired employees) equaled to 1766 yuan, meanwhile for the farming population it was only 14 yuan. Thus, the ratio of urban to rural reached 126 times. Taking into consideration this difference, real income disparity between the urban and rural became much more, and reached in the simple calculation six times (Chinese Academy of Social Sciences, 2005).

(2) Existence of consumption substitution effects Other reasons to decrease purchasing power are to decrease the real estate development boom problem, and the educational and medical problems. If government is not enthusiastic about taking measures against these, the mentality towards consumption of the urban population would receive substantial negative effects. Because of uncertainty in the future, people save more than they consume. In addition, as mentioned previously, such phenomena as a real estate bubble would cause distortion of resource allocation, which might result in a stagnation of macro economic performance. Also, the unfair distribution of social wealth would make Chinese society in transition unstable.

In the second half of the 1990s, of the three leading factors for Chinese macro economy (which were investment, exports and consumption), the leading role of consumption was undoubtedly weak. Actually, at the end of 1999, the personal savings of the population reached six trillion yuan. To expand domestic demand, the national tax bureau decided to collect taxation on interest (implemented on

Table 5.14 Consumption disparity between urban and rural areas in China

	Per capita consumption of whole China		Per capita consumption of rural population		Per capita consumption of urban population		Ratio(Urban/ Rural)
	yuan	index previous year=100	yuan	index previous year=100	yuan	index previous year=100	
1978	184	104.1	138	104.3	405	103.3	2.9
1980	238	109.0	178	108.4	489	107.2	2.7
1985	446	113.5	349	113.3	765	111.1	2.2
1990	833	103.7	560	99.2	1596	108.5	2.9
1995	2355	107.8	1313	106.8	4931	107.2	3.8
1996	2789	109.4	1626	114.5	5532	103.4	3.4
1997	3002	104.5	1722	103.1	5823	102.2	3.4
1998	3159	105.9	1730	101.2	6109	105.9	3.5
1999	3346	108.3	1766	105.1	6405	107.0	3.6
2000	3632	108.6	1860	104.5	6850	107.8	3.7
2001	3869	105.7	1969	104.5	7113	103.2	3.6
2002	4106	106.5	2062	105.2	7387	104.2	3.6
2003	4411	106.5	2103	100.3	7901	106.3	3.8
2004	4925	107.4	2301	103.4	8679	106.4	3.8
2005	5463	107.9	2560	107.6	9410	105.7	3.7
2006	6111	109.3	2848	108.6	10359	107.6	3.6

Source: *Chinese Statistical Bulletin* 2007.

November 1, 1999). However, the collection policy of taxation on interest had no substantial effect on the personal saving behavior of the Chinese population. Table 5.15 shows that the growth rate of the personal saving balance of the population was not only much greater than the GDP growth rate but also much greater than the growth rate of the total retail amount. The statistics indicated that the Chinese tendency of a high propensity to save was fairly consistent with the tendency of a high propensity to invest. Actually, since the beginning of the 1990s (except for 1993), the Chinese propensity to save has been more than the propensity to invest. Since the start of the 1990s (except for the period of inflation in 1993–1995), the general price level in China was relatively stable and China experienced deflation during 1998 and 2001.

Table 5.15 Saving and consumption situation of Chinese population (2001–2006)

	Saving balance at the end of the year (100 million yuan)	Annual growing amount of saving (100 million yuan)	Annual growth rate of saving (%)	Retail amount growth rate of consumer goods (%)	GDP growth rate (%)
2001	73762.40	——	——	——	——
2002	86910.60	13233.20	17.90	8.80	8.00
2003	103617.65	16707.05	19.22	9.10	9.10
2004	119555.39	15937.74	15.38	13.30	10.10
2005	141050.99	21495.60	17.98	12.90	10.20
2006	161587.30	20536.31	14.56	13.70	10.70

Source: Chinese Statistical Office.

Compared with the world average propensity to save, 19.7%, the Chinese propensity to save in 2005 was higher, at 46%. To the contrary, the US propensity to save was around 2%. In addition, for one year, 2005, the total increasing amounts of yuan deposits reached 4.57 trillion, of which 2.15 trillion yuan was occupied by personal saving, but government saving equaled only 176 billion yuan, which meant around 8.19% of personal saving (see *Chinese Statistical Bulletin* 2006). However, what was the main purpose of Chinese personal saving?

According to a questionnaire survey of families who have family registrations in urban areas in the whole of China, in the first quarter in 2006, by the National Bank of China, under the then current level of inflation and interest rate, the ratio of respondents favoring more consumption was 28.6%, which was lower by 0.9% and 1.8% than in the previous quarter and the year before. The ratio of population favoring consumption decreased consecutively in three quarters, reaching the least level in history. Analysis by the National Bank of China pointed out the following important reasons; (i) people are worrying about their future. The questionnaire surveys said that the major reasons of personal saving were educational cost, endowments, housing purchase, and security against unexpected accident. (ii) The boom in houses and automobiles was cooling down. According to the survey, the ratio of people who wished to purchase an automobile within three months was 18.2%, which was 1% and 3.8% less than the previous quarter and the year before (which had been the least in history). Also, the ratio of people who want to purchase a house within three months equaled to 9.8%, which was 0.1% and 1.5% less than in the previous quarter and the previous year respectively. Meanwhile, people were expected to join the stock market. The ratio of people favoring purchasing stocks and funds reached 8%, which was 1.8% higher than the year before.

(3) The problems on participation rights to policy decision procedure It might be impossible for such big countries as China to approach a similar level to Japan regarding economic disparity (such as regional disparity and income disparity). Rather, the US experience would become a more appropriate lesson for China. The Chinese Statistical Office has never announced formerly its Gini coefficients; however, according to the World Bank (2006), the Gini coefficient of China (2001) was 0.45, and USA (2000) and Japan (1993) was 0.38 and 0.25 respectively.

Why have the people of USA a strong unity and strong patriotic spirit, although they have rather a large income disparity? In other words, why has the disparity never caused social instability? We think the reason comes from the democratic policy decision system. People have widely participated in the policy-decision process by voting in parliament and the local autonomy system. Because they have personally participated, they could be patient with the policy results. If the executive situation of the policy is not satisfied for the people, they could correct their selection at the next opportunity. That is to say, because the expression of their intentions and policy decision procedure to the disparity problems has been open, comparatively better policy measures could be established (and attain the equal opportunity), and peoples' dissatisfaction has never been so expanded, which could be adjusted within the system. A democratic policy decision system is the institutional apparatus to internalize the negative externality caused by economic development.

Development is a process to transform a simple society into a complex structured society, through which various socio-economic problems are occurring. People are given actual feelings and share responsibility and tasks with government through participating in the policy decision process. With participating people taking a position not to oppose the government, they share the responsibility with government. For an authoritarian system country, what is particularly stimulating indicates that social stability is the purpose of governance and is secured by introducing autonomy and participation rights that are completely the opposite to authoritarianism.

Interaction effects of institutional change between the economic system and political system

The meanings of Deng Xiaoping's system contributed not only to modernization of the Chinese economy and an improved position in international society, but also – we emphasize – to establishing a newly institutional change mechanism. We call it here 'a fact following mechanism of institutional change'. It means that, China, which has employed a gradual systemic change, has requested an endogenous systemic transition to be compatible with sustainable economic development. Gradually integrating the boundary between the economic system and political system would reach a stage requesting the respective institutional change, whose process is, we think, the real systemic transition (see Figure 5.4).

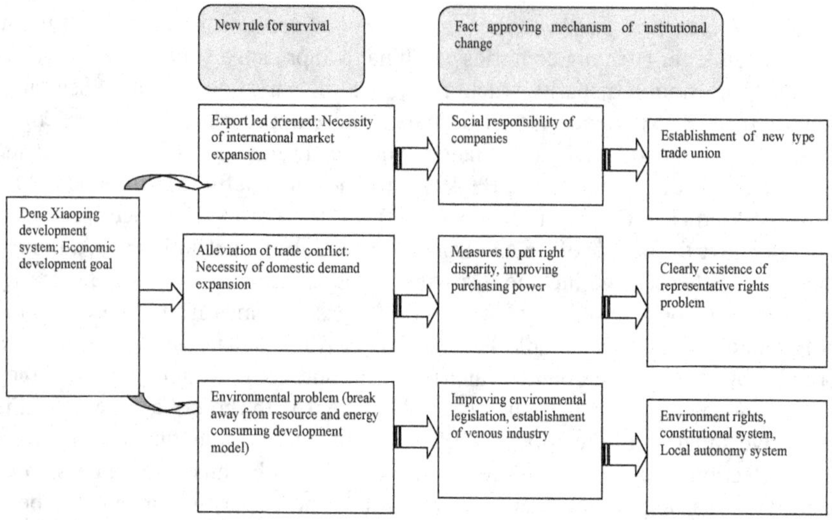

Source: Author.

Figure 5.4 New rule for survival and fact following mechanism of institutional change in the Deng Xiaoping development system

(1) Protection of workers' rights and interests and establishment of new type trade unions Local governments have already been contributing to the protection of workers' rights and interests, in the form of a correction of the lowest wages (as stated above) and as an introduction of institutions to make public illegal enterprises.

For example, Guangdong province, which has lots of farming workers, has started to protect farming workers' rights and interests. Publicity was developed within the province in October 2005 and it was announced that protection for farming workers' rights and interests became an important area of the province's policies. In addition, the Labor and Social Security Division of Guangdong province made public the list of 20 enterprises with serious violations (of which 11 manufacturing enterprises employed lots of farming workers from inland rural areas) and tried not only to have administrative measures but also social surveillance regarding these aspects. By such a new announcement system, enterprises and business organizations whose violations – such as wage non-payment, hard overtime work, non-participation of social insurance for employees – come to light, are made public through the internet, job intermediate organizations, community labor security service organizations, the mass media, and so on.

We can say that, as regards workers' rights and interests, local government policy is an external driving force while an expansion of new type trade unions, which started from privately-owned enterprises, is an internal driving force. It might be probable that such organizations would grow as a kind of political group representative of workers' collective negotiation.

For example, in order to protect workers' rights and interests, Wuxi local government of Jiangsu province made public the 'opinion to promote collective negotiation on wages in enterprises' (Wuxi local government 121st official document in 2005). In particular, they have strongly requested the institutional reinforcement of collective negotiation on wages to foreign-owned and privately-owned enterprises. To be specific, trade union and employee representative meetings of each level advocated the establishment of institutions of collective negotiation about a welfare and wage increase mechanism within enterprises.

More and more people in China have recognized that the foundation of such new-type trade unions (the characteristics of which indicate that the chairperson and committee members are selected by vote) is indispensable for realizing cooperative labor–management relations. Since the days of the central planning system, in China, unions (traditional-type trade unions) existed in enterprises, but while similar to the welfare section or general affairs section of enterprise, they were not trade unions in the correct sense. Hence, this new type of trade union is an indispensable autonomous organization to protect workers rights and interests as representatives of workers in collective negotiation.

The new type trade union in China has been established, which was stimulated by both external factors and internal factors.

(I) External factors As regards external factors, because of the export-led development strategy, international markets have become important for China. International society has a common recognition which says that enterprises should be responsible for workers' rights and interests and environmental protection. On 25, December, 2003, Nanfang Dushi Bao (Southern Metropolis Daily) reported the following case. Yajia Industry Group Company at Yuhang district, Hangzhou city of Zhejiang province, was busy adjusting meters to record the working hours of employees, which was requested by a world famous shoe making company from the USA. The US major company evaluated the situation of workers' rights and interests in the Yajia Industry Group Company in the year concerned. It was satisfied with the wage payment, production circumstances, safety protection for employees etc, however it recognized the trouble with the meters that recorded the working hours of employees, and requested the meters be repaired. This became a precondition for continuing transaction contracts.

External factors upon workers' rights and interests have worked for Chinese domestic enterprises to change their dependence upon the low cost advantage. We should understand that in the current Chinese situation, without a complete legal system external factors are working as a substitution effect. An executive of Yajia Industry Group Company said that such a transaction partner from a foreign country checks the workers' rights and interests more carefully than local government, just as a mother-in-law supervises her daughter in-law. Chinese enterprises are thus now fully conscious of the protection of workers' rights in the light of law and international custom. Also we think those external factors for microscopic viewpoints are concerned with the improvement of legal circumstances all over the nation.

(II) Internal factors Regarding internal factors, a new type of trade union is said to be an endogenous request after an enterprise reaches a certain scale. For the development of the enterprise, it is important to employ stable and skilled labor. Lots of enterprises have high mobility of workers before a new type trade union is established, which has serious effects on production. Enterprises have an immediate need of training for workers. In Guangdong province, the annual mobility ratio of a labor intensive industry is more than 60%. Many enterprises are always recruiting new workers. Once a new-type trade union is established, when workers have problems, they negotiate collectively with management through the trade unions, which work to solve the problems. Thus, workers have few worries and the mobility rate decreases noticeably.

Through such internal and external factors, the new type trade union has been rapidly developed. In Zhejiang province in particular, which has many more privately owned enterprises than other provinces, in 1999 (which was earlier than the others) an experiment was carried out regarding the new type of trade unions and direct election. Statistics from Yuhang district in Hangzhou announced that the number of new-type trade unions selected by direct election in 2003 reached 310, whose ratio to total enterprises and to privately owned enterprises was 36% and 70% respectively. What was the role of the new type of trade union? In the case of Yajia Industry Group Company, the new type of trade union negotiated with management to establish a wage increase agreement, which says that, once the enterprise profit is higher than a certain level, with a 1% profit increase, workers' wage increases by 15%.

According to Guo Wencai, who is an executive of the Chinese national union association, in the coastal area in which foreign-owned enterprises (such as Shenzhen of Guangdong province, Quanzhou of Fujian province and Qingdao of Shandong province) are concentrated, selecting a chairperson by direct election has been tried. Direct election is accepted as a way to reform Chinese trade unions. Actually, in small and medium-sized enterprises of fewer than 200 employees in China, the method of direct election for the chairperson has been accelerated.

Generally speaking, economic globalization expands the movement of social responsibility of enterprises, whose sense of values seem to be common with such political tasks as freedom, equality, human rights, and so on. Is the new type of trade union in China growing to be a political group? What role does it play for Chinese transition? Compared with the Polish Solidarity case (for the Polish case, see for example, Ash, 2002, Eringer, 1982, Kenney, 2003 and 2006, and Osa, 2003), in China – which has employed a gradual way of transition – the role of trade unions we think will be very different.

Clearer signs of peasants' representative rights problems

To correct disparity problems, particularly poverty problems in rural areas, we have to treat the problem of representative rights. It is not enough to solve the problems through the three agricultural policies, because a group that has no representative rights politically cannot advocate its own rights. Under the present peasants' autonomous system, executives of the village are selected by direct election. However, as they do not have financial authority, they have to follow what higher government orders. The executives are not able to be representatives for the peasants' interests (on this topic see Chapter 4). Needless to say, there is a parliamentary system but there could be quite a few representatives of peasants. As a matter of fact, Jinshan district in the suburbs of Shanghai is classified as a rural area. An executive who was working as a head of the district, party secretary, chief member of executive committee of district parliament, etc, also held the post of people's representative in Shanghai, and of representative of the Tenth National Parliament (from 2002 to 2007) and is formerly classified to be a representative of peasants.[15]

It is usually doubted whether peasants could participate in politics, but the author does not agree with this. Peasants should have their rights to advocate their own interests and should have the ability to insist on this. We think such a substantial right to vote is an indispensable institutional apparatus to solve the poverty problems in China's rural areas (see Chapter 4).

Necessity of establishment of environmental rights

For sustainable economic development, China has to change the development model from a resource and energy consumption type. Environmental problems are classified into two kinds, which are (i) problems of environmental pollution and quality of everyday life, and (ii) problems of the restriction of resource and energy input for production. The Japanese lesson, which had a 'catch up' strategy with a similar development system led by government, pointed out that to solve environmental problems one should start by advocating environmental rights. That is to say, the settlement of environmental pollution became the initial driving force.

The main reason for the successful insistence on environmental rights was constitutional government and a local autonomy system in a constitutional sense. The constitutional government system brought about an internal ability to go together with environmental rights presented by the international society (which was formerly presented by the Tokyo Declaration adopted at the international conference sponsored by the International Social Science Council in 1970). To correspond to environmental rights, the law on environmental protection has been improved and regulations on enterprises have been more restrictive. At the same

15 Statement at the interview by the author in 2006.

time, as environmental problems have regional characteristics, it is necessary to respond quickly and at the actual location. In Japan, because of a local autonomy system, advanced local governments (and the head of the local governments) have been elected one after another, which creates a transmission mechanism of environmental protection from the bottom to the top (from people to local government, from local government to central government).

In Japan in 2000, remarkable progress on environmental legislation was carried out, which was to implement the Resource Recycling Promotion Law. Through the legislative regulation, Japan has realized the development of the environmental industry (the venous industry, which means the stage from waste to recycling) as well as the traditional arterial industry (meaning the stage from resource to final product). Japan has thus completed the transformation from an industrial society model of mass production, mass consumption and mass waste to a sustainable society model whose characteristics are '3R' (Reduce, Reuse and Recycle) (Chen Yun, 2007b) (see Figure 5.5).

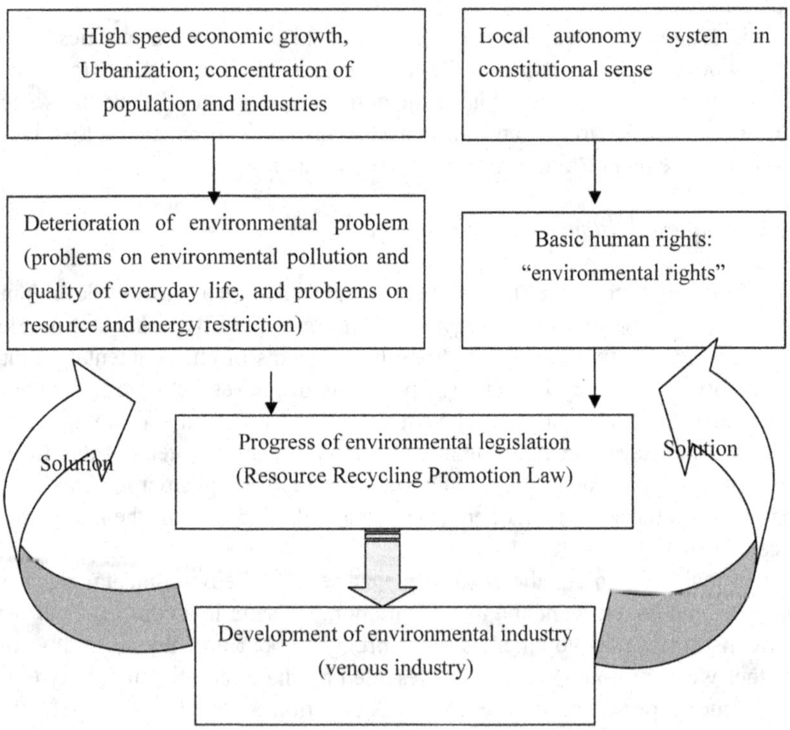

Source: Author.

Figure 5.5 Framework of institutional analysis to build the sustainable society in Tokyo

At the current stage of Chinese environmental problems, attention is focused upon the development from material and energy waste types. However to realize the goal it is necessary to establish environmental rights. Legislative grounds for protesting behaviors by the victims of environmental pollution are given, by which an initial movement to internalize the negative externality by enterprises can be brought about.

Recently in China, analyses – entitled Chinese sustained development and environment problems – have been active; however, deep-rooted circumstances point out industry's priority ways of thinking, taking into consideration the cooperation of development with environment problems. It might be similar to Japan in the 1960s before the Pollution Diet was held. In China, even among scholars, there are very few who insist on environment priority.

It is the current situation in China that the local autonomy system has never been established in a constitutional sense, which is different from Japan (although in China there could be established such institutions as a race autonomous system, the special administration districts of Hong Kong, and Xiamen, are still in the decentralization stage, which means that a local autonomy system has never been established in a constitutional sense). Thus, in the whole society in China, they have no effective measures (such as direct election rights to select the head of a local government, and bottom-up style transmission mechanism centers on direct claim rights) to apply the brake to the development impulse, which is industry's priority. The head of a local government in China is chosen by the local assembly consisting of local representatives who are elected by local citizens in a formal sense, but actually, as candidates are nominated by higher government (or the party organization), local government officials are responsible to higher organizations. At the present stage, whose main purpose has been to improve industrialization, the GDP growth rate should be the appropriate index to show the better performance of local government officials. Substantially, local administration has fallen into a view that 'GDP is almighty'.

As environmental circumstances in China have become serious recently, the movement to make 'green GDP' as a substitute index of GDP has been more active. However, as it is a hard task to find an exact method of measuring 'green GDP', it is expected to have a full-scale change to green GDP. A more fundamental reason is as follows; if the situation of local citizens who have no rights of direct election and direct claim is unchanged, they will not have active local government to try to create better regional circumstances.

We think that, as a serious environment problem usually occurs in specific regional spots, the existence of a mechanism to convey the problem from the actual spot to a higher organization is indispensable. As was shown in the Japanese case to treat the problem, the deterioration of the environmental situation for citizens surrounding the spot (damage to their health and decline of quality for their everyday life) was prime for concerted neighborhood action, and resolving the problems of improving both the production system and the development system became necessary, which finally led to better legislation. Meanwhile, in China, having faced the bottleneck of energy and resources, slogans have been displayed saying ‘circulating economy’, ‘saving energy’, ‘saving society’; however, the main reason why this has never been effective, even when putting greater attention upon improvement of the production system, seems to be due to lack of institutional reform.

Generally speaking, without considering institutional problems, it might be impossible to improve environmental problems. As regards environmental problems, we cannot help say that central government, which remains aloof from the problems can do nothing, compared with local government, which has taken measures rationally under the current institution. The ‘institutional revolution’ (for example the introduction of the local autonomy system) to reform environmental administration without citizens’ opinions will lead to structural reform related to environment problems in China.

Conclusion

In this chapter, in light of various characteristics of the East Asian model, we examine the important topic asking whether China could join the East Asian model countries. In order to realize the sustainable development of the Chinese economy, we observe and analyze that, in China, a compound reform process of the fact following type, involving the reform of the political system has appeared.

Traditionally we have a concept of the advantage of the latecomer, which is favorable for less developed countries. However, the actual situation is not so simple. In improving the development process, the disadvantage of backwardness is gradually appearing. Because of backwardness, various problems related with development started to be associated with each other in a complicatedly way. It might be necessary for less developed countries to complete several stages of economic development in fewer years than for advanced industrialized countries. This is undoubtedly more difficult than a step-by-step development process of advanced industrialized countries. Government is expected to play an important role as both management and a driving force engine for development. Actually, the active intervention of government was one of the characteristics of the East Asian model.

China, located in East Asia, is not an exception. Such concepts as the whole nation’s system, open system, market-oriented economy, have been outstanding characteristics of recent times. However, as indicated by constitutional economics, there are dilemmas between government and market. As a matter of fact, not only between government and market but also in various topics discussed in this book, such as between politics and economy, central and local, internal and external relations, we could recognize similar dilemmas. Because the reason for dilemmas might be coming from unhealthy actors, tasks to evolve should be necessary. If these tasks proceed, regardless of unhealthy circumstances, market failure or government failure would occur. The above-stated pairs seem to be similar to the relations between a blind person and a physically handicapped person. Unless each of them supports the other, both would find it difficult to act.

What is more difficult is that each of them is not a great friend, and they are others who know about nothing of each other. There might be tensions between them because they need each other but they are cautious about each other. Both of the two are in crucial relations toward mutual promotion or toward mutual retrogression. Thus, if their cooperative relations collapse, both of them might be ruined (failure of transition). In that sense, step-by-step progress would be safer for both of them. It could become an explanation for the necessity of a gradual way of transition. When less developed countries take a path towards maturity, learning by doing might be a normal way and a rule.

What is the key to the success of the East Asian model? Could China, after reform and the open door policy, follow the East Asian model? The two problems have been core topics upon which we have paid attention in this book. In this chapter we have focused our attention on the characteristics of the economic aspects of the East Asian model. In Chapter 6 we investigate further, attaching greater importance on the political system of development.

Chapter 6
Political Economy of the East Asian Authoritarian Development System: Lessons Towards Shared Growth

Introduction

Research purpose

Emerging nation states in postwar Asia have faced two tasks, which are economic development and nation state foundation. In such fields as development economics and political economy of development etc, the aims are to investigate development problems of less developed countries and to focus attention upon relations between economic aspects and political aspects.

Since the 1980s, the remarkable economic development of East Asia (whose region is also called as West Pacific Region) has roused experts' interest on authoritarian development systems, particularly on the original meanings of development tools. China is located in East Asia and Chinese ideological and cultural tradition is closely related with East Asia; in addition, Chinese political economic relations with the region have also been closely connected. The purpose of this chapter is to classify various East Asian countries' developments with authoritarian systems into some models, and to analyze the logics of their development from the viewpoints of political economy, to examine their contributions to Chinese development model building.

We classify here authoritarian development models of East Asia into the East Asian NIEs model, a Southeast Asian model and a Chinese model. The main purpose of this book thus is to find several empirical rules that are hidden in authoritarian development systems. Empirical rules indicate the rules that became tangible to some extent in the East Asian region, and are likely to come into existence in China in the near future (and which have universal validity).

There could be differences from one country to another. Special circumstances of respective countries should be added when we investigate the logic of the development model. Even in the same country, there could be also differences from one period to another due to particular characteristics of the respective period, because compared to a democratic political system with a fairly mature separation of the three branches of government, an authoritarian development system undoubtedly has a relatively unstable structure. Such special circumstances come from various factors such as leader's personality, size of nation state, racial and religious complexity.

Concept of East Asia

The concept of East Asia is substantially different according to the discipline involved, the scholar's position, research topic, and so on. In this chapter, East Asia is depicted as countries related via the flying geese model. The countries are Japan, China, Asian NIEs, and Association of Southeast Asian Nations (ASEAN) member countries.[1] However, the area might be dynamically expanding. For example, India could be included. Also, when we refer to the East Asian NIEs model, and the ASEAN model, I will indicate some example countries rather than all member countries.

Structure of this chapter

This chapter consists of seven parts and a conclusion. In the next section, we have a short review of the postwar economic and political development of Asian countries and its four stages. In the third section, we examine the East Asian authoritarian development system from the viewpoints of characteristics of tools. In the fourth section, we classify East Asian authoritarian systems into three kinds, and in the fifth section we understand the Taiwanese experience, especially focusing our attention upon relations between administration and politics under the one-party system and upon roles of technocrats. In the sixth section, we investigate various conditions to realize shared growth with a comparison of the East Asian NIEs model and the ASEAN model. In the seventh section, the Chinese way and Chinese tasks are given. Finally we summarize the conclusions of this chapter.

Postwar economic and political development of Asian countries

The first stage: social instability after independence and economic tasks for development

The Japanese defeat in the Second World War in 1945 did not lead directly to independence of East Asian countries, because former suzerain states returned to colonize them again. Indonesia attained independence in 1949 by winning a

1 The League of Southeast Asia expanded to ten member countries from the initial five, which are Singapore, Thailand, Malaysia, Indonesia, the Philippines (those five are original member countries of the League established in Bangkok, August 8, 1967), Brunei (joined after the independence in 1984), Vietnam (joined in 1995), Myanmar, Laos (joined in 1997) and Cambodia (joined in 1999).

victory against the UK and the Netherlands. Vietnam, after the Japanese defeat, spent nine years in a protest movement to reach independence in 1954.

Emerging countries after independence encountered various troubles. During the reconstruction from the war, it was extremely difficult for them to build their nation states because their economic foundations were fairly weak. Charismatic leaders who led racially independent movements became a core for nation state building. Such leaders as Sukarno of Indonesia, Ho Chi-Minh of Vietnam, Mao Zedong of China were the examples. Lee Kuan Yew of Singapore was not a soldier, but was respected by the people as a leader of a national independent movement.

Just after the nation building, many countries had land reforms. In the Chinese revolution led by Mao Zedong, they promoted a series of land reform and the peasant liberation movement during the revolutionary process. That was because the Chinese revolution had strong characteristics of an agricultural revolution, saying that the urban was surrounded by the rural. However, in China, after lands were distributed for peasants, at the end of the 1950s lands were intensively concentrated again. During the building process of the people's commune, the shock therapy was employed (see Chapter 1). In postwar Japan, a series of economic reconstruction and democratic reforms were promoted by the General Headquarters established by the US government which included land reforms. In Taiwan and South Korea, successful land reforms were supported by the US government. Lots of less-developed countries, such as the Philippines, tried to follow the Taiwanese experience, however, most of these countries were not successful. Postwar land reforms contributed to social stability by raising efficiency of agricultural production and the self-sufficiency ratio. Also, agricultural development contributed for mobility of redundant workers and industrial development.

The second stage: foundation of an anti-communist front in East Asia during the Cold War and US support

The initial US strategy plan for the postwar East Asian region was generally as follows. By providing military assistance with a bilateral security agreement, US supported land reforms to establish a parliamentary system and to assist the transition towards civilian politics. However, soon after that the whole world entered the days of the Cold War. Asia became a strategic region with a border between such socialist countries as China, Vietnam and the USSR.

The Korean War occurred in 1950 and the US carried out military intervention by dispatching an army to the Korean Peninsula. Moreover, the US changed the strategy when the communist party in Japan and Indonesia became more active in order to prevent expanding communism in Asia. It meant the US adjusted its foreign policy to make such autocratic leaders as Sukarno, Chiang Kai-shek, Syngman Rhee retainable. The US thus approved the administrations by autocratic leaders in Asian countries and supported both economic and military aspects. When the Vietnam War started at the end of 1960s, the US had military intervention to adhere to an anti-communist front. Actually, on August 8, 1967, five countries – Singapore, Thailand, Malaysia, Indonesia and The Philippines – established the first Association of Southeast Asian Nations in Bangkok. That had strong political implications of an anti-communist front.

In the development dictatorship system supported by the USA, Asian countries employed priority to industrial development policies, with which their economies were developed, and accelerated successful industrialization. Meanwhile, it was correct to say that bureaucrats and officers supporting an authoritarian system became the privileged classes and had a cozy relationship with the industrial world. Because of corruption, people and students had more complaints which led to frequent occurrence of coup d'états in various places. Afterwards, leaders who were called the founders of promoting the nation came into existence in various countries. In 1960, in South Korea, President Syngman Rhee lost his position because of the April Revolution coming from the students' movement, and one year after in 1961 Park Chung Hee carried out a coup d'état and came into power. In the same year, Singapore, led by Lee Kuan Yew, separated from Malaysia to be independent. In 1966, in Indonesia, Sukarno was deprived of his power and Suharto took up a position of deputy president. In 1978, in China after the death of Mao Zedong and the demise of Cultural Revolution, Deng Xiaoping returned to his political position and started the reform and open door policy. All of the above were called the founders of promoting the nation again.

New leaders were favored with the international circumstances of détente, which could make them concentrate on nation building towards industrialization. Export-oriented strategy was improved and various middle and long term economic plans were carried out, and also active attractive policies for foreign capital were implemented, through which they successfully realized economic development, which they had never enjoyed before. The 'flying geese' development model, through an international transfer of industry, seemed to explain this well (as will be mentioned later).

The third stage: reform and open policy of socialist countries and the demise of the Cold War, and becoming advanced countries of Asian NIEs

The Chinese reform and open door policy was a big occurrence that surprised the whole world.

From the viewpoints of the external environment, Chinese successful reform and open door policy was substantially contributed to by lots of Chinese merchants living abroad who had full entrepreneurial spirit. At present, the number of Chinese people living abroad is around 37 million, most of whom live in Southeast Asia. Foreign direct investment by the Chinese network contributed to the role of pump priming at the initial stage of inward FDI in China. Statistics indicated that almost half of inward FDI in China came from Hong Kong, Macao and Taiwan.

China has actively promoted an export-oriented industrialization and trade strategy with which China has gradually integrated in the international economy.

In December 2001, China participated in the WTO after more than ten years of negotiation.

Since the beginning of the 1990s, Asian NIEs have reached the level of advanced industrialized economies. South Korea also has become a member of the OECD (Organization for Economic Cooperation and Development) which is usually named as an 'advanced economies' club' in 1996. The 'flying geese' development model, which explains the vertical division of labor, has been changed to have, partly, a horizontal division of labor. For example, the deepening of the division of labor among processes, catching up on telecommunication industries by NIEs, etc, can be pointed out.

The fourth stage: economic globalization and East Asian Free Trade Area, internationalized tendency of internal politics and economy in each country and region

East Asia is a region in which the growth rate is the highest in the world. Table 6.1 shows the real GDP growth rate of countries and regions in the world. Undoubtedly the high Chinese rate of economic growth is remarkable. The GDP ratios to the world total in 2003 were 29.8% of the USA, 29.9% of the EU, 11.7% of Japan, 3.9% of China, 3.1% of NIEs, and 1.5% of the ASEAN four.[2] Thus, the Asian GDP total of Japan, China, Hong Kong, Taiwan, South Korea and the ASEAN four occupied 20.2% of the world total GDP.

East Asia was a vacuum region of the Free Trade Association (FTA), however after 2000 the active tendency to establish an FTA has been recognized. Behind the tendency it could be said that, because negotiations on the Doha Round within the

Table 6.1 Real GDP growth rate

	1998	1999	2000	2001	2002	2003	2004	2005
Whole world	2.4	3.4	3.9	1.6	1.9	2.7	4.1	3.4
Japan	-1.0	-0.1	2.4	0.2	-0.3	1.3	2.7	2.7
USA	4.2	4.5	3.7	0.8	1.9	3.1	4.2	3.5
EU 25	3.0	2.9	3.8	1.9	1.2	1.1	2.4	2.2
China	6.0	7.1	8.7	7.3	8.3	9.2	10.0	9.6
ASEAN 4	-9.5	3.2	5.8	2.3	4.6	5.4	5.9	5.1

Note: China includes Hong Kong. ASEAN 4 countries indicate Indonesia, Thailand, the Philippines and Malaysia.

Source: (Japanese) Ministry of Economy, Trade and Industry (2007).

2 World Bank, annual, and Statistical Database of Budget Bureau in Taiwanese Administration Agency.

WTO framework have faced rough going, a bilateral FTA has focused attention. In 2002, an FTA was established between Japan and Singapore and in 2003 the foundation of Southeast Asian FTA was basically agreed. In 2004, among China, Hong Kong and Macao an FTA was established. Also, in November 2004, China concluded the FTA with ASEAN countries. In April 2007, the Japanese cabinet signed the FTA with Thailand, and South Korea concluded the FTA with USA. At present, South Korea is actively negotiating to conclude an FTA with Australia, New Zealand and Canada.

There are other FTA schedules which are negotiating among themselves. For example, negotiations between China and Australia, China and South Korea, Japan and ASEAN, Japan and South Korea, Japan and the Philippines, Japan and Malaysia, Japan and Brunei have been recognized.

Table 6.2 expresses regional trade agreements with which China is concerned.

Development of telecommunications has improved the will towards democratization of the above countries and regions, which has caused exposure of autocratic nation states to serious critics. It means that increased relations of economic interdependence have promoted internalization and liberalization of the Asian countries and isolated political and economic management has never been allowed.

In such economic globalization, we understand that in East Asia new structural change has occurred in which economic performances are rather different. (1) First, in Southeast Asian and South Asian countries, such countries as Indonesia and the Philippines had riots coming from peoples' discontents against the long-term centralized administration. Myanmar, which has never broken with a military system, is exposed to international critical views. India had no stable leader after the open economic policy experienced political disturbance. (2) Meanwhile, in Asian NIEs countries and regions, South Korea and Taiwan progressed towards democratization the top down way, in which they had to carry out a burying the past and a reform of the internal system.

We expect that in the 21st century East Asian countries will attain systemic evolution by having painful experiences in politics and economy. China should have attention focused upon it after joining the WTO.

Characteristics of the East Asian authoritarian system

East Asian Miracle: attractiveness of 'flying geese' development model

After the Industrial Revolution, the international economy experienced four economic cycles. In the cycles, the economic center transferred from Europe to North America, and from the Atlantic coast to the Pacific coast. The center of the world economy thus has consisted of three poles. Accompanied with the above process, the core cities of the three poles are London, New York and Tokyo, which have grown to be three mega cities in the world. This was not the process in

Table 6.2 Development of regional trade agreements with which China is concerned

Type	Process	Member countries
Regional trade agreement (RTA)	Admission and signing	Bangkok agreement (2001.5.23)
Closer Economic Partnership Arrangement (CEP)	Signing	China (continent) and Hong Kong (2003.6.29)
		China (continent) and Macao (2003.10.29)
Free trade agreement (FTA)	Some parts of negotiation on commodity trade, conflict resolution mechanism etc. have been completed	China and ASEAN (2002.11.4); towards FTA conclusion between China and ASEAN in 2010
	Under negotiation	China and Gulf Cooperation Council (GCC)
		China and South African Customs Union (SACU)
		China and Chile China and New Zealand
	Under consideration	China and Australia
		East Asia
		China, Japan and South Korea (private research)
	Making a proposition	China and India
		China and Pakistan
		Shanghai Cooperative Organization
		China and Singapore

Source: Author (based upon the materials given by the spokesperson of the Ministry of Commerce, Long Guoqiang, at the Chinese high ranking forum 2005 sponsored by Chinese cabinet development research center, March 19–21, 2005).

which an advanced region was replaced by a late-comer region through losing the advantages. The economic globalization process has the possibility to expand the market and to raise the efficiency by reasonable resource allocation in the global market. It could be said it was a 'win-win game'. The participation of 130 countries and regions in the WTO might be enough evidence of a positive evaluation. Needless to say, regulation for fair trade has to be a crucial prerequisite.

In the 1960s, the Japanese real GDP growth rate reached 10.2% per annum. Due to the rapid growth of Japan and Germany, the equilibrium situation in economy and trade among advanced economies had to be adjusted. In August 1971, the USA abolished the fixed exchange rate system and finished the conversion of gold into dollars. Since the Nixon shock and the oil crisis in 1973, the Japanese economy carried out a soft landing by experiencing several failures. Japanese average growth rate in the 1970s was 4.5% per annum.

At the end of the 1970s, because of the soaring international oil price, the aggravation of US–Japan trade conflicts, Plaza Accord in 1985 etc, the Japanese yen appreciated. Meanwhile, Japanese per capita income (in terms of US dollars) increased 15.3% in the 1960s, and 17.3% in the 1970s, which was higher than the inflation rate.

Japanese enterprises tried to rationalize with personnel cuts, and also attempted outward FDI, against comparative disadvantages, when they received yen appreciation, wage rise pressure, etc. In addition to outward FDI to such export countries as the US and the European ones, Japanese enterprises had a tendency of transferring exportable goods production of light industry to South Korea, Taiwan, and Singapore and this was accelerated. Transferring the production base of Japanese enterprises, varied from one type to another (wholly owned, joint venture, etc) and, because of the mutual benefits of the host countries' side (receiving relatively advanced technology) and home countries' side (gaining more foreign markets promoted by Japanese enterprises), industrialization through FDI has been rapidly improved.

In South Korea, they concentrated their industries upon enterprise groups such as Hyundai, Samsung and Daewoo, and chose efficient ways of industrialization. Taiwan has had a reasonable base of small and medium sized enterprises, which was established under Japanese rule and employed industrial promotion policy depending upon the base. Singapore had a foreign capital attraction policy at an early stage, and attempted to promote advanced industry, service industry, and soft industry. Thailand in particular attached greater importance upon inward FDI from Japan, therefore Japanese-owned enterprises were observed in industries in Thailand.

The above-mentioned countries and regions enthusiastically tried industrialization to catch up with Japan, which improved its industrialization from the Meiji days. In 1986, both South Korea and Taiwan attained the same growth rate of 11.6%, which were followed by Thailand's 13.3% and Singapore's 11.1% in 1988. Also, in 1989, Malaysia and Indonesia reached a high rate of GDP growth, which was 9.2% and 7.5% respectively. They concentrated their attention upon the rapid economic growth of such other countries as China, Vietnam, and India.

Asian less-developed countries have succeeded in their industrial transfer and participated in an economic development group one after another, a movement which as it looked similar to the 'flying geese' model, was called a 'flying geese development model'. What we should be interested in is that, when the north–south issues on economic disparity have become substantial all over the world, the above-mentioned consecutive development pattern came into existence in Asia and destroyed the dual structure to some extent and attained shared growth.

What is authoritarianism?: authoritarianism as a tool

We could summarize the characteristics of an East Asian authoritarian development system as a combined system of a development oriented one in an economic sense with authoritarianism in a political sense. In this chapter we can put more weight upon characteristics of an authoritarian political system (see Chapter 5 on the characteristics of a development oriented system).

Authoritarianism can be split into two types, which are in a wide sense and a narrow sense. The original meaning of authoritarianism in a wide sense is that the societal members forcibly obey the ruler's will. Thus, as a matter of fact, it is similar to paternalism or totalitarianism. This system is aimed at fully controlling the social economy and political life of the people by using a national violence mechanism and ideology; also, the system presses into duty the people for participating and supporting the political campaign of the government. Therefore, characteristics of authoritarianism in a wide sense are simply summarized to be excessive concentration of power and being free from constitutional restriction. Currently, in which democratic values are universally approved, authoritarianism has undoubtedly got negative connotations. For example, western scholars usually use the term as anti-democratic, autocratic (Adorno *et al*., 1950).

Meanwhile, authoritarianism in a narrow sense expresses a kind of particular non-democratic form of government, which is different from totalitarianism. In modern political science, the term authoritarianism in a narrow sense has a special meaning exemplified by the success of the East Asian model.

When the term is used in that sense, the implication of an autocratic system becomes weaker. For example, in the political aspect, they maintain monopolistic power (they do not allow party politics and seriously restrict freedom of the press) but in the socio-economic aspect, social members and market players are highly independent (in which a market oriented system is kept and developed). That is to say, the power in the political aspect is autocratic and in other aspects society has comparative autonomy to the nation state. The dual structure of political aspects and socio-economic aspects are important characteristics by which authoritarianism in a narrow sense is different from totalitarianism. The characteristics of narrow sense authoritarianism are summarized to be a development system with low political participation and high economic growth.

The authoritarian development model seems to be attractive for lots of less developed countries. They have attached greater importance upon the interesting question of whether an authoritarian system is an important factor to promote economic development. Basically, at present, researchers and research organizations have various assertions on relationships between an authoritarian system and economic development. Those assertions have several complicated relations with such practical models as the East Asian model, Latin American model, former Soviet and East European model, and Chinese model (including Vietnam). From the viewpoints of practical East Asian countries and regions, a gradual systemic transition under the authoritarian system contributed to stable social order and for security against internal and external crises. Therefore, it is called wise authoritarianism, meaning a positive contribution for their economic development. Taiwan and South Korea before democratization were typical examples.

We insist here that, referring to East Asian NIEs countries, authoritarianism has clear characteristics as a kind of example. A kind of tool of the authoritarian system means that, in the institutional evolutionary process of socio-economic development in less developed countries, the authoritarianism is recognized, as a matter of fact, not to be an end but to be a means. The reason why we emphasize 'as a matter of fact' is because leaders of authoritarianism did not promote a development system with full consciousness. However, since a certain logic was established, the phenomenon was one in which a transition process was deepening independent of some officials' and groups' way of thinking. Thus, we conclude that authoritarianism is opposed by authoritarianism. Both Taiwan and South Korea are proven cases.

When we talk about the conclusion, saying that authoritarianism is opposed by authoritarianism, the author of this book remembers the American film entitled *Terminator 2: Judgment Day*. At the end of the film, the T800 robot (played by Arnold Schwarzenegger) went down in the blast furnace of ironworks in order to destroy thoroughly the dangerous chip that was embedded in his head. It was a moving story filled with heroism of the type often enjoyed in American films. The last scene is meaningful in an allegorical sense. Self-extinction is not easy for everyone. If someone carries it out resolutely, it could cause more benefit for human beings. If he or she is not rationalist, self-extinction could never occur. According to the first law of thermodynamics, the total amount of energy in an isolated system remains constant (which states that energy cannot be created or destroyed, it can only be changed from one form to another). Thus, if it is destroyed, it could be restored to life in another form. Self-extinction does not mean in that sense death, but indicates the first step of restoration. A similar story could be said about the authoritarian political system. The parts and materials included in the authoritarian political system are not extinct from systemic transition but are reformed and returned with a completely new form. There could be found in that process the rationality of gradualism by which they proceed in a reformist way, not a revolutionary way.

Three kinds of authoritarian system in East Asia

Initial condition of development and development model differentiation

Thinkers in the Enlightenment, in the 17th century, insisted that self-preservation was the first law of *jus naturale.* We think that is correct not only for persons but also for the nation state. By the ideological opposition, the postwar world was divided into two camps with different political and economic systems. It was particularly remarkable in East Asia and East Europe. Generally speaking, when each country selects a way of development, they attach greater importance upon their own security, which is crucial to recognizing the development model of postwar East Asian countries and regions.

Figure 6.1 shows the characteristics of three kinds of authoritarian system in East Asia and internal and external environments. In Japan, democratic reform in the political system was accomplished and a single party system – the Liberal

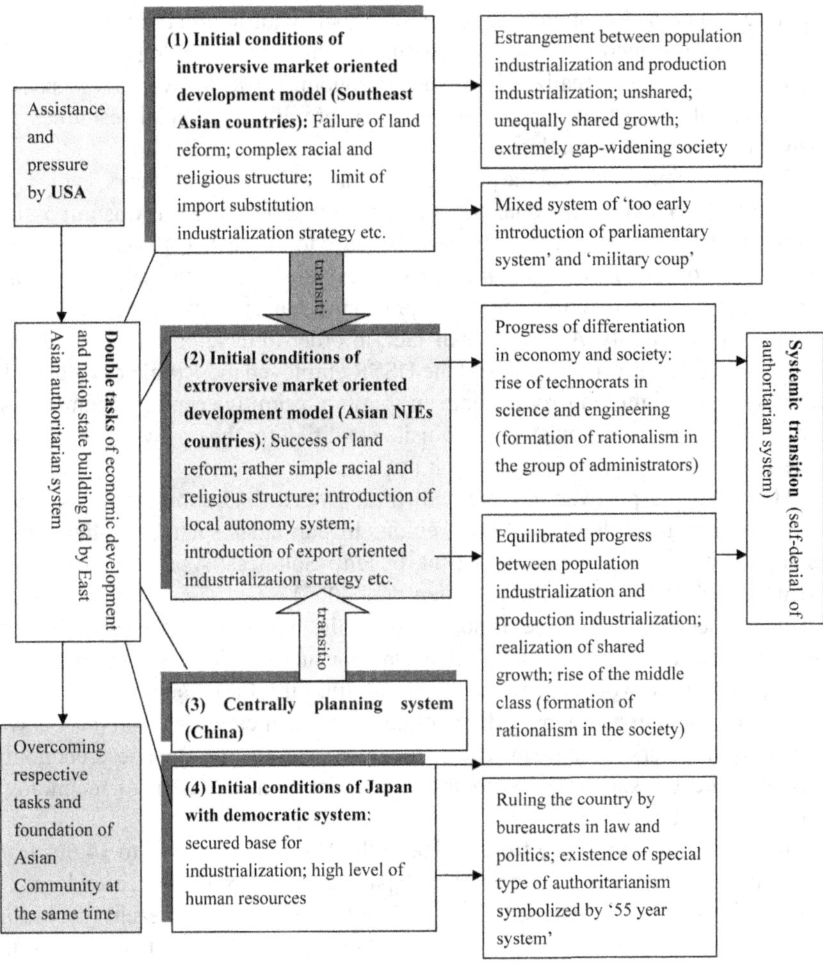

Source: Author.

Figure 6.1 Three kinds of authoritarian system in East Asia

Democratic Party – which was called as the '55 year system', lasted many years. However, it was difficult to say that Japan had an authoritarian system.

(I) Postwar international order led by the USA First of all, what should we understand about the US assistance and pressure shown in Figure 6.1?

In the process of a free trade system led by the USA in the postwar period, the conflict between east and west was an important historical background. The USA and the western countries tried to have a centripetal force through a free trade system, whose results seemed to be successful against the other camp. Western countries combined economic development goals with international cooperation by which they gained reciprocally benefits of a market, technology transfer, raw material trade etc, and realized high-speed economic growth. Needless to say, the US contributed most for providing a market, providing financial resources and providing advanced technology.

In the building process of the postwar international order, most years, in the Cold War, were given over to the dual structure of international order. It was impossible to construct the 'win-win' game structure because for more than 40 years they were in seriously opposed situations and in east-west tensions. At the same time, each camp was probably distorting the development mechanism as they put more weight upon military security. As a matter of fact, in order to develop military industry, which was given priority, China and the USSR employed industrial policy to make agriculture and light industry become an origin of primitive capital accumulation. It meant there could not exist a prerequisite condition for the postwar international order led by the US to globally carry it out.

However, the postwar international trade system had substantial influential power to penetrate the East Asian region. In particular such US allied forces as Japan and South Korea enjoyed the benefit. Southeast Asian countries were included in such beneficiary ones (Chen Yun, 2005).

In the second half of the 1980s, a term 'the days of West Pacific' became popular. East Asia focused greater attention upon an emerging region of one of the three poles in the world economy. In establishing the East Asian miracle, Japan was the production goods providing country for Asian countries, and the US was providing the market for them. Undoubtedly, in the postwar Japanese economic recovery, the US substantially contributed to Japan in the form of technology, finance and market.

In 2005, the import ratio from China of the US total expanded to 14.6% from 6.1% in 1995; contrarily, the ratio from Japan and Asian NIEs decreased by 8.3% and 4.9% respectively (whose ratio in 2005 was 8.3% and 6.1% each) (according to the statistics of the Chinese Ministry of Commerce). Those statistics show that Japan and Asian NIEs utilized China as a production base for export using a cheap labor force. As a result, China has been the biggest partner country in the US trade deficit in place of Japan in the 1980s. Meanwhile the Chinese trade deficit with

South Korea, Taiwan and Singapore has been increasing, which has led China to be the biggest partner country for their trade surplus.

The important role the US has played in trade with East Asian countries has made the US position critical for East Asian economic development, whose influential power has covered not only the economic and trade field but also the military security field.

(II) Choice of East Asian emerging nation states: Southeast Asian way and NIEs way As regards the initial conditions, most East Asian countries and regions have the colonial history against the US, European countries and Japan. They thus established a typical colonial economic structure, which indicated a kind of non-autonomous economic structure with serious distortions. Because they had primary commodities and a dependent economic structure (monoculture economy), they could not basically promote industrialization. They depended upon imports from suzerain states even for daily consumer goods.

A typical example was Malaysia. Malaysia was formerly a colony of the UK, and became independent in 1957. After independence, the Malaysian economy fully depended on such primary commodities as tin and natural rubber. They had almost no industry except tin mining and natural rubber plantations. At the beginning of the 1960s, in Malaysian export industries, primary commodities occupied a dominant position, whose ratio showed that natural rubber and tin reached 50% and 20% respectively. Other exportable commodities were timber and palm oil etc (Bank Negara Malaysia).

In the postwar period, Southeast Asian nation states shared the desire to break away from a subordinate position coming from colonial hardships. Most Asian countries took a protection oriented industrialization strategy which was called the import substitution strategy. They employed therefore such protectionist policies as higher tariff barriers, import quantity regulations. In place of imports, which was reasonable, domestic enterprises had substitute productions. They enjoyed a monopolistic position in the domestic market. It pointed out that the import substitution strategy is a typical introverted strategy. In postwar East Asia, a few countries and regions (which were named later as Asian NIEs) implemented an import substitution strategy for a significantly short period, and they quickly transformed their economies towards an export-oriented strategy (which will be mentioned in the following section). It should be referred that, behind those transformations, NIEs countries and regions had close relations with the USA.

(III) Chinese way: three times transition of the development system Just after the new China was founded, the Korean War occurred, which clearly showed the beginning of the Cold War. Mao Zedong decided to choose a way of 'exclusive to the interests of the USSR'. As regards the economic development model, Mao Zedong entirely introduced the Stalin type development model. The introduction of a Stalin type development model in China continued to the end of the 1950s when Sino–USSR relations worsened. However, after the deterioration of Sino–

USSR relations, such various characteristics of a centrally planned economic system, such as the state planning committee similar to the USSR existed. The Chinese development system after the worsening of Sino–USSR was called a Mao Zedong development system, in which Mao Zedong ideologies – like a populist line, spiritualism, politics priority etc – were thoroughly included.

Both a Stalin type development model and Mao Zedong's development model are closed systems. In those days, socialist international economic integration, such as CMEA (Council for Mutual Economic Conference) led by the USSR, was established, which was the expanded version of a centrally planned system; however, the CMEA could not work well because of the systemic inadequacies. It meant that, in order for a particular institution to be sustainable, all the members could become beneficiaries through everyday life exchanges, whose necessity shows it is necessary for the members to have principles of equality, reciprocity, and non-discrimination.

Mao Zedong's development system in China displayed a central slogan advocating independence and self-reliance. It was a development strategy attaching greater importance upon heavy industry and less importance on agriculture. Although the economic system was different, such an industrialization strategy was similar to a Southeast Asian import substitution strategy. Compared with a Stalinist type development system, which emphasized state-owned, hard planning, centralization, Mao Zedong's development system had characteristics of public owned (meaning state-owned and collective-owned, the former of which was in urban areas and the latter in rural areas) and soft planning and soft centralization (in which local decentralization was attempted twice).

Deng Xiaoping's development system was a reform and open door policy and in the gradual way of transition, which should be called a 'creative destruction' (see Chapter 2 on this concept). Deng Xiaoping's development system has also the characteristics of a development oriented system; however, as it was an open door policy, return of benefit to the society might be possible. Reforms of Deng Xiaoping's era applied such reform measures as multiple proprietary rights, coexistence of planning and market, separation of government from state-owned enterprises in the Chinese economic system, and gradually established market independence by increasing the ratio of privately owned enterprises from year to year. The Deng Xiaoping's reform was started by a local decentralization system; however, it was different from local decentralization of Mao Zedong's era. The decentralization by Deng Xiaoping was supported by at least two systems, whose first was administrative decentralization and second was economic decentralization. Administrative decentralization was carried out among vertical administrative ranks, and economic decentralization was implemented as separation of government from state-owned enterprises. The latter decentralization was a newly established one in the Deng Xiaoping's system. That is to say, the local decentralization in China carried out by Deng Xiaoping reached the stage of being irreversible. The development system post Deng Xiaoping (by Jiang Zemin and, Hu Jintao and Wen Jiabao) has been basically located in the extension of Deng Xiaoping.

(IV) Japanese way: authoritarian development system without authoritarianism
In postwar Japan, a series of democratic reforms led directly by GHQ was carried out. The Japanese political system was also democratized, thus the Japanese system was not an authoritarian government in the strict sense. However, generally speaking, the postwar Japanese political system has had a conservative tradition.

After the Cold War began, the US reform plan for Japan made the traditional system survive in the same way as for Taiwan and South Korea. For example, the Emperor system of Japan has been sustained. In addition, it was a surprised that, after the Purge Directive, primary war criminals like Ichiro Hatoyama, Nobusuke Kishi were restored to the political world and later became prime ministers.

The third Hatoyama cabinet was the start of the '55 year system' (which showed the long-term administrative power by the Liberal Democratic Party, which lasted from 1955 to 1993). The LDP has been a kind of 'department store' including various factions in which they have quite often different political views. On the whole, the LDP has been undoubtedly a conservative political power. In the LDP, many politicians succeed to the network of prewar party members and of prewar bureaucrats.

The start of long-term administrative power by LDP was the starting period of the Japanese miracle. One of the characteristics of a government-led economic development model, which was built to realize a catching up and overtaking strategy was the strong administrative directives. Industrial policy, whose representative was the administrative directive, promoted a Japanese miracle and also indicated the closed part of Japanese society.

Aoki *et al.* (1996) classified governments into four typical types. (i) First is authoritarian government in which authority to control is fully centralized and the separation of the three branches is minimized. (ii) Second is rule-based government, which means that relatively stronger central executives control lower level government regardless of authority to control; however, three branches are strictly separated and the negotiation power of government to the private sector is restrained. (iii) Third is relation-based government, which points out that coordination at the time of policy revision is implemented at lower level government; meanwhile, as the three branches are not clearly separated, legal costs are high. (iv) Fourth is disorganized government, which shows that administrations are cut into pieces.

In the East Asian countries, we could recognize that lots of governments are classified as the first type. The US government is typical of the second type. The most difficult government to be clarified seems to be the third type. According to Okuno-Fujiwara (1993), in Japan, because the bureaucratic system is developed (including preparation of bills), sectionalism is brought about in administrative control and the legislative branch is strongly controlled by the administrative branch. Thus, the Japanese government is classified as the third type. In addition to the above, when administrative litigation is brought, the average number years during a suit at the final judgment of the Supreme Court is ten (Miyazaki, 1986).

The long-term procedure of administrative litigation seems to reach the stronger position of the administrative branch.

Consequence of non-West European type racialism

In the rapid progress of racialism and economic globalization, conflicts between internationalization and racial sentiment have been continued. What are the relations between racialism, which has been a powerful incentive to mobilize people, and economic development under globalization?

(I) Economic racialism Greenfeld (2001) published a book entitled *Spirit of Capitalism: Nationalism and Economic Growth*, whose topic seems to have a kind of spiritual relationship with Max Weber. Greenfeld presents a concept of economic racialism and insists that, each race and each nation state has a different view on the importance of racial dignity and it is difficult to say each racialism has an economic racialism factor, an example of which is France. Other parts of racialism deny the relations between racial dignity and business. Russia is an example of the racialism. According to Greenfeld, economic racialism could be recognized as a racialism accepting economic competition.

Which particular race and nation state comes under the type of accepting economic competition? It is closely connected with the structure of the national state and society. Classification of Greenfeld suggests the following three kinds: (1) first is the kind of 'individualism and citizen' type, (2) second is the 'collectivism and citizen' type, and (3) third is the 'collectivism and racial' type. The most appropriate with economic racialism is the 'individualism and citizen' type (whose typical examples are the UK and USA). The intention of the 'individualism and citizen' type nation state is the intention of most citizens. Government has the right of a representative of them actually or legally, and has respect for human rights, and promotes appropriate institutions. Meanwhile, a collective type of racialism attaches greater importance on shared interest of the nation state and race as a whole than self interest. Elite group members who have particular talents decide shared interest for the nation state; however, they are not selected by ordinary election. All of the contemporary dictatorial systems are the products of collective type racialism. The most popular collective type racialism is the 'collectivism and racial' type nation state (from which in the past Fascism was coming). The second type of 'collectivism and citizen' nation state is a compound existence, which is difficult to recognize.

Behind the racialism mentioned by Greenfeld, a national and social structure came into existence. The starting point of the logic by Greenfeld says a series of the logics that a nation state structure of 'individualism and citizen' type produces economic racialism, and economic racialism might reach economic growth. Undoubtedly it depicts the development logic of a west European type nation state. Anther development model is the East Asian model, which depicted the postwar economic growth of Japan and Asian NIEs. The national and social structure of those countries and regions are basically a collective structure (whose characteristics are authoritarianism in political system and development oriented system in economic system), which could be called the non-west European economic racialism. What should we consider the Southeast Asian countries? As stated before, Greenfeld asserts that each national and racial state has a respective view on the importance of racial dignity and it is difficult to insist that each racialism has an economic racialism factor. Greenfeld illustrates France and Russia for the assertion. Although evidence is not enough (whether or not it is coming from religion and culture, whether or not it is caused by immature consciousness of challenge and counter challenge of civilization by Toynbee), successful examples of Chinese entrepreneurship in Southeast Asian countries gave us suggestive cases compared with local people. It might indicate that racialism in Southeast Asian countries does not reach the stage of economic racialism which East Asian NIEs have already reached.

(II) Can China follow the East Asian NIEs model? Is it possible for China to join the East Asian NIEs model member? We think it might be too early to have a definite conclusion on this at present because the Chinese model has been transforming. However, there could be recognized several heterogeneous characteristics between China and South Korea and Taiwan. Overcoming the heterogeneities seems to be an indispensable prerequisite for China to have the similar development model with East Asian NIEs. They are as follows: (1) in postwar Taiwan and South Korea, they had an authoritarian system in the political aspect; however, in the economic aspect they introduced a market-oriented system. Thus, they could join the postwar free trade system led by the USA, which contributed to their high-speed economic growth. Meanwhile, China has faced serious tasks to transform the dual structure of the Chinese economic system since the reform and open door policy started in 1978. (2) The main job of the elites who have led Asian NIE-style collective nation state are bureaucrats and they have accomplished not only Chinese traditional culture but also western culture. Thus, they have never rejected such crucial values included in West European racialism as rationalism and liberalism. Even in the military system and one party dictatorial system, a certain distance between politicians and bureaucrats could exist. That is to say, through functional separation, bureaucrats who are in charge of economic and social regulation could have relative independence and continuity of policy measures. To the contrary, because of the negative legacy of central planning days, in the bureaucrats' group in China the number of specialist bureaucrats has never been enough. Therefore, as there has occurred recently in China a boom of returnees from studying abroad, we think it is now a great time to reform the bureaucrat system. (3) The Asian NIEs model typically shown in Taiwan and South Korea has successfully realized shared growth. It was especially remarkable in comparison with the Southeast Asian model. In China, which has enjoyed high speed economic growth, shared growth has been the most worried about topic. To measure the degree of shared

Table 6.3 Some indicators of East Asian countries and regions

Group	Country (region)	Population average annual growth (%)	GDP per capita growth (%)	Adult literacy rate (% of people 15 and above)	Population below $1 a day (PPP $, %)	Gini index	Land inequality Gini index
		00-04	03-04	98-04			
1.	Japan	0.2	2.5	—	—	0.25(93)	-
2. Asian NIEs	Taiwan					0.24(00)	-
	South Korea	0.6	4.1	—	<(298)	0.32(98)	0.34(90)
	Singapore	1.9	6.3	93	—	0.42(98)	-
	Hong Kong	0.7	7.7	—	—		
3. South-east Asia	Thailand	0.7	5.4	93	<2(00)	0.40(02)	0.47(93)
	Philippines	2.0	4.3	93	15.5(00)	0.46(00)	0.55(91)
	Indonesia	1.3	3.7	88	7.5(02)	0.34(00)	0.46(93)
	Malaysia	2.0	5.2	89	<2(97)	0.49(97)	-
	Vietnam	1.1	6.4	90	—(98)	0.35(02)	0.53(94)
4.	China	0.7	8.8	91	16.6(01)	0.45(01)	-

Note: (1) Figures in parentheses indicate survey year. (2) Blanc means "not available data".
Source: World Bank (2005).

growth, such indices as disparity between urban and rural, the Gini coefficient, etc, are useful. Table 6.3 points out various indicators of East Asian countries and regions. (1) As regards population growth, Southeast Asian countries usually have higher growth rate than Asian NIEs. In China, because of a special population policy (only one child policy), they attained a similar growth rate with Asian NIEs countries and regions. They are seriously worried about problems of an aging society. (2) Regarding per capita GDP growth rate, China recorded the highest rate. The Japanese rate of 2.5%, and Indonesian rate of 3.7% (2003–2004), were relatively low. (3) As far as adult literacy rate (of people aged 15 and above) is concerned, Asian NIEs have a higher education level, and China and Southeast Asian countries were at the same level. (4) Concerning the population below the poverty line (below one dollar a day of PPP), the Philippines' 15.5% and Chinese 16.6% was substantially higher. (5) As regards Gini coefficient, a higher coefficient was recognized in Malaysia (0.49), China (0.45), and the Philippines (0.46). (6) The Gini coefficient on land disparity was high in the Philippines (0.55), Vietnam (0.53), Thailand (0.47) and Indonesia (0.46).

Table 6.4 shows the population below the national poverty line. Japan and Asian NIEs countries and regions overcame the poverty issue; however, it has been generally serious in Southeast Asian countries. The Chinese population below the

Table 6.4 Population below the national poverty lines (%)

Group	Country (region)	Survey year	Rural	Urban	National	Survey year	Rural	Urban	National
1.	Japan	-	-	-	-	-	-	-	-
2. Asian NIEs	Taiwan								
	South Korea	-	-	-	-	-	-	-	-
	Singapore	-	-	-	-	-	-	-	-
	Hong Kong	-	-	-	-	-	-	-	-
3. South-east Asia	Thailand	1990	40.8	31.2	38.6	00-01	38.7	29.5	35.7
	Philippines	1994	53.1	28.0	40.6	1997	50.7	21.5	36.8
	Indonesia	1996	-	-	15.7	1999			27.1
	Malaysia	1989			15.5				
	Vietnam	1998	45.5	9.2	37.7	2002	35.6	6.6	28.9
4.	China	1996	7.9	<2	6.0	1998	4.6	<2	4.6

Note: Blanc means "not available of data".
Source: World Bank (2005).

national poverty line recorded 6% in 1996 and 4.6% in 1998. The Poverty ratio in rural areas has been without doubt more serious than in urban areas.

What logical characteristics did Asian NIEs need to come into existence? Also what are the relations of the characteristics with an authoritarian systemic transition? We investigate in the following sections.

Relationships between party and administration in one-party political system and roles of technocrats: decipherment of Taiwanese experience

As regards Taiwanese experience, we think it is deciphered by the following logic. By a development-oriented policy with economic priority and influence of the US factor, they established an outward oriented market economy. Deepening the market oriented economy under the reform and open door policy, differentiation of socio-economic aspects and division of labor was fulfilled. Needless to say, in order to manage efficiently the complicated society, they need intellectual elites (initially, technocrats in science and engineering played active roles). When the macro-economy and social management successfully develops, the middle class would emerge and grow. It would coincide with the shared growth. The middle class comes into existence anywhere in society and plays an important role as a rational core to the whole society, in cooperation with bureaucrats in administration and cultured leaders in politics. The shared growth phenomena are surely driving forces for transformation towards democratic institutions closely connected with the middle class in social aspects and with technocrats in administrative leaders.

At this stage of development, bureaucrats from the fields of law and politics are appearing.

Establishment of extroverted market oriented economy: background of the rise of the technocrats

(I) Taiwanese miracle After the Nationalist Party fled to Taiwan in 1949, the Taiwanese economy started to build properly. For 50 years, Taiwan had economic construction with remarkable economic performance leading to high speed economic growth. In particular, for 28 years from 1961–1988, the annual average growth rate in Taiwan reached 9.3%. Compared with the average growth rate of advanced countries, 3.6%, Taiwan had 1.6 times higher growth rate, which was the highest of the Asian NIEs countries and regions.

In 1979, they called the four countries and regions, which were Taiwan, Hong Kong, South Korea and Singapore, Asian NIEs. The Taiwanese GDP in 1987 was ranked 21st in the world. As regards per capita GDP, Taiwan recorded US$8,813, which was 25th in the world ranking. Regarding foreign exchange reserves, they had US$82.4 billion in 1991, which was the most in the world followed by Japan. Over 50 years, Taiwan developed the economy from being less developed and dependent on agriculture to an advanced economy depending upon the tertiary sector with an emerging developed technology. It has promoted a rationalized economic structure and also raised substantially the educational level and human resources. In 2000, Taiwanese GDP reached more than US$300 billion whose per capita GDP was US$14,000. Both exports and imports were more than US$140 billion and foreign exchange reserves recorded US$106.7 billion.

(II) External factors: US influence We could recognize various influential factors by the USA. It seems to be very important to correctly place the US factor in the East Asian international order. All the countries and regions of the postwar East Asian 'flying geese' model – Japan, NIEs, ASEAN and China – have received beneficial opportunities of exports and investment which the USA has provided. At the same time, they have enjoyed public goods given by the USA, one of which was a free trade system.

Japan, Taiwan and South Korea have closer relations with the USA because of special postwar international circumstances. The USA assisted the land reform and democratic reform for them and gave support for their economic reconstruction and development through various aid organizations. Because lots of elites of the countries and regions went to the USA to study, they played the role of an intermediary between the USA and the countries concerned.

The USA appreciated the technocrats group in the Nationalist party as a sound component and assisted them. In those days, elite groups from military forces attached greater importance upon military industry and expansion of armaments, meanwhile the technocrats group insisted that economic development of Taiwanese public welfare should have priority. From the 1950s to the beginning of the 1960s, the US office stationed in Taiwan attempted to control the plan of counterattack on continental China led by Chiang Kai-shek's group and tried to prevent militarization of the Taiwanese economy. In that aspect, US strategy and technocrats' view in Taiwan had common ground (Niu Ke, 2002). The technocrats group had a practical idea on the Taiwanese economy and adopted a stance towards neutral profit, who succeeded to enforce their positions by utilizing their educational background studying in both the US and Europe. Those factors contributed to their successful assertions on economic policy and advantageous international circumstances for Taiwanese economic development were established.

(III) Establishment of an extroverted market oriented economy and rise of the technocrats Experience of Taiwanese economic development suggests to us that formation of reasonable logic in social development was very important. An extroverted market-oriented economy corresponded, we think, to the formation of reasonable logic. What does the extroverted market oriented economy bring about? It is a kind of open system, in which the division of labor asserted by Adam Smith becomes international and is established in a wider area. Efficient allocation of resources in the world is established successfully, which contributes more development for the economies concerned. At the same time it needs more divided and more differentiated socio-economic activities within a country. The more complicated tendency in socio-economic aspects necessarily requests more specialized administration, which leads to an indispensable appearance of bureaucrats.

Technocrats in Taiwan had the following characteristics. First, a higher ratio was occupied by experts with a higher educational background, and higher endowments. The educational background of 44 members in such Taiwanese committees as the management of production and business committee, the economic stability committee, the US aid committee, and the international economic cooperation and development committee showed that only one member was not a university graduate. As shown in Table 6.5, most technocrats had an educational background and had studied in the USA, thus giving them a pro-American tendency.

Table 6.5 Experience of studying abroad of Taiwanese technocrats

Background of education	Number	Ratio (%)
Experience of studying abroad	28	63.63
USA	23	52.27
Western Europe	4	9.09
Japan	1	2.27

Source: Liu Ming (1992), p.195.

Table 6.6 Special fields of Taiwanese technocrats

Special field	Number			Ratio (%)
Engineering	21			47.72
Social Science	15	Economics	12	34.09
		Law	2	
		Administration Management	1	
Natural Science	3			6.82
Military	1			2.27
Other fields	3			9.10

Source: Liu Ming (1992), p.195.

Second, most technocrats with a higher educational background were came from a science and engineering course. Table 6.6 indicates that, as regards special fields of bureaucrats in Taiwan, engineering occupied 47.72%, and social science 34.09%. Moreover, of the 14 ministers of the economy in Taiwan from 1950 to 1990, only Zhang Zikai and Xu Lide had experience of studying economics and politics. Other ministers of the economy had an education from science and engineering. For example, Yin Zhongrong was an electrical engineer, Sun Yunxuan (Sun Yun-suan) graduated from the faculty of electrics, Harbin Institute of Technology and had experience of being a visiting scholar in the USA. Li Guoding (K.T.Li) had a job working for the Institute of Physics, Cambridge University (Long Jianxin and Huang Wenzhen, 1993, pp. 126–127). Chen Lu An, a son of the President of Taiwan province, Chen Cheng, also got a PhD in Mathematics at Massachusetts Institute of Technology and successively held various important posts such as the minister of the economy, minister of defense, and president of the inspection agency etc.

Third, most technocrats in Taiwan come from the Chinese continent. In the 1950s and 1960s, of 29 technocrats working for the three major US aid organizations, only one family record was registered in Taiwan. Also, in the 1970s and 1980s, for most heads of finance and economy sections, their family records were registered in the continent. We point out the backgrounds to the situation: (1) under Chiang Kai-shek and his son, parents and children placed their confidence in elites from the continent. It was a general rule that, in authoritarian system, it is important to gave aides important posts for stability of the system. (2) After liberation from the Taiwanese colony, Japanese bureaucrats returned to Japan and the elites of Taiwan were not enough.

When people talk of the 'Taiwanese miracle', most of them have focused their attention upon lots of gold and machineries, which Chiang Kai-shek's army took from the continent. Actually however, lots of human resources, with higher educational background and who transferred to Taiwan together with Chiang Kai-shek's army, contributed to Taiwanese economic development. To repeat, from the viewpoints of a structural-functionalism approach, the existence of professional technocrats was both for managing a complicated society and for supplementing disadvantages of backwardness.

(IV) Conditions for the rise of technocrats: reform of party affairs and adjustment of relationship between party and administration In the one-party dictatorship in Taiwan, technocrats miraculously became its main actors and established the Taiwanese miracle. Why was it possible?

At the initial period of economic development, the main obstacle to hinder Taiwanese technocrats' activities in the economic policy was traditional power related to Chiang Kai-shek's army. Inside the National party controlling group, it was recognized the three kinds of elite group could be classified by function and power. They are (1) bureaucrats' group from Nationalist party, (2) bureaucrats' group from military forces, and (3) bureaucrats' group from administration. The former two were the political elite and military elite. At the beginning of the postwar period, the position of the technocrats was much lower than professional soldiers and party executives under the authoritarian system. Thus, technocrats had no power to lead policy decision and administrative regulation. However, after the cabinet was established, by promoting an extroverted market-oriented strategy, the division of labor and differentiation of government administrative sections was improved and the importance of technocrats was recognized. In those period, the top ranking government officials gathered around Chiang Kai-shek's and his son, and the President of Taiwan province, Chen Cheng,[3] decided to entrust non-politics oriented elites with the authority of economic policy decision. It is correct to say that the power transformation process was closely related to the reform of party affairs, which started in the Chiang Kai-shek days.

During the two years from 1950 to 1952, the Nationalist party established a reform committee and carried out party administration reform. They accomplished a new organization system by putting in order the party discipline and by dismissing inappropriate party members. The reorganization broke down the long-lasting factional dispute which had continued from the days of controlling continental China to fleeing to Taiwan. It worked to purge the corrupted factions (like the CC group gathered around Chen Guofu and Chen Lifu) and to weaken the power of senior party members. In place of them a kind of balance among party, administration, military forces, and secret service was established. The reorganization gave the opportunity for technocrats to come to the front. When

3 Chen Cheng (1898–1965); the domicile of origin was Qingtian of Zhejiang province. After 1948, he successively held various posts like Chairman of Taiwan province and Commander of the Defense Army, Vice President of the Nationalist Party, Chairman of Administrative Office. Since 1950s, he carried out the land reform and promoted the local autonomy in Taiwan, and earned the esteem of the public of Taiwan. After his death, he was called Chen Cheng Bo in a friendly way.

Chiang Ching-kuo,[4] the son of Chiang Kai-shek, came to power, he promoted lots of bureaucratic human resources to high ranking officials of administration under the slogan of political reforms, which was based upon the speech of Chiang Kai-shek regarding human resources as important at the tenth national meeting of Nationalist party in 1969. Chiang Ching-kuo raised them to be cabinet members around him. For example, such technocrats as Li Guoding (K.T.Li), Sun Yunxuan (Sun Yun-suan), Jiang Yanshi, Yu Guohua were initially given important posts, in which bureaucrats like Li Denghui, Lin Yanggang whose domicile of origin was Taiwan were included. It indicated the tendency towards the Chinese mainland of the Nationalist party was progressing. Through the reorganization, political power gained by senior party members who were party executives and senior party members was gradually shifted to the technocrats group. After a few years, they were replaced by bureaucrats coming from former administrative sections who established a core of new leaders' group. Taiwan was promoted to be the days of governance by experts.

Technocrats in Taiwan took part in decisions of economic policies based upon their higher education and special knowledge with a practical attitude. The national goal of economic development gave the opportunity for the rise of technocrats. Acceleration of the division of labor and internationalization improved the importance of technocrats, which contributed to establishing a class of technocrats.

The party affairs reform brought a new change to relations between party and administration. The basic tendency was the correction of influential power for party organization to administrative sections. After the reform in 1952, reasonable changes of party organization, which became looser, were implemented and unification was strengthened. Each administrative section had various party organizations respectively, and they did not found any single leading system of the party, but administrative executives of each level held additional posts for party affairs (Sun Daiyao, 2002, p. 71). That is to say, they had no leading system which consisted of party committees and party secretaries outside the administrative system. Due to such institutional design, bureaucrats in administrative sections acquired substantial independent rights to decide policy measures and they became

4 Chiang Ching-kuo (1910–1988); when he was 15 years old in 1925, he was an active member of a students' movement called 'May 30th Movement' (which occurred on May 30, 1925) and went to study to USSR, Moscow, at Sun Yat-Sen University in October, 1925. Deng Xiaoping, who was six years older than Chiang Ching-kuo, was his classmate. He graduated from the University in 1927. During his stay in Moscow, he joined the Communist Party of the USSR. In Taiwan, Chiang Ching-kuo successively held various important posts such as Central Executive Committee of the Nationalist Party (1957), Minister of Defense (1965), Head of Administration Office (1972). In 1975, he took office as Chairman of the Nationalist Party as the successor of Chiang Kai-shek. Also in 1978 he took office as the Sixth President of Republic of China, and was reappointed to the Seventh President. In 1988, he died of diabetes, and Vice President Li Denghui was his successor.

the main players of economic construction. In addition, due to improvement of the division of labor system in the public policy section, the party affairs system was reasonably separated from policy decisions, particularly economic policy decisions. Party roles were changed from a 'party leads government' system to policy cooperation, and the autonomous rights of administrative bureaucrats were significantly expanded.

As stated above, the gaining autonomous rights process of technocrats had indispensable prerequisites in which they were given protection and trust by the highest ranking powerful persons, like Chiang Kai-shek and Chen Cheng. In the main economic leading sections at each period of Taiwanese economic development, excellent technocrats contributed to them. The reorganized system and budget was independent of ordinary administrations, which worked to restrict the influence of various interest groups (Sun Daiyao, 2002, p. 178). In addition, in order to prevent corruption and a cozy relationship between the public and business, similar to Singapore and Hong Kong, Taiwan established an institutional mechanism to prevent corruption like a periodical evaluation system for bureaucrats, an asset declaration system, and 'to employ a person of integrity at a high salary' system.

Moreover, because most technocrats were coming from the mainland, they could naturally be separated from such interest groups as the traditional enterprise association, the landowner group of rural area. For example, when the land reform in Taiwan was carried out, they had upright attitudes for the reform, which were completely different from the mainland days (Matsuda, 2006, Chapter 6).

(V) Establishment of a rational core and systemic transition The rational core of Taiwanese society consisted of civilized leaders (like Chiang Kai-shek, Chiang Ching-kuo and Chen Cheng), the technocrats' group, the middle class, and so on. Formation of the middle class was the fruit of the Taiwanese miracle. We recognize the important characteristics of the Taiwanese miracle as shared growth (common to the East Asian model), without which it might be impossible to form the middle class (in contrast to the Southeast Asian model of countries). The middle class has received the benefit of an open market economy and has believed in rationalism (in legislative regulation and contract theory), which a market oriented economy has. The rationalism, which was improved in civil society, corresponded to a civilized elite group (technocrats who were representatives of rationalism), and both of these promoted Taiwanese society to transform peacefully towards a democratic system.

Another important thing to be careful about was the local autonomy in Taiwan. Since the 1950s, the Nationalist party implemented the local autonomy system at the lowest administrative level. In such local parliaments as in cities, counties, and provinces, the members were gradually selected by direct election (Bo Qingjiu, 2001). The direct election system enabled local elites to participate in political activities. The introduction of a local autonomy system as well as land reform seriously contributed to Taiwanese elites to support the Nationalist party. In Taiwan, which had an authoritarian system, they dichotomized politics and economy, and central government and local government, through which they restricted social dissatisfaction and gave them liveliness. Undoubtedly the existence of democratic factors played substantial roles to prevent corruption in Taiwan during high speed economic growth.

Chiang Ching-kuo, a son of Chiang Kai-shek, took office as the Sixth President of the Republic of China in 1978 and was highly evaluated by Taiwanese ordinary people as a person of independence, integrity, and diligence. He gave an order in the early days to Ma Yingjiu[5] to examine Martial Law and Parliament reform issues. On July 15th, 1987, in Taiwan they implemented a new National Security Law and lifted Martial Law which lasted for 38 years. In 1987, they also released people from visiting relatives in the mainland, which was greatly requested by Taiwanese people. The statement by Chiang Ching-kuo, saying that the key for legislative regulation was a law not a person, led the Taiwanese democratic reform in an irreversible direction. In the afternoon of October 7th 1987, when Chiang Ching-kuo was interviewed by Mrs Katherine Graham of *The Washington Post* (USA) at the Presidential Office, he said that the Republic of China lifted Martial Law and opened party politics. At the end of 1980s, Chiang Ching-kuo decided to lift party politics and a press ban and also decided to carry out an ordinary election at each level of government including the national parliament. Taiwan started to move to a constitutional system.

(VI) Consistency between elites of engineering and science and authoritarian system Until the 1980s in Taiwan, why did technocrats of engineering and science occupy leading positions (in contrast with postwar Japan and Taiwan since the 1990s)? It might be interpreted that elites of engineering and science are compatible with an authoritarian system. Because an authoritarian system does not transform it enough to a legislative and democratic system, it is difficult to be compatible with elites of law and politics in the ideological sense. Meanwhile, elites of engineering and science are practically oriented and, even under an authoritarian system, they can play important roles with practical tools, which lead them to be compatible with an authoritarian system. Moreover, the successful results (economic growth)

---

5 Ma Yingjiu (1950–); born in Hong Kong in 1950. His father was also a high ranking official of the Nationalist Party. In 1981, he got a PhD in Law from Harvard University, and started to work for Chiang Ching-kuo as the English Secretary. His personality of being rational, modest and honest was highly praised by Chiang Ching-kuo, which led him to the post of Vice President of the Central Bureau of the Nationalist Party when he was 34 years old, in June 1984. In 1993, he took office as Minister of Justice. In 1998, he was elected to Mayor of Taipei, and was returned in 2002. In 2003, he took office as Vice Chairman of the Nationalist Party and in 2005 he was elected to Chairman of the Nationalist Party by the first direct vote with 72.36% of the vote. In February, 2007, he was charged with misappropriation of special money for the head of local government, and resigned as Chairman of the Nationalist Party. The case has been tried, but it is said that it would be possible to run for President of Taiwan in 2008 as the only candidate from the Nationalist Party.

of elites of engineering and science (partly including economics) give additional legitimacy to authoritarianism, which should undoubtedly be attractive.

After the systemic transformation was carried out, the elites of law and politics might reach the center of power. The experience in Taiwan and South Korea showed this. In Japan, which was democratized in the postwar period, elites of law and politics have occupied the central position of power from the beginning. As there are similar compatible relations between elites of engineering and science and authoritarian systems, in a democratic system the elites of law and politics might have compatible relations.

Tasks for shared growth: comparisons of Asian NIEs model and Southeast Asian model

Postwar East Asian countries attempted a task of economic construction when they had an incomplete nation state. At that stage, the legitimacy of the authoritarian system is given by economic development and progress of national welfare. Both economic development and progress of national welfare are crucial conditions for nation state building. Because integration of the nation state means the progress of everyday life in the cultural area and social network, shared growth gives the base and security.

According to the hierarchy theory of needs by Maslow (1954), human needs are classified into five stages. The first stage needs are subsistence needs (physiological needs and security needs), which are followed by the needs of a sense of belonging, and needs of respect. And the final stage is needs of self realization. In the postwar Asian countries, peoples' level of human needs was limited to be lower, which was the important external condition of the authoritarian system. If an authoritarian system establishes advantageous circumstances for economic development, it could have legitimacy. Economic development satisfies the lower stage needs of people. They are prerequisites for realization of higher stage needs.

We should indicate serious inconsistency between productive industrialization and labor force industrialization as problems with the Southeast Asian model. In the policy aspect, productive industrialization became a purpose in which they attached less importance upon human modernization. It led to expansion of income and asset disparity. There could be recognized not only absolute poverty in rural areas but also serious slums in urban areas. Also, in Southeast Asian countries, as they have had almost always serious racial disputes and religious disputes, it is difficult to secure necessary stable circumstances for sustainable economic development and for correction of disparities. Compared with the above, the East Asian NIEs model is based upon a human-centered development ideology. The quantity and quality of population has been cooperative with economic development, which finally leads to shared growth called an *equivalent ideal situation* (on the explanation of this concept, see Chapter 2). That is to say, in Southeast Asia, population is an external factor for economic modernization, and in the East Asia NIEs model, population is an internal factor for economic modernization. We think that experience of Singapore, which has established a harmonized society even of a multiracial nation state, might be a good lesson for Southeast Asian countries that have suffered from racial and religious disputes.

Southeast Asian model

From the viewpoints of policy evaluation, we could point out the positive role of an import substitution strategy carried out in Southeast Asian countries. After the 1960s, the industrialization ratio of Southeast Asian countries (meaning the ratio occupied by manufacturing industry to GDP) remarkably increased. World Bank

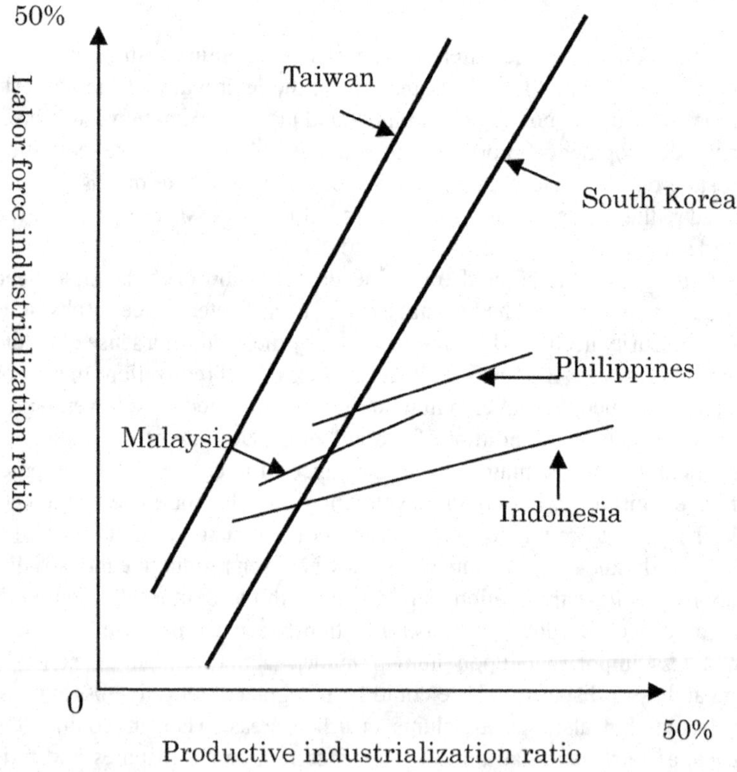

Note: Diagonal line was expressed when both production and employment grow at the same ratio.

Source: Author (based on Watanabe, Toshio (1991), p. 87.

Figure 6.2 Conceptual figure on productive industrialization ratio and labor force industrialization ratio in Asian countries (1960s-1980s)

statistics suggest to us that the industrialization ratio of the Philippines increased from 20% in 1960 to 27% in 1975, and the Thai case showed a more substantial increase from 11% in 1960 to 20% in 1985. Malaysia expanded the ratio from 9% in 1960to 18% in 1985.[6]

Figure 6.2 is a concept figure to compare Asian NIEs' model with the Southeast Asian model. It displays a tendency of relations between productive industrialization and labor force industrialization. The horizontal axis plots the productive industrialization ratio, which shows the similar tendency in both models, however as regards the vertical axis, which plots the labor force industrialization ratio, the ratio of Southeast Asian countries was much lower than NIEs' countries and regions.

Why has such inconsistency occurred in Southeast Asian countries? Two explanations are possible: (1) first, because of a high rate of population growth, population is an external factor for the economy, (2) second is import substitution industrialization and the impact of its trade strategy.

The high rate of population growth in Southeast Asian countries seemed to be coming from a high birth rate and low death rate. The low death rate was caused by three factors, which were (i) during the days of colonialization, suzerain states introduced a modern medical system, roads, and a bureaucratic system and educational system, which contributed to the improvement of medical care, rapid disaster relief and decrease of the death rate; (ii) colonialists tend to restrict conflicts and wars, which existed traditionally in the colonies, in order to keep trade orderly, which caused a substantial reduction of death rates; and (iii) because of assistance of the international society, public health reform was improved in each country and the death rate became much lower.

However, unfortunately, the population explosion in rural areas coming from the above-stated reasons offset the results of the postwar greening revolution. In addition, due to the failure of land reform, large-scale land owners monopolized the results of the greening revolution, which expanded both disparity and inequality.

Meanwhile, the high birth rate could be interpreted by birth economics (to analyze the cost and benefit of having children from micro-economic viewpoints of family and women). At the lower stage of economic development, with a lower level of income, the benefit of giving birth (utility increase by security of aged days, etc) is higher but the cost of giving birth (such as educational cost, opportunity cost etc) is lower. People wish to have more children, which increases the birth rate. However, at the higher stage of economic development, the cost and benefit relations are reversed and the birth rate decreased.

Two factors are working when redundant population in rural areas moves towards urban areas. The first one is the push side factors, which indicate poverty of rural areas and shortage of job opportunity. When we discuss the poverty of the rural area, it is necessary to analyze the failure of land reform and the population explosion. The second one is the pull side factors, which show the attractiveness

6 World Bank, *World Development Report*, annual (see 1960-1980).

of urban areas, particularly job opportunities of industrial sectors. Todaro's theory insists there are employment expectations, which expresses these by multiplying wage income by the employment ratio. When disparity between the urban and rural is large, the effect of the employment ratio is remarkably decreased. Peasants' desire to break away from the current situation works to move them to urban areas regardless of the employment ratio. Todaro thus warns that it is possible for there to occur at the same time an unemployment problem in the urban area and a labor shortage problem in the rural area.

What is the situation of job opportunities in urban areas of Southeast Asian countries? Different from Asian NIEs countries and regions, which took an export oriented strategy after the 1960s (whose initially developed industry belonged to labor intensive industry), an import substitution strategy taken by Southeast Asian countries was supported by capital intensive industry. Capital intensive industry requires fewer laborers and more advanced quality of labor.

The main purpose of an import substitution strategy is to replace the imported goods by domestically produced goods and to establish a more independent national economic structure.

The characteristics of an import substitution strategy are as follows. (1) First, it is domestic market oriented. The market to absorb the products is mainly located in the country, which displays a monopoly of the domestic market by national enterprises. However, as they are fully protected by the government, enterprises have never become competitive with foreign rivals and it has been very difficult to export the products. (2) Second, they import parts, intermediate products, and machinery and equipment from advanced countries. (3) They develop a trade policy advantageous for the above purpose. For example, they establish a favorable exchange rate system for machinery import (more appreciated exchange rate than market level) and customs duties (lower customs duties than ordinary level). As mentioned above, an import substitution strategy means an inward-looking industrialized strategy. Ironically enough, an import substitution strategy needs independency, but as they cannot produce parts and machineries, etc, they have to be fully dependent upon importing them. It points out that an import substitution strategy does not need fewer imports.

Less developed countries have at the beginning stage of industrialization neither the capacity of production of high quality production goods nor enough entrepreneurship. Therefore, they depend on the joint ventures of domestic enterprises and foreign owned enterprises. In addition, enterprises of advanced countries have incentives to invest directly. For example, (1) they want to avoid import restriction measures of less developed countries, and to enjoy a monopolistic position of their domestic markets, and (2) they receive various advantageous measures for foreign investors and the merit of cheap labor forces and cheap land prices.

Because of the compatibility for both sides, Asian countries have received a very active FDI boom. The Philippines developed the import substitution industrialization strategy, whose core was the Philippine zaibatsu and US-owned enterprises, from the middle of the 1950s. Thailand, which depended upon primary commodities from the middle of the 19th century, experienced the first industrialization of the country in the middle of the 1960s, taking the Vietnamese War as an opportunity. It meant that the Vietnamese War caused the inflow of foreign investment into Thailand. Malaysia also started the import substitution industrialization strategy at the middle of the 1960s, whose core industries were textiles and electrical machinery (the export ratio of such raw materials as tin and natural rubber to the export total was gradually decreased). After the four dragons in 1970s' Asia, at the end of the 1980s the above three countries and Indonesia were called the 'four little dragons' in Asia.

As is well known, machinery becomes a substitute for labor. Thus, import substitution strategy with development of capital intensive industry means a workforce substitution strategy. For Southeast Asian countries that have redundant labor, an import substitution strategy might make unemployment issues more serious. Lots of inflowing population from rural areas cannot find any job opportunities in formal sectors in the urban area and have to find jobs in unstable informal sectors, such as a stallkeeper, a day laborer, or a repairer, which are

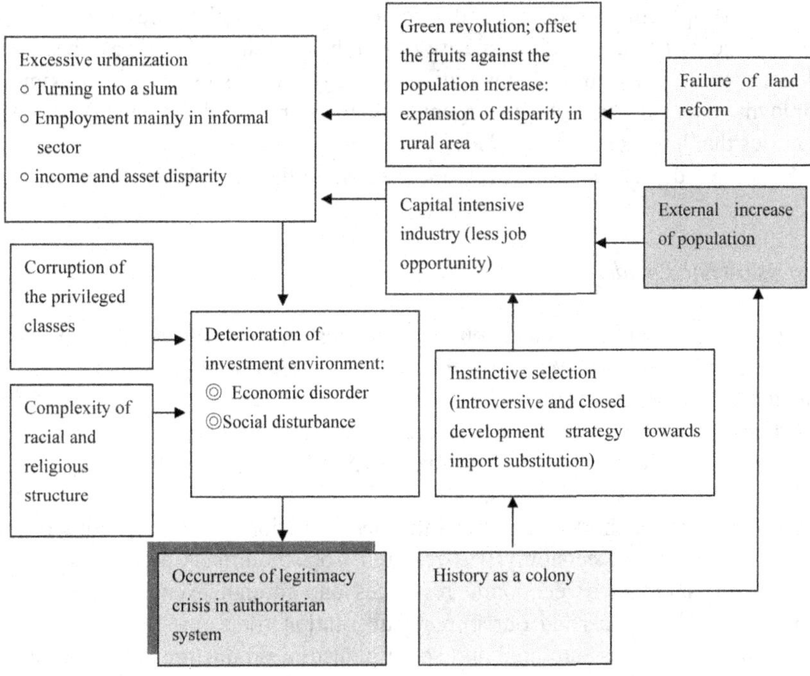

Source: Author.

Figure 6.3 Concept of the trap in Southeast Asia

usually under private management. According to research on the informal sector in Manila's metropolitan area by the University of the Philippines in 1977, 61% of employees were from outside Manila's metropolitan area. The informal sector played the role of a safety device for the expanding metropolitan area. However, the income level of the people living there is low and unstable, and their places of residence, the slums, were studded in every corner of the metropolitan area. People living in the slums of Prime Cities of less developed countries are particularly serious. For example, at the end of the 1980s, the population ratio of the slums in Bangkok metropolitan area to the total metropolitan population reached 20%, in Jakarta metropolitan area 26% and Manila 35% (NHK, 1984).

The informal sector in the job opportunity sense and the slums phenomena in the living aspect displayed actual circumstances of excessive urbanization (excessive urbanization is a phenomenon that occurs when the growth rate of the urban population is higher than the expansion rate of urban employment and the increasing rate of infrastructure construction like housing, schools, roads, sanitation facilities etc). Poverty in the rural area cannot be resolved by moving the population towards the urban area, moreover the poverty might spread over the urban area.

The unemployment problem and income disparity problem are both sides of the same coin. The economic disparity of Southeast Asia might have substantial relations with the import substitution strategy. The strategy to maximize employment is undoubtedly an urgent task to be resolved for less developed countries that have lots of redundant workforces.

Figure 6.3 depicts the logic in various factors of the 'trap' in Southeast Asia.

East Asian NIEs model

Compared with Southeast Asian countries, why can Asian NIEs countries provide more job opportunities? We think this has close relationships with an export-oriented development strategy. From the middle of the 1960s, NIEs countries and regions have provided subsidies, income tax exemption, and export finance for export-oriented companies. The main exportable goods of those days were typically labor intensive products.

First, we have a short look at the Taiwanese situation. At the beginning of the 1950s, the Taiwanese economy was restored from the effects of war; however, it faced the shortage of economic resources and foreign exchange. Thus, the Taiwanese authority carried our import substitution for a few years. After the market of Taiwan was saturated and some industrial production capacities were excessive, the Nationalist party government submitted a reform plan on foreign exchange and trade policy, and established the investment promotion act. The Taiwanese authority founded three processing export districts, concentrating upon spinning and electronic industries, and created the export oriented development strategy. In the 1970s, due to the oil crisis, the Chiang Ching-kuo government

Table 6.7 Some indicators on export products of South Korea (1970)

		Export amount (1,000 US$)	Labor density coefficient	Relative wage
1.	Clothes	232,530	0.35	0.67
2.	Household products	119,499	0.35	0.80
3.	Wooden products	96,596	0.32	0.74
4.	Spinning	50,904	0.18	0.76
5.	Textiles	46,772	0.31	0.76
6.	Electric products	44,637	0.19	1.03
7.	Food industry	44,634	0.20	1.09
8.	Rubber products	18,016	0.28	0.75
9.	Metal products	12,781	0.33	0.91
10.	Steel products	9,901	0.16	1.36
11.	Transport machines	9,645	0.15	1.41
12.	Machineries	7,923	0.33	0.94
13.	Other chemical products	7,578	0.13	1.29
14.	Non iron ore products	6,651	0.23	1.22
15.	Chemical fertilizer	6,333	0.05	1.15
16.	Nonferrous metals	5,627	0.12	1.13
Total manufacturing		737,182	0.20	1.00

Note: Labor density indicates the workers reward per product, and relative wage shows the ratio of wage of industry concerned to the average.

Source: Economic Planning Board (EPB), *Korean Statistical Bulletin*, 1970, Seoul.

Table 6.8 Comparison of employment inducement in manufacturing export of Asian NIEs and Southeast Asia (1975)

	South Korea	Taiwan	Thailand	Philippines	Japan
A(1000 workers)	886	511	150	129	2265
B(1000 workers)	2107	1501	1356	1326	14364
A/B	42.05	34.04	11.06	9.73	15.77

Note: A indicates number of workers induced by exports, and B total number of workers.

Source: Watanabe, Toshio (1991), p.91.

quickly adjusted economic development strategy to become the second import substitution strategy, where great importance was placed on the ten construction plans, which led Taiwanese heavy industries to develop. Those ten construction projects have supported the contemporary Taiwanese economy. At the same time, Taiwan followed the US experience which established the first High-Tech development district (Xinzhu Science and Engineering development district) in the less developed countries. In the development district, electronic information industries have been accumulated, which led to the third or fourth rank in

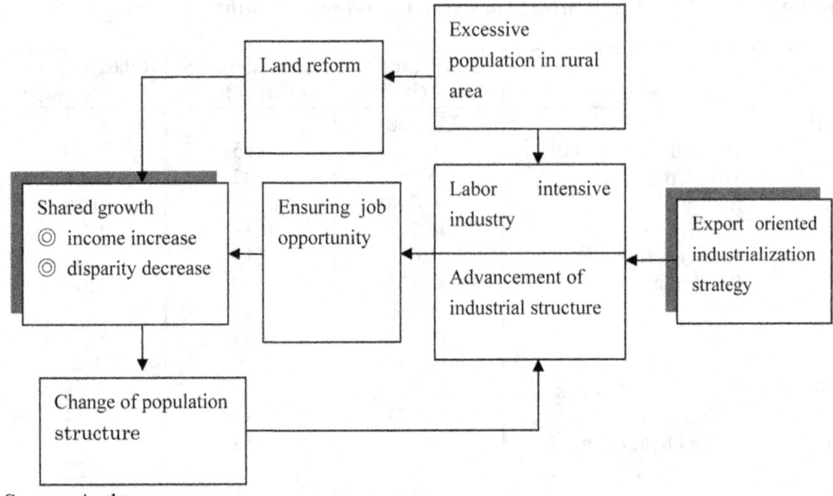

Source: Author.

Figure 6.4 Realization of shared growth in East Asian NIEs model

production of electronic related products. The market share in more than ten electronic products has been the highest in the world.

South Korea had a similar development experience. Table 6.7 shows that, as of 1970, the total export amount of the three goods (clothes, wooden products, household products) occupied 60% of the total export amount. Labor density (meaning the workers reward per product) of the three goods shared the top three of all the products. In addition, relative wage (the ratio of wage of industry concerned to the average) clearly indicated that those three were low wage sectors. The labor intensive industry contributed to earning foreign currency as a major industry when South Korea was a redundant workers' country and also contributed to increasing job opportunity.

Table 6.8 displays the job creation of manufacturing exports of some countries in Asian NIEs and Southeast Asia. *A* indicates the new number of employees caused by exports and *B* points out the total number of employees. As regards the ratio of *A* to *B*, as of 1975, South Korea and Taiwan showed 34.04% and 42.05% respectively, which was much higher than Thailand (11.06%) and the Philippines (9.73%). The export industry in Asian NIEs created 30–40% of the total job opportunities. In addition, this table also shows figures for Japan. Although Japan is said to be a trading nation, the ratio occupied 15.77%, which was not so high. Japan, therefore, records a large amount of trade but also has a substantially large domestic demand.

In the Asian NIEs countries, the job creation policy (export oriented industrialization strategy) to absorb redundant workers led both to income expansion and success of restraining the population explosion (which happened in Southeast Asian countries) as explained by the principles of 'birth demographic economics'.

Generally speaking, therefore, we could say that the key to the success of the East Asian model in Japan and East Asian NIEs is shared growth, of cooperating modernization of human beings and modernization of industry (see Figure 6.4).

Chinese way and Chinese tasks

Establishment of an outward-looking market-oriented economy (economic nationalism): transformation of the initial logics

Deng Xiaoping's policy, which started in 1978, gave the logic of an outward-looking market-oriented economy to China. During the days of a centrally planned economy, as China was caught in the vortex of the Cold War and had deteriorating relations with USSR, China had to attach greater importance to security matters. It was thus the necessary choice to give priority to military and heavy industries. After the 1970s, China preferred détente with the USA in order to compete with the common enemy, the USSR, and established diplomatic relations with Japan. Emergencies around China radically changed and economic modernization and improvement of peoples' everyday life became the main task for them.

Around 15 years after the Deng Xiaoping strategy started in 1978, the Third Plenary of Fourteenth Communist Party Meeting held in November 1993 declared the establishment of a market socialist system. The term *market socialism*, we think, should be recognized as an expression of a kind of authoritarian system of a Chinese version. The term socialism indicates the political system of one-party control and the term *market* shows the goal of reform, which has been a transformation. Thus, we could understand that the Chinese development system in the transition period might become the authoritarian system of the East Asian model towards high-speed economic growth with a low degree of political participation.

At the end of the 1970s, important factors to transform the Chinese development model were détente of the international situation and the existence of a civilized and rational leader like Deng Xiaoping. The basic goals of Deng Xiaoping's development model were (1) modernization of the national economy (at the end of the 1970s the four modernizations were presented), (2) promotion of a Chinese position in international society, and (3) improvement of peoples' everyday lives. Meanwhile, as a short-term goal, social stability was important. Social stability has been an indispensable task when such super big countries as China transform their economic system. It was one of the basic reasons for China to employ a gradual way of transition. According to Huntington, when we examine the social stability, the following relations are important whose relations are 'social stability = ability of institutional security / degree of social mobility'.

The denominator, the degree of social mobility, means the degree of growth of peoples' demand and consciousness. The hierarchy theory of needs by Abraham Maslow classifies the peoples' demand into five stages from the low stage to the high stage. When the numerator, the ability of institutional security (which points out the institutional providing ability to meet the physical and mental demand of the people) cannot catch up with the degree of growth of peoples' demand and consciousness, the original balance is lost and social instability occurs.

We cannot deny the view, saying that, in the Deng Xiaoping strategy, there exist contradictions between long-term goals and short-term goals. Actually, after the open door policy started in China, they experienced social instabilities. Through the reform and open door policy, much more information becomes available and the degree of social mobility might be rapidly raised. Needless to say, economic

Table 6.9 The ratio of urbanization in China (100 thousand, %)

	Total population (end of the year)	Population in urban areas		Population in rural areas	
		Number	Ratio	Number	Ratio
1978	96259	17245	17.92	79014	82.08
1980	98705	19140	19.39	79565	80.61
1985	105851	25094	23.71	80757	76.29
1989	112704	29540	26.21	83164	73.79
1990	114333	30195	26.41	84138	73.59
1991	115823	31203	26.94	84620	73.06
1992	117171	32175	27.46	84996	72.54
1993	118517	33173	27.99	85344	72.01
1994	119850	34169	28.51	85681	71.49
1995	121121	35174	29.04	85947	70.96
1996	122389	37304	30.48	85085	69.52
1997	123626	39449	31.91	84177	68.09
1998	124761	41608	33.35	83153	66.65
1999	125786	43748	34.78	82038	65.22
2000	126743	45906	36.22	80837	63.78
2001	127627	48064	37.66	79563	62.34
2002	128453	50212	39.09	78241	60.91
2003	129227	52376	40.53	76851	59.47
2004	129988	54283	41.76	75705	58.24
2005	130756	56212	42.99	74544	57.01
2006	131448	57706	43.9	73742	56.1

Source: *Chinese Statistical Bulletin* 2007.

development contributes largely to the ability of institutional security; however, liberalism and individualism in the market-oriented economy is inconsistent with an authoritarian system. Also, corruption – usually accompanying an authoritarian system – would damage the government's confidence and legitimacy.

In the light of experiences and lessons of East Asian NIEs model and Southeast Asian model, tasks related with Chinese transition could be summarized as the following. (1) In the economic aspect, could China realize shared growth? Is China likely to be caught in the 'trap' of the Southeast Asia? (2) In the political aspect, could they improve the symbol of rational authoritarianism (technocrats group)? According to Taiwanese experience, which accomplished one-party control, it undoubtedly depends upon a civilized leader and reform of party administration.

We investigate the above two tasks in the following section.

Is China impossibly caught in the 'trap' of Southeast Asia?

As mentioned before, the legitimate bases of the authoritarian system are high speed economic growth and shared growth. We think that, when China accomplishes high speed economic growth, it might be dangerous to be caught in the trap of Southeast Asia, because (1) there are differences between the ratio of productive industrialization and labor force industrialization. Due to the difference, many workers cannot enjoy their industrialization and the benefit of economic growth. Unless the situation is changed, the difference between them might be expanded. In addition, (2) the land reform in China has reached halfway, although land reform in rural areas is an effective measure to break away from poverty. In order to resolve the present three agricultural problems (agriculture, rural area and peasants), further policies of land reform are necessary in addition to promotion policies towards non-agricultural jobs for redundant workers in rural areas.

(I) *The difference between the ratio of productive industrialization and labor force industrialization* Table 6.9 clarifies the ratio of urbanization (which tells the ratio of town and village population to total population, both of them are population with family registration) in China. The Chinese ratio of urbanization increased to 43.9% in 2006 from 17.9% in 1978. Since 1999, urbanization has been accelerated and raised by 9.12% for the seven years, by the tendency of which they expect that the Chinese ratio of urbanization will reach 65% in 2020.

As pointed out in Table 6.10, the ratio of labor force industrialization was much less than the ratio of productive industrialization. As of 2006, 25.2% of the workforce produced 48.9% of total production. This ratio was, however, calculated by the population of family registration, and, as a matter of fact, redundant workers in Chinese rural areas have started to move to urban areas. The fifth national population census in 2000 indicated that mobility population in China equaled 121,070,000 in which mobility population within provinces displayed 78,650,000 and across provinces 42,420,000. Most provinces, which have a large outflow population are located in inland areas. Particularly for such

Table 6.10 Comparisons of labor force industrialization with productive industrialization in China

	Structure of employment			GDP structure		
	Agriculture	Industry	Services	Agriculture	Industry	Services
1952	83.5	7.4	9.1	50.5	20.9	28.6
1957	81.2	9	9.8	40.3	29.7	30.1
1962	82.1	8	9.9	39.4	31.3	29.3
1965	81.6	8.4	10	37.9	35.1	27
1970	80.8	10.2	9	35.2	40.5	24.3
1975	77.2	13.5	9.3	32.4	45.7	21.9
1978	70.5	17.3	12.2	28.2	47.9	23.9
1979	69.8	17.6	12.6	31.3	47.1	21.6
1980	68.7	18.2	13.1	30.2	48.2	21.6
1981	68.1	18.3	13.6	31.9	46.1	22.0
1982	68.1	18.4	13.5	33.4	44.8	21.8
1983	67.1	18.7	14.2	33.2	44.4	22.4
1984	64	19.9	16.1	32.1	43.1	24.8
1985	62.4	20.8	16.8	28.4	42.9	28.7
1986	60.9	21.9	17.2	27.2	43.7	29.1
1987	60	22.2	17.8	26.8	43.6	29.6
1988	59.3	22.4	18.3	25.7	43.8	30.5
1989	60.1	21.6	18.3	25.1	42.8	32.1
1990	60.1	21.4	18.5	27.1	41.3	31.6
1991	59.7	21.4	18.9	24.5	41.8	33.7
1992	58.5	21.7	19.8	21.8	43.4	34.8
1993	56.4	22.4	21.2	19.7	46.6	33.7
1994	54.3	22.7	23	19.8	46.6	33.6
1995	52.2	23	24.8	19.9	47.2	32.9
1996	50.5	23.5	26	19.7	47.5	32.8
1997	49.9	23.7	26.4	18.3	47.5	34.2
1998	49.8	23.5	26.7	17.6	46.2	36.2
1999	50.1	23	26.9	16.5	45.8	37.7
2000	50	22.5	27.5	15.1	45.9	39.0
2001	50	22.3	27.7	14.4	45.1	40.5
2002	50	21.4	28.6	13.7	44.8	41.5
2003	49.1	21.6	29.3	12.8	46.0	41.2
2004	46.9	22.5	30.6	13.4	46.2	40.4
2005	44.8	23.8	31.4	12.5	47.5	40.0
2006	42.6	25.2	32.2	11.7	48.9	39.4

Source: *Chinese Statistical Bulletin* 2007.

Table 6.11 Job structure of the migrant population in Shanghai (100 thousand, %)

	Number	Ratio
Technical skill	10.77	3.8
Clerical work	1.54	0.5
Commercial service	77.89	27.4
Agriculture, forestry and fishery	20.74	7.3
Manufacturing	73.47	25.9
Construction	55.53	19.5
Others	44.35	15.6
Total	284.28	100

Source: Chen Yingfang (2006).

provinces as Henan, Sichuan, Shandong, Anhui, workforce outflow has been one of the main industries.

The main goals for outflow population have been big cities located in coastal regions. Beijing received more than three million and Shanghai more than four million redundant people. According to the calculation of the local town and village reform center in China, there are more than 270 million redundant workforces in Chinese rural areas, who have to get non-agricultural jobs. We have no statistics on the employment situation in urban areas of outflow workforces from rural areas; however, we easily expect the following. (1) A stable growing situation of the industry sector suggests to us that a fairly large number of the outflow population work in factories. They strongly contribute to Chinese factories all over the world and are usually enforced by low wage and low social security. Needless to say, there are some people who learn labor skills and raise their careers to be engineers. Also, there are some people who return to their hometowns after enough training to become entrepreneurs. There have never been large scale slums in Chinese urban areas, which shows that the industrial sector gives job opportunities for the outflow population from rural areas (Chinese industry and the construction sector provides the workers with their housing). (2) Meanwhile, in the Chinese urban areas, they cannot give enough jobs for regular employees to redundant workers in rural areas. Some of the mobile population from rural areas are working as day laborers, stallkeepers. In particular, there are lots of people of middle age and lots of women who work for fast-food restaurants, stallkeepers, tricycle services etc.

Those situations are testified to some extent by the situation in Shanghai. A research on the mobility of the population in the fifth population census in Shanghai in 2000 pointed out that the outflow of population in the whole city reached 3.87 million, in which people with family registration in rural areas became the largest at 85.3%. Of the reasons to reach Shanghai, engaging in economic activities was the most cited, which shared 73.6% with 2.8 million (see Table 6.11).

According to Table 6.11, manufacturing (25.9%) and commercial service (27.4%) had the largest share; also, the total of manufacturing and construction shared 45.4%. Commercial service means a fast-food restaurant managed by a family, stallkeepers etc. The clerical work occupied only 0.5%, who seemed to move from other cities.

As stated above, in the China population, mobility has been very active between urban and rural areas, and between industries. What problems then have occurred with the mobility?

(i) Some barriers against population mobility

At present in China, when peasants mobilize among regions, they have to overcome three barriers, which are the family registration system, economic cost, and mental cost. The family registration system has eased recently and they easily purchase daily provisions, daily necessities etc, at the market. However, the accompanying barriers in such a system with family registration include education and social welfare, which are deeply ingrained in regions. Each city has a system to receive a mobile population from rural areas for economic development, however, they have still had long distance to go for equal treatment. We have much information about mental distress of a mobile population, and various miserable events are reported by the mass media. For example, suicides of workers from rural areas because of non-payment of wages occurred rather often. Lots of brothels are founded near construction sites. Regarding the school for children of the farming population, which was established voluntarily by them, the local government ordered to remove the school because the school could not meet basic conditions. Nobody could take care of aged parents who stayed in rural area and nobody knew the aged parents who died from natural causes.

(ii) Reasons for accumulated redundant population in rural areas

Table 6.9 shows that, in 1980, 68.7% of all workers occupied the agricultural sector. Why were such a huge number of redundant population accumulated in rural areas before the Deng Xiaoping strategy? The reasons seemed to be the following (see Chapter 1 about the detail). First, at the end of the 1950s, arable land in China reached its limit. Because of low productivity in agriculture, labor input expansion was necessary to produce more. However, some portion of redundant workers worked for the communes farming companies (which were the forerunner of TVEs). Such commune farming companies provided simple production goods for agriculture and were embodied as the way of self-reliance.

Second, because the first priority was given to national security, military industry development became the central target and modernization of human resources was never the target of nation building. Three major institutions (the family registration system, the unification of foodstuff purchase and sale, and the national regulation system on employment) were established and the free mobility of workers was prohibited. At the end of 1956, the reform of public owned property rights was finished and public property rights were established in China.

Most enterprises thus became state owned and collectively owned. The separation system of agriculture and industry was established by formerly implementing the family registration system in 1958.

Ironically, although the dialectic which occupied an important position in the Mao Zedong's ideology is a philosophy advocating universal relations among things and phenomena, the philosophy was not applied to the relations between agriculture and industry in central planning China. As a matter of fact, in 1956, Mao Zedong presented the well known article entitled Ten Important Relations, in which Mao Zedong indicated cooperative relations between agriculture and industry as important relations in the national economy and social development. However, unfortunately, such relations were not actually realized in the logic of central planning.

Centrally planned economies have similar characteristics with war-time economies and so they might not be sustainable. Heavy industry led the development strategy, which enforced hard burdens upon peasants and rural areas, and extended the distortion of the national economy and social structure. Thirty years after the beginning, the system reached its demise.

In contemporary China, they have recognized that building the cooperative development strategy between agriculture and industry is very important. Also, when it is built, they have to attach greater importance upon the 'modernization' of human beings. In order to realize the 'modernization' of human beings, deregulation on labor mobility is indispensable. In addition, we think that employment promotion policies are also important tasks.

(II) Tasks on land reform in China Without overcoming the three agricultural problems, it might be impossible for industrialization in China to be successful. We should recognize also that, when the three agricultural problems are attempted to be resolved, not only are the employment promotion policies for non-agricultural sectors in rural areas crucial but so are the land reform policies.

Industry and agriculture are interdependent with each other, and modernization of agriculture and modernization of industry also have twin-like relationships. Raising productivity in agriculture makes it possible to save on the labor force and land which can be provided for industrial use. In addition, developing industry can allocate more machineries, chemical fertilizers and agricultural chemicals etc, into agriculture. Industry and agriculture are thus promoted interdependently. In postwar Japan, Taiwan, and South Korea, they carried out land reform and established advantageous external circumstances for industrialization. As regards the Taiwanese case, they succeeded in rapidly decreasing the ratio of peasants without land to less than 10%, which became the base for shared growth.

In the Taiwanese case, after the land reform, the ratio of landed peasants to the all the peasants substantially increased, which reached 51.8% in 1953, 65.7% in 1963, and 84.7% in 1979, although before the land reform the ratio was only 26.2%. Meanwhile, both ratios of half-landed peasants and of peasants without land sharply declined, and also landowners whose land areas were large nearly disappeared (Li

Fei, 2004, p. 247). The land reform in Taiwan, which occurred from the end of the 1940s to the beginning of the 1950s, however, was implemented moderately and gradually, in three separate stages. The land area which landowners could hold (about three hectares) was around three times more than the average arable land area occupied by ordinary peasants (about one hectare) (Dong Zhenghua et al., 1999, p. 36). The success of land reform caused considerable repercussions, which established the base (social, economic and political base for the authoritarian development system) for shared growth realized later in Taiwan (see Li Guoding (K.T.Li), 1996; Lin Qing, 2001; Huang Junjie, 1991; Li Ren and Li Songlin, 1992; and Yang Muxi, 2001). For example, (1) labor incentive for peasants was raised so that the high-speed growth rate of agricultural production recorded that expanding production for 16 consecutive years from 1953 to 1968 (whose annual average growth rate reached 5.2%) was realized because of the land reform. (2) Due to the structural change of rural society, the base for political support became more firm. The land reform played the role similarly to the substitute of revolution, and the peasants were moved from potential revolutionary power to basic social conservative power, as insisted on by Huntington (1968). (3) We could recognize the light of wisdom of persons to design the institution by observing the wise transformation from agricultural capital to industrial and commercial capital, which was, we think, substantially contributed to by Nong Fu Hui (meaning the association for agricultural restoration), the US aid organization.

Meanwhile in Southeast Asia, although they had success through the assistance of international society in the 1960s and 1970s,[7] because of delayed land reform, disparity among social strata became more serious. In such aspects as finance, market share, tax revenue, public service etc, big land owners have more advantages than tenant peasants. In the countries without successful land reform, there have existed powerful interest groups such as landowners and they have effectively controlled not only land policies but also various economic policies to be advantageous for them. It can be said that the land reform policy at the early stage of the postwar period was a touchstone of the ability of policy measures for the countries concerned.

Arable land is only one production good for the majority of Chinese peasants. However, is land really an asset of Chinese peasants? The answer could be negative. We can have a look at the land policies from three viewpoints of (1) current land requisitioned policy, (2) asset value of land, and (3) possibility of land privatization.

(i) Bad effects of current land requisitioned system

7 In the second half of the 1960s, the IRRI (International Rice Research Institute) founded by the Rockefeller Foundation and the Ford Foundation succeeded in improving a species, HYV, meaning high yield crops. After that, in the rice producing area in Asia the HYV was introduced to raise the productivity. In addition to rice, wheat was also an improved species.

On March 1, 2002, the Land Contract Law of the People's Republic of China came into effect. With the law peasants have the right to use land, the right to manage land, the right to have earnings, and to transfer the right to use land, for the first time in the legal sense. However, in the process of urbanization, accompanying land requisition, the asset rights on the land of peasants have never been actually admitted. The legal base of the current way of land requisition is the Land Control Act of 1998, which might however be used to exclude peasants' rights. There are several laws related to land in China, which for example are the Constitution of the People's Republic of China (which had the fourth revision in 2004), the Agricultural Act (which was set up in July, 1993 and revised in 2002), the Land Control Act (which was established in 1998), the Enforcement Ordinance of Land Control Act (which was implemented on January 1, 1999), the Peasants' Committee Organization Act (which was set up in 1998). The above-mentioned constitution and acts spelled out the farm land as collectively owned by peasants, based upon which, when land is requisitioned, it is resold to local lower rank government as public assets. The legal ambiguity of land asset rights might become institutional reasons which damage peasants' rights and interests.

According to the joint research carried out by the Secretariat of the Central Supervising Group for Chinese Agricultural Policy and Ministry of National Land and Resources, through the current system for compensation (meaning land compensation cost, planting compensation cost, workforce outflow compensation cost etc), the amount of compensation money for peasants reached around 10,000 yuan per furrow (one furrow equals to 6.667 ares), and as regards land requisition for infrastructure construction like railways and roads (public interests), the amount of compensation money would become much less, to be around only 5–8000 yuan per furrow.[8]

The most serious problems regarding the land requisition system are as: (1) the area becomes too large (reflecting development boom) and arable land destruction becomes remarkable; (2) amount of compensation money for land requisition is too small to protect peasants' rights and interests; (3) such policy supports as mobility, non-agricultural job opportunity and social security policy for peasants who lose their lands are not enough; (4) because the policies are led by administration, illegal procedures of land requisition are universally acknowledged and no right to know, no right to participate, and no right to make an objection is secured.

Any problems mentioned above are caused by the local government's activity to maximize their self interest. For example, the Formula 1 racing circuit, established in Jiading district in Shanghai, started construction on October 17, 2002, and whose land area of the first stage reached 2.5 square kilometers. Even if this was land for commercial use, local government ordered land requisition from peasants and sold the land to Shanghai International Race Circuit Ltd, with

8 Office of Central Commission of Supervising Group for Chinese Agricultural Policy and the Ministry of Land and Resources (2002), which carried out a special investigation for the Sixteenth National Meeting of the Communist Party. Also see Xinhua website.

Photo 6.1 Actual situation of 'the most terrible case of Dingzihu, eviction rejected family, in history'

Note: The person who took this photo seemed to be a citizen of Chongqing, and the photo was prevalent through the internet started in Chongqing in February 2007. The situation was as following; In order to provide urban redevelopment at a certain commercial facility development project located at the center of Chongqing, they started to remove people in 2004. However, even three years after they began, they could not reach agreement in the negotiation with the family of a shop owner (whose shop was located at Jiulongban district, Hexing Road), a married couple of Yang Wu and Wu Ping. Thus the three-story shop (with housing) was changed to be an 'island' surrounded by a moat, ten meters in depth, and they continued to confront each other. On March 19, three days after the real right law was signed, Chinese central TV broadcasting station reported the progress of this case in the program (Chinese constitutional state report). When the media both abroad and in China paid attention, at the beginning of April the case was finally finished. The married couple entered into a contract on the condition that they would receive the shop with the same area in the center of Chongqing.

an extremely low price of 152.1 thousand yuan per furrow. It showed that local government exclusively authorizes the public interest and no right to know, no right to participate, and no right to make an objection is secured. The compensation cost for land requisition of the seventh land ('seven' here means the number of the land, each of which was sold at auction by local government) in the same area of Juyuan at the Jiading district equaled 250 thousand yuan per furrow, and the contract price at the auction in September 2003 reached 1.2 million yuan per furrow (contracted by the Shanghai Sansheng Real Estate Company). Local government easily gained 950 thousand yuan profit per furrow. Moreover, peasants living there did not know the fact that their lands where they lived were already sold. They knew it for the first time just when they had to move, and they protested.[9]

In the revision of the Constitution in 2004, article ten was revised to say that the nation can requisition land (meaning collectively owned land of rural areas and state-owned land of urban areas) for public interests and grant compensation for it. Although it strongly emphasizes 'public interests' and 'compensation', the actual procedures in land requisition were often carried out illegally everywhere, which caused people in rural and urban areas to rebel.

In April 2007, 'the most terrible case of Dingzihu,[10] eviction rejected family, in the history', happened in Chongqing and was sensationally reported by the media both abroad and in China and was symbolically meaningful (see Photo 6.1). As regards the case in Chongqing, although it would be difficult to say who were responsible, it would be easy to say that the legal system has been substantially delayed in establishment. Any governments, any citizens, and any developers have their self-interest, but when the establishment of a legal system is remarkably delayed, the situation becomes greatly disrupted, which might lead to a vicious circle. As a matter of fact, since 1999, complicated cases caused by requisition accompanied by urban redevelopment have become aggravated. Self-immolation was the most violent case. Such a serious social situation we think has led to the revision of the Constitution in 2004 (the fourth revision of 1982 Constitution) and also to establish the real right law in March 2007 (whose draft started to be prepared in 1998).

(ii) Peasant's land is not a living asset

Peasant's land has ambiguous provision of collective property rights. It has the danger to be taken by force at anytime and also it cannot be used as security for bank loans, thus it has no actual asset value. At the same time, it is prohibited institutionally to sell it for residential use. Peasants have no initial asset in the market-oriented society. They have only one way to change their circumstances in rural areas, which is to move to urban areas to find work.

9 According to the author's interview at Jiading district in Shanghai.

10 Dingzihu indicates the family which does not agree with a developer on the conditions of requisition and stays there.

They have had discussions of 'pros and cons' for a long time on reform plans of land problems in rural areas, particularly arguing that the contract land for peasants could be used as security for bank loans and farm land could be allowed to sell for residential use. The Real Right Act of the People's Republic of China, which was signed in March 2007, gave no permission on the above two. The Deputy chair of the legal committee of the National Parliament, Hu Kangsheng explained that the financial difficulties of peasants should be resolved by establishing sound financial service in rural areas (*Xinhua* website, http://www.xinhuanet.com, August 22, 2006).

For China as an agricultural country, it is reasonable to say that land reform is an important task to be adjusted carefully. However, if such a current situation continues for a long time, farmland cannot be helpful for improvement of peasants' circumstances. On the contrary, farmland is illegally taken by force in the expansion process of urban areas, which has led to wider disparity between urban and rural areas.

(iii) Possibility of land privatization

Since the beginning of the 21st century, accompanying the progress of urbanization, farm land was destroyed and food production decreased. Such crises gave an opportunity for Chinese people to think about land reform. At the end of 2004, a big agricultural province, Anhui province, carried out a questionnaire survey on land privatization, which was intended for 2070 farming families living in 15 cities, 60 counties and districts, 219 towns and villages, of the province. The result showed that 46.09% of farming families were 'against' the land privatization, 28.7% of farming families were 'for', and others were 'indifferent' or 'without knowledge' (Xinhua website, http://www.xinhuanet.com, December 28, 2004).

No advanced country implements a collectively owned land system in rural areas. What are the problems to hinder land privatization in China? The views of the opponents are generally as follows.

First, in order to implement land privatization, it is indispensable to carefully consider differences among land quality and to decide family population to fairly allocate the land. It is questionable if lowest rank executives of rural area can keep fairness in the procedure.

Second, security is more important than efficiency. In China, the total population equaled 1.3 billion in 2002 whose per capita arable land reached only 1.2 furrows. Moreover, as population is distributed with an imbalance, per capita arable land in one third of provinces and cities does not reach one furrow. In 666 counties it is less than 0.8 furrows, and in 463 counties it is less than the dangerous line of 0.5 furrows. In the present situation in China, as regards the immature social security system, farmland is important to meet the basic living necessities, and so should not be viewed from the viewpoint of efficiency. If farmland is privatized and if parents have to part with the land due to gambling etc, what do their children do?

Third, when privatization is advanced, it is necessary for large-scale land owners to come into existence. That expands the income disparity.

Fourth, a land cooperative organization system can improve transferring the right to use it. At present, the right to use of contracted land can be transferred (with conditions of making agricultural land unchanged, within the period of the remaining years in the 30 contracted years). According to the regulation, specific transfer conditions are decided by peasants and peasants can get the revenue. However, when peasants wish to transfer the land to others due to going to urban areas to find work, it is difficult to find partners (such as other peasants and agricultural companies) and to secure the rights and interests. Thus the idea of establishing an organization such as a land cooperative organization system to intermediate to transfer the right to use came into existence. In order to improve the idea, establishing the cooperative economic act in farm land was necessary. When the above-stated questionnaire survey in Anhui province was implemented, 55.75% peasants were for establishing a land cooperative organization by selecting their representatives in a democratic way.

To the contrary, some scholars have advocated land privatization in farming areas when such progresses as a market-oriented economy, privatization, and institutional reforms on asset property rights of state-owned enterprises have been improved. Kuai Zheyuan, the chief of the Chinese Research Center for National Economy, has been one of the representatives. He insisted on the following assertions when he was interviewed (Ji Shuoming, 2005).

The first assertion was about the efficiency of land use. The peasant economy under the contract system has never efficiently allocated the land resources. Because of the ambiguous property rights, peasants do not take care of the land. Also, due to low productivity, some portions of land have gone to ruin (as peasants went to urban areas to find work). Privatization makes large scale farms possible whose efficiency becomes higher. Some peasants who part with the land are absorbed by urbanization and industrialization. To make land use more efficient needs unambiguous property rights of land.

Second, because peasants have no property rights, when land is requisitioned they cannot have influential voices, and they cannot stop local government from illegal activities. Through land privatization, peasants can get the profit by land price increase and also they can hinder the irregular invasion of public authority.

The third assertion was about the fictitious existence of collective property rights of land. Collectively-owned farmland (and land located in suburban areas) has limited rights to carry out land management collectively. For example, selling land is undoubtedly prohibited and to have a contract with organizations and individuals except collective organizations needs the consent of more than two thirds of peasants or representatives of peasants and also needs the permission of town and village governments. Owing to incomplete authority on the land of individual peasants and collectives, revenues from land are received by some governmental sections to maximize their own self interests.

The fourth assertion was on the meaningful effects to reform in urban areas. Economies in urban areas have been active mainly coming from privatization. We think the similar mechanism might be necessary in rural areas to resolve thoroughly the three agricultural problems. Although such policy measures after 2005 as abolishing agricultural tax and providing subsidies to peasants contribute to agricultural promotions, the three agricultural problems cannot be radically solved.

As indicated above, few experts are opposed to farm land privatization from the viewpoints of ideology. Opponents' views are concentrating upon side effects or the too serious preparations when such radical reforms are carried out. To be sure, from the origin of the political party system, although they are just friendly parties to maximize their self interest, the indispensable existence of party management has been a change of institutional environments to give norms to party activities like the Political Party Act. Similarly, when land privatization is progressed, such an institutional environment might be necessary. It should be cautious that careless implementation of land privatization will cause the above-stated side effects. Side effects should not hinder institutional construction. International experiences such as the Taiwanese lesson of land reform and historical perspectives in China surely seem to give any helpful suggestions. The reform and open door policy in China, led by Deng Xiaoping started in 1978, was much more difficult to carry out than it would be nowadays (see Chapter 2 on this leadership by Deng Xiaoping).

(III) Conclusion: the future of the three agricultural policies towards shared growth Chinese development strategy was based upon the labor intensive type as shown in the Guangdong model and Jiangzhe model in the 1980s. Also, the 'Big Cycle of International Economy' discussion in 1988 came into existence in an extension of the idea. After the 1990s, the High-Tech industrial development districts were established one after another all over China, by attaching greater importance upon High-Tech industry from a viewpoint of industrial policy. The ratio of High-Tech products to whole export products has steadily been increased. As there is the reciprocal demand between light industry and heavy industry, the remarkable development of light industry in 1980s caused the development of heavy industry. Actually, the ratio of heavy industry production to GDP was extended after 2000 (on the detail see Chapter 5). Heavy industrial development seemed to be closely related with reforming and promoting state-owned enterprises, which was accelerated from the second half of the 1990s (see Chapter 3 for the details).

Also in China, many redundant workers in rural areas have to be moved. Taking into consideration the Chinese population structure in both quality and quantity, non-agricultural employment promotion policies have been crucial political tasks. It seems to be indispensable to found some organizations to take responsibility for non-agricultural job opportunities in rural areas (like TVEs) and to expand job opportunities in the formal sector in urban areas. We think, from the current situation, which has a large number of restructuring unemployed workers, employment promotion policies have to be resolved.

It is also necessary to have policy measures to change peasants' attitudes from passive to positive. For example, peasants' autonomous attitudes could be created by land reform, and peasants should be given the right to organize (to establish self-reliant organizations like an agricultural cooperative) and the right to representation (to have seats of agricultural representatives in a correct sense to national and local parliaments). Such measures mean the institutional security to defend peasants from infringing their rights, which we think leads to carrying out a local autonomy system in a constitutional sense.

Relations between party and administration and transforming the bureaucrats group in the transition period

A centrally planned economic system has a leading ideology, in which a leader is a kind of almighty being. A highly centralized system in a political aspect covers the economic aspect, which produces state-owned enterprises and a unified government and company. The division of labor theory insisted upon by Adam Smith emphasizes efficiency improvement by the division of labor. We think the idea could be applied to the field of social management. In order to manage a society, which has become a complicated system efficiently, it is indispensable

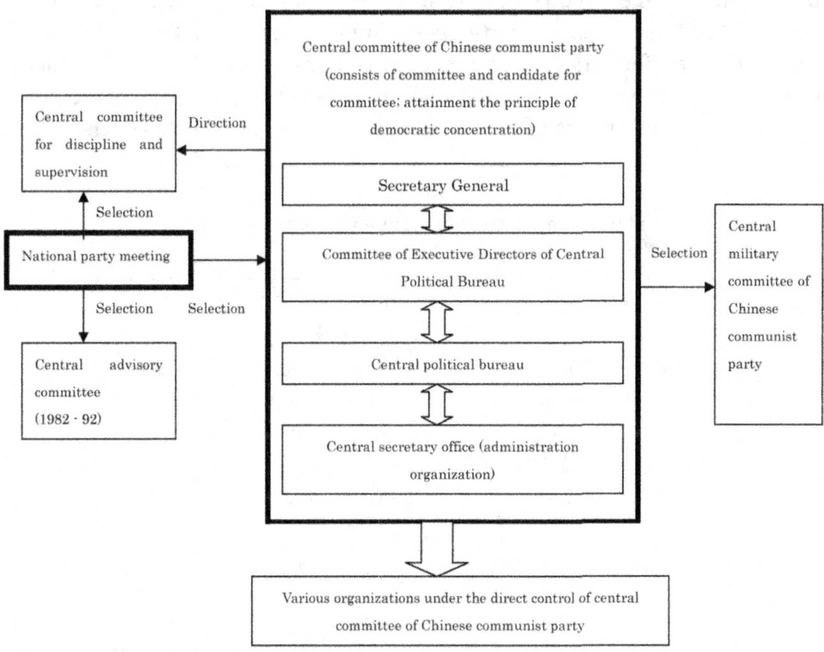

Source: Author.

Figure 6.5 Central organization system of the Chinese communist party

to establish a system of division of labor and cooperation, not to establish an 'almighty' system.

After 1978, transition towards an open market oriented system has caused Chinese society and economy to have a division of the labor system. Separation of government from enterprises, meaning reform of state-owned enterprises has steadily been carried out. The division of labor in the market necessarily needs the division of labor in the political and administration aspect, which will let the separation of party and administration come to the surface as a serious task. The separation of party and administration in China has been a task to be examined for a long time since the 1980s. However, in the 1980s, although it was recognized as an ideology to need the separation of party and administration, because the economy and society were not developed enough, the task had no reality and urgency. Such social and economic circumstances contributed to party executives keeping their power.

We think it is not necessary to emphasize the separation of party and administration in an organizational and functional sense. From the lesson of Taiwanese history on such a separation, we think it is indispensable to have the transformation of the logic coming from the external environment. The Chinese failure on the separation of party and administration until the 1990s surely impeded the transformation. Meanwhile, after 1999, based upon such events as the acceleration of urbanization, the real estate boom, the Chinese participation in the WTO, China's needs of experts in social and economic management have

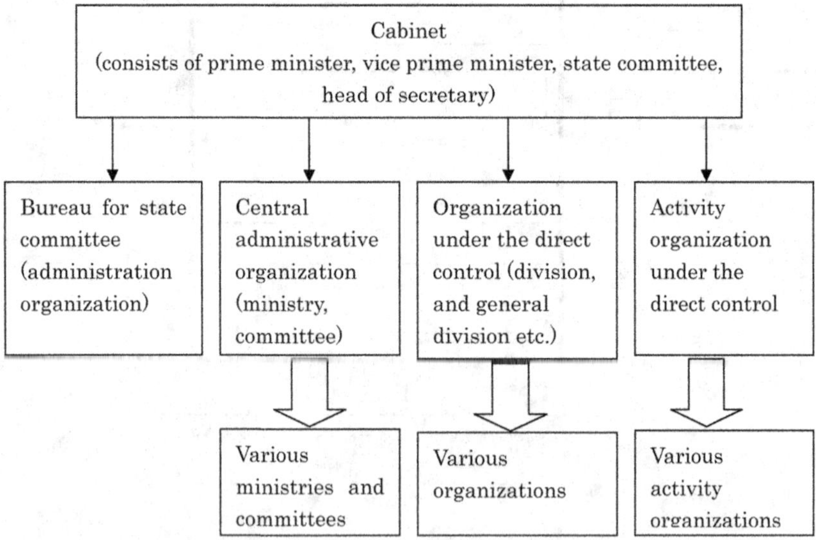

Source: Author.

Figure 6.6 Organizational system of Chinese cabinet

Table 6.12 Number of graduates of Universities (prime minister, vice prime minister, state committee, chairperson, ministers)

	At the end of March, 1996				First meeting of Eighth National Parliament ('93.3)				First meeting of Seventh Ntional Parliament ('88.3)				First meeting of Sixth National Parliament ('83.6)			
University, Vocational College etc.	Prime minister, Vice prime minister, State committee	Economy and industry section	Others	Natioal total	Prime minister, Vice prime minister, State committee	Economy and industry section	Others	National total	Prime minister, Vice prime minister, State committee	Economy and industry section	Others	National total	Prime minister, Vice prime minister, State committee	Economy and industry section	Others	National total
USSR (studying abroad)	5	0	3	6	5	1	3	7	4	7	4	11	1		1	2
GDR (studying abroad)	1			1	1			1			1	1				
Czechoslovakia (studying abroad)									1		1	1				
Tsinghua University	4	1	3	6	3	3	4	7	1	2	3	5	3	2		4
Renmin University of China		1	2	3		1	1	2		1		1				
Peking University		1		1		1		1	1			1			1	1
University of Finance and Economics		1		1												
Foreign Affairs College			1	1			1	1								
Beijing Vocational School of Economis		1		1		1		1								
Beijing University of Mining and Technology		1		1		1		1								
Beijing Iron and Steel Engineering Institute		1		1		1		1								
Beijing Petroleum Institute		1		1		1		1								
Beijing Agricultural Machinery and Chemical Institute		1		1		1		1								

Table 6.12 *Continued*

	At the end of March, 1996				First meeting of Eighth National Parliament ('93.3)				First meeting of Seventh Ntional Parliament ('88.3)				First meeting of Sixth National Parliament ('83.6)			
University, Vocational College etc.	Prime minister, Vice prime minister, State committee	Economy and industry section	Others	Natioal total	Prime minister, Vice prime minister, State committee	Economy and industry section	Others	National total	Prime minister, Vice prime minister, State committee	Economy and industry section	Others	National total	Prime minister, Vice prime minister, State committee	Economy and industry section	Others	National total
Beijing Institute of Posts and Telecommunications		1		1		1		1								
Beijing Aeronautical and Astronautical Institute			1	1			1	1						1		1
Nankai University														1		1
North China University						1		1								
Zhangjiakou Industrial Junior College										1		1				
Shenyang Mechanical and Electrical Engineering Junior College		1		1		1		1								
Shenyang Institute Of Light Industry (Junior College)		1		1		1		1								
North-East Railway Institute										1		1				
Dalian Maritime University										1		1				
Dalian Technical Institute										1	1	2				
Harbin Institute of Technology			1	1			1	1								
Harbin Foreign Languages University										1		1				
Fudan University	1			1	1			1								

Table 6.12 ***Continued***

	At the end of March, 1996				First meeting of Eighth National Parliament ('93.3)				First meeting of Seventh Ntional Parliament ('88.3)				First meeting of Sixth National Parliament ('83.6)			
University, Vocational College etc.	Prime minister, Vice prime minister, State committee	Economy and industry section	Others	Natioal total	Prime minister, Vice prime minister, State committee	Economy and industry section	Others	National total	Prime minister, Vice prime minister, State committee	Economy and industry section	Others	National total	Prime minister, Vice prime minister, State committee	Economy and industry section	Others	National total
Shanghai Shipping College		1		1		1		1								
Shanghai Second Medical University			1	1			1	1			1	1				
Shanghai Jiaotong University										1		1		2		2
Tatong University														1		1
Nanjing University			2	2			1	1			1					
Nanjing Military Institute	1		1	1	1		1	1	1			1				
Nanjing Geological School		1		1												
Anhui Agricultufal College		1		1		1		1								
Shandong Institute of Technology		1		1		1		1								
Beijing Language & Culture University	1			1												
East China Textile College										1		1		1		1
China Textile University										1		1				
Zhongshan University										1		1				
Franco-Chinoise de Lyon											1	1			1	1
Jinan University									1			1	1		1	1
Guangxi University										1		1		1		1

Table 6.12 ***Concluded***

	At the end of March, 1996				First meeting of Eighth National Parliament ('93.3)				First meeting of Seventh Ntional Parliament ('88.3)				First meeting of Sixth National Parliament ('83.6)			
University, Vocational College etc.	Prime minister, Vice prime minister, State committee	Economy and industry section	Others	Natioal total	Prime minister, Vice prime minister, State committee	Economy and industry section	Others	National total	Prime minister, Vice prime minister, State committee	Economy and industry section	Others	National total	Prime minister, Vice prime minister, State committee	Economy and industry section	Others	National total
Chongqing Institute of Architecture and Engineering		1		1												
South-West Associated University															1	1
Yan'an University											1	1				
Chinese Resisting Japanese Aggression University of Military and Politics													2	2	2	4
Xinjiang Agricultural Institute		1		1		1		1								
local normal school											1	1	2	1	1	4
equals junior college students														1		2
none	2	3	4	8	2	2	5	8	4	2	4	8	6	14	10	25

Note: "Study abroad" includes practice at the factories, and the "graduates of university" includes quiting university and correspondence courses. Blank means he or she did never enter university nor vocational college. The number of people is the same as the source below indicates.

Source: Mitsubishi Research Institute (ed.) (1996), pp.56–57.

rapidly been raised. It should happen that the position of technocrats and party executives of the nation will be reversed. The bureaucratic system in China has been experiencing peaceful revolution. Generally speaking, in the transformation process, it is important to need the necessary circumstances. As a matter of fact, in the gradually reforming China, they have followed such a fact-following mechanism of institutional change (see Chapter 5 on the logic of a fact-following mechanism of institutional change).

As regard the characteristics of the bureaucrats' group in China after Deng Xiaoping's reform in 1978, they were still in the days of technocrats from science and engineering courses. However, significant change could be recognized, which says that traditional technocrats in science and engineering have been replaced by bureaucrats in economics and finance since the end of the 1990s (especially at the Sixteenth National Communist Party Meeting in 2002). We expect the remarkable tendency cannot be reversed. We investigate the expression, reasons, and new direction regarding the tendency.

(1) The days of ruling a country by engineers Before the end of the 1990s, China could be said to be in the days of ruling a country by engineers. The characteristics of those days say that it is easier for technocrats coming from a background in science and engineering to promote their positions from the top to the bottom. Most of the technocrats have experience of studying in such former socialist countries as the USSR, GDR, Czechoslovakia, and have an academic background of graduating from distinguished universities in science and engineering in China. Table 6.11 shows universities (educational level and special subject) from which they (meaning the Prime Minister, Vice Prime Minister, State Committee, High Ranking Government Officials of Administrative Vice-Minister level, at the Sixth, Seventh, and Eighth National Parliament, up to the end of March, 1996) graduated. Before examining Table 6.12, we will take a short look at structures of the central organizational system of the Communist Party and administrative system of the People's Republic of China.

Figure 6.5 indicates the central organizational system of the Communist Party. (1) In the National Communist Party, they select members of each committee, which is the Central Committee of the Chinese Communist Party (which consists of committee and candidate committee, within which the principle of a democratic concentration system is accomplished), the Central Committee of Inspection of Discipline, Central Advisor Committee. (2) In the Central Committee of the Chinese Communist Party, when the National Party Meeting is closed, the Highest Leaders Organization select members of Central Military Committee of the Communist Party, which indicates that party fully controls military forces. In the administration system of the PRC they have another Central Military Committee of the PRC. They are not contradicted because members of them are the same. (3) When the Central Meeting of the Political Bureau is closed, the state committee implements the authority. (4) The Central Committee of Inspection of Discipline carries out the policy measures led by the Central Committee, and it has an authority to control the activities of the lower rank committee of inspection of discipline. (5) The Central Advisor Committee existed for ten years from 1982 to 1992, whose roles were assistance and advice of political activities for the Central Committee. Members of the committee were chosen from the party members who had 40 years experience of party membership, enough experience as leader's activities, and received the confidence of people regardless of the party. Deng Xiaoping established this committee, which took the responsibility for the retired party executives who were replaced by younger executives, but it was dismissed in 1992.

Meanwhile, Figure 6.6 shows the organizational system of the cabinet. (1) The cabinet consists of the Prime Minister, the Vice Prime Minister, State Committees, and the President of Secretaries. (2) The State Committee is a newly established position, according to the 1982 Constitution, and is a cabinet minister with the same rank as the Deputy Vice Prime Minister. The state committee can hold the posts of the respective minister or the head of committee, and also can be in charge of special duties entrusted by the executive meeting of the cabinet. In addition, the state committee can work on diplomatic activities on behalf of state committees.

Table 6.12 explains the following. A remarkable existence is given to one of the most distinguished universities of science and engineering, Tsinghua University. As a matter of fact, besides the top ranking officials, there are many graduates of Tsinghua University among medium-rank and lower-rank executives (especially of the central government section in Beijing), and this was called the Tsinghua University phenomena. A the end of 1980, graduates of Tsinghua University occupied around 40% of the total number of executives of ministers and provincial governors level (Wang Qian, 2007).[11] The data presented by Tsinghua University shows that for the past ten years the total number of executives at minister and provincial governor level reached about 300.

The People's Republic University also has an increasing number of the posts. Interestingly enough, the People's Republic University was originally established to develop executives for the nation; however, the numbers of graduates who have been promoted to top executive positions of the nation are much fewer than Tsinghua University. We think the reason for the superior position of Tsinghua University (which specializes in science and engineering) over the People's Republic University (a university with every faculty) might be greater importance being attached to the science and engineering field in the authoritarian system.

Compared with the graduates of Tsinghua University, the graduates of Peking University are said to have stronger personality, whose general image is thus idealistic. The graduates of Peking University entered political society (as in China, both political organizations and bureaucratic organizations are united, both are difficult to distinguish between) but were actually late being promoted. The

11 Statement by Xu Xianglin, Vice Dean of the Faculty of Management, Peking University, at the interview by *Nan Fang Zhou Mo* (*Southern Weekend*). Also see Wang Qian (2007).

phenomena were closely related with external circumstances (that is to say, the Chinese development stage).

However, as stated later, even the technocrats who graduated from science and engineering might gradually change their special fields according to actual jobs. Such technocrats who can change their special fields during the hard days of a market-oriented economy can successfully take positions at the time of bureaucrats in economy and finance. Accompanying the change, the original technocrats who graduated from economy and finance will occupy more important seats. At the same time, since the Sixteenth National Communist Party Meeting, the 'Peking University phenomena' has appeared and the graduates of Peking University seemed to rising quickly (see later).

(2) Appearance of bureaucrats' group in economy and finance and reshuffling tendency of the personnel of the Central Bank The bureaucrats' group in economy and finance are classified into technocrats in a wider sense. However their characteristics are different from traditional engineers who graduated from science and engineering faculties. The bureaucrats' group in economy and finance who are interested in economic rationality, efficiency, social welfare, economic globalization etc, have fairly common characteristics with bureaucrats in law and politics. The appearance of a bureaucrats' group in economy and finance therefore might be a prelude of the appearance of bureaucrats in law and politics.

After the Sixteenth National Meeting of the Chinese Communist Party in November, 2002, the bureaucrats' group in economy and finance have steadily started to appear in Chinese central administration. The bureaucrats' group members are distributed in the following party and national organizations. As regards the party organization system, it mainly indicates the central leadership group of economy and finance, and as far as the national organization system is concerned, especially important positions are the Prime Minister, the Vice Prime Minister, State Committee, Ministry of Commerce, Bank of the People's Republic of China (Central Bank), Ministry of Finance, Committee of National Development and Reform, Committee of National Economy and Trade, Committee of Security Supervision and Management, Committee of Insurance Supervision and Management, Ministry of Information and Industry, and Ministry of Transformation. In the following section we investigate the appearance of a bureaucrats' group in economy and finance with two cases.

(i) The prelude: the Sixteenth National Meeting of the Communist Party

At the Sixteenth National Meeting of the Communist Party, held in November, 2002, which was the prelude of the days of Hu Jintao[12] and Wen Jiabao,[13] many

12 Graduated from Tsinghua University (1964), Department of Hydraulic Engineering.

13 Graduated from Beijing University of Mining and Technology (1968). Masters Degree in Engineering. Engineer.

bureaucrats in economy and finance were promoted. For example, Prime Minister Wen Jiabao who is in charge of economy and finance and Wu Bangguo[14] who manages state-owned enterprise reform were promoted to the executive committee of political bureau. State committee Wu Yi[15] and Head of National Planning Committee Zeng Peiyan[16] were promoted to the committee of political bureau. Head of National Committee of economy and trade Li Rongrong,[17] President of Bank of People's Republic of China Dai Xianglong,[18] Minister of Finance Xiang Huaicheng,[19] Committee of Security Supervision and Management Zhou Xiaochuan,[20] Minister of Agriculture Du Qinglin,[21] Minister of Labor and Social Security Zhang Zuoyi,[22] Minister of Transportation Zhang Chunxian,[23] Head of General Bureau of National Tax Affairs Jin Renqing,[24] General Bureau of

---

14 Graduated from Tsinghua University (1966), Department of Electronic Engineering. Engineer.

15 Graduated from Beijing Petroleum Institute (1962). Engineer.

16 Graduated from Tsinghua University (1962), Department of Electronic Engineering. Engineer.

17 Graduated from Tianjin University (1968), School of Chemical Engineering. Engineer.

18 Graduated from University of Finance and Economics (1967). Economist.

19 Graduated from Shandong University (1960), School of Chinese Literature. He took office as Minister of Finance from March 1998 to March 2003, and now is the Mayer of Tianjin.

20 Zhou Xiaochuan (1948~); born in 1948, and graduated from Tsinghua University (1985), PhD (in Engineering). He was a member of a leading group for systemic reform of the Chinese cabinet, and Vice President of the Systemic Reform Research Institute of the Chinese Economy from 1986 to 1987. From 1986 to 1989, he was a Deputy Minister of Foreign Trade, and from 1986 to 1991 he was a member of the Systemic Reform Committee of Chinese National Economy. He was a Vice President of the Bank of China from 1991 to 1995, and the Head of Foreign Exchange Management Bureau in 1995. In 1996, he took office as a Vice President of the People's Bank of China. In July 1997, he was the First Member of the Chinese Monetary Policy Committee. In 1998 he was the President of the Chinese Construction Bank, and in February 2000 he was the Chairman of the Supervising and Management Committee of Chinese Security. In December 2002, he took office as the President of the People's Bank of China, and now he is the Party Secretary and a member of the Sixteenth Central Committee of the Communist Party in China.

21 In 1994–96. He got a masters degree in Economic Management at Jilin University.

22 Graduated from Heilongjiang University (1966), School of Foreign Language (specialized in Russian Language). In April 2003, he took office as the Head of Heilongjiang Province.

23 Completed Masters Course in Management Science of the North-Eeast Mechanical Science. He took office as the Minister of Transportation in October 2002. In December 2005, he was the Party Secretary of Hunan Province and was transferred to the Chief of Executive Committee of Hunan Provincial Parliament.

24 Graduated from University of Finance and Economics (1966). Economist.

National Customs House Mou Xinsheng,[25] Minister of Science and Technology Xu Guanhua,[26] President of the National Board of Audit Li Jinhua,[27] and Minister of Construction Wang Guangtao[28] were promoted or reappointed to be members of the Central Committee.

Moreover, party secretaries and technocrats in the central management organization of economy and finance like Wang Xudong,[29] Lu Fuyuan,[30] Hua Jianmin,[31] Yan Haiwang,[32] and Head of the General Bureau of Civil Aviation in China Yang Yuanyuan[33] were selected as members of the Central Committee. Also, the presidents of the four big state-owned commercial banks – the president of the Bank of China, Liu Mingkang;[34] the president of the Bank of Agriculture, Shang

---

25 Graduated from North-West University in Politics and law (1968), Department of Law.

26 Graduated from Beijing Forestry University (1963). Member of the Chinese Academy of Science.

27 Graduated from the University of Finance and Economics (1966), Masters Degree in Finance and Economics.

28 Graduated from Tongji University, got the Masters Degree in Roads and Bridges. He took office as the Minister of Construction in December 2001, and was reappointed in March 2003.

29 Graduated from Tianjin Institute of Science and Technology (1982), Department of Systems Engineering. He took office as the Party Secretary of Hebei Province from December 2001 to November 2002. From November 2002, he was the Party Secretary of the Ministry of Information Industry. In January 2003, he was the Vice Minister of Information Industry, and in March 2003 took office as the Minister of Information Industry.

30 Graduated from Jilin University (1970), Department of Physics. From September 2002 to March 2003, he was the Vice Minister of Foreign Trade, and from March 2003 he took office as the Minister of Commerce and Party Secretary. In August 2006, he died of an illness.

31 Graduated from Tsinghua University (1963), Department of Automotive Engineering. Engineer. In 1998, he was the Vice Head of the Central Leaders Group of Finance and Economy, and in March 2003 he took office as the Executive Committee and the Head of Cabinet Bureau.

32 Graduated from Harbin University of Architecture (1965). In April 1998, he was the Vice Secretary of the Executive Committee of the Central Monetary Policy, and the Vice President of the People's Bank of China. In March 2003 he took office as the Party Secretary of the Supervising and Management Committee of Chinese Banks, and as the Vice President of the People's Republic of China.

33 In 1966, enlisted in the People's Liberation Army. He studied as a pilot in the second reserve school in the People's Liberation Army, and in 1968–1969 also studied at the high ranking school of Chinese private civil aviation. In May 2002 he took office as the General Chairman of the Chinese Civil Aviation Agency.

34 In 1987, got an MBA at City University of London. In February 2000 to April 2003, he was the Chairman and the President of the Bank of China. Since April 2003 he has taken office as the Chairman of the Supervising and Management Committee of Chinese Banks.

Fulin;[35] the president of the Bank of Industry and Commerce Jiang Jianqing;[36] and the president of the Bank of Construction, Zhang Enzhao[37] – and the persons in charge of the big three oil companies and large-scale state-owned enterprises were placed in the name list of Central Committee and Central Candidate Committee and Central Committee of Inspection of Discipline (Yi Ming, 2002).

In China, their duty in the party secures their own administrative duty. Bureaucrats in economy and finance who participated in the ranks of Central Committee and Central Candidate Committee might have a change of duty but secured their important posts. After the Party Meeting in 2002, the average age of bureaucrats in economy and finance decreased to 56 years old from 60 years old.

(ii) Extra time: a reshuffling tendency of the personnel of the Central Bank, from a practical business type to scholarly type

When the bureaucrats' group in economy and finance appeared, particular attention was focused upon the reshuffling tendency of the personnel of the Central Bank. Needless to say, the central bank plays an important role to maintain the value of the currency, which is closely related with monetary policy. For such transition economies as China, the change happening in the central bank reflects the degree of progress in market oriented reform. According to the revised version of the Bank of the People's Republic of China Act in 1994, a division in function was carried out between the central bank and commercial banks. In the 21st century, the four state-owned commercial banks were steadily reformed to be stock companies, which were listed in domestic and foreign stock exchanges. Meanwhile, the central bank has been attaching greater importance upon macro economic adjustment policies, particularly monetary policy. Therefore, the central bank needs more scholarly type human resources than practical business type human resources.

Zhou Xiaochuan, who took office as the president of the Bank of the People's Republic of China in December 2002, actively reshuffled the personnel of the Bank to have a more scholarly flavor. In order to carry out the tasks of the central

35 From 1978 to 1982, he studied at the Beijing Institute of Finance and Trade, PhD.

36 Graduated from Shanghai University of Finance and Economics (1984), got a Masters Degree and PhD at the Shanghai Jiao Tong University. Since February 2002, he took office as the President of Industrial and Commercial Bank of China.

37 Graduated from Fudan University (1964), School of Economics. In January 2003, he was the Party Secretary and the President of the Construction Bank of China, and the Party Secretary of the Chinese Security and Asset Management Company. In November 2003, he was a member of the Central Committee of Discipline and Supervision, also in September 2004 he took office as the Chairman of the general meeting of stockholders for the Construction Bank of China and the Party Secretary. On March 16, 2005, he resigned from the posts of the Construction Bank of China and Chinese International Finance Co Ltd., due to personal affairs. On June 20, 2005, he announced on the website of the Construction Bank of China that Zhang Enzhao was investigated by the Party Committee of Discipline and Supervision about illegal activities.

bank to adjust to the macroeconomic situation, particularly through monetary policy, such new sections as monetary stability section, financial market section, Zhengxinguanliju (credit and confidence management section – founded in November 2003 to manage the markets as a whole in evaluation of the maximum amount of loan money, and whose main aims are (i) to supervise unfair competition in credit evaluation, (ii) to supervise overestimation, (iii) to restrain bank risks, (iv) to secure enterprise information and national security etc), and an anti-money laundering section, were established. In October 2003, the scholarly type bureaucrat Xie Ping[38] was promoted from the head of the research section of the central bank to the head of the monetary stability section, and Yi Gang[39] from vice head of monetary policy section to the head of it. When Zhou Xiaochuan took office, the main tasks of the central bank were to eliminate financial risk, which had accumulated over long years, and to develop the economy in a stable and open environment. The monetary stability section was established to carry out these tasks. After the Supervising Management Committee on the Commercial Bank was founded, the task of the central bank has been concentrating on monetary policy; thus, the job as the head of the monetary policy section is said to be the core of the central bank.

On December 29, 2003, the Vice Head of the Budget Policy Committee of the Executive Committee in the National Parliament, Su Ning,[40] took office as Vice President of the Central Bank. They said it was an extraordinary personnel change. Traditionally, it is usual that a bureaucrat changes the position to be National Parliament organization. However, the reverse course change happened in a few case. Su Ning is an expert who has a thorough knowledge of macro economic policy. With Zhou Xiaochuan, and Guo Shuqing,[41] who is the Head of National Foreign Currency Management Section, in the managing executives, the three experts on macro economic policy took office.

In May 2004, Zhang Xin,[42] Li Bo, and Zhang Tao,[43] all of whom have a career to study abroad, took office as the Vice Head of the Monetary Stability Section,

---

38 He got a PhD (Economics) at the Renmin University of China.

39 He got a PhD (Economics) in the USA in 1986–1994. From 1994 to 1997, he was a Professor of Chinese Economic Research Center of the Peking University. In 2003 he was the Head of Monetary Policy Office of the People's Bank of China, and in July 2004 he took office as the Vice President of the People's Bank of China.

40 He obtained certification as an engineer, and was the Chairman of the Macroeconomic Research Office of the cabinet.

41 He has been a well known scholar in economics, and since the second half of 1980s he has investigated Chinese economic reform.

42 He got a PhD (Finance) in the USA (Columbia Business School) in 1996. After he worked for the Financial Division of World Bank, in January 2005, he took office as the Head of Financial Stability Office of People's Bank of China.

43 He worked for the Asian Development Bank as the Senior Economist during 1997–2004. Since 2004, he has been Vice Chairman of the Research Office of People's Bank of China.

the Vice Head of Treaty and Legal Section, the Vice Head of the Research Section respectively, without the normal procedure.

On August 9, 2004, the Vice President of the National Board of Audit, Xiang Junbo,[44] took office as Vice President of the Central Bank. One week later, on August 16, 2004, the other three of Vice President and President Aides were decided, which led to a fundamental framework of a reshuffling tendency of the personnel by Zhou Xiaochuan, which showed a President (Zhou Xiaochuan), five Vice Presidents (Wu Xiaoling,[45] Guo Shuqing, Su Ning, Xiang Junbo, Li Ruogu[46]), and three President Aides (Liu Shiyu,[47] Yi Gang, and Hu Xiaolian[48]).

On August 11, 2006, when the cabinet approved, Fan Gang – who is a scholar in macroeconomics and transition economies – was appointed to the post of a member of the monetary policy committee of the central bank.

The above-mentioned procedure indicates that the characteristics of structural reshuffling of the personnel at the central bank by President Zhou Xiaochuan was to transform it from a practical business type to a scholarly type. In order to carry this out, traditional personnel networks in which personnel promotions were implemented within the central bank or introduced from commercial banks were radically cut off, and various personnel promotions were carried out without normal procedure.[49]

(iii) Analysis

When we analyze the change of bureaucrats' group in China, we should be careful about the following situations.

First, as stated above, many bureaucrats in economy and finance, who were promoted by Zhou Xiaochuan, graduated from science and engineering faculties. However, they were involved in jobs related with economy and finance and

44 Graduated from Renmin University of China (1985), Department of Finance, and got a Masters Degree (Economics) at Nankai University, also he got a PhD (Law) at Peking University. In 2002, he took office as the Vice Head of the National Board of Audit.

45 Graduated from the Research Institute of the People's Bank of China, which is called the Huanpu Military Academy in the financial circle. He successively held various posts like the Head of Research Office of the Central Bank, the Chairman of the National Foreign Currency Management Office.

46 After he got a Masters Degree (Law) at Peking University, he was on the teaching staff at Peking University in 1984–1985. Since June 2005, he has been Chairman and President of the Export and Import Bank of China.

47 Graduated from Tsinghua University, Department of Hydraulic Engineering, also he got a Masters Degree (Economic Management) at Tsinghua University. In 2002–2004, he was the Head of Administration Bureau of People's Bank of China, and in July 2004 Assistant President and n June 2006 Vice President.

48 Graduated from Research Institute of the People's Bank of China (1981), and got a Masters Degree.

49 Nanfang Zhoumo (Southern Weekend) February 20, 2004, and Jingji Guanchabao (The Economic Observer) August 22, 2004 etc.

Table 6.13 The executive committee of the central political bureau in the communist party started in 2002

Name	Post	Graduated	Career
Hu Jintao	President of PRC, General Secretary of the Communist Party of China, Chairman of the Central Military Commission	Tsinghua University, Department of Hydraulic Engineering	Engineer
Wu Bangguo	Chairman of the Standing Committee of the National Parliment	Tsinghua University, Department of Electronic Engineering	Engineer
Wen Jiabao	Prime minister	Beijing University of Mining and Technology	Engineer
Jia Qinglin	Chairman of the National Committee of the Chinese People's Political Consultative Conference	Hebei University of Technology, Department of Electric Power	Engineer
Zeng Qinghong	Vice President of PRC	Beijing Institute of Technology, The Automatic Control Department	Engineer
Wu Guanzheng	Secretary of central discipline inspection commission	Tsinghua University, Department of Automotive Engineering	Engineer
Li ChangChun	Head of the central group for propaganda and ideological work	Harbin Institute of Technology	Engineer
Luo Gan	Secretary of parliament commission for politics and law	Beijing Iron and Steel Engineering Institute	Engineer
Huang Ju (died in June 2007)	Vice Prime minister (in charge of financial sector)	Tsinghua University, Department of Electrical Engineering	Engineer

Source: Author and *Sankei Shimbun* (August 4, 2007).

Table 6.14 Leaders of next generation

Name	Post	Graduated	Degree and Career
Li Keqiang	Secretary of Liaoning Province communist party committee	Graduate School of Peking University	Doctor's degree (in Economics)
Bo Xilai	Minister of commerce	Graduate School of Chinese Academy of Social Sciences	Master's degree (in Literature)
Zhang Dejiang	Secretary of Guangdong Province communist party committee	Kim Il-sung University (North Korea), Department of Government and economics	Bachelor's degree (in Economics)
Liu Yandong	Minister of Unified Front Operation	Graduate School of Jilin University	Doctor's degree (in Public Administration)
Li Yuanchao	Secretary of Jiangsu Province communist party committee	Graduate School of Central Party School	Doctor's degree (in Laws)
Zhou Yongkang	Minister of Public Safety	Beijing Petroleum Institute	Engineer
Xi Jinping	Secretary of the Shanghai Municipality communist party committee	Graduate School of Tsinghua University	Doctor's degree (in Laws)

Source: Author and *Sankei Shimbun* (August 4, 2007).

accumulated lots of practical experiences. They got enough knowledge on macro economic policy by what is said to be 'learning by doing', often observed in less developed countries.

Second, behind the appearance of bureaucrats in economy and finance, a balance between party and administration has been attempted to be kept. Some important posts have been occupied by party executives. For example, of the posts after the Sixteenth Party Meeting in 2002 was closed, the Minister of Information Industry Wang Xudong came from the Organization and Personnel Management of the Party, the Minister of International Economy and Trade Zhang Chunxian came from Party Secretary of the Ministry of Transportation, and the Head of Insurance Supervision and Management Committee Wu Dingfu was the person in charge of the Discipline and Supervision Group, which is in the Board of Audit of the Central Committee of Discipline and Supervision.

Third, the new Chinese tendency to be managed by the bureaucrats in economy and finance has been expressed by the introduction of a job manager system to managers of state-owned enterprises. The tendency in which a royalty index has been replaced by an expert index has become remarkable. However, another problem has occurred. It is often reported that, because of the inappropriateness to the tradition of state-owned enterprises, they reluctantly resigned their posts.

(3) The reshuffling tendency of the personnel at the Seventeenth National Meeting of the Communist Party: demise of engineer governed state days? The National Meeting of the Communist Party, which is held every five years, is very important in telling the future of the Chinese political system. It is quite reasonable that the attention of internal and external society would be paid to the trend of personnel at the Seventeenth National Meeting of the Communist Party. Of the personnel affairs of the communist party, the executive committee of the central political bureau in the communist party occupies the central part. As shown in Table 6.13, all members of the executive committee of the central political bureau in the communist party, which started in 2002, were originally engineers. Meanwhile, many posts would be occupied by leaders of the next generation who graduated from the humanities course faculties, such as economics and law. Advanced level educational backgrounds, such as master's degree and doctor's degree are remarkable (see Table 6.14).

Accompanied by market oriented transition and WTO affiliation of China, the needs of experts in socio-economic management have been growing and the 'calm revolution' has been caused in the leader system, which has traditionally consisted of model workers, party affairs executives and engineers. In the Chinese bureaucratic system, we should pay attention to both the tendency of a shift from 'engineer' to 'graduate from the humanities course' (including finance and economics, law, and politics) and the appearance of a 'Peking University phenomena'. The details are as follows.

(4) Appearance of a 'Peking University phenomena' in the arena of Chinese politics According to the *NanFangZhouMo* (Southern Weekly), June 14, 2007, the bureaucrats whose educational backgrounds are cultural science and social science, at such positions as incumbent provincial governors and incumbent party secretaries, occupied 75% of the total (coming from open materials to the public till May 2007). What was paid most attention to was the 'Peking University phenomena', which indicated the expanding positions and activities of the graduates of Peking University and by which traditional 'Tsinghua University phenomena' might be replaced.

The information presented in May 2007 showed that incumbent executives in higher positions than that of vice provincial governors and vice ministers with the educational background of graduates of Peking University (both undergraduates student and graduate student) total 57. In particular, 16 recently promoted are minister-level executives, including Shanxi provincial governor, Yuan Chunqing, The first secretary of Central secretariat of young people's association of Communism, Hu Chunhua, Shanxi province party secretary, Zhao Leji, Hebei

Table 6.15 Comparison of high ranking executives of graduates of Peking University and Tsinghua University

	Executives of minister level (total)	Born in the 1960s	Born in the 1950s	Born in the 1940s	Born in the 1930s
Peking University	16	1	7	7	1
Tsinghua University	36	0	5	29	2

Source: Wang Qian (2007) and Author.

provincial governor, Guo gengmao. Ninety percent of the 57 executives graduated from humanities courses such as literature, history, philosophy, law, economics, and politics, only two graduated from science courses such physics and chemistry.

Of the 57 bureaucrats higher ranking than vice minister level, 39 were born in the 1950s (from 48 years old to 57 years old), most of whom have appeared at the time of the Sixteenth National Communist Party Meeting in autumn of 2002. Meanwhile, of the 36 executives in a higher position than minister level, whose educational background were graduates of Tsinghua University, 29 were born in 1940s and only five were born in the 1950s. Current executive ordinance regulates that the retirement age of executives higher than minister level is 65 years old, and of executives higher than vice minister level is 60 years old, thus within the coming five years of those high ranking executives of graduates of Tsinghua University, at least half will retire. Table 6.15 shows what is mentioned above.

The Chinese University OB net announced the top ten universities from which prominent politicians graduated. The Peking University phenomena could be recognized from the list, which shown in Table 6.16. At present, the number of prominent politicians is occupied the most by graduates from Tsinghua University, however, sooner or later, Tsinghua University will be replaced by Peking University. Needless to say, the rising phenomena of politicians graduating from the humanities courses would not stop at the Peking University phenomena and the phenomena would spread over the general universities (particularly the faculties of the humanities course) all over the nation. The *Zhongguo Xinwen zhoukan* (*China News Weekly*), January 2005, analyzed the personnel changes of 18 minister level executives in the whole of China, which proved the rising tendency of executives graduating from the humanities course. Of the 18, 14 (of which 70% graduated from the humanities) were changed to new positions and four retired (of whom one was from physical education and three were from science courses).[50] It seems to us that executives who graduated from science courses have shifted to be executives from humanities courses.

50 See Zhongguo Xinwen Zhoukan (*China News Weekly*), January 10, 2005.

Table 6.16 Top ten universities from prominent politicians were graduated

	University	Location of university	Number of prominent politician
1	Tsinghua University	Beijing	41
2	Peking University	Beijing	34
3	Renmin University of China	Beijing	25
4	Jilin University	Changchum	18
5	Harbin Institute of Technology	Harbin	17
6	Fudan University	Shanghai	14
7	Shandong University	Jinan	9
8	Shanghai Jiaotong University	Shanghai	9
9	China University of Petroleum	Beijing	8
10	Nanjing University	Nanjing	7
11	Chinese Institute of Science and Technology	Hefei	7
12	Beijing University of Education	Beijing	7

Note: Definition of prominent politician is as following; incumbent minister and vice minister level executives, provincial governors and ministers level government executives, the Fourteenth, Fifteenth, Sixteenth Communist Party Central Committee member and candidate member.

Source: Chinese University OB net http://www.cuaa.net/, Research report on evaluation of Chinese Universities in 2007 jointly held by 21st century human resource report and University (journal), University, No.2, 2007, etc.

(5) Attaching importance to raise human resources outside the communist party

In 2007, Chinese politicians coming from the Democratic Party group were appointed to cabinet ministers after a 35-year vacancy. After the Communist Party administration was established in the 1950s, the talented politicians of the Democratic Party were once appointed to ministers. For example, Huang Yanpei was appointed to minister of light industry, Zhang Bojun minister of transportation, Shi Liang minister of justice.

There have been eight politicians from the Democratic Party group in China, each of which has his own history; however, after the new China was established, each of them has accepted the leading position of the Communist Party and has agreed with supporting the nation building plan of the Communist Party. The Democratic Party group in China was in the position as a party of participation in government, and the party offered its opinions at such opportunities as political agreement conferences. Table 6.17 indicates the details of the Democratic Party group.

After the 'anti-right movement' in 1957, the eight Democratic Party group suffered from serious damage, by which members of the Democratic Party group

Table 6.17 Details of eight Democratic Party group

Title of the party	Established	Remarks
Chinese Nationalist Party Revolutionary Committee	1948.1	Established by a reformist group of the Nationalist Party opposed to dictatorship of Chiang Kai-shek
Chinese Democratic Union	1941.3	The forerunner was the Chinese Democratic Politics Union. Most of the members are intellectuals who contribute for cultural and educational circles
Chinese Democratic Nation Building Party	1945.12	Racial industry and commercial business persons, and intellectuals who are closely related with the business persons
Chinese Democracy Promotion Party	1945.12	Established by proposals of teachers of elementary school and junior high school, and intellectuals in publishing business circles those days. At present, the majority of the members are intellectuals of cultural and educational circles who are trying to promote patriotic democratic campaign
Chinese peasants Democratic Party	1930.8	The forerunner was the Chinese Nationalist Party Extraordinary Activity Committee. In 1935 they changed the name to be Chinese Democratic Liberation Activity Committee, and in 1947 the present name was given. The majority of the members are high ranking intellectuals in the circles of medical and health, science and technology, and cultural and education
Chinese Zhigong Party	1925.10	In May 1947 the party was reformed. Majority of the members are returnee overseas Chinese
9.3 Democratic Science Party	1944.11	The forerunner was the Democratic Science Party, whose name was changed to be the present in September 1945. The majority of the members are high ranking intellectuals in the circles of cultural and education, and science and technology, who are chiefly promoting democratic movement
Taiwan Democratic Autonomous Union	1947.11	Consisted of compatriots whose domicile of origin are Taiwan and who live in the Chinese continent and promote patriotic democratic campaign

Source: Author.

could be appointed as only vice governor level executives under the 'political arrangement'. From the year of 2005, the situation has been gradually changed, when the central communist party promulgated the Fifth Official Document prescribing that qualified executives from outside the communist party could take office as the head, which was the new prescription to break the traditional practice. In July 2006, the central unified front section conference indicated the guidelines to enforce the bringing up and promotion of executives outside the communist party. Since the second half of 2006, in each level of government, the section arrangement of personnel changes has been proceeding. During the period of the Chinese National Parliament and Political Agreement Conference in March 2007, a government spokesperson asserted that minister level executives coming from the Democratic Party group would be appointed in the near future. In the first half of 2007, the prediction came true. First, on April 27, 2007, the Tenth executive committee of the National Parliaments appointed Wan Gang[51] to be the minister of science and engineering. Wan Gang is the first minister coming from the Democratic Party group 35 years after Fu Zuoyi resigned as the minister of hydroelectric power generation in 1972.

Two months after that, on June 29, 2007, the 28th executive committee of the National Parliament appointed Chen Zhu[52] to be the minister of health, who is not a member of any party. We could recognize lots of similarities between Wan Gang and Chen Zhu, of which their broad outlook on international affairs is closely connected with their background of studying abroad and could be considered to be their outstanding advantage.

Generally speaking, the Chinese executive system has been exposed to the trend of the time, and it has been necessary to reform it. It might be probable that a power struggle between the old and new power will continue for the time being. However, since Chinese reform and the open door policy has gone into an irreversible orbit, the days of ruling the country by experts will surely come sooner or later. In the Chinese Communist Party National Meeting held every five years, they have steadily carried out reshuffling personnel, even if they have no slogan, like the reform of party administration in Taiwan in 1950s.

(6) The dual structure phenomena of a bureaucrats group in the transition period

Under the authoritarian system in China, when they select bureaucrats, the traditional criterion to select them attached greater importance to royalty and not expertise. It became a traditional practice to select executives among basic governments, state-owned enterprises, ex-soldiers, and model workers.[53] Thus, traditional practice economy and the traditional practical way of selecting

---

51 President of Tongji University and Vice Chairman of Zhigong Party, expert in automobiles; born in 1952, from 1985 studied in Germany and after then stayed in Germany for 15 years.

52 Vice Chairman of the Chinese Science Association, expert in medical science; born in 1953, from 1984–1989 studied in France and got a PhD.

53 For example, both Li Ruihuan, the Mayer of Tianjin City Directly under the Central Government in 1980s, and Zhang Baifa, the Vice Mayor of Beijing City Directly under the Central Government also in 1980s, were model workers of the nation in 1950s. In addition, Li Ruihuan took office as the member of Executive Committee of the Central Political Bureau.

executives established causal relationships. After the 1980s, because such selected executives had weak knowledge on a market oriented economy and modern method of management, the inappropriateness to adjust regional economy and to manage regional society became clearer. Also, because a market-oriented economy has developed, the necessity for expertise has been higher and bureaucrats in economy and finance have occupied important positions in place of bureaucrats in science and engineering.

Such observations suggest that the Chinese bureaucrats group might have a dual structure. It would be a good situation for China in the transition period that the traditional bureaucrats' group has changed to be a dual structure. Countries in systemic transition have to experience a dual structure in various aspects. In the ferry boat called dual structure, relations between the new and old system are the same situation as the 'bitter enemies in the same boat'.

The details of a dual structure in the bureaucrats' group are as follows. (1) In the aspects of domestic politics and administration, particularly in the monetary and financial aspects (as mentioned above), a civilized bureaucrats' group with enough international sense has gradually came into existence, which has usually been called a scholarly type of bureaucrats and has corresponded to the Taiwanese technocrats from the 1950s to the 1980s. Meanwhile, however, (2) in local politics and the regional economy, the traditional way to select bureaucrats is kept unchanged. The quality of the local bureaucrats' group might not be enough. In order to have a well managed regional economy and society, as they have a serious shortage in logical minds and knowledge, there could quite often occur wrong affairs. Local government's case in which, neglecting public welfare problems, they are busy to get money from the development boom, is a typical example. Also, ignoring the central government's position attaching greater importance upon the three agricultural problems, high ranking local government officials usually know nothing about the helpful way to use money to eliminate the three agricultural problems.[54]

Why have such differentiated phenomena occurred? In the international aspects, when China has progressed in the way of an extroverted market economy, central government's politics and economic policy (particularly upon financial aspects) have been linked with and suffered from the international economy. As a matter of fact, therefore, in China there have already been unmanageable situations without experts. However, in the internal aspects, China has still been at the stage of an industrialized development, in which manufacturing has been a major industry in each regional economy. Also, the main industry of Chinese manufacturing has been the processing industry, whose characteristics are low value added productivity. Based upon cheap labor and cheap land cost, attracting capital can easily contribute to increased GDP, which secures the promotion of

54 According to the author's interview at several places in coastal areas, a certain head of local government said with complaints that the hardest work every year was to use up too much of the budget.

local government's bureaucrats. The above-stated actual management of the regional economy could be dealt with by traditional bureaucrats.

The situation changed substantially at the end of the 1990s. Urbanization was accelerated, and various social contradictions (such as land requisitioned problems) clearly existed, and institutional reform has become indispensable. Acceleration of the economic growth has promoted differentiation of social strata, and the propertied classes have been coming into existence in China. In order to deal with the new situation, the fourth constitutional amendment was carried out in 2004. The Real Right Act was signed at the National Parliament on March 2007. With the evolution of urbanization after 1999, a real estate bubble has occurred all over the nation. Price soaring phenomena of housing were closely connected with corruption by bureaucrats, which was a serious cause of dissatisfaction of Chinese people.

Economic development has become a driving force of social mobility and it is necessary for keeping social stability to promote capable bureaucrats. However, because the organizational structure of bureaucrats is established with a pyramidal shape, the number of bureaucrats at the top is relatively smaller. Although, therefore, when the president, like Zhou Xiaochuan, displayed leadership and reshuffling personnel of a particular organization was possible, in the local area there are an enormous number of bureaucrats and it might be impossible to reform the bureaucrats' group by the head of governmental organization. In China, which has the dual structure phenomena of bureaucrats group, it is indispensable to reform radically the executive selection system.

(7) Possibility of success of bureaucrats in law and politics: a symposium on the role of lawyers in the political reform in China On June 2, 2005, a joint symposium of the Carnegie Endowment for International Peace and Asian Foundation entitled 'the role of lawyers in the political reform in China' was held. The head of the International Cooperation Section of the Chinese Ministry of Justice, Gong Bing, indicated after his retrospective on the role of lawyers in USA that, in the phenomena of ruling the country by technocrats in China, there are many wrong recognitions about the role of lawyers (the number of professional lawyers in China is around 120,000) and mentioned a critical view that many political leaders have negative opinions on the lawyers who are unrelated with politics or are politically heterogeneous.

Also, Jerome Cohen, who is a Professor of New York University and an expert of legal problems in China, gave comments as follows; not only the USA but also the former USSR had political leaders coming from professional lawyers. Lenin appeared in court as a lawyer. In the early stage of Soviet administration, there were leaders from the judicial world. Gorbachev was also from the judicial world (he also had a degree in agricultural economics). However, of the Chinese leaders group, nobody is from the judicial world and nobody is knowledgeable about the law. Recently, when the members of the Central Political Bureau were adjusted, the Chief Justice of the Chinese Supreme Court, Xiao Yang,[55] could not become the member of Central Political Bureau, whose place was occupied by an executive[56] in charge of National Security.

An interesting thing for us as regards the argument was that the bureaucrat of the Chinese Ministry of Justice emphasized his own views at the symposium held in the USA. In the authoritarian system, because the Ministry of Justice has been under various restrictions originally given by the Chinese Constitution similar to the National Parliament, they have been longing for judicial independence. It is uncertain for us whether or not the aim of participation in the symposium of the bureaucrat of the Chinese Ministry of Justice was to make use of the pressure from abroad. However, we might say that, in the process of Chinese economic development, their consciousness which was suppressed for long years started to be awakened. Similarly, the executive committee of the parliament in Chinese local areas (Chinese people's representatives hold additional posts and they participate in the National Parliament once a year, whose session lasts less than ten days; thus, the executive committee has been established as a standing organization) has become more self-assertive. The more advanced the region, the more self-assertive. For example, in Wenling city of Zhejiang province, in which a market-oriented economy fairly developed, the implementation of a democratic conference system, which was established to supervise the government budget, is paid attention.

There were other interesting things discussed at the conference. As stated earlier, the phenomena of ruling the country by technocrats would be an inevitable result of the authoritarian system. In China, they started with the days of ruling countries by technocrats, and also have now a shifting tendency from technocrats to bureaucrats in economy and finance, which raises a question of whether technocrats' days at the stage without enough successful results will result in challengers, bureaucrats in economy and finance? Expectations for lawyers to play roles in political reforms in China means rapidly promoting institutional democratization. What warnings are there behind it?

First, in the world of globalization, domestic economy and politics are necessary to deal with international difficulties resulting from environmental changes. As regards economic aspects, China has to overcome both the tasks of industrialized days (substantial everyday life for the people) and post-industrialized days (environmental protection). From the viewpoints of politics, contemporary China

55 Graduated from Renmin University of China (1962), Department of Law. He was the Minister of Justice from March 1993 to March 1998. In 1998 he took office as the Chief Justice of the Supreme Court.

56 Guo Boxiong, General of the People's Liberation Army, and the Vice Chief of Staff of Executive Director in the People's Liberation Army. In 1999, he was the member of the Central Military Committee of the Communist Party, and the member of the National Military Committee. He was selected as the member of the Central Political Bureau in 2002.

cannot have enough time, as Taiwan and South Korea had previously, and whose procedure indicates that first they developed with authoritarianism and technocrats, and then transformed towards a democratic and constitutional state. As stated before, the authoritarian systems of Taiwan and South Korea were tolerated by the USA because of the Cold War. Undoubtedly, China has its own advantage and is stronger against pressure from abroad than Taiwan and South Korea. However, everything has its limit. When China was the target of economic sanctions due to the Tian'an'men Affairs Incident in 1989, the sanctions worked substantially against China. After China participated in the WTO, such kind of sanctions will work more seriously.

With economic development in China, it might be recognized there is a deterioration of political corruption, economic disparity, environmental disruption, human rights problems, etc, but not everywhere. Those internal political events might damage the legitimacy of the authoritarian system. The Tian'an'men Affairs Incident in 1989 was the typical example, and the *Falungong* Affair at the end of 1990s had a serious effect on Chinese society.[57] Behind the above two affairs, various social problems are closely related. The bureaucrats' group which grew corrupt caused people's weak desire to have good government.

As regards internal and external pressure, Chinese politics at present needs more wisdom than before. In order to prevent corruption, the following reforms seem to be indispensable.

i. First is the reform of the selection system for executives. It is necessary to become free from dogmatic authority of party organizational division and to transform towards a more transparent system. Deficiency of the

57 Falun Dafa is a large-scale private organization whose aim is to practice a way of training the body and the spirit (it is said that membership reaches more than 10 million), which propagates the idea of a main doctrine of code and truth, goodness and patience, also which has also carried out openly opposite actions against the Chinese Communist Party (for example, on April 25, people were surprised to look at the protective activity when more than 10,000 believers sat down and surrounded the Zhongnanhai (the center of Chinese politics and place of residence of top ranking officials of the Chinese Communist Party). In July 1999, it was convicted of diabolical religion by the Chinese government (according to the announcement of the Chinese government, before July 1999, the number of dead persons of Falun Dafa from various reasons reached more than 1,400, of whom 136 Falun Dafa believers committed suicide because of the doctrine for disregarding life and death. In addition, Falun Dafa believers actively organized movements against the Chinese Communist Party to deviate from social order like surrounding governmental organizations and news media). Many believers, such as Li Hongzhi, the founder of Falun Dafa, defected to foreign countries. However, at present, Falun Dafa believers have carried out organized hostile actions against the Chinese Communist Party in foreign countries. For example, from June 2002 to August 2003, Falun Dafa organizations in foreign countries were jamming the satellite broadcasting of Chinese central TV, educational TV, and more than other ten local TVs, which was widely reported both at home and abroad.

current selection system for executives indicates the lack of a corruption prevention system. As shown in Figure 6.5, a committee for party discipline was established; however, because corruption events by secretaries of the committee for party discipline occurred rather often, the failure of this system might be clear to everyone.

ii. Second is the necessity of judicial independence to prevent corruption. We think it is not admissible that judicial judgment is replaced by the disciplinary punishment by the party.
iii. Third is to establish the self-assessment system of civil servant's asset. Because of the resistance of the vested interest group, the Chinese Public Servant Act revised in April 2005 could not include an article on the self-assessment system, which has rather shown the importance of it.
iv. Fourth is the necessity to establish an anti-corruption organization. In China, at present, there are several separate anti-corruption organizations, such as the Supervising Committee of Discipline, which is part of the Communist Party, Anti-Corruption and Anti-Bribe Agency which belongs to the Public Prosecutor's Office, and other divisions and agencies, like the Public Security Division and Inspection Agency, which take part in investigations of corruption. We think it is necessary to establish a high ranking unified anti-corruption organization for which only the supreme director is responsible, like the Independent Commission Against Corruption (ICAC) of Hong Kong. The ICAC of Hong Kong carries out investigation and collects evidence against corruption; however, ICAC has no authority to charge whose responsibility is given to another governmental organization, The Agency of Judging Politics. Thus, the power of ICAC is quite limited. Moreover, a reciprocal checking power system with another agency effectively works. Also, such an anti-corruption organization should be supervised by society (with establishing an institution to report to parliament, ombudsman and a supervising committee of citizens).
v. Fifth is to advocate the 'zero tolerance culture against corruption' in Chinese society. Nowadays in China, a current saying that corruption is a Chinese culture might be recognized. That way of citizens' attitude promotes corruption. A good way to change the current thinking is, we think, that school education should include anti-corruption education.
vi. Sixth is to have guidance for detailed regulations covering the execution of government official's duties. Citizens should pay careful attention to the corruption.

The legitimacy of an authoritarian system in China might be seriously damaged by corruption rampant in the society. Effective anti-corruption methods should be established. Meanwhile, however, introducing the above-mentioned anti-corruption measures might change the characteristics of the authoritarian system, which would lead to a result saying that an authoritarian system is opposed to an authoritarian system.

Conclusion

Suggestions by the two authoritarian development models

The legitimate bases of an authoritarian system are (1) high speed economic growth and (2) shared growth. In this chapter we compare the inward-looking Southeast Asian model with the outward-looking Asian NIEs model. The latter succeeded both in high speed economic growth and shared growth, meanwhile, the former succeeded in high speed economic growth but is still far away from shared growth. It is also worried about income disparity expansion, which might hinder more economic development. For example, lack of enough domestic demand becomes an obstacle for production increase. As is well known, shared growth is not only the final goal of development but also the necessary condition for sustainable development.

East Asian NIE countries and regions realized the peaceful transformation of a power structure, which became possible by rational authoritarianism of high ranking officials and by the support of the middle class. The creation of lots of middle class citizens was the result of shared growth. How was the shared growth realized to make modernization of human beings and industry coexist? It is indispensable to carry out a rational development strategy (such as an outward-looking strategy towards a market oriented economy) and institutional reform (such as land reform at the initial stage). Those successful strategies were established by rational leaders and rational technocrats. They acquired lots of experiences, knowledge and culture in domestic and foreign societies, which led them to a flexible way of thinking, coordinated with the external world. Bureaucrats in Taiwan and South Korea implemented a successful export-oriented strategy harmonized with the international economy, and they succeeded in the appropriate position of them in the postwar international order led by the USA (see Figure 6.7). It was the exact opposite of Southeast Asia in which they were worrying about their dependent position. Even though there were some rational leaders and rational technocrats in Southeast Asia, they basically failed to open their economies due to complex religious and racial conflicts.

We mentioned in Chapter 5 various characteristics of economic aspects in the East Asian model, and in this chapter we stated various characteristics of political and administrative aspects in the East Asian model by explaining the Taiwanese experience. The following two are the most important.

We could recognize that both agricultural land reform and a local autonomy system at the early stage of development (1950s) were the bases to make an authoritarian system in Taiwan stable. Compared with Taiwan, South Korea was similar in carrying out agricultural land reform; however, as regards a political system, a direct election of the President was put into effect in an earlier period

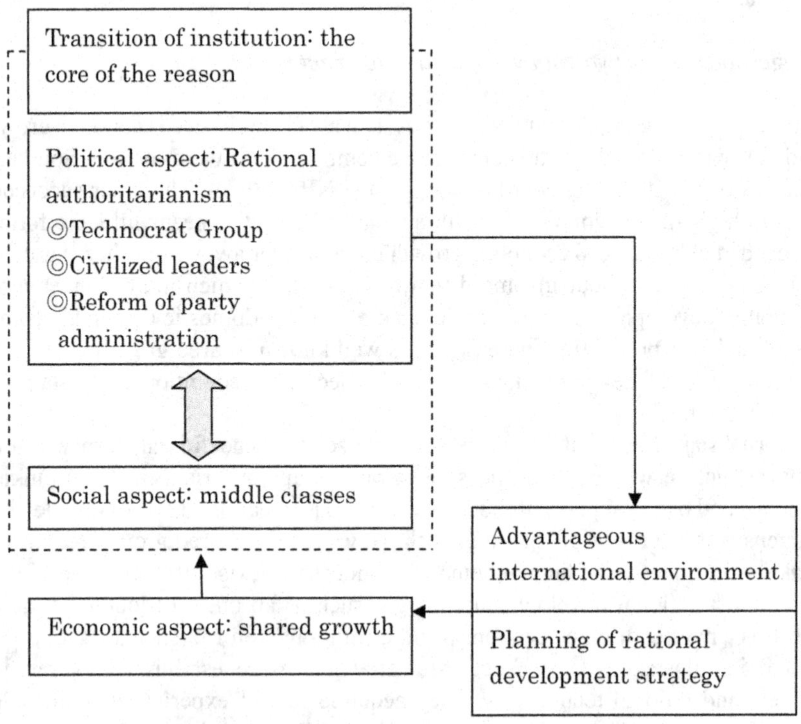

Source: Author.

Figure 6.7 Economic development and systemic transition in East Asian NIEs model

(1987) but direct elections in the local area were realized at a later period (1991).[58] The process of democratization in South Korea 'from the top to the bottom' was the opposite of the Taiwanese democratization process of 'from the bottom to the top' (what is called a direct election of the President in Taiwan was implemented in 1996 for the first time). The difference of democratization process of South Korea from Taiwan might be related with an economic development model in which

58 On February 25, 1988, Roh Tae Woo was installed as the Thirteenth President. During his term of office, several changes in political structure appeared. For example, although the authority of Parliament and independence of the Supreme Court was reinforced, the authority of the President was reduced. A local autonomy system was restored. A local autonomy system, which was established in the Syngman Rhee administration was left abandoned since the Park Chung Hee administration started. In May and June in 1991, two locally autonomy government level parliament elections were carried out.

the chaebol (South Korean zaibatsu) played the central roles. That is, because at the election of the President, the chaebol could work better than inconsistent ordinary people, and also because the chaebol contributed to the relative stability of the political situation and for the maintenance of an authoritarian system. To the contrary, the Taiwanese model of economic development could be said to be small and medium sized enterprises, which played important roles, and which might be related with a local autonomy system. However, even though we could recognize significant causal relationships between an authoritarian system and industrial structure, it might be difficult to judge scientifically the cause and effect of the two (for example, according to the Marxist theory they say the economic structure decides the political structure, which might be plausible). Moreover, we would continue to ask reasons why the industrial structure of each country and region has been different?

Under the outward-looking market-oriented system, a group of technocrats were promoted to political leaders and administrative executives. At the institutionally less developed stage, those technocrats demonstrated their institutional rationality and moral independence, which played a kind of substitute of an immature institution. Accompanied by the evolution of a socio-economic system to be more complicated, in order to have better governance, the wisdom of the technocrats' group was never enough, which led to the active involvement of civil society for public policy. It could be recognized as a prelude to political democratization. In line with the social tendency, institution building, particularly the establishment of legal order, became a central task for the society, also in concert with which characteristics of top leaders and bureaucrats transformed from science and technology to law and politics.

In addition to the above, the East Asian NIE countries and regions have some similar social characteristics, examples of which are as following.

- They are racially homogeneous countries and regions, which seemed to contribute to promotion and maintenance of social centripetal force.
- They have polytheism. It might come from Confucian supremacy, which contributed to social generosity.
- They are small sized countries and regions, which became easier for them to sustain social uniformity. For example, as symbolized by 'all Japanese belong to the middle class', it is easy to realize shared growth. However, it might actually not be natural. There are many countries that are small sized and have substantial disparity. Moreover, Japan is not, as a matter of fact, a small sized country, because Japan has around 130 million population (but compared with China, Japan is much smaller).

As regards external environments for East Asian NIE model countries and regions, we could recognize common characteristics.

In particular, they have been supported by the USA directly or indirectly. Both South Korea and Taiwan have been directly supported by the USA, to the contrary

Hong Kong and Singapore were contributed to by the USA for their export market and for developing their technocrats.

Chinese tasks

Can China become a member of the East Asian model? Analysis of two Asian models gave China careful suggestions indicating that, without establishing a human being centered model of economic development, it is impossible to have successful modernization and successful systemic transition.

By Deng Xiaoping's reform and open door policy, China gained the initial logic towards an outward-looking market economy. However, it was only a necessary condition but not a sufficient condition. In this chapter, in light of a shared growth concept we have analyzed the problems of Chinese society from the viewpoints of (1) relations between the urban and rural, and (2) characteristics of bureaucrats, which lead us to the following concluding remarks.

First, as stated before, there are serious differences in the industrialization ratio between production and employment. We should emphasize a necessity to introduce an industrial policy attaching greater importance to employment, and policies related to rural areas to make peasants more active and freer (by such measures as land reform and a local autonomy system).

Second, since Deng Xiaoping's reform in 1978, China has still been a country ruled by technocrats in science and engineering. However, we could recognize substantial change from the end of the 1990s. Compared with the traditional ruling country by technocrats, bureaucrats in economy and finance have occupied their significant position in the Chinese administration. We think it has been caused by the development ideology towards an open economy and society. In China, an important necessity is to have experts in economics and social management and this has been recognized as an irreversible tendency. Meanwhile, at the same time, China has serious tasks to be overcome, which are (1) the dual structure of bureaucracy in a vertical administration strata and (2) corruption.

Third, in the days of globalization, inward-looking management of the economy and politics has become impossible. Internal problems might be received by international pressure. In addition, we could understand that, when China tries to solve the above stated problems, the logic saying an 'authoritarian system is opposed to authoritarian system' comes into existence.

Future of political systemic transition in China: open system and 'Birdcage fable'

In this book as a whole, we investigate the logics of transition and development in China. The priority of Chinese transition has extended one after another from the urban to rural, from coastal to inland, from private owned to state owned, from economy to politics. Taking into consideration the East Asian model, every scholar would pursue the future of Chinese development model by asking 'could economic liberalization lead to political democratization?' We do not avoid the crucial problem in this book and insist on the fact following mechanism of institutional change, in which the reset of the initial condition called an open system has been particularly important.

It reminds the author of this book of a short story he read many years ago, whose title he is unsure about but a tentative title could be 'a birdcage'. The hero of the story bought a wonderful birdcage and was satisfied with looking at it, but he did not intend to raise a bird. However, all the friends, neighbors, mail carriers etc, who visited his home always asked him; 'What did the bird do? Did the bird die?' He responded politely one by one at the beginning; 'No. I have never raised a bird'. The visitor then asked; 'Then, when will you raise a bird?' He answered; 'No. I do not have a plan to raise a bird' The visitor asked; 'Why don't you? Why have you bought such a wonderful birdcage even you don't intend to raise a bird?' The hero of this story who was tired from responding to the same questions finally reached a solution. He bought a bird. Since then he was never asked the persistent questions about a bird.

The birdcage fable we think might seem to connote a plausible explanation and future forecast of political democratization of China. 'What will the future of Chinese democratization be?' Or to be more concrete, 'What will the future of a Chinese parliamentary system be?' By looking back on the past, as regards democratic system design in China, we recognize that China has already had lots of fine birdcages. For example, they have such fine birdcages as a 'parliamentary system', and 'judicial system'. However, we could not find any suitable birds in respective birdcages yet. It is different for the years before 1978, at the present time when China opened the door for the external world, lots of guests and friends have visited China. They have always asked the question about 'that bird' taking into consideration various fine birdcages. Then what kind of response does China give to the visitors and what kind of behavior does China take? There are some possibilities. For example, (1) they authorities are tired of responding to the same questions and finally get angry, and turn the visitors away. After then nobody visits. (2) They are tired of responding to the same questions, and finally hide the birdcage or throw it away. However, the guests who know that China had the birdcage will wonder and ask; 'where is the birdcage?' (3) They are tired of responding to the same questions, and finally get birds, as that story says.

If the response is (1) above, it means that China would be back to the closed country (to be back before 1978). Chinese people are no longer interested in the Mao Zedong's era. Thus, it could not be chosen. If the response is (2), in China all institutions and organizations except administration offices and party organizations would be abolished. Chinese society would fail to function properly and would be completely paralyzed. Thus, if China selects the way of (2), it means China would run out of control and be ruined. If the response is (3), it indicates that China would establish more harmonized relations with international society. Because Chinese transition and development started by resetting the initial condition of the reform and open door policy, option (3) could be most probable.

Needless to say, it is not enough to infer so simply. In each chapter of this book we try to develop a concrete way of the process. Although the fact following mechanism of institutional change in the Chinese society has undoubtedly been caused by external pressures (like the influence of WTO affiliation), much deeper-rooted pressure has come from internal society. Such institutions as an executive committee of basic level parliament and a law court have the awakening of their logic for existence and have started to assert themselves. In the light of original institutional design, the birdcages, which have no reasonable contents thus far, have started to seek their own birds. Taking into consideration the open system, it should be careful that both internal pressure and external pressure have been unified.

Concluding Remarks: Gradual Way of Transition in China

After the new China was founded in 1949, China experienced the central planning system for around 30 years, and since the reform and open door policy (market oriented system) started, China has promoted it for about 30 years. There is a proverb in China, saying 'Sanshinian Hedong, Sanshinian Hexi' ('east of the river for 30 years, and west of the river for the next 30 years'), which means that prosperity or decline, and victory or defeat, fortune changes with time. China employed the gradual way of transition for 30 years after 1978, i.e. from 1978 to 2007, and if it has been the 30 years of compensation, starting again from the ultra leftist way for the previous 30 years (from 1949 to 1978), in the new 30 years, which starts in 2008 China, will approach a new world. In this book, we are very much aware of such a situation and analyze the pattern of transition and development China has followed.

The most important characteristic of the Chinese development model might be 'gradualism'. In this book we call the gradual way of transition in China the 'wisdom of creative destruction', and investigate the concrete evolution.

In this final chapter, as concluding remarks, we will touch various topics related to the Chinese gradual way of transition.

Characteristics of Chinese civilization and culture

China has, by itself, the 'feminine' aspects of a country of the East. In addition, during the period of high speed economic growth, there have appeared 'masculine' aspects in China, which look aggressive as a big country with significant energy and resource consumption. Actually, in the long history of China, there have been inside Chinese culture opposite ways of thinking (or philosophies), Confucianism and Taoism (or Buddhism), which have been in harmonized coexistence with each other.

The author left China for several years in the second half of the 1990s, and visited foreign countries such as Japan and other places. In comparison with other countries, China looked – even for the author – rather an enigmatic country. China was one of the four ancient civilization countries, and only China has inherited an ancient civilization (on the same earth and of the same races and of the same cultural tradition), which might be surprising. In the modern period, in Mao Zedong's era, the country accumulated lots of political failures; however, although China reached the very limit of collapse, it did not end in failure. We think China has a structure that is difficult to fall apart. Because China is a big country, substantial diversity could be accumulated, which might naturally cause a kind of law such as 'balance of power'.

It seems to be certain, when any power is increasing, an opposite power and a neutral power are raised in other places. For example, when Mao Zedong was alive, Zhou Enlai and Deng Xiaoping were also alive. In ancient days, Chinese dynasties continuously changed, and tragic and comic histories were repeated. Unless a nation state has its own spiritual adjustability, that nation state will become weak and die from high blood pressure. Then how can such spiritual adjustability be created?

The author has a way of thinking that Confucianism and Taoism (or Buddhism) has given not only a well balanced spiritual structure to China but has also supported the microscopic spiritual structure of the Chinese people, and the latter is looked at as the composition of the former. A Chinese person (particularly an intellectual) is usually a believer in Confucianism when he or she is younger, but after he or she ages, a Chinese person changes to be also a believer in Taoism (or Buddhism) as well as Confucianism. To be also a believer in Taoism (or Buddhism) plays a role to harmonize his or her excessive desire of success in life (led by Confucianism). Chinese people recognize that harmonization of positive and negative aspects (publicly and privately) is the key to improving health. From ancient days, Chinese people have a custom that they decorate the desk of a drawing room with a bottle on the left and a mirror on the right, to pursue 'peace of mind' (the same sound as a bottle and mirror in Chinese language). Thus, in another way of saying, it explains why Confucianism and Taoism (or Buddhism) were developed in ancient China; that is to say, because there is a necessity, then invention, development, and a more exact tendency is brought about.

If in one race (or one country) a positive spirit becomes too powerful, it might easily run out of control (for example, plunge into war). On the contrary, if a negative spirit becomes too influential, it might be too weak and easy to mistreat, which would easily lead to collapse (for example, the country is easy to occupy and to be colonize). As regards China, being an independent nation for some thousand years shows the nation's ability to adjust to surrounding environments.

The Chinese people, who live with Chinese civilization and a culture based upon the above spiritual structure, have enough ambitions to succeed in the world, which could reach the 'Spirit of Capitalism' as insisted upon by Weber. They have discussed the reasons why, in China, capitalism has never been developed all over the nation, although from dynastic days the bud of capitalism was recognized. We think the main reason for this is the transformation from an open system to a closed system (for example, the transformation from Song dynasty to Ming dynasty brought about systemic change).

Necessity and possibility of the gradual way of transition in China: comparisons with Central and Eastern Europe

It is not easy how to evaluate the adaptability of the gradual Chinese way of transition compared with the former socialist countries in Central and Eastern Europe. China has employed a gradual way of transition and such former socialist countries in Central and Eastern Europe as Poland and Czech Republic have selected a radical way of transition. What are the main reasons for each way of transition? We consider here the reasons why China has needed a gradual way and why, in China, it has been possible to choose the gradual way.

On the necessity of a gradual way of transition

As a social scientist, the author of this book positively evaluates the Chinese way of gradual transition. We could recognize various fundamental judgments on the necessities of a gradual way of transition. First of all, the transition pattern is closely related with the complexity and urgency of the surrounding circumstance. The more complex, the less urgent, the more gradual way of transition would be necessary. China is an ultra-big country, with 9.6 million square kilometers land area and a population of 1.3 billion. In addition, China is the biggest less developed and transition country in the world and so there could be recognized large scale variety – China has been suffering from an inconsistency problem. Thus, in the development pattern, we think a gradual way of transition could be applicable in China; however, at the same time, a radical way of reform was partly employed and in a timely way (as far as the urgent sector was concerned, the introduction of a family contract system in farming areas at the end of the 1970s was an example of radical reform).

Second, as regards the speed of transformation, the gradual way is undoubtedly slower than the radical way. However, even if the country proceeds with transition slowly and feebly, it proceeded steadily on its own. Progress might be more sure than a rapid step forward of countries, flying separately from the ground supported by a giant on both sides. There are two reasons we could indicate. (i) As China is the biggest giant country, it might be unrealistic for it to be supported by others on both sides. For smaller size countries, it is more probable to be supported by foreign countries and international society towards more a radical way of transformation. Examples might be postwar Japan and Taiwan. However, if the Japanese start towards modernization was recognized as beginning in 1868 (the Meiji Restoration), Japan it should be said was in the gradual way of reform. As far as Taiwan is concerned, due to the cession of territory after the Sino-Japanese War, Taiwan has developed as one country with Japan. Thus, the Taiwanese history of modernization could be dated back to the prewar period. In China, however, it might be impossible to carry out the systemic transition without self-reliance (meaning without internal incentive). No country could support the biggest size giant country enough, and self-reliance would be the only one way for China. (ii)

Human beings could neither regain their health nor undergo rehabilitation in the true sense unless they train their own muscles. The gradual way of transition might be parallel to a rehabilitation procedure. Although it is not beautiful to look at (for example, as stated in Chapter 6, industrialization with regard to the labor force industrialization ratio index is important, along with an authoritarian political system), it is surely indispensable in regaining one's health. By a gradual way of transition, China has been in the procedure to plant the incentive for transformation within Chinese society little by little, it is not good for the external world to let China employ radical measures.

Third, it is difficult to say that even the government has enough recognition about the way and the measures of transition. The central planning economy period gave us enough evidence of insufficient recognition of the government. The wise remarks by Deng Xiaoping, saying 'cross the river by finding out stones', seems to be thus the reasonable choice left for China. There have never existed any blueprints on the Chinese way of gradual transition. Although it is said to be the common recognition of Chinese people, it should be said as the desire to break away from the current situation with all their might. We think that such thoughts based on feelings are usually observed among people whose circumstances might be the worst, as the Todaro hypothesis asserts (indicating that rural workers in an absolute poverty situation move to urban areas regardless of the rate of employment in urban areas). It might be uncertain if there is something certain for them at the opposite side of the world. The future possibility depends upon such factors as an agreement between leaders and people in the transition process, and validity of the process of reform. During the procedure, full of uncertainty, we could always recognize the game between the players of reform and the targets of reform.

As stated above, we expect Chinese reform based upon gradualism would take many years, and due to the different conditions, other transition countries could have their own rationalities of the transition process.

On the possibility of a gradual way of transition

On the details we mentioned in Chapter 2 about the transformation of the start of the logic and the beginning of gradual reforms, complicated factors were working on them; in particular, the following three should be emphasized. (1) The huge disparity between China and the world, which came from the implementation of a central planning system for 30 years, from the new nation's establishment to the reform and open door policy. It means both crises of survival as the nation was placed in the predicament, and of serious rural areas inside the nation. (2) The slackly centralized system is the characteristic nature of China, and (3) the wisdom of Deng Xiaoping.

What are other reasons for successful Chinese gradual transition? The following two are remarkable in comparison with the situation of Central ad Eastern Europe.

First, there are large differences in traditional culture or popular culture between them. Gradual reform automatically displays the maintenance of an authoritarian system (led by a communist party). There are substantial differences in patience in authoritarianism between east and west. As regards Central and Eastern Europe, they had the popular feudal system before the Middle Ages, under which local decentralization had a long tradition. Thus, a socialistic centralization system was heterogeneous for them from the beginning. In particular, from the practical stage of socialism not the stage of theory, immaturity or figment of the system was exposed much more clearly, and the admired utopia was ruined. In Central and Eastern Europe, they tried to break away from socialism in the early days from the end of the Second World War, like Hungary in 1956.

Meanwhile, in China around the period of the third century BC (after the Qin dynasty and the Han dynasty built large empires), they established the history in which people endured an autocratic system. People were apt to understand not that liberty was given from birth but that authority was given from birth. Needless to say, they desired to have wise authority, like the saying of Qingtian Dalaoye (wise bureaucrats like a blue sky), and lots of traditional plays described such wise governors and bureaucrats as Bao Zheng (999–1062) and Hai Rui (1514–1587) whom every Chinese knows.[1] Even in these days such plays gain the sympathy of the Chinese people.

A contemporary tendency in China, emphasizing more sovereignty than human rights, has been closely connected with the historic characteristics. The main reason for European countries to be independent from the Roman Empire was to emphasize racial self-determination rights (which gave a broad interpretation of human rights). In addition, we could recognize a similar reason for the American Revolutionary War against the United Kingdom. As the saying goes, 'no taxation without representation', emphasizes individual rights for a colony formed to be independent. Meanwhile, in China, the foundation of a unified dynasty has been looked at as the inviolable rule (as the appropriate form), and they have recognized that unification has been normal and, independence and separation have been abnormal, a way of thinking that has reached these days. Under a giant centralized unified nation, we would not be surprised if individual human rights might be weak. However, there are still various problems to be investigated. For example, why must China be a centralized unified nation (necessity)? Why could China always be unified (possibility)? We will examine these later.

Second, in Europe, each country's size is not big, and most of them have land borders. In such an environment, they have a substantial learning effect or one another. A rebellious mind and radical way of transformation is easily diffused throughout Europe when they are caused in one country or region. There have existed environments in which people are mutually encouraged. However, in

1 As indicated in note 15 of Chapter 2, Bao Zheng (999–1062) was a prime minister of the Song dynasty (1271–1368), and Hai Rui (1514–1587) was of the Ming dynasty (1368–1644).

the biggest scale unified nation (China), it is difficult to have such effects. When they have the biggest scale unified nation for many years, a kind of super stable structure has been established. According to Jin Guantao and Liu Qingfeng (1984), a structure among peasant economy, Confucian culture, and political authoritarianism has been created to support one another. Thus, even dynastic changes were carried out every several decades or every several hundred years without exception; a newly established dynasty had no new basic framework and was the copy of the previous dynasty.

We could recognize in Chinese society a strange mix of a super stable structure and revolutionary spirit (as symbolically shown in the peasant uprising at the end of the dynastic period). There seems to be a kind of causal relation between the two. If there is, we could estimate some deficiencies in the Chinese super stable social structure. We will investigate them later.

The reasons to make a Chinese way of gradual transition possible and different from the European way of radical transition are as stated above, the difference of traditional culture and public culture to the European one, also the lack of substantial learning effects (caused by equal sized countries located on the borders of each other). Generally speaking, therefore, the Chinese gradual way of transition should not be recognized as an autonomous preference, but be recognized as a result caused by several factors.

Some remarks on the gradual way of transition

The legitimacy of an authoritarian development system could be coming from the realization of shared growth and institutional secured ability to meet people's needs.

There might be a few who make a protest against the Chinese gradual way of transition. However, the majority of Chinese people we think tacitly consent to the pattern of institutional transition. Most of the people who make a protest have experience in living out of China and, in the light of various ideas for development, they could not stand the conservative way of reform, called the gradual transition; to the contrary however, almost all Chinese people living within Chinese society are usually satisfied with a better situation compared with the past. High speed economic growth contributes to the improvement of everyday life of the Chinese people (meaning it contributes to Pareto improvement). 'To contribute always for social progress' (which indicates Pareto improvement) is the responsibility for leaders of the Communist Party, and is the roots of the legitimacy of administration. As regards contemporary China, because they have employed a gradual way of transition and have contributed to the improvement of Chinese people compared with the past, internal pressure to support a radical way of transition would fail. To contribute to an improvement of the everyday life of the Chinese people is, as a matter of fact, a fairly difficult task. As symbolized by the slogan of harmonized society, the main content of improvement should be to realize shared growth not only GDP growth, which is well recognized by the present Chinese leaders as of

2007. Also, serious tasks to be resolved are to prevent corruption and to harmonize growth with the environment.

We should understand correctly that because China is a big country, it causes more difficulties of Chinese transition on the one hand and also it enables Chinese strength to endure external pressure on the other. It might be better for external society to watch China with a warm heart and to give helpful external pressure. For human beings, when there is no pressure, there is no growth with them. Similarly, external pressures are necessary for nation states and races to grow. To keep up helpful external pressures to promote reform should be meaningful. As far as Chinese society after 1978 (especially after 2001) is concerned, as China has been closely connected with international politics and the economy, China has to receive external pressures. In Chapters 4, 5 and 6 of this book, we argue in detail that the characteristics of the Chinese development model and the fact following mechanism of institutional change are a compound type of internal politics and external relations. From the very beginning, the reform and open door policy at the end of 1978 was begun jointly by tremendous pressure, both internal and external.

Few years have passed since China made a comeback to international society. Thus, China has never actually been the giant it looks; rather, it has been immature psychologically. This unbalance between the physique and mentality has been closely related with the current situation as it is said to be immature in nation state building and immature in racialism. However, in the Chinese soil, which has four thousand years of history (of repetition of unification and division), there have been lots of hidden sources of wisdom. After the appearance into international society, China has been promoted to grow with various stimuli.

The future of Chinese national structure: rebuilding of the relations between central and local government

Ancient Chinese culture has been fascinating for many people. Meanwhile, contemporary China was less developed, and socialist ideology worked for China to be blocked from external eyes. China disappeared for many years from the international scene, which veiled China in mystery. At the same time, in the Chinese four thousand year history, with many complications, lots of problems, which are attractive for many people, were hidden. For example, as stated previously, why must China be a centralized unified nation (necessity)? Why could China always be unified (possibility)? Also could Chinese traditional repetition of unification and division be broken? Those problems are closely connected with one another.

Problem one: why must China be a centralized unified nation?

In China, they understand that a unified state is normal and independence and separation is abnormal, a recognition that has lasted till nowadays. In Chinese language, the process of dynastic change is described as 'Zhiluan Xunhuan' (meaning peace, war, and circulation). A unified state points out the 'peace', independence and separation indicates the 'war'. There are various explanations on the reasons why such concepts are made.

First, there were workings as the model of a giant empire which was established by the First Emperor of Qin dynasty in the third century BC, which were closely related with the following two reasons.

Second, such soft power as weights and measures, unification of languages, Confucian culture became the base for the centralized unified nation, which worked as an intermediary between the two dynasties. Inside the country, there are always powers for separation; however, culture in a wide sense works as a centripetal force and adhesive. The previously mentioned super stable structure theory explains roughly the same thing. There could be indicated a similar example, when in Western Europe in the 17th and 18th century, a movement developed towards nation state building, in the center of which culture played a main role (Nakamasa, 2006).

Third, a more deep-rooted reason might be given by tasks for survival, which means that independence and separation indicate more risk for the outbreak of war. A unified nation would surely be wishful to avoid risks. A unified nation thus plays a role as a safety-net similar to collective military security. In West European society, on the contrary, sovereign nations could defend their security by the power balance strategy. In other words, ancient China implemented the hegemony theory. It might not be a matter of right or wrong; the Chinese continent and European continent undoubtedly employed a different development pattern under different circumstances. On the Chinese continent, because they selected a centralized unified nation as a means of collective military security, the delayed development of human rights could be interpreted as the cost paid to the selection (as discussed previously).

Problem two: why could China always be unified?

China has huge land area, about the same as Europe as a whole, in which the country finally reached unification even though it experienced a cycle of unification and division. These results were led by which power and in which framework? Although flood control theory could explain the necessity of a centralized unified nation in China to some extent, could the possibility be secured by any theory? When there is a demand, a market would certainly produce supply (for example, a national hero of the period). Could such a simple explanation be satisfactory?

In contemporary society, they could control floods by technological development to some extent. Therefore, is a centralized unified system unnecessary? In the ancient world, a centralized unified nation was preferred to various separated small nations due to the purpose of collective military security. However, in contemporary society, as the right of belligerency has been taken away by the United Nations based upon the international treaty, small nations could secure their safety. Such various factors might suggest ways of change in Chinese national structure in the future.

Problem three: could the Chinese traditional repetition of unification and division be broken?

There is an expression in China saying 'Daluan Dazhi' (meaning a repetition of greatly disordered days and greatly prospered days). It could be interpreted that greatly disordered days were followed by greatly prospered days, or, to the contrary, it could also be interpreted that greatly prospered days were followed by greatly disordered days. The meaning of 'Daluan Dazhi' thus might be similar to the meaning of 'east of the river for 30 years, and west of the river for the next 30 years'. Could what those expressions symbolize be broken by evolution of an institutional apparatus?

We should here explain a little more about a revolutionary way and reformist way. In the United Kingdom, a reformist way or revolution without bloodshed (like the Glorious Revolution) was preferred. We recognize that in the United Kingdom, civilization and culture have been handed down to contemporary society, during which civilization and culture have been accumulated and have evolved. On the contrary, the evolution of Chinese civilization and culture has always been interrupted by revolution, which occurred at the end of dynastic days (peasant uprising), which has been just like the repetition of construction and destruction of building blocks. It should be pointed out that the height of the building blocks remained the same as before although various culture factors were changed. As the result, the Chinese civilization and culture surely developed; however, it could not break away unaided from the ancient agricultural civilization before the Opium War occurred. What were main reasons?

A highly centralized unified nation could have an ability to survive if the nation could have certain openness. The openness has two aspects. The first is an external openness. Historically, all the prospered dynasties (like the Han dynasty and the Tang dynasty) were open. The moving environment necessarily requests the advanced ability to govern and to make policy; however, the governor's group with no competition has no incentive to do this. The first monarch of the new dynasty who could survive in these disorderly days and who won a victory had enough ability and sufficient wariness and also had enough insight and courage to construct an open system. Because the right of succession system was based upon blood (especially given priority to the eldest son) it was a non-competitive institutional arrangement, and the successor therefore could not necessarily have such insight, courage, ability as the first monarch. Accompanied by an open system, the easiest way to confront challenges was to withdraw tasks, just as an ostrich supposedly hides its head in the sand when an enemy is chasing.

The second aspect of openness is the necessity of openness between basic level society and the higher level governing group. The *Keju* (meaning the imperial examinations) started from the Sui dynasty, and the Tang dynasty worked for many years as an institution to select talented persons from Chinese society and contributed to the stable governance of premodern Chinese society. Simultaneously, as stated in Chapter 4, the autonomous space lower than county level could be recognized as a certain wisdom for governance (indicating that utilizing the social capital of 'Xiangshen', local administrative institution, contributed to the maximum benefit with cost minimization). Needless to say, 'monopoly', which could be an attribute of a centralized system, would be certainly confronted with 'openness'. The occurrence of excessive tax collection and corruption, etc, suffocated the inside of Chinese society and, as a result, China alwayss suffered from a cycle of disorderly days and prosperous days.

In that sense, the peasant uprising at the end of dynasty period could be recognized as a general cleaning of a passage that was suffocated till then. We think Eckstein's assertion was plausible, saying that, although the peasant uprising in the dynastic period in China was called a peasant revolution, it was not so revolutionary (Eckstein, 1977). How could China break away from the cycle of disorderly days and prosperous days?

As China could not secure openness, the Chinese pattern had to be classified as an accumulated pattern of building-block type civilization. In order to break away from the accumulated pattern of building-block type civilization whose building blocks' height remained the same as before, we think rebuilding of a national structure (relations between central and local) should be indispensable. The wisdom of an accumulated pattern of bamboo-type civilization (reformism) of the United Kingdom could be a helpful lesson for China.

Generally speaking, the repetitive drama of unification and division seems to be coming from a lack of institutional innovation. To be specific, the possibilities of a national structure of the Chinese continent are not only bipolarization patterns, either a centralized united nation or variously separated small nations (unfortunately they have been actual so far). For example, we recognize the views, held for a long time, that a federal system was adaptable to a big country's governance. Also, many countries, of both a federal system and single system (countries such as the United Kingdom, Germany, and France) have introduced a constitutionally locally autonomous system since the 17th century and 18th century. Such wisdom upon governance causes both positive aspects coming from a united community on the one hand and harmony between central and local coming from local autonomy on the other. Also, in ancient China, even if it might not be conscious, we surely understand the existence of such wisdom (see Chapter 4). It would be crucial, we think, that in order to rebuild the nation state to contribute to the harmonized society, China could put such wisdom to practical use.

Conclusion

The transition and development in contemporary China has evolved rather compositely because of the restriction on time and space. A great variety of colors can made using combinations of only the three primary colors: similarly, a great variety of researches regarding China is possible by considering the circumstances with which China has been confronted. Because research topics have been composite, scholars on Chinese problems find it necessary to investigate more creatively and with more interdisciplinarity. For example, intellectual ability comes and goes regardless of time, space, and traditional academic discipline, and analytical ability to see through phenomena correctly, easily disturbs ordinary people's viewpoints. When we ask the question of what systemic transition is, a much deeper-rooted answer might be the 'transition of human beings' (including scholars themselves).

The author is reminded of Sisyphus, a tragic ancient Greek God. In the face of extremely difficult tasks, e.g. Chinese systemic transition, the author's actual feeling might be similar to that of Sisyphus who could not reach the top of the mountain. However, the author has kept on challenging, like Sisyphus. There is one significant difference between the author and Sisyphus. Sisyphus pushed stones passively under the penal code. The author understands the life of a scholar as a providence and has pushed up stones voluntarily. However, is what we say correct in a true sense? Such instinct of scholars might be a kind of penalty. Human beings call for something from society, which constitutes the 'original sin'. All human beings compensate for the original sin by various forms (by their jobs). Human beings are both demanders and suppliers; rather, human beings should be suppliers.

According to the Greek mythology, Sisyphus could find a way to be extricated from the penal code. He pushed up stones in different ways each time and on his way back he played with butterflies. With such ways he was able to enjoy the endless penalty. It is not important whether or not it is a passive or voluntary, providence or penalty. Let us understand a penalty as a providence and let us make our own life as a scholar enjoyable.

Selected Bibliography

Adorno, Theodor W., Frenkel-Brunswik, Else, Levinson, Daniel J. and Sanford, R. Nevitt (1950) *The Authoritarian Personality*. New York: Harper & Row.

Aoki, Masahiko, Kim, Hyung-Ki and Masahiro Okuno-Fujiwara (eds) (1996) *The Role of Government in East Asian Economic Development: Comparative Institutional Analysis*. New York: Oxford University Press.

Ash, Timothy Garton (2002) *The Polish Revolution: Solidarity*. New Haven: Yale University Press.

Aslund, Anders (1994) Lessons of the first four years of systemic change in Eastern Europe. *Journal of Comparative Economics*, 19.

Bank Negara Malaysia, *Quarterly Economic Bulletin*, Kuala Lumpur, quarterly.

Baran, Paul A. (1968) *The Political Economy of Growth*. New York, Monthly Review Press.

Berliner, Josef S. (1994) Perestroika and the Chinese model. In Robert Campbell (ed), *The Postcommunist Economic Transformation*. Colorado: Westview Press.

Bo Qingjiu (ed) (2001) *Difang Zhenfu Yu Zizhi* (*Local Government and Autonomous System* (5th edn)). Taibei: WunanTushu Chubanshe Publishing.

Brus, Wlodzimierz (1972) *The Market in a Socialist Economy*. London: Routledge and Kegan Paul.

Cao Jinqing (2000) *Huanghebian De Zhongguo* (*China on the bank of Yellow River*). Shanghai: Shanghai Wenyi Chubanshe Publishing.

Carter, Jimmy (2003) From May 4th Movement to village Elections: China's quest for democracy Speech at the Peking University, September 9.

Central Commission of Supervising Group for Chinese Agricultural Policy and the Ministry of Land and Resources (2002) *Guanyu Wanshan Zhengdi Zhidu De Diaoyan Qingkuang Ji Zhengce Jianyi* (*Investigation and Policy Proposal on Land Requisition System*). Beijing.

Chen Shaofang (2006) Qingdai Difang Xiangcun Zhili De Chuantong Tezheng (The Traditional Features of the Local Administration of Rural Society in Qing Dynasty). *Jingang Xuekan* (*Academic Journal of JingYang*), No.3.

Chen Xiwen (ed) (2003) *Zhongguo Xianxiang Caizheng He Nongmin Zengshou Wenti Yanjiu* (*A Study on the Chinese Local Government Budget and the Problem of Income Increase of Peasants*). Shanxi: Shanxi Jingji Chubanshe Publishing.

Chen Yingfang (2006) Shanghai ni okeru kosekiseido to toshi hinkon (Family registration system and poverty in urban area in Shanghai). In Shindo Muneyuki (supervisor) and Goishi Norimichi (eds), *Higashi Ajia Daitoshi no*

Global ka to Nikyoku bunka (*Globalization and Polarization of the East Asian Big Cities*). Tokyo: Kokusai Shoin Publishing.

Chen Yuanxie (1951) Woguo Gongye Quwei Peizhi Wenti De Tantao (An analysis of regional allocation of industrial district in China). *Zhongguo Gongye* (*Chinese industry*), 3 (new version), No. 8.

Chen Yun (2005) Dongya Zhixu Zhong De Meiguo Yinsu He Dongya Guojia De Neixiangxing (American factors in Asian order and introversion of Asian countries). In Dai Xiaofu and Dingping Guo (eds), *Dongya Fazhan Moshi Yu Quyu Hezuo* (*East Asian Development Model and Regional Cooperation*). Shanghai: Fudan University Press.

Chen Yun (2006a) Guoji Maoyi Zhong De Huilv Zhendang Jiqi Dui Guonei Chanye Jieguo De Yingxiang (Exchange rate fluctuation in international trade and the impacts on domestic industrial structure. *Shijie Jingji Wenhui* (*World Economic Papers*) (Fudan University), 7.

Chen Yun (2006b) The economic development and regional disparity of the Yangtze River Delta. *Economic Papers* (Warsaw School of Economics), 40.

Chen Yun (2007a) Shangai ni okeru Jyutaku Seido no Kaikaku (Reforms of Housing System in Shanghai). In Shindo Muneyuki (supervisor) and Goishi Norimichi (eds), *Higashi Ajia Daitoshi no Boucho to Kanri* (*Expansion and Management of megalopolis in East Asia*). Tokyo: Kokusai Shoin Publishing.

Chen Yun (2007b) Tongzhi Yu Zizhi:Dongjingdu Goujian Xunhuanxing Shehui De Zhidu Fenxi (Central regulation and autonomy: an institutional analysis of circular type society building in Tokyo). In Su Zhiliang (ed), *Dongjing Yu Shanghai De Dushi Wenhua* (*Urban Culture of Tokyo and Shanghai*). Shanghai: Cishu Chubanshe Publishing.

Chen Yun (2008) Political Economy of the Chinese Development Model: The Fact Approving Mechanism of Institutional Change in Chinese Society. Economic Papers (Warsaw School of Economics), 43.

Chen Yun and Ken Morita (2005) Chugoku no Taiseiikou ni okeru Kaihatsu model no hensen to Shotoku kakusa: Chuou no Taiseiikou Keiro to no Hikaku Bunseki (Changes of development model and income disparities in systemic transition in China: comparative analysis with Central Europe). *The Hiroshima Economic Review*, 29(2).

Chen Yun and Ken Morita (2006) Development strategies and income disparities in China: comparisons with Central Europe. *Economic Papers* (Warsaw School of Economics), 40.

Chen Yun and Ken Morita (2009a) *Chugoku no Taisei Ikou to Hatten no Seijikeizaigaku (Political Economy of Transition and Development in China*), Tokyo, Taga Shuppan Publishing.

Chen Yun and Ken Morita (2009b) *Political Economy of Development in China: Comparisons with Japan, New Jersey,* World Scientific Publishing.

Chen Yun and Tsuneichi Toda (2001) Yangtze River Delta no Keizai Kaihatsu to Chiiki Kakusa ni kansuru Jisshoteki Bunseki (The economic development and regional difference of the Yangtze River Delta). *Chiiki Kenkyu* (*Regional Studies*) 31(3).

Chen Zongshen (1995) *Jingji Fazhanzhong De Shouru Fenpei* (*Income Distribution and Economic Development*). Shanghai: Shanghai Renmin Chubanshe Publishing.

Chinese Academy of Social Sciences (2005a) *2005nian Jingji Lanpishu* (*Blue Book on Chinese Economy in 2005*). Beijing: Shehui Kexue Wenxian Chubanshe Publishing.

Chinese Academy of Social Sciences (2005b) *Guanyu Xibu Diqu Jingji Jiegou Tiaozheng He Tese Chanye Fazhan De Yanjiu* (*A Study on Western Region Economic Structural Adjustment and the Development of Special Characteristic Industries*). Beijing, Western Region Development Research Center (Chinese Academy of Social Sciences).

Chinese Bank Regulatory Commission (2007a) *Zhongguo Yinghangye Duiwai Kaifang Teji* (*Special section about the opening to external world of Chinese banking sector*). http://www.cbrc.gov.cn/chinese/info/twohome/index.

Chinese Bank Regulatory Commission (2007b) *Zhonnguo Yinhangye Duiwai Kaifang Baogao* (*A Report on the opening to external world of Chinese banking sector*) (March) http://www.cbrc.gov.cn.

Chinese Cabinet Development Research Center (1995) *Chugoku no Chiiki Kaihatsu Senryaku ni kansuru Kenkyu: Chugoku no Chiiki Keizai Kaihatsu (1)* (*A Study on Regional Development Strategy in China: Regional Economic Development in China (1)*). Tokyo: National Institute for Research Advancement (NIRA).

Chinese Cabinet Development Research Center (The Eleventh Five Year Plan Research Group) *Guanyu Dishiyige Wunian Guihua Dao 2020 niajian, Zhongguo Jingji Shehui Fazhan Zhongde Tuchu Maodun, Jiben Renwu, Weilai Fangxiang He Zhengce Zouxiang De Baogao* (*Inside Report on prominent contradiction, basic duties, future aim and policy orientation during the period of the Eleventh Five Year Plan and 2020*). Beijing: Chinese Cabinet Development Research Center.

Chinese Entrepreneur Research Association (1997) Dangqian Woguo Qiye jingyingzhe Dui Jili Yu Yueshu Wenti Kanfa De Diaocha (A Research about the views of Chinese enterprise managers on the problems of incentive and restraint: Special research report on growth and development of Chinese enterprise managers 1997). *Guanli Shijie* (*Management World Monthly*), 4.

Chinese Ministry of International Economy and Trade (ed) (1985) *Zhongguo Duiwai Jingji Maoyi Nianjian* (*Chinese Bulletin of International Economy and Trade*). Beijing: Zhongguo Shuili Dianli Chubanshe Publishing.

Chinese Statistical Office (Annual) *Zhongguo Tongji Nianjian* (*Chinese Statistical Bulletin*). Beijing.

Chinese Statistical Office (Annual) *Zhongguo Chengshi Tongji Nianjian* (*Chinese Urban Statistical Bulletin*). Beijing.

Chinese Statistical Office (Annual) *Zhongguo Jinrong Nianjian* (*Chinese Financial Bulletin*). Beijing.

Chinese Statistical Office (Annual) *Zhongguo Laodong Tongji Nianjian* (*Chinese Labor Statistical Bulletin)*. Beijing.

Dangdai Zhongguo Jihua Gongzuo Bangongshi (Bureau of Contemporary Chinese Planning Policy) (ed) (1987) *Zhonghua Renmin Gongheguo Guomin Jingji He Shehui Fazhan Jihua Dashi Jiyao 1949-1985* (*History of Socio-Economic Development Plan of People's Republic of China 1949-1985*). Beijing: Hongqi Publishing.

Deng Xiaoping (1983) *Deng Xiaoping Wenxuan* (*Collective Works of Deng Xiaoping) Vol.2*. Beijing: Renmin Chubanshe Publishing.

Deng Xiaoping (1987) Banhao jingji Tequ, Zengjia Duiwai Kaifang Chengshi (Towards better construction of special economic zones and more establishment of open cities and towns: lecture in 1984). In Deng Xiaoping, *Jianshe You Zhongguo Tese De Shehuizhuyi* (*Construction of the Chinese Socialism (revised version)*). Beijing: Renmin Chubanshe Publishing.

Deng Xiaoping (1993) *Deng Xiaoping Wenxuan* (*Collective Works of Deng Xiaoping) Vol.3*. Beijing: Renmin Chubanshe Publishing.

Dickens, Charles (1989) *Tale of Two Cities*. New York: Bantam Classics.

Dobb, Maurice (1946) *Studies in the Development of Capitalism*. London: Routledge.

Domar, Evsey D. (1957) *Essays in the Theory of Economic Growth*. Westport: Greenwood Press.

Dong Zhenghua, Ziyong Zhao *et al*. (1999) *Toushi Dongya De Qiji* (*Readings on the East Asian Miracle*). Shanghai: Xuelin Chubanshe Publishing.

Du Runsheng (1998) *Du Runsheng Wenji (1980-1998)* (*The Collected Works of Du Runsheng (1980-1998))*. Shanxi: Shanxi Jingji Chubanshe Publishing.

Eckstein, Alexander (1977) *China's Economic Revolution*. Cambridge: Cambridge University Press.

Economic Planning Board (EPB) (1970) *Korea Statistical Yearbook 1970*, Seoul.

Eringer, Robert (1982) *Strike for Freedom: The Story of Lech Walesa and Polish Solidarity*. New York: Dodd Mead.

Fan Gang (1993) *Jianjin Zhilu:Dui Jingji Gaige De Jingjixue Fenxi* (*Gradual Way of transition: An Analysis of Economic Reforms*). Beijing: Zhongguo Shehui Kexue Chubanshe Publishing.

Fan Gang (1997) *Jianjin Gaige De Zhengzhi Jingjixue Fenxi* (*Political Economy of Gradual Reforms*). Shanghai: Yuandong Chubanshe Publishing.

Fang Weizhong (ed) (1984) *Zhonghua Renmin Gongheguo Jingji Dashiji (1949~1980)* (*On the Details of the Economy of the People's Republic of China (1949~1980)*). Beijing: Zhongguo Shehui Kexue Chubanshe Publishing.

Fe'ldman, Grigorii A. (1928) On the theory of rates of growth of the national income. *Planovoe Khozyaistvo* (*Planned Economy*).

Fei Xiaotong (1988) *Xiangtu Zaijian* (*Reconstructing Hometown*). Tianjin: Tianjin Renmin Chubanshe Publishing.

Fei Xiaotong (1998) *Xiangtu Zhongguo* (*Hometown China*). Beijing: Peking University Press.

Fei, John C.H., Ohkawa Kazushi and Gus Ranis (1986) Keizai Hatten no Rekishiteki Perspective: Nihon, Kankoku, Taiwan (Historical Perspective of Economic Development: Japan, South Korea and Taiwan). In Ohkawa Kazushi (ed), *Nihon to Hattentojyoukoku* (*Japan and Less Developed Countries*). Tokyo: Keisoshobou Publishing.

Georgescu-Roegen, Nicholas (1971) *The Entropy Law and the Economic Process*. Cambridge: Harvard University Press.

Glushkov, Victor and Vitali A. Moev (1976) *Computer to Shakaishugi* (*Computer and Socialism*) (Japanese edition, translated by Yuzo Tanaka). Tokyo: Iwanami Publishing.

Greenfeld, Lian (2001) *The Spirit of Capitalism: Nationalism and Economic Growth*. Cambridge: Harvard University Press.

Gu Wenfeng (2006) *Yige Xiangzhen Shuji De Meng Yu Tong* (*Dream and Distress of a Certain Secretary of Town and Village-level Local Party*). Beijing, Xinhua Chubanshe Publishing.

Guo Wenjia (2003) Songdai Shehui Baozhang Jigou Jianlun (A theory of social security system in Song era). *Guangxi Shehui Kexue* (*Guangxi Social Science*), September.

Hamashita, Takeshi (1995) Chugoku Chiikikeizai Kaihatsusenryaku no Hensen (On the change of development strategy of regional economy in China). In National Institute for Research Advancement (Japan), *Chugoku no Chiikikaihatsu Senryaku ni kansuru Kenkyu: Chugoku no Chiikikeizai Kaihatsu (2)* (*A Study on Regional Development Strategy in China: Regional Economic Development in China (2)*). Tokyo: NIRA.

Hayami, Yujirou (1995) *Kaihatsu Keizaigaku* (*Development Economics*). Tokyo: Sobunsha Publishing.

He Xuefeng (2003) *Xin Xiangtu Zhongguo* (*New Hometown China*). Guangxi: Nanning Normal University Press.

Hicks, John R. (1969) *A Theory of Economic History*. Oxford: Clarendon.

Hirschman, Albert O. (1958) *The Strategy of Economic Development*. New Haven: Yale University Press.

Huang Junjie (1991) *Nongfuhui Yu Taiwan Jingji (1949–1979)* (*Agricultural Reconstruction Society and Experience in Taiwan (1949–1979)*). Taibei: Sanmin Shuju Publishing.

Huang Zongzhi (1994) *Huabei De Xiaoning Jingji He Shehui Bianqian* (*Peasant Economy and Social Change in Chinese Northern Region*). Hong Kong: Oxford University Press Hong Kong.

Huntington, Samuel (1968) *The Political Order in Changing Society*. New Haven: Yale University Press.

Imai, Satoshi (1985) Bouekitaisei Kaikaku no Genjyou to Kadai (Current situation and tasks of the reform of international trade system). In JETRO (Japan External Trade Organization), *Chugoku: honkakuka suru keizai kaikaku (China: towards full scale economic reform)* Tokyo: JETRO Publishing.

Institute of Developing Economies (1982) *International Input–Output Table for ASEAN Countries 1975*. Tokyo: Institute of Developing Economies.

Ishikawa, Shigeru (1980) *1980nendai no Chugoku Keizai* (*Chinese Economy in the 1980s*). Tokyo: The Japan Institute of International Affairs.

Ishikawa, Shigeru (1990) *Kaihatsu Keizaigaku no Kihon Mondai* (*Basic Problems of Development Economics*). Tokyo: Iwanami Publishing.

Ishikawa, Shigeru *et al.* (1974) *Chugoku no Kagakugijyutsu ni kansuru Ichikousatsu: Kagakugijyutsu Shigen no Jyuyou to Kyoukyu no Mechanism* (*An Analysis of Science and Technology in China: On a Mechanism of Demand and Supply of Science and Technology Resources*). Tokyo: Japan Economy Research Center.

Japan Institute of International Affairs (1974a) Chihou ni Dokuritsu shita Kougyoutaikei wo Uchitaterukoto ni tsuiteno Mao Zedong shuseki no danwa (The comments of the President Mao Zedong on establishment of independent industrial systems in local areas). *Chugoku Daiyakushin Seisaku no Tenkai (jyou)* (*The Great Leap Forward in China (first volume)*). Tokyo: The Japan Institute of International Affairs.

Japan Institute of International Affairs (ed) (1974b) *Shin Chugoku Shiryou Shusei5* (*Compilation of Materials on Contemporary China 5*). Tokyo: Japan Institute of International Affairs.

Japan-China Geographical Association (ed) (1992) *Ajia no Toshi to Jinkou* (*Asian Metropolis and Population*) (translated by Japan-China Geographical Association). Tokyo: Kokinshoin Publishing.

Jefferson, Gary and Inderjit Singh (1997) Ownership reform as a process of creative reduction in Chinese industry. In Joint Economic Committee (ed), *China's Economic Future: Challenges to U.S. Policy*. New York: M.E. Sharpe.

Ji Shuoming (2005) Tudi Siyuhua Jiejue Sannong Wenti (Privatization of Land can resolve the three agricultural problems), Phenix Net Site. http://www.phoenixtv.com, February 14.

Jiang Shijie (1951) Xinzhongguo Jingji Jianshezhong de Gongye Quwei Wenti (On the problem of regional allocation of industrial districts in the new economic construction of China). *Zhongguo Gongye* (*Chinese Industry*), 2(10).

Jin Guantao and Qingfeng Liu (1984) *Shengshi Yu Weiji: Lun Zhongguo Fengjian Shehui De Chaowending Jiegou* (*Prosperity and Crisis: Super Stable Structure of Chinese Feudal Society*). Changsha: Hunan Renmin Chubanshe Publishing.

Johnson, Chalmers (1982) *MITI and Japanese Miracle: the Growth of Industrial Policy, 1925-1975*. Berkeley: University of California Press.

Kahn, Herman (1979) *World Economic Development: 1979 and Beyond*. New York: William Morrow.

Kaneko, Masaru (1995) Toshi Kakusa no Kenshou (An Investigation of Disparities among cities). *Chugoku no Chiiki Kaihatsu Senryaku ni kansuru Kenkyu: Chugoku no Chiiki Keizai Kaihatsu (2)* (*A Study on Regional Development*

Strategy in China: Regional Economic Development in China (2)). Tokyo: National Institute for Research Advancement (NIRA).

Kawachi, Jyuzou, Fujimoto, Akira and Hideo Ueno (1987) *Henbou suru Ajia* (*Transforming Asia*). Tokyo: Sekai Shisousha Publishing.

Kawai, Shinichi (1996) *Chugoku Kigyou no Kenkyu: Kokka, Kigyou, Jyugyoin no Kankei* (*An Analysis of Chinese Enterprises: Relations among Nation State, Enterprises and Employees*). Tokyo: Chuoukeizaisha Publishing.

Ke Yan (2002) Goujian Xinxing Juguo Tizhi De Jige Guanxi (Some relationships about building a new type whole nation system). *Tiyu Wenhua Daokan (Sports Culture Guide)*, 3.

Kenney, Patrick (2003) *A Carnival of Revolution: Central Europe 1989.* New Jersey: Princeton University Press.

Kenney, Patrick (2006) *The Burdens of Freedom*. London: Zed Books.

Kobayashi, Kouji (1990a) *Chugoku no Sekai Ninshiki to Kaihatsu Senryaku* (I) (*Chinese Recognition of the World and Development Strategy* (I). Tokyo: Institute of Developing Economies, 9.

Kobayashi, Kouji (1990b) Jinminkousha no Kaitai to Nouson no Saihensei (I) (Dissolution of Communes and Reorganization of Rural Areas) (I). *Ajia Keizai (Asian Economies)*, 9.

Kobayashi, Kouji (1990c) Jinminkousha no Kaitai to Nouson no Saihensei (II) (Dissolution of Communes and Reorganization of Rural Areas (II). *Ajia Keizai (Asian Economies)*,10.

Kojima, Reiitsu (1986) Chugoku ni okeru Toshi no Kaikaku: Chushin Toshi Kousou (Urban Reforms in China: Central Municipality Plan). *Ajia Keizai (Asian Economies)*, 11.

Koopmans, Tjalling C. and John M. Montias (1971) On the description of economic systems. In Alexdander Eckstein (ed), *Comparison of Economic Systems*. Berkeley: University of California Press.

Kornai, Janos (1986) The soft budget constraint. *Kyklos*, 39.

Kornai, Janos (1990) *The Road to a Free Economy*. New York: W.W. Norton.

Kuribayashi, Sumio (1993) Chugoku no Chikikaihatsu Senryaku no Kadai (Problems of Regional Development Strategy). In Maruyama Nobuo (ed), *Choukou Ryuuiki no Keizai Hatten: Chugoku no Shijyouka to Chiiki Kaihatsu* (*Economic Development of Yangtze River Delta Area: Market Economy and Regional Development in China*). Tokyo: Institute of Developing Economies.

Kuznets, Simon S. (1955) Economic growth and income inequality. *American Economic Review*, 45(1).

Lal, Deepak (1985) *The Poverty of Development Economics*. Cambridge, MA: Harvard University Press.

Lang Youxing and Yougen Lang (2005) Cundangzhibu Yu Cunmin Xuanju Guanxi Zhi Tantao (An analysis on the relations between village branch of the party and peasants' election). *Zhonggong Ningbo Shiwei Dangxiao Xuebao* (*Journal of the Party School of CPC Ningbo Municipal Committee*), 1.

Lange, Oskar (1967) The computer and the market. In C.H. Feinstein (ed), *Socialism, Capitalism and Economic Growth*. Cambridge: Cambridge University Press.

Lewis, William A. (1954) Economic development with unlimited supplies of labor. *Manchester School of Economics and Social Studies*, 22.

Li Fei (2004) *Taiwan Jingji Fazhan Tonglun* (*Theory of Economic Development in Taiwan*). Beijing: Jiuzhou Chubanshe Publishing.

Li Guoding (K.T.Li) (1996) *Taiwan De Gaoxin Jishu He Xiandaihua* (*High-Tech Technology and Modernization of Taiwan)*. Nanjing: Dongnan University Press.

Li Honggu and Jiayao Wang (2005) Shanxi Meitan Fuhao De Caichan Diaocha (An investigation on the property of coal millionaire in Shanxi). *Sanlian Shenghuo Zhoukan* (*Sanlian Life Weekly*) December 23.

Li Liming (2004) Yanghang Banzi Tiaozheng Wancheng (Completion of Personnel Adjustment of Central Bank). *Jingji Guancha Bao* (*Economic Observer Report*), August 22.

Li Peilin and Yi Zhang (2003) *Guoyou Qiye De Shehui Chengben Fenxi* (*An Analysis of Social Costs of State Owned Enterprises*). Beijing, Shehui Wenxian Chubanshe Publishing.

Li Ren and Songlin Li (ed) (1992) *Taiwan Sishinian* (*Taiwan Forty Years*), Taiyuan, Shanxi Renmin Chubanshe Publishing.

Li Yang (ed) (2006) *Zhongguo Jinrong Fazhan Baogao 2006* (*Report on Financial Development in China 2006*). Beijing: Shehui Kexue Wenxian Chubanshe Publishing.

Liang Xiaolong, Bao Mingiao and Lin Zhang Lin (2006) *Juguo Tizhi* (*Whole Nation System*). Beijing: Renmin Tiyu Chubanshe Publishing.

Lin Qing (2001) Taiwan Nongdi Zhidu Gaige De Fenxi Yu Qishi (Analysis and Suggestion about the institutional reform of agricultural land in Taiwan). *Taiwan Yanjiu* (*Taiwan Study*), 1.

Lin Yifu (1992) *Zhidu Jishu He Zhongguo De Nongye Fazhan* (*Institution, Technology and Agricultural Development in China*). Shanghai: Shanghai Sanlian Shudian Publishing.

Lin Yifu (1999) Woguo Jinrong Tizhi Gaige De Fangxiang Shishenme (Which course should the reform of financial system in China be?). In Hai Wen and Feng Lu (eds) *Zhongguo: Jingji Zhuanxing He Jingji Zhengce* (*China: Economic Transition and Economic Policy*). Beijing: Peking University Press.

Lin Yifu, Cai Fang and Zhou Li (1999) *Zhongguo De Qiji: Fazhan Zhanlue Yu Jingji Gaige* (*Chinese Miracle: Development Strategy and Economic Reform (revised edition)*). Shanghai: Shanghai Renmin Chubanshe Publishing and Shanghai Sanlian Chubanshe Publishing.

Liu Hanping (2002) *Difang Zhengfu Caizheng Nengli Wenti Yanjiu* (*A Study on the Financial Ability Problem on Local Government*). Beijing: Zhongguo Caijing Chubanshe Publishing.

Liu Junde (ed) (1996) *Zhongguo Xingzheng Quhua De Lilun Yu Shijian* (*Theory and Practice of Chinese Administrative Divisions*). Shanghai: Huadong Normal University Press.

Liu Ming (1992) *Bi'an De Qifei: Taiwan Zhanhou Sishinian Jingji Fazhan Licheng* (*Leading of the Opposite Shore: Economic Development Process for 40 years in Taiwan*) Harbin: Heilongjiang Renmin Chubanshe Publishing.

Liu Tachung and K.C. Yeh (1965) *The Economy of the Chinese Mainland: National Income and Economic Development, 1933-1959*. New Jersey: Princeton University Press.

Liu Zenwei and Zenyao Wang (ed) (1987) *Xiangcun Tizhi Gaige* (*Systemic Reforms of Township and Village in China*). Beijing: Zhongguo Nongye Chubanshe Publishing.

Long Jianxin and Wenzhen Huang (1993) *Taiwan Jingji Jieping* (*An Analysis of Taiwanese Economy*). Bieijing: Zhongxin Chubanshe Publishing.

Lu Huilin (2004) Laorenhui De Gushi (A story of the aged club). *Zhongguo Gaige (Nongcunban)* (*Chinese Reforms (Rural Area Version)*), 4.

Lu Zhongyuan and the Eleventh Five Year Plan research group (Chinese Cabinet Development Research Center) *Shiyiwu Guihua Jiben Silu He 2020nian Yuanjing Mubiao Yanjiu* (*Inside Report on the Study of Basic Plan of the Eleventh Five Year and Long Run Goals by 2020*). Beijing.

Ma Chengsan (1995) *Chugoku Keizai no Kokusaika* (*Internationalization of Chinese Economy*). Tokyo: Simulshuppansha Publishing.

Ma Guochuan (2005) Shuoxiao Pinfu Chaju Bixu Pochu ZhongziQinglao De Guannian (Abolishing the strict rules of attaching greater importance on capital and less importance on labor is necessary to reducing the disparity between rich and poor). *Guoji Jinrongbao* (*International Finance Report*) (October 21).

Maddison, Augus (2001) *The World Economy: a Millennial Perspective*. Paris: OECD.

Mao Zedong (1974) *Mao Zedong Shisou Banzai (1)* (*Hurrah for Mao Zedong Ideology: Vol. 1*) (translated by Research Association on Contemporary Chinese History of Tokyo University). Tokyo: Sanichishobou Publishing.

Mao Zedong (1977) Zhonggong Qijie Liuzhong Quanhui Kuoda Huiyi Zongjie, 1955.10.11(Summary of the Enlarged Meeting of Seventh National Meeting of Chinese Communist Party,1955.10.11) In Mao Zedong (1977), *Mao Zedong Xuanji* (*Selected Works of Mao Zedong*) *Vol. 5*. Beijing: Renmin Chubanshe Publishing.

Maruyama, Nobuo (ed) (1993) *Choukou Ryuiki no Keizai Hatten: Chugoku no Shijyouka to Chiiki Kaihatsu* (*Economic Development of Yangtze River Delta Area: Market Economy and Regional Development in the China*). Tokyo: Institute of Developing Economies.

Maruyama, Nobuo (ed) (1994) *90 nendai Chugoku Chiiki Kaihatsu no Shikaku* (*Viewpoints of Chinese Regional Development in the 1990s*). Tokyo, Institute of Developing Economies.

Maslow, Abraham (1954) *Motivation and Personality*. New York: Harper & Row.

Matsuda, Yasuhiro (2006) *Taiwan ni okeru Ittoudokusaitaisei no Seiritsu* (*Establishment of one-party dictatorship system in Taiwan*). Tokyo: Keio University Press.

McKenzie, Richard (ed) (1984) *Constitutional Economics: Containing the Economic Powers of Government*. Maryland: Lexington Books.

Meadows, Dennis L. *et al.* (1972) *The Limits to Growth*. New York: Universe Books.

Mi Jianguo, Li Yang and Jinlao Huang (2001) *Zhongguo Yinghangye Fuwu Shichang Kaifang Mianlin De Tiaozhan* (*Challenges of the Opening of Banking Service Market in China*). Beijing: Guowuyuan Fazhan Yanjiu Zhongxin (Chinese Cabinet Development Research Center).

Minami, Ryoshin and Akira Ono (1987) Senzen Nihon no Shotoku Bunpu (Income Distribution of Prewar Japan). *Keizai Kenkyu* (*Economic Studies*), Vol.38.

Ministry of Economy, Trade and Industry (Japan) (2005) *Tsusho Hakusho 2005* (*White Paper on International Trade and Industry 2005*). Tokyo: Ministry of Economy, Trade and Industry.

Ministry of International Trade (China) (1985) *Zhongguo Duiwai Jingji Maoyi Nianjian 1985* (*Chinese International Economy and Trade Bulletin 1985*). Beijing: Zhongguo Guanggao Youxian Gongsi Publishing.

Ministry of Labor and Social Security, and Chinese Statistical Office (2007) *Laodong Yu Shehui Baozhang Shiye Fazhan Tongji Gongbao 2006* (*Statistical Bulletin on the Development of Labor and Social Security Projects*). Beijing.

Mitsubishi Research Institute (ed) (1996) *Chugoku Saikou Shidousha Who's Who* (*Chinese Top Ranking Leaders Who's Who*). Tokyo: Sousousha Publishing.

Miyazaki, Yoshio (1986) Gyouseifufuku Shinsaseido no Unyou to Mondaiten (Inspecting system on the protect against administration: operations and problems). *Shakaikagaku Kenkyu* (*Social Science Study*), Vol.38, No.(2).

Morita, Ken and Yun Chen (2008) A Sociological Study of Transition: China and Central Europe, *Economic Papers* (Warsaw School of Economics), 43.

Morita, Ken and Yun Chen (2009a) *Chugoku no Keizai Kaikaku to Shihon Shijyou* (*Economic Reforms and Capital Markets in China*), Tokyo, Taga Shuppan Publishing.

Morita, Ken and Yun Chen (2009b) *Transition, Regional Development and Globalization: China and Central Europe*, New Jersey, World Scientific Publishing.

Murrell, Peter (1992) Evolutionary and radical approaches to economic reform. *Economics of Planning*, Vol.25.

Myint, Hla (1964) *The Economics of the Developing Countries*. London: Hutchinson.

Myint, Hla (1971) *Economic Theory and the Underdeveloped Countries*. New York: Oxford University Press.

Myrdal, Gunnar (1968) *Asian Drama: An Inquiry into the Poverty of Nations*. New York: Pantheon Books,1968.

Nakagane, Katsuji (1979) Chugoku: Shakaishugi Keizai Seido no Kouzou to Tenkai (China: structure and development of socialist economic institution). In Iwata Masayuki (ed) (1979), *Kouza Keizaitaisei Vol. 4: Gendai Shakaishugi* (*Series Economic System Vol. 4: Contemporary Socialism*). Tokyo: Touyoukeizai Shinpousha Publishing.

Nakagane, Katsuji (1999) *Chugoku Keizai Hattenron* (*Theory of Economic Development in China*). Tokyo: Yuikaku Publishing.

Nakamasa, Masaki (2006) *Nihon to Deutschland: Futatsu no Zentaishugi* (*Japan and Germany: Two Kinds of Totalitarian State*). Kobunsha Publishing.

National Institute for Research Advancement (NIRA) (1995) *Chugoku no Chiiki Kaihatsu Senryaku ni kansuru Kenkyu: Chugoku no Chiiki Keizai Kaihatsu (1), (2)* (*A Study on Regional Development Strategy in China: Regional Economic Development in China (1), (2)*). Tokyo: National Institute for Research Advancement.

NHK (1984) *21 seiki wa keikoku suru (2)* (*21st century is warning (2)*). Tokyo: NHK Publishing.

Niu Ke (2002) Meiyuan Yu Zhanhou Taiwan De Jingji Gaizao (US Assistance and Economic Reforms of Postwar Taiwan). *Meiguo Yanjiu* (*USA Study*), Vol.3.

North, Douglass (1990) *Institutional Change and Economic Performance*, Cambridge: Cambridge University Press.

North, Douglass and Barry Weingast (1989) Constitutions and commitment: the evolution of institutions governing public choice in seventeenth-century England. *Journal of Economic History*, XLIX.

Nurkse, Ragnar (1953) *Problems of Capital-Formation in Underdeveloped Countries*. New York: Oxford University Press.

Office of Central Commission of Supervising Group for Chinese Agricultural Policy, and the Ministry of Land and Resources (2002) *Guanyu Wanshan Zhengdi Zhidu De Diaoyan Qingkuang Ji Zhengce Jianyi* (*Investigation and Policy Proposal on Land Requisition System*). Beijing.

Ogawa, Kazuo and Hiroshi Watanabe (1995) *Kawariyuku Russia, Touou Keizai* (*Transforming the Economy in Russia and Eastern Europe)*. Tokyo : Chuoukeizaisha Publishing.

Ohkawa, Kazushi and Hirohisa Kohama (1993) *Keizai Hattenron: Nihon no Keizai to Hattentojyoukoku* (*Economic Development Theory: Japanese Economy and the Less Developed Countries*). Tokyo: Touyoukeizai Shinpousha Publishing.

Okuno-Fujiwara, Masahiro (1993) Government business relationship in Japan: a comparative institutional analysis. Manuscript.

Osa, Maryjane (2003) *Solidarity and Contention: Networks of Polish Opposition*. Minneapolis: University of Minnesota Press.

Peng Min (ed) (1989) *Dangdai Zhongguo De Jiben Jianshe* (*Fundamental Construction of Contemporary China*). Beijing: Zhongguo Shehui Kexue Chubanshe Publishing.

Perkins, Dwight (1969) *Agricultural Development in China 1368-1968*. Houston: Aldine Publishing Company.

Ping Xinqiao (1995) *Caizheng Yuanli He Bijiao Caizheng Zhidu* (*Principle of Finance and Comparative Financial System*). Shanghai: Shanghai Sanlian Chubanshe Publishing.

Pipes, Richard (1999) *Property and Freedom*. New York: Random House.

Pu Shanxin *et al*. (1995) *Zhongguo Xingzheng Quhua Gailun* (*An Introduction of Chinese Administrative Districts*). Beijing: Zhishi Chubanshe Publishing.

Qin Hui (2003) *Chuantong Shilun:Bentu Shehui De Zhidu, Wenhua Jiqi Biange* (*Ten Points at Issue on the Tradition: Institution, Culture and Their Changes in Chinese Traditional Society*). Shanghai: Fudan University Press.

Ranis, Gustav and John Fei (1961) A theory of economic development. *American Economic Review*, Vol. 57.

Research Group on the Peasants' Autonomous System in Chinese Rural Areas, (1995) *Zhhongguo Nongcun Cunmin Daibiao Huiyi Zhidu (Peasants Representative parliament System)*. Beijing: Zhongguo Shehui Chubanshe Publishing.

Rifkin, Jeremy (1980) *Entropy: A New World View*. New York: Viking Press.

Sasaki, Nobuaki (1993) *Chugoku Keizai no Shijyouka Kouzou* (*Market Oriented Structure of Chinese Economy*). Tokyo: Sekai Shisousha Publishing.

Shanghai Statistical Office (annual), *Shanghai Tongji Nianjian* (*Shanghai Statistical Bulletin*), Shanghai.

Shannon, Claude Elwood (1948) A mathematical theory of communication. *Bell System Technical Journal*, Vol.27.

Shen Hong (1994) *Fengong Yu Jiaoyi* (*Division of Labor and Transaction*). Shanghai: Shanghai Renmin Chubanshe Publishing.

Shiozawa, Yoshinori (1990) *Shijyou no Chitsujyogaku* (*An Analysis of Order of the Market*), Tokyo: Chikuma Shobou Publishing.

Sigurdson, John (1977) *Rural Industrialization in China*. Cambridge: Harvard University Press.

Smith, A. (1776) *An Inquiry into the Nature and Causes of the Wealth of Nations*. London: Methuen.

Suehiro, Akira (1998) Hattentojyoukoku no Kaihatsushugi (Developmentalism in less developed countries). In Institute of Social Science (Tokyo University) (ed), *20 Seiki System 4: Kaihatsushugi* (*20th Century System 4: Developmentalism*). Tokyo: Tokyo University Press.

Sugimoto, Nobuyuki (2006) *Daichi no Houkou* (*Roar of the Earth*). Tokyo: PHP Kenkyujyo Publishing.

Sun Daiyao (2002) Guomindang Baitui Taiwan Hou Dangzheng Guanxi Tiaozheng Sumiao (An Overview of Relationship Adjustment between Party and Administration after Nationalist Party Defeat into Taiwan). *Yanhuang Chunqiu* (*History of Chinese Race*), Vol.6.

Sun Daiyao (2003) *Taiwan Quanwei Tizhi Jiqi Zhuanxing Yanjiu* (*Authoritarian System and Transition in Taiwan*). Beijing: Zhongguo Shehui Kexue Chubanshe Publishing.

Sun Huairen (ed) (1990) *Shanghai Shehuizhuyi Jingji Jianshe Fazhan Jianshi (1949–1985)* (*A Short History of Socialist Economic Construction and Development in Shanghai (1949~1985)*). Shanghai: Shanghai Renmin Chubanshe Publishing.

Takai, Kiyoshi and Akira Fujino (eds) (1996) *Shanghai to Choukou Keizaiken* (*Economic Region of Shanghai and Yangtze River Delta*). Tokyo: Akishobou Publishing.

Tanaka, Hiroshi (1993) *Kisokara yoku wakaru seiji keizai* (*Easier Introduction to Politics and Economy*). Tokyo: Obunsha Publishing.

Tang, Anthony (1968) Policy and performance in agriculture. In Eckstein Alexander *et al.* (eds), *Economic Trends in Communist China*. Houston: Aldine Publishing.

Tang An'zhong (2004) Fanxing Fenshuizhi (Reconsideration about the tax sharing system). *Zhongguo Jingji Shibao* (*Chinese Economic News*), September 24. Vol. 3.

Tang Jun (1950) Gongye Quwei De Peizhi Wenti (On the problem of regional allocation of industrial district). *Zhongguo Gongye* (*Chinese Industry*), 2(5).

Tang Yonglun (1952) Zhongnanqu Gangtie Gongye Shengchanli Peizhi De Yanjiu (An analysis of steel manufacturing production allocation in Central-Southern district). *Zhongguo Gongye* (*Chinese Industry*), Vol.3 (new edition), No. 9.

Taylor, Lance (1994) The markets met its match: lessons for the future from the transition's initial years. *Journal of Comparative Economics*, 19.

Terrill, Ross (1999) *Mao: A Biography*. Stanford: Stanford University Press.

Tiebout, Charles M. (1956) A pure theory of local expenditures. *Journal of Political Economy*, 64 (October).

Todaro, Michael P. (1969) A model of labor migration and urban unemployment in less developed countries. *American Economic Review*, 59.

Toynbee, Arnold J. (1957) *A Study of History* (Abridgement of Volumes VII-X by D.C. Somervell). Oxford: Oxford Publishing.

Ueno, Kazuhiko (ed) (1993) *Gendai Chugoku no Gouchin Kigyou* (*Township and Village Enterprises in Contemporary China*). Tokyo: Taimeidou Publishing.

UNESCO (2003) *Global Education Monitoring Report*. Paris: UNESCO Publishing.

Wada, Yoshio (1997) Chugoku Kokuyukigyou Kaikaku no Bunseki: Keizaikaihatsu to Kigyou (An Analysis of State Owned Enterprise Reforms in China: Economic Development and Enterprise). *Kaihatsuenjyo Kenkyu (Development Aid Studies)*, 4 (4).

Wang Chuncai (1991) *Peng Dehuai Zai Sanxian* (*Peng Dehuai at the Third Front*). Chengdu: Sichuan Renmin Chubanshe Publishing.

Wang Jian (1988) Xuanze Zhengque De Changqi Fazhan Zhanlue: Guanyu'Guoji Daxunhuan' Jingji fazhan Zhanlue De Gouxiang (Choose a correct long run development strategy: on the international big cycle development strategy). *Jingji Ribao* (*People's Daily*), January 5.

Wang Qian (2007) Zhengzhi WutaiShang De Beida Biyesheng (graduates of Peking University on the political stage). *Nanfang Zhoumo* (*Southern Weekend*), June 14.

Wang Shaoguang (1997) *Fenquan De Dixian* (*Limit of Decentralization*). Beijing: Zhongguo Jihua Chubanshe Publishing.

Wang Yukun *et al.* and Guowuyuan Fazhan Yanjiu Zhongxin (Chinese Local Area Development Research Group in Chinese Cabinet Development Research Center) (1992) *Zhongguo: Shiji Zhijiao De Chengshi Fazhan* (*China: Regional Development of 20th and 21st Century*). Shenyang: Renmin Chuanshe Publishing.

Wang Zhenyu (2006) *Fenshuizhi Caizheng Tizhi Quexianxing Yanjiu* (*A Study on the Deficiency of the Tax Sharing System*). Shenyang: Research Institute of Finance in Liaoning Province.

Watanabe, Toshio (1991) *Ajia Keizai wo dou toraeru ka? (What do we think about Asian Economy?)*. Tokyo: NHK Publishing.

Watanabe, Toshio (1995) *Shinseiki Ajia no Kousou* (*A Plan of Asia in the new century*). Tokyo: Chikuma Shobou Publishing.

Watanabe, Toshio (1996) *Kaihatsu Keizaigaku: Keizaigaku to Gendai Ajia* (*Development Economics: Economics and Contemporary Asia*). Tokyo: Nihon Hyoronsha Publishing.

Weber, Max (1958) *The Protestant Ethic and the Spirit of Capitalism*. New York: Scribner.

Weber, Max (1964) *The Religion of China* (translated by Hans H. Gerth). New York: Free Press.

Weber, Max (1968) *Economy and Society: An Outline of Interpretive Sociology*. New York: Bedminster Press.

Weber, Max (1993) *Rujiao Yu Daojiao* (*Confucianism and Taoism*) (Chinese edition). Nanjing: Jiangsu Renmin Chubanshe Publishing.

Wei Guangqi (2004) *Guanzhi Yu Zizhi:20 Shiji Qianbianqi De Zhongguo Xianzhi* (*Central Regulation and Autonomy: Chinese County System at the beginning of the 20th Century*). Beijing: Shangwu Yinshuguan Publishing.

Williamson, Jeffrey G. (1965) Regional inequality and process of national development: A description of the patterns. *Economic Development and Culture Change*, 13 (4).

Winiecki, Jan (1993) Cost of transition that are not costs: on non-welfare reducing output fall. In Mario Baldassarri and Robert Mundell (eds), *Building a New Europe: Eastern Europe's Transition to a Market Economy*. New York: St. Martin's Press.

Wittfogel, Karl August (1957) *Oriental Despotism: A Comparative Study of Total Power*. New Haven: Yale University Press.

World Bank (1987) *World Development Report 1987*. New York: Oxford University Press.

World Bank (1993) *The East Asian Miracle*. New York: Oxford University Press.

World Bank (2005) *World Development Report 2006: Equity and Development.* New York: Oxford University Press.

Wu Chuanzhen and Yuan Li (2005) Zhongguo Wanyi Buliang Zichan Chuli Neimu (Inside story on the disposal of huge amount bad loans in China). *Nanfang Zhoumo* (*Southern Weekend*), January 27.

Wu Junhua (1995) Kaikakuki ni okeru Seichou Chiiki no Ruikeika (Classification of Development Regions at the Reform Period). In National Institute for Research Advancement, *Chugoku no Chiiki Keizai Kakusa to Chiiki Keizai Kaihatsu ni kansuru Jisshou Kenkyu: Chugoku no Chiiki Keizai Kaihatsu (2)* (*A Positive Analysis of Regional Economic Disparity and Regional Economic Development (2)*). Tokyo: National Institute for Research Advancement.

Wu Yi (2002) *Cunluo Bianqian Zhongde Quanwei He Zhixu* (*Authority and Order in the Change of Rural Area*). Beijing: Zhongguo Shehui Kexue Chubanshe Publishing.

Xiao Tangbiao (2004) Xiangzhen Gongzuo De Yali He Tiaozhan: Hongguan Tizhi He Zhengce Dui Nongcun Jianshe Jiqi Zhili De Fumian Yingxiang (Pressures and challenges of town and village policies: a study of negative effects of the macro system and policies against rural area construction and governnance). Zhongguo Cunmin Zizhi Xinxiwang (autonomous information net of Chinese rural area and peasants) http://www.chinarural.org.

Xie Lizhong (2001) Hui Shehui Lilun: Yige Chubu De Fenxi (Sociological theory of grey society: some early stage analysis). *Shehuixue Yanjiu* (*Analyses of Sociology*), 1.

Xie Ping and Xiaoling Wu (1992) *Zhongguo De Jinrong Shenhua He Jinrong Gaige* (*Financial Deepening and Financial Reform in China*). Tianjin: Tianjin Renmin Chubanshe Publishing.

Xu Dixin (ed) (1988) *Dangdai Zhongguo De Renkou* (*Population of Contemporary China*). Beijing: Zhongguo Shehui Kexue Chubanshe Publishing.

Yan Hao (ed) (1988) *Dangdai Shanghai Dianzi Gongye* (*Contemporary Electronic Industry in Shanghai*). Shanghai: Shanghai Renmin Chubanshe Publishing.

Yan Ruiqin *et al.* (1988) *Zhongguo Gongnongye Chanpin Jiage De Jiandaocha* (*The Schere for Agricultural Products with Industrial Products*). Beijing: Zhongguo Renmin University Press.

Yang Deyin (ed) (1993) *Bianjing Maoyi Shiyong Shouche* (*Practical Handbook of Border Trade*). Beijing: Zhongguo Shangye Chubanshe Publishing.

Yang Muxi (2001) Taiwan De Tudi Gaige He Shehui Zhuanxing (Land Reform and Social Transformation in Taiwan. *Taisheng* (*Voice of Taiwan*), September.

Yang Wu and Lei Cao(1991) *Zhongguo Jingji Dili* (*Chinese Economic Geography*). Beijing: Minzu University of China Press.

Yang Xiaokai (2001) Haode Zibenzhuyi He Huaide Zibenzhuyi (Good capitalism and bad capitalism). *Yang Xiaokai Wenji* (*The Collected Works of Yang Xiaokai*), http://www.gongfa.com/yangxiaokaiwenji.dwt.

Yang Xiaokai (2004) Tudi Siyouzhi He Xianzheng Gonghe De Guanxi (On the Republic Relations between Private Ownership of Land and Constitutional

Relations). *Yang Xiaokai Wenji* (*The Collected Works of Yang Xiaokai*), http://www.gongfa.com/yangxiaokaiwenji.dwt.

Yi Ming (2002) Zhongguo Disidai Caijing Guanliao Dengchang (Appearance of the Fourth Generation Bureaucrats of Finance and Economy). *Singapore Lianhe Zaobao* (*Singapore Allied News*), December 23.

Yin Huimin (2004) *Shandongsheng Caizheng Fenpei Jiegou Yanjiu* (*An Analysis of Financial Distribution Structure in Shandong Province*). Beijing: Jingji Kexue Chubanshe Publishing.

Yokohama Industrial Office (1996) *Saishin Chugoku Data Book (Newest Data Book of China)*. Tokyo: Kokonshoin Publishing.

Yu Jianrong (2001) *Yuecun Zhengzhi* (*Politics of Rural Area in China*). Beijing: Shangwu Yinshuguan Publishing.

Yu Yingshi (1991) *Chugoku Kinsei no Shukyourinri to Shouninseishin* (*Religious Ethics and the Spirit of Merchant in Modern Times of China*) (translated by Noriko Mori). Tokyo: Heibonsha Publishing.

Yu Yongzhen (2006) *He Kuaguo Yinghang Jingzhen: Zhongguo Yinghangye De Xiaolv He Jinrong Anquan* (*Competition with Multinational Banks: Efficiency and Financial Safety of Chinese Banking Sector*). Beijing: Zhonggong Dangxiao Chubanshe Publishing.

Yuan Yuanyuan (2007) Shututonggui: Sida Guoyou Zichan Guanli Gongsi De Jiannan Zhuanxing (Different ways and the same goal? Difficult transition ways of the four state owned asset management companies). *Dangdai Jinrongjia* (*Contemporary Bankers*), 5.

Zhang Jie (1998) *Zhongguo Jinrong Zhidu De Jiegou He Bianqian* (*Structure and Change of Chinese Financial System*). Taiyuan: Shanxi Jingji Chubanshe Publishing.

Zhang Shuguang (1995) Fangkai Liangjia, Quxiao Liangpiao: Zhongguo Liangshi Gouxiao zhidu Bianqian Yanjiu (Liberalization of food prices and abolishment of food coupons: a case study of the change of food purchasing and sales system in China). *Zhongguo Shehui Kexue Jikan* (*Quarterly Journal of Chinese Social Science*), 13 (Winter).

Zhang Xiangdong and Xinyu Gou (2006) Gedi Zhujingban Mianlin Shengcun Zhengsu Fengbao (Like a storm towards orderly adjustment of Beijing Representative Bureau). *Jingji Guanchabao* (*Economic Observer Report*), September 3.

Zhang Xinguang (2004) Zhongyang Caizheng Zhuanyi Zhidu: Haogang Yongzai Daorenshang (Central budget transfer system: good steel is used for making a sword). *Xuexi Yuekan* (*Study: Monthly*), August.

Zhang Xinguang (2006) Nongcun Shuifei Gaigehou De Xiangzhen Zhengfu Tizhi (Systemic reform of town and village level government after the introduction of agricultural area tax reform). *Kaifang Daobao* (*Open Policy Report*), (December 27, 2006).

Zhang Xiuying and Jinling Liu (2004) *Zhongguo Xibu Diqu Xiangzhen Fuzai Wenti Yanjiu* (*A Study of Debt Problems of Town and Village Level Regions in Chinese Central Area*). Beijing: Renmin Chubanshe Publishing.

Zhang Yi (ed) (1988) *Zhongguo Xiangzhen Qiye Gailun* (*An Introduction of Township and Village Enterprises in China*). Shanghai: Shanghai Shehui Kexueyuan Chubanshe Publishing.

Zhang Yi (1991) *Zhongguo Xiangzhen Qiye: Jiannan De Fazhan Guocheng* (*Township and Village Enterprises in China*). Beijing: Falv Chubanshe Publishing.

Zhong Jiayong (2004) Xuezhe Zhuzheng,Yanghang Nengfou Yingdui Tiaozhan? (Could the Chinese Central Bank led by Scholars be well managed?). *Nanfang Zhoumo* (*Southern Weekend*), February 20.

Zhongyang Wenxian Yanjiushi (ed) (2003) *ZhonGong Shisanjie Sizhongquanhui Yilai Lici Quanguo Daibiao Dahui Zhongyang Quanhui Zhongyao Wenxian Xuanbian* (*Selected Important Documents of respective National Representative Conference Since the Fourth Meeting of Thirteenth Chinese Communist Party*). Beijing: Zhongyang Wenxian Chubanshe Publishing.

Zhou Feizhou (2006) Cong Jiquxing Zhengquan Dao Fuyouxing Zhengquan: Shuifei Gaige Dui Guojia He Nongmin Guanxi De Yingxiang (From taken up type administration to floating type administration: on the impacts of tax system reform to the relations between the nation and the peasants). *Shehuixue Yanjiu* (*Analyses of Sociology*), Vol.3.

Zhou Taihe (ed) (1984) *Dangdai Zhongguo De Jingji Tizhi Gaige* (*Contemporary Systemic Reform of Chinese Economy*). Beijing: Zhongguo Shehui Kexue Chubanshe Publishing.

Zhu Rongji (1955) Congfen Liyong Yanhai Diqu De Gongye (Satisfied level of utilization of industry in coastal district). Jihua Jingji (Planning Economy), 6.

Index

accumulated debt, 106, 171, 200, 204
administration management cost, 248
administrative decentralization, 306
administrative district, ix, 24, 25, 27, 31, 32, 35, 37-39, 54, 55, 79, 81, 84, 85,107, 108, 172, 173, 189
administrative economic district, 25, 54, 55, 76, 80, 81
administrative permission law, 199
administrative reform, 146
administrative structure, 81, 110, 200, 219
adventurism, 17
agricultural tax, 74, 107, 201, 205, 207, 233, 340
anti-communist front, 295, 296
appropriate technology, 52
asset bubble, 243, 271
Asset Management Corporation, x, 141-144
asymmetric information, 246, 255, 265
attempted ordinance of public service, 250
authoritarian system, vii, 1, 71, 115, 166, 206, 236, 239, 248, 250, 253, 255, 283, 293, 294, 296, 298, 301-303, 304, 309, 311, 314, 315, 317, 318, 319, 327, 329, 348, 361, 364, 365, 366, 367, 369, 370, 377
authoritarianism tax sharing system, 221
autocratic system, 115, 275, 301, 373

bad loans, x, 127, 132, 136, 139, 140, 141-145
balance of power, 374
Beijing representative bureau, 171, 197-199, 396
big scale economic cooperation district, vii,22, 54
biggest scale unified nation, 378
black cats and white cats assertion, 75
border trade, 88, 91-93, 95, 399
Boxer Rebellion complex, 67
bureaucrats group in economy and finance, 348, 351

central region promotion strategy, 91, 93, 97-99, 135, 242
central tax, 183, 215
charismatic leader, 274
Chiang Ching-kuo, 315-318, 324
Chiang Kai-shek, 229, 295, 313-318, 360
Chen Cheng, 315-317
Chinese people living abroad, 296
collective labor, 30, 42, 51
Confucian society, 245
communes, ix, 33, 45, 48, 51-53, 64, 72, 149, 233, 332
constitutional government, 5, 169-171, 232, 235-236, 246, 287
constitutional one-party system, 235, 236, 237
consumption city, 33
comfortable society, 63-64, 73
corruption perception index, xi, 200, 251-253
CMEA (Council for Mutual Economic Assistance), 66, 305
cozy relationship, 265, 296, 317
creative destruction, v, 59, 61, 112, 113, 234, 306, 307, 373

Daqing model, 56
day of consumers, 265
Dazhai model, 56
Democratic Party Group, 359-361
Deng Xiaoping,
- on wisdom, 59
- on ability as a leader, 68
- on speech in the southern tour, 70 175, 182
- on collective works, 61, 383

dependence on a low production cost path, 243

development strategy of equilibrating arrangement, 17
development strategy with inland priority, 17
development strategy with priority, 74
development zone boom, 174-177, 205
disadvantages of a late comer, 151
dual economy model, 109, 264, 265
dual structure of government, 248
dual structure of wage rates, 259, 260

economic decentralization, 306
egalitarian (Datong) ideal, 63
election by popular vote, 225
emerging nation state, 241, 293, 305
Emperor system, 307
employment expectation, 322
Enlightenment, 229, 302
enterprises in the communes, ix, 40-42, 48
environment costs, 243
environmental industry, 288
excessive distribution problem, 158
export oriented, 86, 244, 246, 296, 305, 322, 324, 326, 367
export processing zone, 84

fact following mechanism, v, vii, 8, 115, 239, 240, 243, 276, 277, 283, 284, 347, 371, 372, 379
fallacy composition, 8, 165-166
Falun Dafa, 365
family contract system, 51, 72-75, 112, 117, 179, 233, 236, 375
family organization system (Bao Jia Zhi Du), 229
family registered system, 16, 29, 72
fangnu, 255
Fel'dman – Domar model, 50, 51, 53
55 year system, 304, 307
financial contract system, 80, 171, 178-180, 218
financial decision authority, 208
financial transfer, vii, x, 171, 183, 186, 188, 190-194, 196-199, 201-203, 206, 217, 221
five principles of peaceful coexistence, 64
five small industries, 28, 40, 49, 53
floating type government, 207
flood control theory, 376
flying geese development model, 296-298, 300
forced sending back home system, 221
founders of promoting the nation, 296
four modernizations, 65, 327
four windows, 83, 89
free discretion rights, 195
free movement of population, 220
funds outside the national budget, 200

GHQ (General Headquarters) , 295, 307
Gini coefficient, 111, 283, 310
Glorious Revolution, 275, 276, 381
government looking after system, 242
go-west development strategy, 94, 97, 103
gradual way, v, xv, 112-115, 171, 172, 203, 234, 286, 291, 306, 327, 373, 375-376, 388
gradualism, 149, 242, 302, 373, 376
Great Leap Forward, 17, 29, 31, 33, 38, 40, 45, 52, 390
greening revolution, 321
Guangdong model, 340

harmonized society, 64, 320, 378, 382
hegemony theory, 380
hierarchy theory of needs, 319, 327
high accumulation model, 51-52
High-Tech development district, 325
horizontal division of labor, 297
Hu Jintao, 306, 349, 355
human-governed system, 242

imperial examination, 382
imperial politics, 228-229
import substitution, 4, 86, 240, 242, 305, 306, 319-324
impulsive developments, 176
independent cities from provincial plan, 84
ICAC (Independent Commission Against Corruption), 366
independent directors, 120
independent organizations, 148
independent movement, 295
industrial region promotion strategy in northeast area, 93, 97-98, 135
informal sector, 111, 323

initial condition, 13, 14, 55, 67, 172, 274, 302, 305, 371
inland civilization, 113
inseparable from administration, 54
institutional evolution, 184, 246, 274, 275, 277, 302
institutional imitation, 275
intermediate technology, 52, 53
international strategic development plan for the big circle, 85
inverted-U shaped hypothesis, 244

Jiang Zemin, 94, 306
Jiangzhe model, 112, 340
joint-stock commercial bank, 129, 130, 132, 133, 137, 145
judicial independence, 364, 366

Korean War, 29, 243, 295, 305
Kuaikuai, 54, 55

land
  cooperative organization, 91, 229, 339
  finance, 171, 204, 205, 208, 213, 218
  requisitioned policy, 334
  requisitioned problems, 363
large scale and public owned, 30
law-governed system, 224, 225, 242
Lewis model, 109
little empire economy, 80, 98, 177, 180, 227
local autonomy system, vii, 169, 170-172, 203, 208, 218, 219, 224-228, 231, 235, 236, 283, 287-290, 317, 340, 368-370
Local Government Act, 170, 225
local politics, 9, 228, 229
local tax, 182-185, 188, 191, 193, 198, 215

management of enterprise groups, 121
Mao Zedong,
  on slogan, 33, 42, 53, 56, 64
  on type of social system, 57
  on lecture, 247
  on selected works, 393
  on ten important relations, 19, 56, 332, 333
Marx, K., 14, 69, 369
MBO method, 123, 125
menace by China, 269
middle class, 311, 317, 367, 369
migrant workers, 261
military industry, 27, 28, 48, 87, 98, 304, 312, 332
minimum wage rates, 261
Minor Third Front, 28, 29, 54, 98
modern bureaucratic system, 245
modernization of human beings, 327, 333, 367
multi-tiers dual economic structure, 45, 83, 86
Municipal Corporation Act, 225
Myrdal, G.
  on circular accumulative causation, 107
  on soft state, 251
  on speed money, 254
  on Asian Drama, 390

national ability, 127, 236
national control system of labor works, 16, 29, 30
national council for social security fund, 155
national development and reforms commission, 147
Neo-Confucian countries, 245
new type of trade union, 240, 285, 286
Nixon shock, 300
non-agricultural population, 31, 32, 81
non-agricultural production, 32
non-tradable stocks, 122, 164, 165

omni-directional open strategy, 59, 75, 83, 87
one item and one discussion, 202
open coastal strategy, 59
Opium War, 5, 381

party affairs reform, 249, 316
peasant liberation movement, 295
peasants' representative rights, 240, 287
peasant's self-governing committee, 201-204, 207
political agreement conference, 361
population explosion, 49, 155, 321, 326

power balance, 380
private property report system, 250
production city, 33
professional technocrat, 203, 245, 314
pro-Soviet model, 243
public servant law, 199
Public Service Law of the People's Republic of China, 250

QFII (Qualified Foreign Institutional Investors), 121

racial self-determination rights, 377
radical way, 114, 275, 375, 377, 378
radicalism, 242
ratio of labor force industrialization, 329
ratio of heavy industry, 23, 269, 340
ratio of productive industrialization, 328, 329
Real Right Act, 338, 363
Redundant workforce, 52, 53, 86, 103, 106, 324, 331
reformist way, 302, 381
regional protectionism, 180
revolutionary way, 302, 381
Ricardian trap, 73, 74
ruling the country by technocrats, 363, 364

Schere, 33, 47
self-reliance, 30, 36, 56, 113, 114, 141, 306, 332, 375
self-sufficient financial power, 198
separation of party and administration, 248, 342
shared tax, 183, 185, 188, 215, 217
Shoup, C., 226
 on three principles, 226
 on recommendation, 226
slackly centralized system, 60, 61, 75, 115, 231, 246, 376
small township system, 37
socialist reform movement, 33
soft budget constraint, 52, 150, 159, 208, 248, 391
soft budget system, 52, 171, 198, 221, 237
Solidarity, 286, 384
special economic zone, ix, 77, 84-85, 89, 90, 107, 112, 121, 134, 175, 388
Stalin, J., 66, 69, 305, 306
SASAC (State-owned Assets Supervision and Administration Commission of the State Council), 120-123, 125, 126, 130, 148, 165
state-owned mind, 265
Sun Yat-sen, 14, 61, 64, 232, 316
super stable social structure, 378
supervising cost, 51
symmetry of information, 240

taken up type government, 206
tax collection authority, 171, 208
tax sharing system, vii, x, 169-171, 177-179, 181-186, 190, 192, 193, 197-199, 205, 208, 209, 215, 216, 218-221, 234, 237, 398
technology imitation, 275
the harder the richer system, 242
theory of induced technology and institutional innovation, 277
theory of water, 232
Third Front, 17, 20, 26-29, 35, 42, 44, 48, 54, 98, 103
three agricultural problems, 100, 105-107, 111, 219, 247, 329, 333, 340, 362, 390
three border open cities, 88
three capital enterprises, 86
three institutions, 29, 30
three strategies, 17
Tian'an'men Affairs, 69, 70, 71, 254, 365
Tiaotiao, 54, 55
Todaro, M. P., 109-110, 222, 322, 376, 397
 on Todaro model, 110, 222
two bombs and one satellite, 256
two-tiers dual economic structure, 45

ultra leftist way, 373
unification of economy and administration, 13, 30, 36, 42, 43, 105
unified party and administration, 248
unified purchase and unified sale system, 33
Universal Declaration of Human Rights, 278
variety of dual structures, 48
venous industry, 288

vertical division of labor, 297
Vietnam War, 295

waste management society, 276
Weber, M., 228, 229, 245, 308
on spirit of capitalism, 245, 308, 374, 385, 398
on protestant ethic, 393
on Confucianism, 245
on patrimonial bureaucracy, 251
on religion of China, 398
on Economy and Society, 398
on Confucianism and Taoism, 398
Wen Jiabao, 97, 98, 201, 306, 349, 350, 355
whole national physical education system, 256
whole nation's system, 240, 241, 255, 256, 266, 272, 277, 290
wise authoritarianism system, 169, 218, 246
Wuchang Uprising, 232
workers' interests, 240
working division system, 37, 51

Zhou Enlai, 61, 62, 65, 224, 374

Printed in the United States
by Baker & Taylor Publisher Services